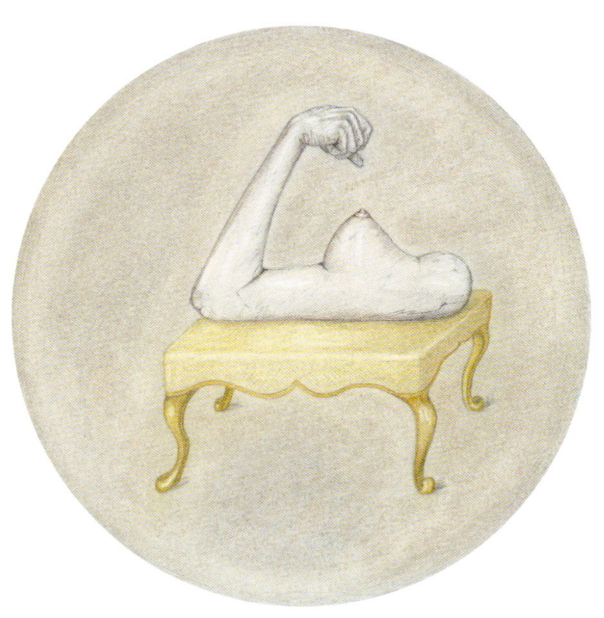

Birgit Jürgenssen

I am.

Edited by
Natascha Burger
Nicole Fritz

PRESTEL
Munich · London · New York

Contents

p. 7
Foreword
Natascha Burger & Nicole Fritz

p. 19
Birgit Jürgenssen: *I Don't Know*
Natascha Burger

p. 67
I am. An Act of Self-Assertion
Gabriele Schor

p. 77
A Natural History
Lorenzo Giusti

p. 95
The Circuits of a Riddle
Melissa Destino

p. 117
I am – Bicasso
The Transformation of Cultural Traditions
in the Work of Birgit Jürgenssen
Nicole Fritz

p. 143
Grave Waters
Jessica Morgan

p. 151
Vertigo
Patricia Allmer

p. 173
Femishism: Birgit Jürgenssen
in conversation with Maurizio Cattelan
Maurizio Cattelan & Marta Papini

p. 187
Birgit Jürgenssen,
Seen through the Anthropocene
Abigail Solomon-Godeau

p. 207
The Rat in the Bed
Louisa Buck

p. 215
The Woman Does (Not) Exist
Marta Dziewańska

p. 223
Freed from Any Constraint
On Birgit Jürgenssen's
Photographic Experiments
Ninja Walbers

p. 267
»There is more advantage to separate
home and body«
Heike Eipeldauer

p. 275
Narcissus and Echo
Jasper Sharp

p. 285
Trans-Europe Express
Michael Bracewell

p. 305
Biography

p. 309
Catalogue of Works

p. 323
Selected Exhibitions

p. 327
Bibliography

p. 331
Authors' Biographies

p. 335
Acknowledgements

Foreword

[1] Ulrich Beck, Elisabeth Beck-Gernsheim (eds.), *Das ganz normale Chaos der Liebe*, (Frankfurt/M.: 1990), S. 37 [translated].
[2] Birgit Jürgenssen in conversation with Heidemarie Seblatnig, in Seblatnig, *Einfach den Gefahren ins Auge sehen: Künstlerinnen im Gespräch* (Vienna, 1988), pp. 158–61.

When asked to explain the precise meaning of individualization, sociologist Ulrich Beck replied that we might say »I am I,« but not »I am Swiss or I am Catholic,« as these traditional ties are revocable.[1] One particular work by Birgit Jürgenssen can be seen as an illustration of this thesis—it also gives this retrospective its title.

In 1995, the artist wrote the words »Ich bin« (I am) in Latin characters on a school slate, thereby poetically condensing a single moment in the here and now. This was a minimalist expression of selfhood, not only symbolizing the fleeting nature of the experienced moment but also referring—by means of the sponge hanging next to it—to the transitory, processual, and ultimately finite nature of our being.

Jürgenssen's artistic career began back in the 1960s and spanned over four decades, during which time she developed an individual repertoire of images by sounding out her own emotional range. Her way of life as an artist is encapsulated not just in this one work but rather in her entire oeuvre, which is an impressive testimony to this approach. She herself said, »I am much more [interested] in experimenting […] than in devising a brand,«[2] and she had no need to work on developing a style or formal criteria but rather embodied the utopia within her own self.

One of several crucial elements in the work of Birgit Jürgenssen is the body. It is not just an object but also the medium of experience from which she developed her works. In more than a thousand drawings, Jürgenssen captured her own seismographic intuitions of realms prior to the conceptual and conscious; relations between people, sexuality, socially determined notions of beauty, and gender roles are all mirrored and deconstructed with subversive humor and self-irony, as are deeper layers of the artist's own identity. Hers is a diverse body of work that derives so clearly from the very intimate, and it gains a new relevance and potency today, in an age when digitalization means that perceptions of our everyday lives are becoming ever »flatter.«

Perhaps the diversity and discontinuity of the artistic means deployed is one reason why Jürgenssen's work has hitherto been received primarily only in Austria. The exhibition *I Am.*, developed by Kunsthalle Tübingen and the Estate of Birgit Jürgenssen in Vienna, is the first comprehensive posthumous retrospective of the artist's work outside of Austria. We are delighted that after Tübingen, this exhibition will go on to GAMeC – Galleria d'Arte Moderna e Contemporanea di Bergamo in Italy and the Louisiana Museum of Modern Art in Humlebæk, Denmark, in summer 2019.

Jürgenssen's work has often been seen primarily in terms of her exploration of relations between the sexes, whereas we now endeavor to open up the perspective and present the impressive range of her entire oeuvre. This exhibition and also the contributions to the accompanying publication look at lesser-known groups of work and at the artist's later output. The selection of works and the texts also show that Jürgenssen's intuitive sensitivity prefigured both today's discourse of the body and the greater awareness we now have of relations between people and the environment. As an expression of an integrated and empathetic consciousness, Jürgenssen's work was not just highly topical in her own time, it was visionary—and this is why her work has such remarkable presence.

We would like to thank all the people who participated in this ambitious project: Hubert Winter, the head of Birgit Jürgenssen's estate, for his trust and support; Philipp Wagner for his meticulous attention to detail and for his editorial work; Marie Artaker for her wonderful design concept and for the tireless energy she applied to the task of implementing it; the authors for their texts and the staff at Galerie Hubert Winter and at Kunsthalle Tübingen for their enthusiasm; and all the private and public lenders of works, the gallery owners, sponsors of Kunsthalle Tübingen, and the directors of participating museums and institutions for their commitment and their own interest in presenting the work of Birgit Jürgenssen.

Natascha Burger, Estate Birgit Jürgenssen
Nicole Fritz, Kunsthalle Tübingen

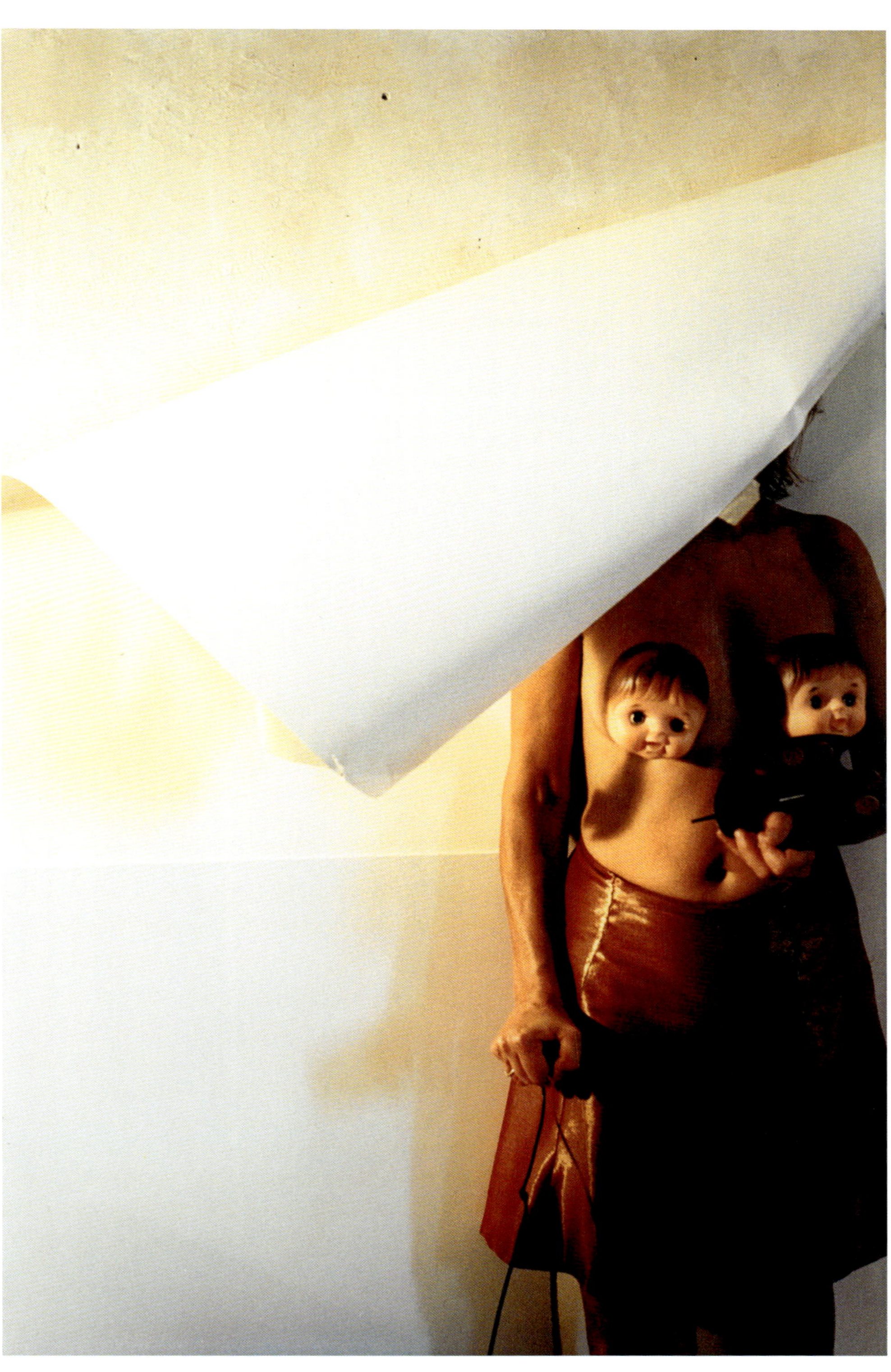

1   *Ohne Titel* 1997
     Untitled

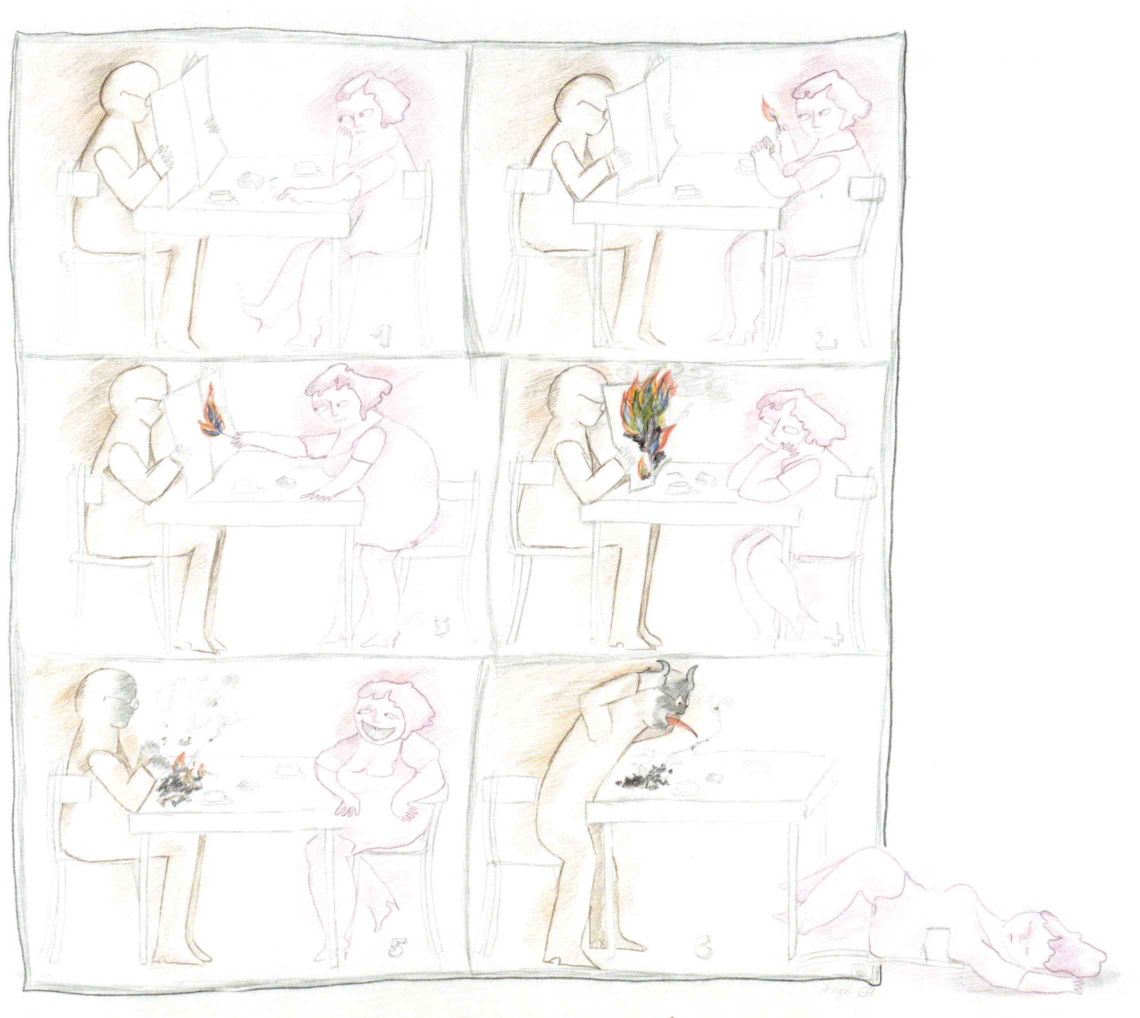

2 *Ohne Titel* 1969
Untitled

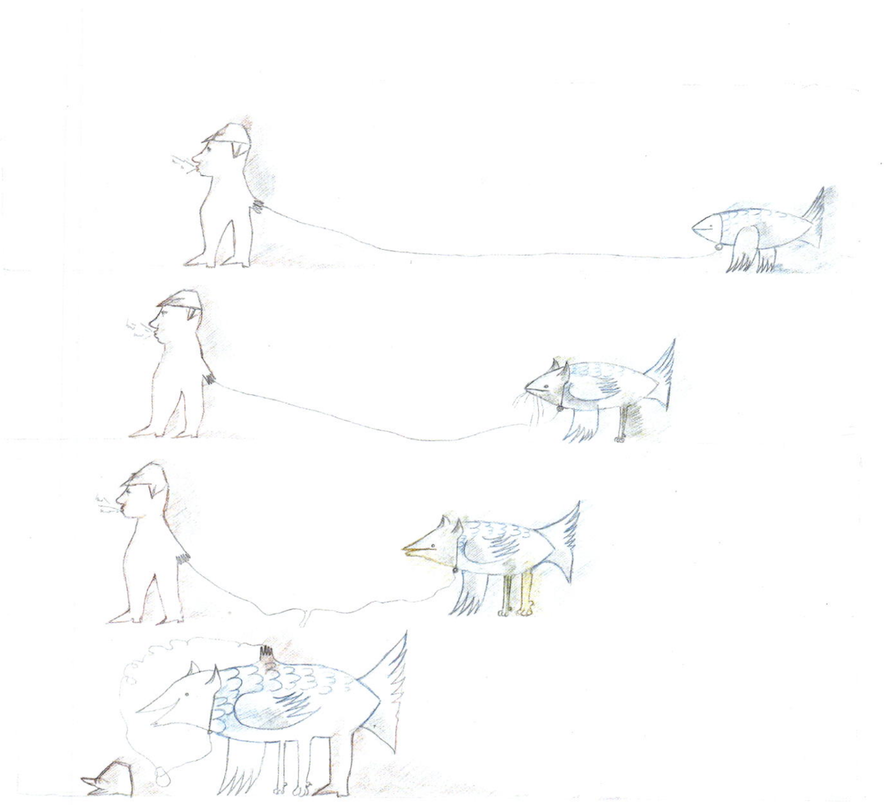

Ohne Titel 1969
Untitled

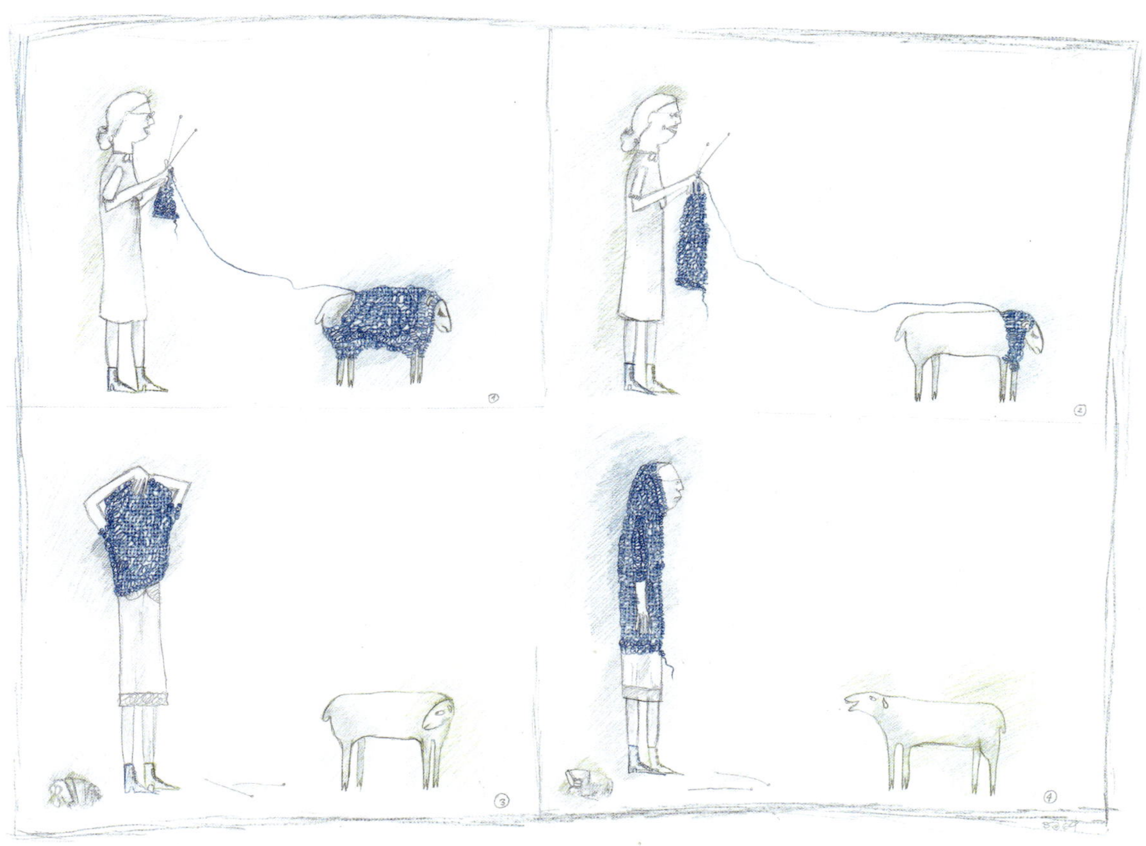

<u>4</u>   *Ohne Titel* 1969
     Untitled

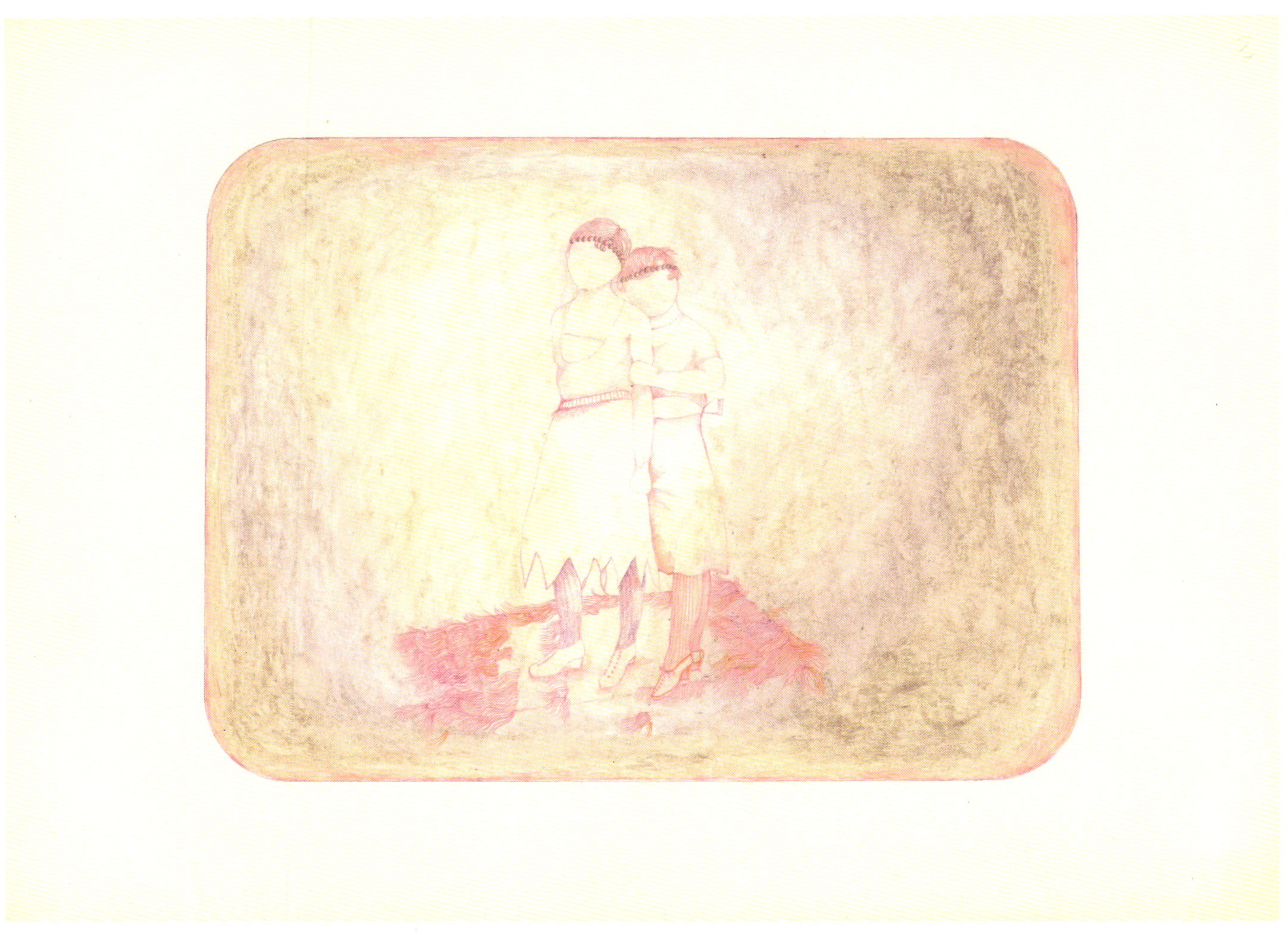

5   *Ohne Titel* 1971
    Untitled

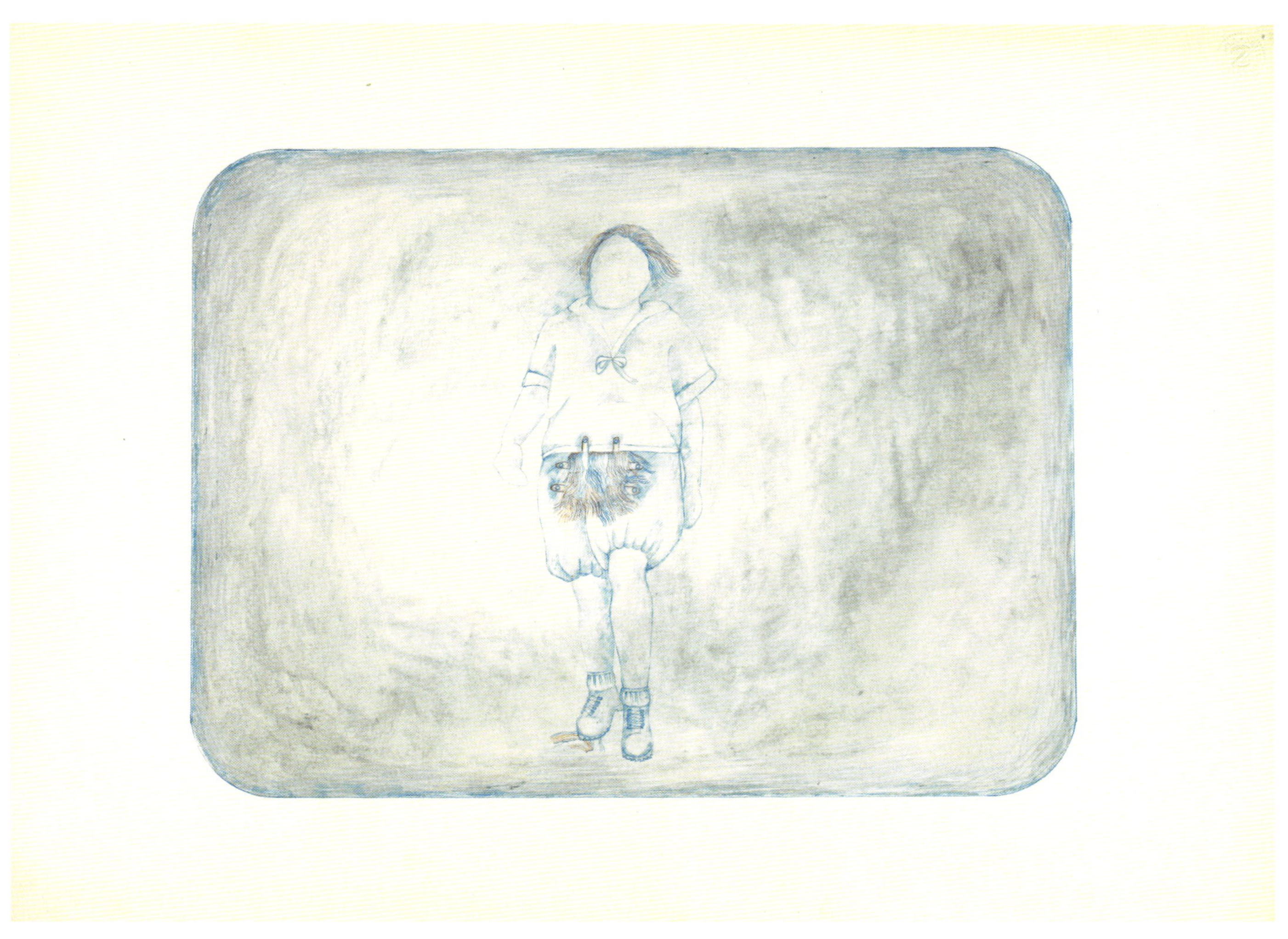

<u>6</u>   *Ohne Titel* 1971
Untitled

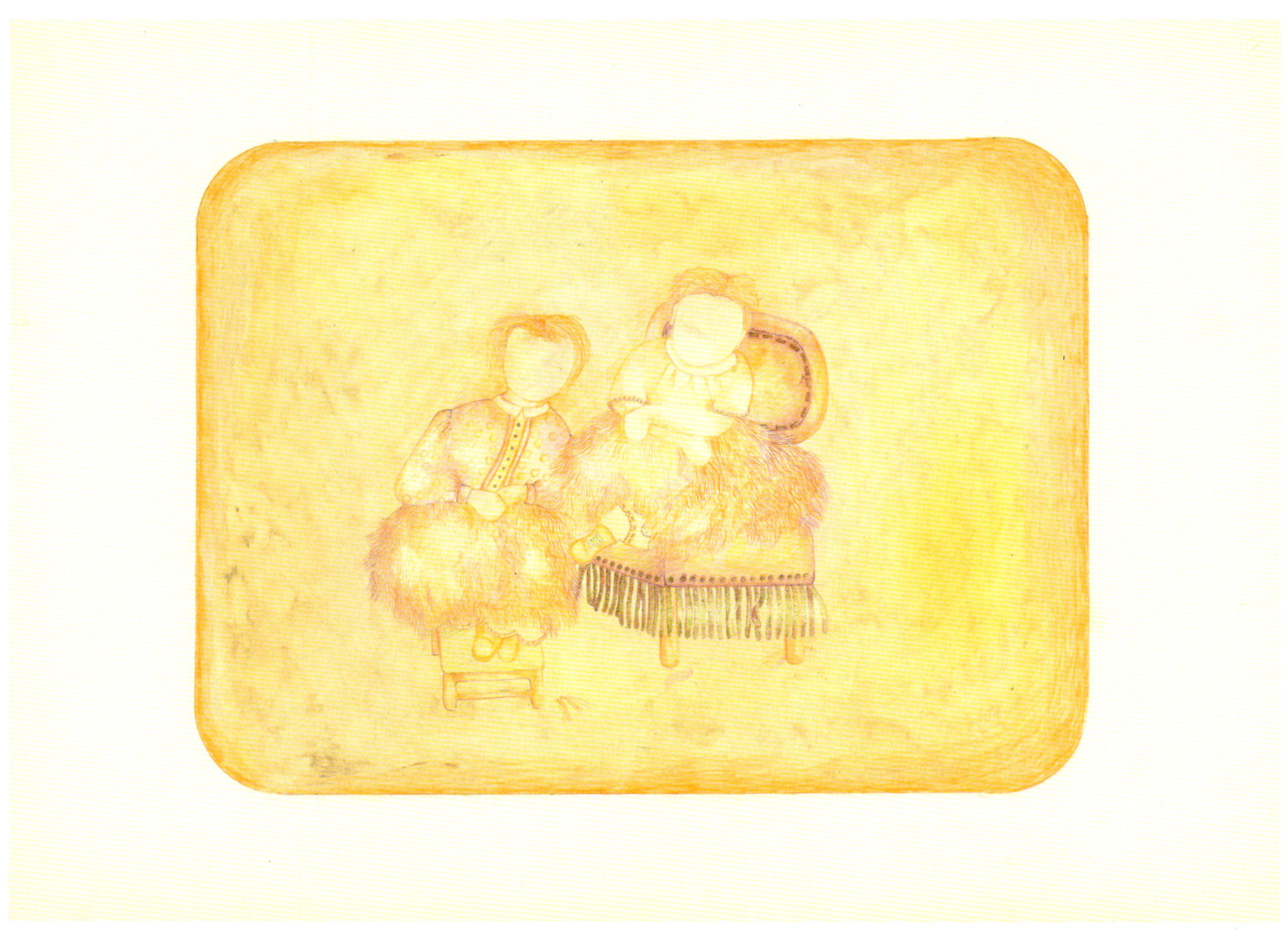

7   *Ohne Titel* 1971
     Untitled

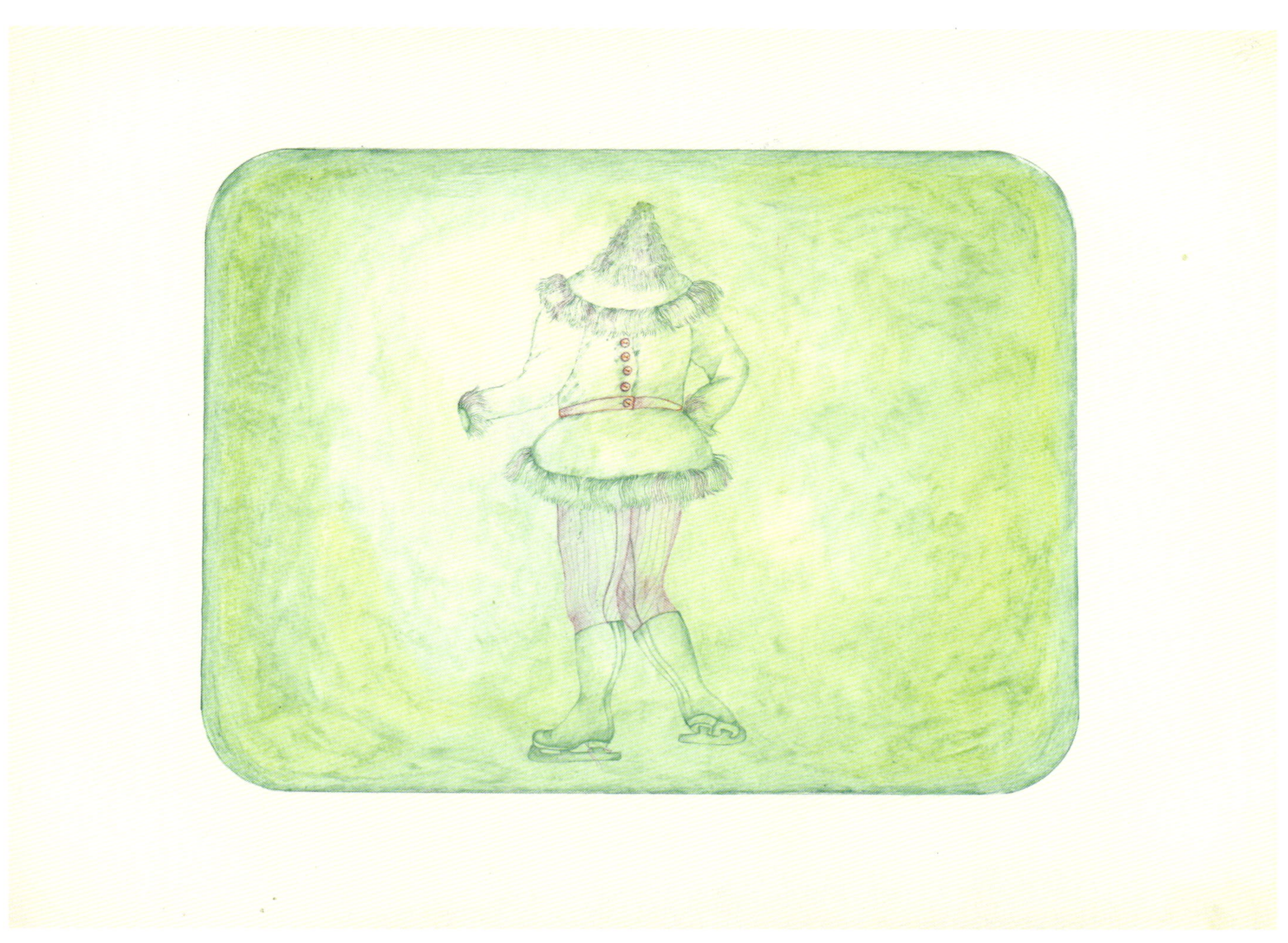

8 *Ohne Titel* 1971
Untitled

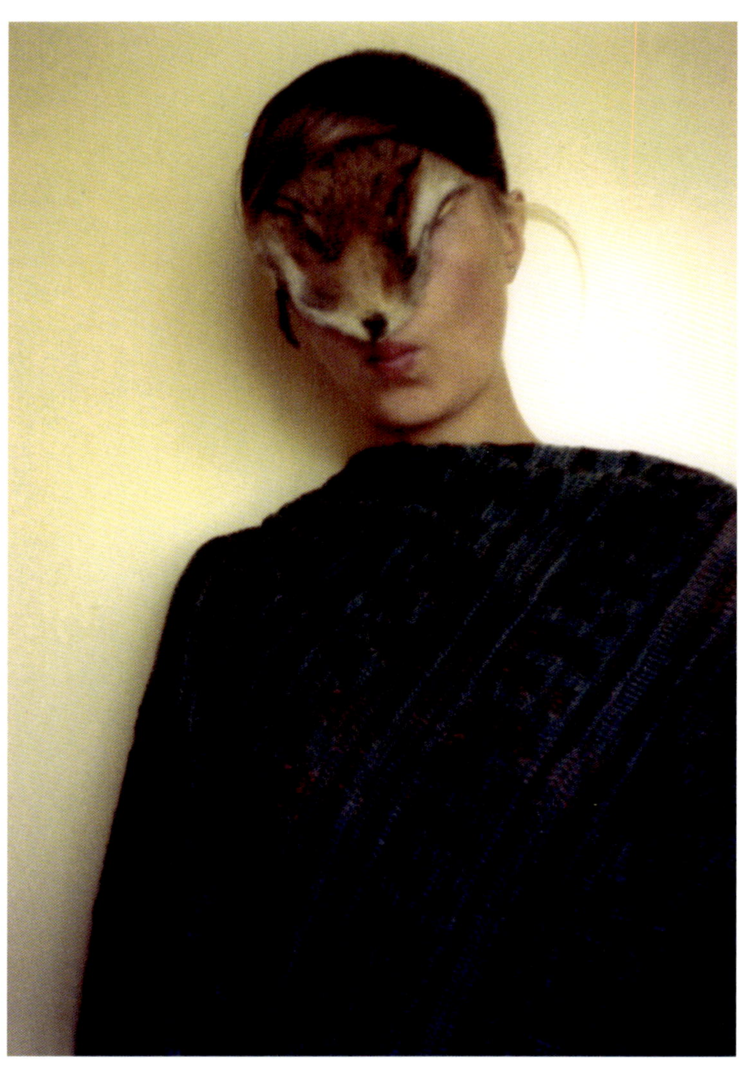

    Ohne Titel (Selbst mit Fellchen) 1974/1977
Untitled (Self with Little Fur)

Birgit Jürgenssen: *I Don't Know*

Natascha Burger

über den Blick + das Unsichtbare

Das Licht das Spuren hinterlässt

Photo → „Intimität" → bezieht sich

auf das Verhältnis von Betrachter +

Objekt der Phantasie → Puzzle über

die Ursprünge erotischer Manipulation

Selbstbewusstsein

DAS SELBST → DAS ANDERE
SUBJEKT → OBJEKT
PRIVATES → ÖFFENTLICHES

Mit den Augen hören!

Sujets:
STOFF → HAUT
LAPPEN → AUGEN → LICHT

White. A blind pupil. Inside the optic vault, desires roll out their rime.
For the first time we had gone to the north or the west; the clearing awaited
our first steps ...[1]

[1] From the invitation card for the exhibition *I Don't Know*, Galerie Hubert Winter (Vienna, 2001); from Michel Butor, *Fenêtres sur le passage intérieur* (Bois-de-Champs: Aencrages, 1982) [translated].
[2] On Jürgenssen's work with this title, see the text by Gabriele Schor in this publication, p. 67.
[3] Georges Didi-Huberman, *Ähnlichkeit und Berührung: Archäologie, Anachronismus und Modernität des Abdrucks* (Cologne: DuMont, 1999), p. 17 [translated].

I Don't Know was the title Birgit Jürgenssen gave to her last solo exhibition at Galerie Hubert Winter in Vienna in 2001. Two years later, in September 2003, the artist died at the age of only fifty-four, leaving a large and impressive estate. Based on her inexhaustible wealth of ideas, shrewd observation, and an incessant internal monologue, Jürgenssen created a multidimensional work that to this day exudes refreshing irony, provocative elegance, and a self-effacing presence.

To manage an estate, and particularly this estate, is a very sensitive challenge. It means understanding and decoding the complexity of a real person (or trying to do so), seeing her in terms of her local and aesthetic history, and gradually coming to understand the contexts in which she operated. *I Am.* (ill. 48)[2] as a confident artistic statement by Birgit Jürgenssen and the title of this retrospective, the comprehensive precision of this sentence stands symbolically for the obligations that managing this estate entails. Who is Birgit Jürgenssen?

This privileged view of an artistic oeuvre and its complex image, which Jürgenssen's multifaceted approach certainly deconstructed, has to be reconstructed and then made visible. And she bequeathed us a remarkable image, a strong imprint. As Georges Didi-Huberman puts it:

»It is not possible to understand a technology—and thus also not an art—unless one attempts to grasp its anthropological dimension. In terms of its procedures and uses, the imprint is doubtless a product of ›that science of the concrete‹ of which Lévi-Strauss writes in the first chapter of *The Savage Mind*. Why? Because making an imprint always means creating a network of *material relations*, from which a concrete object emerges [...], but which link up with a whole array of *abstract relations*, myths, phantasms, knowledge, etc.«[3]

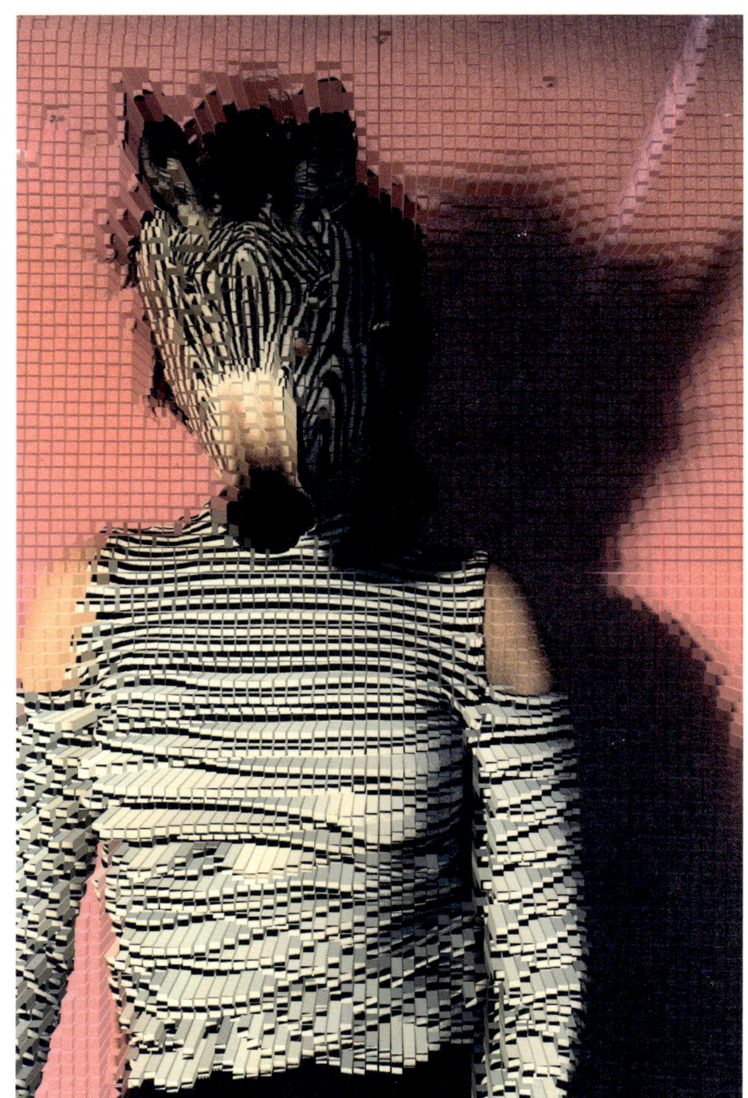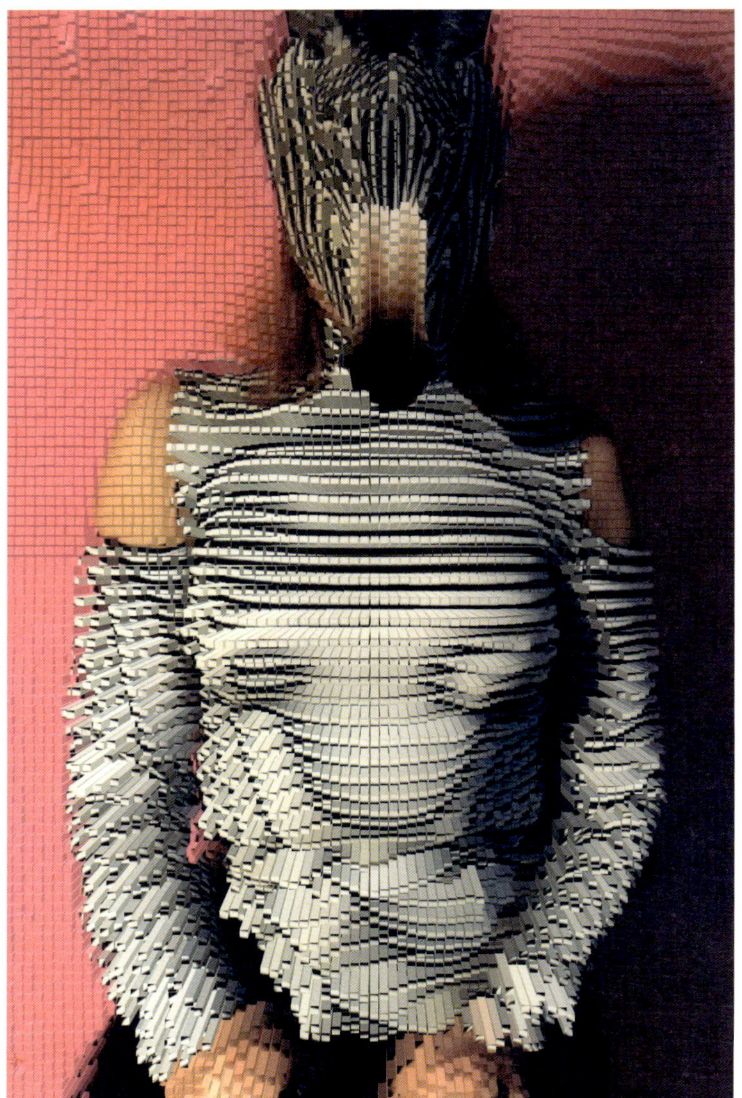

10   *Zebra 1* 2001
11   *Zebra 2* 2001

[4] Rainer Metzger, »Birgit Jürgenssen: ›Wie erfährt man sich im anderen, das andere in sich?‹: Ein Gespräch mit Rainer Metzger,« *Kunstforum International* 164 (March–May 2003), pp. 234–47, here: p. 245 [translated].
[5] On this, see the text by Ninja Walbers in this volume, pp. 223–50.
[6] Birgit Jürgenssen, »Pulsschlag einer Sinnlichkeit,« in *Schmuck: Zeichen am Körper*, ed. Linzer Institut für Gestaltung (Vienna: Falter, 1987), p. 234 [translated].

[7] Birgit Jürgenssen in conversation with Doris Linda Psenicnik on December 21, 1998, unpublished, Estate Birgit Jürgenssen, Vienna.
[8] See ibid.
[9] On this, see *Dreamers Awake*, exh. cat. White Cube (London: White Cube, 2017), p. 10. The significance of fur in art history is characterized there as follows: »Obsessive use of fetishistic objects or materials (hair, stockings, gloves, velvet and fur) to empower the female self and queer desire, as well as their irreverent playful dare to the spectator to ›please touch.‹«
[10] S. Thäsler, »Metamorphose,« *Wechselwirkung: Technik Naturwissenschaft Gesellschaft* 7, no. 25 (May 1985), accessed September 11, 2018, www.e-periodica.ch/cntmng ?pid=wsw-001:1985:7::303. Thanks to Melanie Wagner.

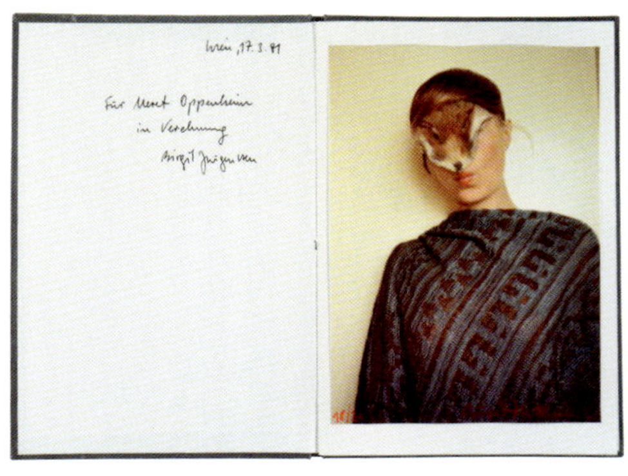

12   Dedication to Meret Oppenheim, 1981
Fotobibliothek Diessenhofen Schweiz
Courtesy Photobibliothek.ch

Jürgenssen's »savage mind« and the »net of material and abstract relations« she spun, her system of coordinates consisting of references, ideas, traces, resources, reversions, and preemptions, were not all immediately apparent in her final solo exhibition. Shifting meanings and enigmatic overlaps can only be grasped after a second look—as so often in this artist's work. Jürgenssen knew how to manipulate the gaze and the act of seeing, and how to surprise. Defining her way of working and her emancipated thinking in terms of this (final) moment reveals connecting lines right through her entire oeuvre and all the way back to her earliest works. This creates a framework that we can use to sharpen our awareness of her work and thought processes, allowing us, first and foremost, to explain them. It is right here that the irresistible quality of this artist becomes apparent; the art of multilayered transformations and the poetic transfer into her own language, her visual idiom, run through her entire work and clearly distinguish her from her contemporaries. Jürgenssen realized very early on that she did not want to create any kind of trademark or clearly recognizable brand: »I was not interested in complaining. I did not want to join any feminist group as the opportunities there seemed too one-dimensional to me. The only thing to do seemed to be to use all the media that were available.«[4]

Substituting boldness and curiosity for simulation and strategy, Jürgenssen made use of »all the media that were available.« She began to draw at the young age of eight, and she soon also became interested in analogue photography, which she would pursue right to the end of her artistic career. »All the media that were available« also included painting, various photographic techniques,[5] sculpture, and installations, culminating in the »new media« of video and digital photography. For Jürgenssen, »new« technologies and the new opportunities they presented as a means to implement her ideas artistically, preferably independently, were a permanent stimulus for almost four decades, and they were, above all, a constant challenge to the artist herself. It thus seems noteworthy that in the early 1980s, while a student in Franz Herberth's graphic arts class, she became assistant to Maria Lassnig, subsequently taught in Arnulf Rainer's master class, and also established the teaching of photography at the Academy of Fine Arts Vienna, before eventually teaching there in the media class.

Regardless of the artistic medium employed, much comes together in the last exhibition that Birgit Jürgenssen designed, entitled *I Don't Know*, initially suggesting doubts but in fact making her approach and mindset crystal clear. »Everything begins with seeing. The secret is what is visible, not the invisible.«[6] Jürgenssen developed her ideas in series, constantly referring back to earlier work. The two-part photographic piece *Zebra* (ill. 10, 11) is an excellent example of backward references in her oeuvre, both temporal and in terms of content. A work from the 1970s, clearly influenced at the time by surrealism, is taken up anew nearly three decades later and further developed for exhibition. Jürgenssen worked in the »loop«, everything was in motion.[7] Motifs could be put aside, repeated, rejected, reinterpreted.

The surreal approach to the mask in a computer-animated digital photograph of 2001 represents a clear return to one of the icons of Jürgenssen's work, and in fact one of her earliest self-portraits: *Untitled (Self with Little Fur)* (ill. 9). Back in the 1970s, and heavily influenced by French surrealism as a result of her early trips to Paris (which acted as a form of inspirational poetry),[8] she photographed herself as a hybrid creature. Half human, half animal. Jürgenssen did not, however, fully implement this apparent shift of identity. The transformation was restricted to her face only, as a medium of expression, with a clear formulation of a human-animal antagonism. This comes across both in the performative photograph itself and also very consciously in the work's title: »Self« (human), »with Little Fur« (animal). Years later, the feminine, elegant, and surreal fur[9] was transformed into a »stubborn and untamable« zebra.[10] The framing is again constrained by the vertical format, with the grid pattern showing the head and torso of the artist in the clear act of transforming once again into an animal. The difference is that this time the transformation is not restricted to the face and a mask, as Jürgenssen includes her whole upper body in the transformative masquerade.

Twenty-seven years of creative output lie between these two works. Whenever we speak of a unifying thread or rather a web interconnecting the works of Birgit Jürgenssen, then contrasting these two photographic works is a good way of understanding the organic principles of her work. Determined and consistent testing of the limits, by means of experimentation, questioning, and reworking.

It is not surprising that Birgit Jürgenssen revisits the theme of metamorphosis in a digitally reworked version, and in the form of an analogy to the »little fur,« as this photographic work was particularly important to her. Compared to many female artists of her generation, who seemed to be bolder, more expressive, and louder in drawing attention to themselves, Jürgenssen saw herself more akin to Meret Oppenheim and Louise Bourgeois, who were »more poetic, less direct, and more subversive.«[11] She expressed her personal appreciation and conceptual kinship in the form of a dedication to Meret Oppenheim (ill. 12).[12]

Horror Vacui: The White Surface

»I Don't Know.«

What does Birgit Jürgenssen not know? What is making her unsure? She announces her doubts very directly, deciding on an exhibition title that makes us, the audience, ask questions, and gives rise to confusion and curiosity. The works shown in the exhibition at the time did not seem to offer any clear answers. Their apparent insecurity may relate to her choice of the »new media« of video and digital photography, which Jürgenssen used for the first time in an exhibition in this show. Is it the new forms of expression that perhaps made Jürgenssen doubt? Asked in an interview whether she liked to focus in her work on one or several themes, she answered that she was working on the theme of analogue and digital photography for the exhibition at Galerie Hubert Winter, and for the first time was using digital photography in combination with 16:9 film in an exhibition context.[13]

Notwithstanding this formulation of insecurity and expression of doubt, quite intentionally referencing Socrates (»I know that I know nothing«) and perhaps Kierkegaard, who saw irony as a means of creating distance, this doubting and ignorance that Jürgenssen attempts to have us accept by means of a careful choice of exhibition title nonetheless culminates in irony. In fact, the artist operates skillfully and *free of doubt* between the media of analogue and digital photography.

Even if *Purkersdorf*, *Venice*, and *Madison Avenue* (to name the titles of just a few works) initially appear to have no connection with each other and seem to be shown as autonomous pieces within the exhibition, akin to Foucault's concept of heterotopias, which bring together at one and the same location several different spaces that are actually irreconcilable,[14] there could be no mere experimenting and certainly no coincidences and uncertainty whenever Birgit Jürgenssen planned an exhibition. Every presentation was thought through down to the very last detail in advance, and meticulously sketched and written down. In this process, Jürgenssen's notebooks were of great importance. As someone who never ceased thinking and working, she put down a large corpus of ideas in her many notebooks and sketchbooks. Alternating between drawing and writing, she formulated rough concepts for current works, ideas for her students at the academy, and even fully developed plans for upcoming exhibitions. There are more than eighty of these notebooks, workbooks, and sketchbooks in Birgit Jürgenssen's estate today; they are remarkable documents of her way of working and thinking, permitting subjective and personal insight into her mental processes. Reading them, it quickly seems »as if the notebook provides the ›inside story,‹ the ›inside track‹ to the soul of the person keeping the notebook, and likewise the inside track as to the genesis of their ideas and achievements. It is like being privy to the secrets of an alchemist's laboratory, enlivened by their all-too-human foibles and weaknesses.«[15] These notebooks define Jürgenssen as an incredibly well-read, book-loving thinker, and they show her individual

[11] Metzger, »Birgit Jürgenssen« (see n. 4), p. 245.

[12] See the cover of this book, which shows a further multilayered version of Birgit Jürgenssen's »little fur.«

[13] Unpublished interview with Christine Braunersreuther on the exhibition *Product Mother's Day* in the Museum of Ethnology, Vienna, 2001.

[14] See Michel Foucault, »Of Other Spaces: Utopias and Heterotopias,« in *Rethinking Architecture: A Reader in Cultural Theory* (London: Routledge, 1997).

[15] Michael Taussig, *Fieldwork Notebooks / Feldforschungsnotizbücher*, 100 Notizen – 100 Gedanken, no. 1 (Ostfildern: Hatje Cantz, 2011), p. 8.

[16] Cited in Felicitas Thun-Hohenstein, »›Everything Flows, Conditions and Permeates Itself …‹ Felicitas Thun-Hohenstein in an Interview with Birgit Jürgenssen,« in *Let's Twist Again: If You Can't Think It, Dance It; Performance in Vienna from 1960 until Today,* ed. Carola Dertnig and Stefanie Seibold (Gumpoldskirchen: de'A Buch- und Kunstverlag, 2006), pp. 272–79.

[17] Ludwig Wittgenstein, *Remarks on Colour / Bemerkungen über die Farben,* ed. G. E. M. Anscombe, trans. Linda L. McAlister and Margarete Schättle (Berkeley: University of California Press, 2007), p. 15.

[18] From a Birgit Jürgenssen notebook: »Three Subject Notebook,« 2000, Estate of Birgit Jürgenssen (sk43), n.p.

[19] Bernd Behr, Eckhard Diesing, Vito Orazem, and Peter Zec, eds., *Welt als Pattern* (Drensteinfurt: Huba, 1984), p. 96.

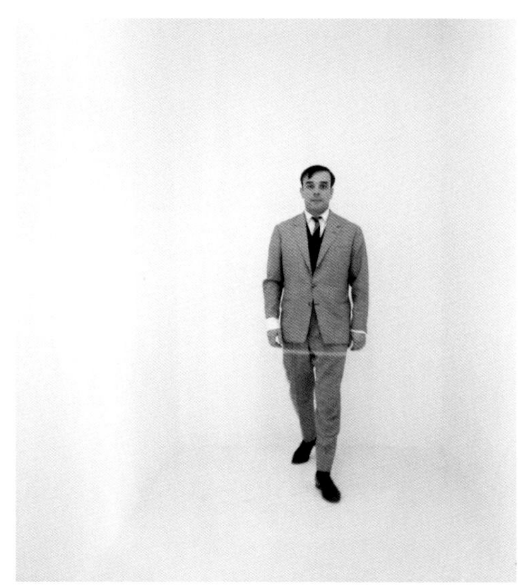

13   Yves Klein *Void Room* at the Museum Krefeld 1961
© The Estate of Yves Klein / Bildrecht, Vienna 2018

way of accumulating knowledge. Looking in depth at this personal archive reveals Jürgenssen's incessant exploration of literature, philosophy, ethnology, and theory. Citations and poems are noted down alongside passing thoughts. For Jürgenssen, literature was an insatiable passion and it was an essential part of her art: »I started very early to spend my time with surrealistic literature and art. My work emerged from an exchange between literature and daily life. It was impossible for me to draw without keeping a piece of literature in mind.«[16]

Today, these personal notes are an impressive source giving a remarkable picture of the complexity of Jürgenssen's intellectual and artistic interests. Readers can sense how the artist's thinking developed and gain insight into her evolution and »rituals« as an artist. This was a free, chaotic, and poetic process, evidence of Jürgenssen's sharp mind and great sensitivity.

For the exhibition *I Don't Know* Birgit Jürgenssen began by noting a seemingly fleeting idea, which ultimately led to the title: »die Farbe WEISZ,« meaning both »the color white« and »the color knows,« whereby the German word *weiß/Weiß* is »misspelled« as »WEISZ«. Jürgenssen was always working with puns and shifting meanings, aphorisms and homonyms, a surrealist approach that utilized different levels of meaning in words and terms for her artistic work. As well as the theme of analogue and digital photography (as »one« possible strategy), Jürgenssen also took the color white as a key starting point in her thoughts on planning this exhibition, and a clear »intermediary« that would directly interconnect her discursive works. »Isn't white that which does away with darkness?«[17]

The color white gains a special value, creating a *vade mecum* for visitors to the exhibition. In connection with this, one very noticeable motif in the images in the exhibition is snow, a medium that cloaks and conceals, a frozen transparency. It appears directly in the title of the video *Snow Storm* (ill. 14) or as a leitmotif in the digital photograph *X-Mahl* (ill. 15), which is printed on linen and directs and misdirects our gaze. We can see two snow-covered »white« birch logs, forming an X on the ground. They are photographed from above, presented tilted up and in large format, with the perspective confusing the viewer's gaze. This digital photograph assumes a painterly quality, as it is printed slightly out of focus and can only really be seen as a whole from a certain distance. This is a snow sculpture, as Birgit Jürgenssen commented,[18] with two perspectives. A forked path, offering two options, but no direction. Uncertainty? *I Don't Know.* To Jürgenssen these were »new« media and her use of them is manipulative. She creates unclear digital photographs, deliberately out of focus, with a disturbing dynamism and impossible to clearly define. A lack of clarity in motion, reflections—which Jürgenssen was fascinated by and whose deceptive illusion of doubling had an alienating effect, as for example in *Venice* (ill. 16).

There is a further note made in the context of preparing this exhibition: »Yves Klein, the empty surface.« In 1961, Klein used empty white surfaces to create a radical white-walled space at Museum Haus Lange in Krefeld (ill. 13). A room that also irritates and confuses our seeing, even to the point of snow blindness. A white cube that dissolves the borders between walls and corners and makes it only possible to experience what is seen or not seen in the void through pure emotion alone. Horror vacui, the fear of nothingness, of the void. Jürgenssen was clearly fascinated by the idea of the white empty surface and derived her own version of a white »pictorial surface« from this, developing it in her video *Snow Storm*. Looking out from the protected space of her studio, she filmed the snow falling, heavy, cold, and loud. The window »offers protection, on the one hand, and gives rise to feelings when we open it and gaze out of the protected space; on the other hand, this is the deep repeated experience that has become our chosen image of the other, of the outside, of the new.«[19]

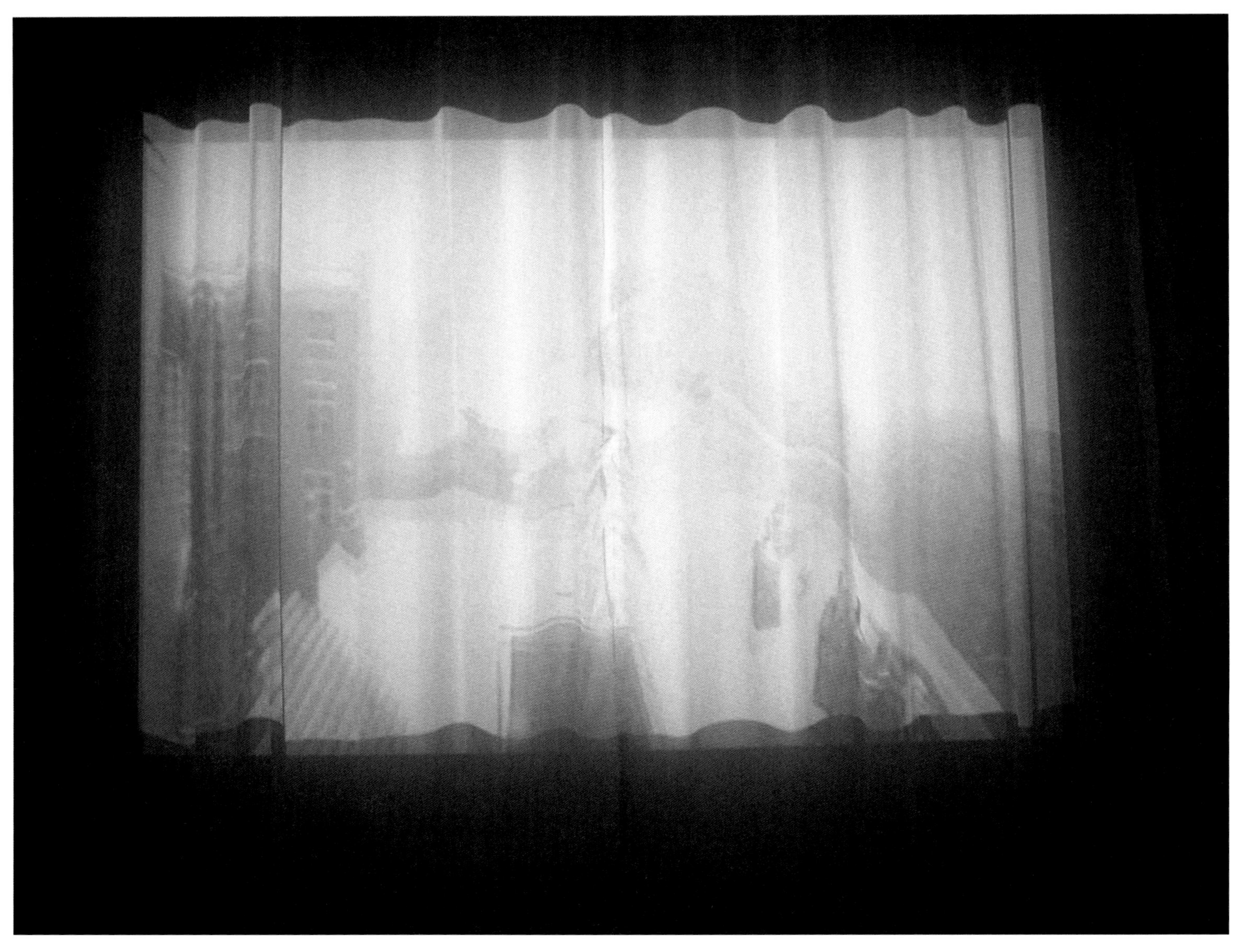

14 *Schneegewitter* 2000/2001
Snow Storm

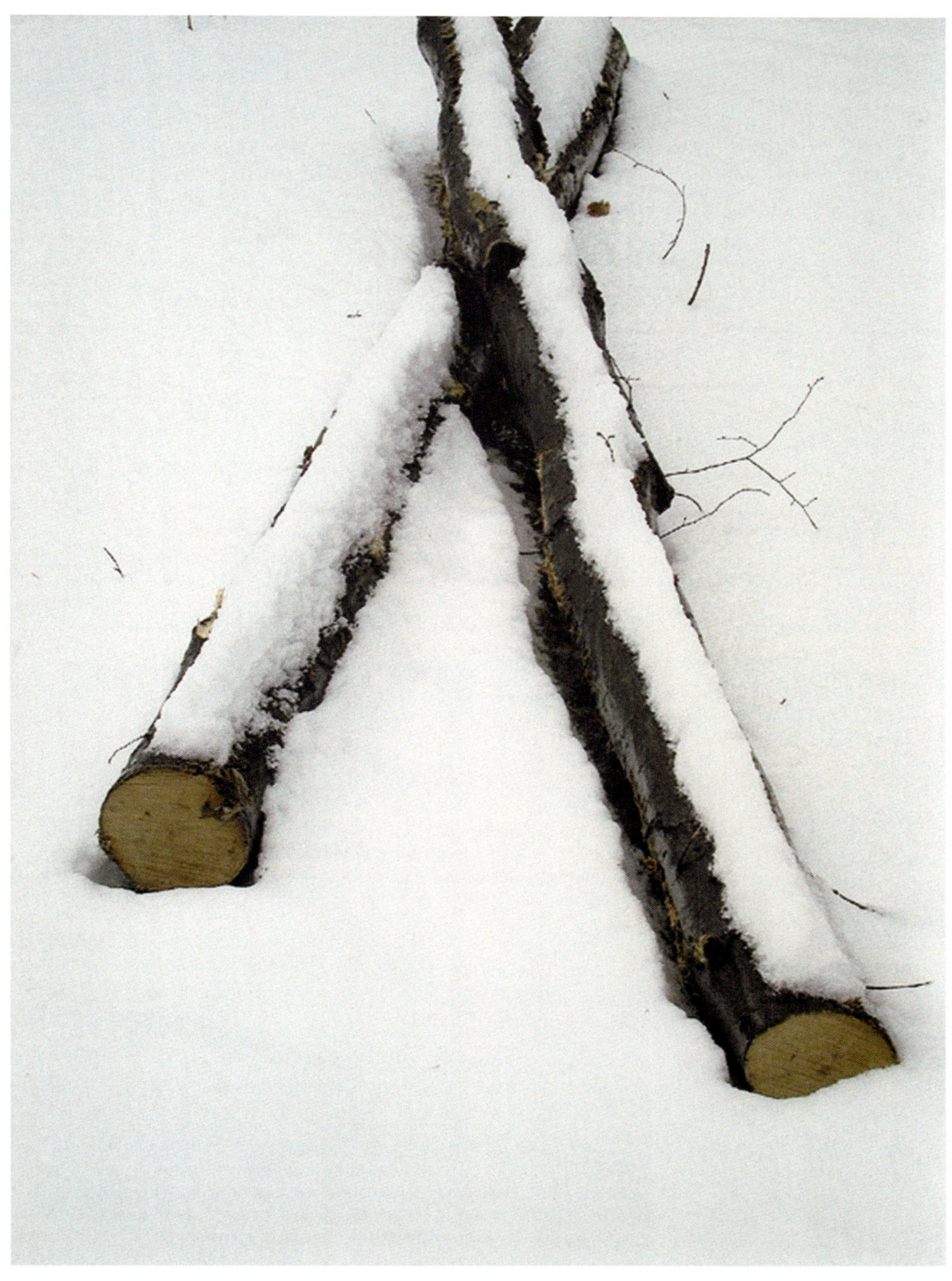

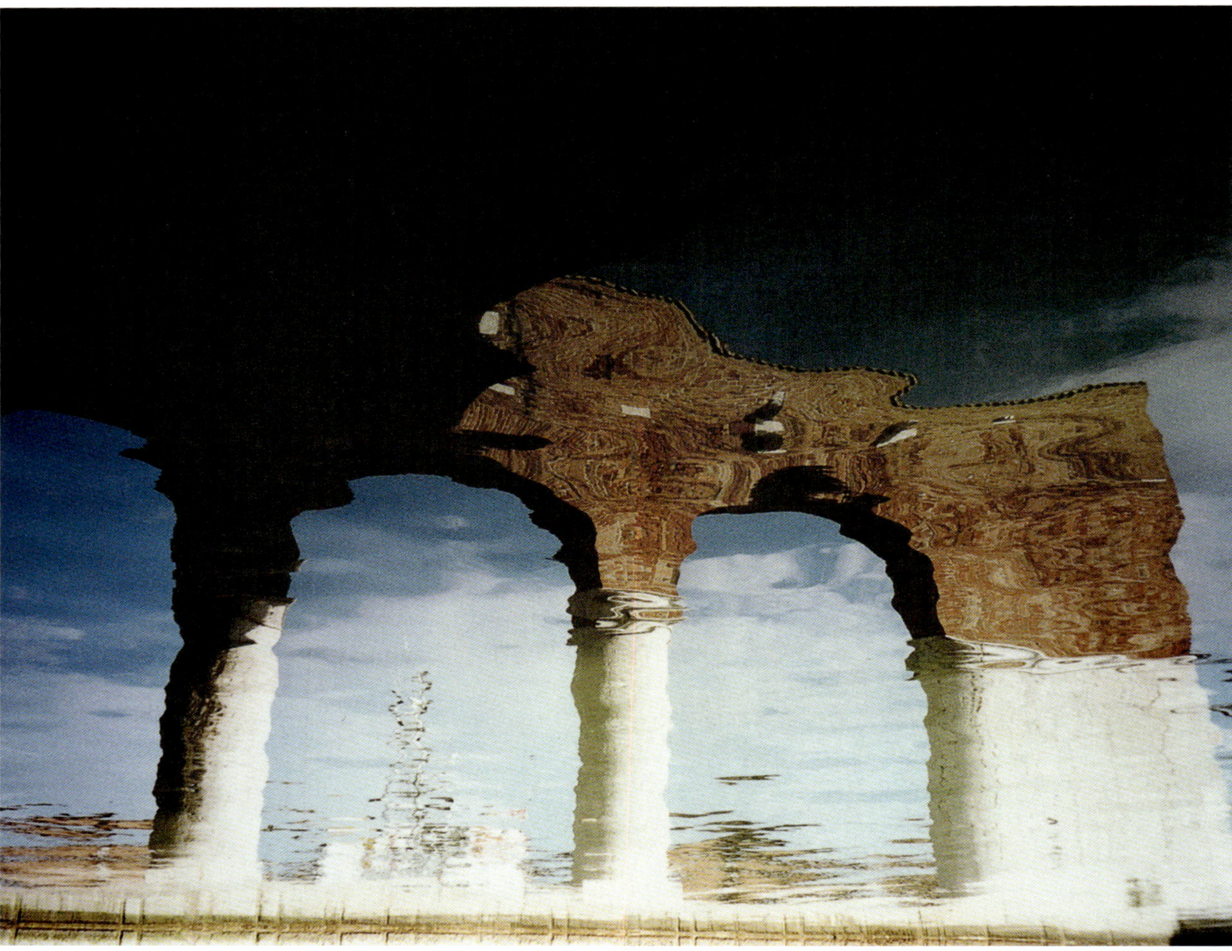

16   *Venedig* 2001
     Venice

Tactility, Textuality

Video emerged as a medium around 1970—Birgit Jürgenssen first used it in 1997.[20]
»The picture we see, of course. It is a moving picture; but just as with movies, the motion
isn't apparent, an optical illusion and not real. This motion is produced by the rapid
succession of slightly different still frames. In television, according to PAL standard, these
frames succeed each other at the rate of 25 per second. In other words, 1 second 25 individual pictures pass before the eyes. At this rate we are left with the impression of con-
tinuous motion.«[21]

    In her video *Snow Storm*, Jürgenssen seems to completely reverse the technical
achievement of »the rapid succession of slightly different still frames« to produce the
illusion of movement: instead, she deliberately provokes a contrary effect. The frame
remains fixed, and movement only takes place as the flurry of driving snow. The image
shown remains unchanged. In the exhibition, this video was projected onto a white

[20] *Angel*, 1997, video; made
for the exhibition
Angel:Angel at Kunsthalle
Wien, 1997.
[21] Wulf Herzogenrath and
Evelyn Weiss, *Kunst bleibt
Kunst: Aspekte inter-
nationaler Kunst am Anfang
der 70er Jahre; Projekt
'74* exh. cat. (Cologne:
Kunsthalle, 1974), p. 70.

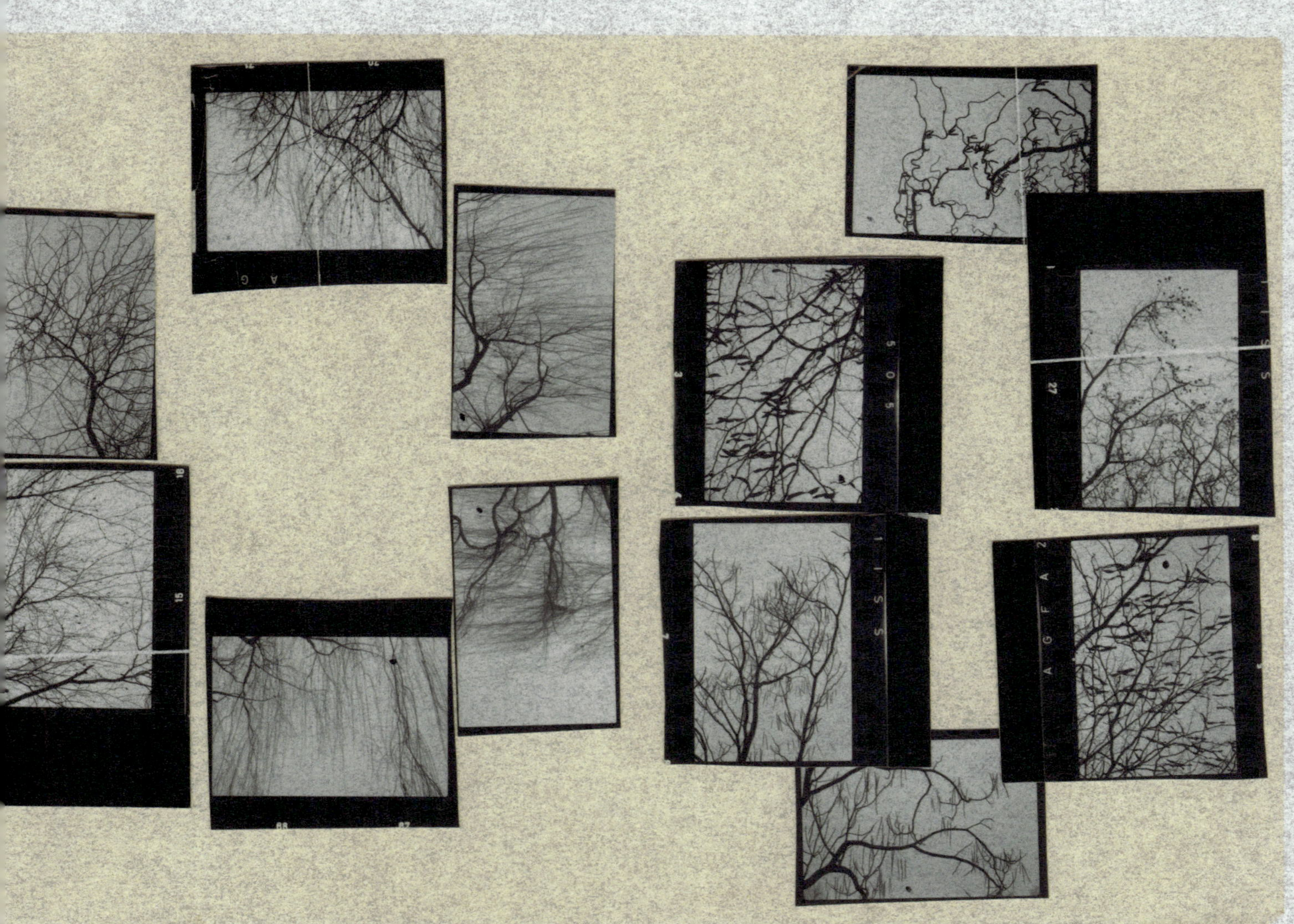

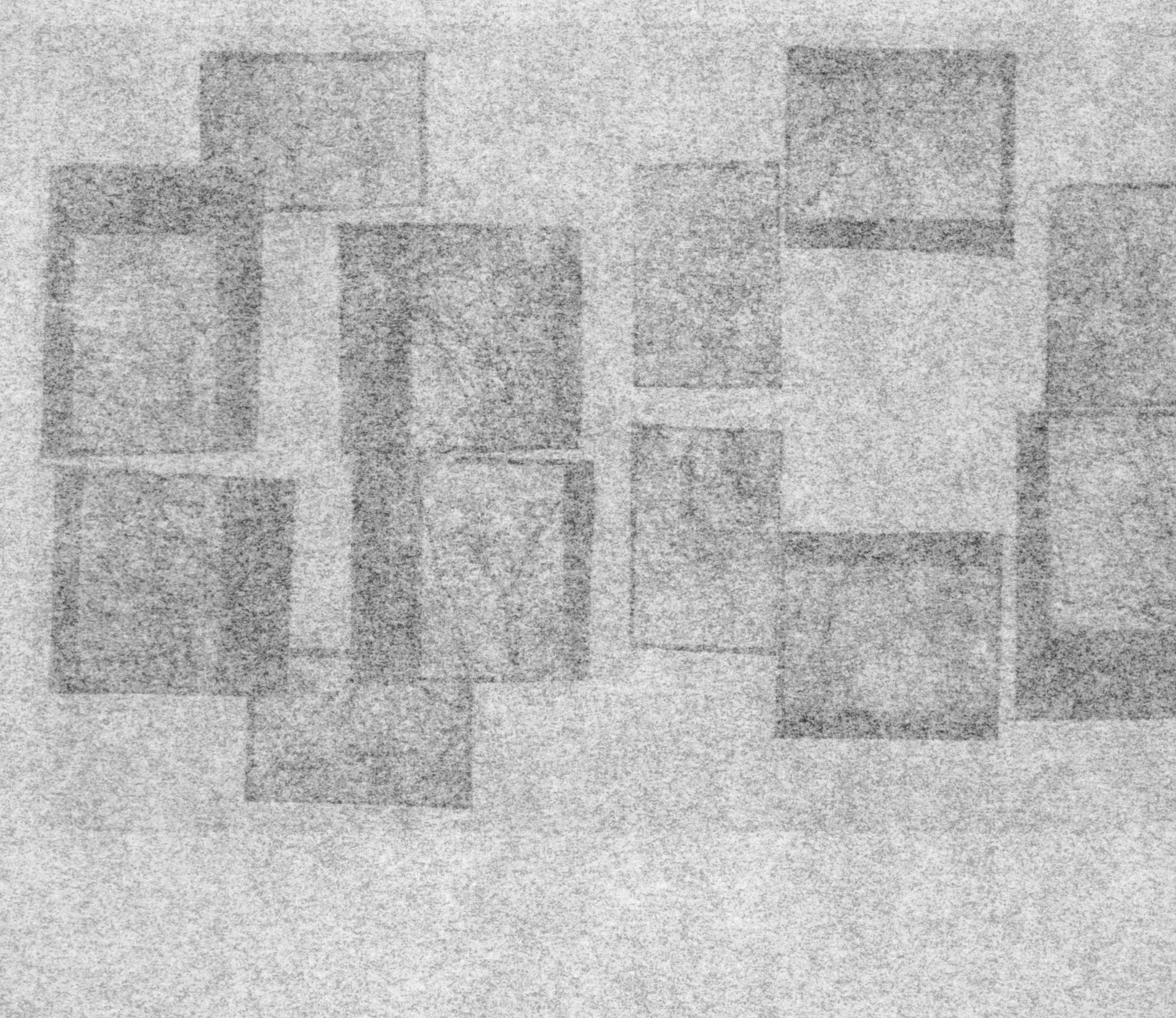

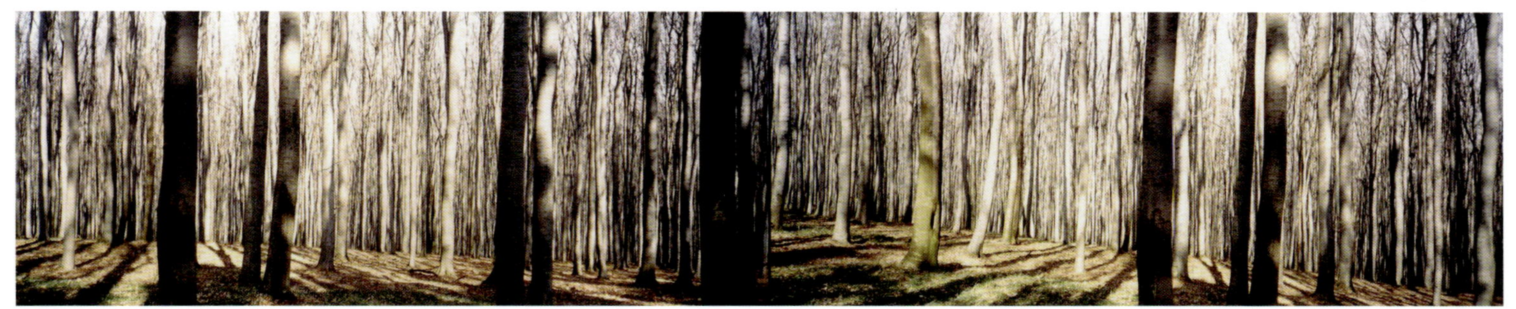

<u>17</u>   *Purkersdorf* 2001

22 *Winter* is part of a six-poem cycle of poems on winter by Friedrich Hölderlin (here translated by Michael Hamburger). In Birgit Jürgenssen's video the poem is read by Simon Frearson. **23** Cited in Thun-Hohenstein, »Everything Flows« (see n. 16), p. 15.

curtain, an installative element the artist used to construct a further visual layer through which the impression of the white image surface was reinforced. A static frame, a still image, street noise, a white snowstorm, filmed from the artist's studio window. Eight minutes long. After around four minutes, a voice-over. We hear Friedrich Hölderlin's poem *Winter*:

> When past, unseen the season's images are,
> Winter's duration comes to us again;
> The field is bare, the view seems milder far,
> And gales blow round about and showers of rain.
>
> A day of rest, such is the year's conclusion,
> A question's tone that seeks a complement.
> Then to our eyes the Spring's new growth is lent—
> So nature shines on earth in her profusion.
>
> Your humble and obedient servant
> Scardanelli
> April 24th 1849 **22**

The poem announces the halt of time, a temporality that is completely absent from the video. The viewer stares out of a window onto a white wall of snow. Nothing happens. There is no story to follow, no narrative. »It is the peace of nature,« of which Hölderlin writes in another poem, the peace of nature in snow-covered birch logs on the ground, the peace of the forest that we can also find in Jürgenssen's photographs *Purkersdorf* (ill. <u>17</u>) and *X-Mahl*, shown in this exhibition. The »exchange between literature and daily life«**23** cited above, an important tool in the thought and work of Birgit Jürgenssen, is recognizable in this video.

By presenting the video as a projection on a white curtain, Jürgenssen elicits a tactile (textural) pleasure, while the male voice gives the video an additional textual layer.

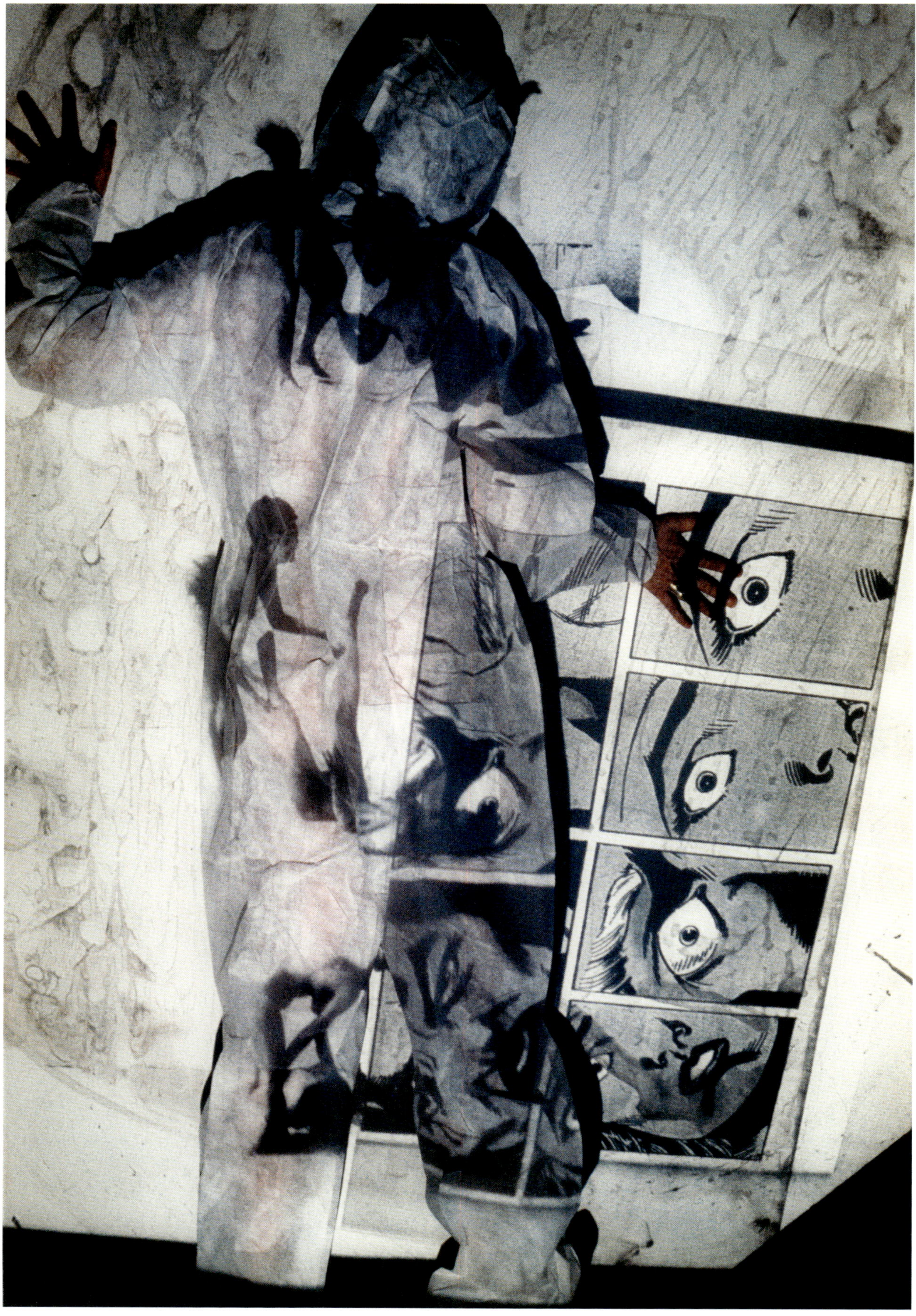

18 *Ohne Titel* 2001
    Untitled

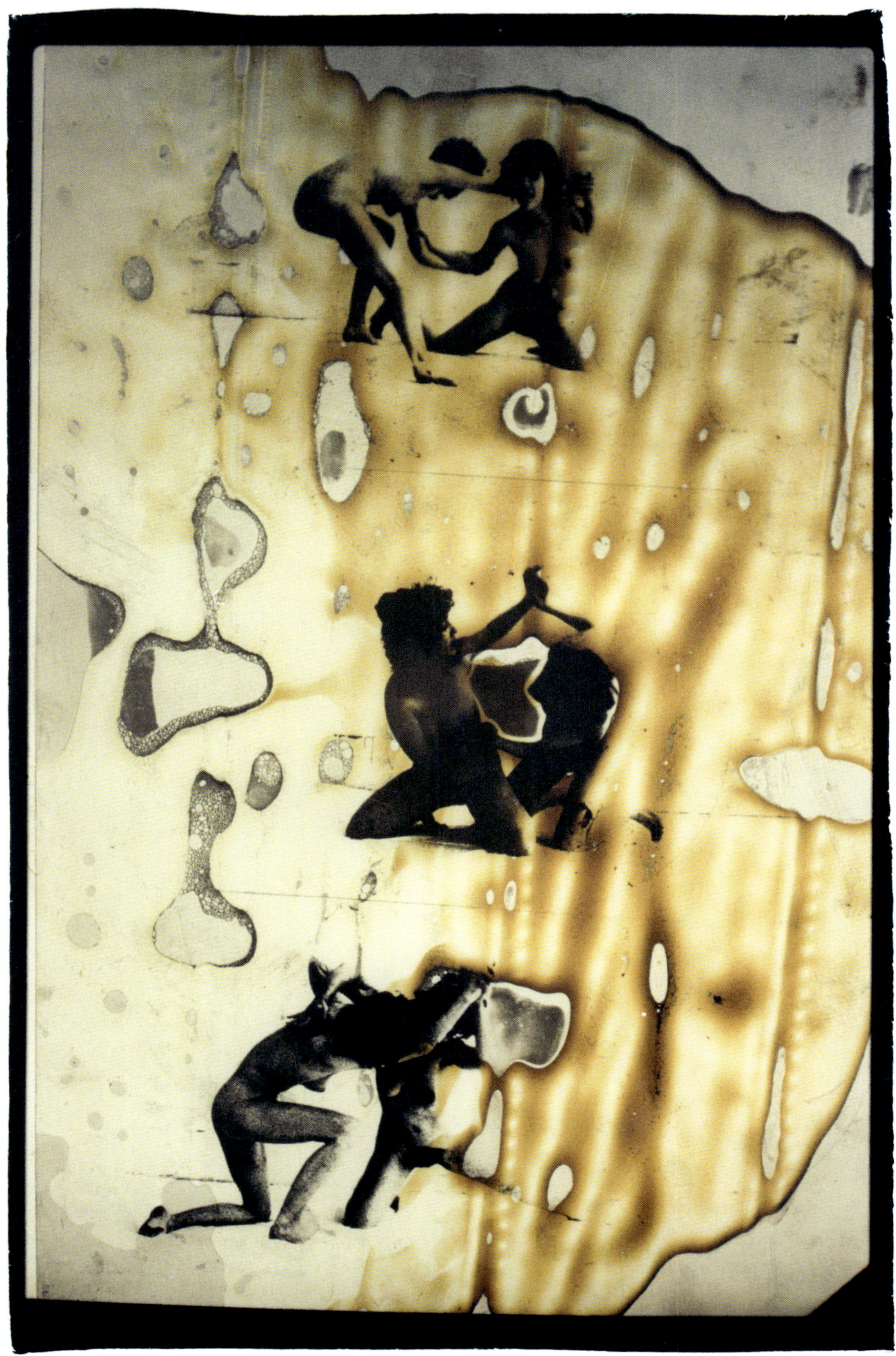

19   *Ohne Titel (Ranking)* 1999
        Untitled (Ranking)

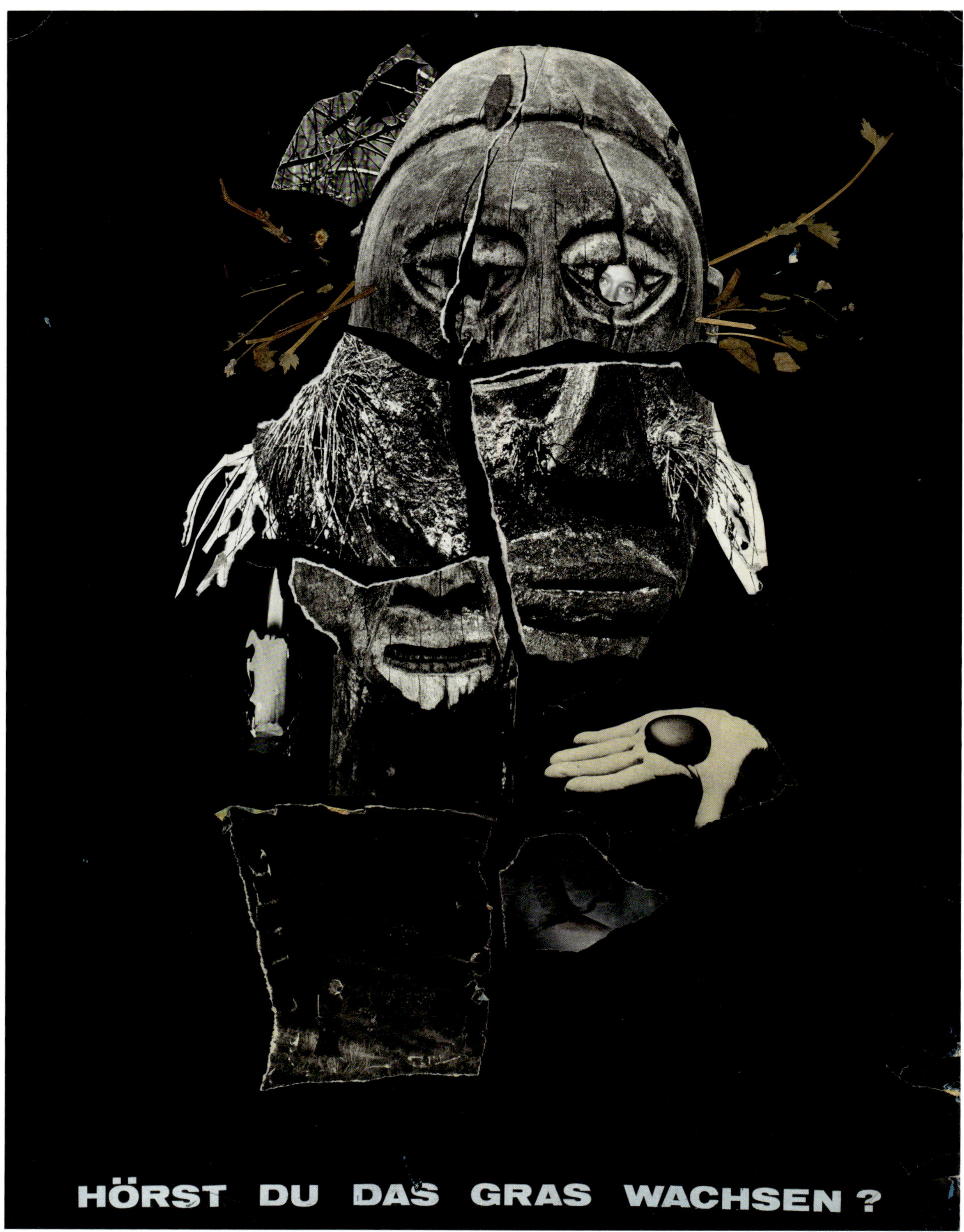

20   *Hörst du das Gras wachsen?* 1968
     Can You Hear the Grass Grow?

[24] From a text by Birgit Jürgenssen, »Dolce Tocco,« 2002, Estate Birgit Jürgenssen.
[25] Birgit Jürgenssen in conversation with Doris Linda Psenicnik (see n. 7).
[26] From a conversation on the art of Birgit Jürgenssen, »Birgit Jürgenssen: Kunst aus dem Zwischenreich …,« in *9 & 9*, exh. cat. Galerie Hubert Winter (Vienna, 1982), n.p. [translated].

Seeing, Hearing, Feeling.

Work with different layers was an important means of expression for Jürgenssen. Using light and dark, projection onto the body, liquids, or collages, she overlapped different layers. Covering a photograph with latex or textiles creates an optical, erotic, and above all tactile stimulation. Covering a photograph—the cool surface of photographic paper—with transparent gauze engenders a voyeuristic element and creates illusion in the face of reality. It would be good to push the curtain aside and take a look behind it.

Physical contact is the basic precondition for touching. »What we touch appears to be our sole reality. In this regard, the sense of touch has more significance for our belief in an external reality than the other senses. To touch is to make contact, *do not touch* is the greatest temptation.«[24]

For Birgit Jürgenssen, the use of several layers and levels leads to a focus of perception onto the nucleus.[25] One of these »condensed« photographs (which was also on show in the solo exhibition and still retain an air of mystery) is the digital photograph *Untitled* (ill. 18), which refers specifically back to an earlier series of works. *Rankings* (ill. 19) was made three years previously and shows naked women fighting; it is repeatedly drawn upon and cited in performative photography. In the new work, Jürgenssen does not project the fighting via overhead projector onto the wall and then photograph the projection; this time she herself enters the picture. Her white overalls turn her into a neutral »screen,« and the women's fighting takes place on her back. This is an agglomeration of levels and projection surfaces. In addition, Jürgenssen underlays the fighting scene with a comic strip showing pairs of eyes open wide in astonishment. Horrified, suffering, and afraid, these eyes mirror the emotions of the fight and stare directly at the viewers. Projections laid on top of one another, a collage technique that is ultimately concentrated into one photographic layer.

Interpretations and meanings of images and a narrative thread are not really clearly recognizable in Jürgenssen's final solo exhibition; hidden clues surprise viewers and develop initially an unexpected multifacetedness, both in terms of media and in terms of content. A diversity of media, the color white, and nature are the interconnecting elements throughout the exhibition, and the visual presence of the works and the restless gaze that Jürgenssen prompts are both quite powerful. »Art from the intermediary realm, privacy as the stumbling block, games as the challenge, symbolism with the key given only later and then taken away again.«[26] One key in the work of Birgit Jürgenssen is no doubt nature.

Can You Hear the Grass Grow?

If we take Lévi-Strauss's principle that archaic societies are superior to their Western counterparts due to their connectedness to nature, then it can be noted that this very awareness is an important and constant point of reference in the work and thought of Birgit Jürgenssen. Nature is not simply a connecting element in the exhibition: it is rather also the narrative, the inspiration, and the constant—the beginning and the end in Jürgenssen's work.

In 1968 Jürgenssen created, *Can You Hear the Grass Grow?* (ill. 20), one of her very earliest works. *Untitled* (ill. 22), the last photograph by Birgit Jürgenssen, was taken just six days before she died in 2003. These two works can be seen as the parenthesis within which the artist's oeuvre sits. In the collage *Can You Hear the Grass Grow?* we can already see Jürgenssen's formal interest in bringing together different levels of image, a practice that she was to explore right to the end of her career. In later years, this no longer manifested in sticking together images from her rich store but in bringing individual image layers together on one and the same visual level—the level of the photograph. The collage, one of modernism's most characteristic and influential techniques, was already used in synthetic cubism in 1912—a stylistic means initiated by Pablo Picasso and Georges Braque. A connection between Jürgenssen and Picasso is not in any way surprising,

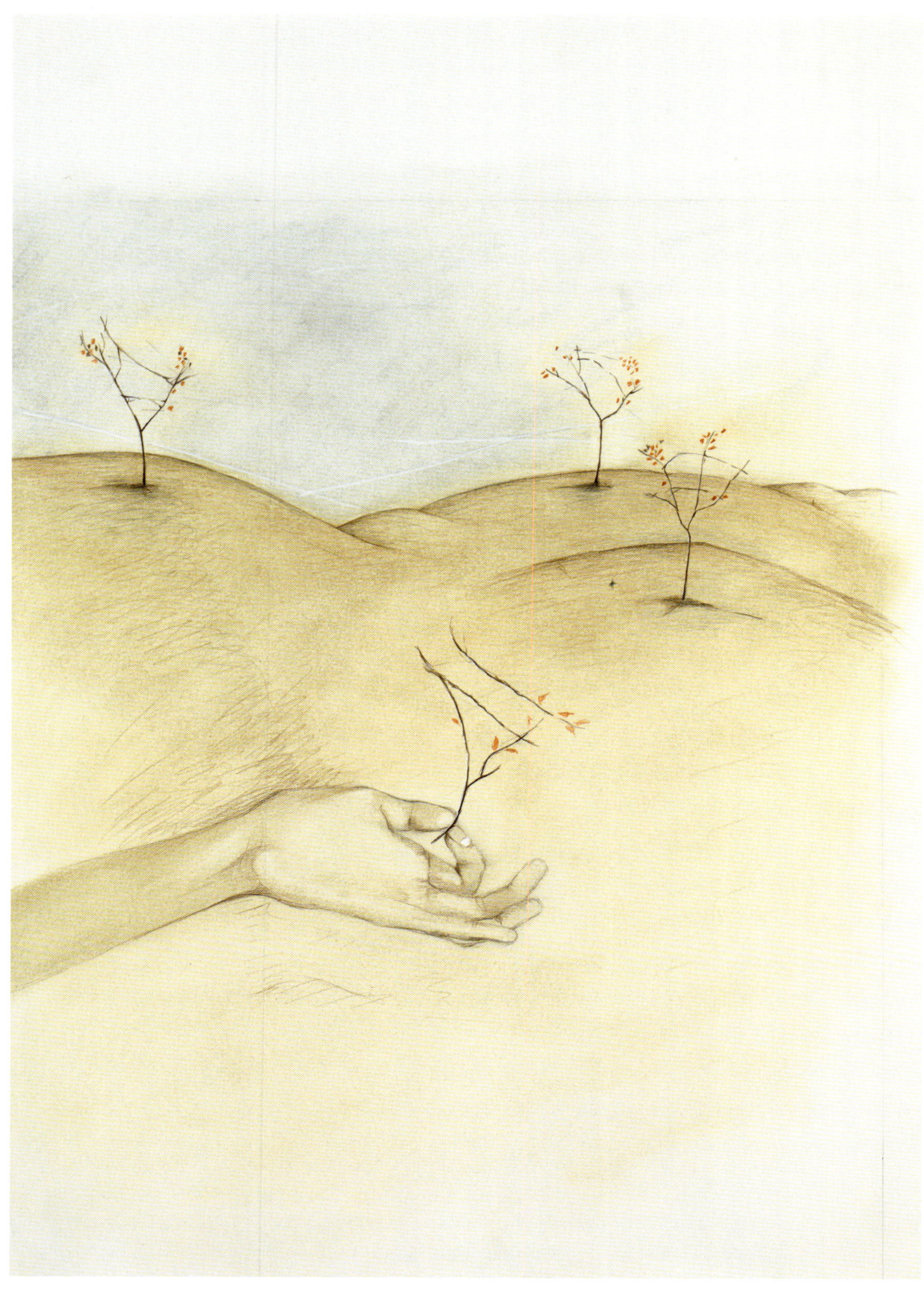

21 *Lebenslinien – Bäumchen* 1977
Lifelines – Little Trees

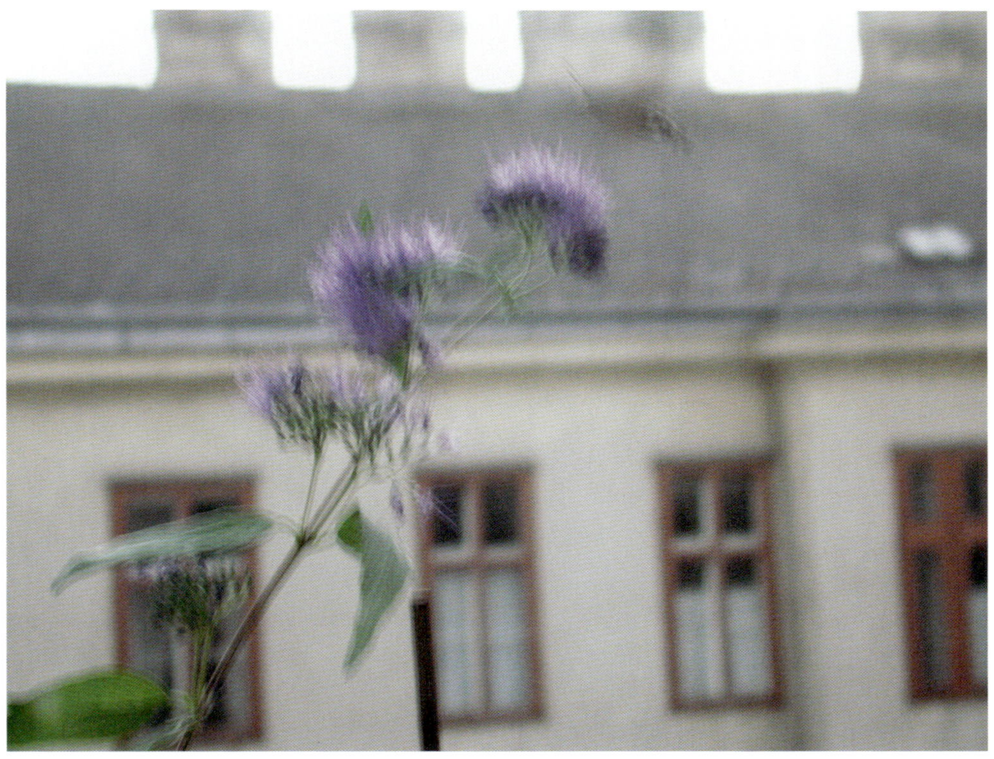

22   *Ohne Titel* 2003
        Untitled

27 Didi-Huberman,
Ähnlichkeit und Berührung
(see n. 3), p. 28.

as she got to know his work at an early age and began to imitate it. In her childhood she drew her first sketches in a school exercise book, the fascinating work of an eight-year-old that she light-heartedly called *BICASSO Jürgenssen* (see p. 117). As a child she had the nickname »Bi,« enjoying a playful symbiosis with the name Picasso, and she filled the pages of this thin school book with visual citations from the work of the Spanish painter. This was the first Jürgenssen sketchbook, later published as a facsimile.

The multilayered nature of the collage together with the absolute silence implied by the title *Can You Hear the Grass Grow?* is a very clear illustration of Jürgenssen's connection to and inspiration from nature. A self-portrait alongside various other cutouts, put together from her own stock of images, allows us to sense the artist's points of reference and interests at this time. It is the »the morphological features, the accidents, and the individual solutions«[27] that Jürgenssen's artistic work brings forth, making any reading of it highly complex. The burning candle can be seen as an iconographic symbol of life, the flying crane is a holy bird in Japanese mythology and honored as a symbol of happiness and longevity. Stones are seen as symbols for endurance, strength, and power. Jürgenssen opted for a favorite stone of Georgia O'Keeffe, which the latter displays in her open palm. This American painter and her symbolic and deep relationship with nature must have greatly impressed Jürgenssen, and O'Keeffe figures a second time on the lower margin of the picture.

Human palms are unique and mysterious. Drawn by nature. In O'Keeffe's case covered over by nature. Birgit Jürgenssen was also fascinated by these so-called lifelines and brought these *lines* to *life* in her drawing *Lifelines – Little Trees* (ill. 21). Little blossoming trees that are planted in nature grow from a sensitive spot. The inside of the outstretched hand remains empty and open. These lines, which are supposed to reveal a person's fate, are passed on and over to nature. The drawing of the lines of the hand follows no logical pattern. In the black-and-white photograph these fateful lines seem to be covered up by nature, and in the fragmentary drawing of 1978 *Palm Lines / Lifelines / Map for the Fortune Tellers* the work's title gives a name to this mythical place (ill. 42).

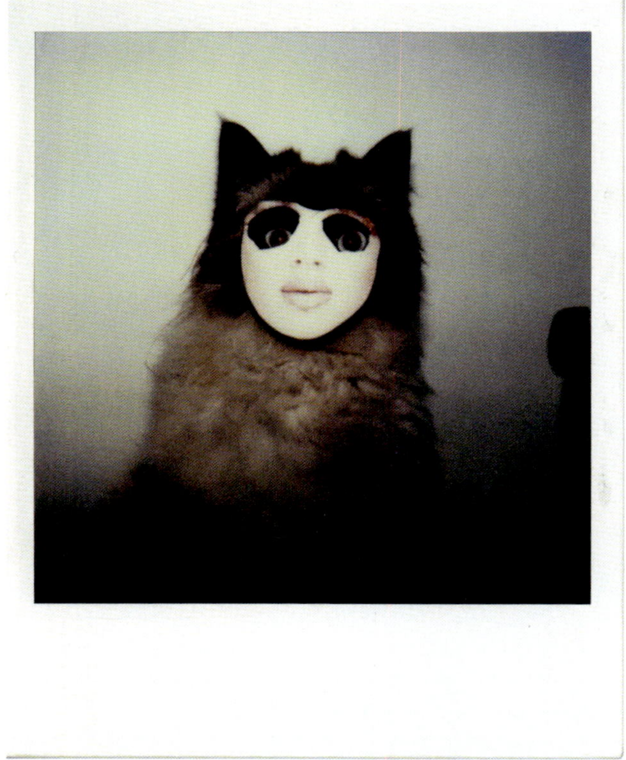

<u>23</u> *Ohne Titel (Olga)* 1979
Untitled (Olga)

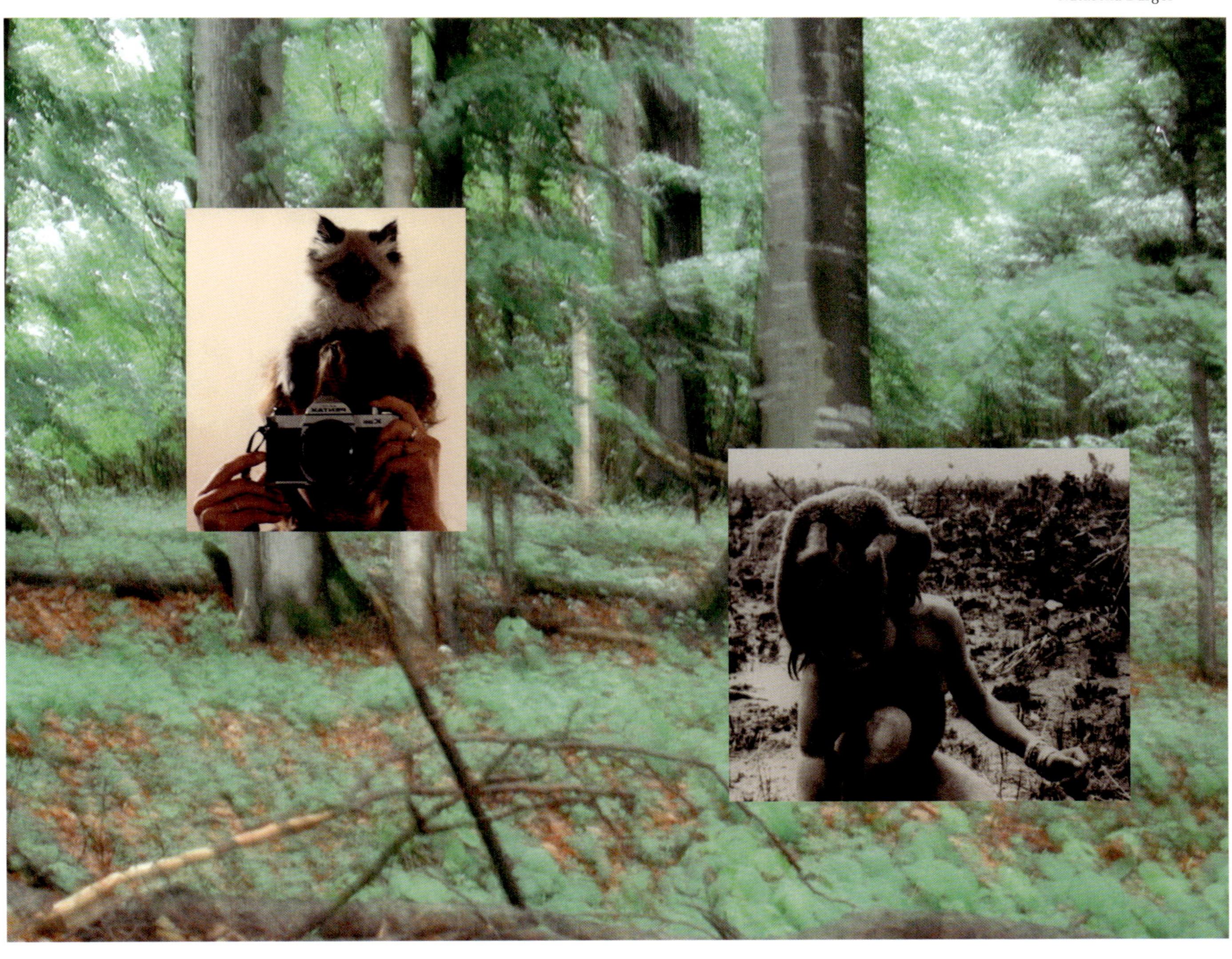

<u>24</u>   *Ohne Titel* 2002
       Untitled

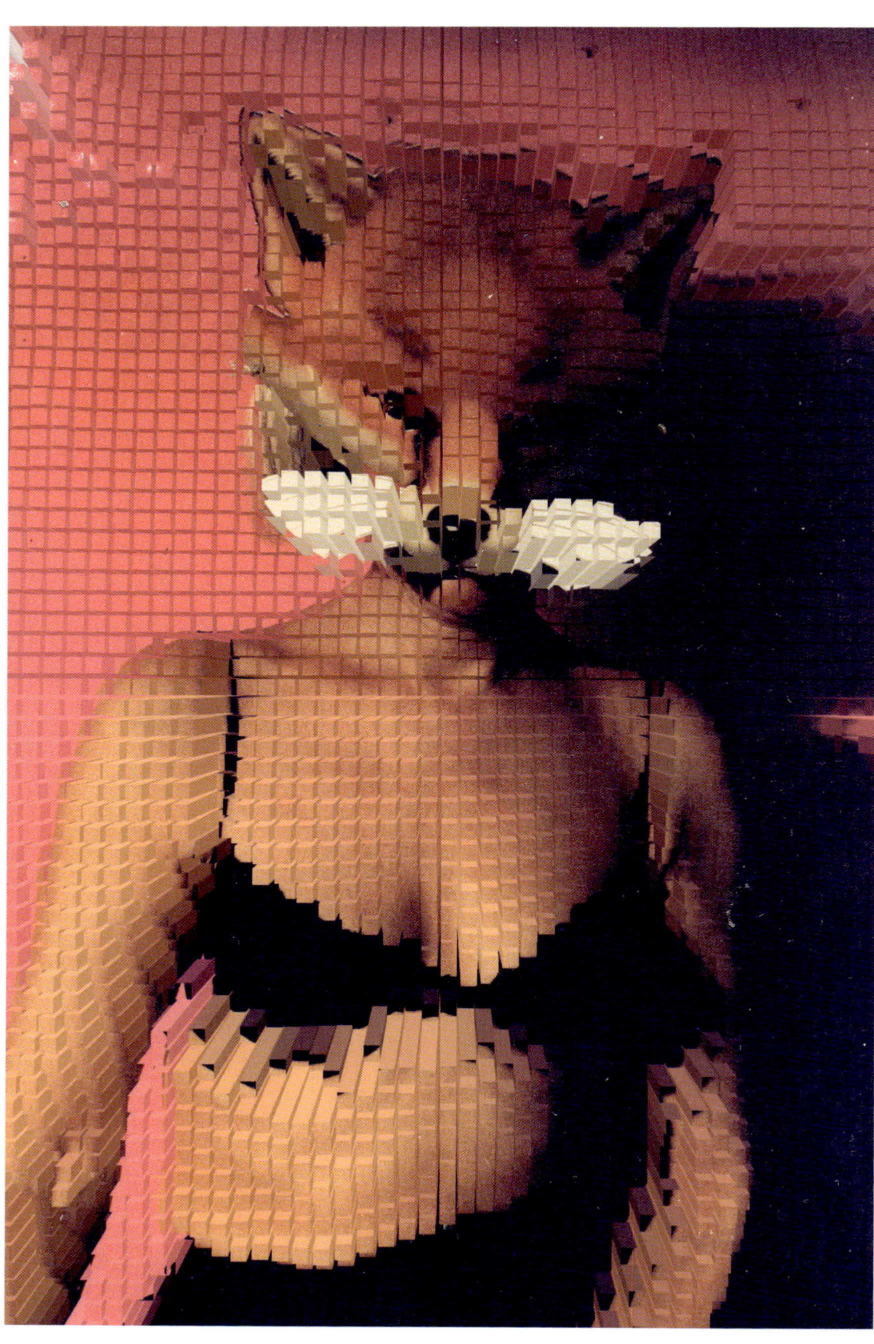

25 *Ohne Titel* 2001
    Untitled

The Savage Mind

28 Claude Lévi-Strauss,
in Adalbert Reif, ed.,
Anworten der Strukturalisten
(Hamburg: Hoffmann
und Campe, 1973),
pp. 118–19 [translated].
29 An indigenous
tribe in the Amazon.
30 See Claude Lévi-Strauss,
*Saudades do Brazil:
A Photographic Memoire*
(Seattle: University of
Washington Press, 1995).
31 Birgit Jürgenssen
in conversation with Doris
Linda Psenicnik
(see n. 7).
32 Birgit Jürgenssen,
in Manfred Schmalriede,
*Erfundene Wirklich-
keiten*, exh. cat. 2. Internationale Foto-Triennale,
Esslingen, 1992
(Stuttgart: Cantz, 1992),
p. 19.

»What I have defined as the ›savage mind‹ cannot be specifically ascribed to anyone in particular, be that any part or type of civilization. It has absolutely no predictive use. I would rather say that I intended the idea of the ›savage mind‹ to identify the system of postulates and axioms that are needed to justify a code that would permit translating the *other* into *our* and vice versa, with the least possible loss—the entirety of conditions, therefore, under which we can best understand each other; of course there remains a residue.«[28]

Birgit Jürgenssen's »savage mind,« which she used to justify her own codes, can be explained in terms of her talent for detailed observation, her highly reflective critical approach, and her explorative way of working. Throughout her career, Jürgenssen was fascinated by Claude Lévi-Strauss's *Tristes Tropiques* of 1955 and *The Savage Mind*, and she used these ideas in her work as a recurring source of inspiration. Her system of coordinates, discussed above, consisting of a strong bond with nature, poetic visual layers, her unique and inspired collage technique and her fascination with ethnology and anthropology, photography as her strongest medium, the motif of the human-animal, and the mask as a recurring means of expression—also as a symbol of the camera taking a photograph—can be clearly seen in a hitherto unpublished digital collage (ill. 24) in the artist's estate. Jürgenssen wrote about this in one of her notebooks:

Cat portraits: Olga+I+camera
Olga+mask
I+fox mask
C.L.Strauss > child + monkeys
THE CAMERA AS MASK – Fichte

One starting point to be found in Jürgenssen's large collection of materials is a set of photographs documenting Claude Lévi-Strauss's journey to the Amazon in 1939. A detailed view of a black-and-white photograph shows a small girl from the Nambikwara people[29] with her pet, a small woolly monkey, on her head.[30] Jürgenssen also portrays herself with her own pet on her head, her cat Olga, which features in many other works as a transmitter of the artist's uncanny hybrid creatures (ill. 23). She also notes down »I+fox mask« as a further focal point of her 2002 collage. Did she perhaps mean her self-portrait with the little fur? That is certainly a starting point for her »savage mind,« but here she really is referring to a self-portrait with a fox mask. Preparing her exhibition *I Don't Know*, Jürgenssen once again deployed the digital grid graphic technique she had used for the image of a zebra in an experiment that was not to end in a finished digital photograph and in this case, too, was merely to serve as a written guide for the »use of masks« (ill. 25).

The final comment, »THE CAMERA AS MASK – Fichte,« opens up a further trace that can be pursued Jürgenssen's work. This leads to Hubert Fichte, a German author and ethnologist. Jürgenssen was interested here in a photo portrait by Leonore Mau (ill. 26) showing Fichte with an African mask. His face is half covered, and he is holding the mask in front of it like a camera. The ethnologist presents himself half masked, his identity thus not completely gone. Jürgenssen does not use the mask as a camera but rather the camera as a mask, the piece of optical equipment that is inserted between the observed and the observer. The camera as a key competence in her work is deployed self-reflectively and self-ironically. The subject is reminiscent of early Jürgenssen photo series, taken in front of the bathroom mirror and intended as a means of self-analysis (ill. 27). In this late work, she is more interested in the act of masking, hiding oneself behind the camera, and it is also »interesting to reflect on the identity of photography.«[31]

The comparison of these two photographs does not merely illustrate Jürgenssen's interest in Lévi-Strauss; »it is also the confrontation of a reality with another version of the same reality.«[32] Integrated into nature, the two photo excerpts attain their common level, basis, and origin. As had been the case in *Purkersdorf*, made for the *I Don't Know*

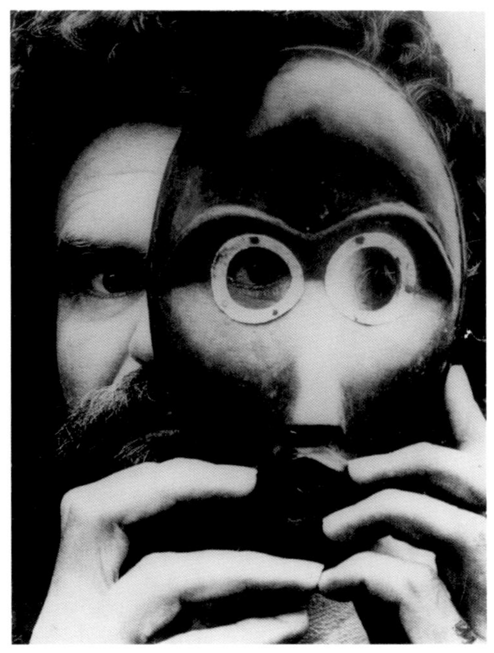

26   Leonore Mau *Hubert Fichte with Dan-Mask* 1979
© bpk / S. Fischer Stiftung / Leonore Mau

exhibition, Jürgenssen concentrates solely on the presentation of a section of forest, and here, with an interest in different vanishing points, confusion, and an anthology of seeing, she uses the »piece of forest« for further computer-generated collages (ill. 28, 29). With erotic and voyeuristic moments, Jürgenssen applies an ironic and critical eye as she integrates her black-and-white images into the forest scene.

»But, whether one deplores or rejoices in the fact, there are still zones in which savage thought, like savage species, is relatively protected. This is the case of art, to which our civilization accords the status of a national park, with all the advantages and inconveniences attending so artificial a formula; and it is particularly the case of so many as yet ›uncleared‹ sectors of social life, where, through indifference or inability, and most often without our knowing why, primitive thought continues to flourish.«[33]

Birgit Jürgenssen's last exhibition is »sure« evidence of her irresistible quality and the multifacetedness of her use of media and means of expression. Unpredictably and knowingly, Jürgenssen operated in her own time. What remains is: »I am.«—»It is personal achievements that count. In the end, there is only the good drawing, the good photo, the good piece of work.«[34]

[33] Claude Lévi-Strauss, *The Savage Mind* (London: Wiedenfeld and Nicolson, 1966), p. 219.
[34] Birgit Jürgenssen in conversation with Heidemarie Seblatnig, in Seblatnig, *Einfach den Gefahren ins Auge sehen. Künstlerinnen im Gespräch* (Vienna: Böhlau, 1988), pp. 158–61, here cited from the website Estate Birgit Jürgenssen, accessed September 7, 2018, https://birgitjuergenssen.com/bibliographie/interviews/seblatnik1986.

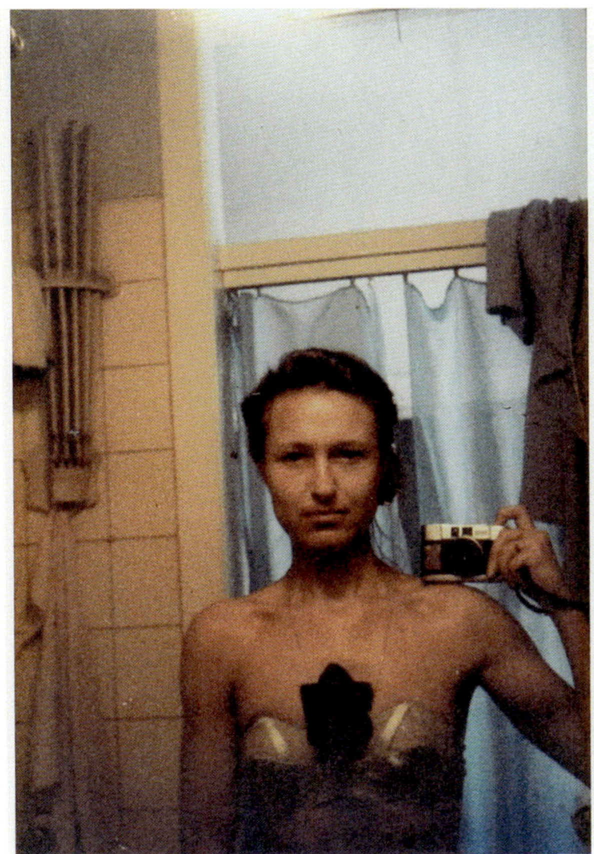 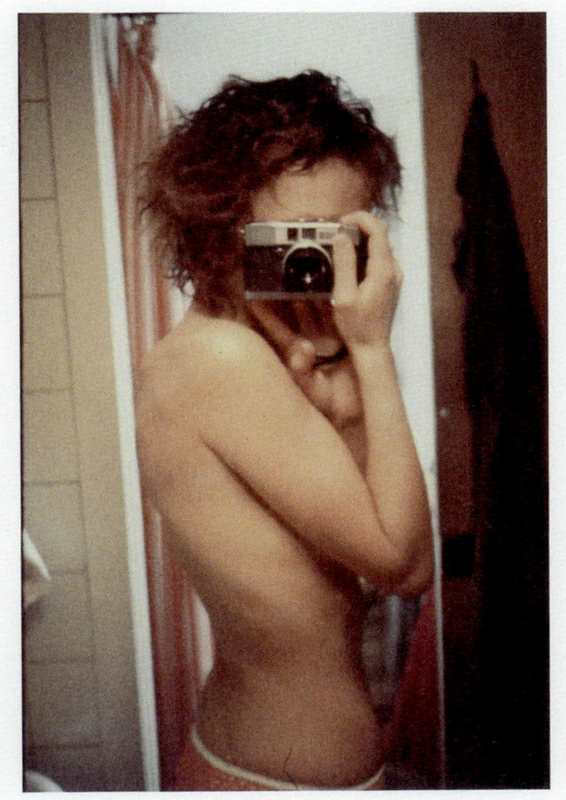

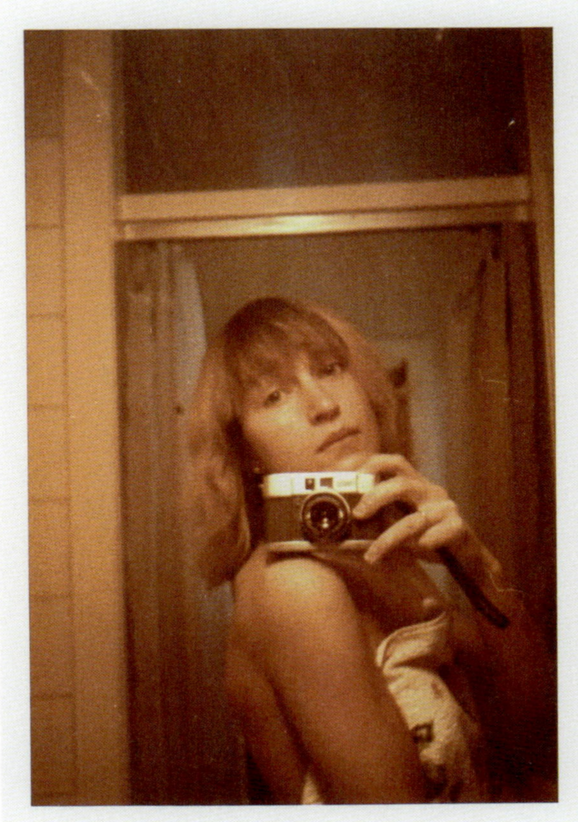 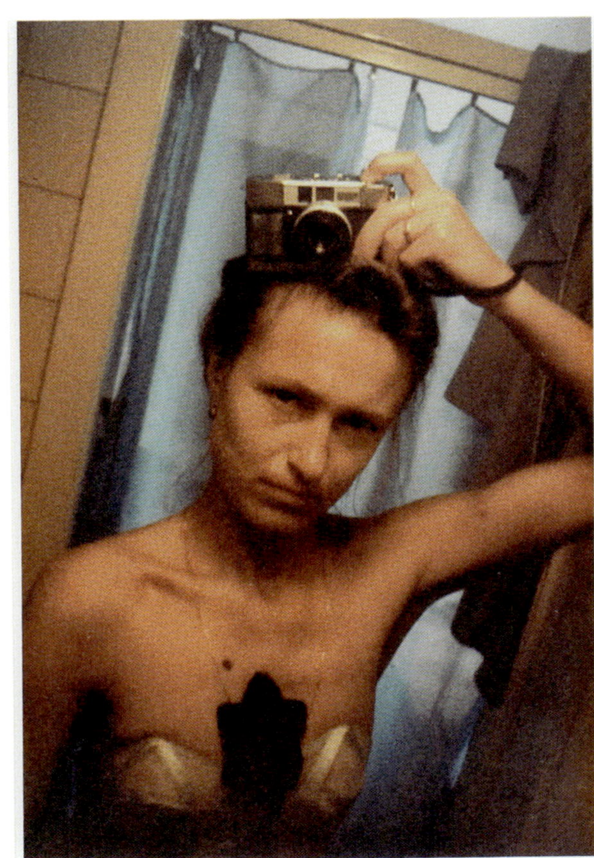

27   *Ohne Titel* 1973
     Untitled

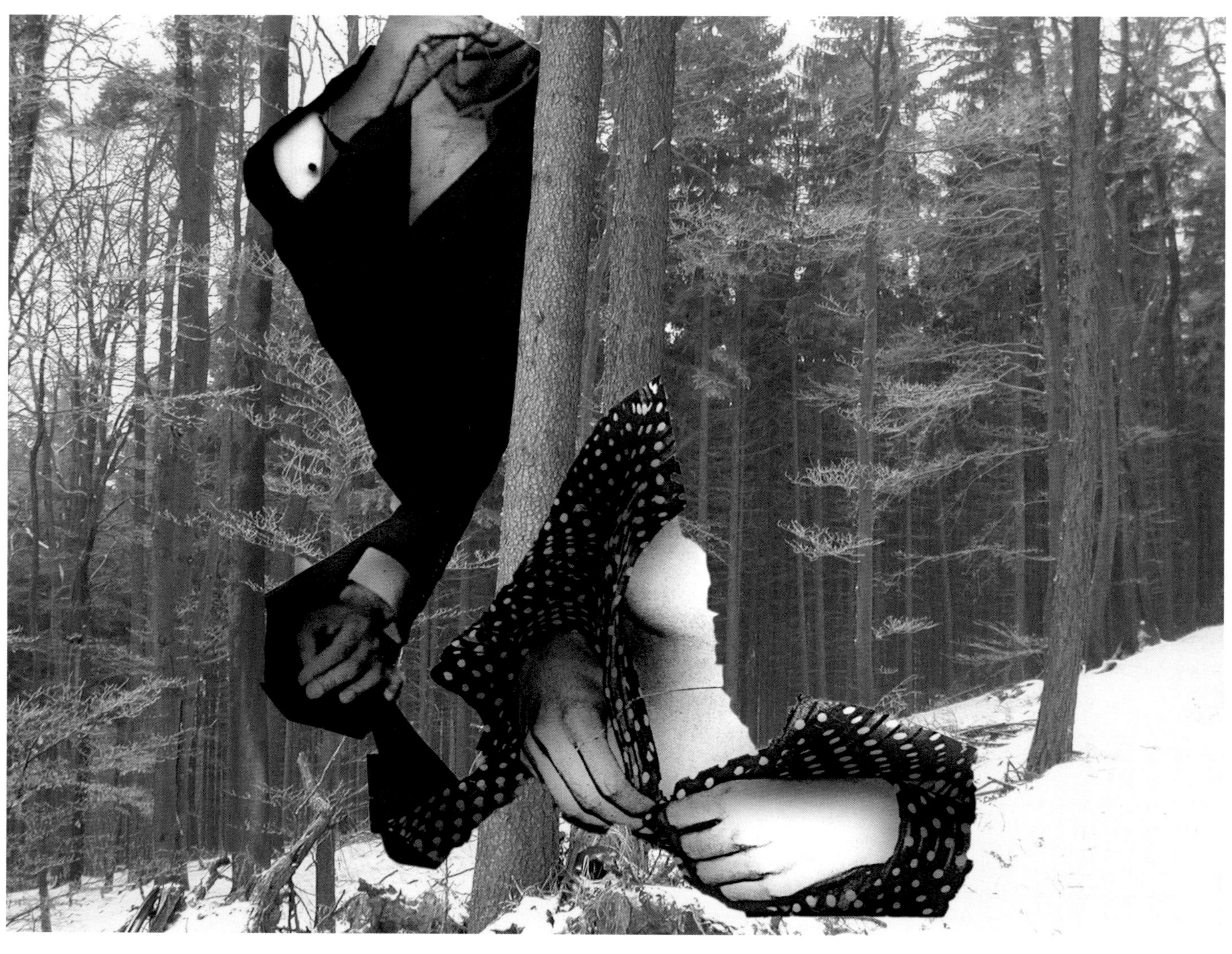

28   *Ohne Titel* 2002
     Untitled

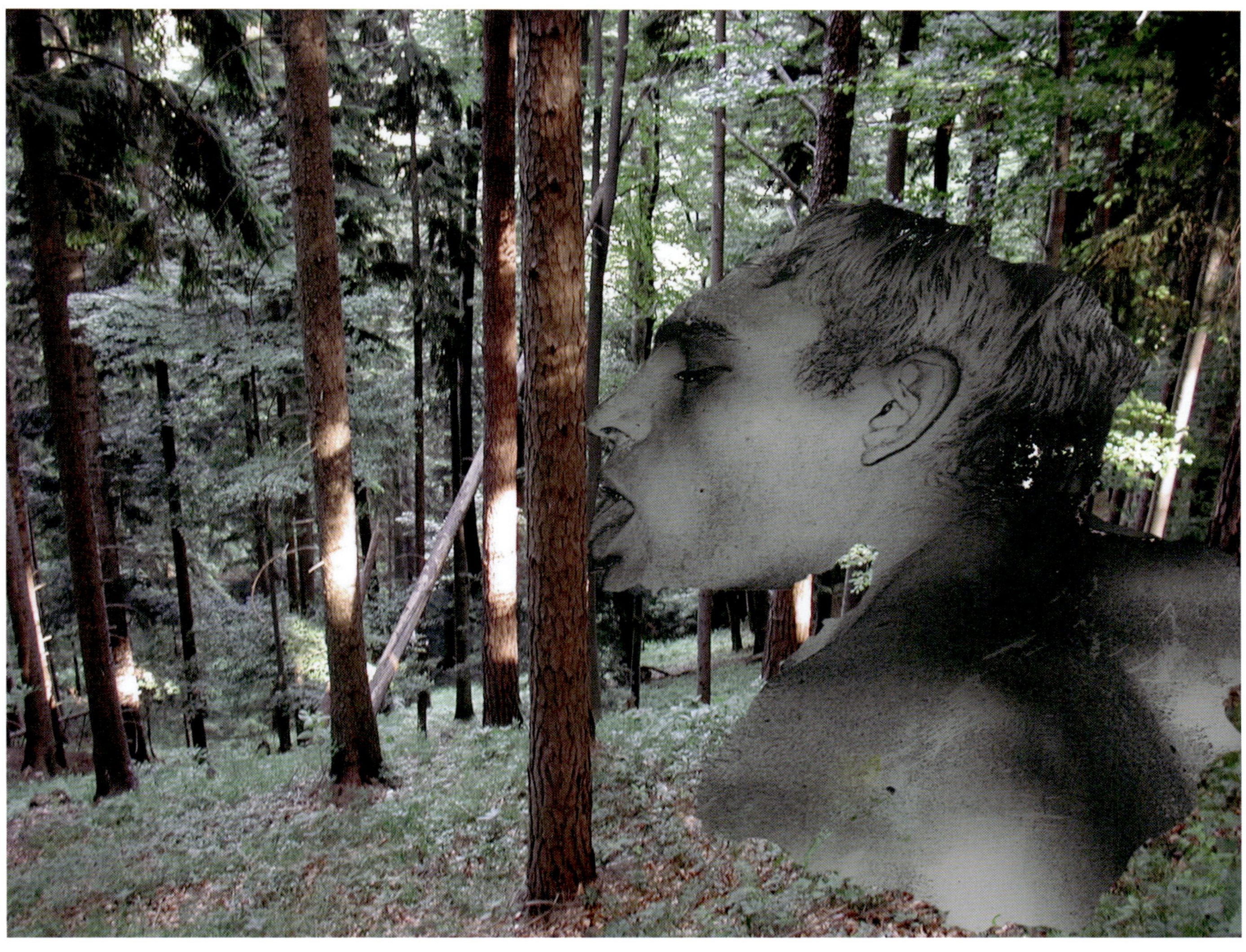

29   *Ohne Titel* 2002
      Untitled

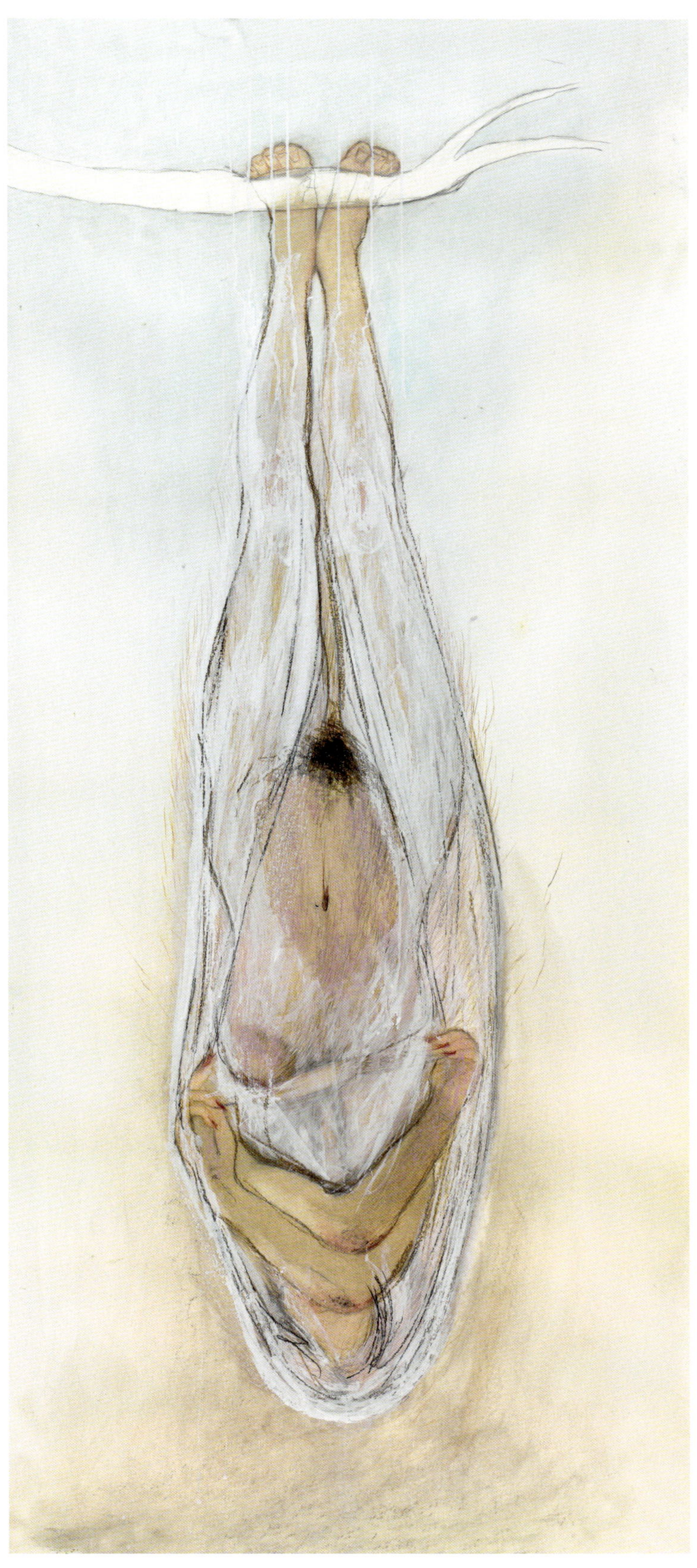

<u>30</u>   *Ohne Titel* 1979
      Untitled

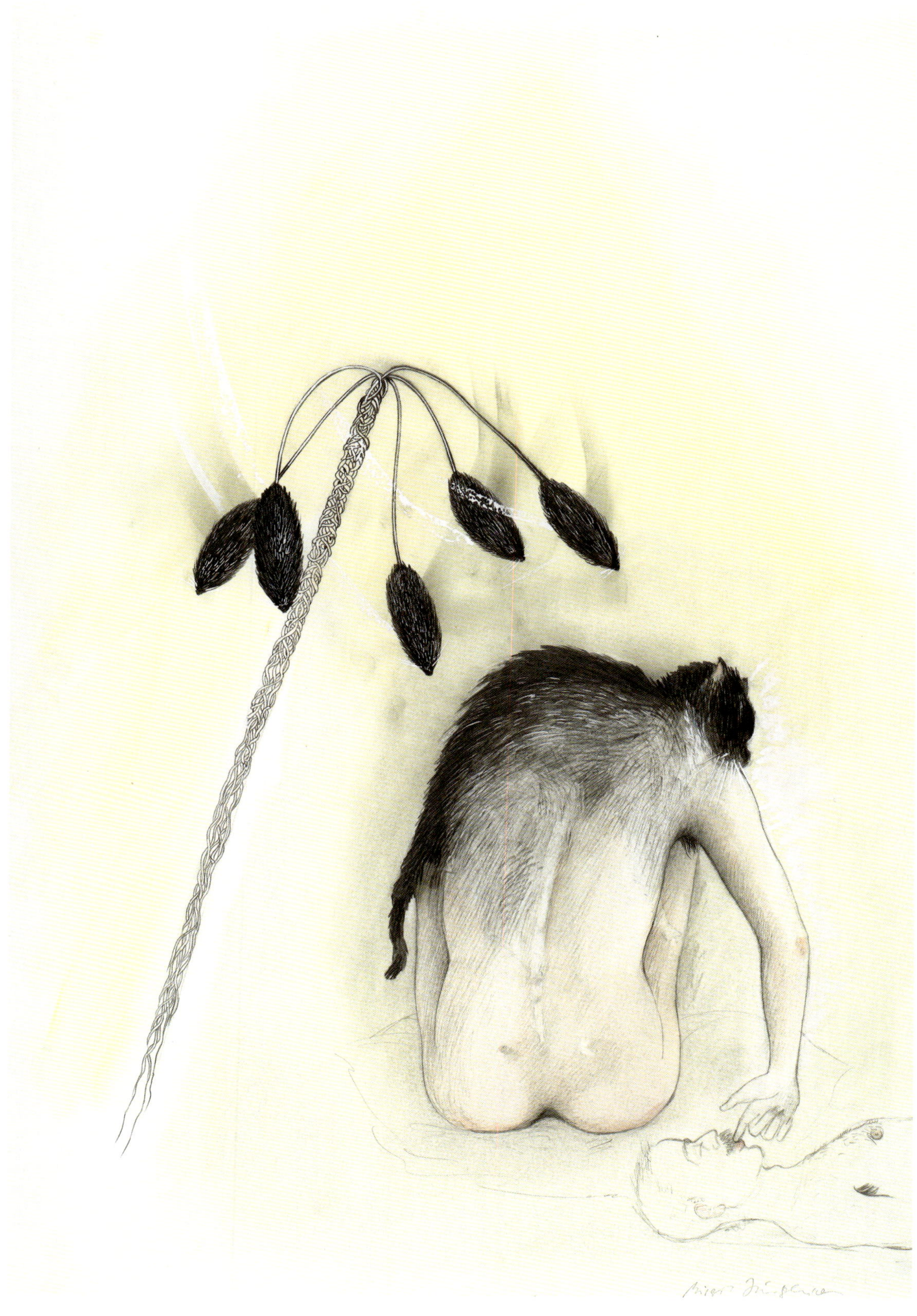

31 *Ohne Titel* 1977
Untitled

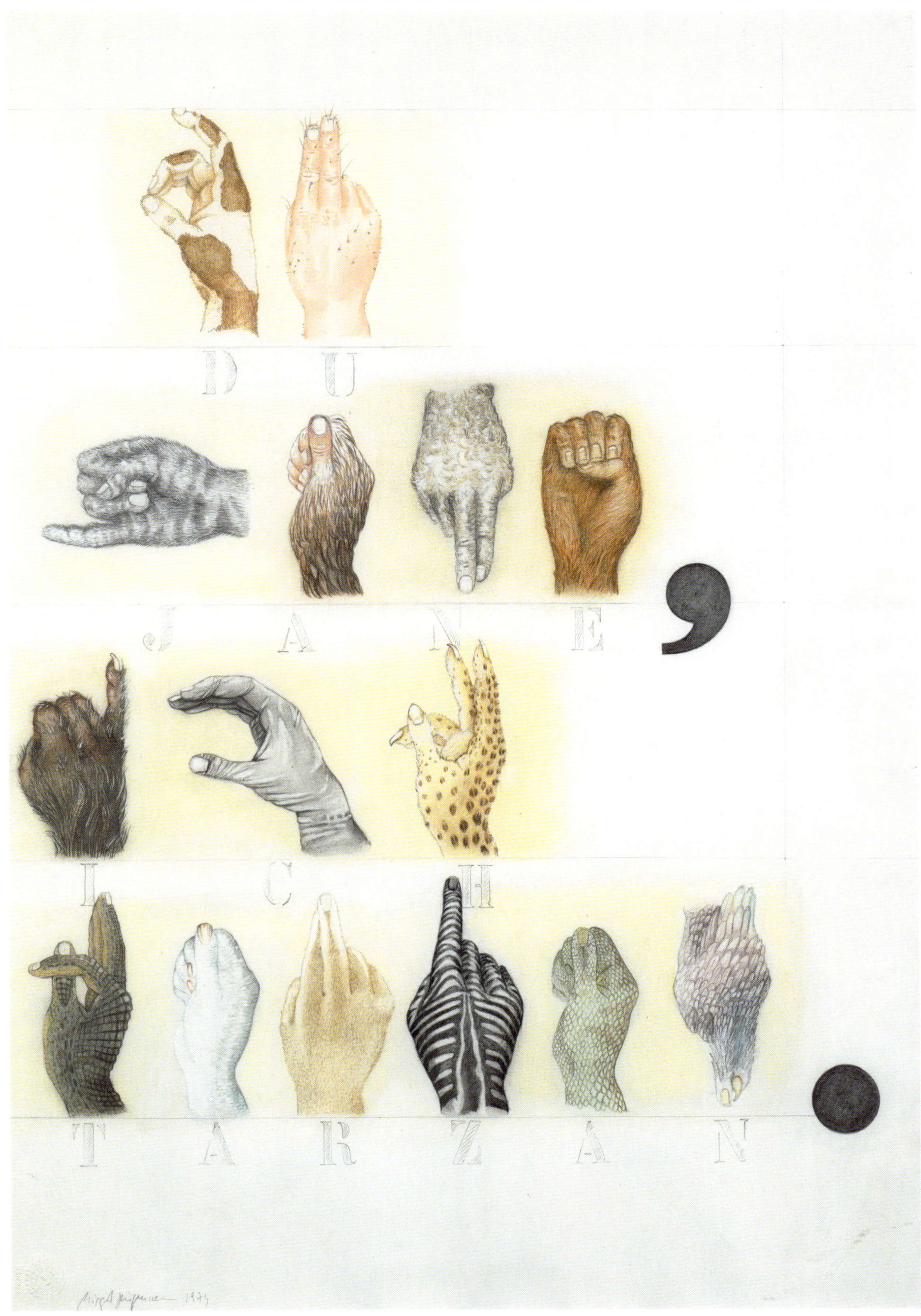

32 *Du Jane, Ich Tarzan 1974*
    You Jane, Me Tarzan

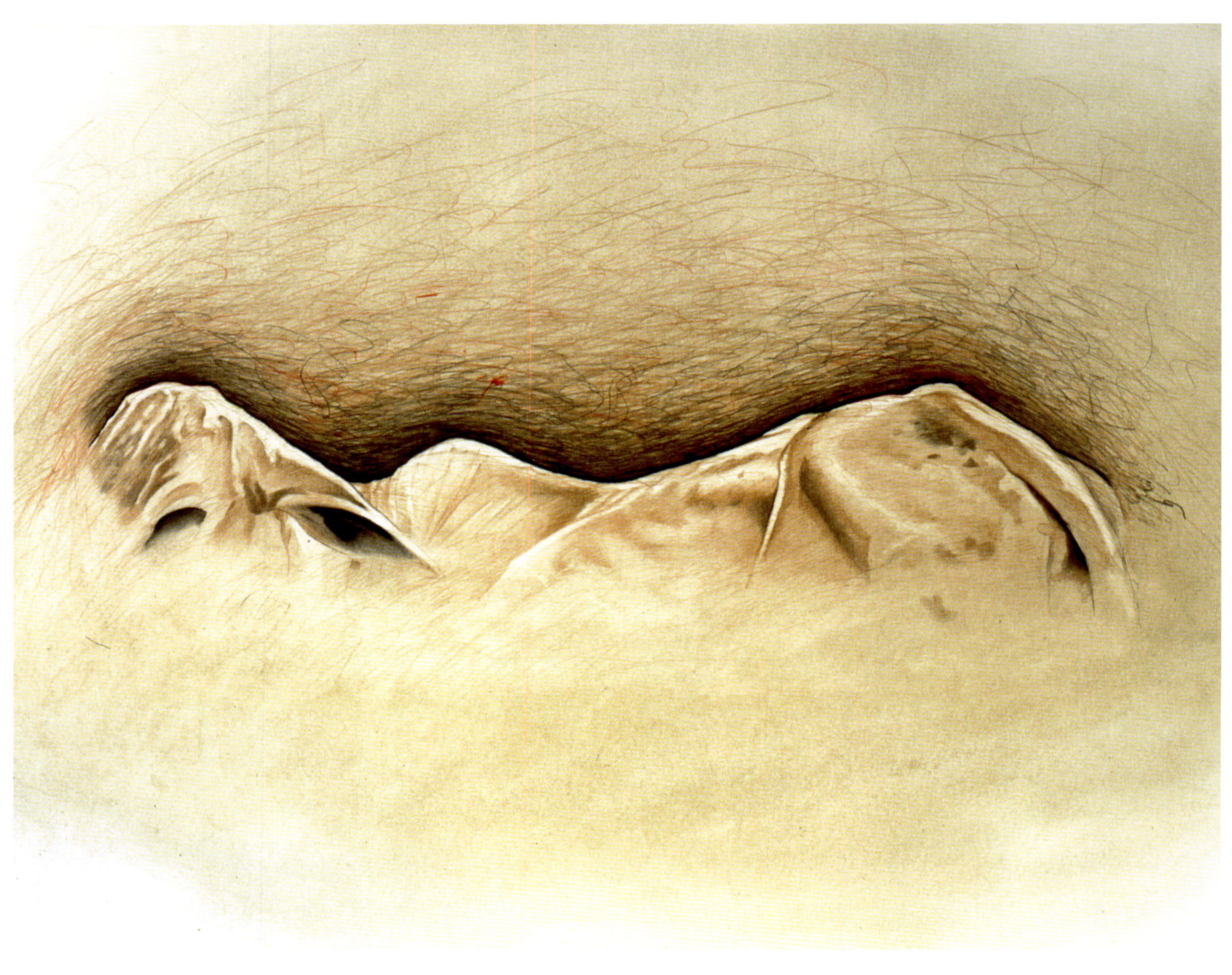

33   *Rückenlinie eines Tieres* 1978
     Dorsal Line of an Animal

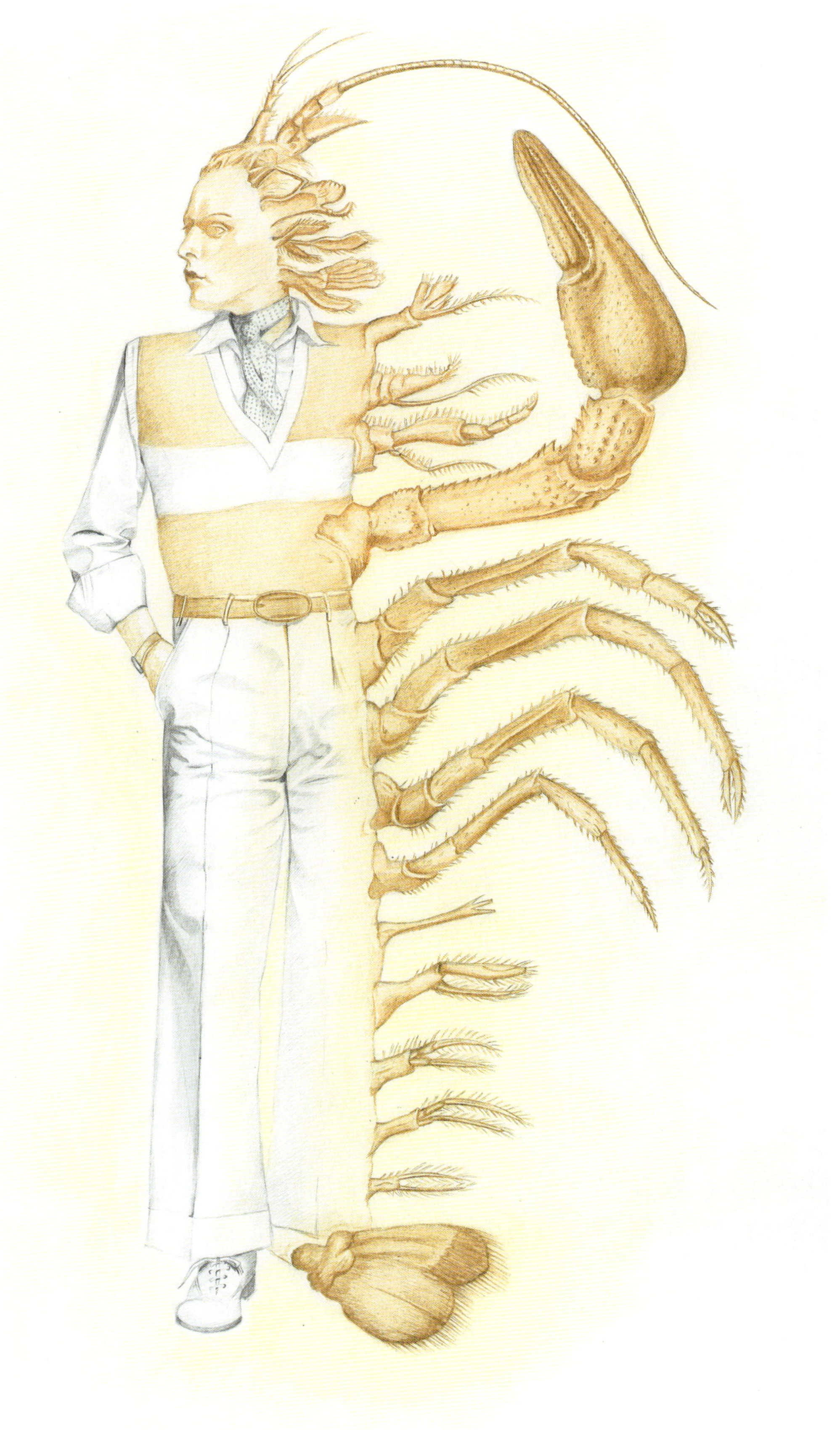

<u>34</u> *Fehlende Glieder* 1974
Missing Limbs

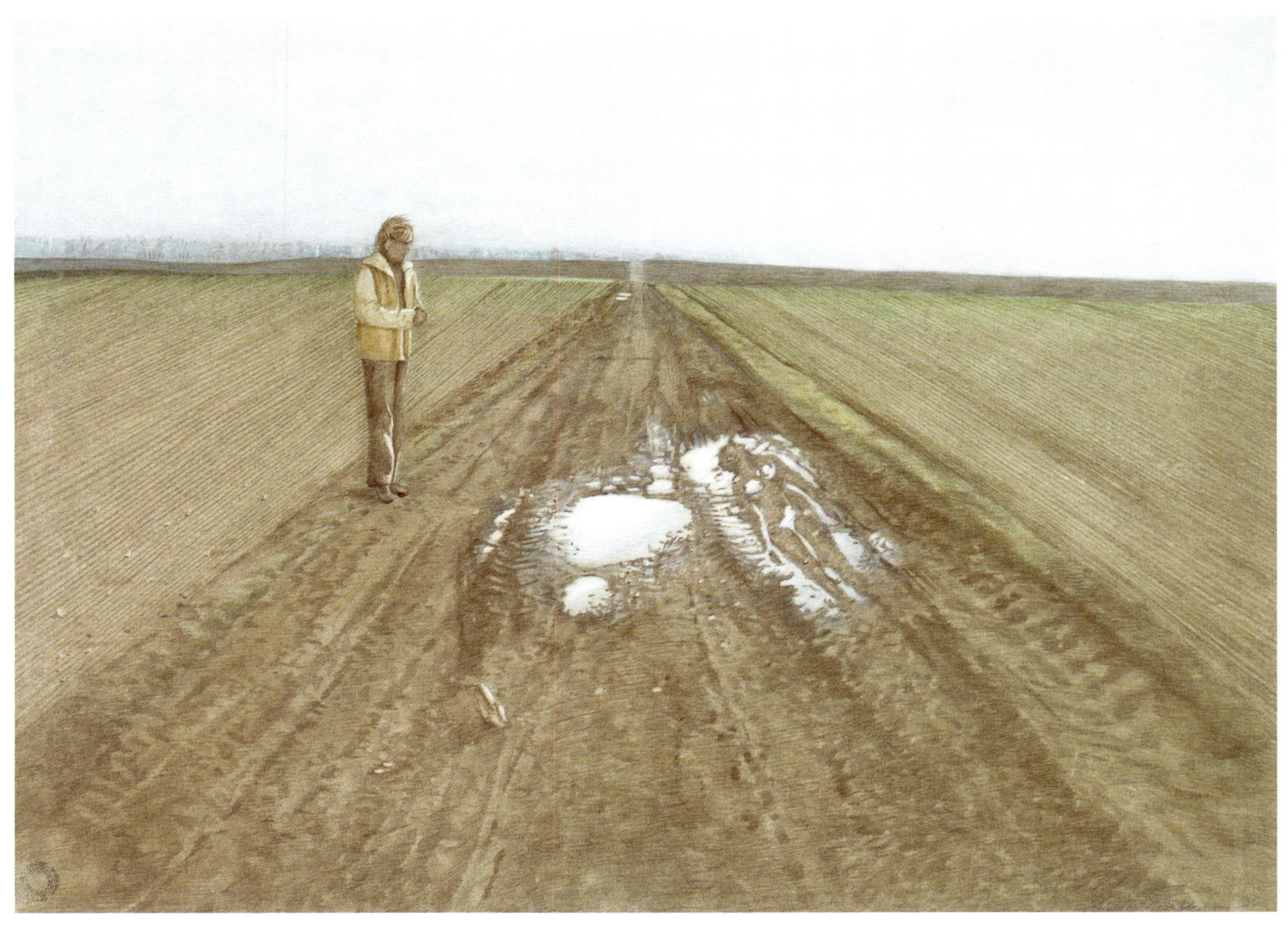

35 *Ohne Titel* 1977
    Untitled

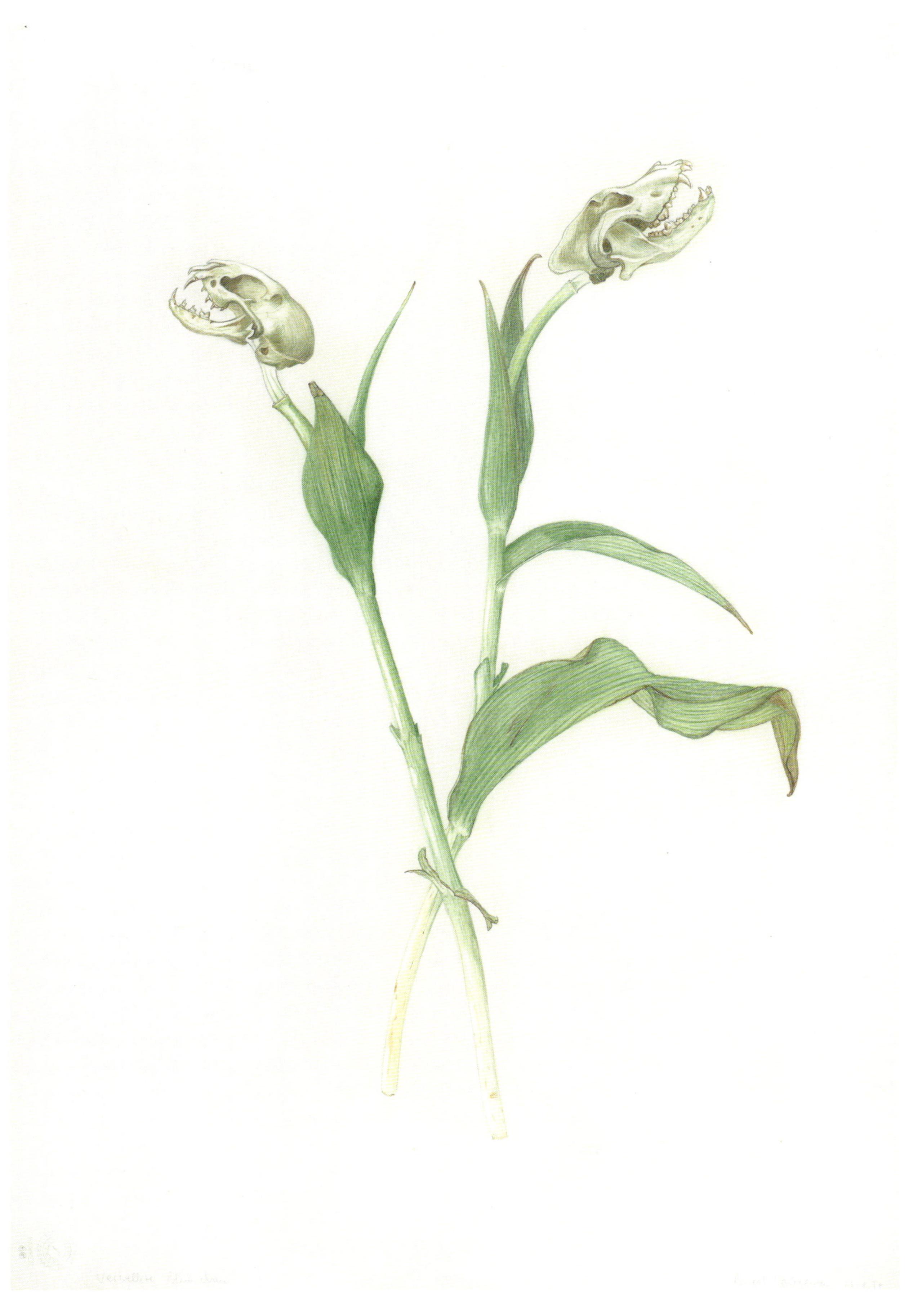

36 *Verwelkte Blümchen* 1974
Withered Little Flowers

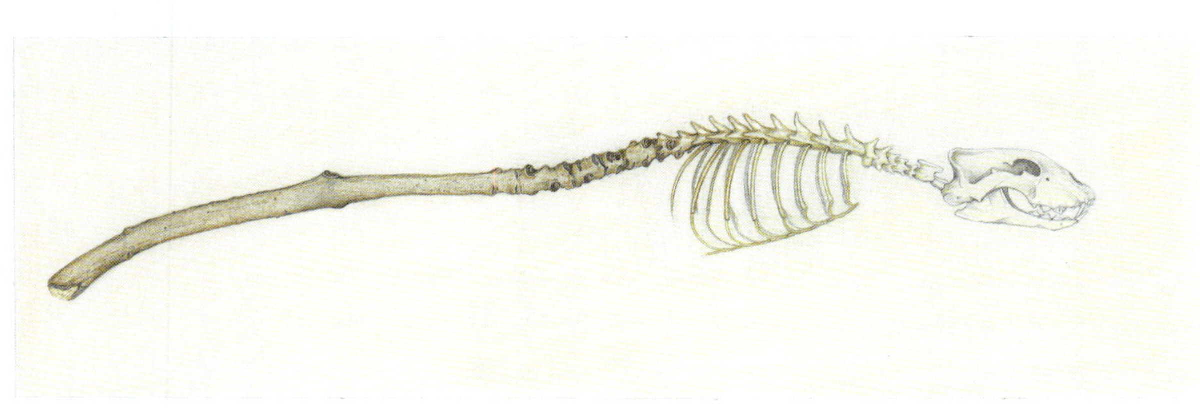

 Metamorphose I 1974
Metamorphosis I

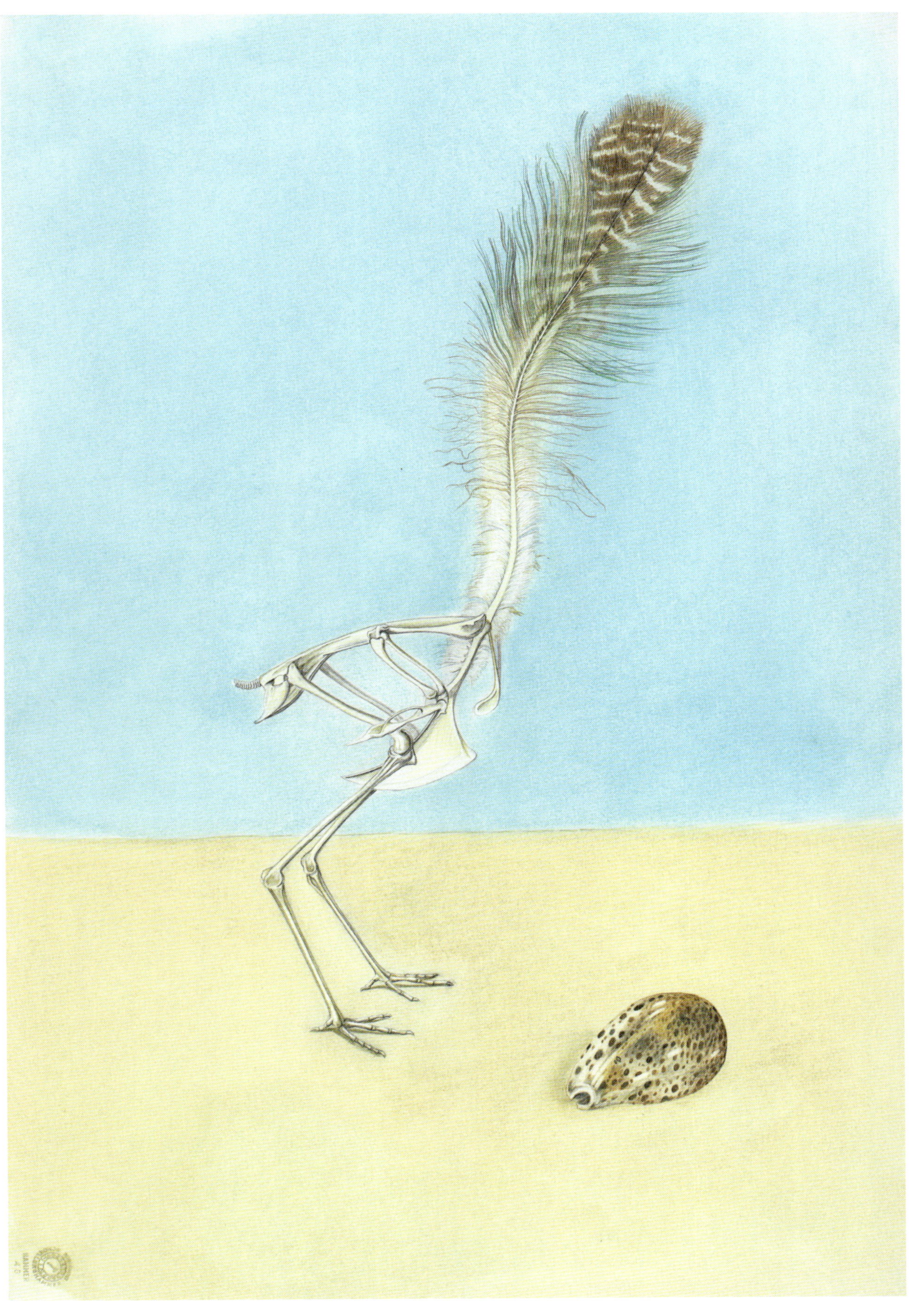

38   *Ohne Titel* 1974
      Untitled

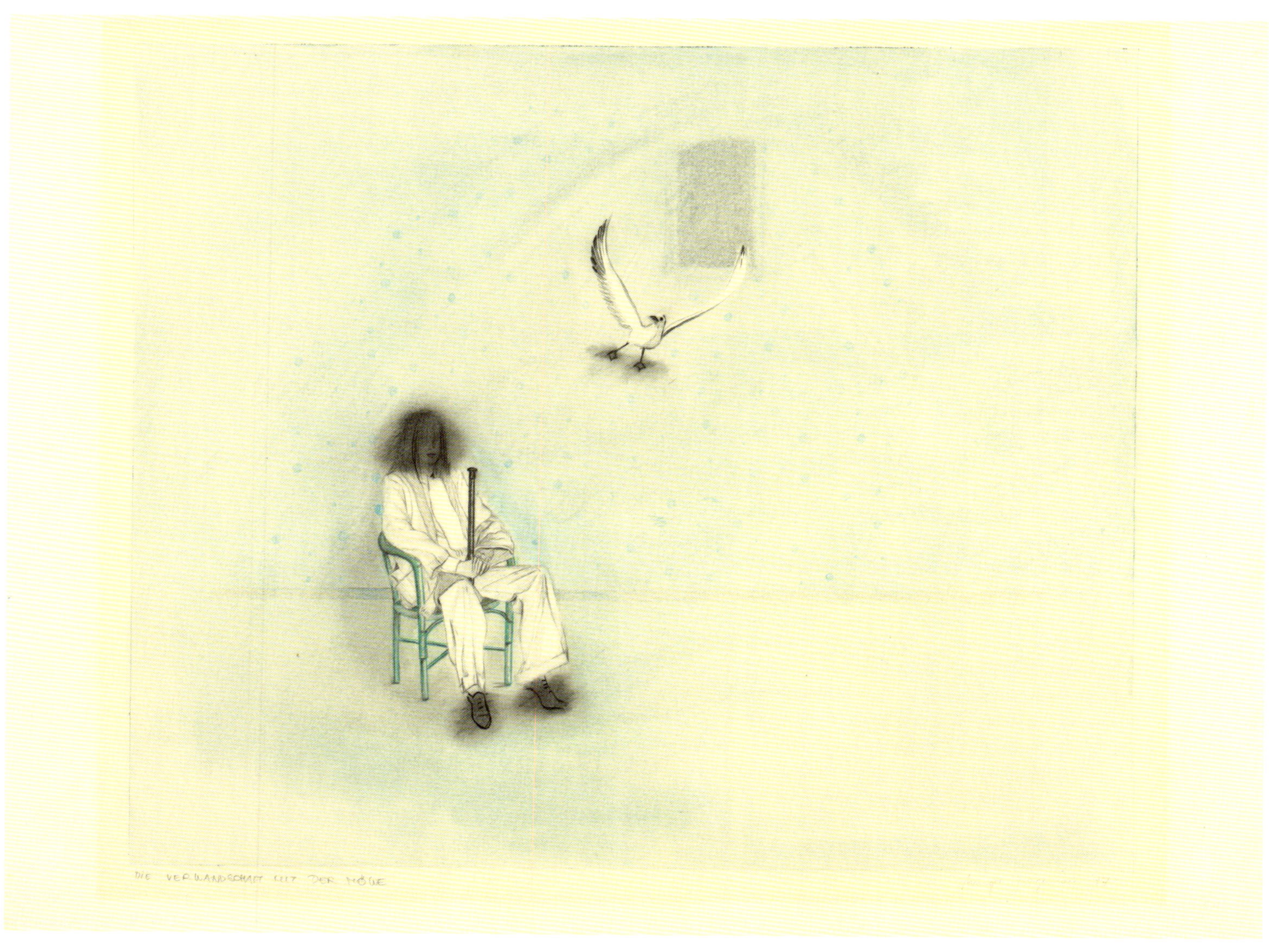

39 *Verwandtschaft mit der Möwe* 1977
Kinship with a Seagull

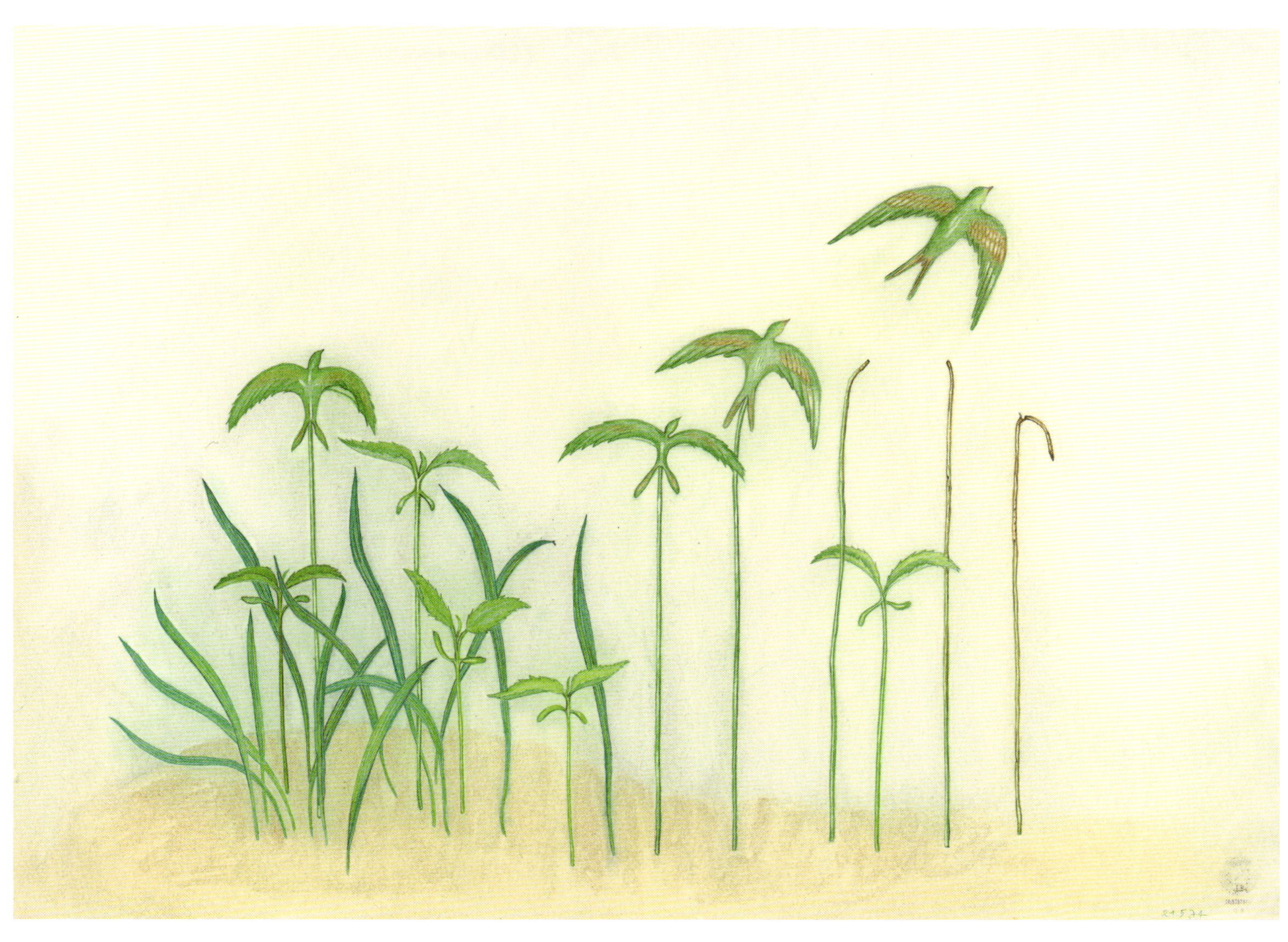

40 *Ohne Titel* 1974
Untitled

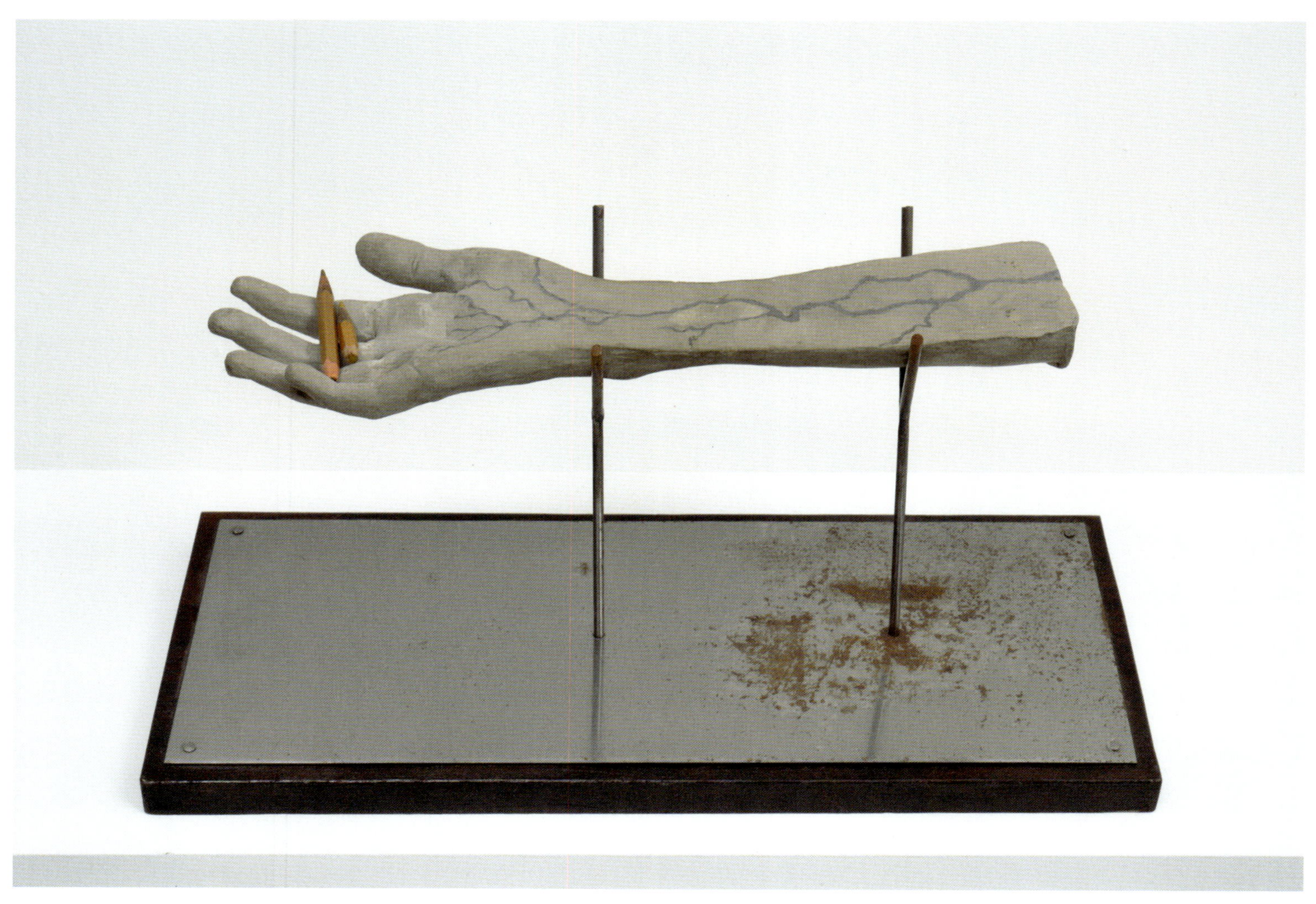

41   *Ohne Titel* 1974
      Untitled

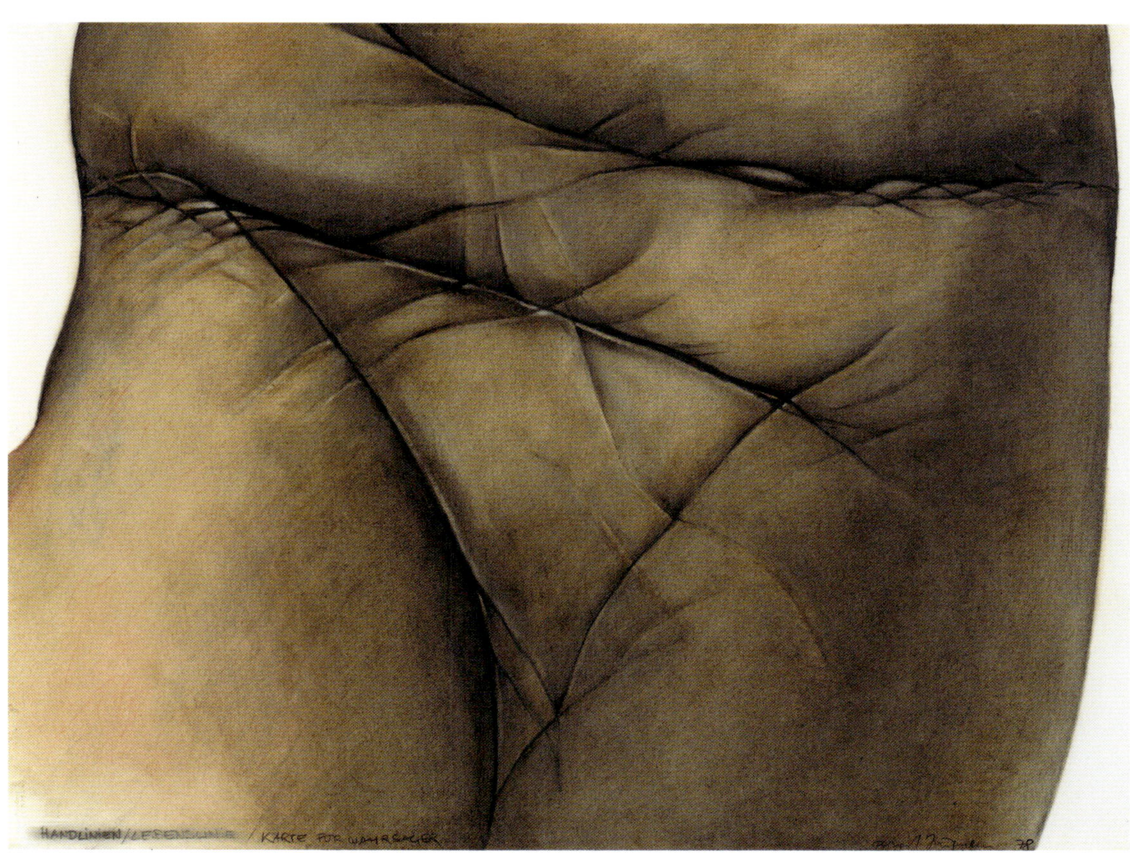

42 *Handlinien / Lebenslinie / Karte für Wahrsager* 1978
Palm Lines / Lifeline / Map for the Fortune Tellers

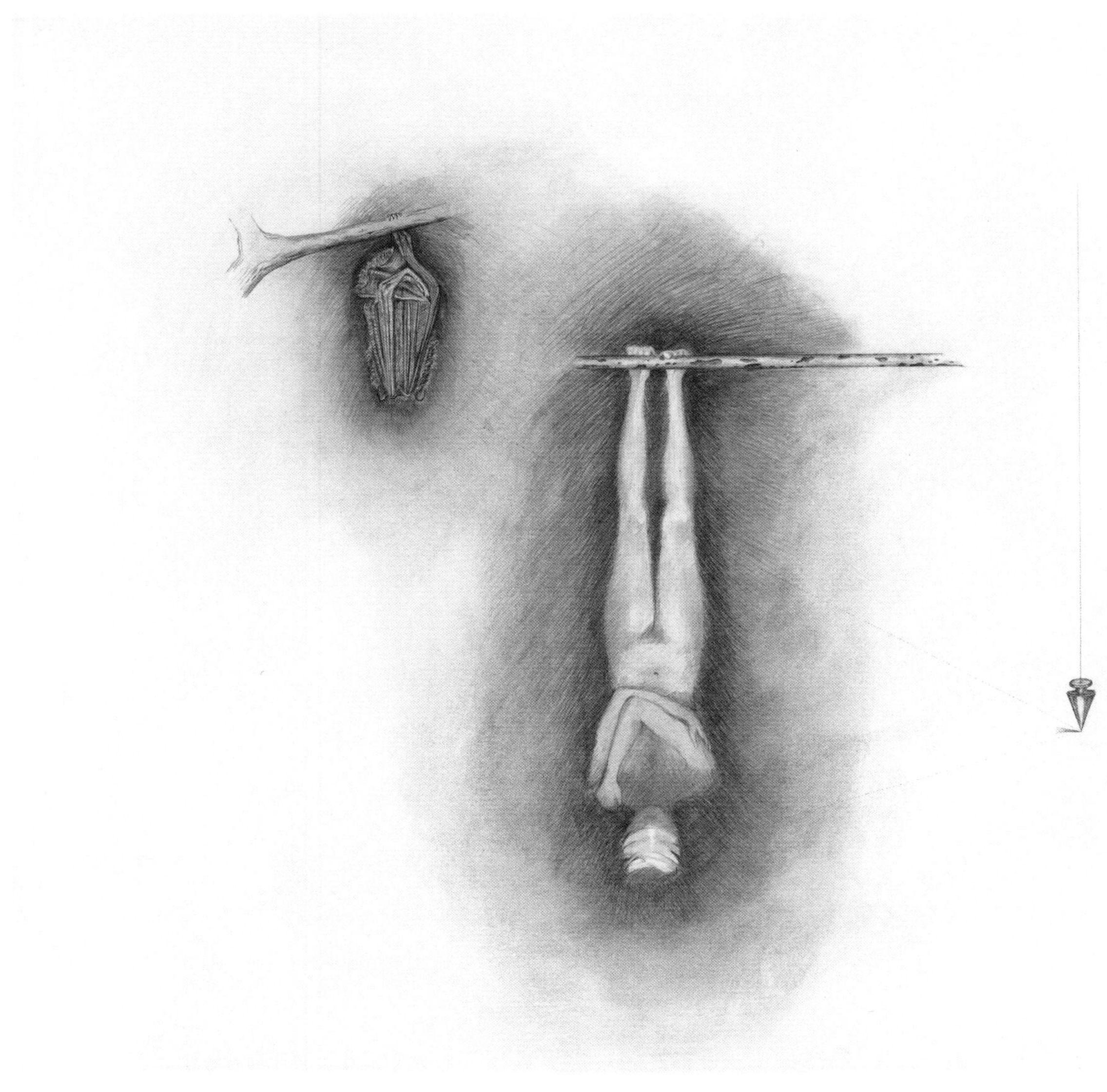

43   *Ohne Titel* 1975/1976
     Untitled

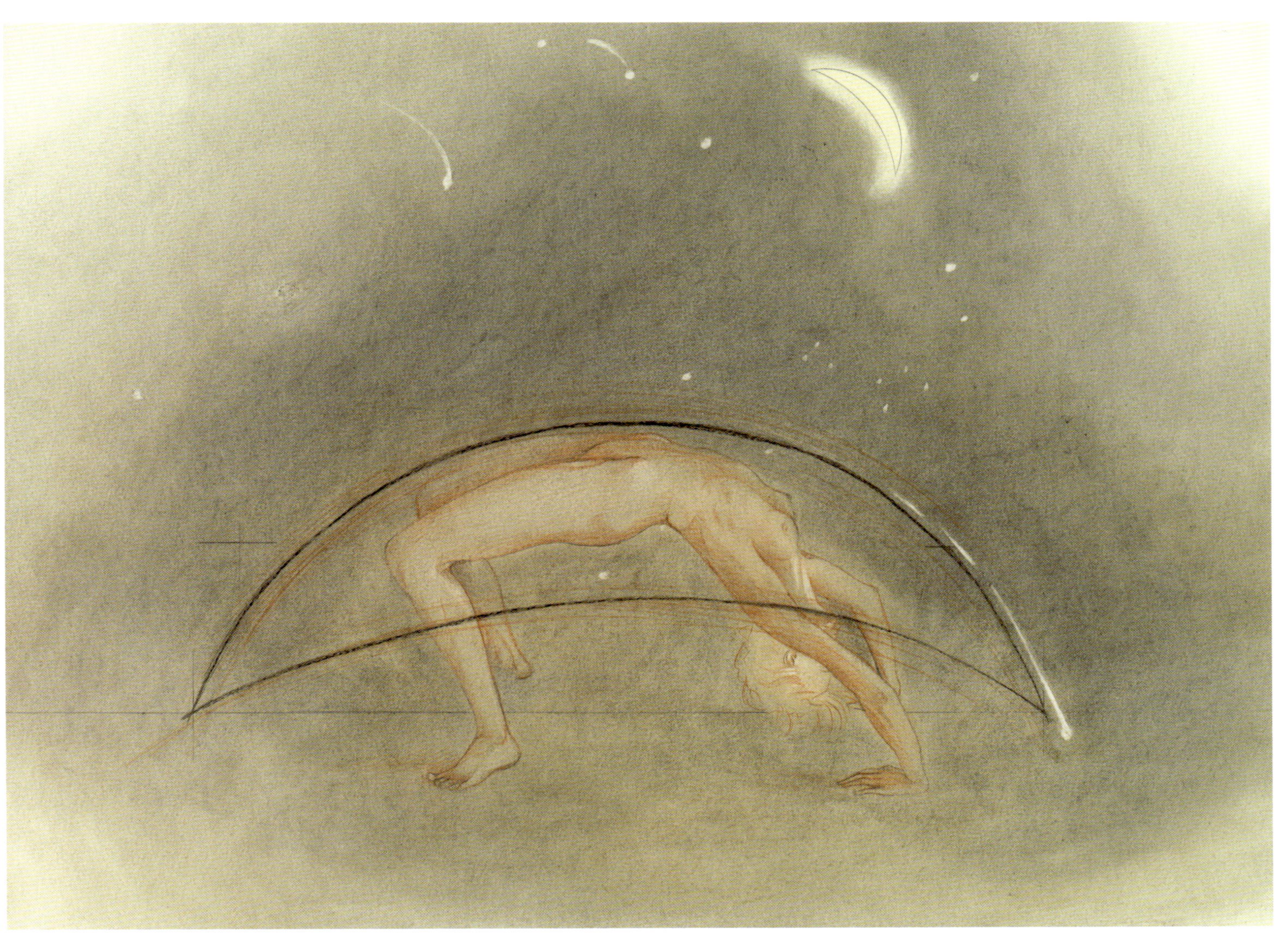

44 *Fluglinie der Sterne* 1978
Trajectory of the Stars

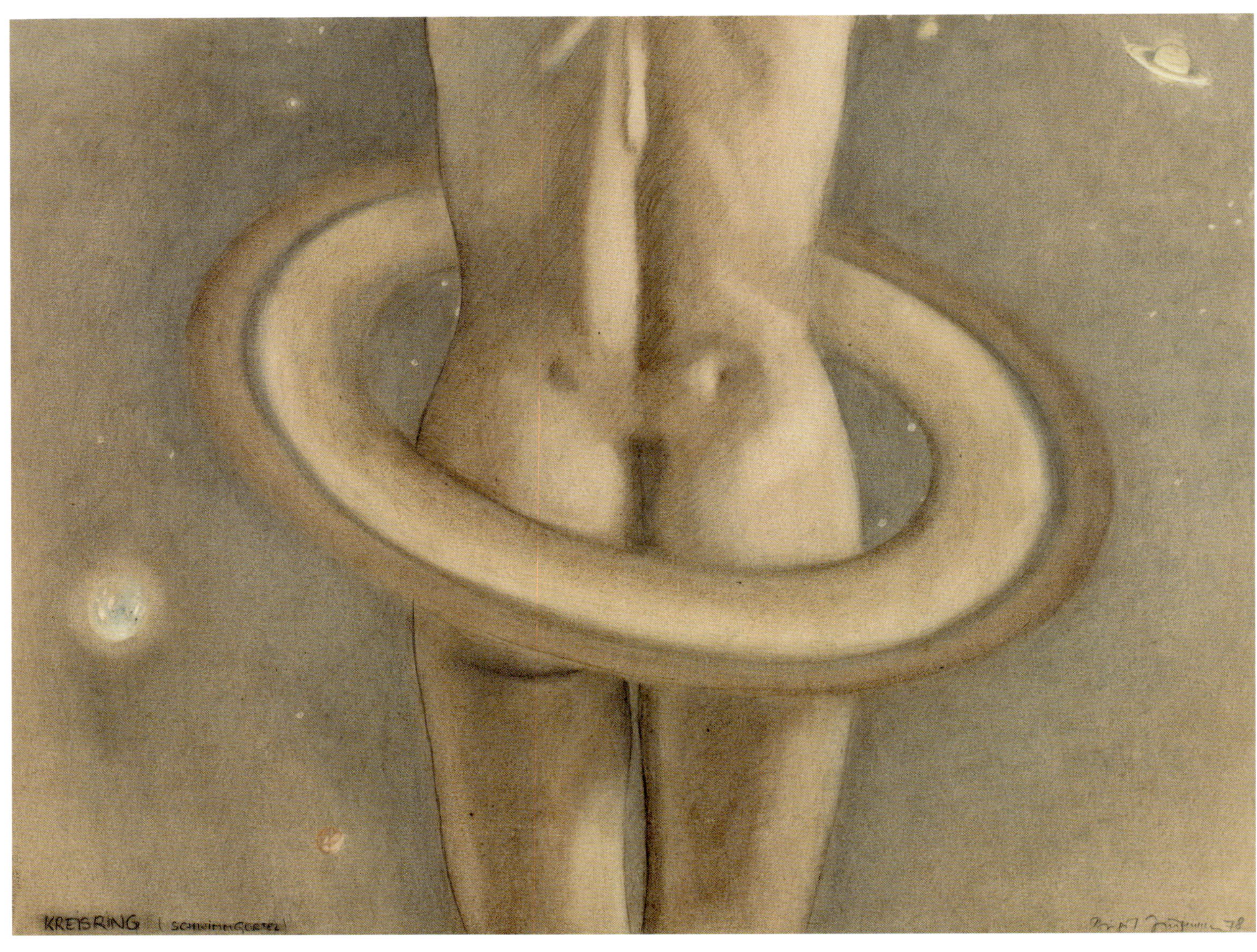

45 *Kreisring (Schwimmgürtel)* 1978
    Annulus (Life Belt)

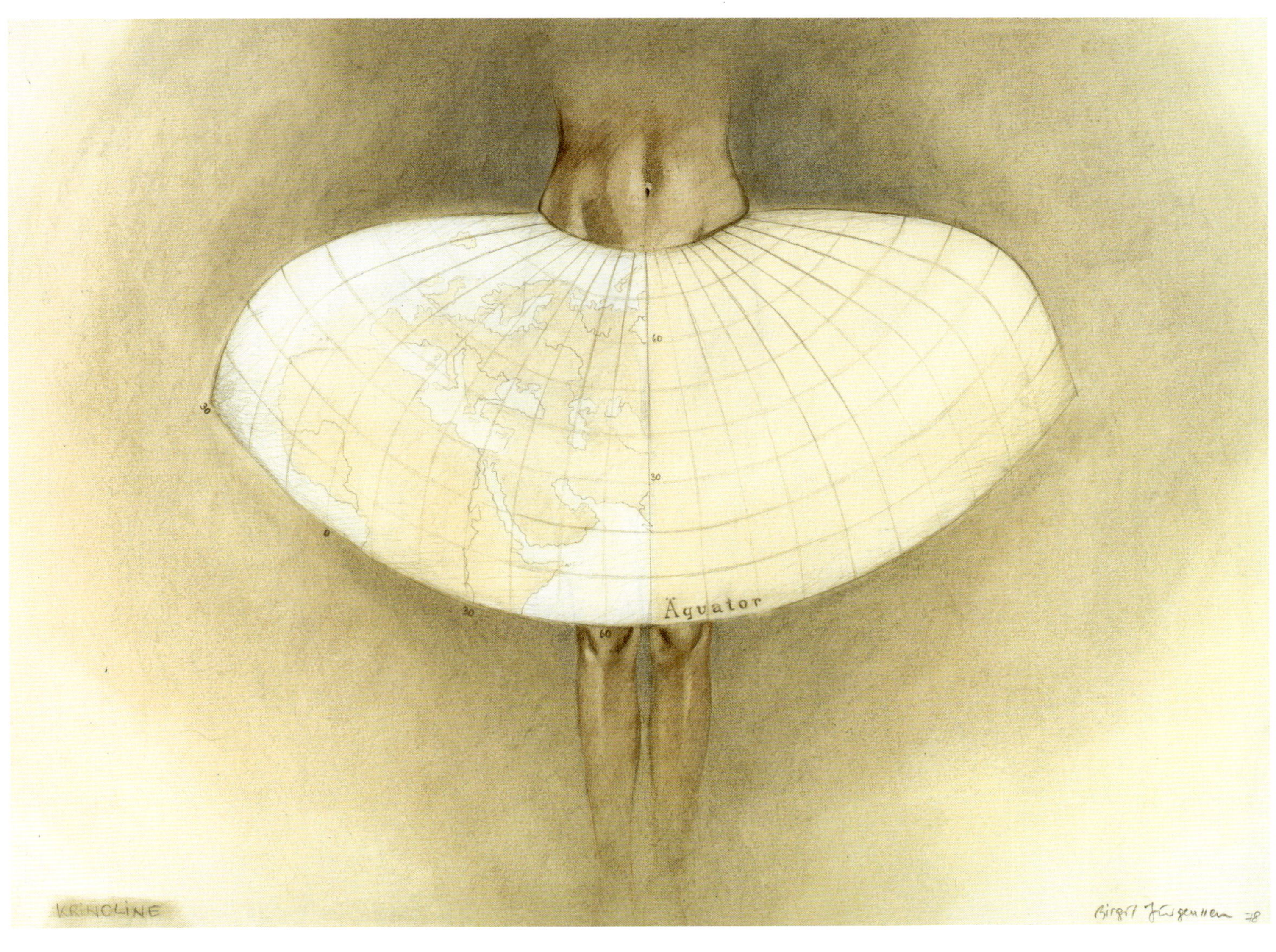

46   *Krinoline* 1978
     Crinoline

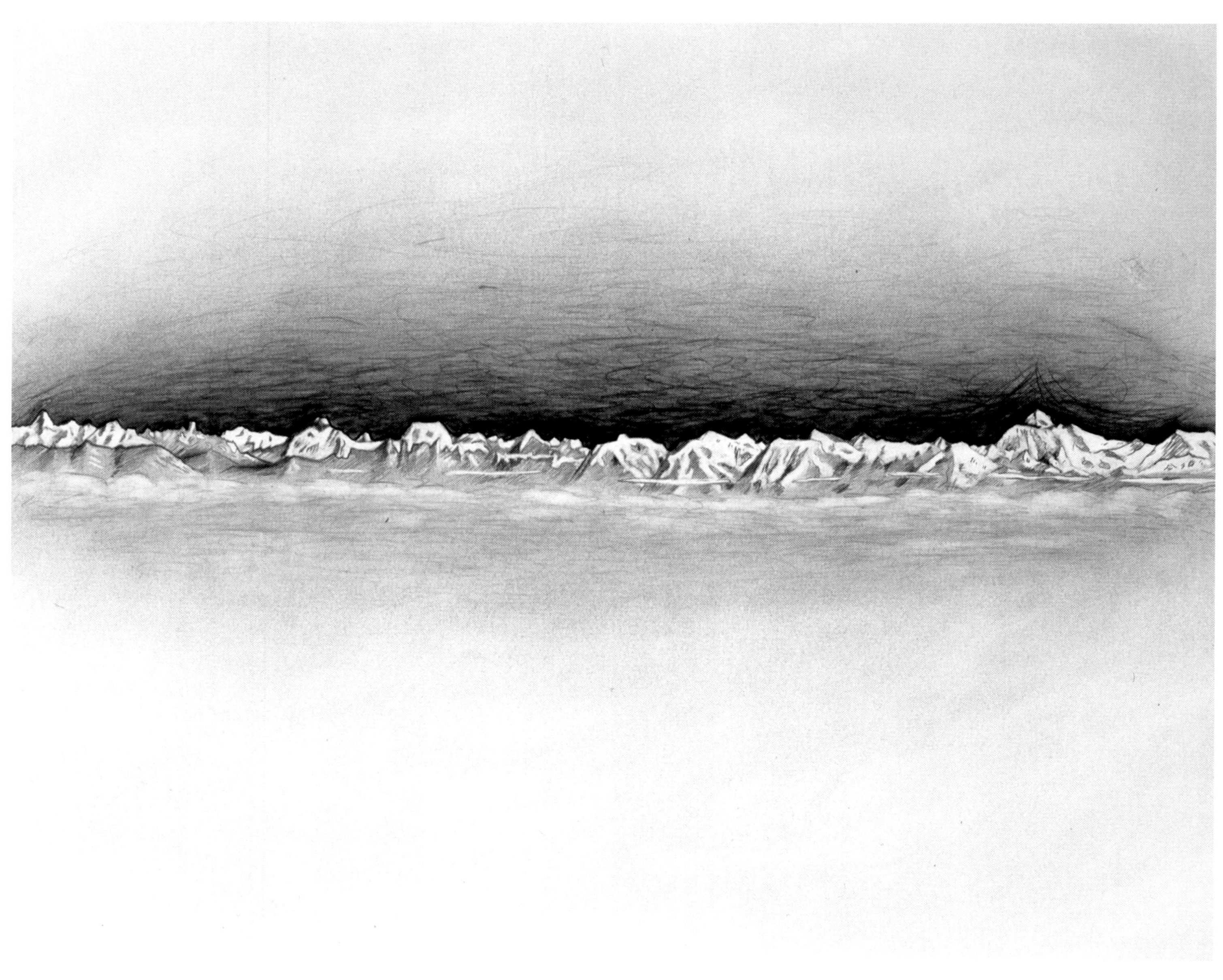

47 *Ohne Titel* 1978
Untitled

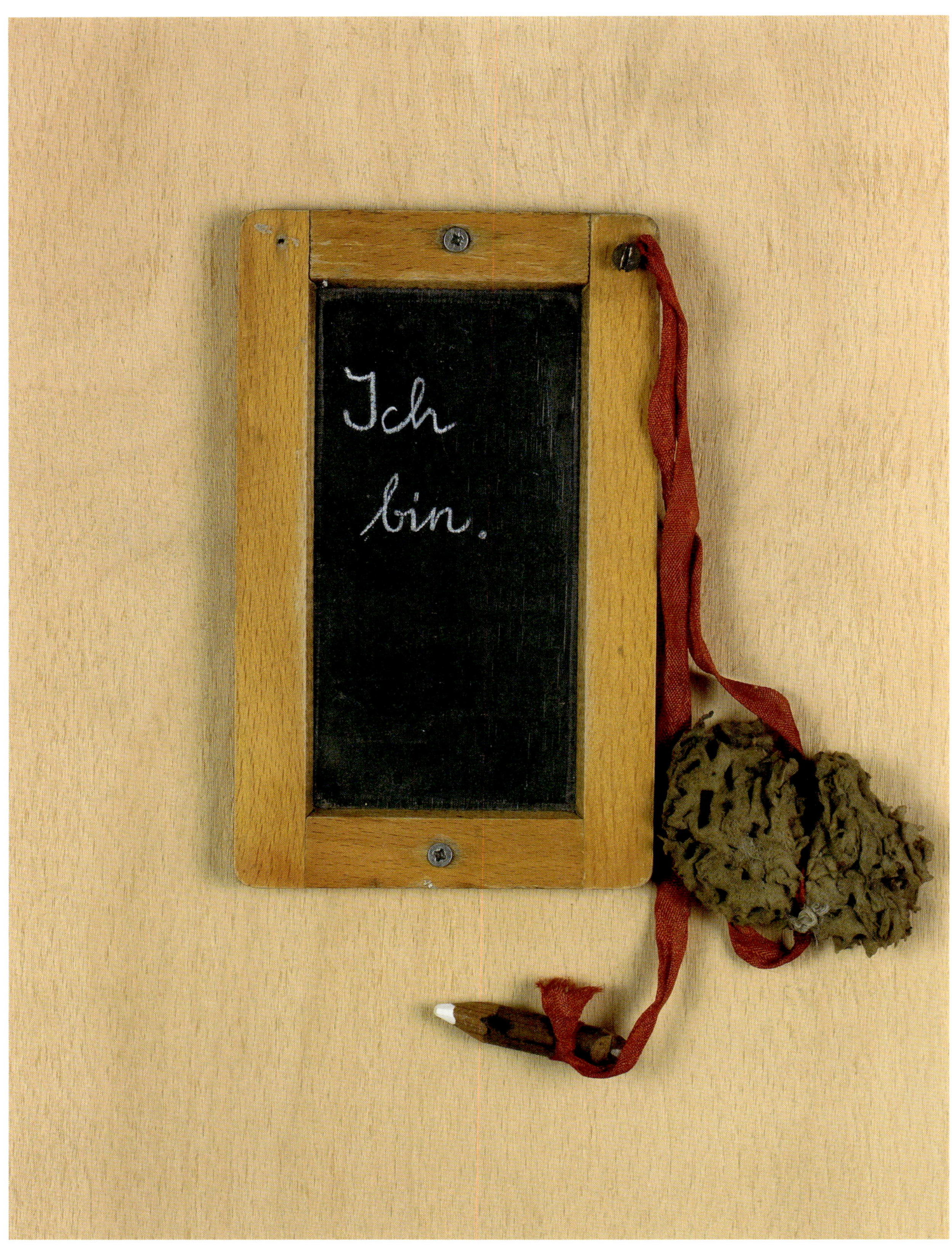

48   *Ich bin.* 1995
      I am.

I am.
An Act of Self-Assertion

Gabriele Schor

In 1995 Birgit Jürgenssen created a small work; on a school slate she wrote *Ich bin* (I am) in chalk (ill. 48). These Latin letters seem to be quite self-contained, determining in their own way the essence of the first person singular. Even the sponge on a strip of red cloth does not detract in any way from the clarity of these pure white letters. This *Ich* wants to be. This *Ich* is asserting itself. It has gotten to where it wants to be. Period.

This was not always the case. In her 1976 photograph *I Want Out of Here!* (ill. 165), Jürgenssen enacts a very moving cry for help. Get me out of this dilemma. Out of the role which has been forced on me, that of being a mere housewife, wife, and mother in this world. »Be really creative, refuse your role,« Jürgenssen wrote in her notebook, and she plunged into a whole range of possible egos and identities. There followed enactments of herself as a Maori woman, as *Batwoman*, as a cool woman who *Pulls Herself Up by Her Own Hair*, as *A Big Girl* (ill. 83), whom no man can compete with, no matter how hard he tries, and as *Faust's Gretchen*, declaring war on her role as a victim. All those oppressive feelings and states of mind are—at long last—swept away, as in the drawings *Bootjack* (ill. 75), *Auto-transfusion*, *Support* (ill. 76), and *Shoe Mask* (ill. 74). Jürgenssen wrenches these stifling female identities out of the corset of a pitiful patriarchy.

She overcame her own shyness of the early years, and between 1988 and 1994 she staged many public performances with the women artists' group *DIE DAMEN*. In 1995, then, she coolly writes the words *Ich bin* on a school slate, in an act of self-assertion. The view from outside and the confrontation with an audience has helped her find a new key to determining her own existence. Turning the interior outward. As early as 1985, she entitles her exhibition in the Galerie Hubert Winter: *How Does One Experience Oneself in the Other, the Other in Oneself?* You can experience yourself in the other by opening up. And how does Jürgenssen experience the other in herself? By unfolding different constructions of the self, by facing up to these, then casting them off again and living with the knowledge that »I am.«

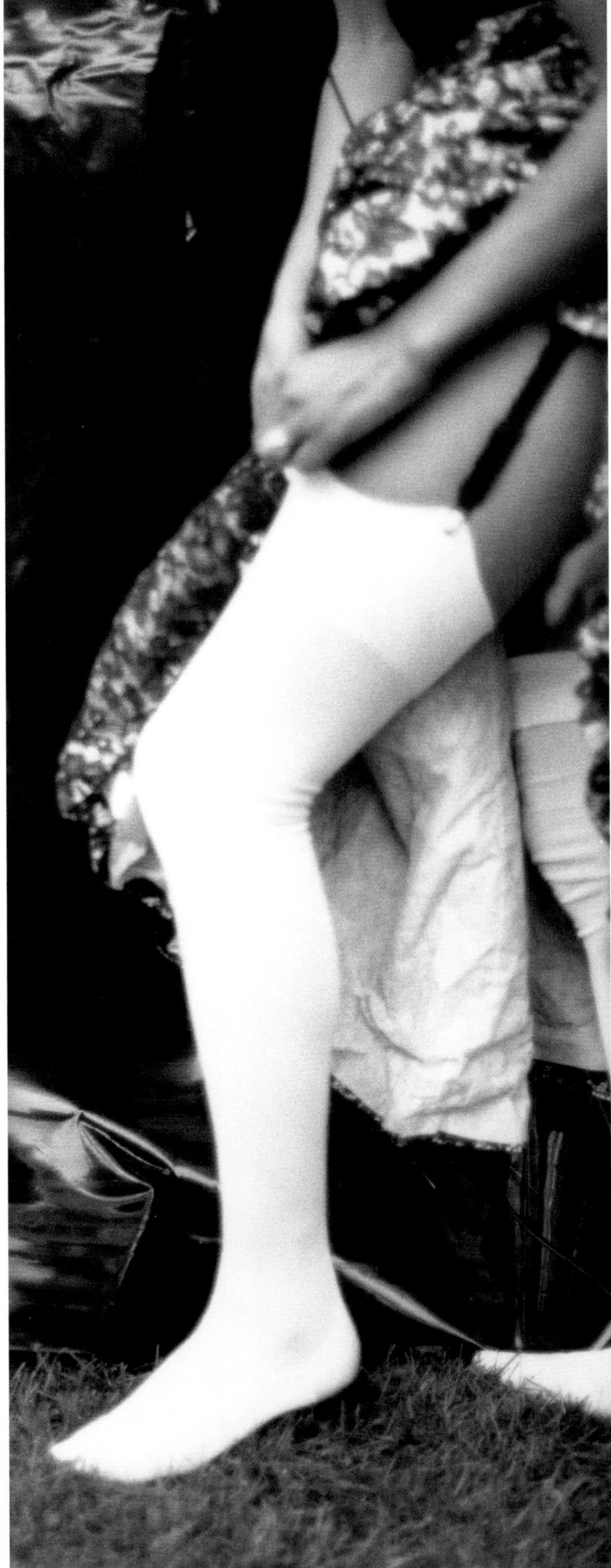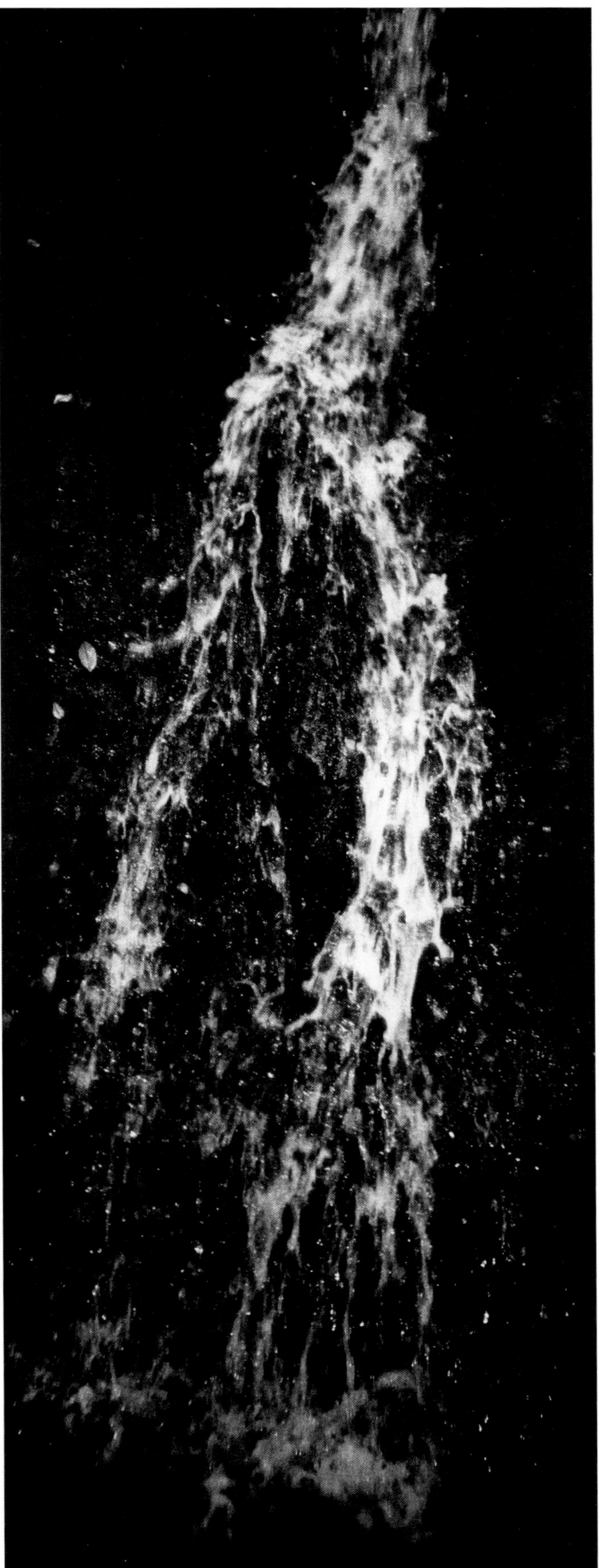

<u>49</u>   *Ohne Titel (Sonderbare Regenfälle)* 1992
Untitled (Peculiar Rainfalls)

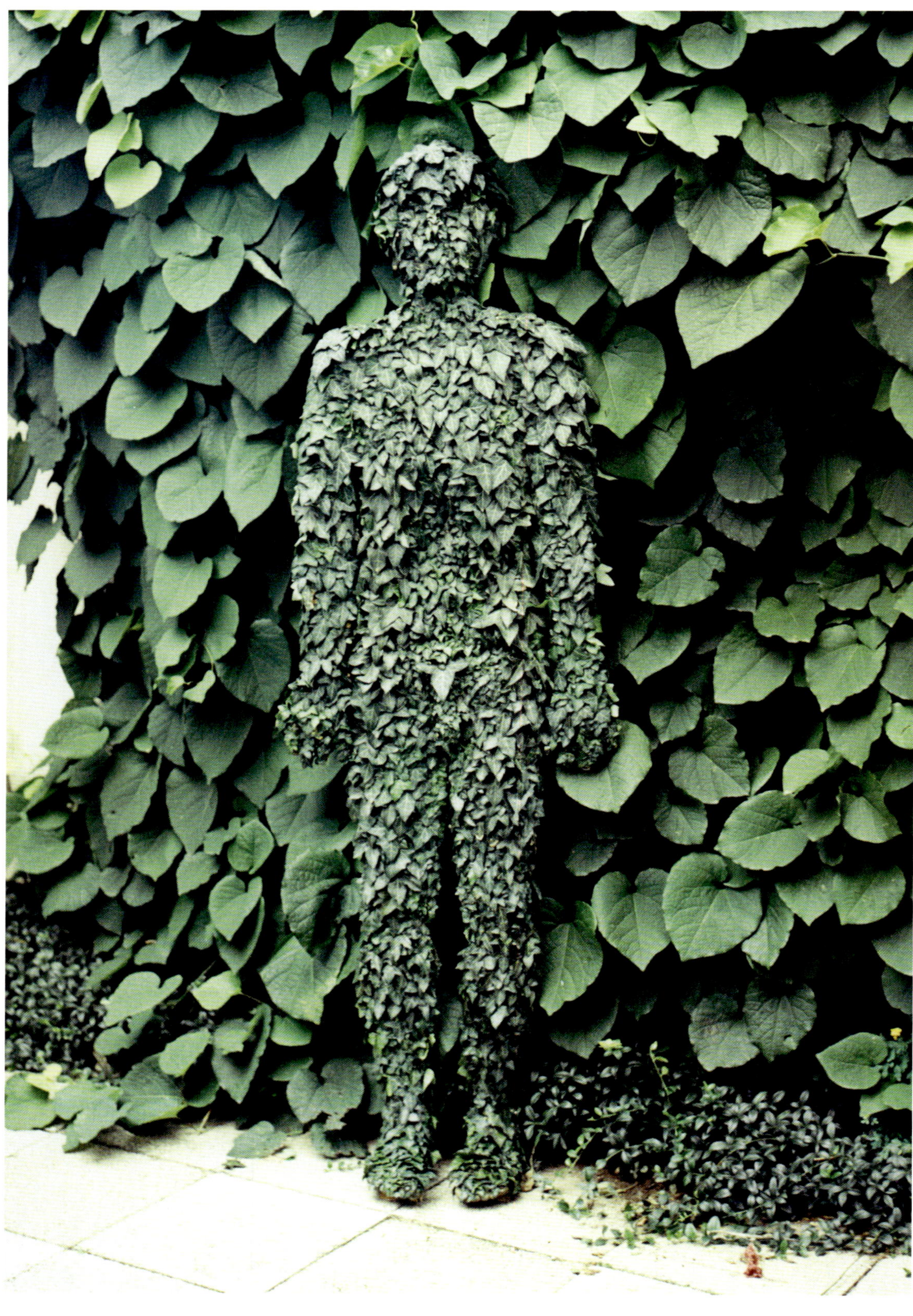

50 *Ohne Titel* 1979
    Untitled

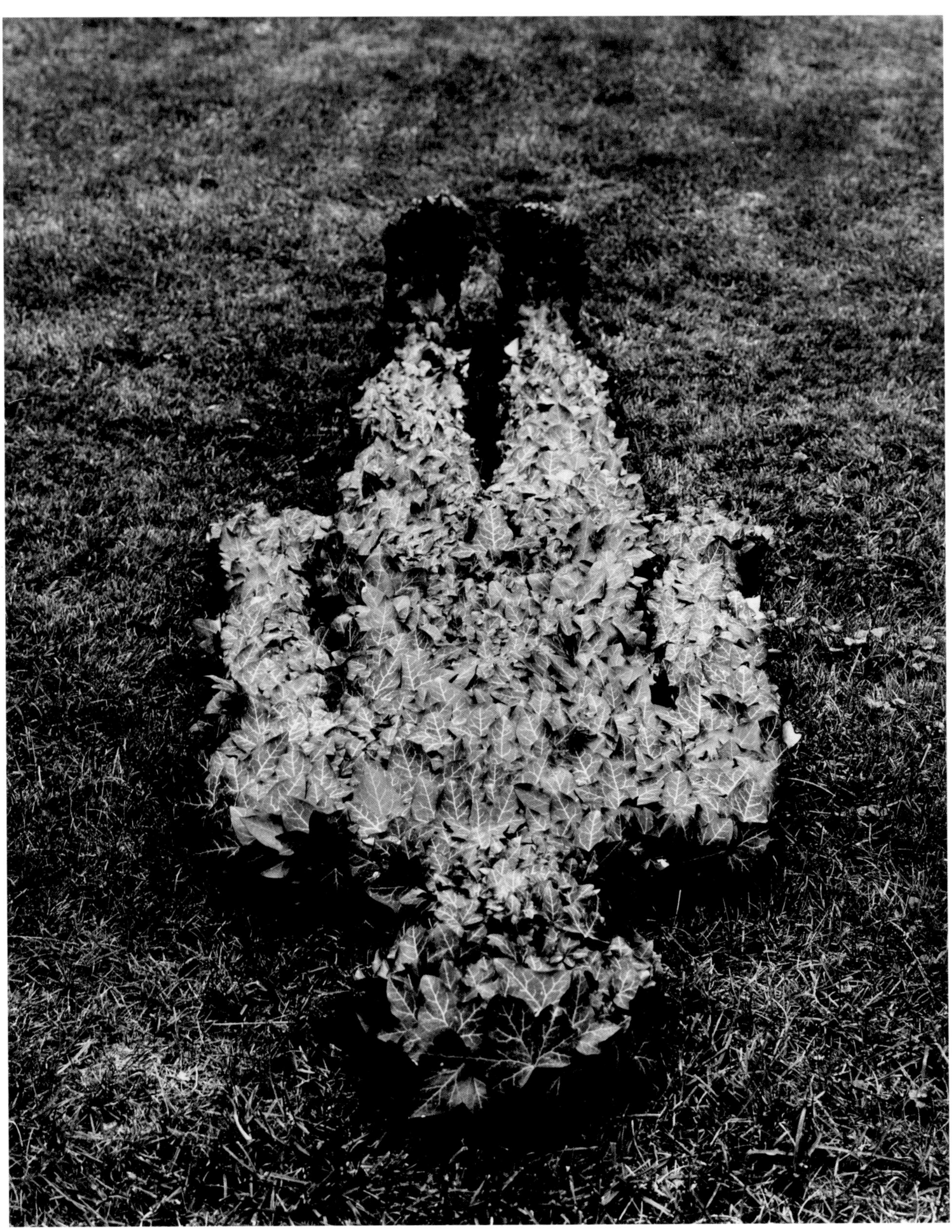

<u>51</u>   *Ohne Titel* 1979/1980
      Untitled

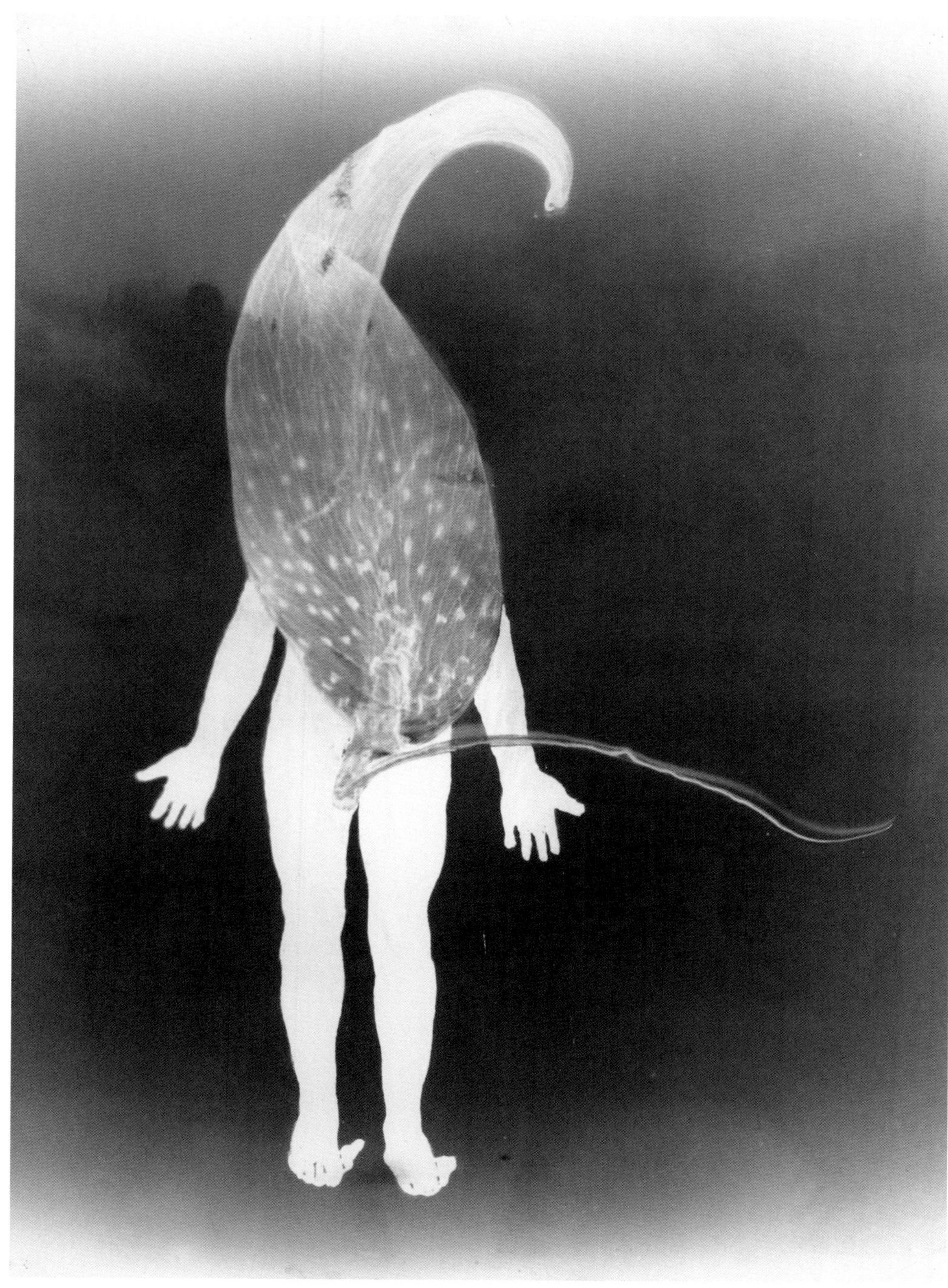

52   *Ohne Titel (Naturgeschichte)* 1975
     Untitled (Natural History)

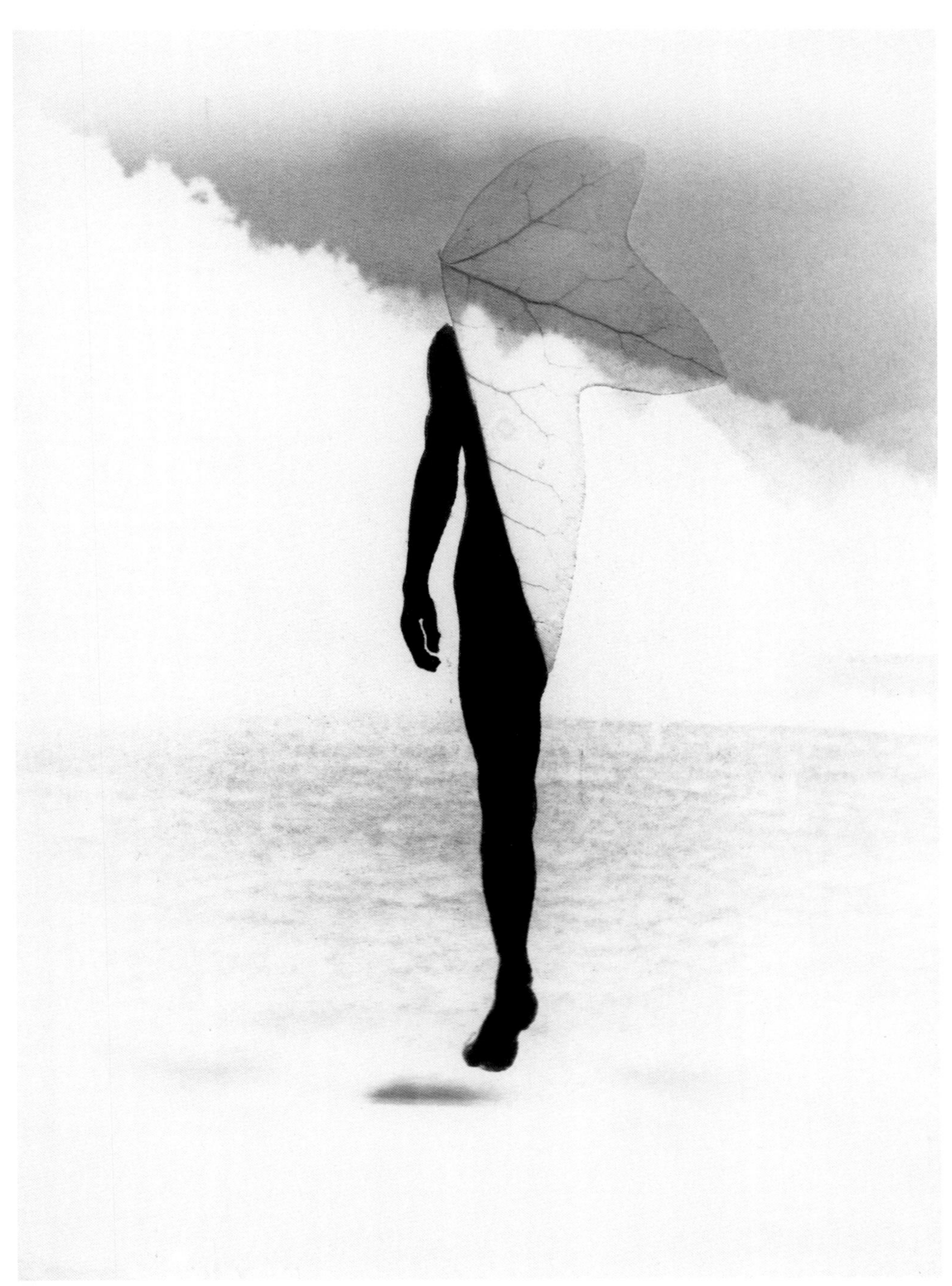

53   *Ohne Titel (Naturgeschichte)* 1975
Untitled (Natural History)

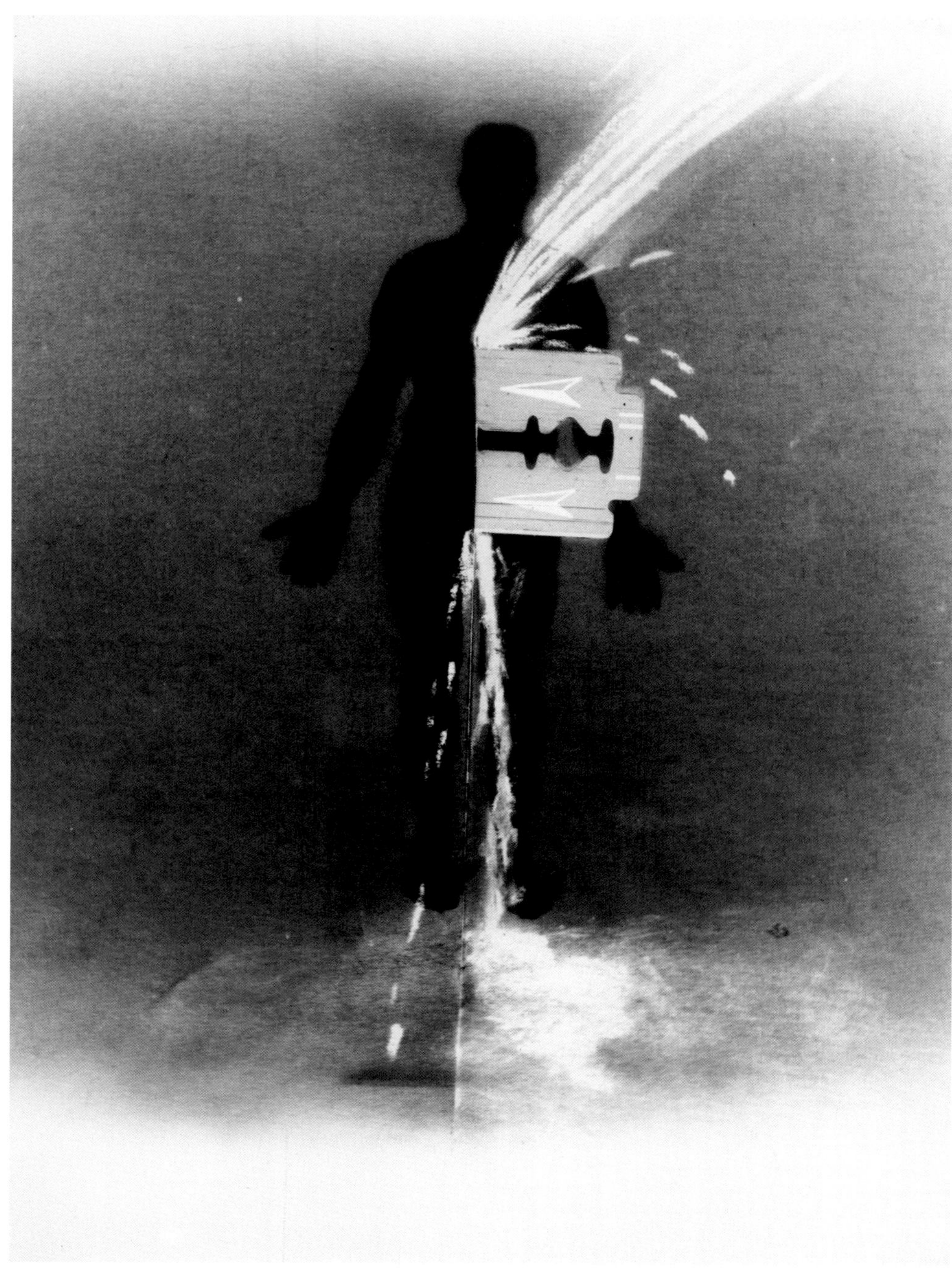

54   *Ohne Titel (Naturgeschichte)* 1975
      Untitled (Natural History)

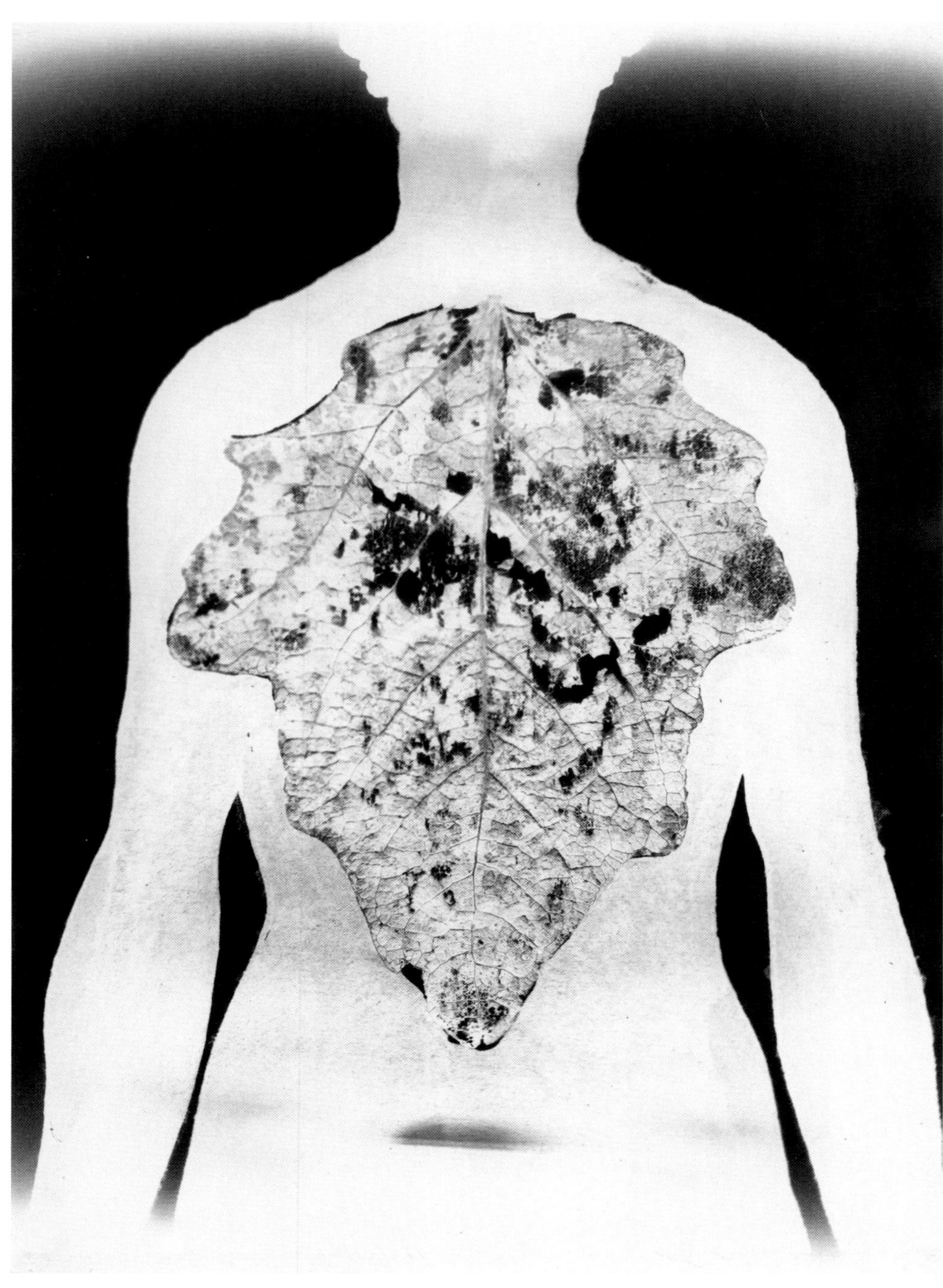

  Ohne Titel (Naturgeschichte) 1975
Untitled (Natural History)

A Natural History

Lorenzo Giusti

»These images are oxidized residues, fixed by light and chemical elements, of living organisms« said Man Ray when defining the photographic technique that bears his name in the dictionary of surrealism. And Birgit Jürgenssen must have been attracted precisely by this dynamic active principle, this concrete—living—element, when she made use of the rayogram to create the series *Untitled (Natural History)*.

Before this, research related to gender issues had been undertaken almost alone and this series opened a wider discussion on the relationship between human and nature, and around the processes of living. A general, intuitive topic that does not exclude the former but rather includes it, encompasses it.

The images represent human bodies integrated with plant elements. In one example the plant grows upward from the bust, in another it occupies half of the figure, including the head and shoulders; in yet another, two leaves serve as wings on the back of a body. The simplest, the most succinct, overlaps a female half-length with an ivy leaf occupying the chest and stomach. The white body against the black background and the leaf in the center: the beating heart of the whole composition (ill. 55).

This image is the most representative of the organicist thinking that permeates the poetics of Birgit Jürgenssen. Humankind is fully integrated into the processes of the living. A total fusion. Leaf and human are a unique element, a single body, subject to Nature's regeneration processes, between birth, death, and rebirth.

The leaf, which in Christian iconography covers genitals, distinguishing the sins of the human race from the rest of Creation, in these works becomes a constitutive element of the body itself. A single, unitary body in which gender is but a variation, a particular element of a total reality that is not the sum of its parts but something more vast and complete.

Bodies not as forms, therefore, but as »formations,« living organisms that promote a »deep« ecological sensitivity, an attention to the intrinsic value of the species, systems, and natural processes. The next step was then to cover the body entirely with leaves (ill. 50, 51). A radical gesture that fuses and integrates. Full physical adhesion to the »whole natural.«

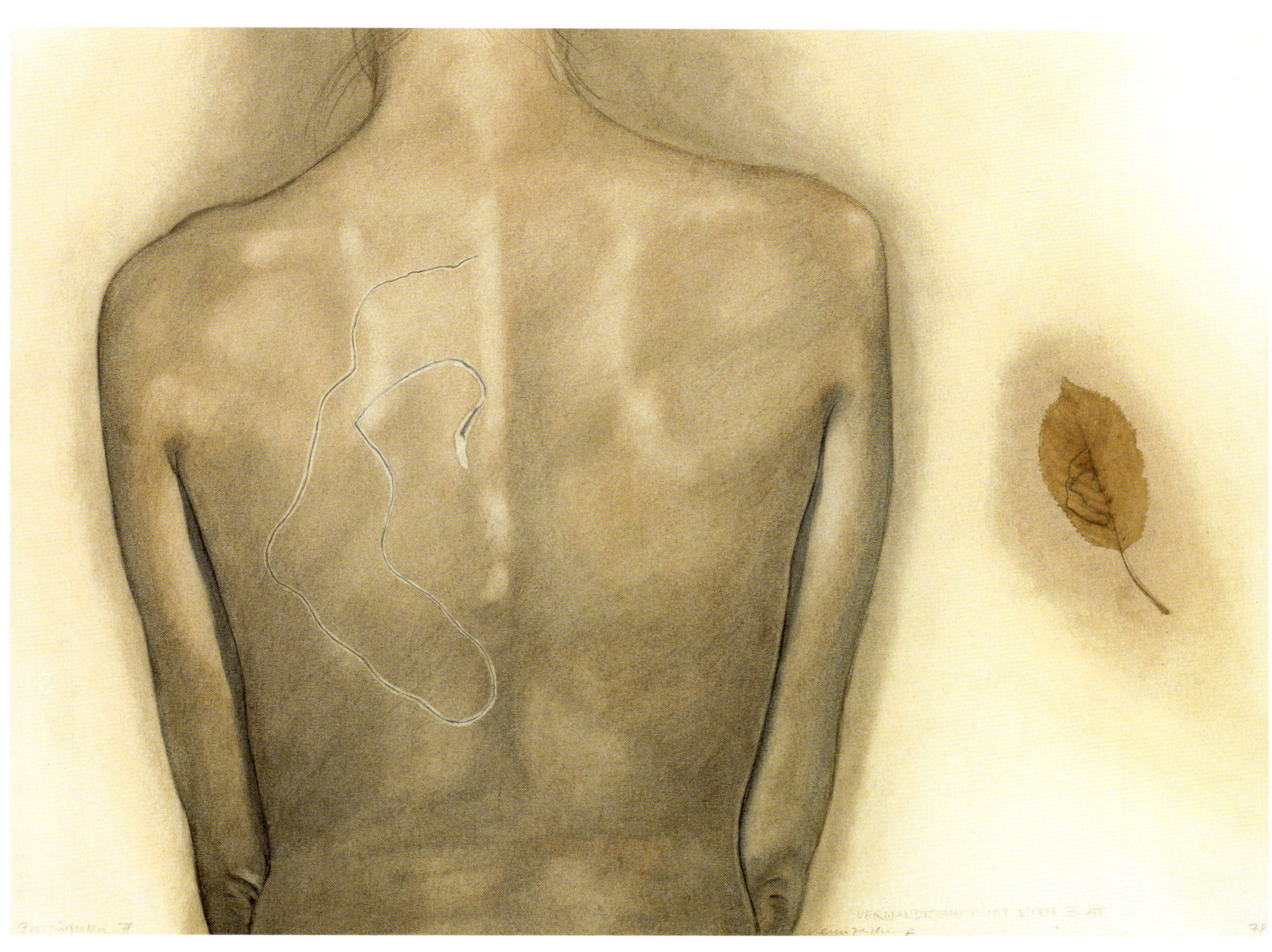

56   *Verwandtschaft mit einem Blatt. Keimzeichnung 1978*
Kinship with a Leaf: Germ Drawing

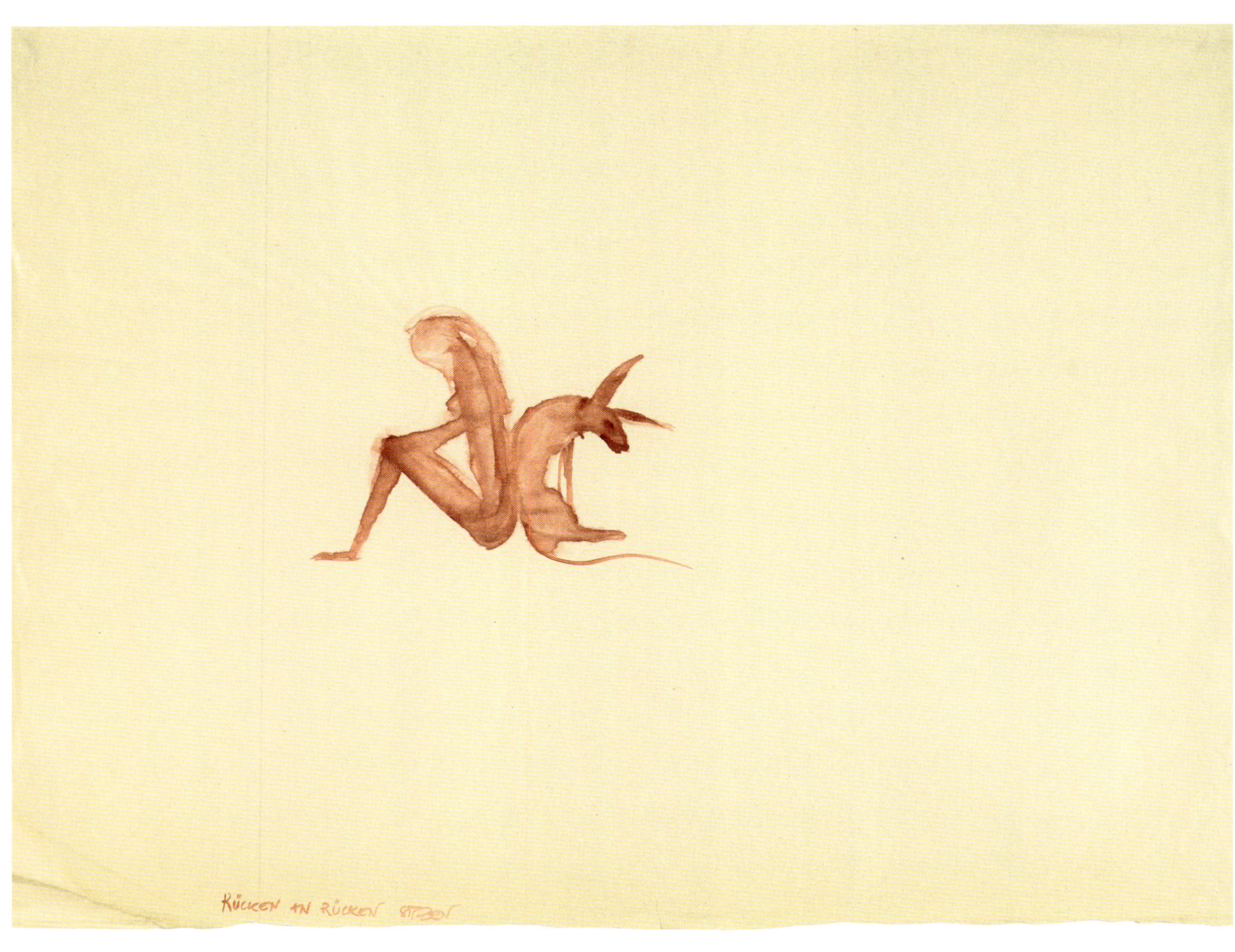

57   *Rücken an Rücken sitzen* 1978/1979
     Sitting Back to Back

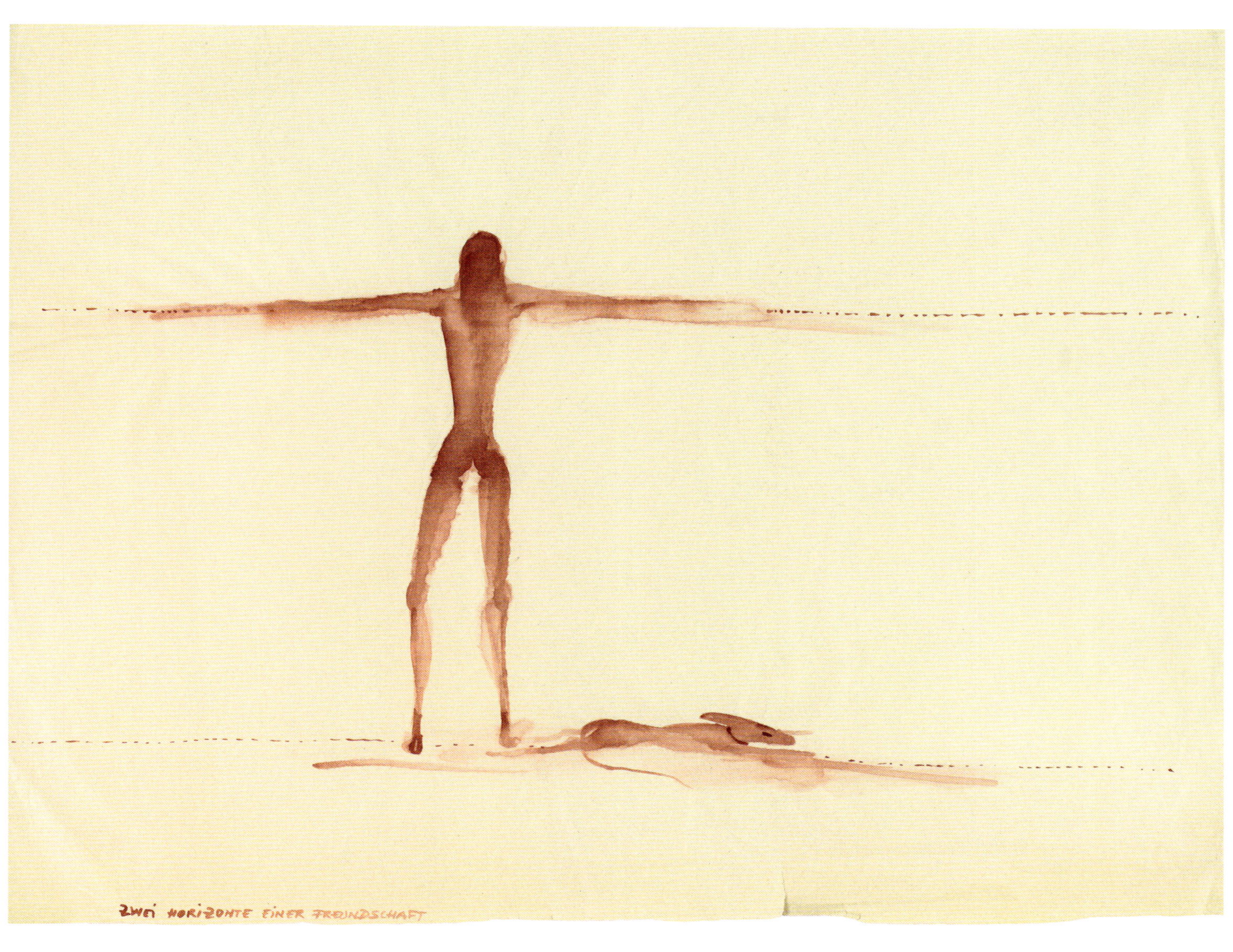

58   *Zwei Horizonte einer Freundschaft 1978/1979*
     Two Horizons of a Friendship

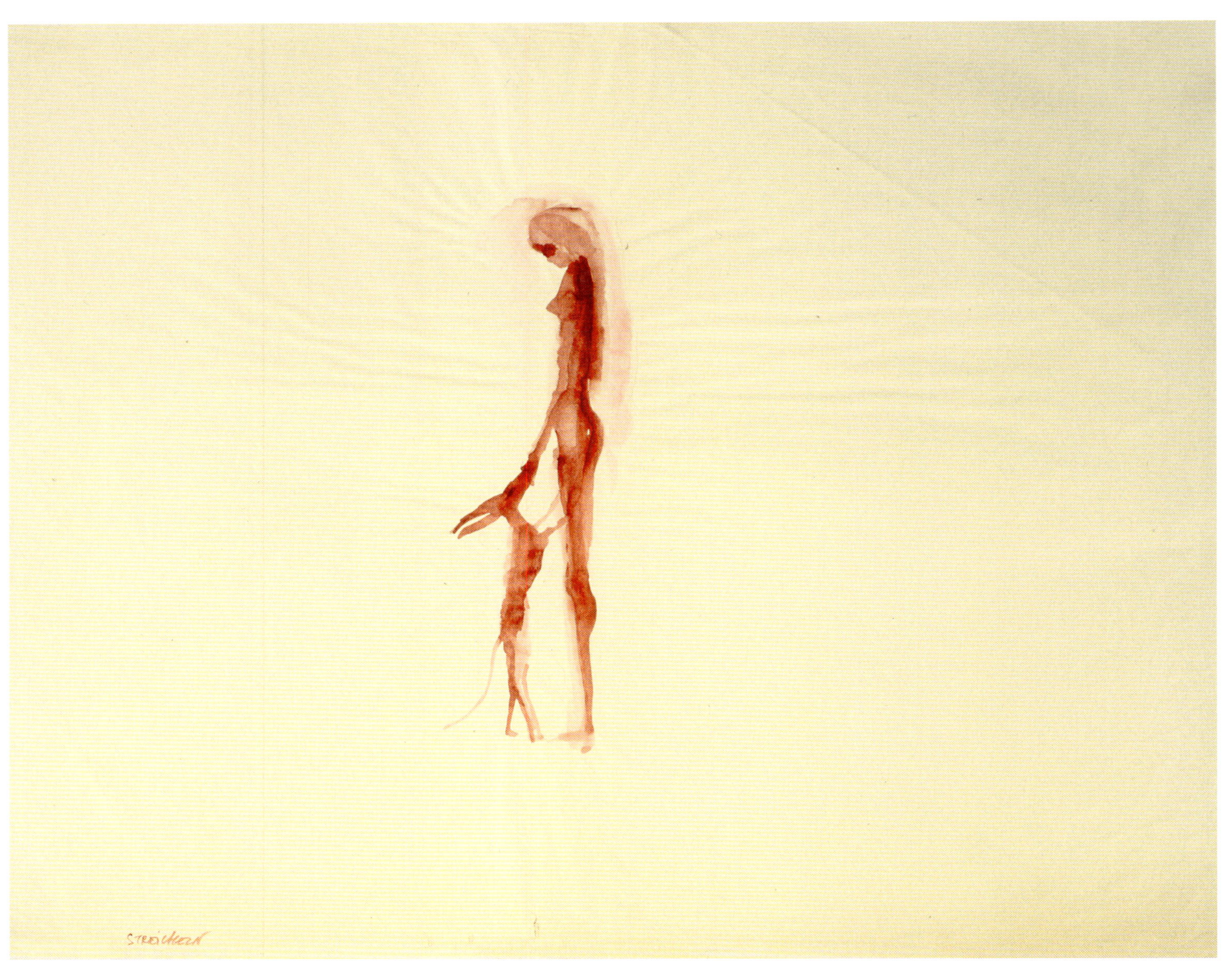

<u>59</u> *Streicheln* 1978/1979
Caressing

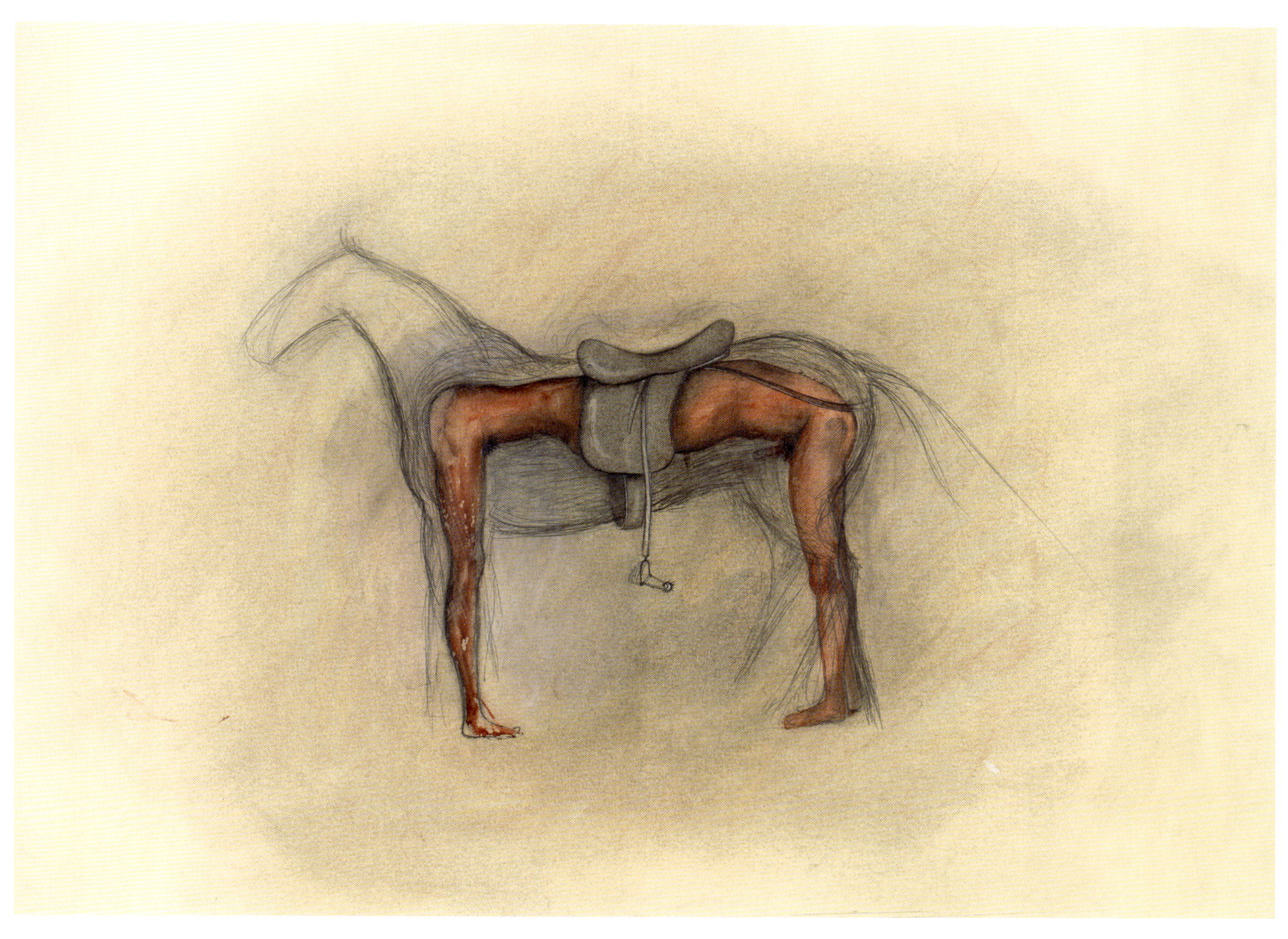

60 *Ohne Titel* 1978
Untitled

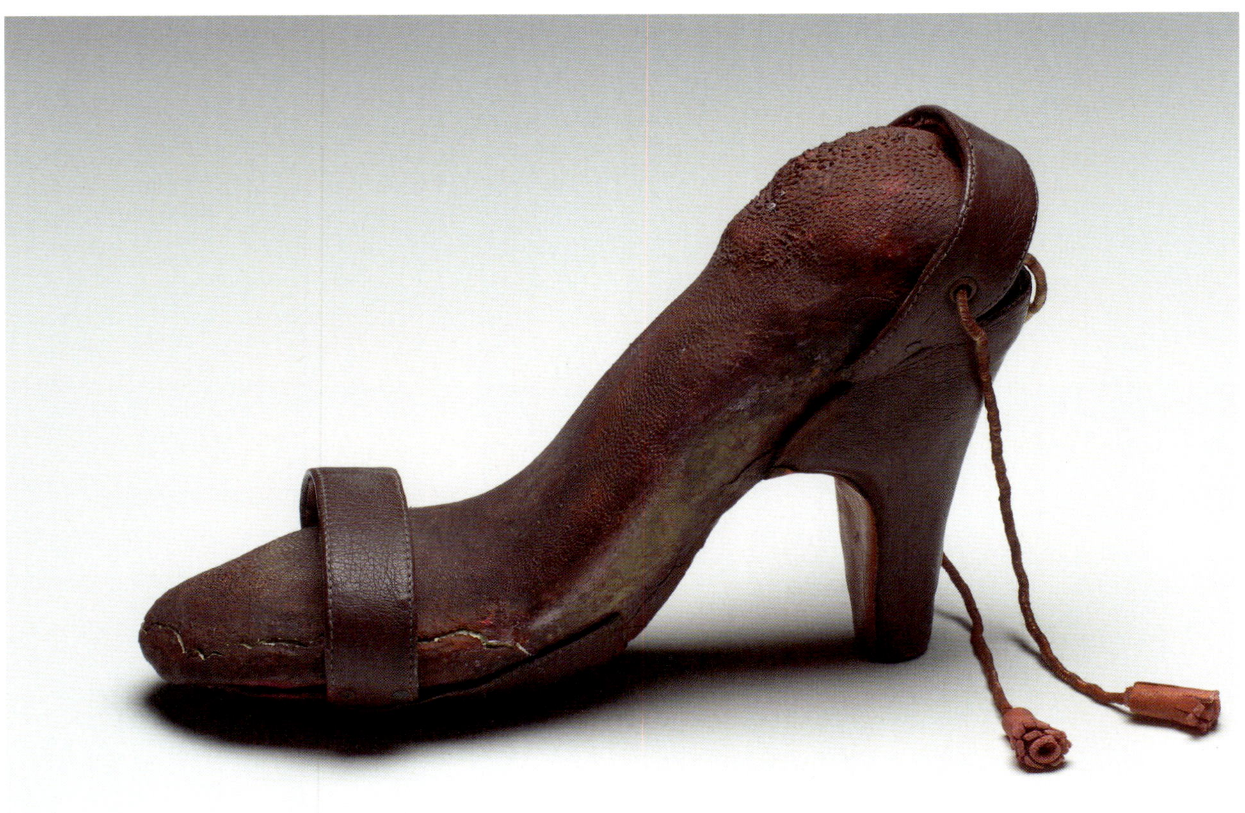

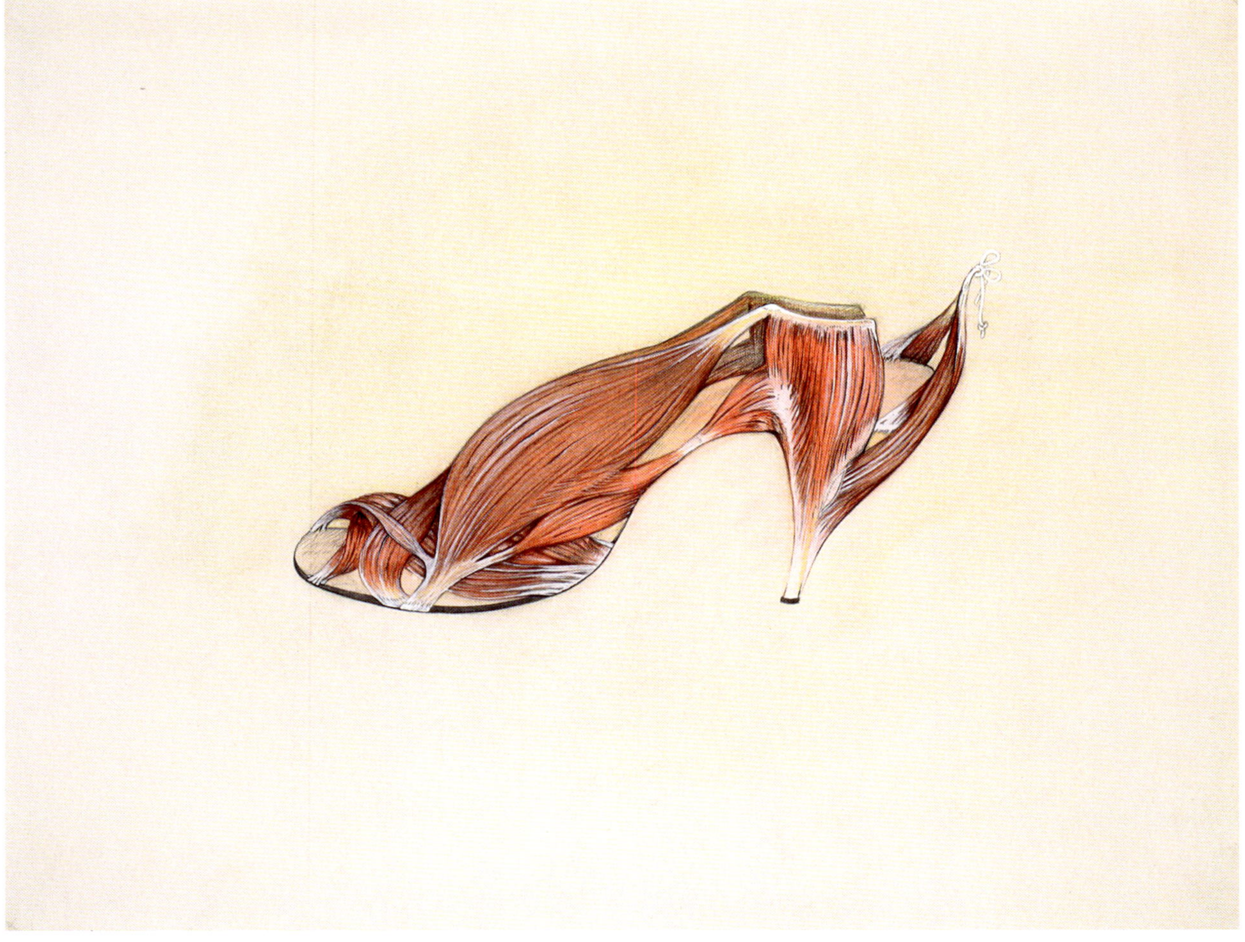

61 *Zungenleckschuh* 1974
    Lick-Tongue Shoe
62 *Muskelschuh* 1976
    Muscle Shoe

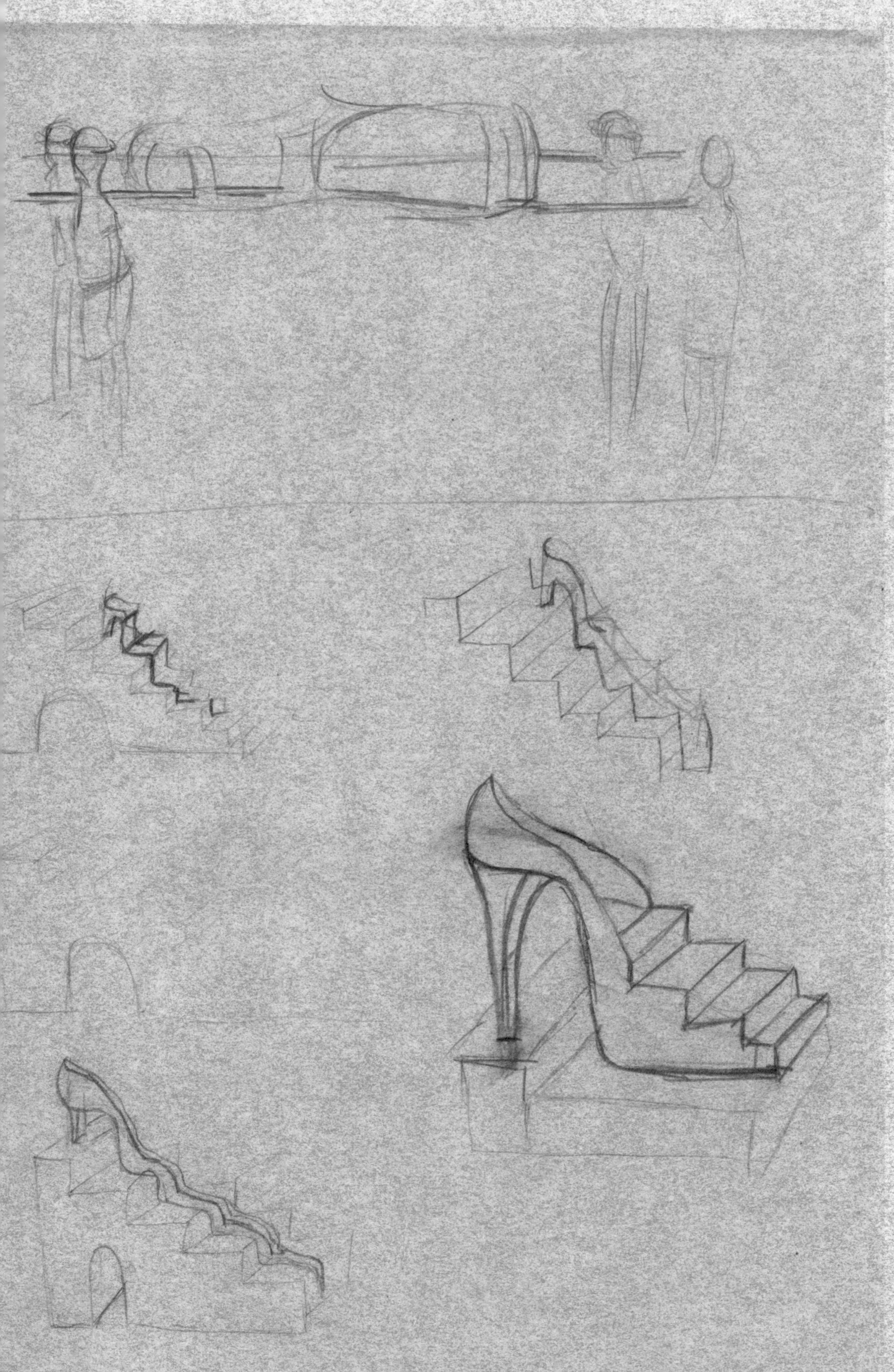

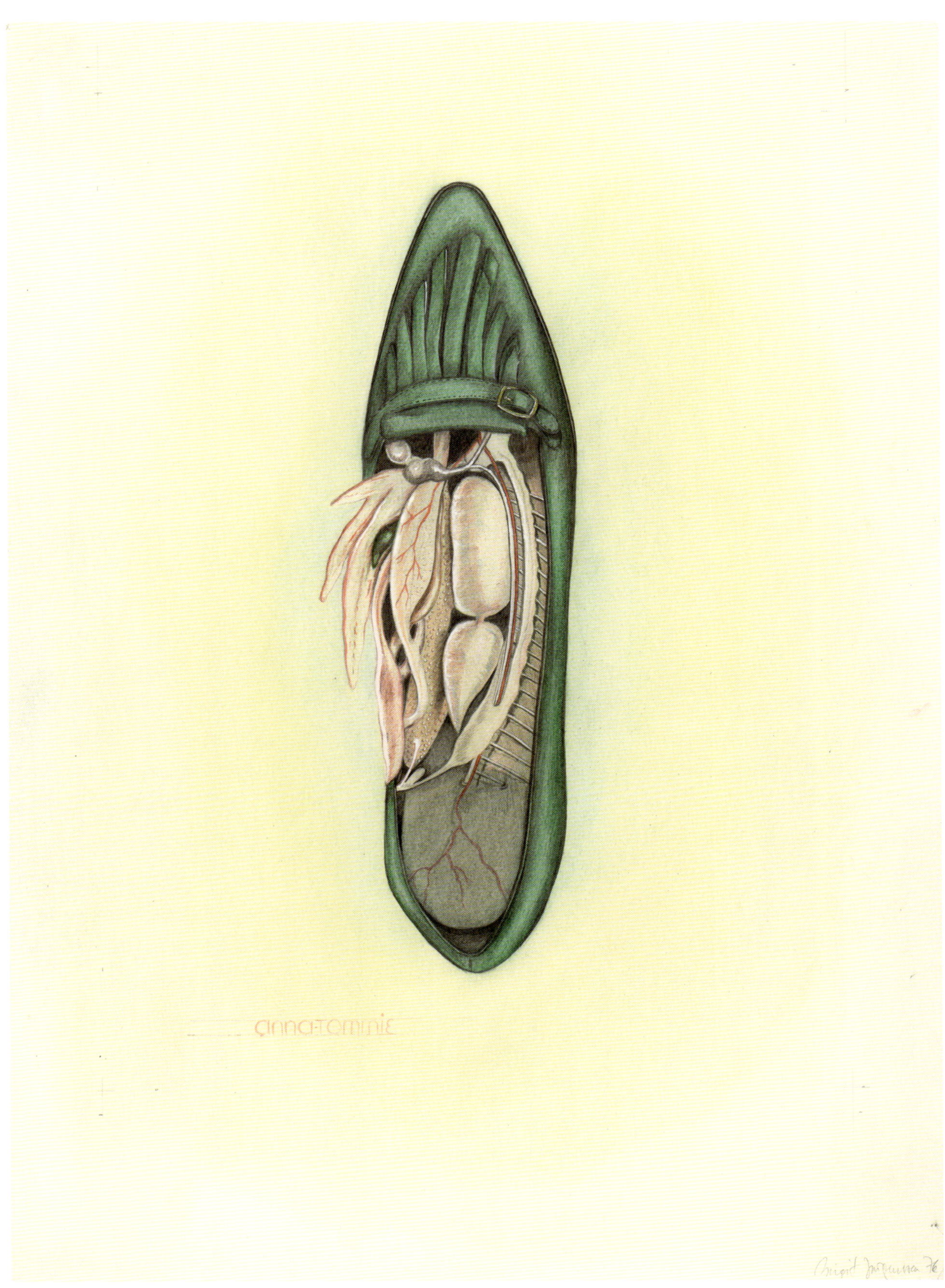

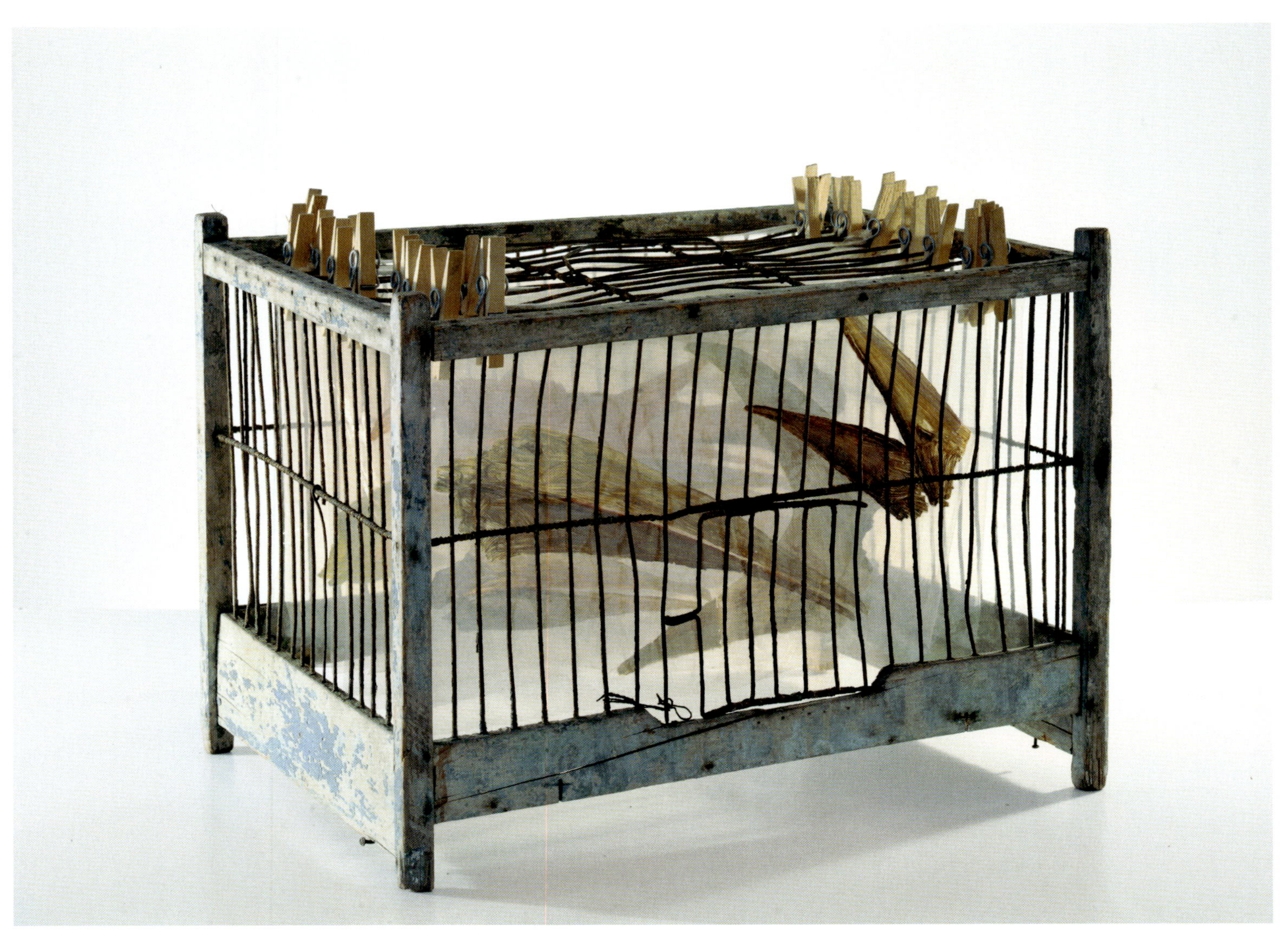

64 *Gefangene Fröhlichkeit* 1982
Caught Happiness

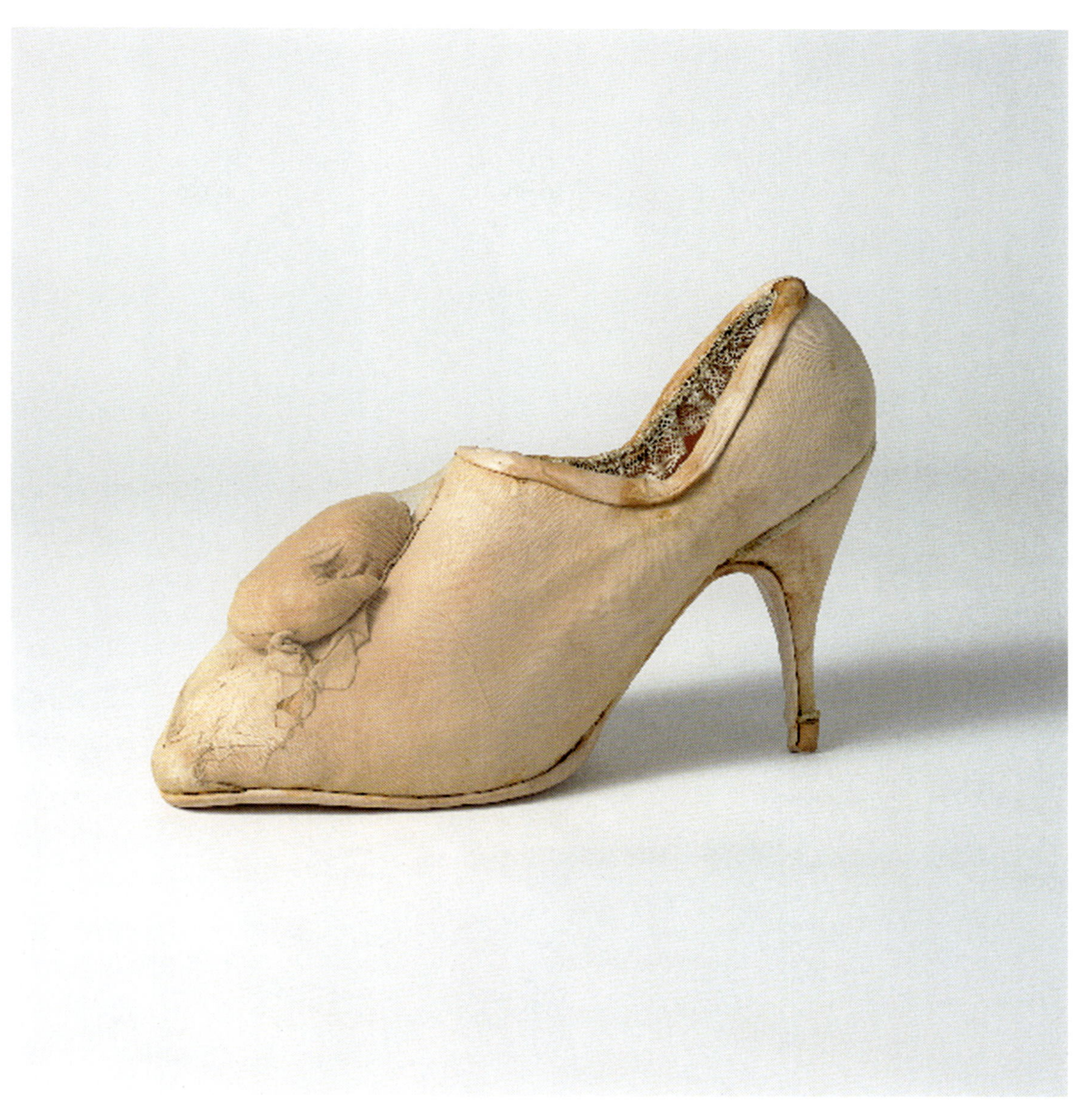

65 *Schwangerer Schuh* 1976
Pregnant Shoe

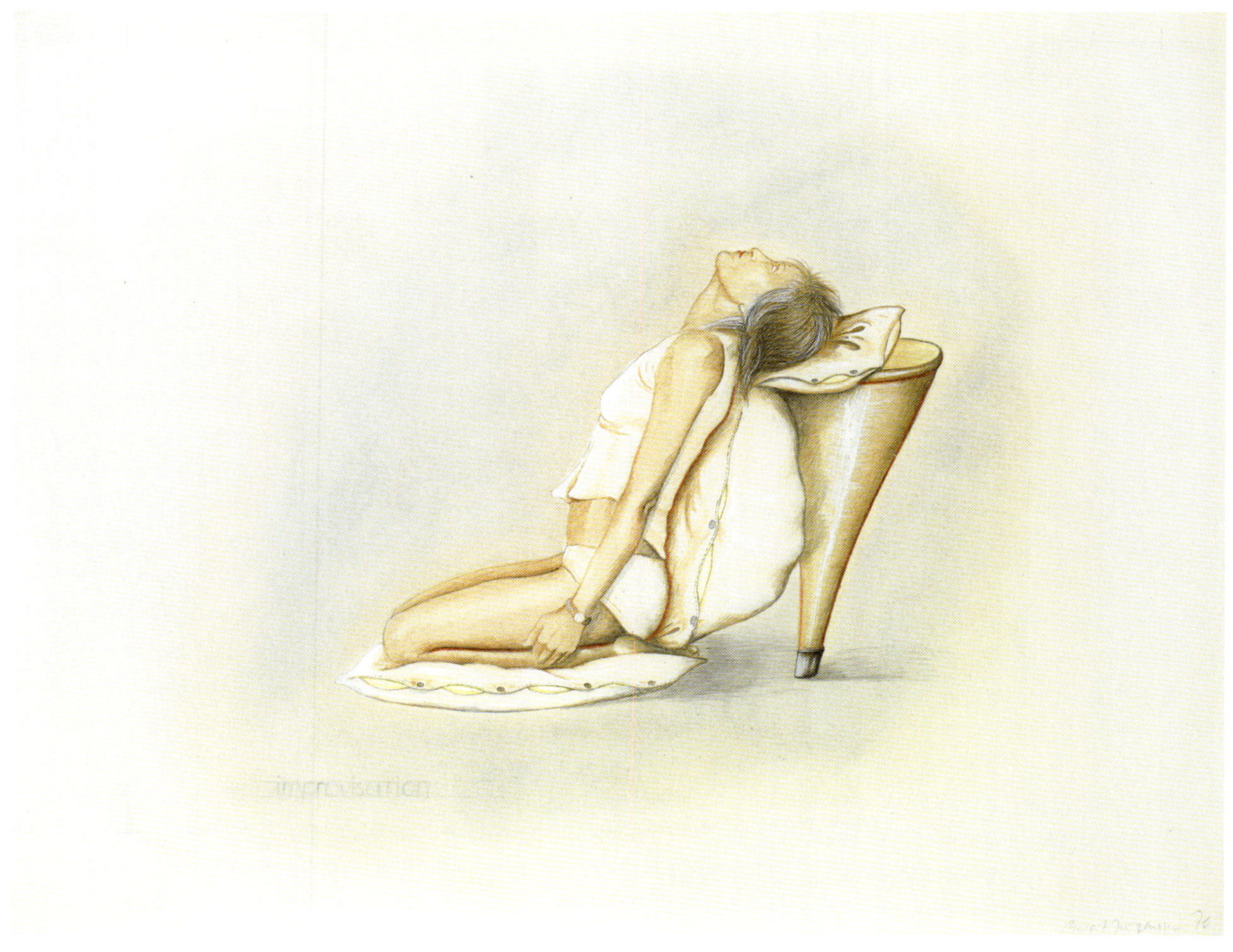

66   *Stütze (Improvisation)* 1976
Support (Improvisation)

2

zwitter

zwitter

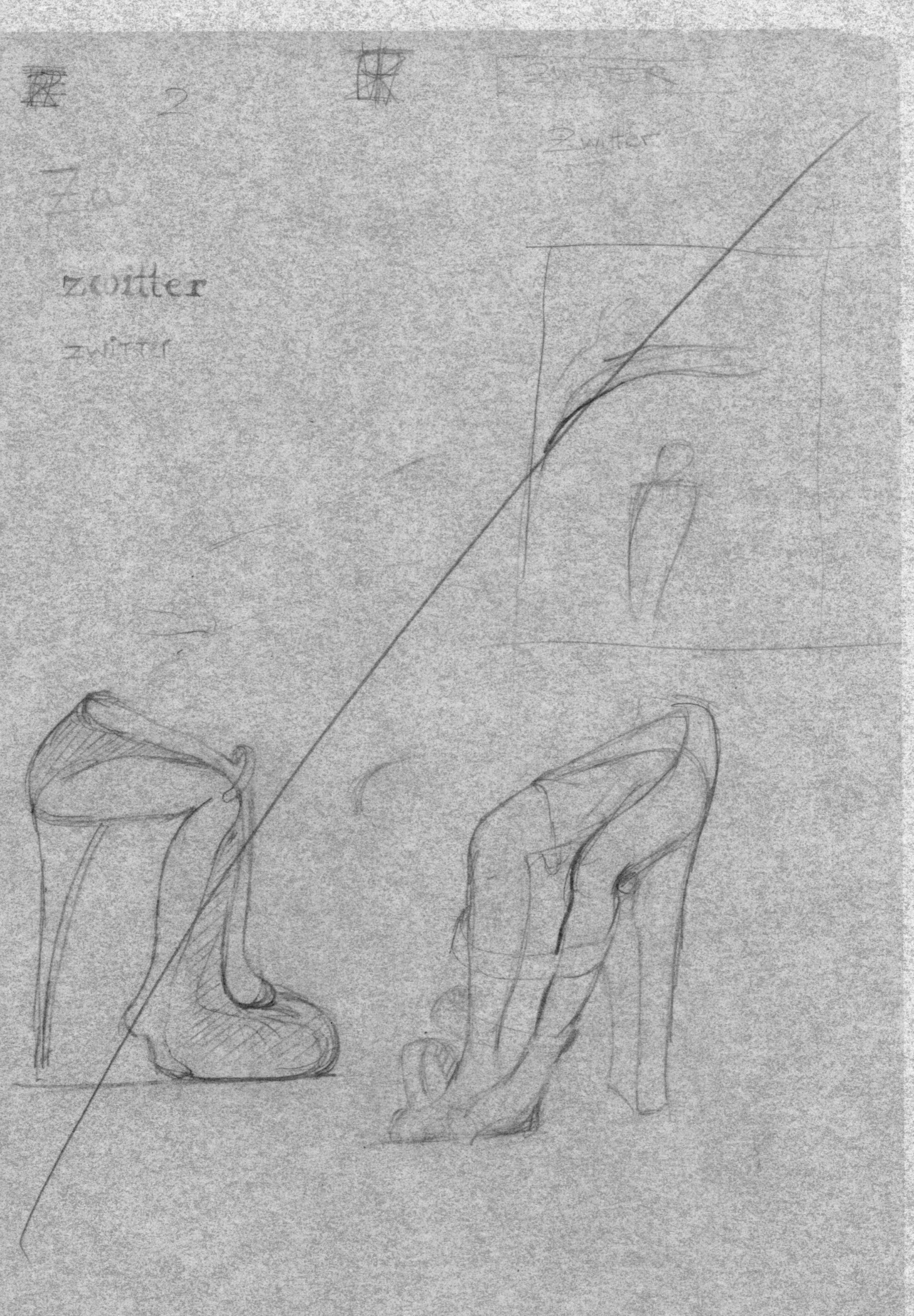

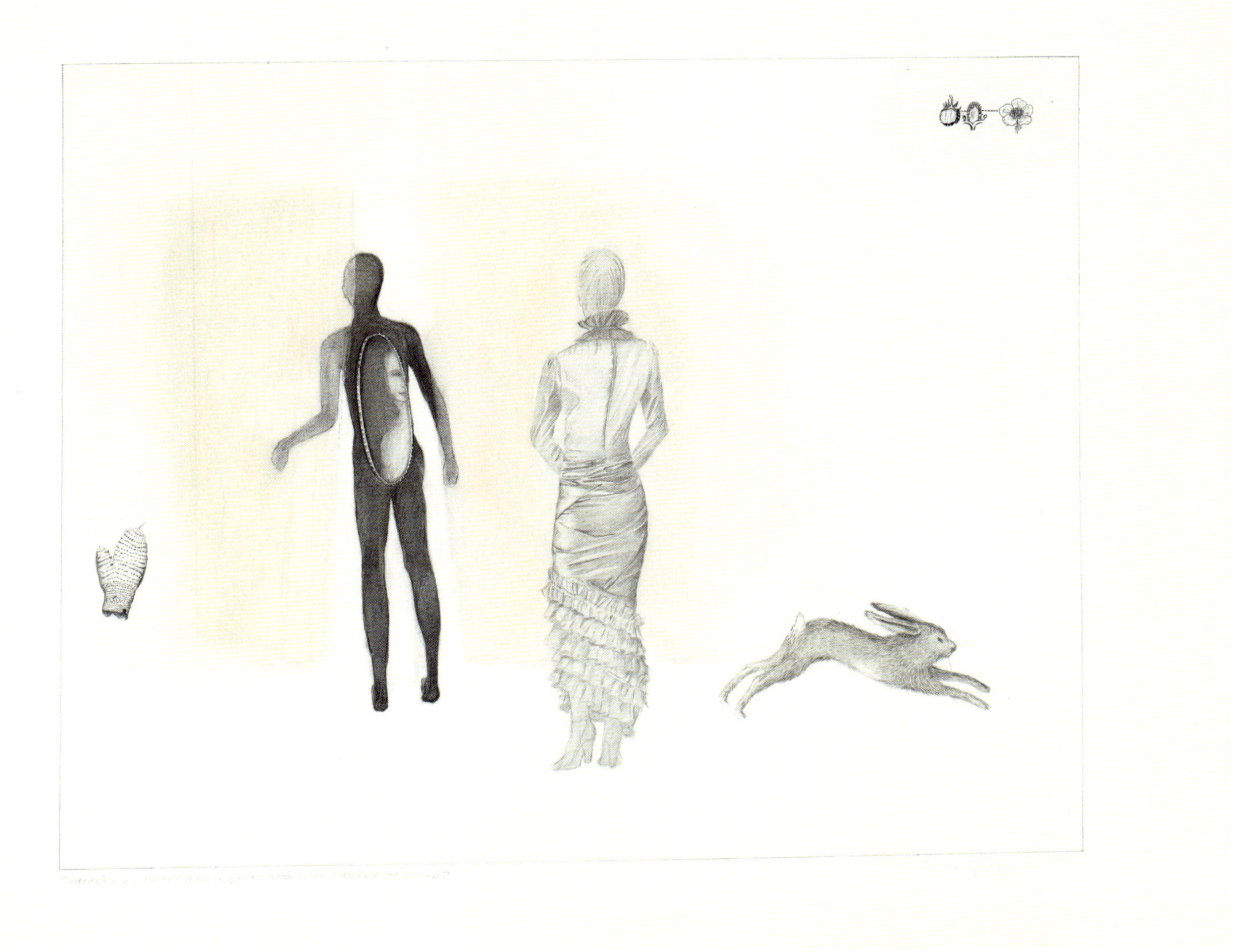

67 *Spiegelblick – Häschenerlebnis – Wem gehört der Mädchenhandschuh?* 1977
Mirror Gaze – Bunny Experience – Who Does the Girl's Glove Belong To?

The Circuits
of a Riddle

Melissa Destino

As sea foam I would like to be frivolous.[1]

[1] Translated from the Italian »Come schiuma del mare vorrei essere frivola.« Excerpt from the poem by Carla Lonzi, »Gita in macchina,« Rome, July 14, 1958. in Carla Lonzi, *Scacco Ragionato. Poesie dal '58 al '63*, Milano, Rivolta Femminile, 1985.

[2] Apart from Lewis Carroll's *Alice in Wonderland and Alice Through the Looking Glass*, Alice appears as reference, both implicit and explicit, in numerous movies, songs, and books. For the purposes of this text, let us mention two specific references: *Radio Alice*, the Italian independent radio of the 1970s, and the song »White Rabbit« by Jefferson Airplane.

[3] As reference for the notion of »circuit,« see Gruppo A/Dams, *Alice disambientata*, ed. Gianni Celati (Milan: L'erba voglio, 1977).

[4] Ibid., p. 7.

[5] »Sense is a nonexisting entity, and, in fact, maintains very special relations with nonsense,« in Gilles Deleuze, *The Logic of Sense*, trans. Mark Lester (New York: Columbia University Press, 1990).

[6] »›Which way? Which way?‹ asks Alice, sensing that it is always in both directions at the same time,« and »Paradox is initially that which destroys good sense as the only direction, but it is also that which destroys common sense as the assignation of fixed identities,« in ibid p. 3.

[7] It seems precisely the moment when the subject, having spiraled the dress's frills toward the front, is pausing before turning them to the back again in a (frivolous) dance. Another discrepancy is apparent here: the subject's hair is short, which means that if the scene takes place in the Victorian era, most likely the subject is not a woman; if it does, instead, happen in the present—the mid-1970s—the dress appears anachronistic. In both cases one can imagine a carnivalesque disguise, which I argue to be a pivotal way of reading the piece, as the carnival is not only a temporary social space where everyone is equal and free but also a subversive force capable of making social order collapse (see Mikhail Bakhtin's notion of »carnivalesque«).

[8] See, in this regard, the linguistic notion of »opaque context.«

Spiegelblick – Häschenerlebnis – Wem gehört der Mädchenhandschuh? (Mirror Gaze – Bunny Experience – Who Does the Girl's Glove Belong To?, ill. <u>67</u>) is a riddle, frivolous and yet very serious. It is impossible not to think of the adventures and worlds of Alice:[2] more than being a symbol, she is a figure within a circuit where everything has to be connected in order to function.[3] »Alice is everywhere but is also what sends us here and there, she gets [us] to embark on great journeys«;[4] she flies as radio signals in the ether, she is uncatchable.

Reading this work seems like a search for holes to fall into to enter (un)imaginable worlds; it is a search for sense, which never exists without its contrary.[5] Jürgenssen makes evident the paradoxes—that is to say, the affirmation of the existence of several senses at once.[6]

Things are not given in their individuality and can only be perceived through a simultaneous intelligence of the *relations between* them. A clue to this might be the interconnected yet inverted temporal processuality indicated by the triad of fruit-plant-flower (top right). Like an interwoven fabric, the drawing unravels via its missing parts: the reassuring possibility of pairing is repeatedly discarded: as we take up our Miss Marplesque pursuit, one glove and the front of the two subjects present in the scene remain mysterious.

The depth of the mirror purposely mismatches the expected reflection. Furthermore, its *shape resembles* a hole or a pond or a portrait frame, but in all three cases it does not quite correspond to the respective category: its contours are too precise to be a hole, its reflection too sharp to be a pond, its width too squeezed to be a portrait frame. And it is this very same discrepancy that leads the flow of thought further.

An imaginary transverse line connects the viewers' coordinates with the ones outlined behind the curtains, passing through a plane that hosts a subject who, dressed in Victorian fashion, is depicted in a suspended movement.[7]

The drawing is an opaque context: it is like a linguistic expression where it is not always possible to preserve the »truth« of the whole when the terms are replaced with other terms.[8] It only works precisely because it is a circuit, of paradoxes.

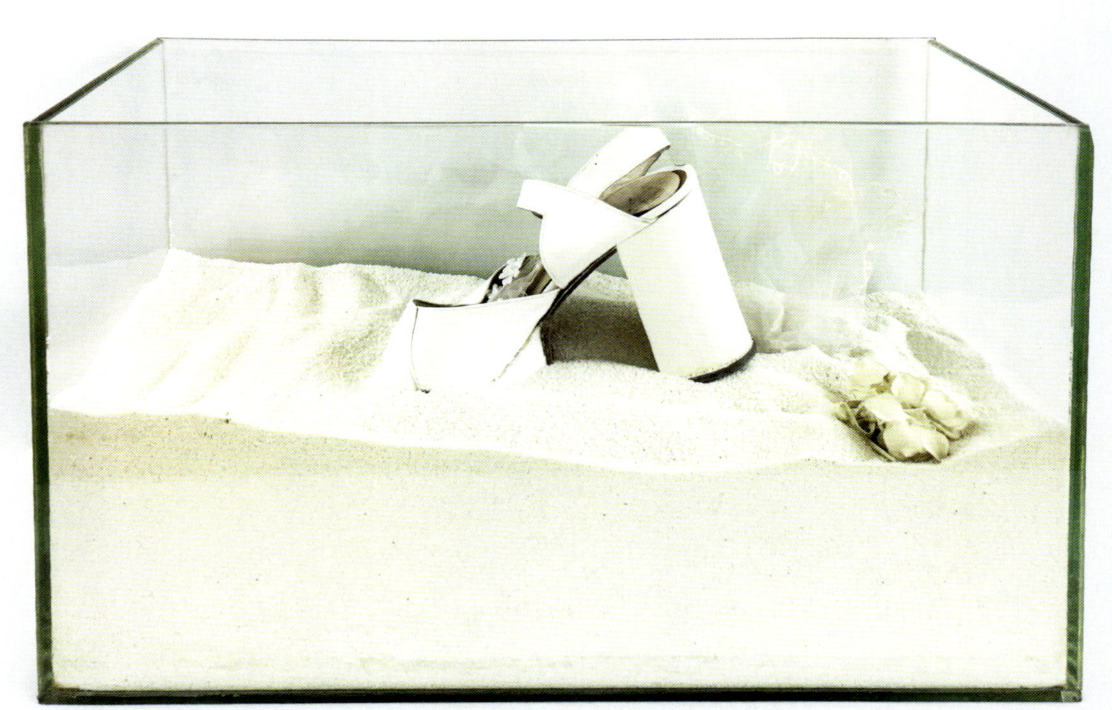

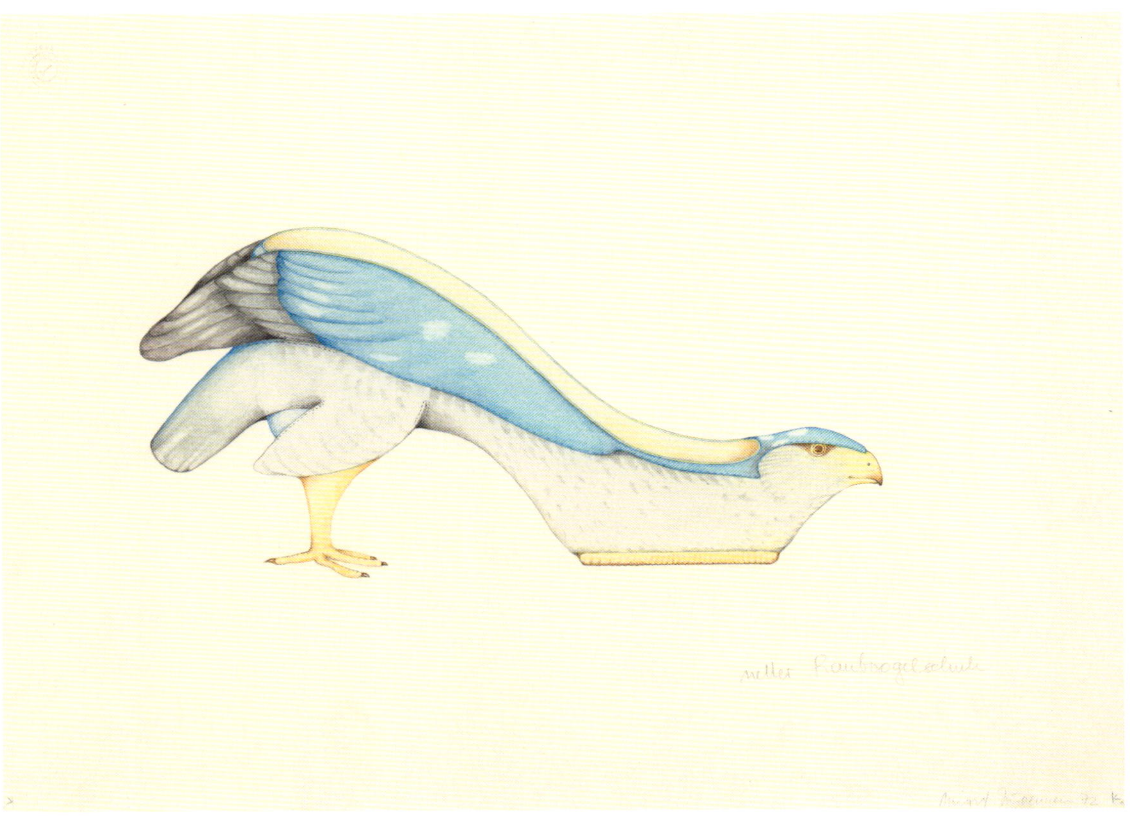

68   *Ohne Titel (Hochzeitsschuh)* 1976
       Untitled (Wedding Shoe)
69   *Netter Raubvogelschuh* 1972
       Nice Bird of Prey Shoe

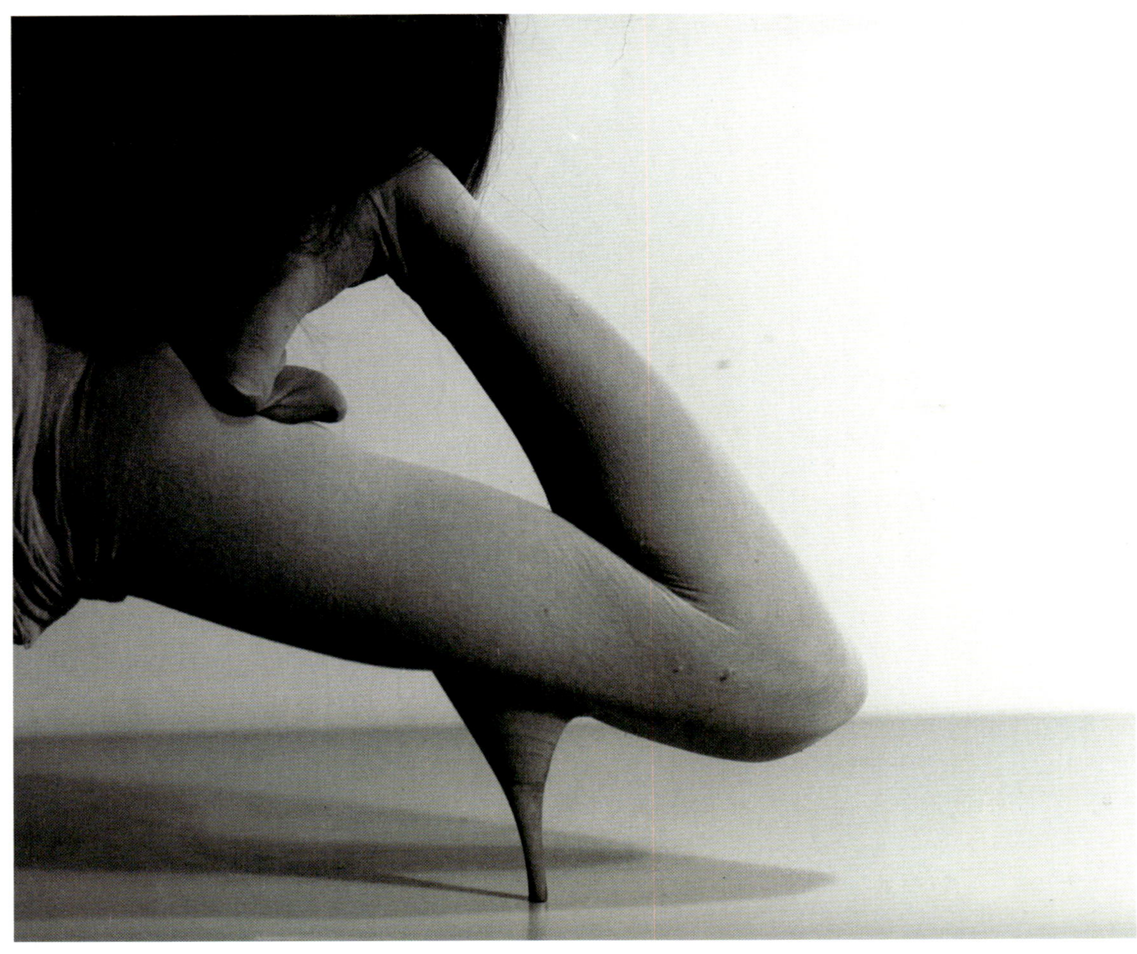

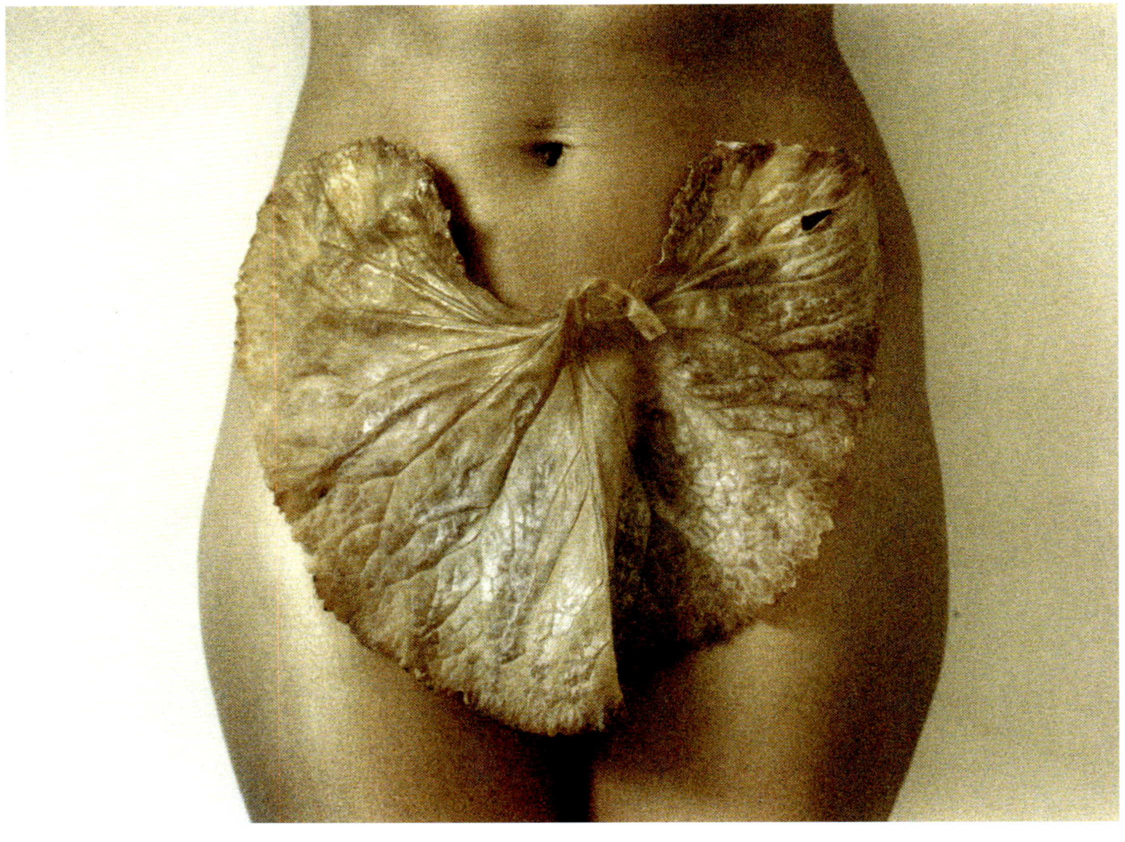

70 *Schuhroulade* 1977
    Shoe Roulade
71 *Ohne Titel* 1988
    Untitled

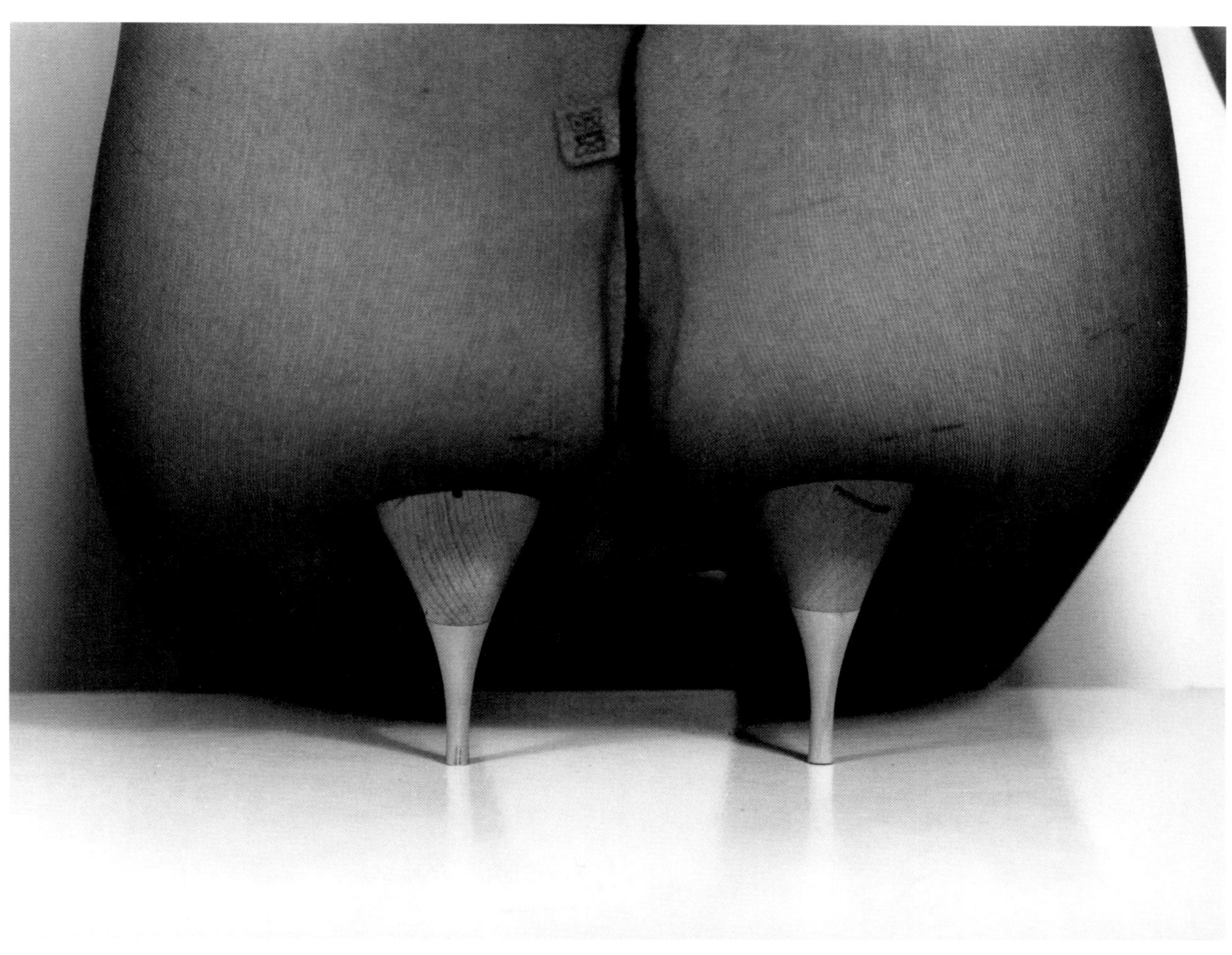

72 *Ballonschuh* 1976
Balloon Shoe

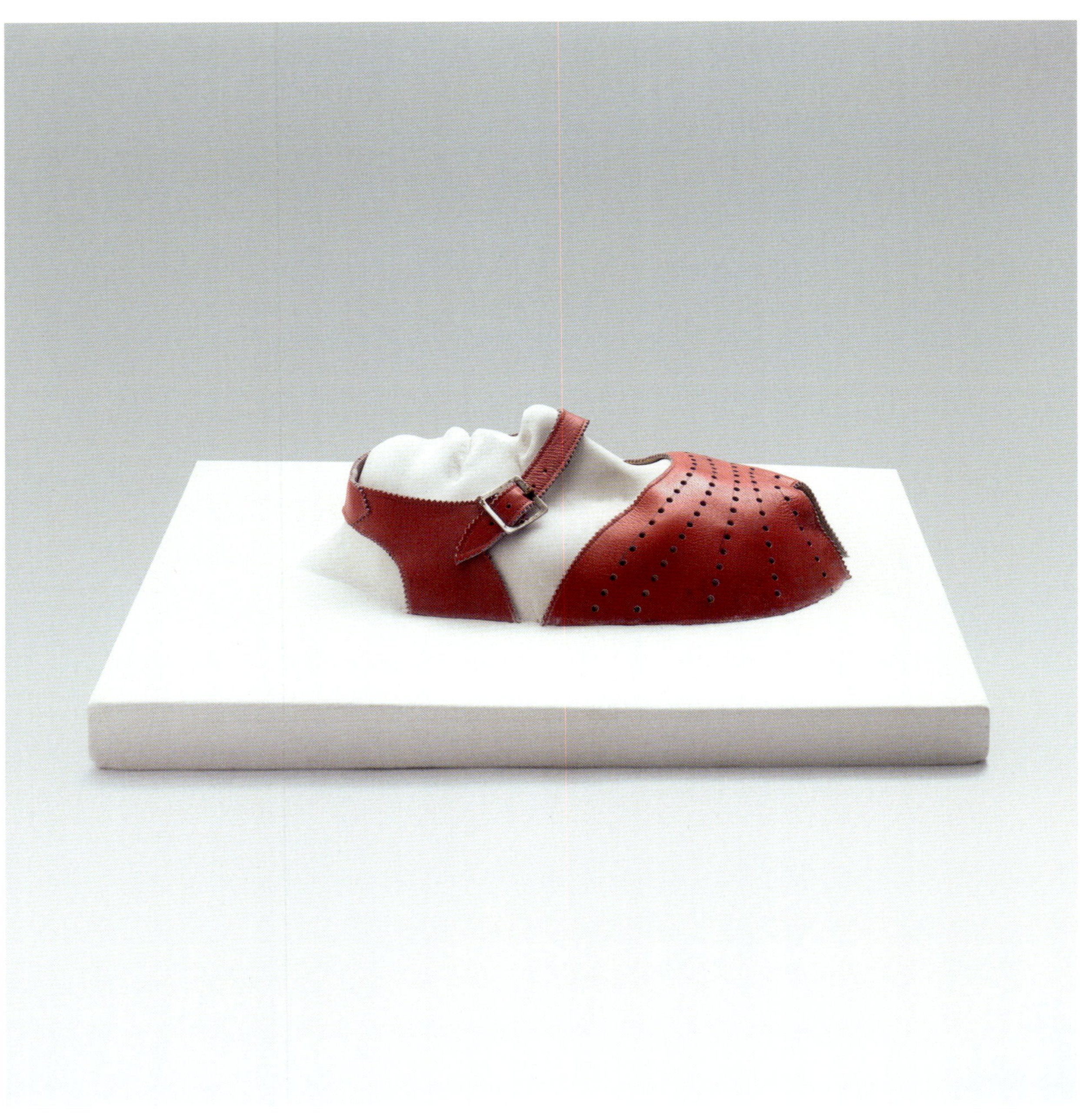

73 *Kopfsandale* 1976
Head Sandal

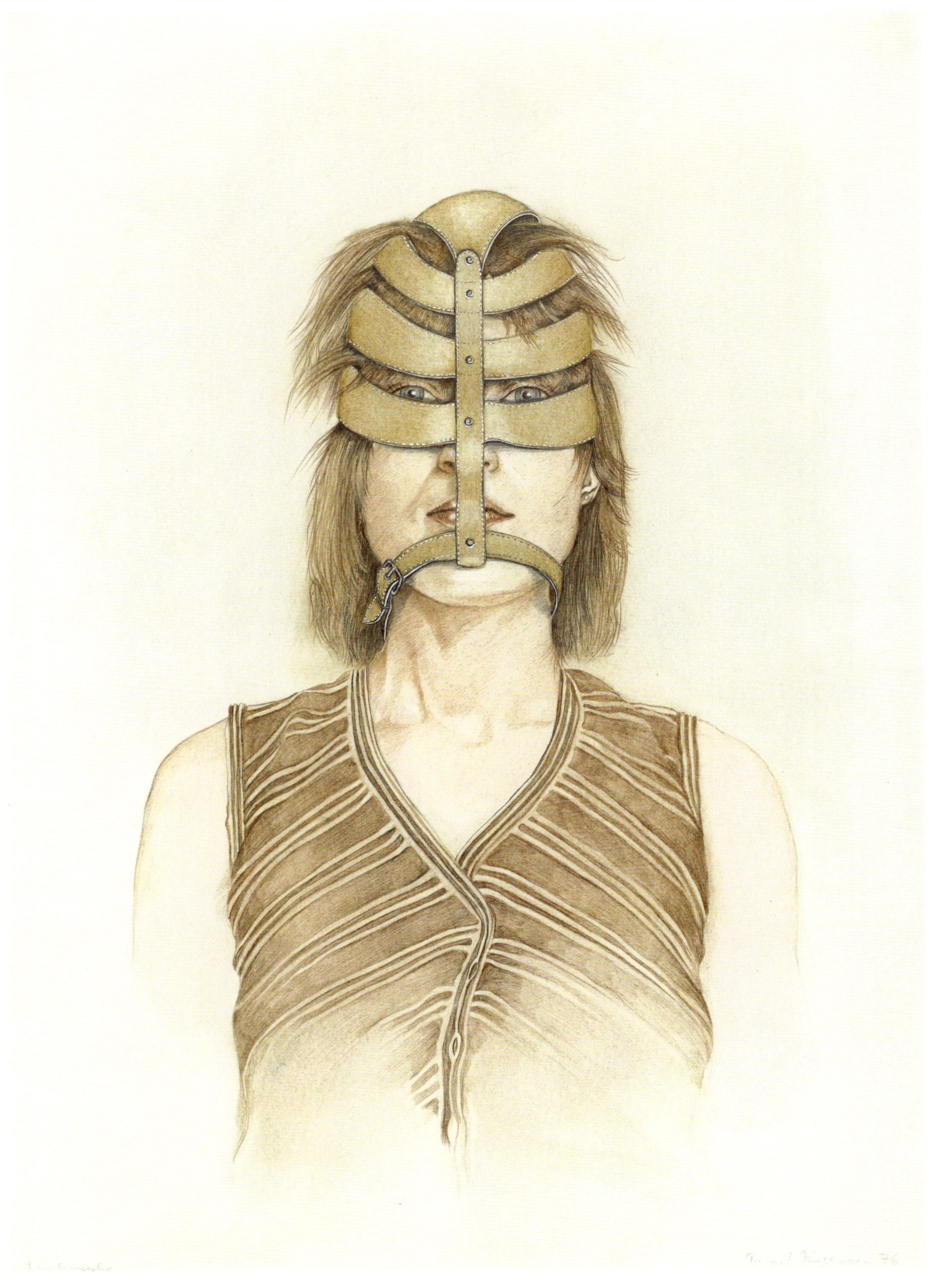

74 *Schuhmaske* 1976
Shoe Mask

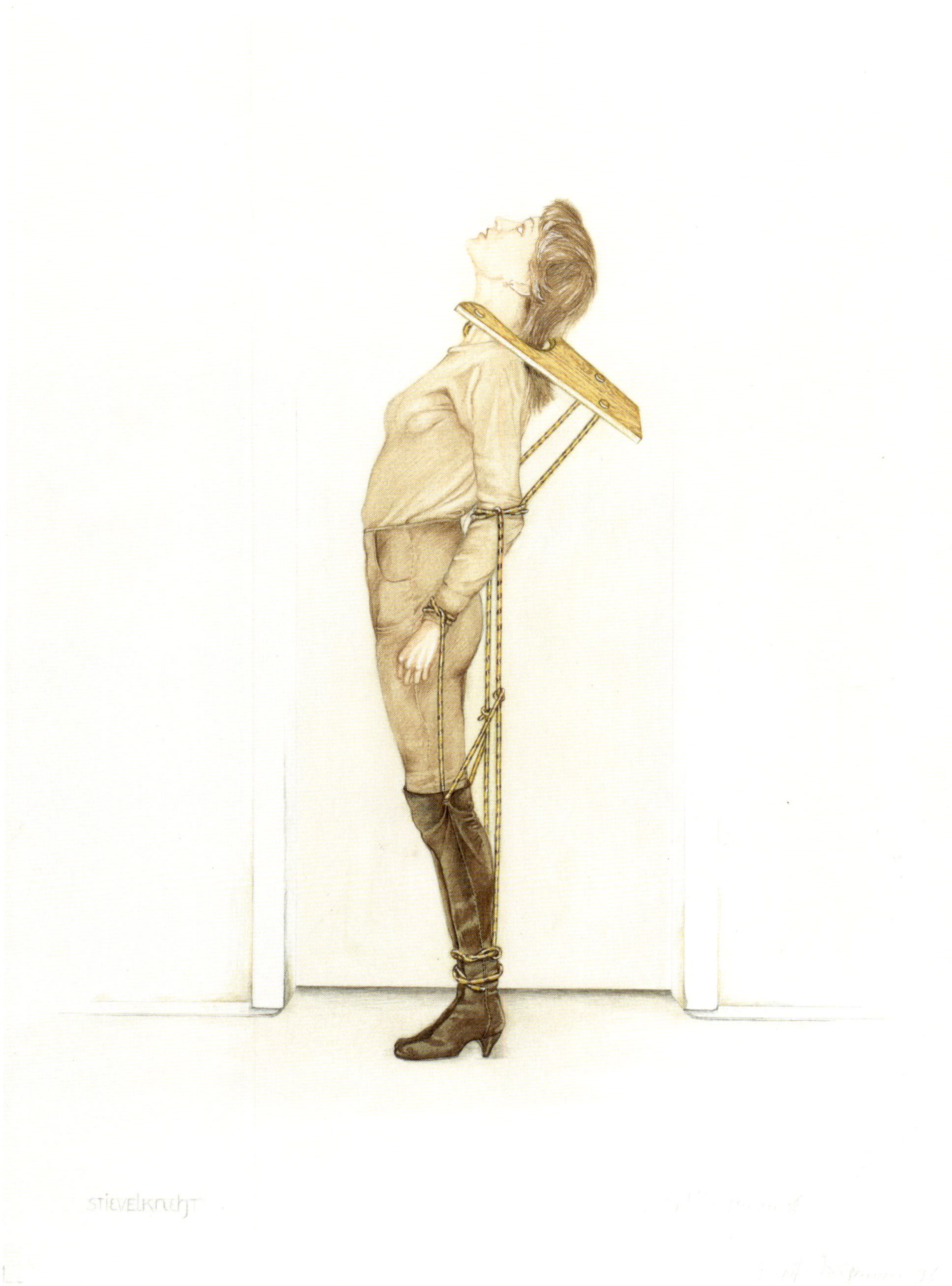

75 *Stiefelknecht* 1976
Bootjack

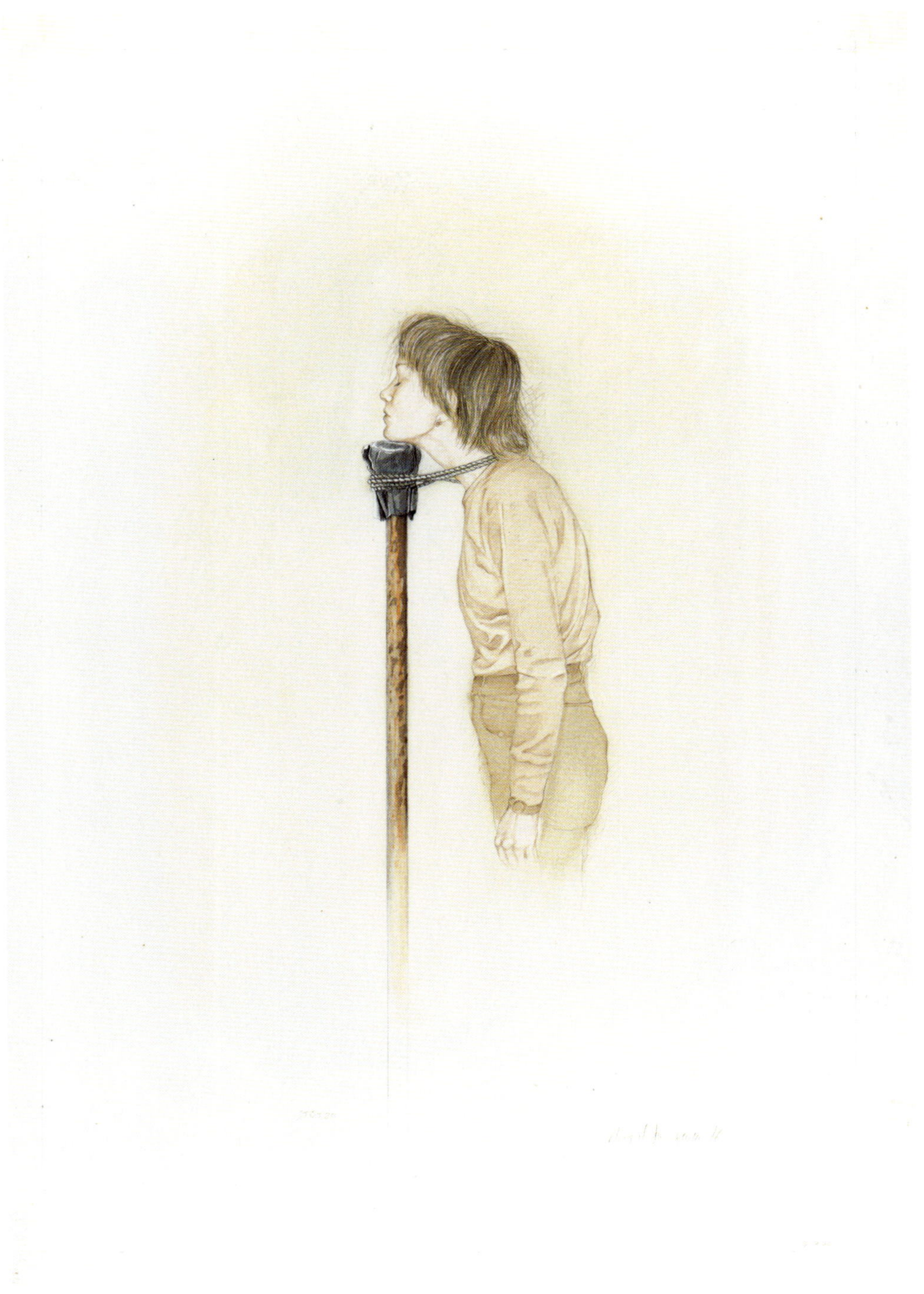

76   *Stütze* 1976
      Support

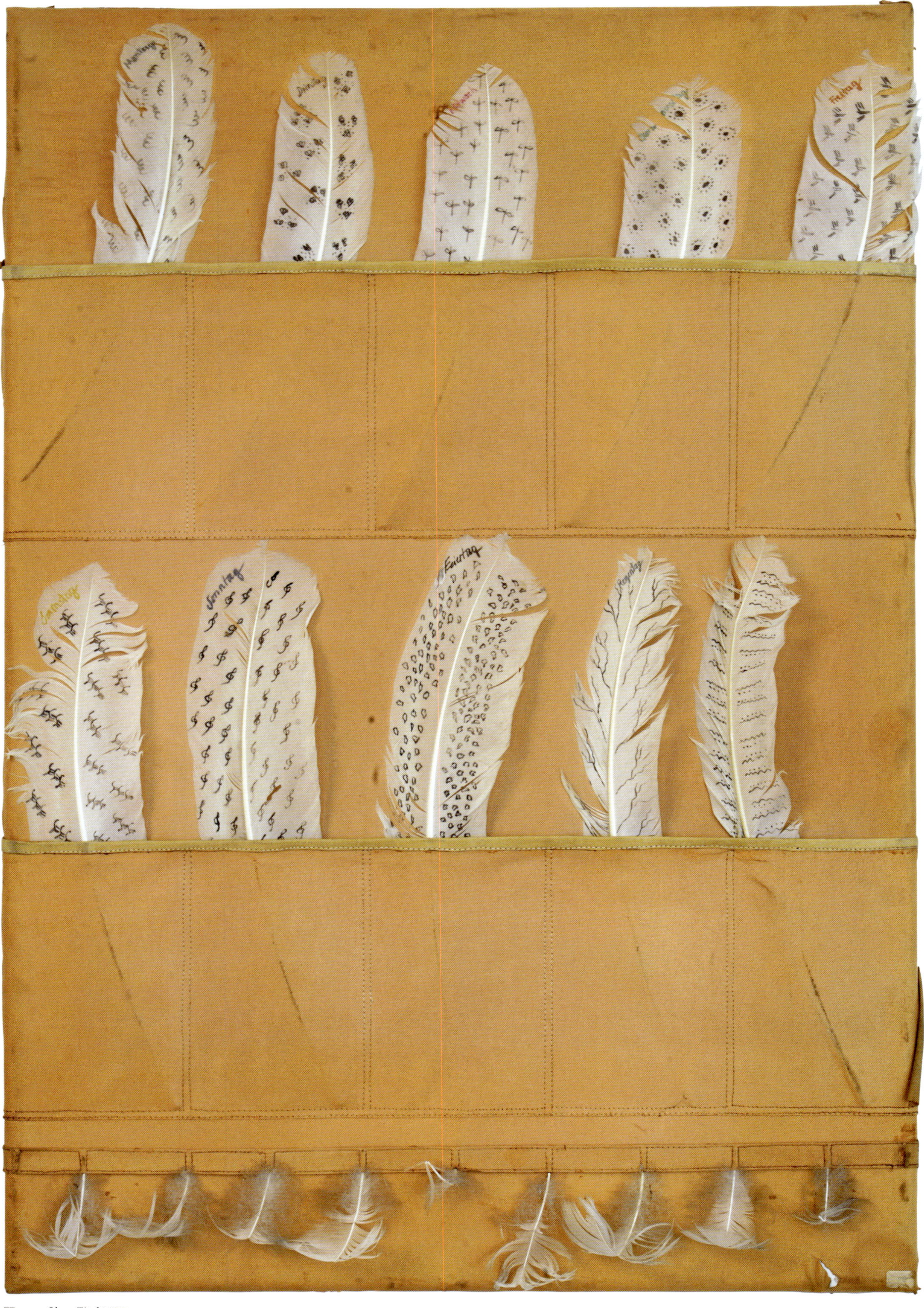

77   *Ohne Titel* 1975
      Untitled

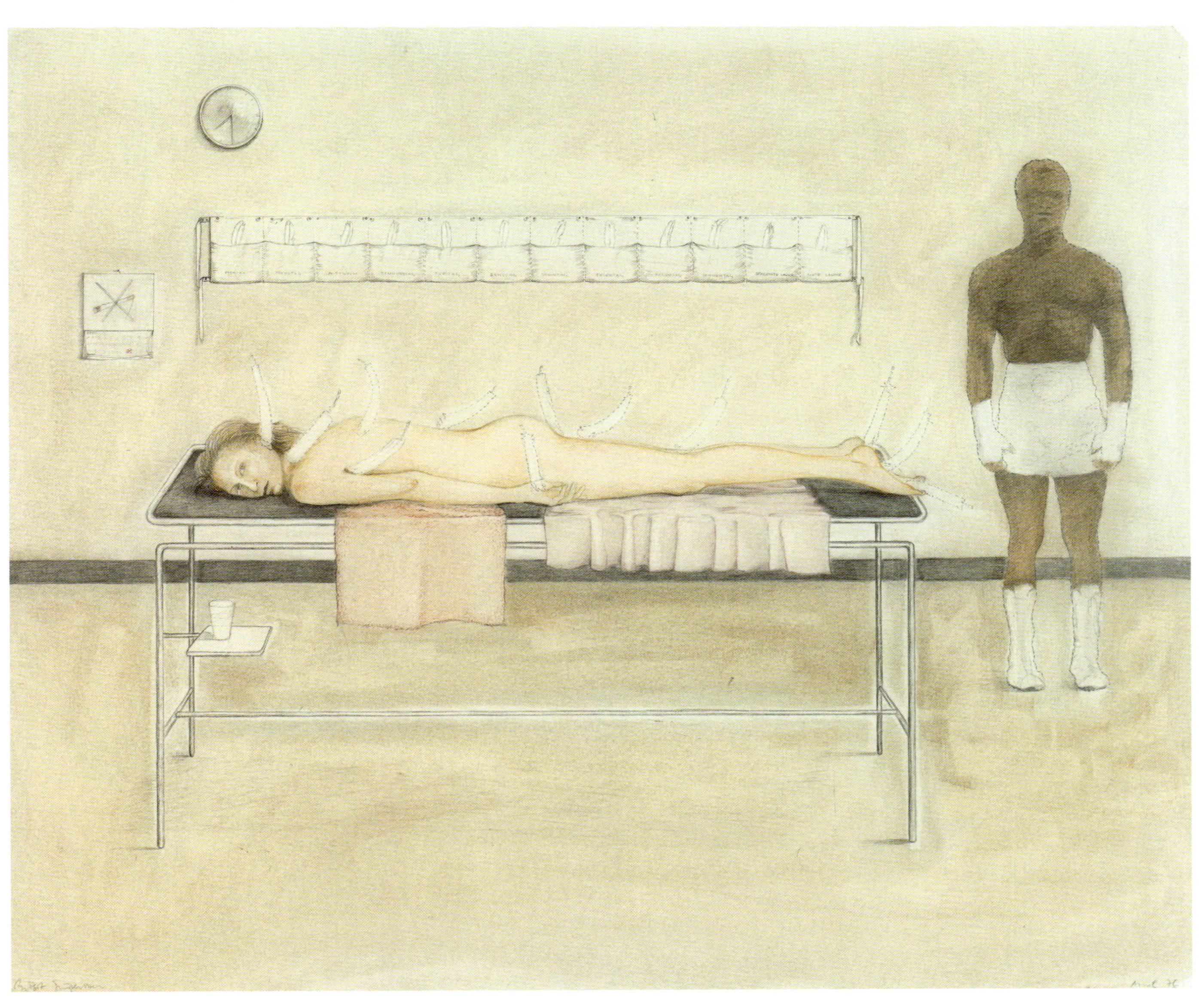

78 *Ohne Titel (The Hour of the Feather)* 1976
Untitled (The Hour of the Feather)

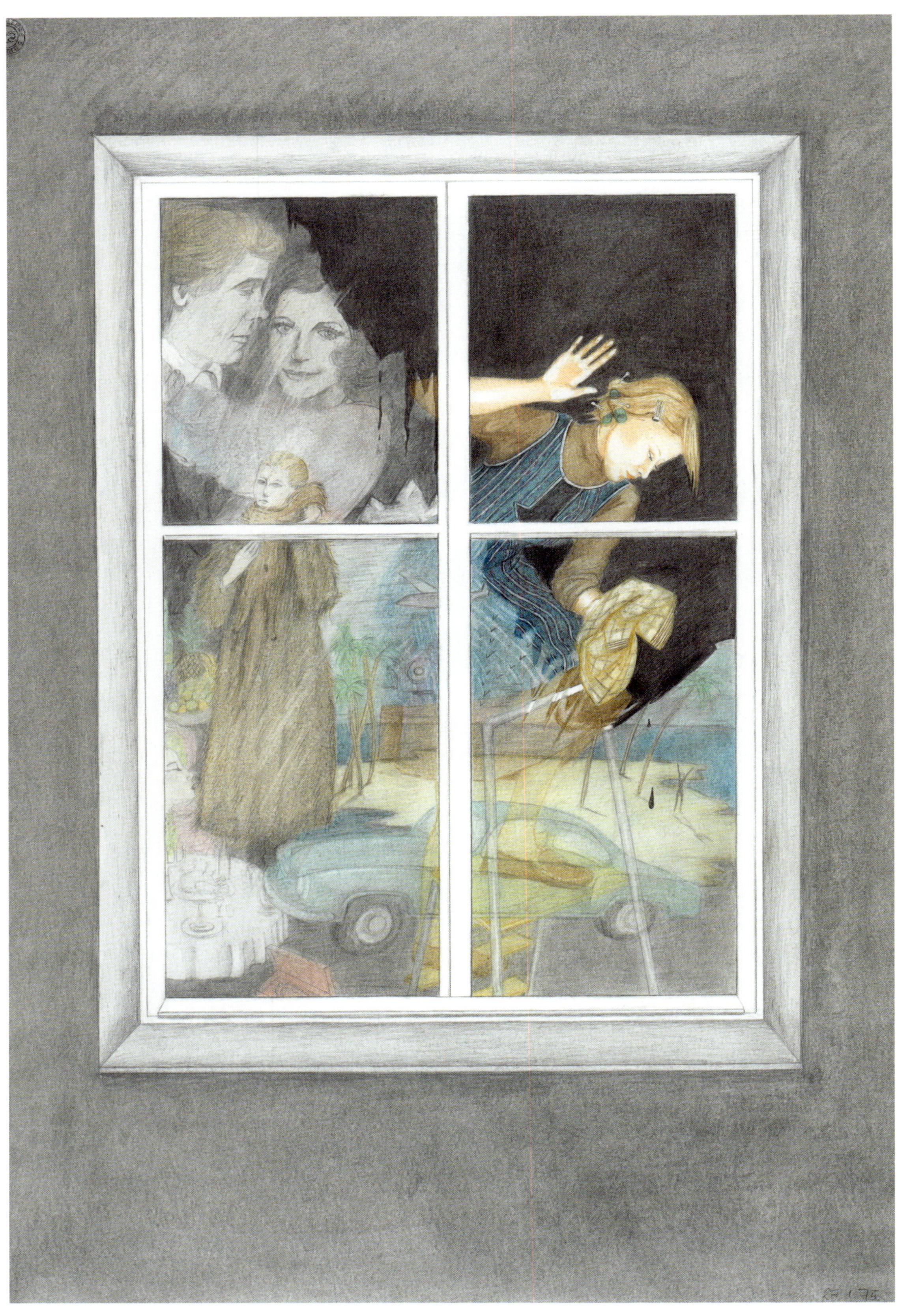

79 *Fensterputzen* 1975
   Window Cleaning

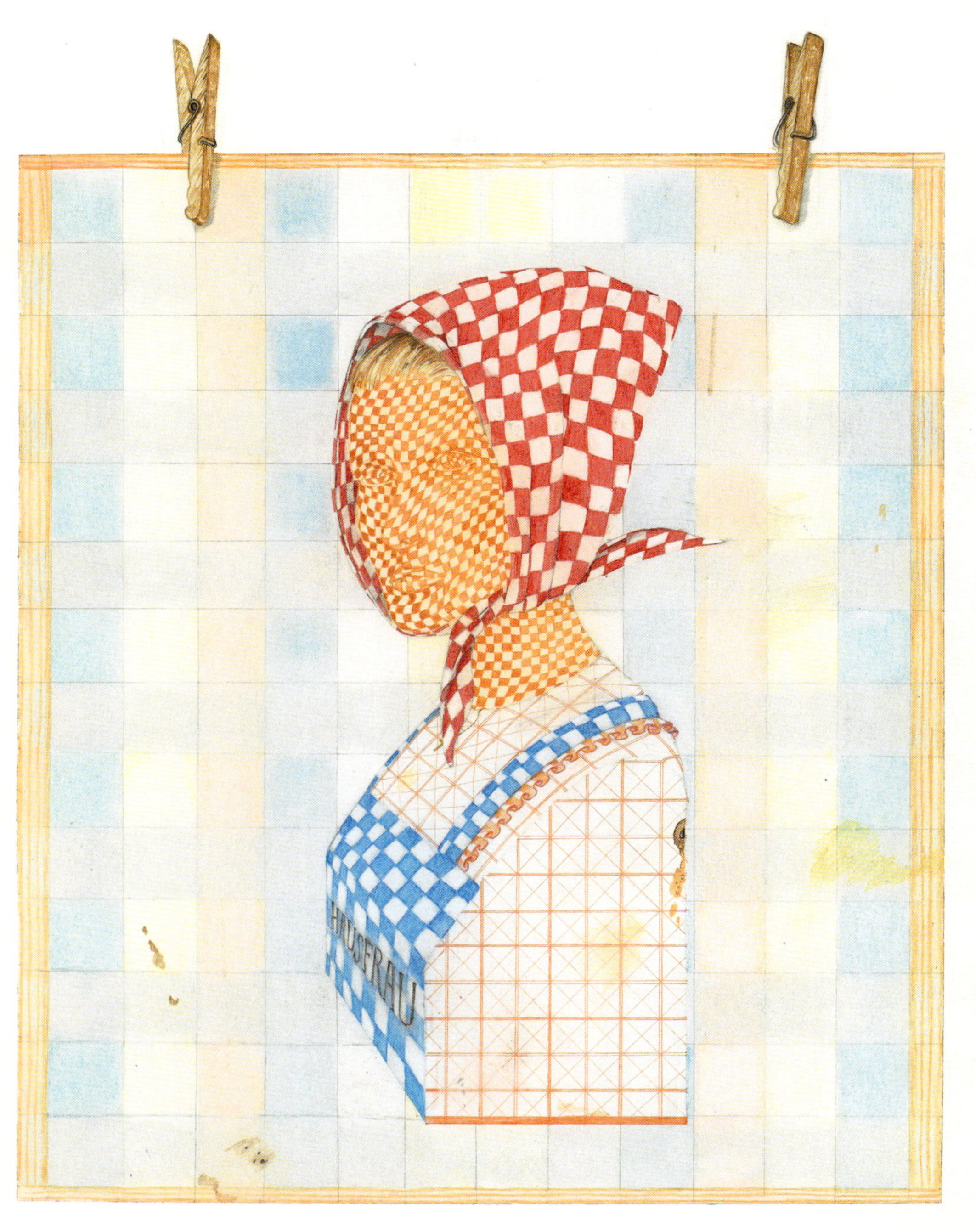

80   *Hausfrau* 1974
      Housewife

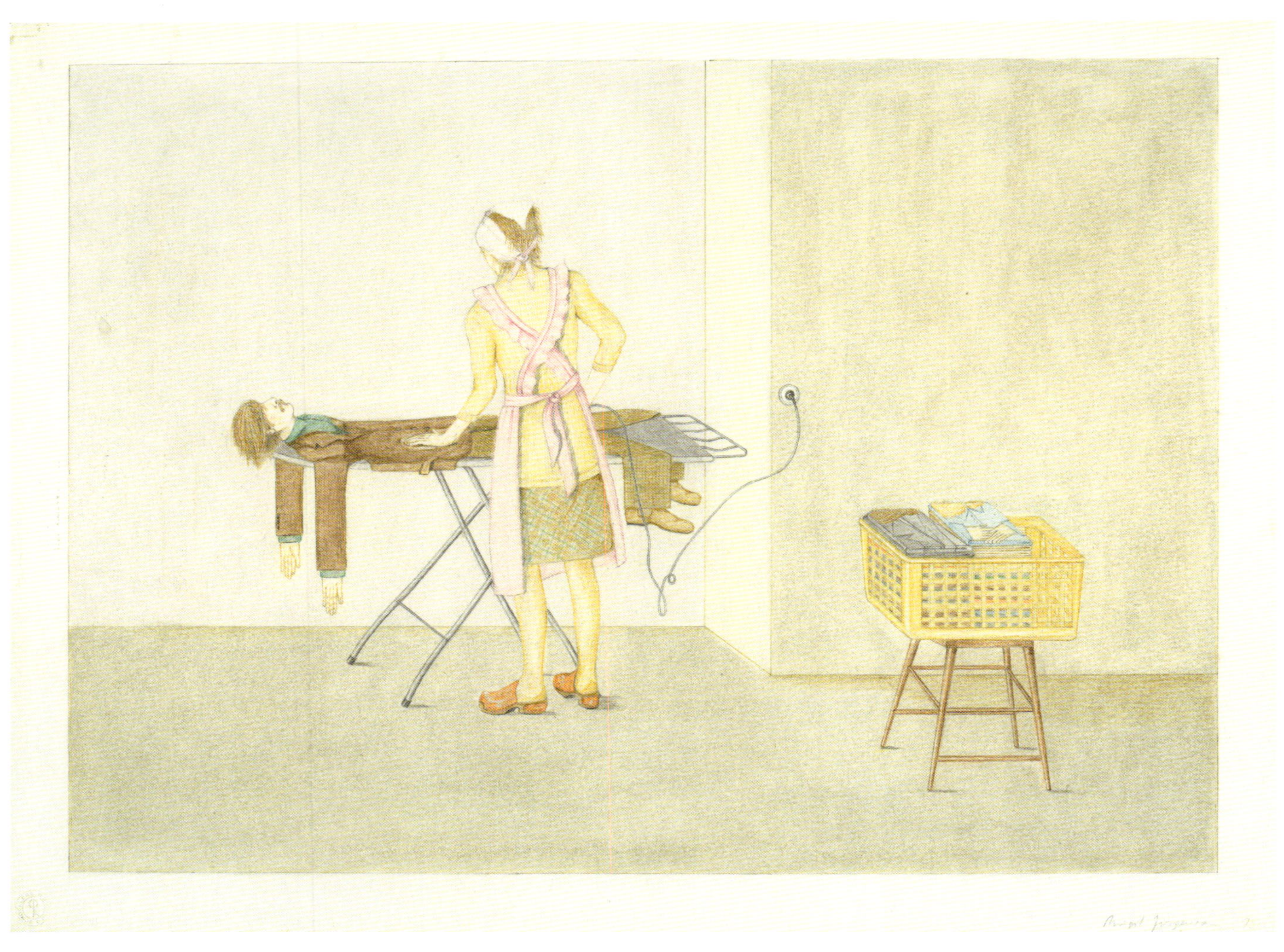

81 *Hausfrauenarbeit* 1973
Housewives' Work

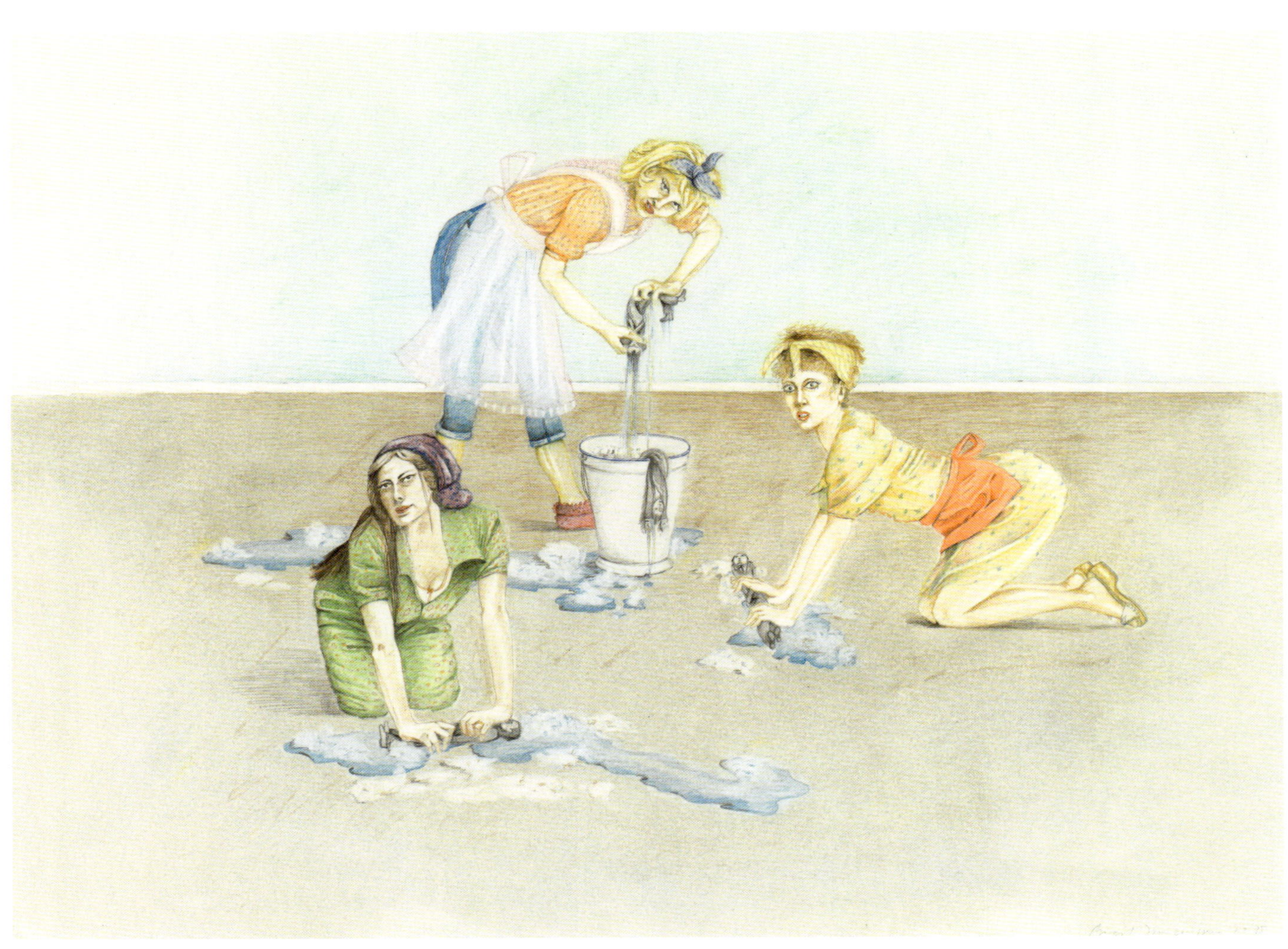

82   *Bodenschrubben* 1975
    Scrubbing the Floor

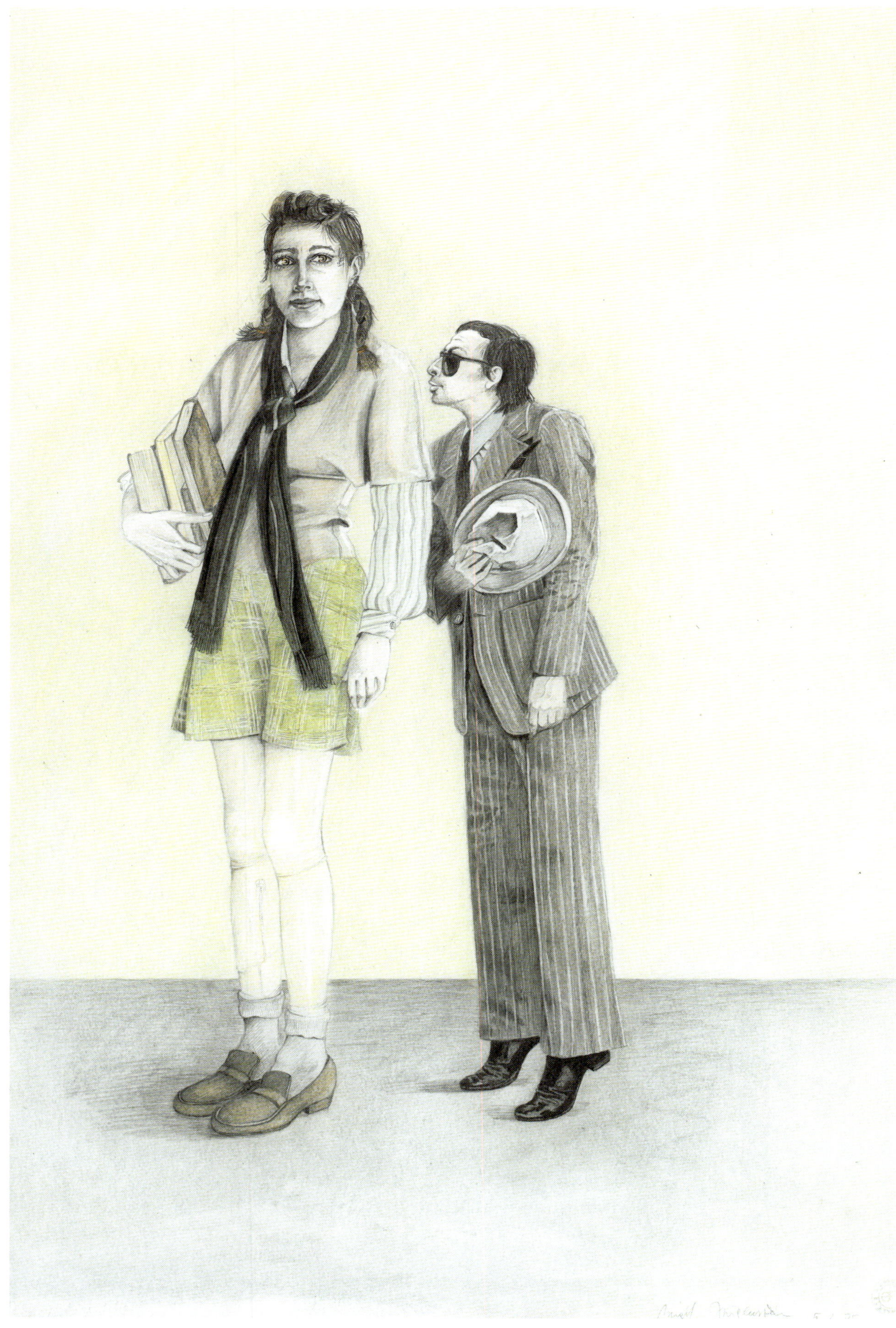

  Großes Mädchen 1975
Big Girl

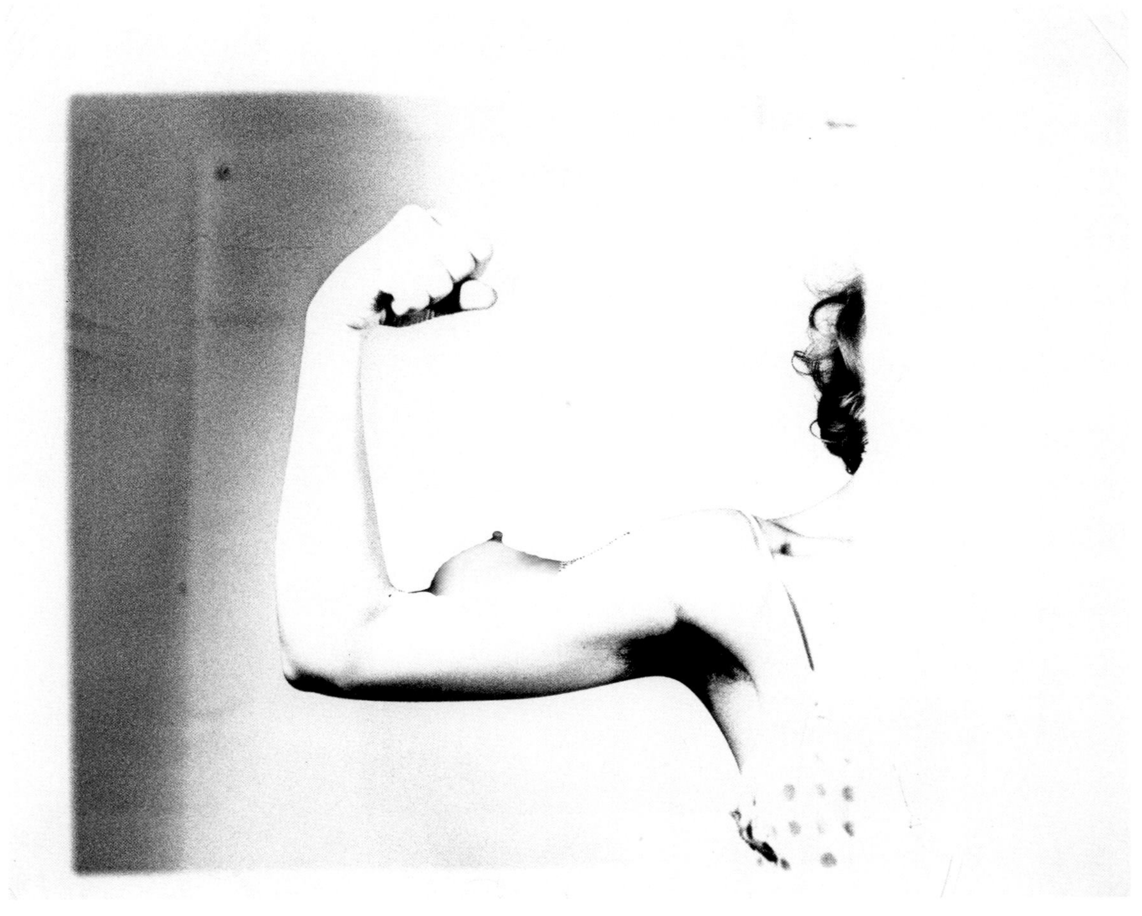

84   *Ohne Titel* 1979
Untitled

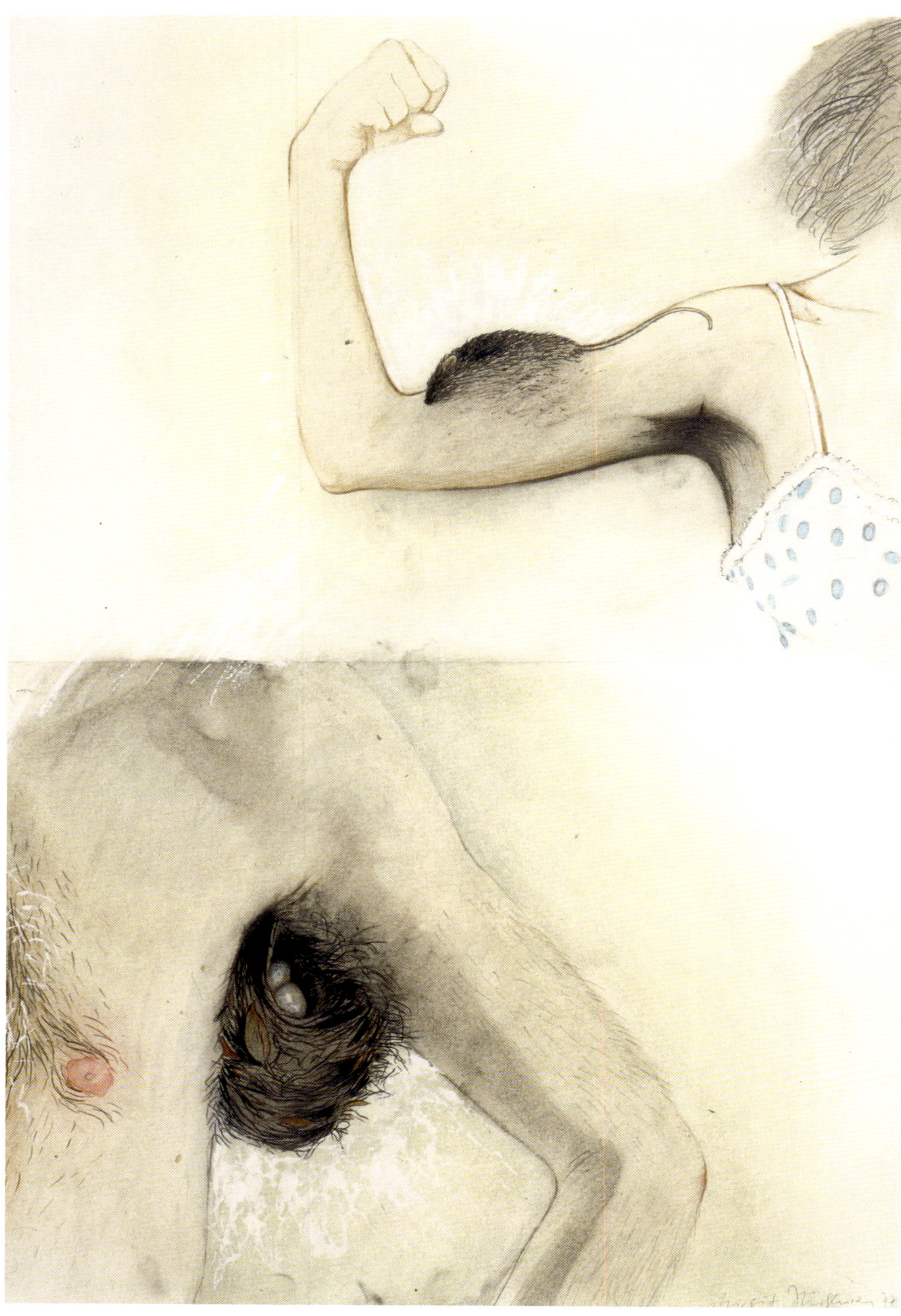

 Ohne Titel 1977
Untitled

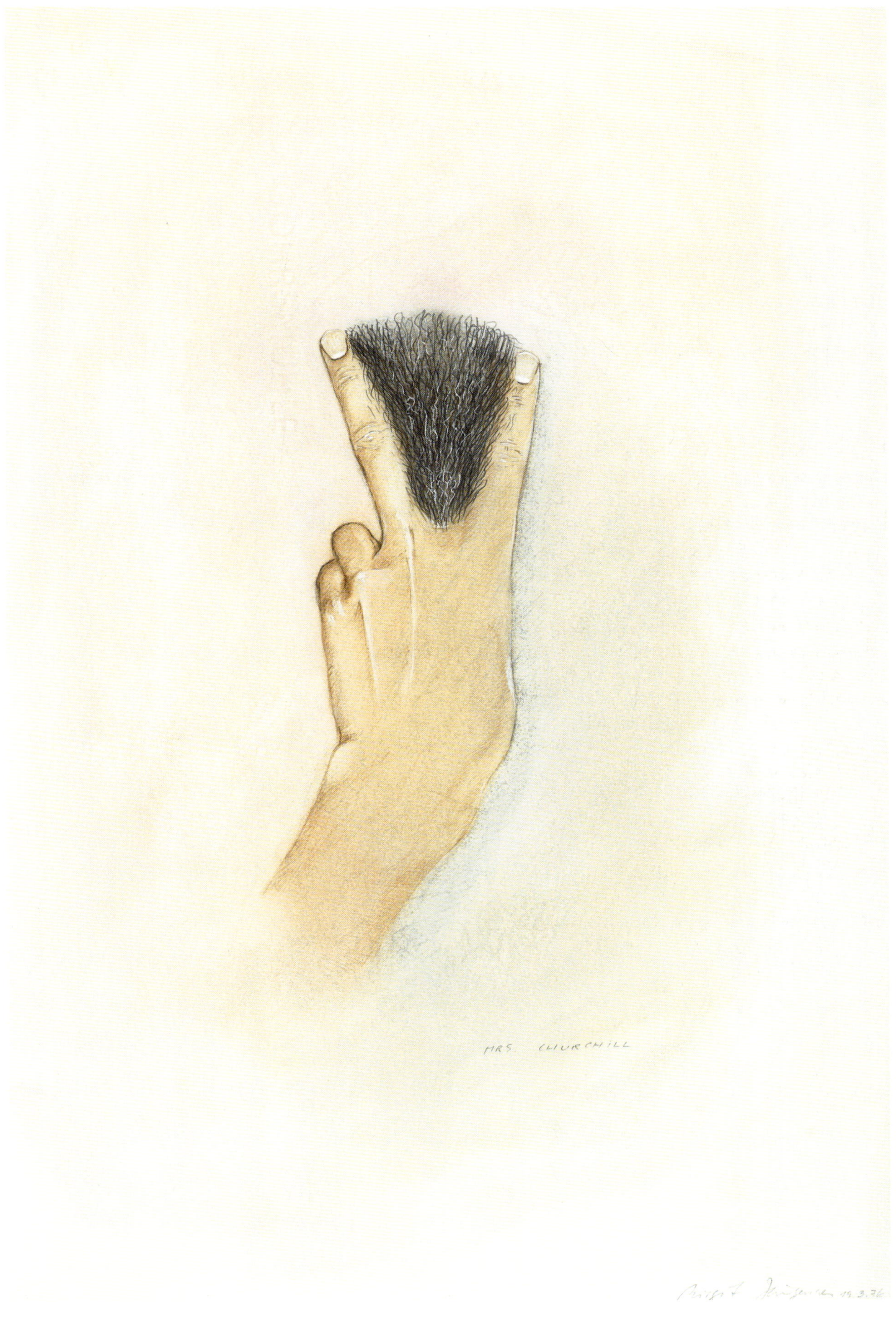

86   *Mrs. Churchill* 1976

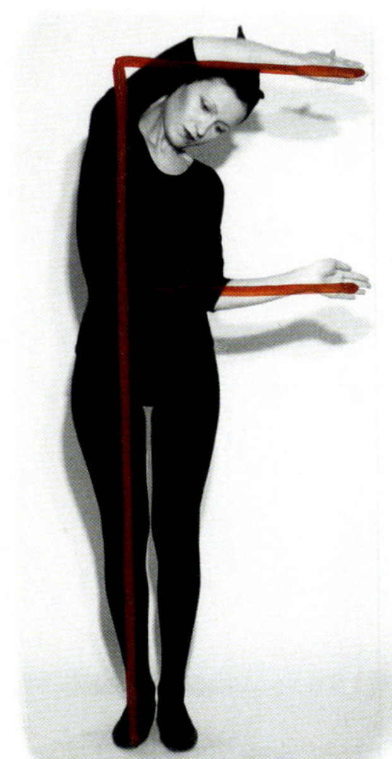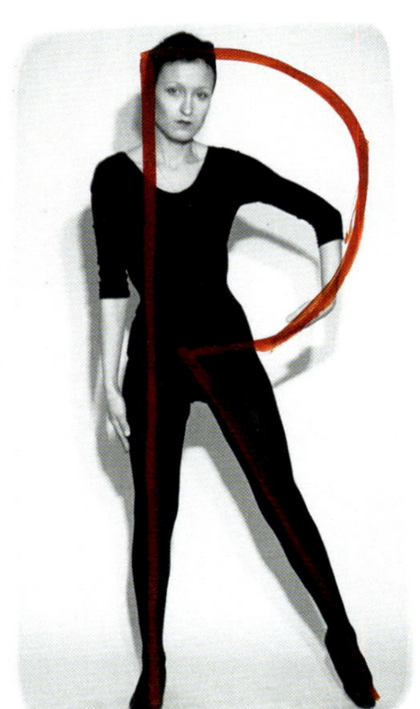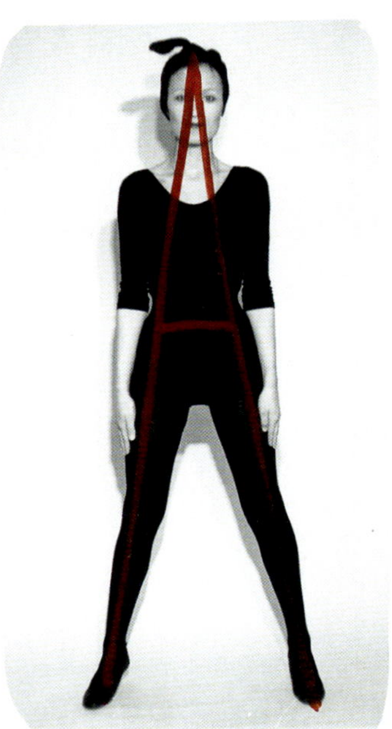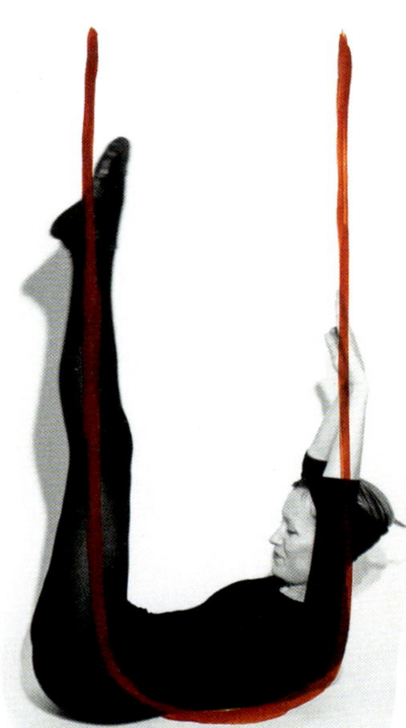

87   *Ohne Titel (Frau)* 1979
Untitled (Woman)

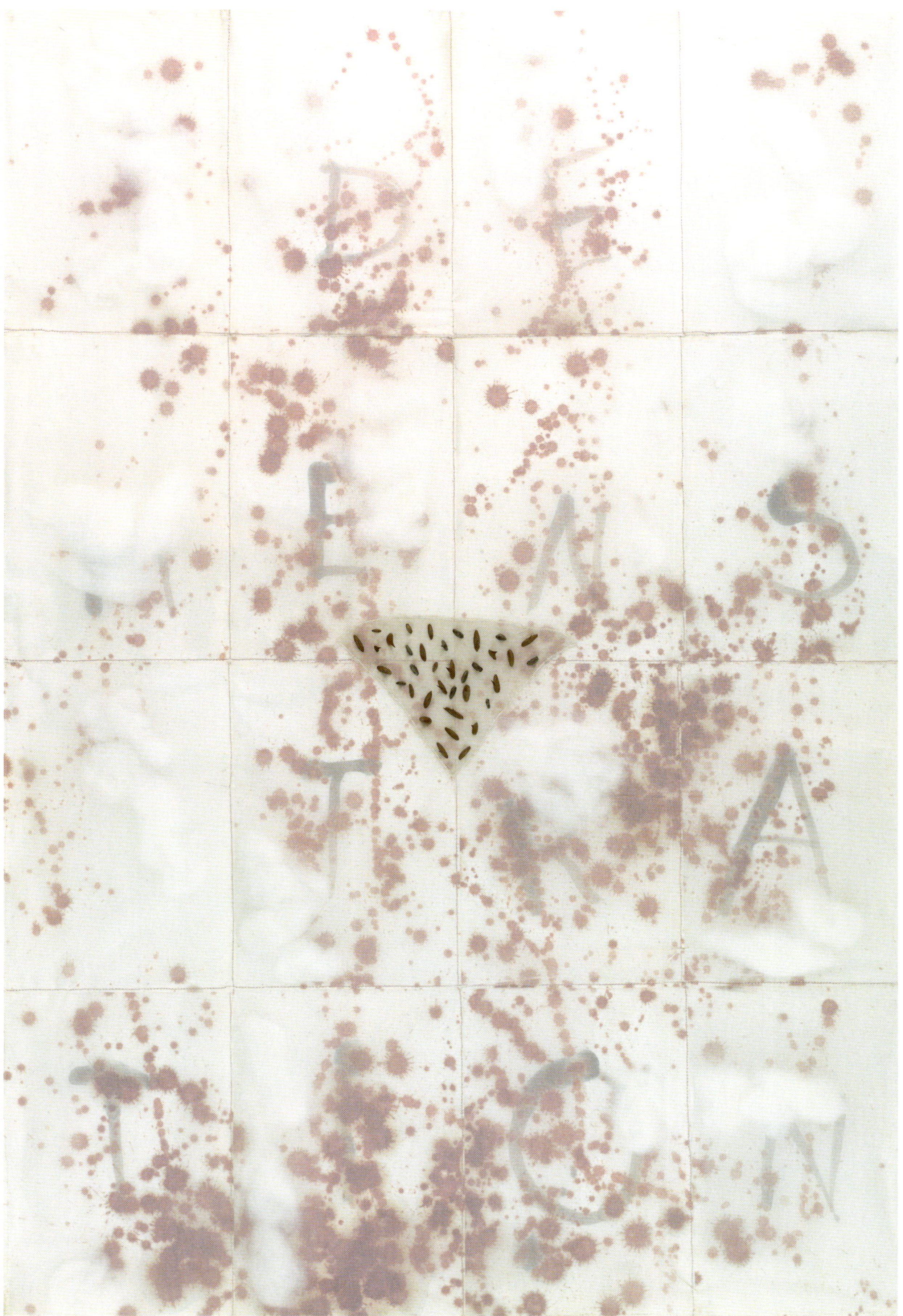

88   *Demenstration* 1978/1979

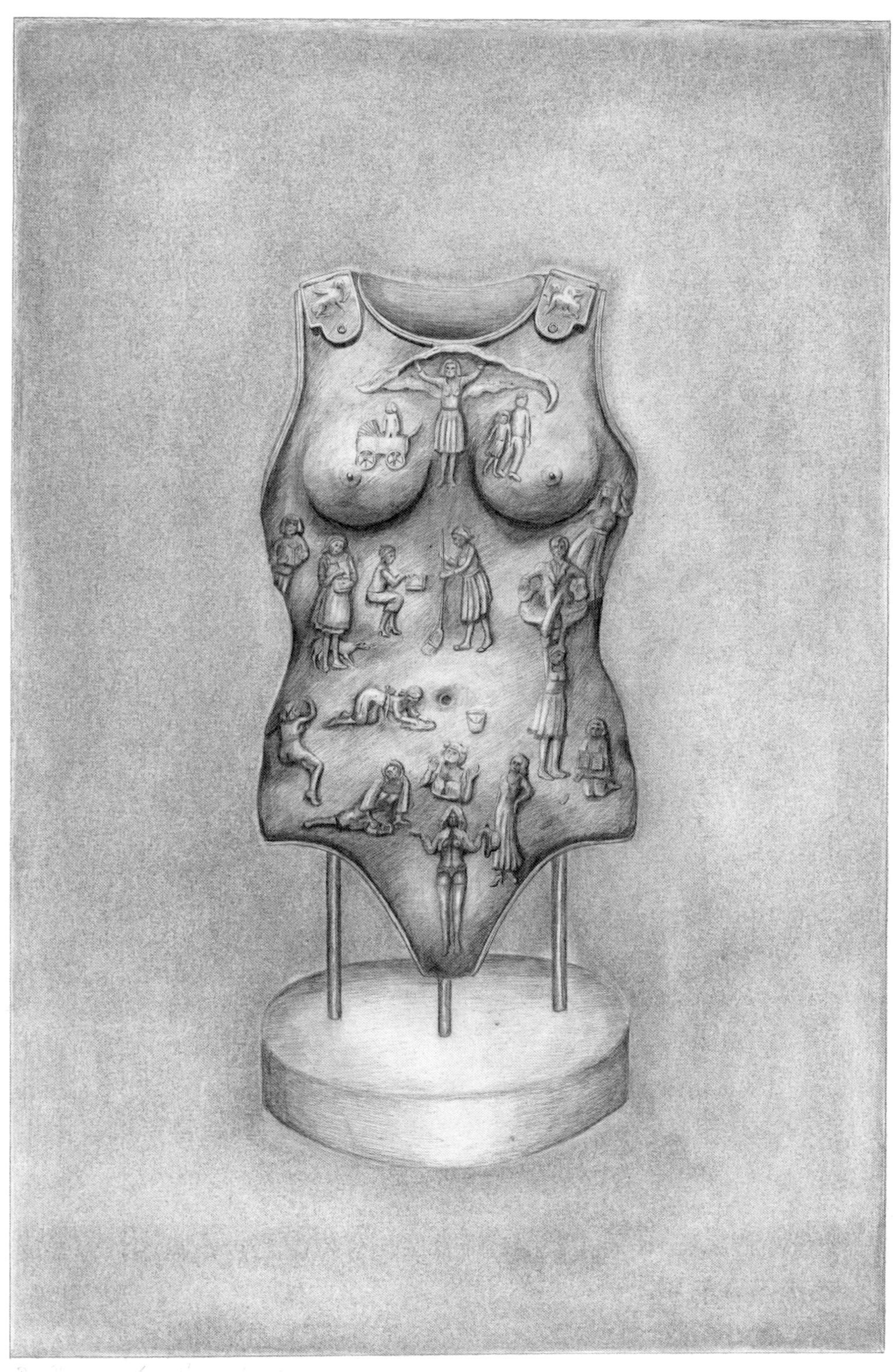

89 *Der Panzer der Augustina* 1974
Augustina's Armor

I Am – Bicasso
The Transformation of Cultural Traditions in the Work of Birgit Jürgenssen

Nicole Fritz

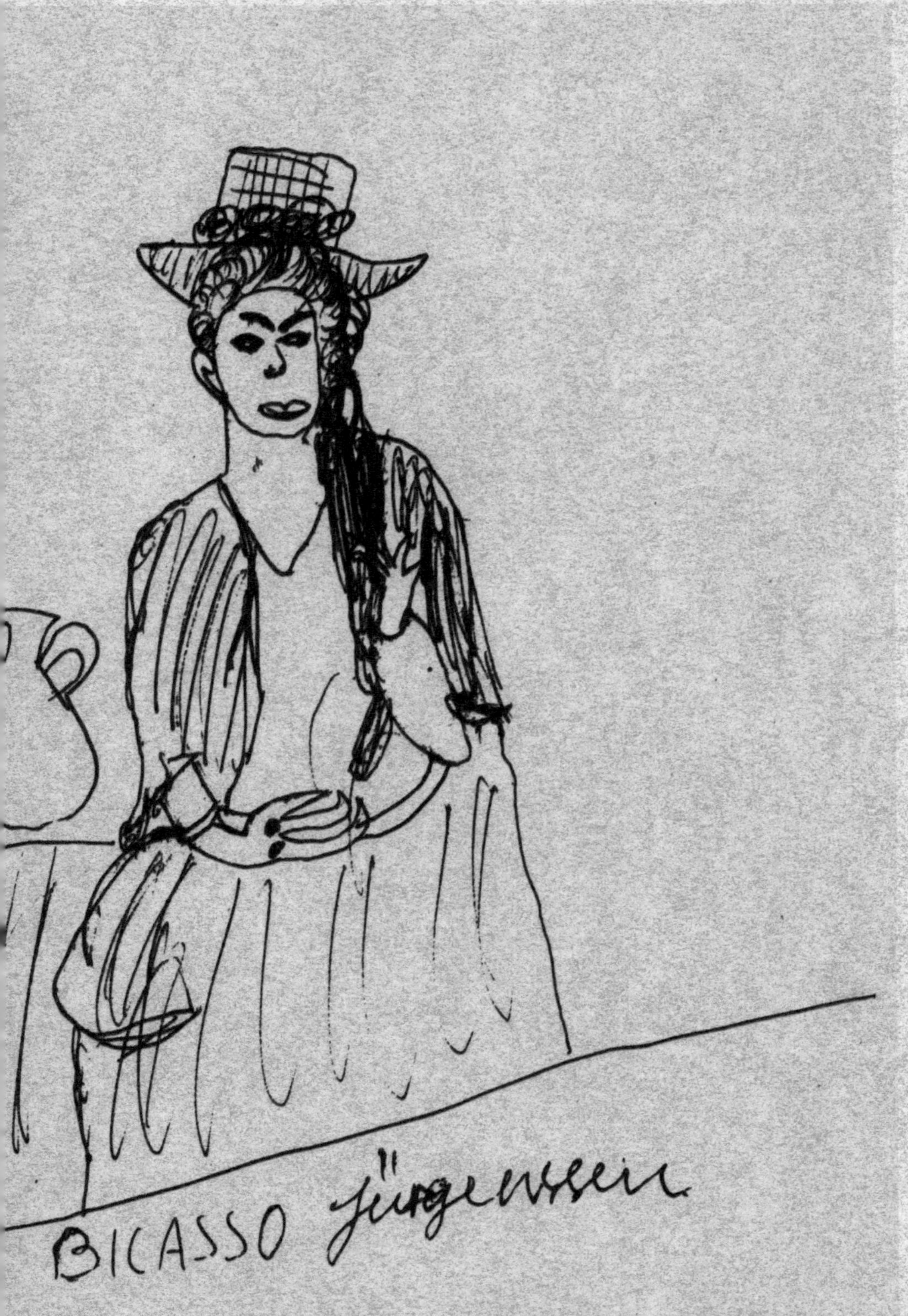

[1] The term *Spurensicherung*, or securing traces, harks back to an exhibition at the Hamburger Kunstverein in 1974. The exhibition was entitled *Spurensicherung: Archäologie und Erinnerung* and subsumed under that term works by the artists Anne and Patrick Poirier, Didier Bay, Christian Boltanski, Nikolaus Lang, Jürgen Brodwolf, and Claudio Costa. The term finally became established thanks to the book *Spurensicherung: Kunst als Anthropologie und Selbsterforschung; Fiktive Wissenschaften in der heutigen Kunst*, edited by Günter Metken in 1977, which expanded the circle of artists further.

[2] On symbol research in cultural science, see Gottfried Korff, »Anti-symbolik und Sym-bolanalytik in der Volks-kunde,« in *Symbole: Zur Bedeutung der Zeichen in der Kultur*, ed. Rolf Wilhelm Brednich and Heinz Schmitt (Münster: Waxmann, 1997), pp. 11–31.

[3] See Victor Turner, *From Ritual to Theatre: The Human Seriousness of Play*, (New York: PAJ Publica-tions, 1982).

Periods of upheaval and disorientation create a desire for preservation, manifestation, and permanence—for cultural memories. Based on this cultural studies hypothesis, the art of the 1970s was accompanied by renewed interest in the culture of the past. Artists slipped into the roles of shaman, priest, priestess, and healer to revive long-buried myths and religious traditions of cultural memory—to remind us of our lost ties to nature. The »securing traces« movement[1] re-established for the future the connection to symbols and myths of centuries gone by, while contemporary feminist artists in the USA and Europe also subjected them to close scrutiny. It is in this feminist context that we also find the work of Birgit Jürgenssen, who was born in Vienna in 1949. On the basis of selected works from Jürgenssen's comprehensive oeuvre, the following essay will adopt an »icon-graphic«[2] perspective to study in detail the strategies the artist developed within her inspiring art universe in her efforts to critically examine, from a contemporary conscious-ness, experiences of cultural history embedded in art's »liminoid system of symbols«[3] and myths, and in her own unique style, to render them productive for modern times.

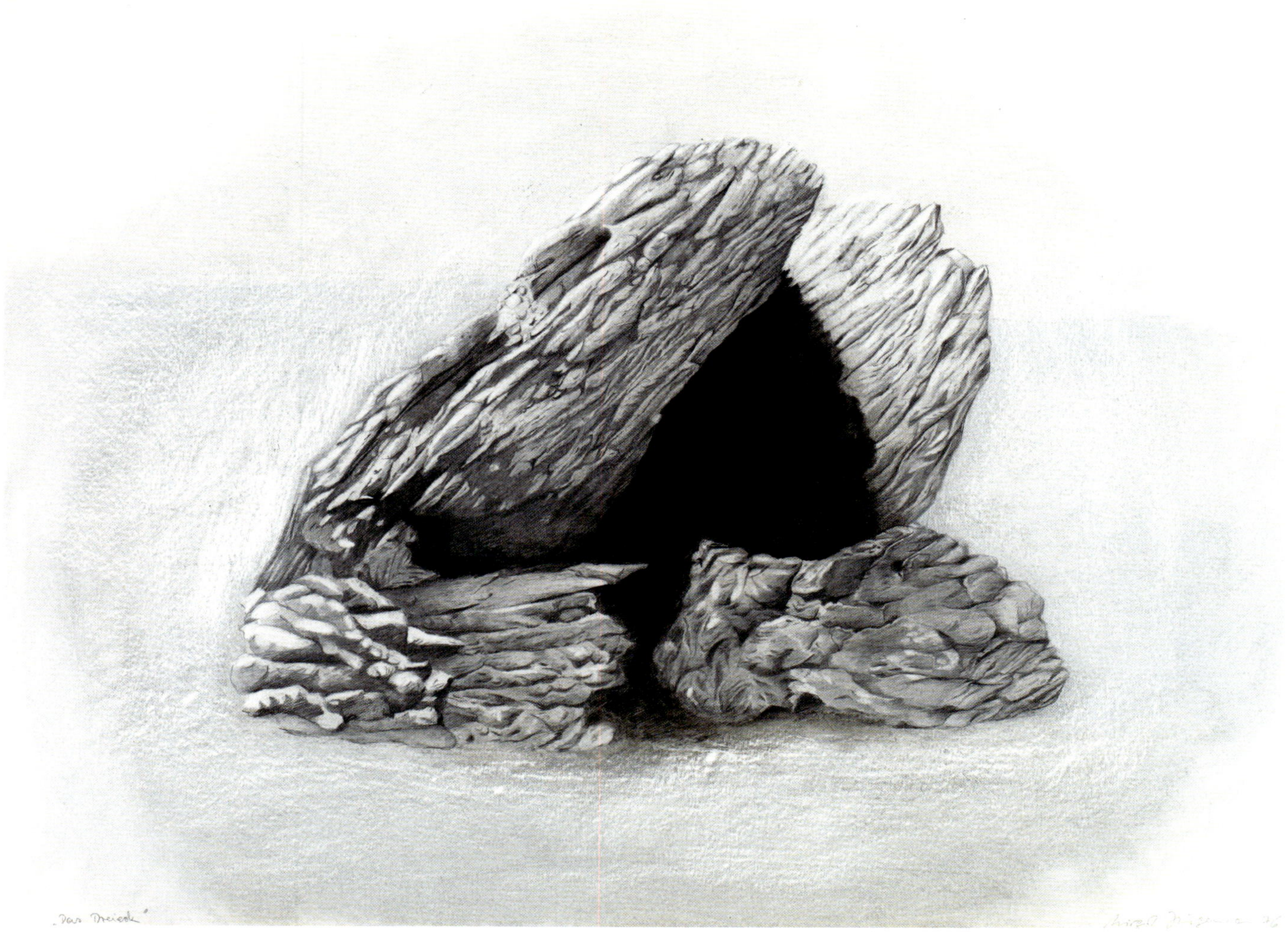

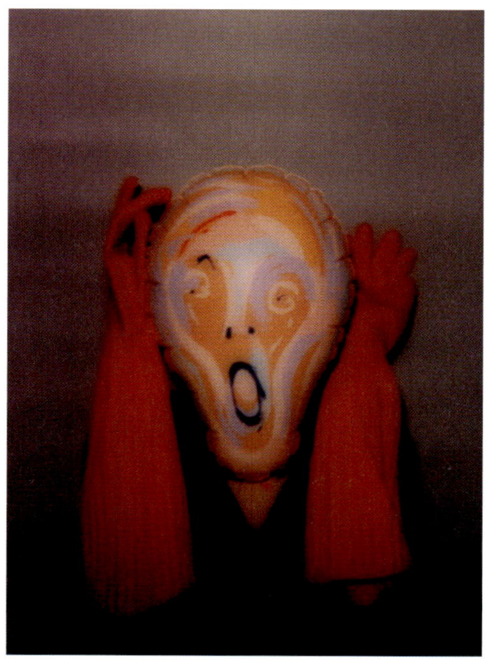

90   *Das Dreieck* 1976
     The Triangle
91   *Ohne Titel* 1994/1995
     Untitled

Siegfriede, St. Sebastine, and *Bicasso*—Feminine Adaptations

4 See Gabriele Schor, »›I Am‹: On the Flux of the Artistic Self in the Works of Birgit Jürgenssen,« in *Birgit Jürgenssen*, ed. Gabriele Schor and Abigail Solomon-Godeau (Ostfildern: Hatje Cantz 2009), pp. 13–64.
5 This debate also involved the reception of, above all, Judith Butler, *Gender Trouble: Feminism and the Subversion of Identity*, (New York: Routledge, 1989); see Heike Eipeldauer, »›Wie erfährt man sich im Anderen, das Andere in sich?‹: Aspekte des (Un)Heimlichen im Werk von Birgit Jürgenssen,« in *Birgit Jürgenssen*, ed. Gabriele Schor and Heike Eipeldauer, exh. cat. Kunstforum Vienna (Munich: Prestel, 2010), pp. 29–44.

It was apparent at an early age that Birgit Jürgenssen, who was born into a bourgeois Viennese family, did not want her identity forged within the framework of traditional systems of order, but wanted instead to develop herself as an independent person. »Bicasso Jürgenssen,« she wrote in her school notebook at the age of eight, not only adopting for herself the reduced linear style of the famed Spanish artist Pablo Picasso but at the same time promptly turning this historical artist role model into something of her own by blending his name into hers to form her signature (see p. 117).[4]

A kind of childish appropriation strategy—even before art history had invented the term »appropriation art« as such at the end of the 1970s. Taking on familiar motifs and styles from art history is a theme that winds its way through her entire work like a unifying thread. In the early 1970s—when Birgit Jürgenssen was in her early twenties—she primarily referenced surrealist predecessors, such as Giorgio de Chirico, and employed surrealist motifs and techniques like decalomania or collage (*The Triangle*, 1976; see ill. 90).

An untitled black-and-white tempera drawing (*Untitled*, 1973, ill. 111) in the style of a metaphysical painting depicts, for example, the interior of a room—a kind of painting gallery—that moves toward a picture in the distance, as if toward its vanishing point. In contrast, however, to the mysterious quality of *pittura metafisica*, this visual space is not void of people: we see a faceless woman in a long black dress who appears to be lost. This same figure also appears in two untitled photographic works from 1994/95, which Birgit Jürgenssen created by superimposing several photographs. These refer to *The Scream*—an icon of expressionism painted in four versions by Norwegian artist Edvard Munch at the end of the nineteenth century. Jürgenssen's two adaptations of the original work focus on the skull-like face of a man who holds his hands pressed against his head with his mouth and eyes wide open in an expression of fear. However, Jürgenssen subverts the iconic representation of the expressionist model in her versions by feminizing the scream motif in her photos and grounding it in everyday imagery.

In one of her photos, for example, she has simply placed the hands of her skull-like figure in arm-length rubber cleaning gloves, as if to give the impression that the horror expressed is brought about by everyday chaos that has to be cleared up (ill. 91). In her second version, Jürgenssen transplants the scream that Munch originally painted in a landscape setting to a single-family housing estate in which a storm is momentarily raging. Contextualizing the fear expressed by the full figure of a woman in a black dress in this version gives us as viewers an empirical explanation for such an expression of terror. In this manner, Jürgenssen ironically fractures the enigmatic aura associated with Munch's work.

It is not only modern masterpieces that Jürgenssen subjects to revision. Long before the gender-based approach[5] and the associated widespread discussion in Europe on awareness of the social construction of identity, she applied her archaeology of memory, which was critical of systems, to the body of imagery and myths transmitted throughout human history, reversing their polarity in the truest sense of the term. An early print from 1977 entitled *Growing with a Tree* (ill. 94) is her interpretation of the beginnings of humanity from a »feminine« perspective. Jürgenssen's concept of evolution in the Romantic tradition is interpreted not as a historiography of male heroic deeds but in analogy to biological growth processes and vacillating between the biological and the social body.

Closely related to this theme are her drawings from the 1970s, in which she depicted the evolution of primitive humans into modern humans by means of the figure of a woman rising up in the truest sense of the word as a feminine process of self-realization. Referring back to this in a print made in 1987, Jürgenssen portrayed the idea of a person attempting to rise up from a crouched monkey on an image of her own body (ill. 95). Imaginary hands, however, prevent the female being, whose body is covered in hair like an animal, from properly walking upright. In creating this work, Jürgenssen

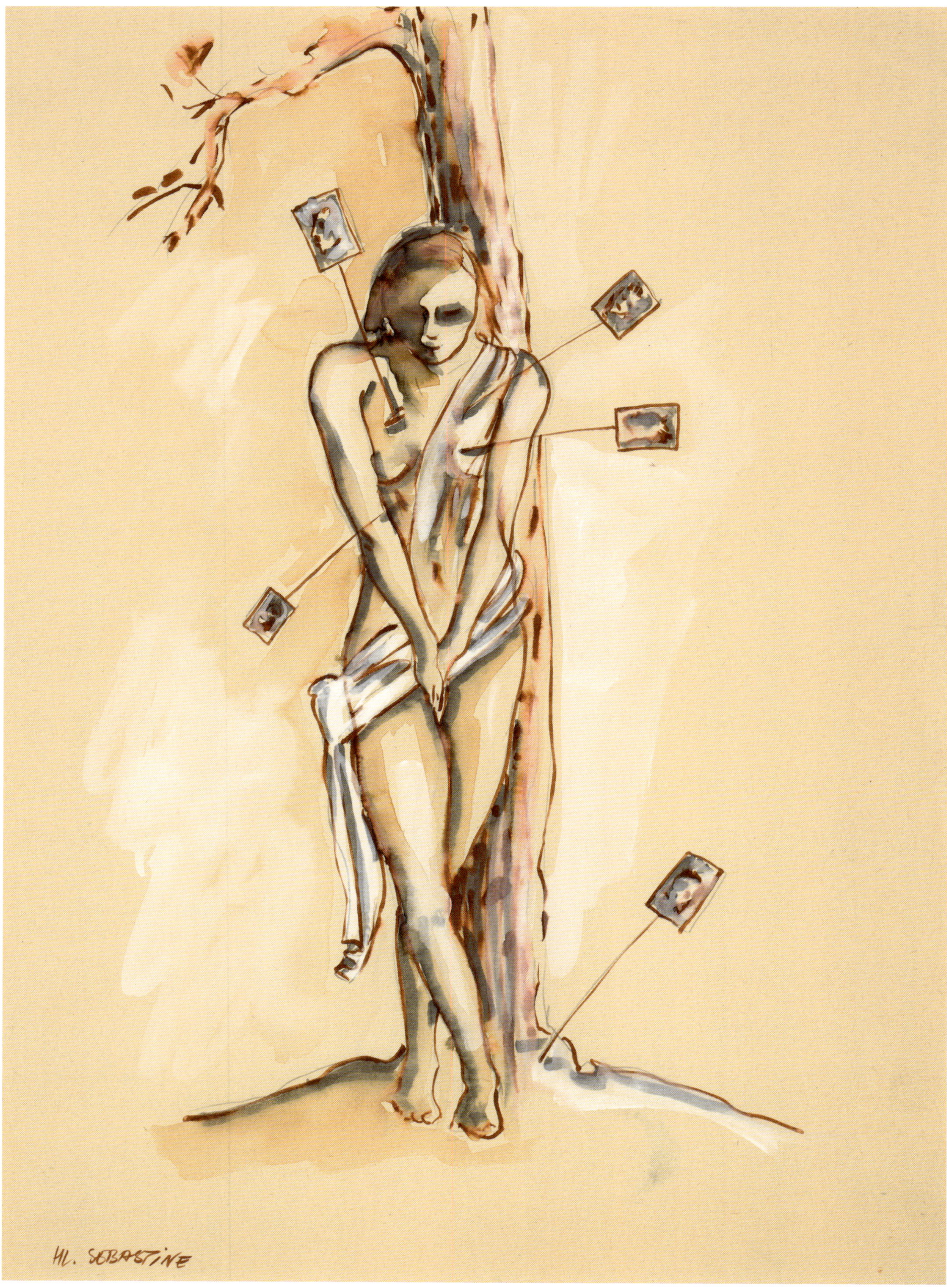

<u>92</u>   *Hl. Sebastine* 1983
St. Sebastine

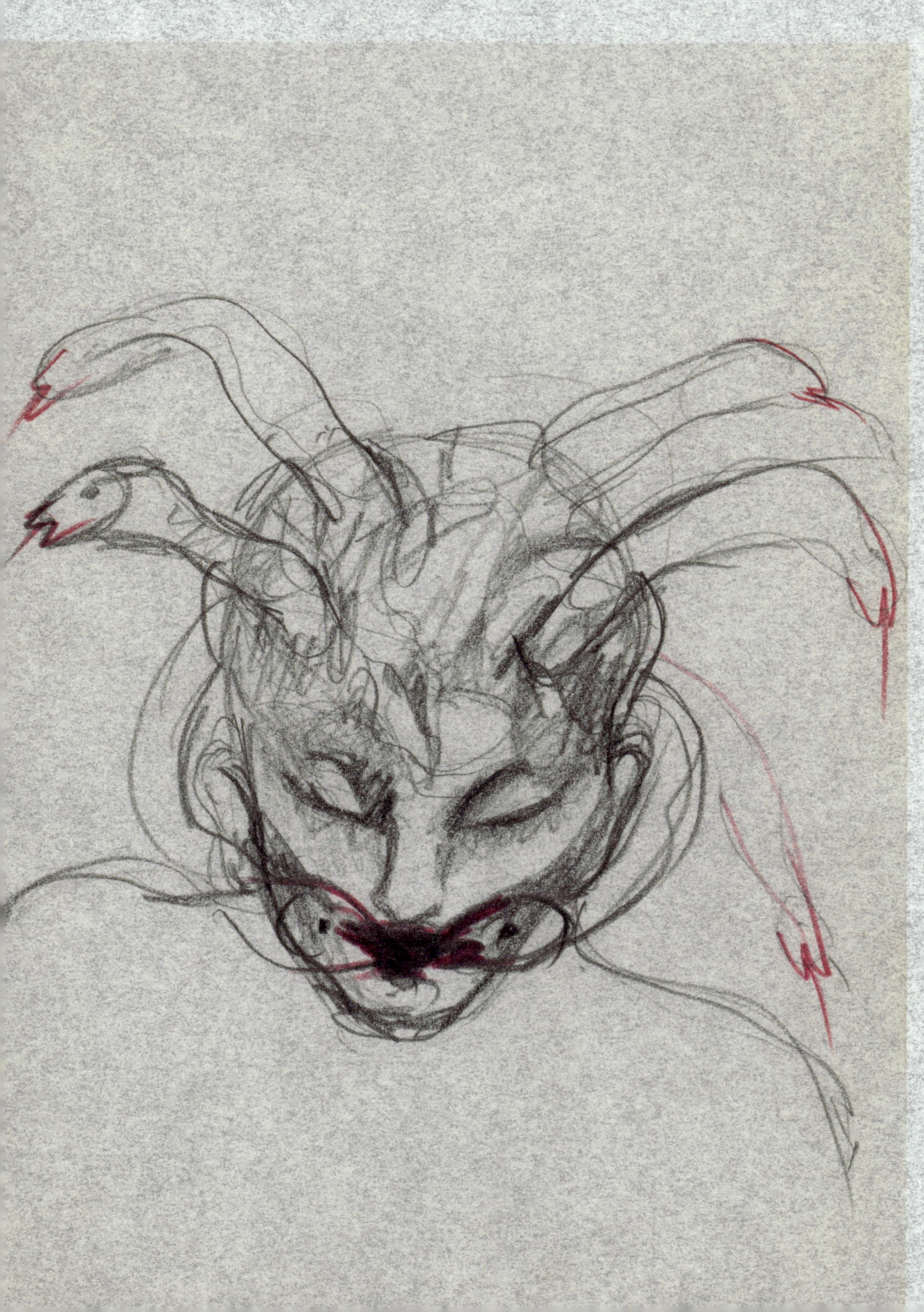

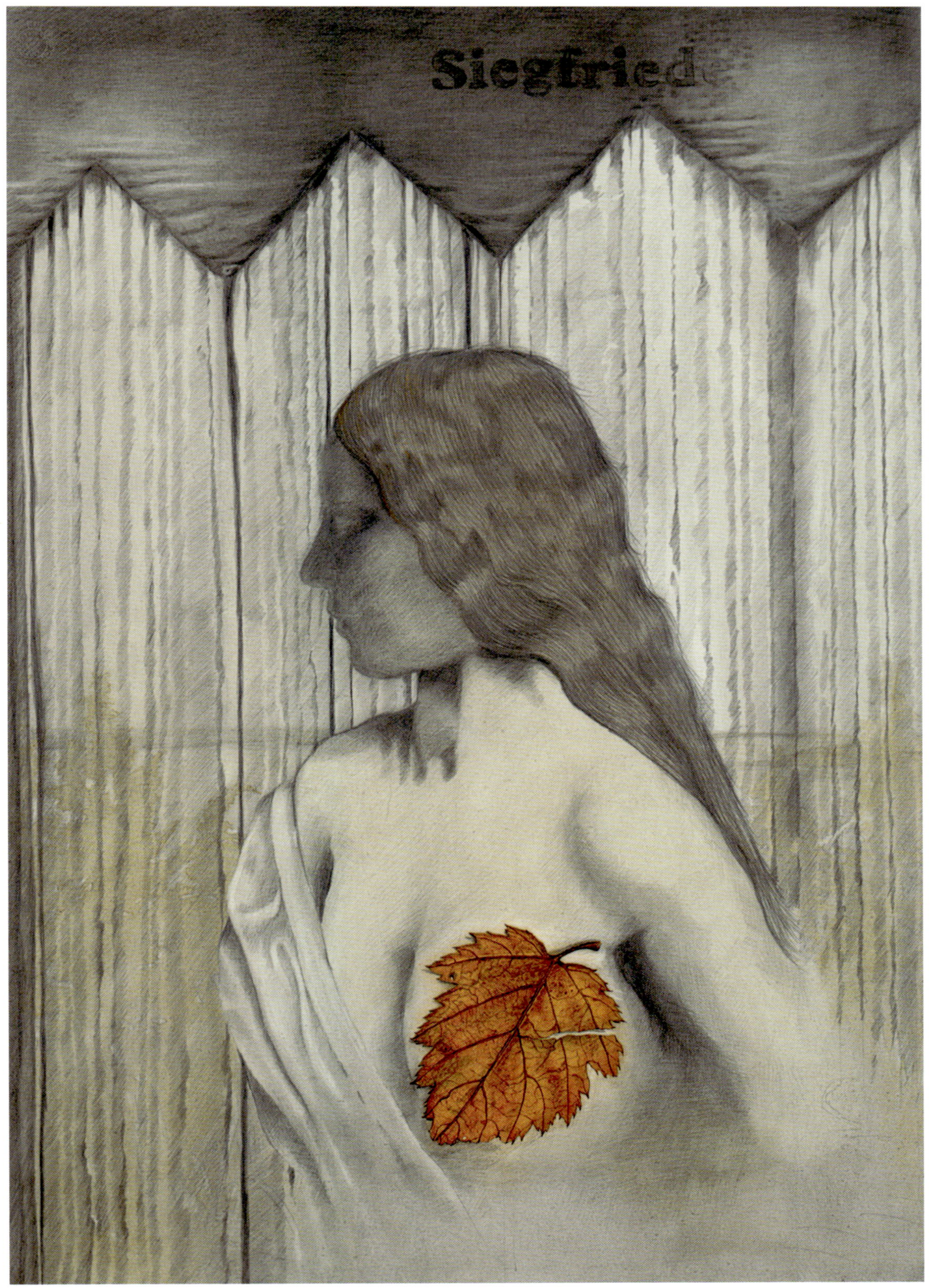

93   *Siegfriede* 1975

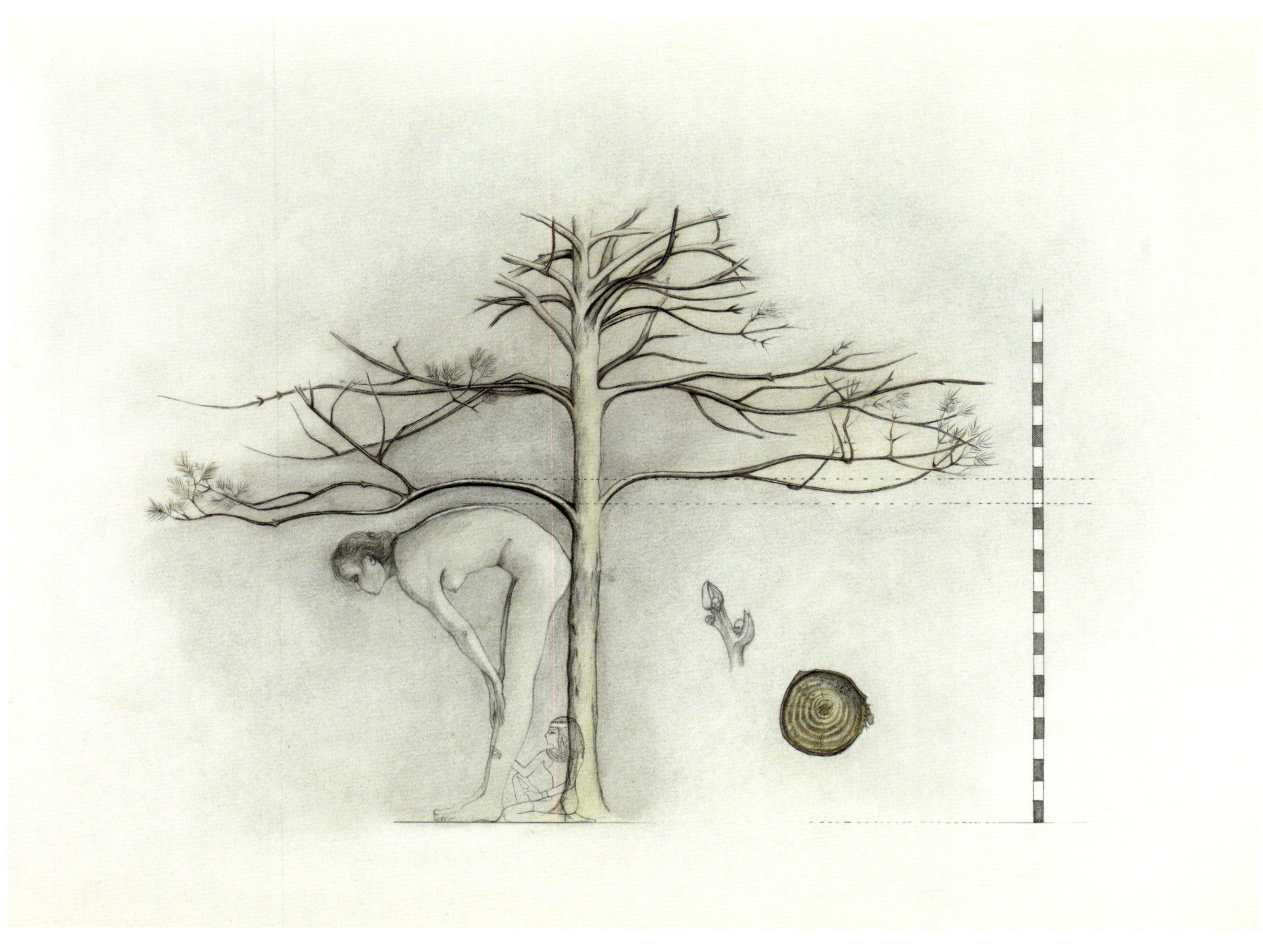

94 *Das Wachsen mit einem Baum* 1977
Growing with a Tree

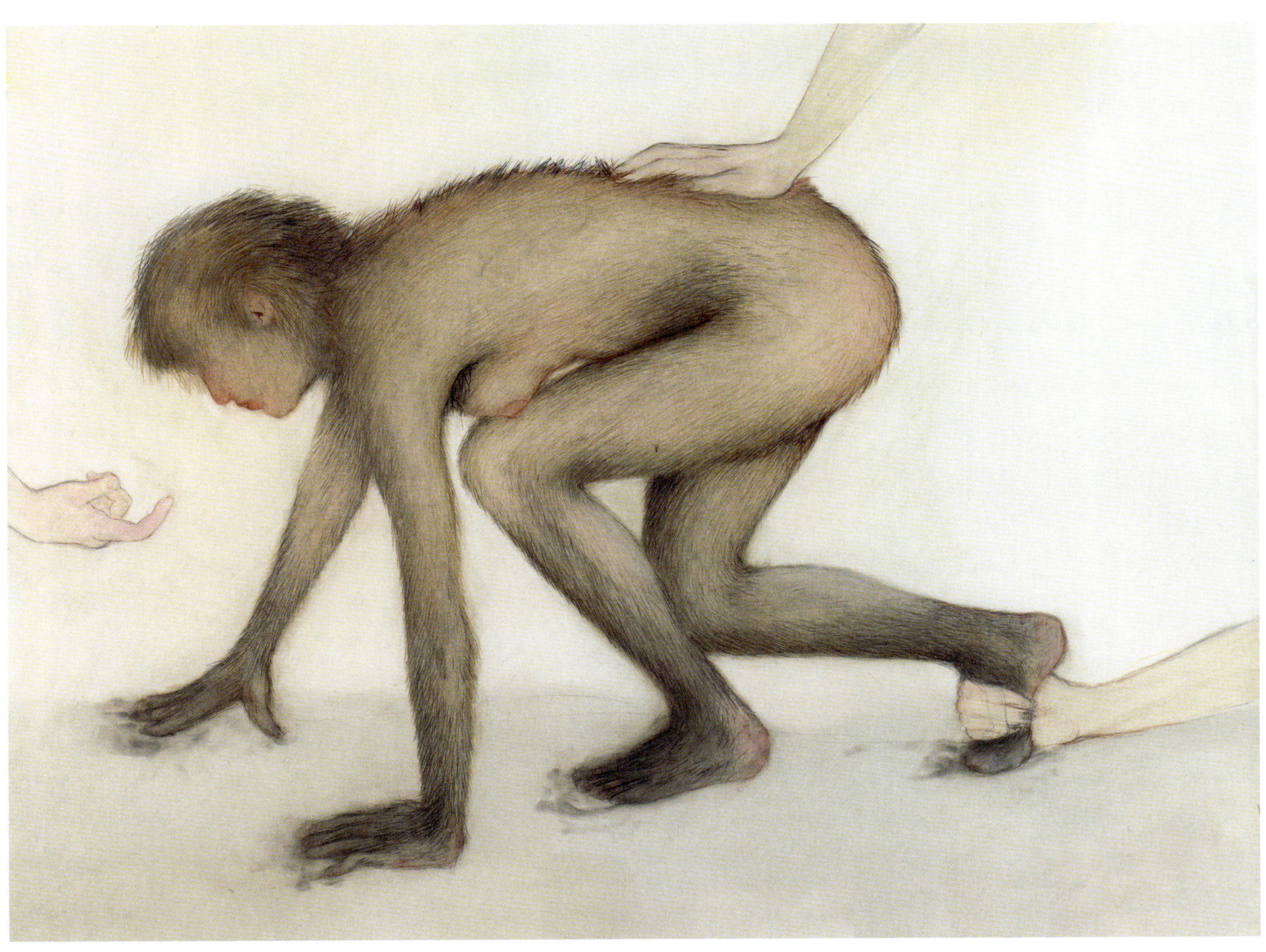

95   *Ohne Titel* 1978
       Untitled

appears to have expressed her need at the peak of the feminist movement to supplement evolutionary history, which, as she saw it, was focused on homo sapiens, with a feminine counterpart in the form of a femina sapiens. She also recreated the archaic image in an autobiographical manner by reflecting in it the emotional blockades and external resistance associated with her own personal development.

Jürgenssen also took a feminist point of view and supplemented antique and Christian tradition with female martyrs and heroines. For example, she placed a figure of *St. Sebastine* beside St. Sebastian, the male Christian patron saint of plague victims. Jürgenssen portrayed her female saint in a sepia, water-colored felt-marker drawing (1983, ill. 92) in accordance with traditional iconographic details—a beautifully shaped body wearing only a loincloth bound naked to a tree and martyred with arrows.

In Jürgenssen's artistic cosmos, there is also a female counterpart to Siegfried, the Germanic mythical hero to whom superhuman powers were attributed. However, she deviated from the traditional account in her work by altering an important iconographic detail. She portrayed her female *Siegfriede* in a pencil drawing dated 1975 (ill. 93) as a long-haired young woman in semi-profile based on the classical Renaissance ideal of beauty. However, the artist did not depict her heroine's back as the vulnerable part of her body—which legend locates between the shoulder blades of the otherwise invincible Siegfried—but at the level of her heart and protected by a linden leaf.

Even if Jürgenssen rendered her heroine in this drawing as emotional and vulnerable, when her work is viewed in its totality, she did not fall into the binary mental trap of categorizing the sexes on the basis of »thinking man and feeling woman.«[6] She did not polarize her protagonists per se into rational-male and emotional-female, as did artists like Joseph Beuys and representatives of the spiritual feminist movement. The »artist shaman« Beuys, for instance, depicted his archaic female figures in harmony with nature and, according to a polarity philosophy now considered outdated, as life-giving and emotional in contrast to the analytical male principle.[7] Like Beuys, feminist artists such as Judy Chicago, Ana Mendieta, and Mary Beth Edelson also used symbols and myths of pre-Christian religions to remind us of women's hidden spiritual powers. In actions such as *Woman Rising* (1973/1974), for instance, American artist Edelson not only modernized archaic rituals in imagery but enacted them on her own body as well, as a means of reestablishing lost relationships to nature. Such positions often followed an ideologically based religious narrative pattern that propagated the integration of female powers in order to offer the world the prospect of renewal and ultimately redemption.[8] Jürgenssen's reception of myths, in contrast, requires no such ideological meta-narrative. Nor did she give any indication that her aim was to permit herself to be conquered by the inherent power of symbols and to awaken the goddess within.

[6] See Ingrid Tomkowiak and Dietmar Sedlaczek, »Denkmann und Fühlfrau: Zur Mythologisierung des Weiblichen in Esoterik und New Age,« in *Männlich – Weiblich: Zur Bedeutung der Kategorie Geschlecht in der Kultur*, ed. Christel Köhle-Hezinger, Martin Scharfe, and Rolf Wilhelm Brednich (Münster: Waxmann, 1999), pp. 325–35.

[7] See, in particular, the chapter »Frauengestalten« in Nicole Fritz, *Bewohnte Mythen: Joseph Beuys und der Aberglaube* (Nuremberg: Verlag für moderne Kunst, 2007).

[8] See Heide Göttner-Abendroth, *Die tanzende Göttin: Prinzipien einer matriarchalen Ästhetik* (Munich: Frauenoffensive, 1982).

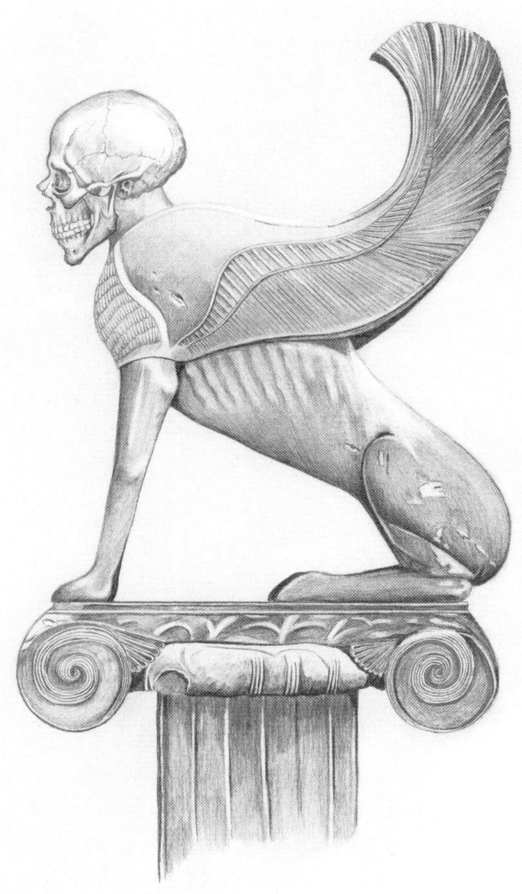

96 *Auch das ewig Rätselhafte kann seinen Reiz verlieren* 1974
Even the Eternally Mysterious Can Lose Its Attraction

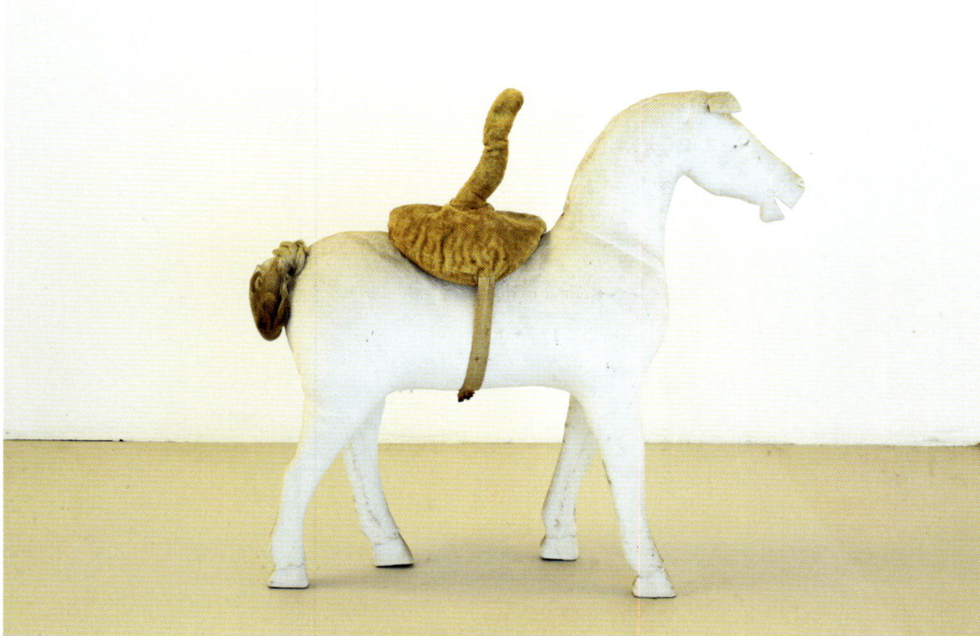

<u>97</u>   *Ohne Titel (Pferd)* 1973
        Untitled (Horse)

Angel, Demon, Muse—Ironic Deconstructions

Maintaining a certain safe distance, Jürgenssen limited herself instead to exploring the meaning and directives that traditional images and symbols transmit, in accordance with the postmodern dictum, and to playfully and humorously deconstructing the view of the world they encompass. The drawing *Even the Eternally Mysterious Can Lose Its Attraction* (ill. <u>96</u>) is an example that supports this thesis. In this small drawing, Jürgenssen destroyed the myth of the enigmatic sphinx commonly considered as female by undermining the symbolic figure's claim to eternity and depicting it as a mortal human being.

However as Jürgenssen herself said, she preferred to deconstruct »the myth of power and male wishful thinking.«[9] »I wanted to reveal the typical prejudices and role models that society assigns to women and with which I was always confronted, and to represent everyday misunderstandings.«[10] A particularly impressive testimony of such artistic reflection of male self-portrayal is her horse made of paper mâché in 1973 (ill. <u>97</u>). This is one of the sculptural works with which she subversively parodied the stereotype of the equestrian statue—and thus the claim to power associated with it—by placing a phallus instead of a rider on the saddle to visually symbolize concentrated masculine strength.

The irony that she displayed in works such as these »has to do with my having grown up heavily surrounded by clichéd roles,« Jürgenssen explained in an interview.[11] She then chose, as an adult artist, to take the liberty of critically questioning and exposing the power structures consolidated in symbols and myths and, in particular, exposing the female roles attributed by men and male projections onto women. She accomplished this in the *Untitled (Angel, Demon, Muse,* collage, 1981, ill. <u>98</u>) by combining two opposing concepts of femininity with one another: the aloof Virgin Mary and the erotic femme fatale that surrealists such as Man Ray had reduced to a pair of seductive lips. By superimposing and thus neutralizing images hardened into clichés in collage form, she ultimately renders them absurd.

[9] Cited in Schor and Eipeldauer, *Birgit Jürgenssen* (see n. 5), p. 240 [translated].
[10] »Felicitas Thun-Hohenstein in an interview with Birgit Jürgenssen,« in *Let's Twist Again. If You Can't Think It, Dance It. Performance in Vienna from 1960 until today,* ed. Carola Dertnig and Stefanie Seibold (Gumpoldskirchen/Vienna, 2006), pp. 272–279, here: p. 274.
[11] Rainer Metzger, »Birgit Jürgenssen: ›Wie erfährt man sich im anderen, das andere in sich?‹; Ein Gespräch mit Rainer Metzger,« *Kunstforum International* 164 (March–May 2003), pp. 234–47, here: p. 234 [translated].

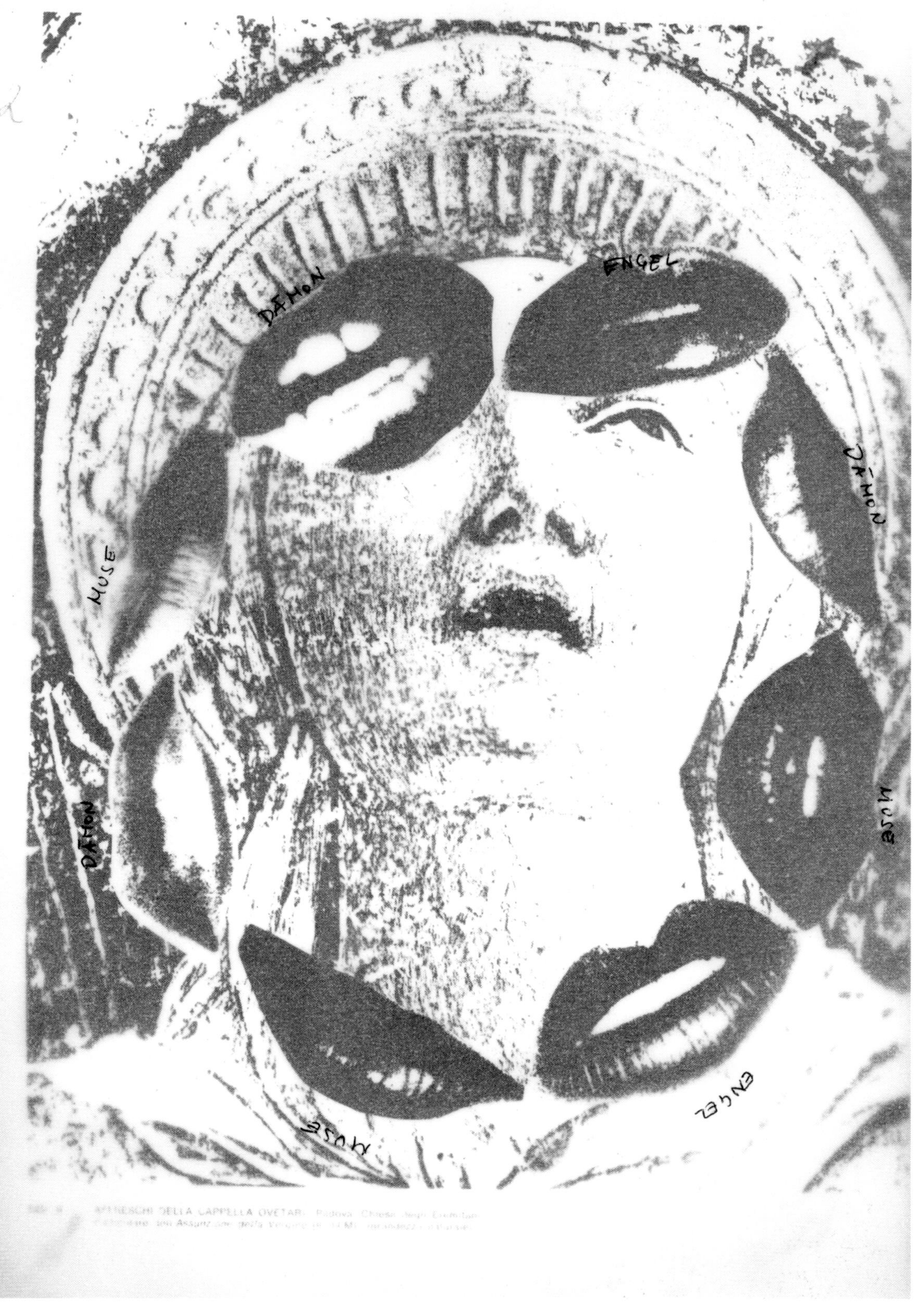

<u>98</u>   *Ohne Titel (Engel, Dämon, Muse)* 1981
Untitled (Angel, Demon, Muse)

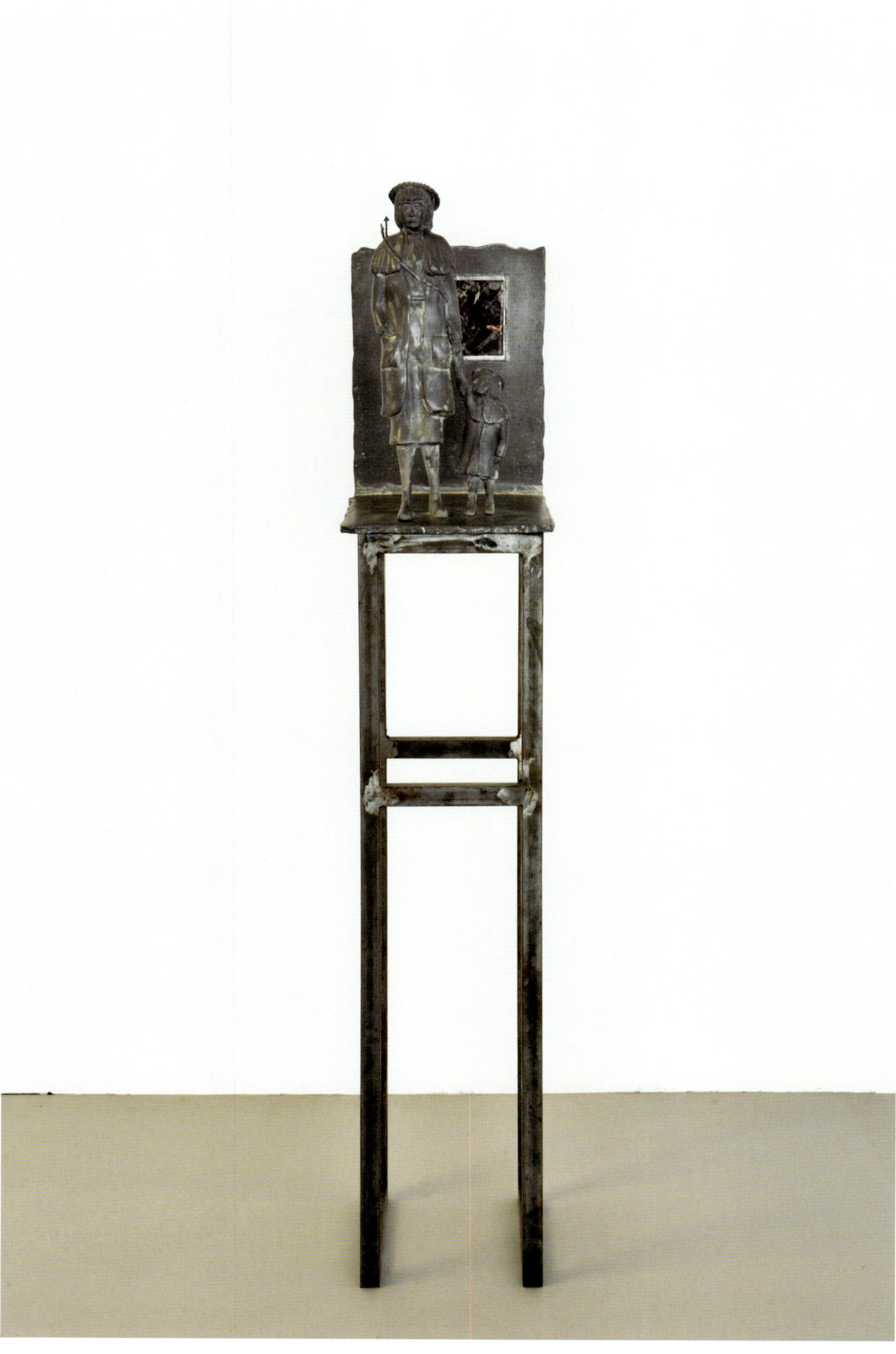

<u>99</u> *Amazone (Mutter und Kind)* 1974
Amazon (Mother and Child)

¹² See Meike Rotermund, *Metamorphosen in inneren Räumen: Video- und Performancearbeiten der Künstlerin Ulrike Rosenbach* (Göttingen: Universitätsverlag, 2012), p. 73.
¹³ Cited in Gabriele Schor »I Am« (see n. 4), p. 36.
¹⁴ Wolfgang Lipp, *Kultur-typen, kulturelle Symbole, Handlungswelt: Zur Plurivalenz von Kultur*, (Berlin: Duncker and Humblot, 1994), pp. 33–74, here: p. 47 [translated].

¹⁵ The figure of thought *fest und flüssig*, or solid and liquid, stems from Aleida Assmann, who, with reference to the philosopher Georg Simmel, exploited the expression fruitfully for the cultural sciences to describe different aggregate states of culture . The »solid« refers to the material form, the artifact or object; the »liquid« by contrast describes the immaterial—the productive individual power of imagination or the language that liquefies the solidified forms by reflecting them. See Aleida Assmann, »Fest und flüssig: Anmerkungen zu einer Denkfigur«, in *Kultur als Lebenswelt und Monument*, ed. Dietrich Harth (Frankfurt am Main: Fischer, 1991), pp. 181–98.
¹⁶ See Sigrid Schade, »›Der Leichnam lebt‹: Bildtradition und Geschlechterkonstruktion in den *Totentanz*-Serien von Birgit Jürgenssen,« in Schor and Solomon-Godeau, *Birgit Jürgenssen* (see n. 4), pp. 179–89.

In a similar manner and at the same time as Birgit Jürgenssen, the German artist Ulrike Rosenbach also dealt with political and social power structures manifest in cultural traditions. Like Jürgenssen in the *Angel, Demon, Muse* collage, Rosenbach also combined two traditionally contradictory clichés of femininity in her video performance *Do Not Believe That I Am an Amazon* (1975, ill. 100)—that of the Madonna and that of the Amazon warrior. In this work, Rosenbach superimposed her own face on a reproduction of Stefan Lochner's *Madonna of the Rose Bower* (1451), at which she then shot fifteen arrows. By identifying herself as an artist with the contradictory women's roles and clichés experienced on her own person, she, like her Austrian counterpart, revealed her own feminine body as a trope of the male projection of cultural codes. Here she was calling not least for a new understanding of femininity far removed at the time from a way of thinking dominated by patriarchal polarization.¹²

One year before Rosenbach took up the Amazon myth in her spectacular action, Jürgenssen had put the symbolic figure of the Amazon to sculptural use in her reserved manner in 1974, allocating it a contemporary place in the truest sense of the term (ill. 99). She conceived her Amazon in a small sculpture of a modern mother and housewife with a child and placed her on an iron chair. The contemporary Amazon holding a child by the hand appears in a »masculine« way warrior-like and worldly, preparing to leave, while the man, portrayed in the role of the passively suffering Ophelia, guards the home.

Once again, in this ensemble Jürgenssen thwarts the orders established in myths by undermining the associated attributions of a strong male and a weak female sex by reversing gender roles. Thus transposed into the present, the symbolic figure also becomes a sociopolitical symbol that, in keeping with the spirit of the 1970s, critically questions the social situation of women and the gender roles that applied at that time.

Jürgenssen's work *Augustine's Armor* (ill. 89) likewise blends history and the present. In the 1974 drawing, she designed a suit of armor like an archaeological find. Instead of historical masculine heroic deeds, however, the armor portrays everyday scenes of women busy with their domestic duties, such as taking care of children and cleaning, and cosmetic rituals, corresponding to the masculine ideals of beauty and gender roles. In the way in which Jürgenssen updated the mythological material by remapping it onto the twentieth century, she anticipated the reanimation strategies of contemporary artists such as Brigitte Maria Mayer, Marc Quinn, and David Nicholson, who are now increasingly exploring our cultural past against the backdrop of the present.

Seducing as the Seduced—Performative Liquefaction of the Cultural

»Be really creative, refuse your role,« Jürgenssen wrote in one of her notebooks¹³ In accordance with this maxim, she visually deconstructed by means of drawing and photographs more than just the cultural stereotype of the sexes transmitted in symbolic orders. Rather, she also employed her »cultural power of interpretation«¹⁴ much more at the end of the 1980s and during the 1990s to performatively »liquefy«¹⁵ set pieces of male-dominated cultural history with a playful anarchy and using her own bodyscape—in this manner she expanded existing iconography by adding her own ideas and self-developed images.

Just as she reconstructed, for example, the popular art motif »death and the maiden« on her own body in a series of staged photographs in the late 1970s and, as Sigrid Schade has demonstrated, added further semiotic concepts to death beyond the topos of the maiden, Jürgenssen also created her own completely new images of cultural traditions in the 1990s (ill. 166).¹⁶

In her modern renditions of the Pygmalion and Ophelia myths or her treatment of the motif of Bathsheba at her bath, she seems to have been particularly interested in visualizing the emotional and physical moments of experience described and preserved in mythology. As the seduced, she seduces, as she herself said, again using visual means and creates, from a self-determined perspective beyond clichés, new sensual

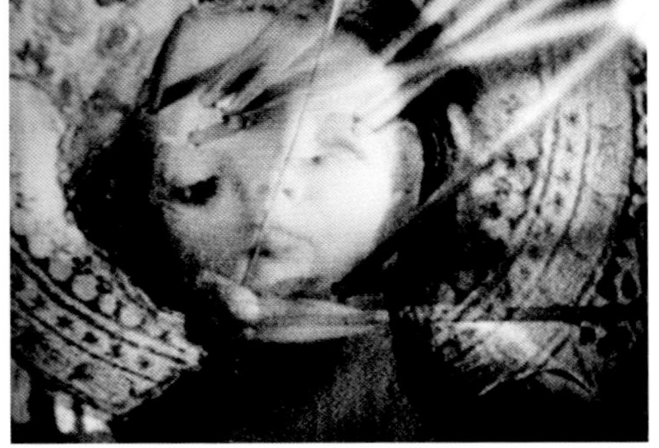

<u>100</u>　　Ulrike Rosenbach *Do You Think I am an Amazon* 1975 © Bildrecht, Vienna 2018

images of male and female corporeality. This is exemplified by the photographic diptychs and tableau-like fabric images of classic sculpture, which she dissected into detailed photographs in order to reveal their sensual radiance to us even more clearly. In what she titled the *Angel* series—staged photographs with the angel motif—she convincingly revived for the present an abstract spiritual impression beyond all tradition (ill. 101). She recreated the angel encounter as a photographed shadow of the body and thus as a physical contact in such a way that the idea of transcendence is not only apparent to us but also spontaneously moves physically closer to and touches us anew.

Throughout her entire oeuvre Jürgenssen also appropriated—as she had done as a child with the name and works of Picasso—the cultural tradition of European visual memory. In her creative process, she charged images from our entire cultural history with her own spiritual and emotional energy, informed by postmodern self-reflexive I.[17] In this way, the empty and sometimes clichéd images of our cultural memory are rendered meaningful again for the present.

Since she did not revive the traditions within the framework of an ideological world view—as the utopian-oriented historical avant-garde movements or current neoconservative movements have done—her works remain topical today. Birgit Jürgenssen's resulting subjective pictorial mythology captivates without manipulating us: applying the metaphor of her water-themed *Bath* series, let us submerge ourselves in her works in order to emerge that much more aware.

[17] The cyber-theorist Donna Haraway describes this postmodern subjectivity, which opens itself to other identities transformationally, as a kind of dismantled and reassembled postmodern collective and personal »I« explicitly committed to partisanship, irony, intimacy, and perversion. See Donna Haraway, *Simians, Cyborgs, and Women: The Reinvention of Nature* (New York: Routledge, 1991), pp. 160 and 163; cited in Amelia Jones, »Survey,« in *The Artist's Body*, ed. Tracey Warr (New York: Phaidon, 2000), pp. 16–48, here: p. 42.

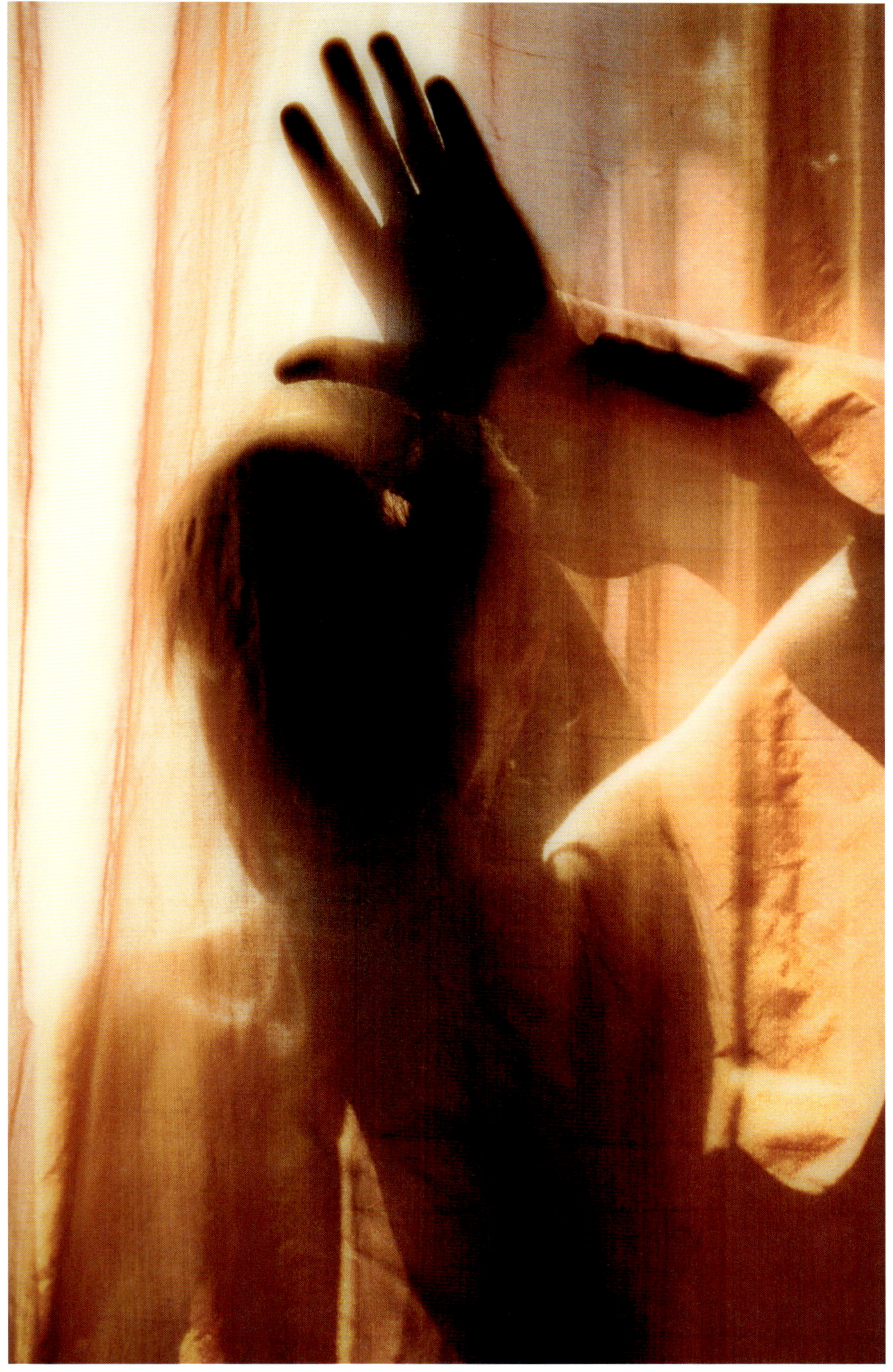

101   *Ohne Titel (Engel)* 1996/1997
       Untitled (Angel)

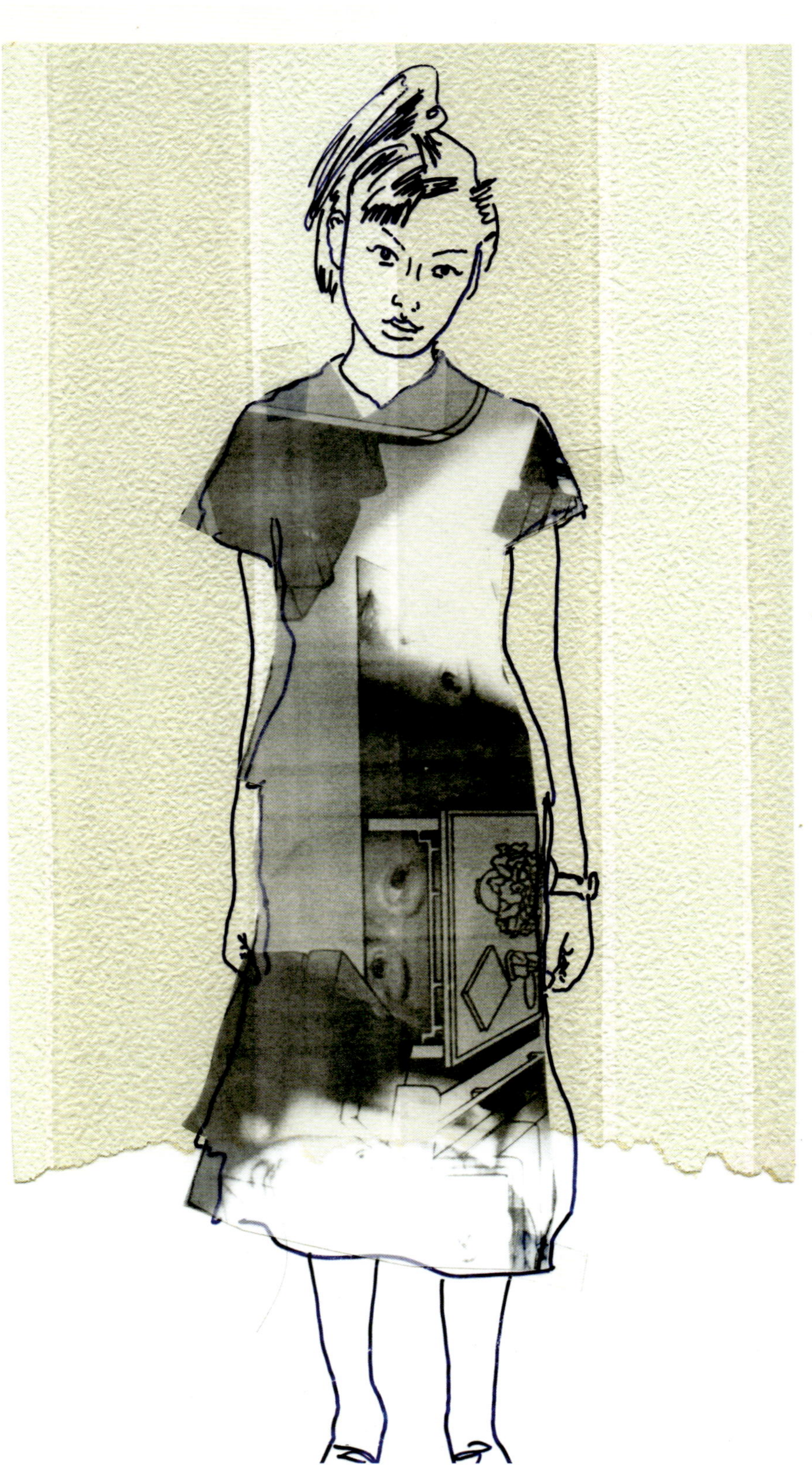

102 *Ohne Titel* 1997
Untitled

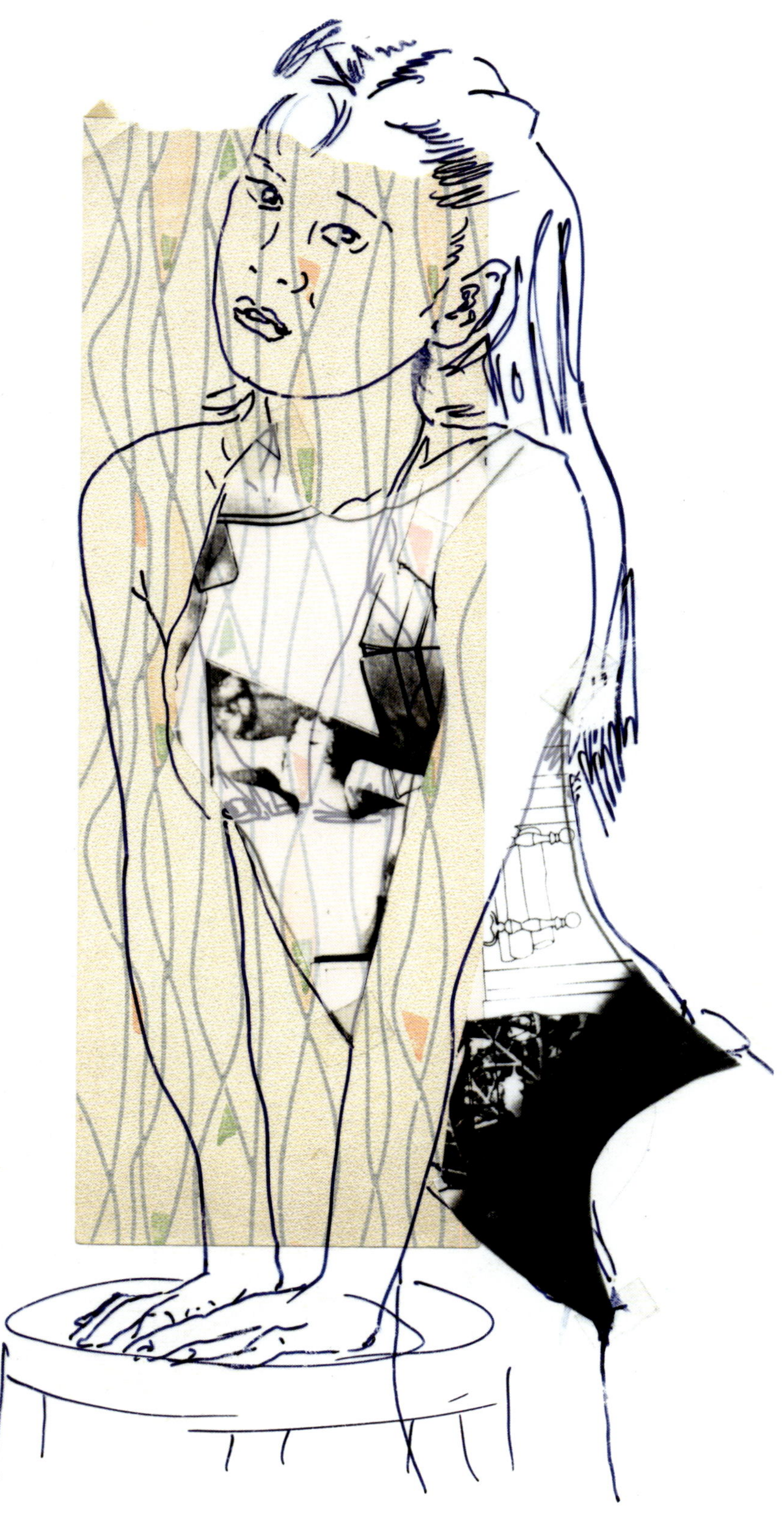

103 *Ohne Titel* 1997
Untitled

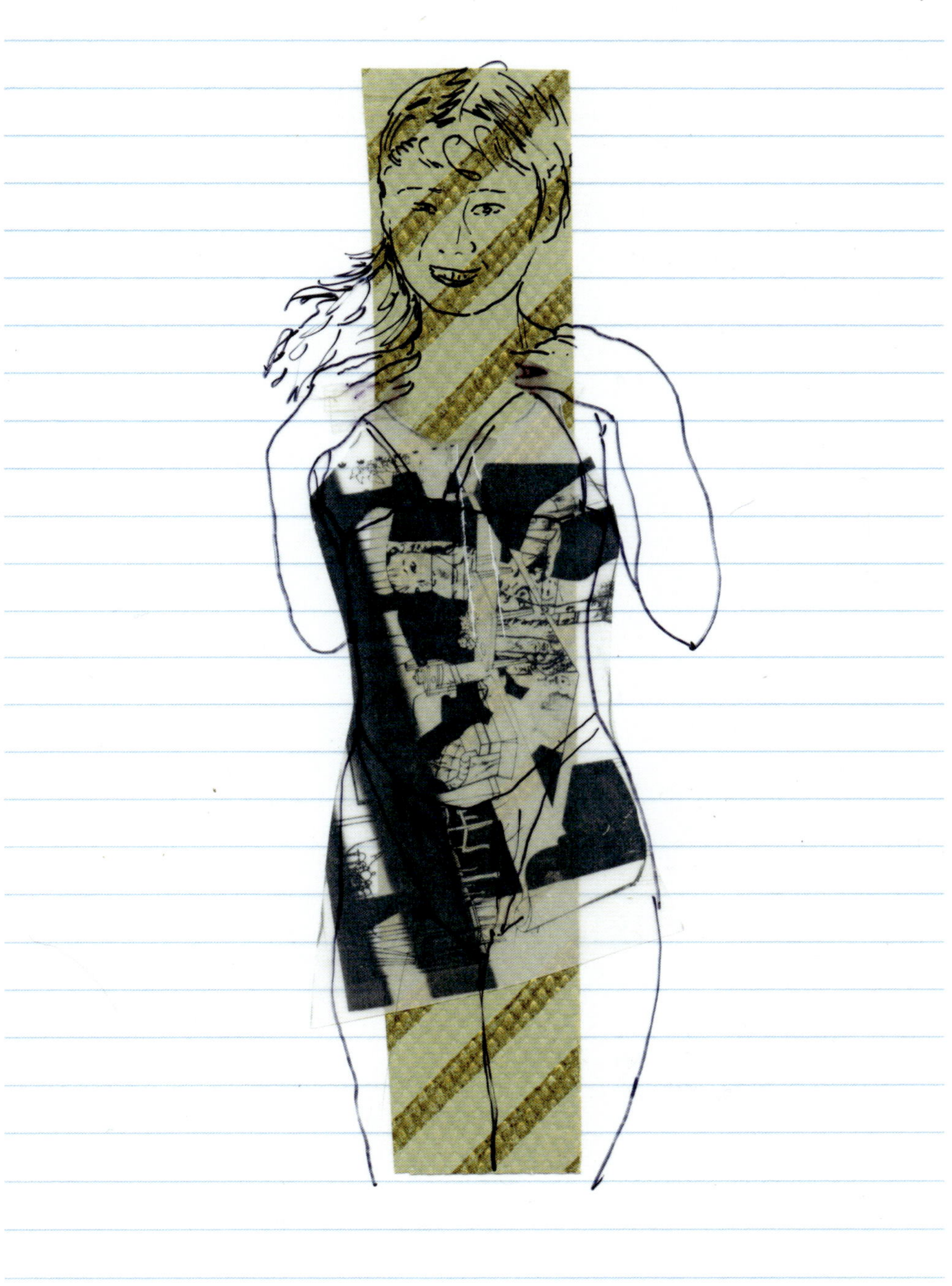

<u>104</u>   *Ohne Titel* 1997
       Untitled

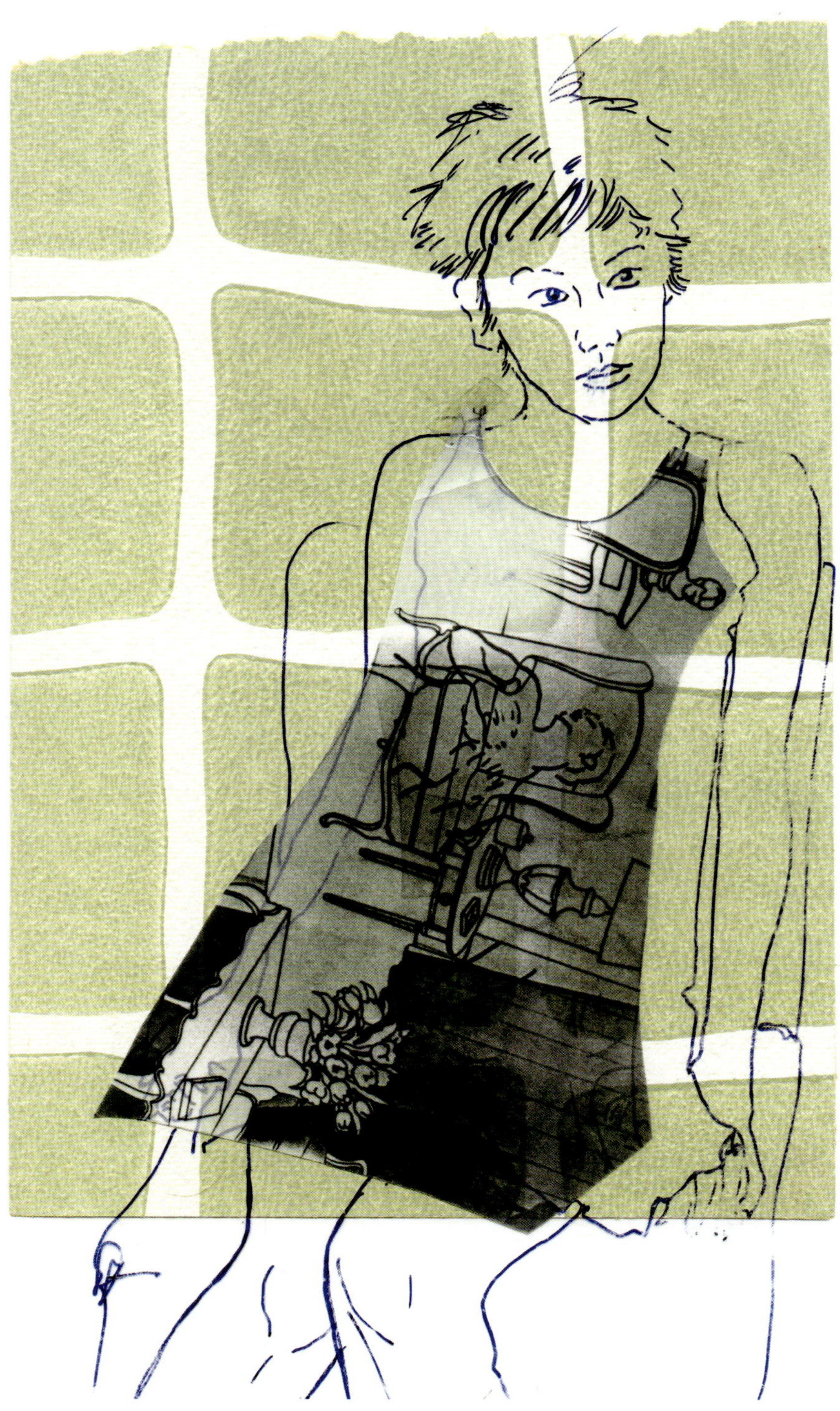

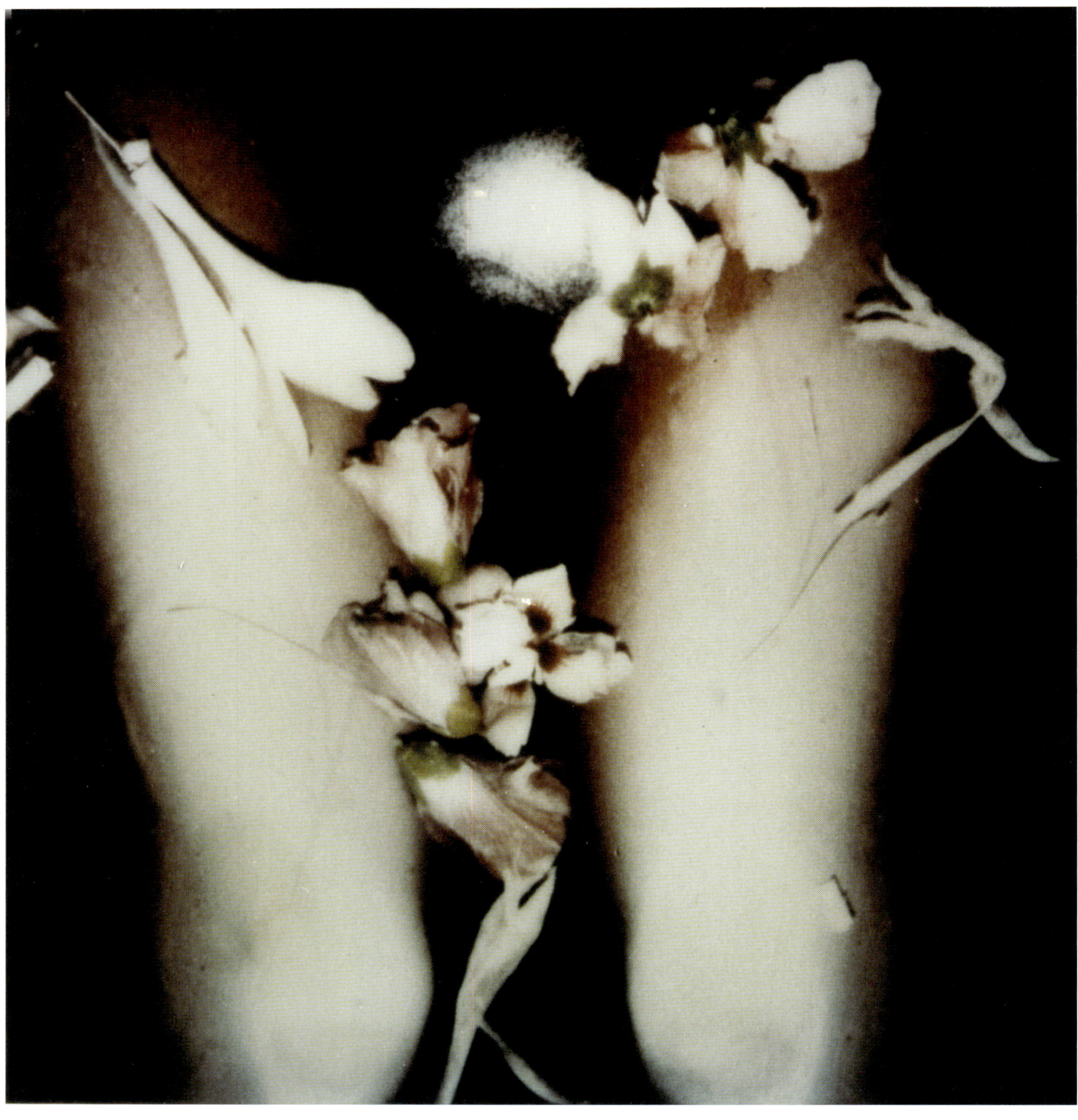

Grave Waters

Jessica Morgan

[1] »Felicitas Thun-Hohenstein in an interview with Birgit Jürgenssen,« in *Let's Twist Again. If You Can't Think It, Dance It. Performance in Vienna from 1960 until Today*, ed. Carola Dertnig and Stefanie Seibold (Gumpoldskirchen/Vienna, 2006), pp. 272–279.

Ophelia, an image that was produced both as a Polaroid and, inverted, as a photographic print on a larger scale, a repetition that perhaps suggests Jürgenssen's affection for the work, depicts two bare knees and thighs emerging from a reddish black watery surround, scattered with flowers. The subject of Ophelia is an appropriate choice for the artist, representing one of the most psychologically complex female characters in a Shakespeare play, given that Jürgenssen's oeuvre is known for its poetic (though also humorous) use of feminist and psychoanalytic tropes. Shakespeare's Ophelia, the would-be lover of Hamlet, is spurned by her lover, who then kills her father, and finally appears in the play to be driven mad by grief. In her last appearance, Ophelia hands out flowers, citing their symbolic meanings. The only herb that Ophelia gives herself is rue: »There's rue for you, and here's some for me.« Rue is well known for its symbolic meaning of regret. Soon after, we learn that she has fallen to a watery death, a presumed suicide. The literary reference is not unusual for Jürgenssen, who once said, »My works have been created [...] out of the interplay between literature and everyday life,«[1] but she was also no doubt familiar with the romanticized representation of Ophelia by the Pre-Raphaelite John Everett Millais. Millais's model was the poet and artist Elizabeth Siddall who posed for the painting in a bathtub—just as Jürgenssen's own image was created. As the only female artist associated with the Pre-Raphaelites, Siddall's own artistic development and ultimately tragic death could, perhaps, have been of interest for Jürgenssen.

Jürgenssen's portrayal of *Ophelia*, though enacted by herself, masks her identity. A highly enigmatic but sexually charged image, the frame is dominated by the pinkish white thighs that emerge from her *Schwarzes Bad* (or Black Bath, as the entire series of Polaroids from which this image is taken are titled). As in her better-known image *Nest* (ill. 220, also 1979), the crotch, in this case absent or occluded by the dark water (ill. 106), is the focus of the image—scattered here with flowers that sit on the water's surface and draw further attention to the hidden depths below.

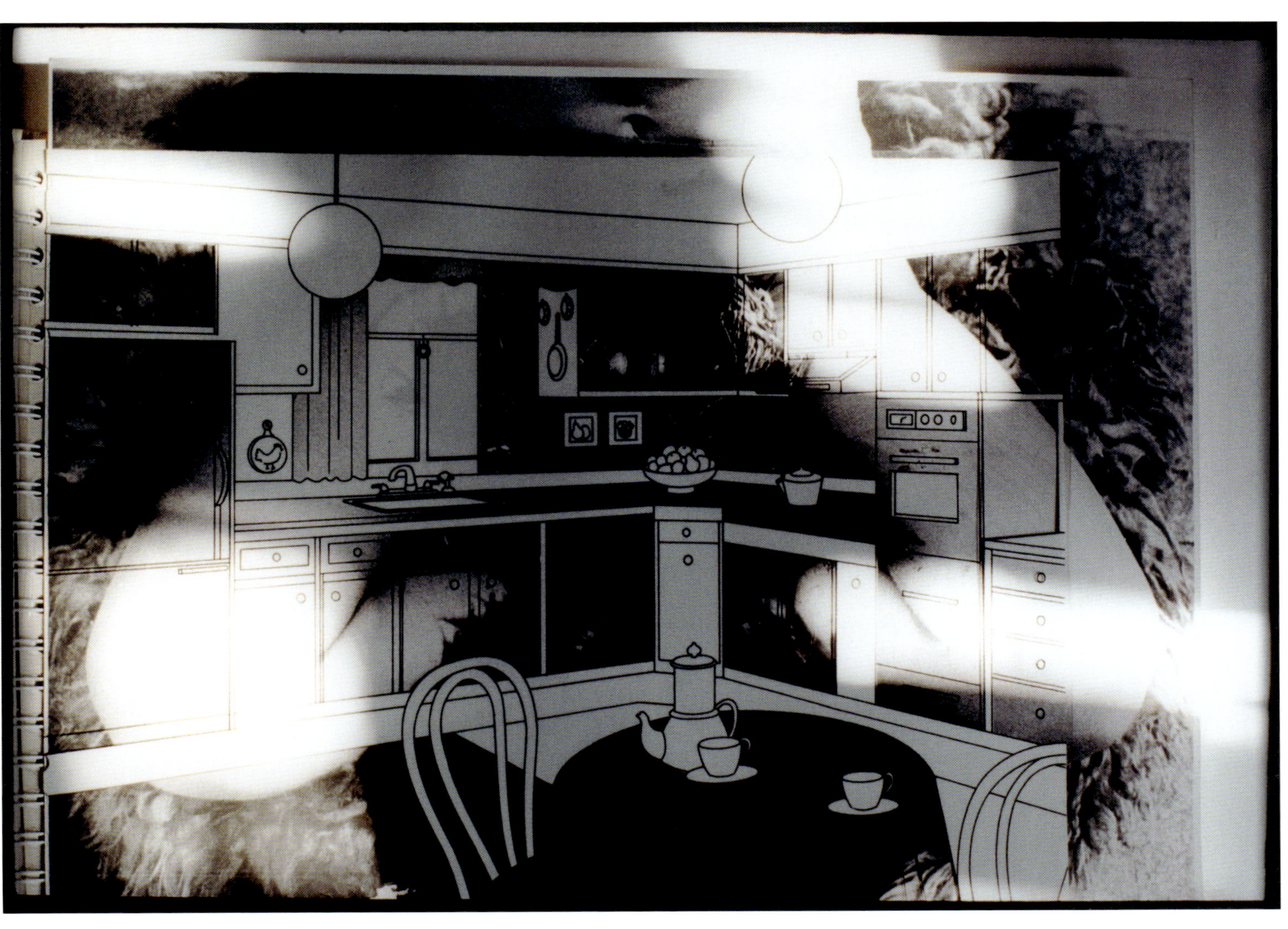

107   *Interieur 5* 1998/2003
Interior 5

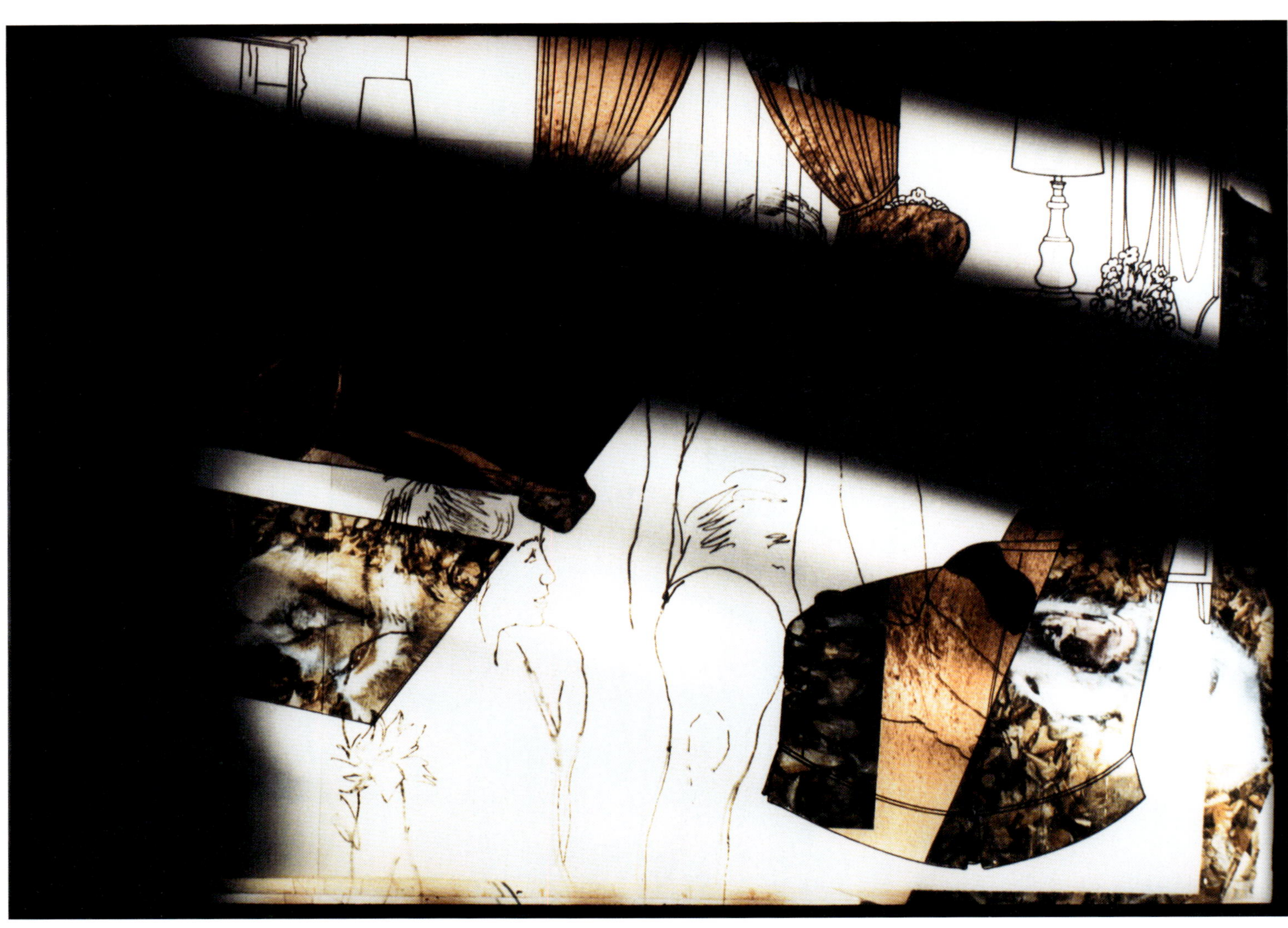

  Interieur 2 1998/2003
Interior 2

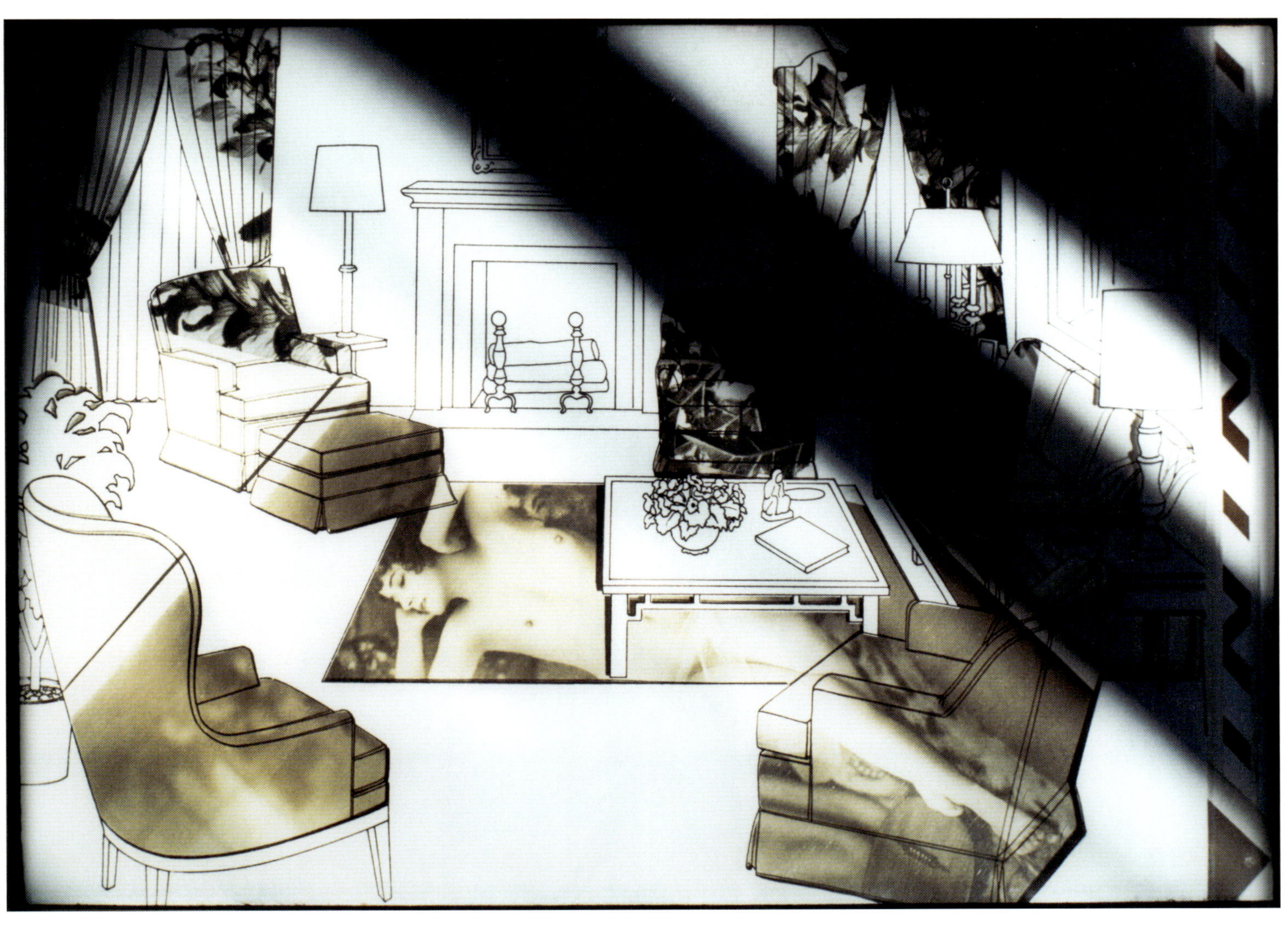

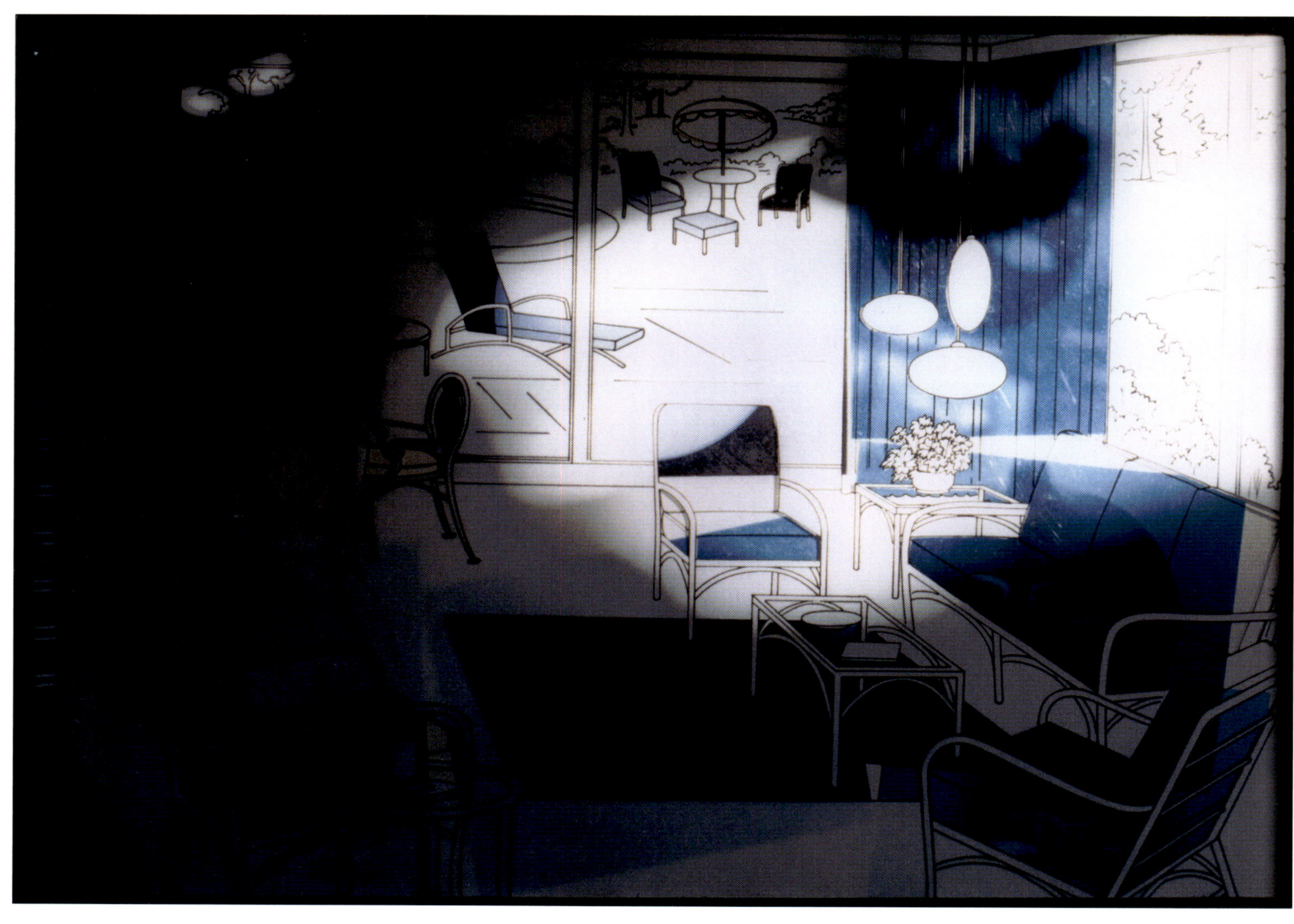

110   *Interieur 1* 1998/2003
      Interior 1

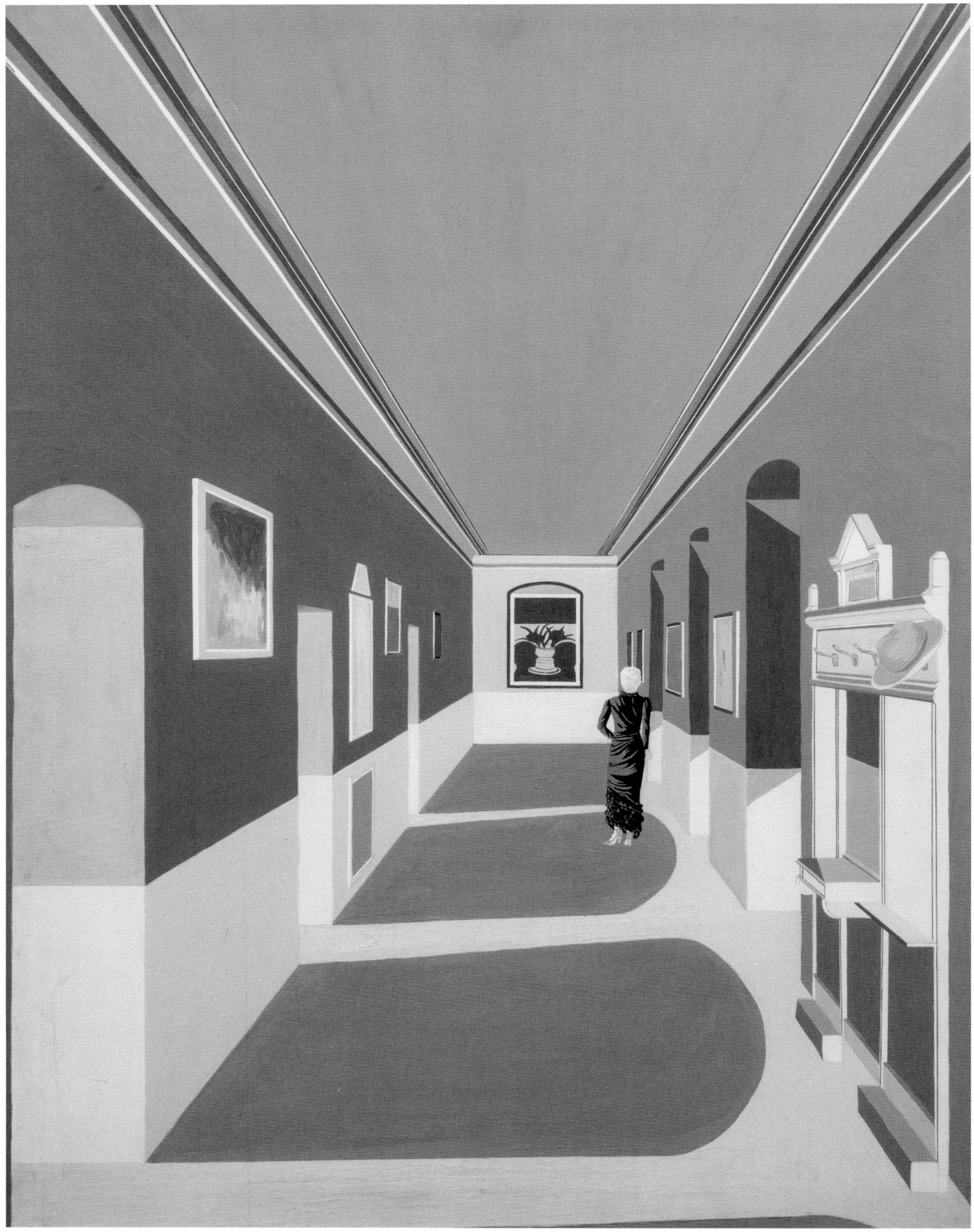

111 *Ohne Titel* 1973
Untitled

Vertigo

Patricia Allmer

Untitled (ill. 111) evokes the surrealist architectural spaces of de Chirico and the suspense of Hitchcock. Through the disconcertingly mismatched de Chirico-esque shadows on the floor, with their resemblance to a film reel, Jürgenssen uses the tropes of interior architectural visualizations to create a space of suspense in which we witness a slice of narrative, a film still perhaps, previsioning Cindy Sherman's film-still photographs of 1977–80. The cinematic mise-en-scène invites us to turn our voyeuristic gaze to the seemingly unaware heroine, evoking the rear view of an archetypically Hitchcockian blonde *femme fatale*. *Untitled* draws, in particular, on a near-monochrome scene in *Vertigo* (1958) in which Kim Novak walks down an apartment corridor. The two faces in the vase illusion, seen at the end of Jürgenssen's corridor, play on *Vertigo*'s exploration of a woman's performance of two different identities, and the fedora hanging to the right evokes that worn by the film's protagonist, Scottie (played by James Stewart). These Hitchcockian allusions extend to the dress in Jürgenssen's piece, which recalls the gothic Mrs. Danvers in *Rebecca* (1940).

Hollywood heroines like Marlene Dietrich and Mae West are recurrent reference points in Jürgenssen's work, and she would have grown up watching Hitchcock films on television (which was first broadcast nationwide in Austria in 1954, during her childhood). Hitchcock's TV series and movies were often televised (*Vertigo* was dubbed into German in 1958, and *Rebecca* in 1951, the latter subsequently broadcast as a radio play on Österreich 1 in 1973, the year *Untitled* was painted), and the *Krimi* (crime narrative) was a favorite genre among Austrian audiences. The monochrome grayscale of Jürgenssen's work thus evokes both her photographic practice (which she began in 1973) and the grayscale of monochrome television and the Austrian TV testcard (with color television only being properly accessible countrywide after 1972). *Untitled* thus combines a variety of allusions to different visual media into a haunting image of suspended action.

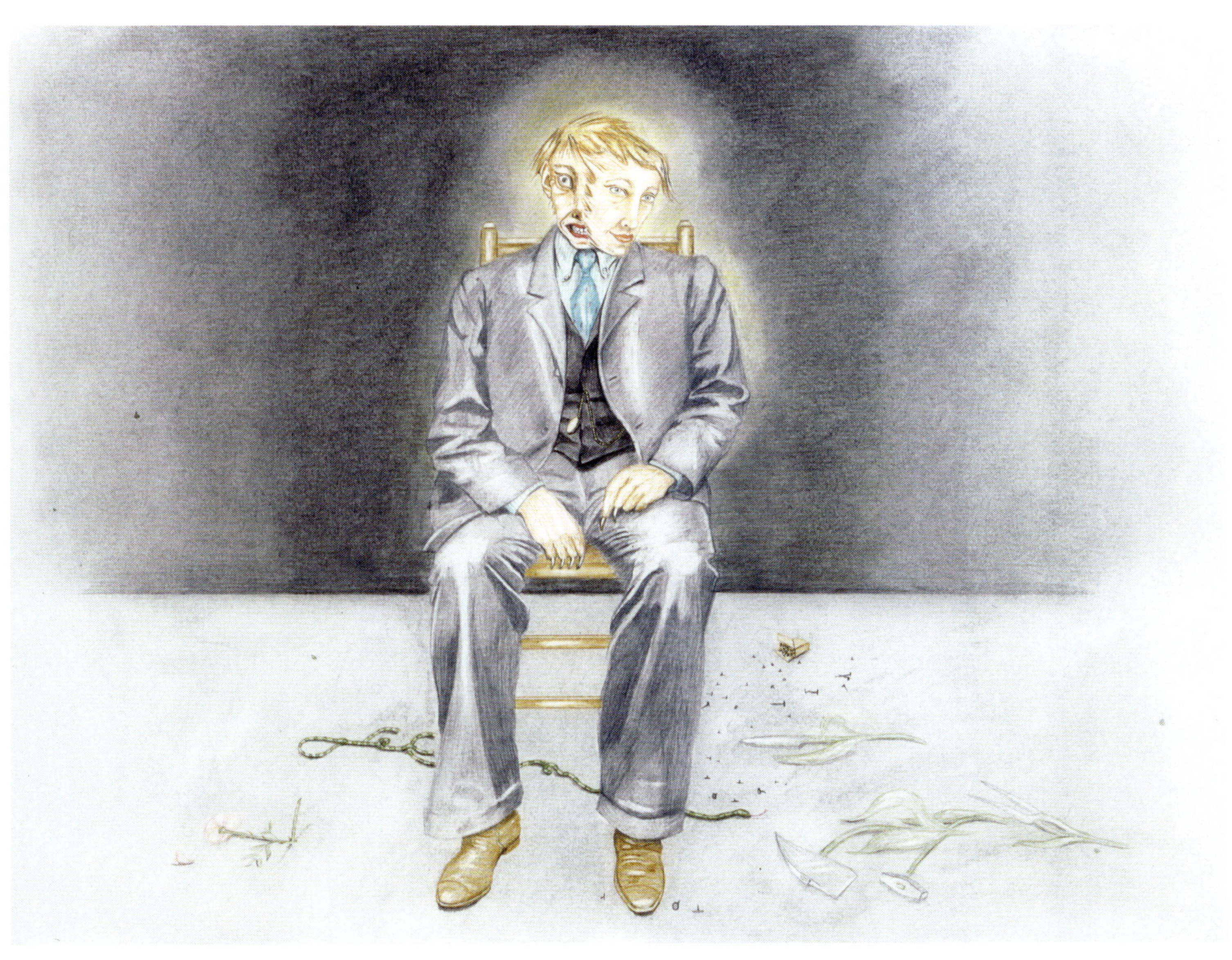

112   *Demaskierung* 1974
       Unmasking

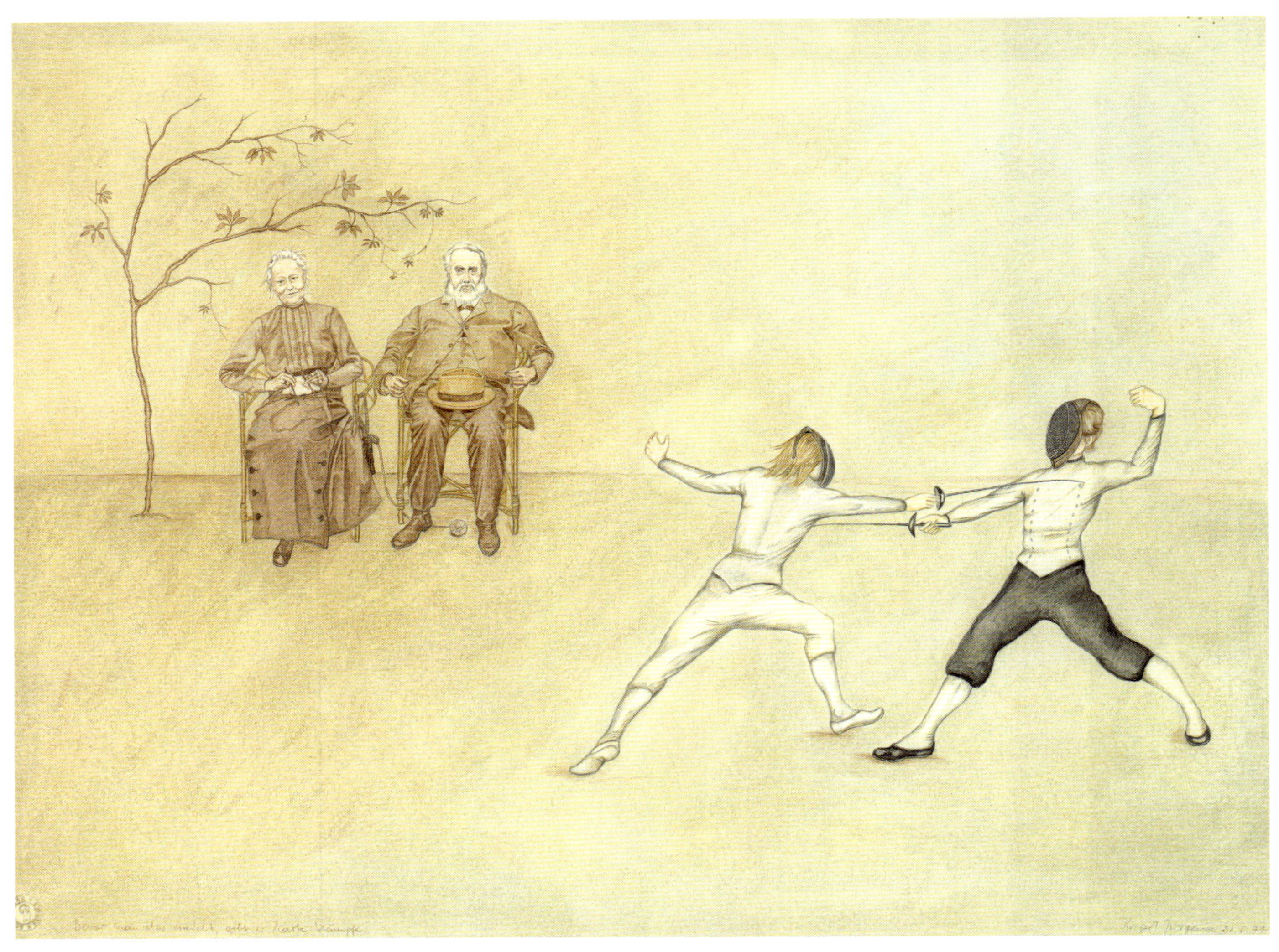

113 *Bevor man das erreicht, gibt es harte Kämpfe* 1974
     You Have a Tough Struggle on Your Hands Before You Get There

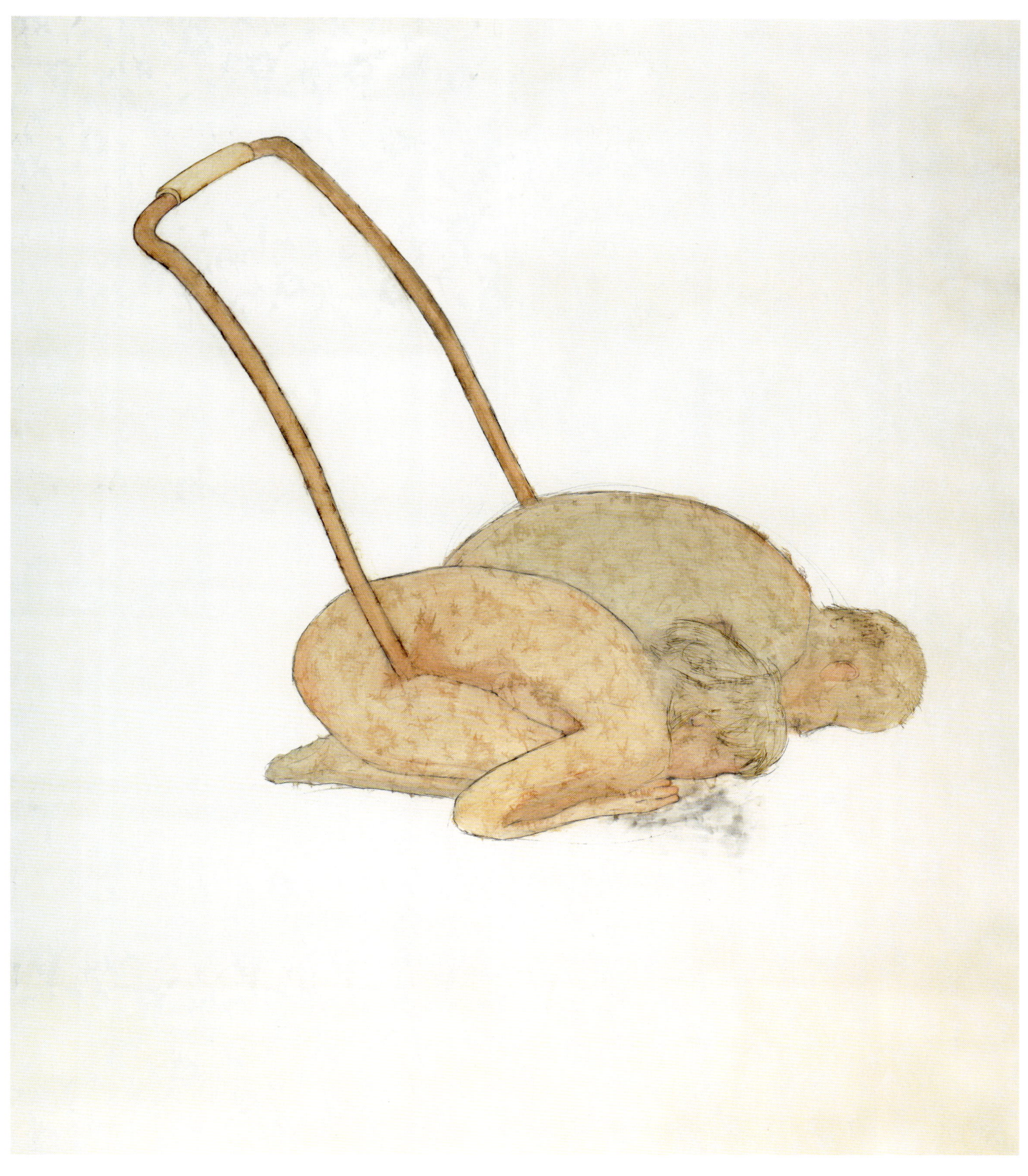

114   *Ohne Titel* 1972
      Untitled

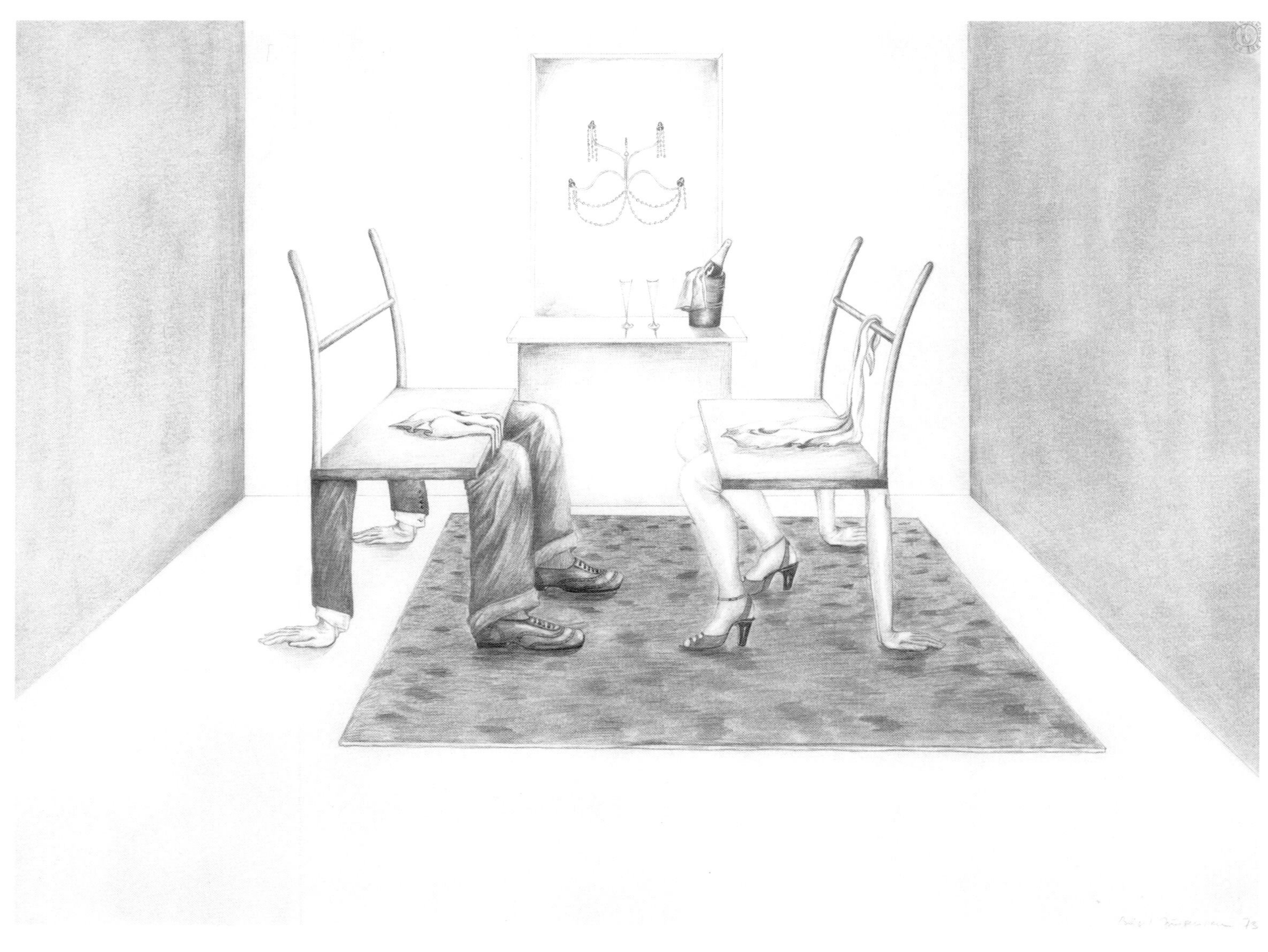

115   *Ohne Titel (The Party)* 1973
       Untitled (The Party)

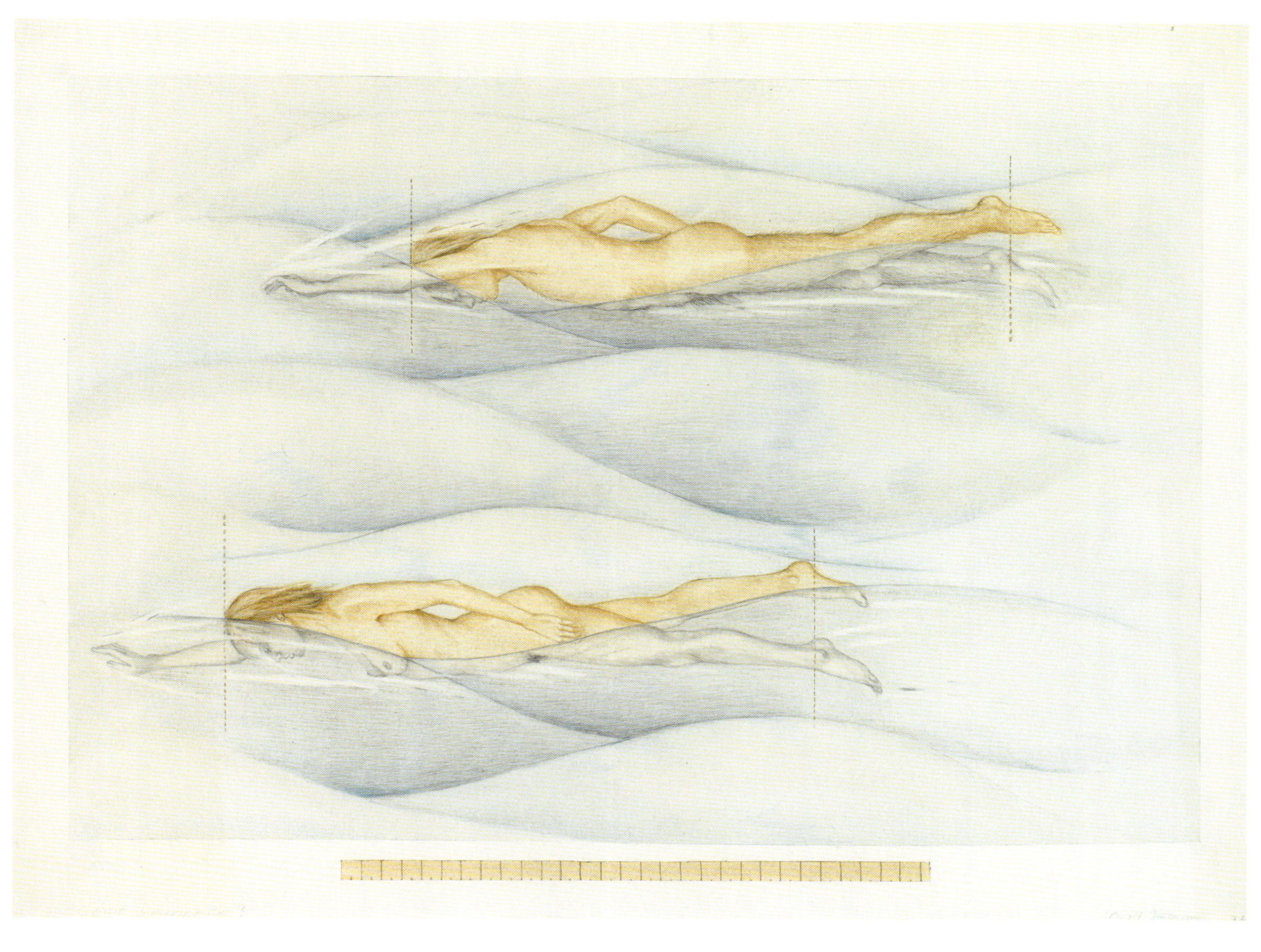

116   *Gleiche Wellenlänge? 1976*
       On the Same Wavelength?

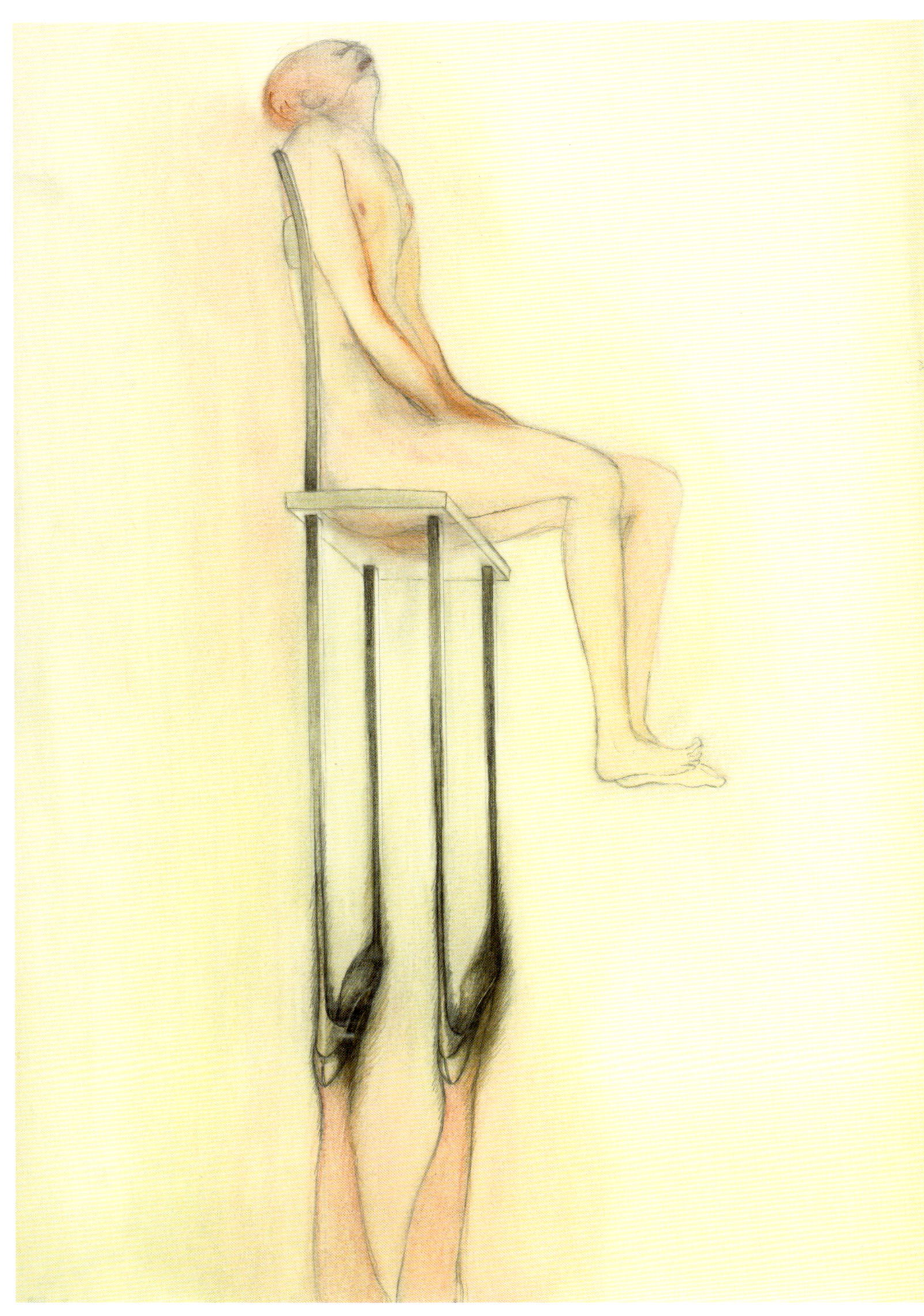

117   *Ohne Titel* 1979/1980
       Untitled

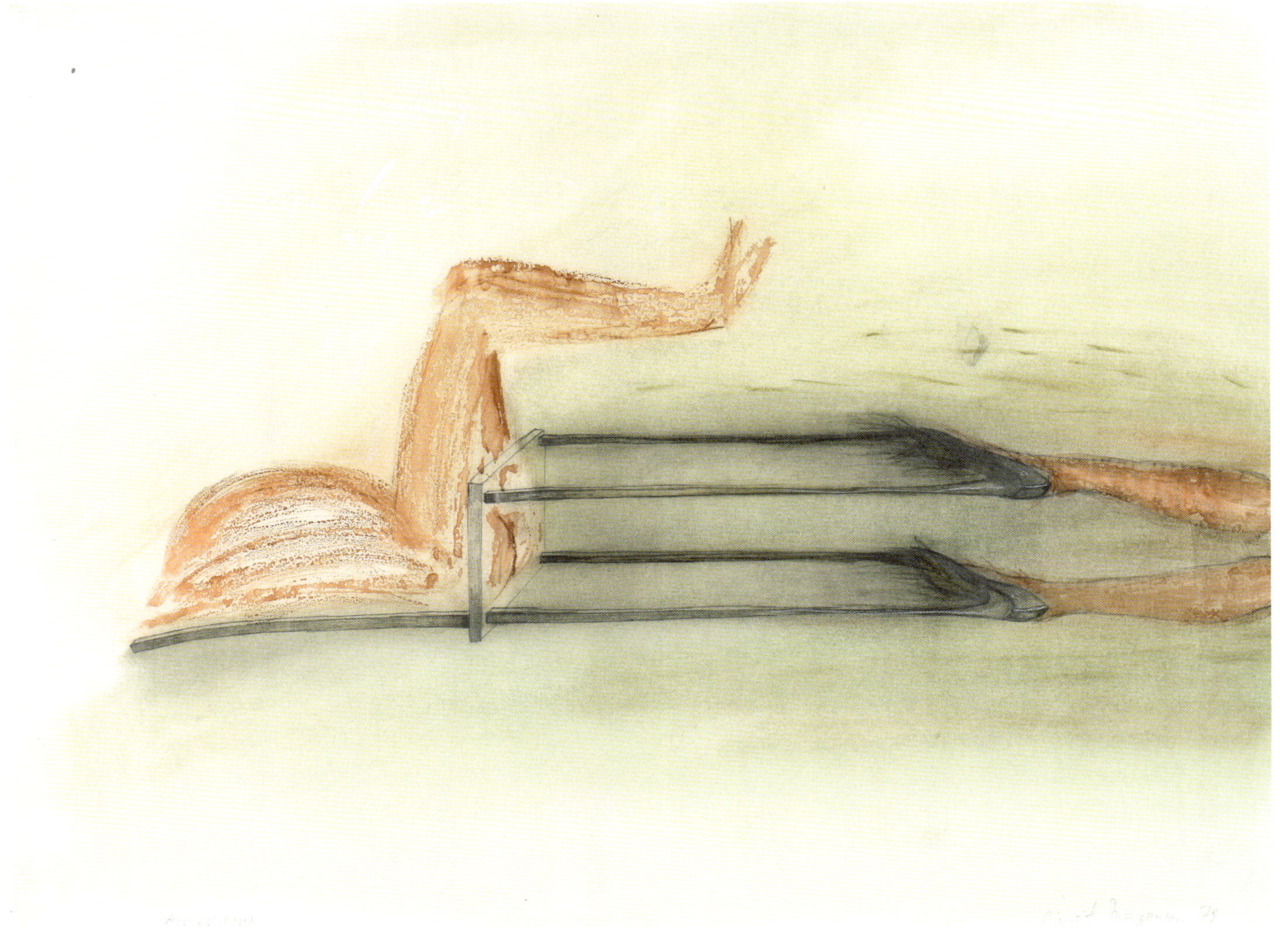

118   *Andersrum* 1979
The Other Way Round

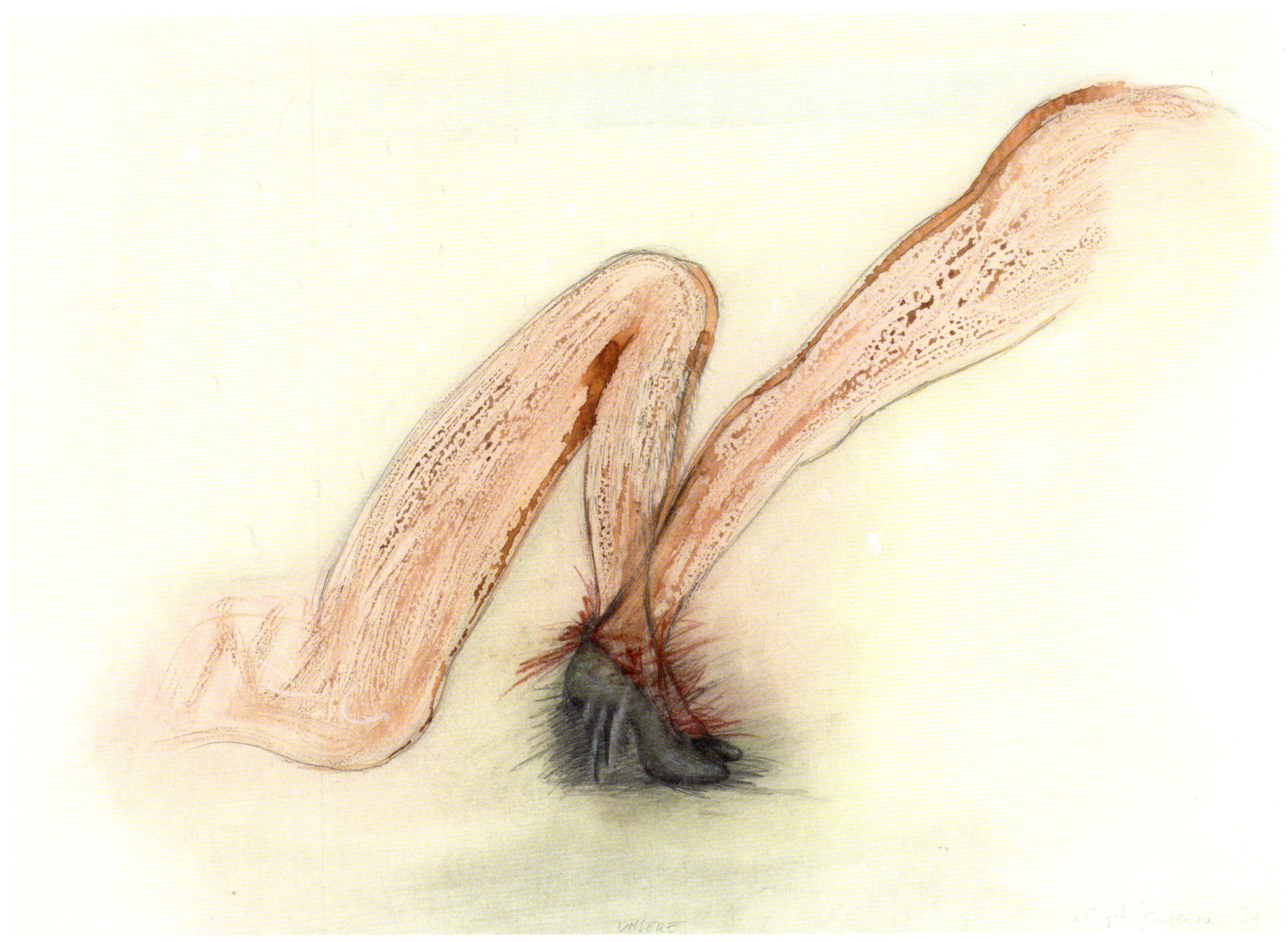

119   *Unsere* 1979
       Ours

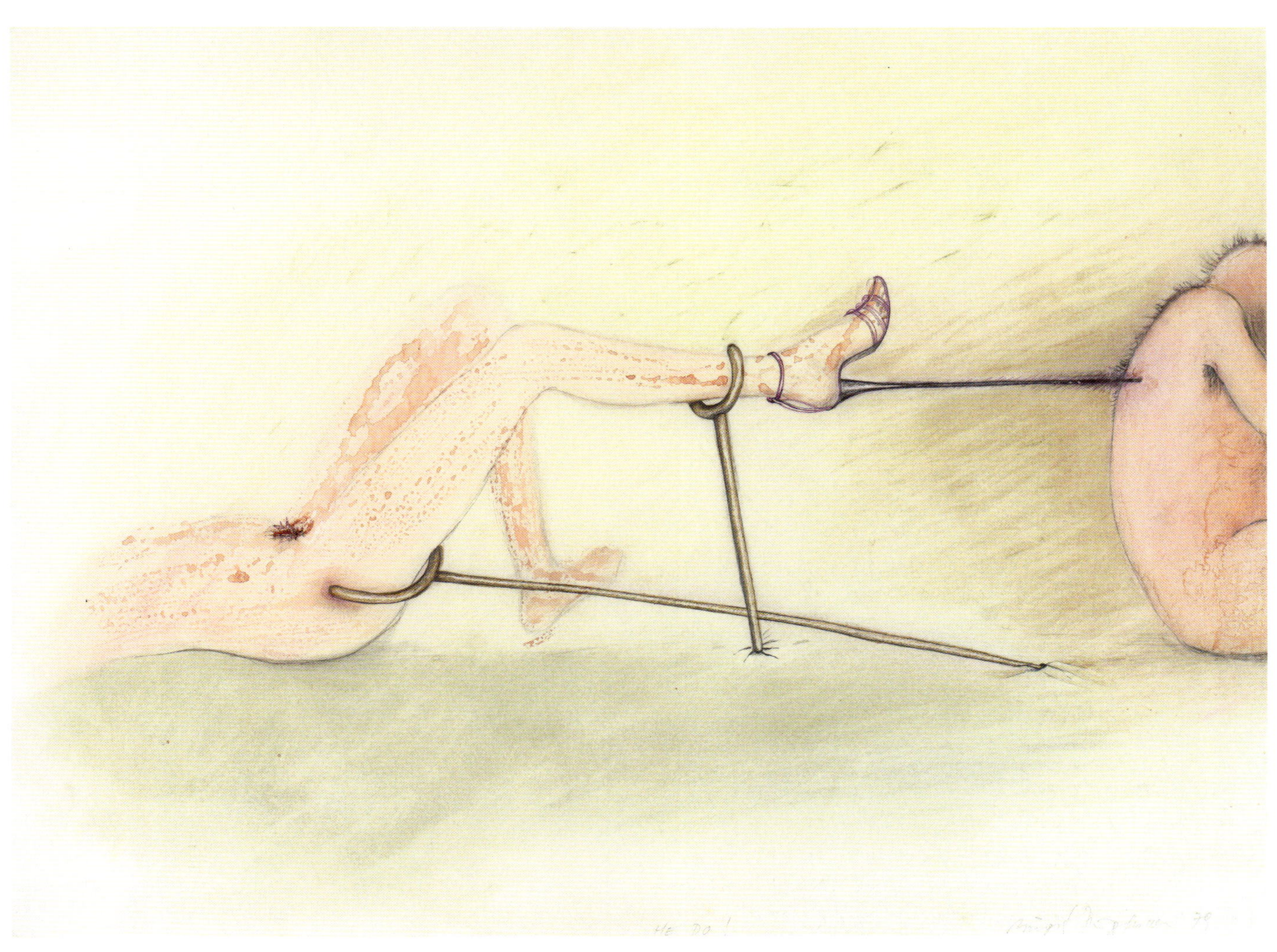

120   *Me Do!* 1979

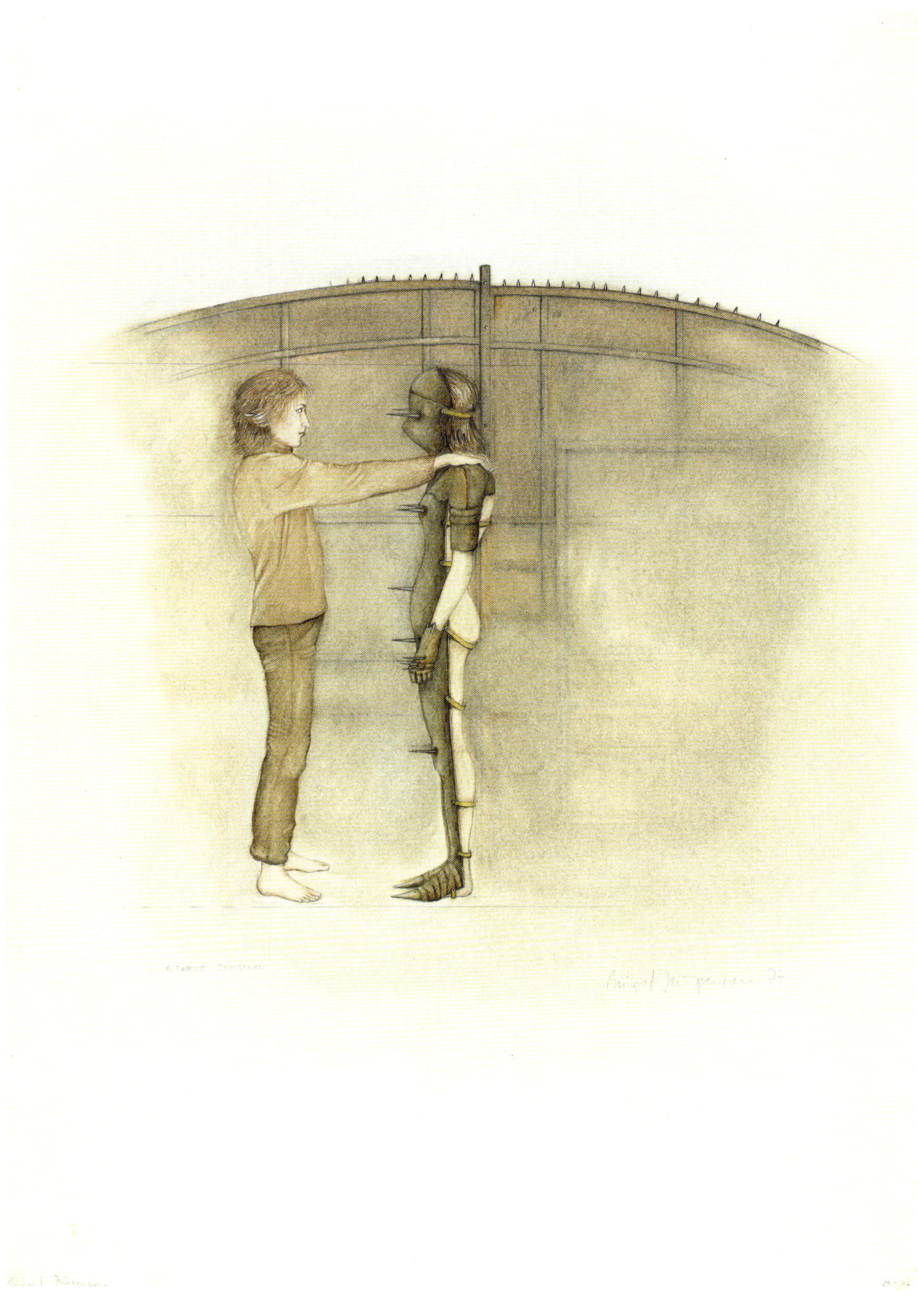

121 *Eiserne Jungfrau* 1976
    Iron Maiden

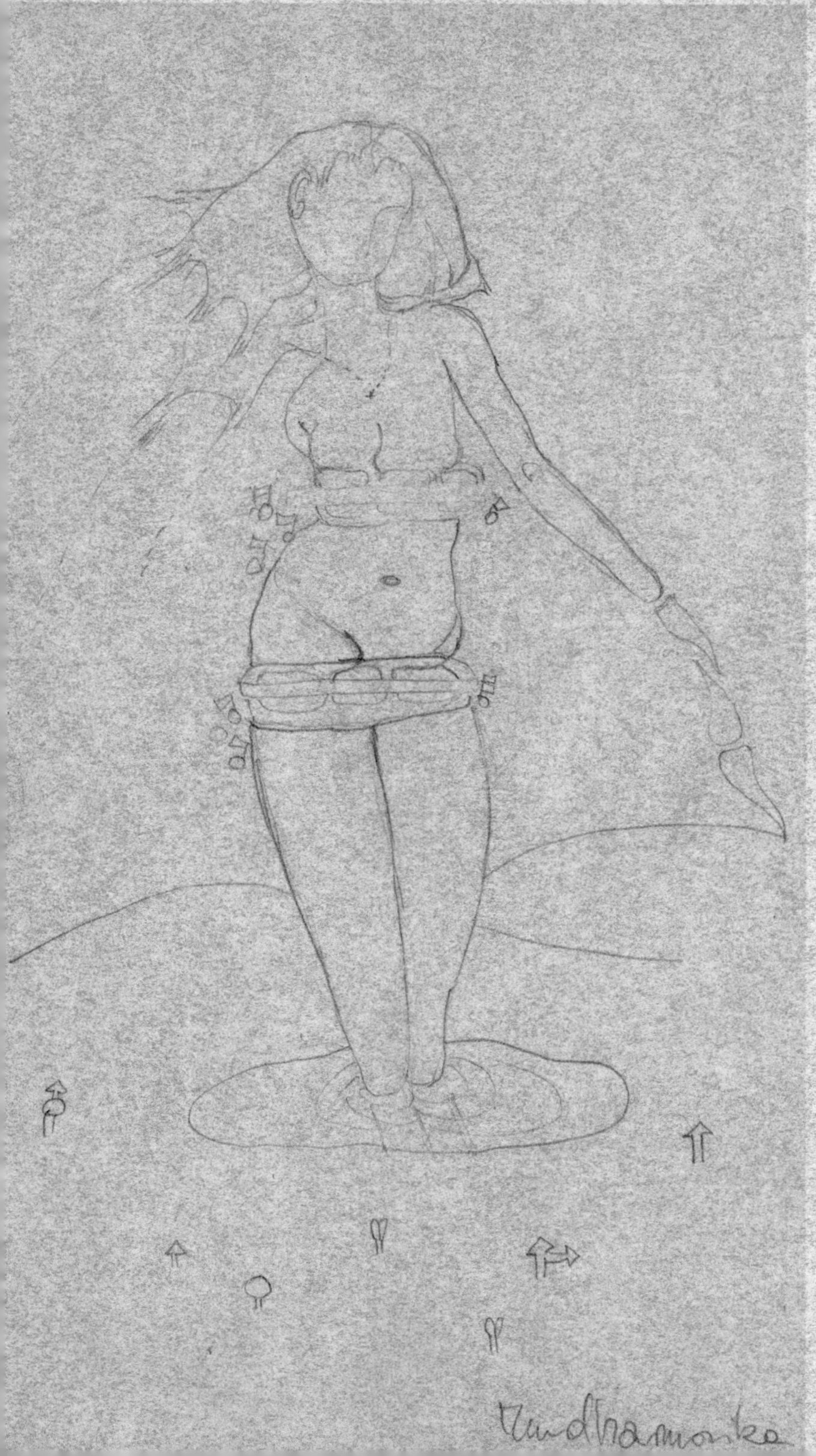

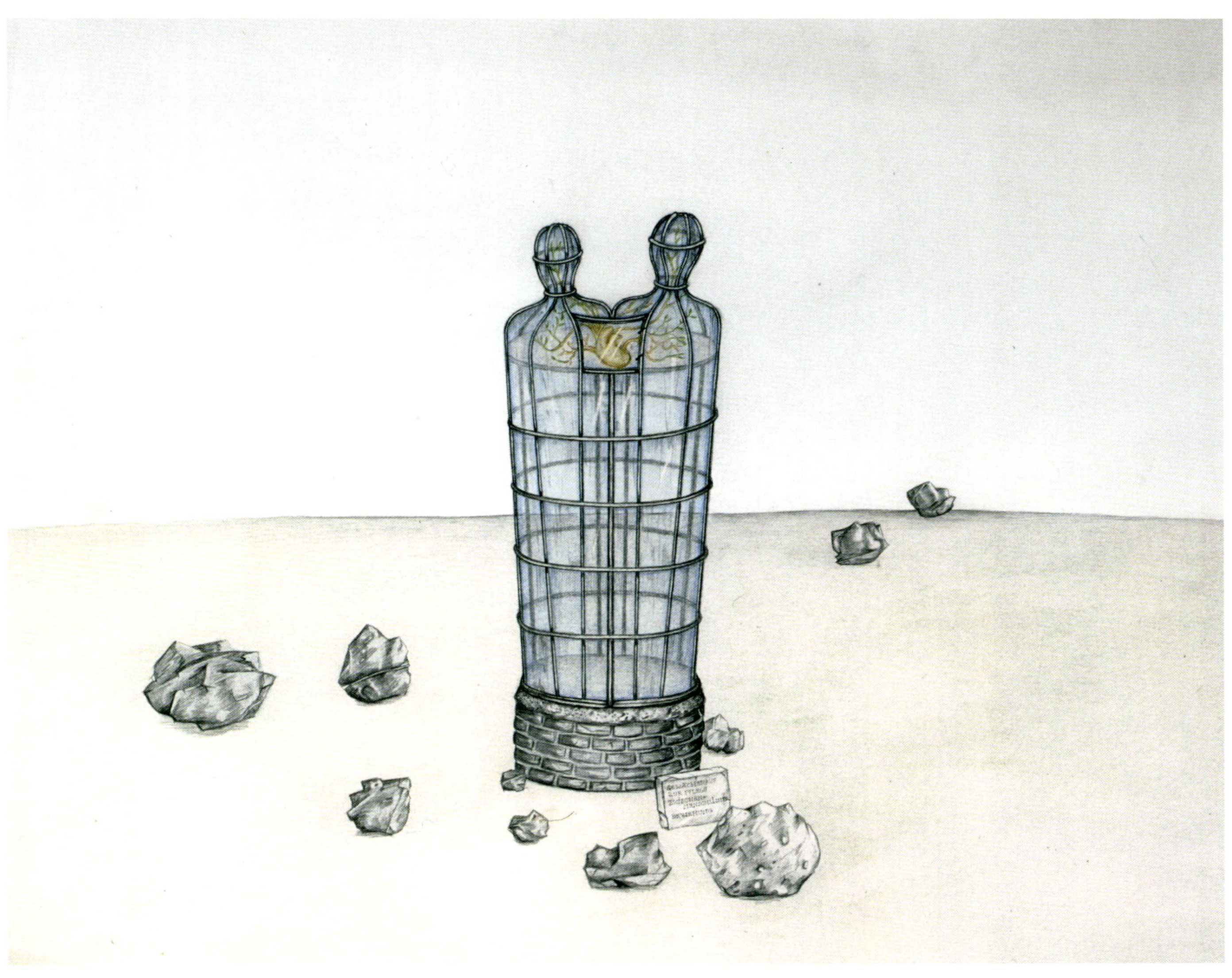

122 *Gewächshaus zur Pflege zwischenmenschlicher Beziehung* 1974
Greenhouse to Nurture Interpersonal Relationship

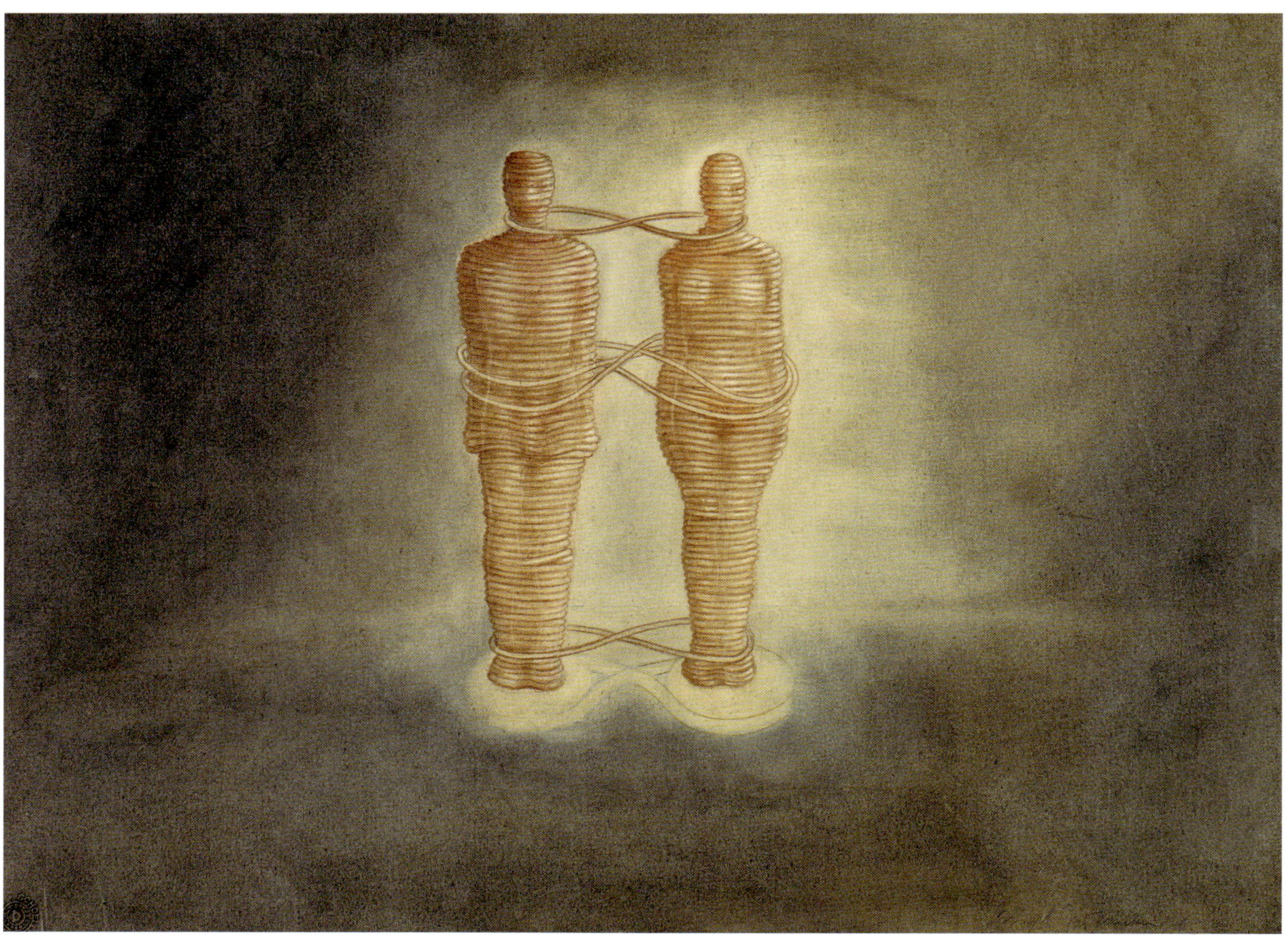

123   *Ohne Titel* 1978
       Untitled

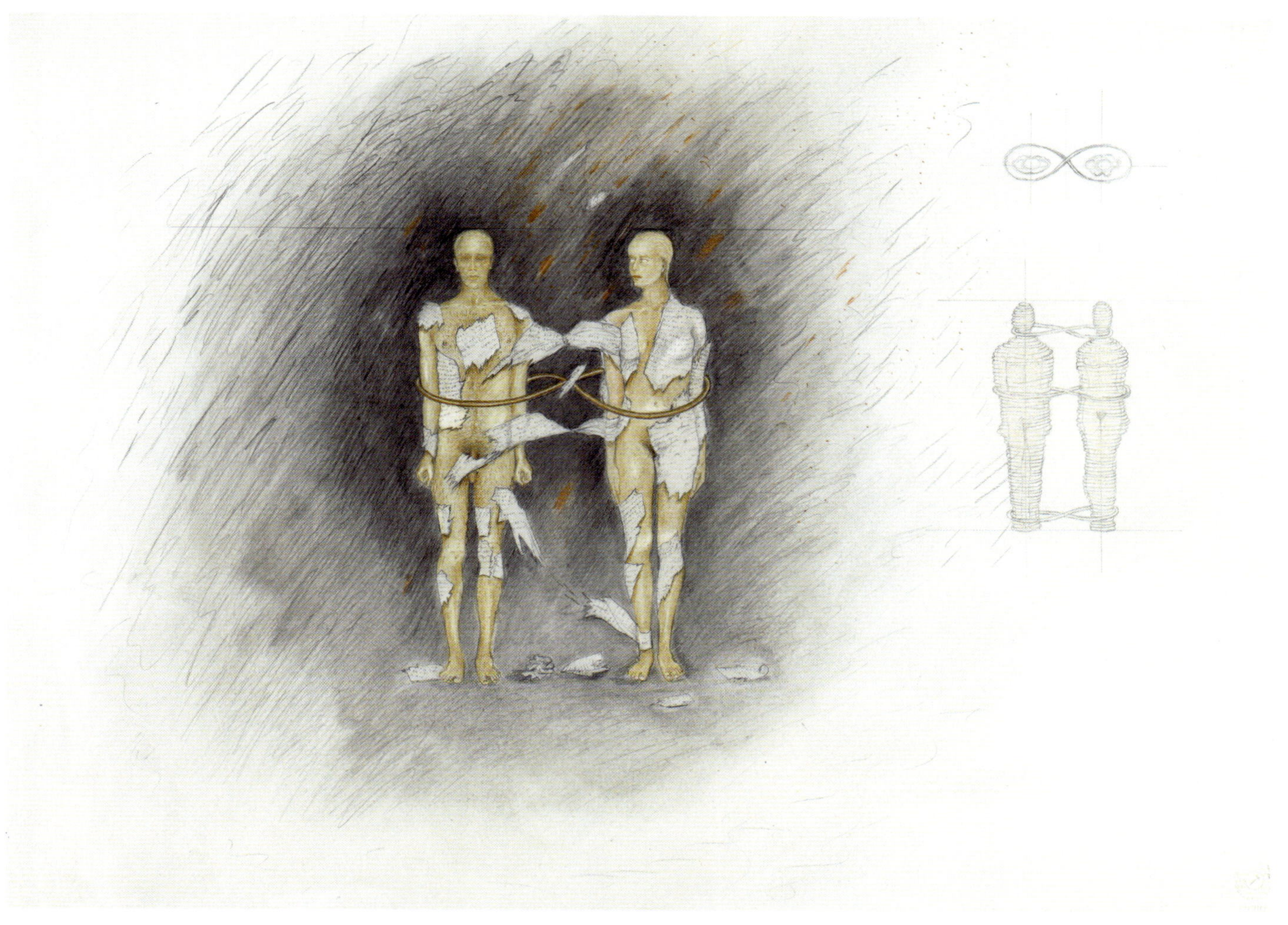

124 *Ohne Titel* 1975
Untitled

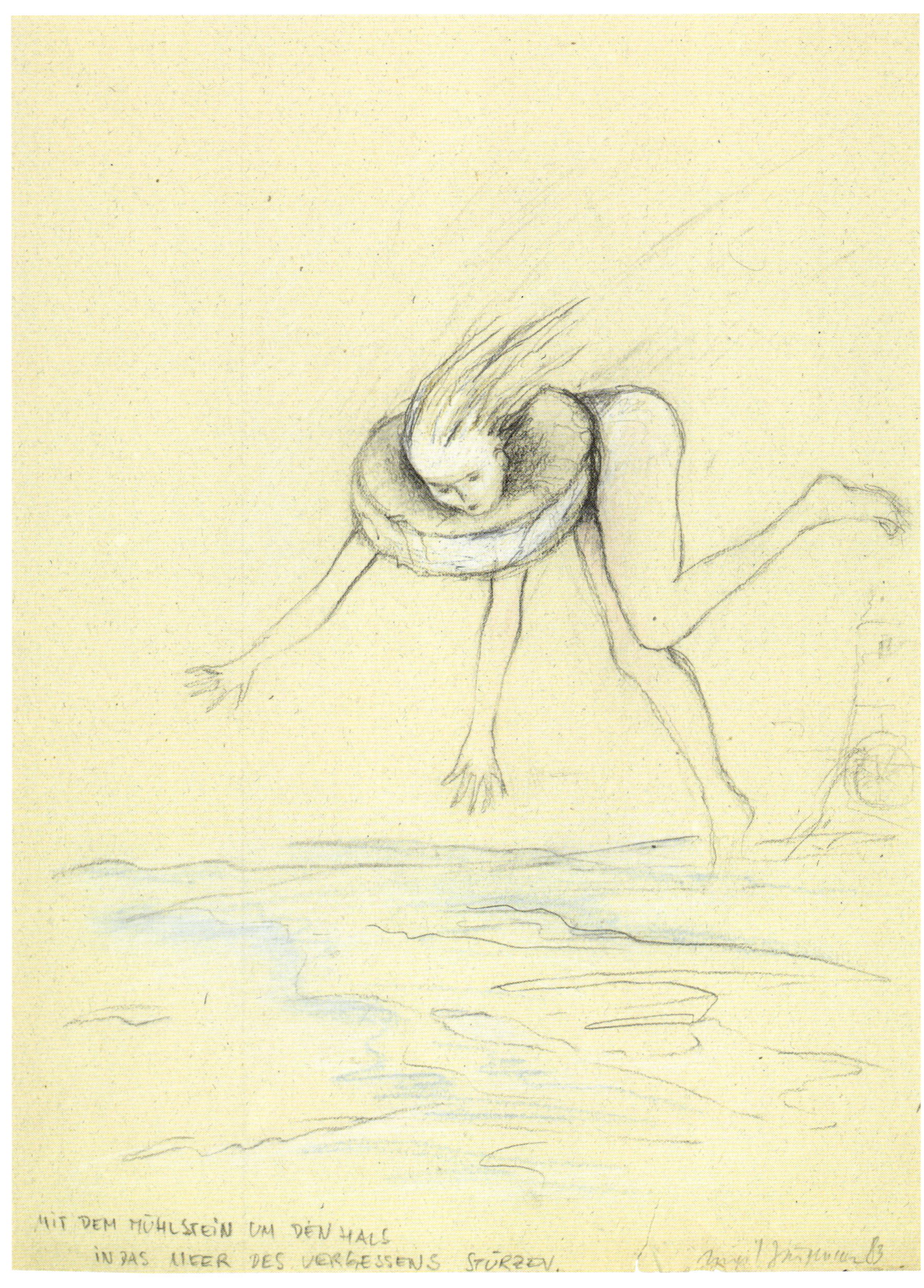

125 *Mit dem Mühlstein um den Hals in das Meer des Vergessens stürzen* 1983
Plunging into the Sea of Forgetfulness with a Milestone around One's Neck

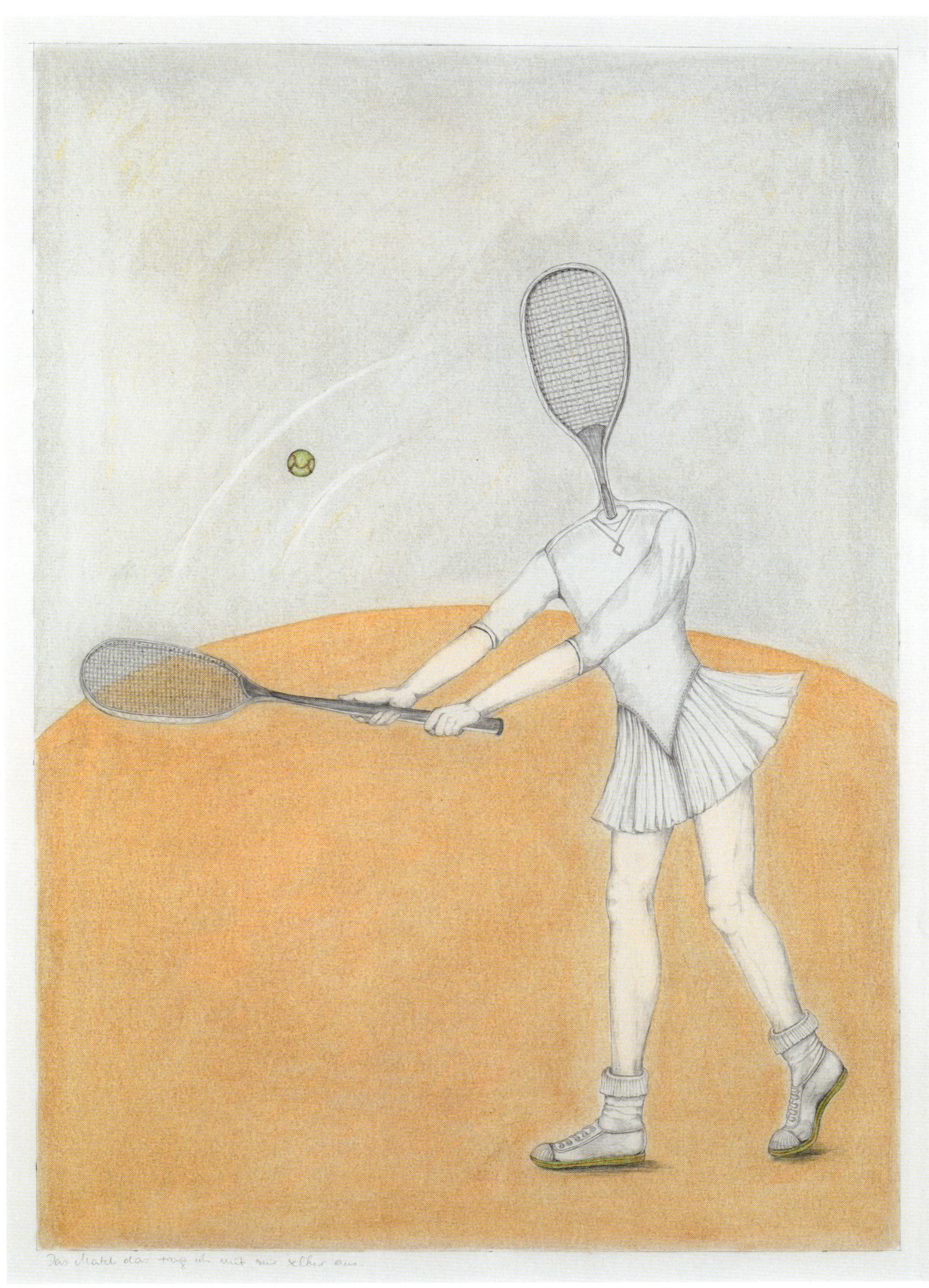

126   *Das Match das trag ich mit mir selber aus* 1973
I'll Play the Match with Myself

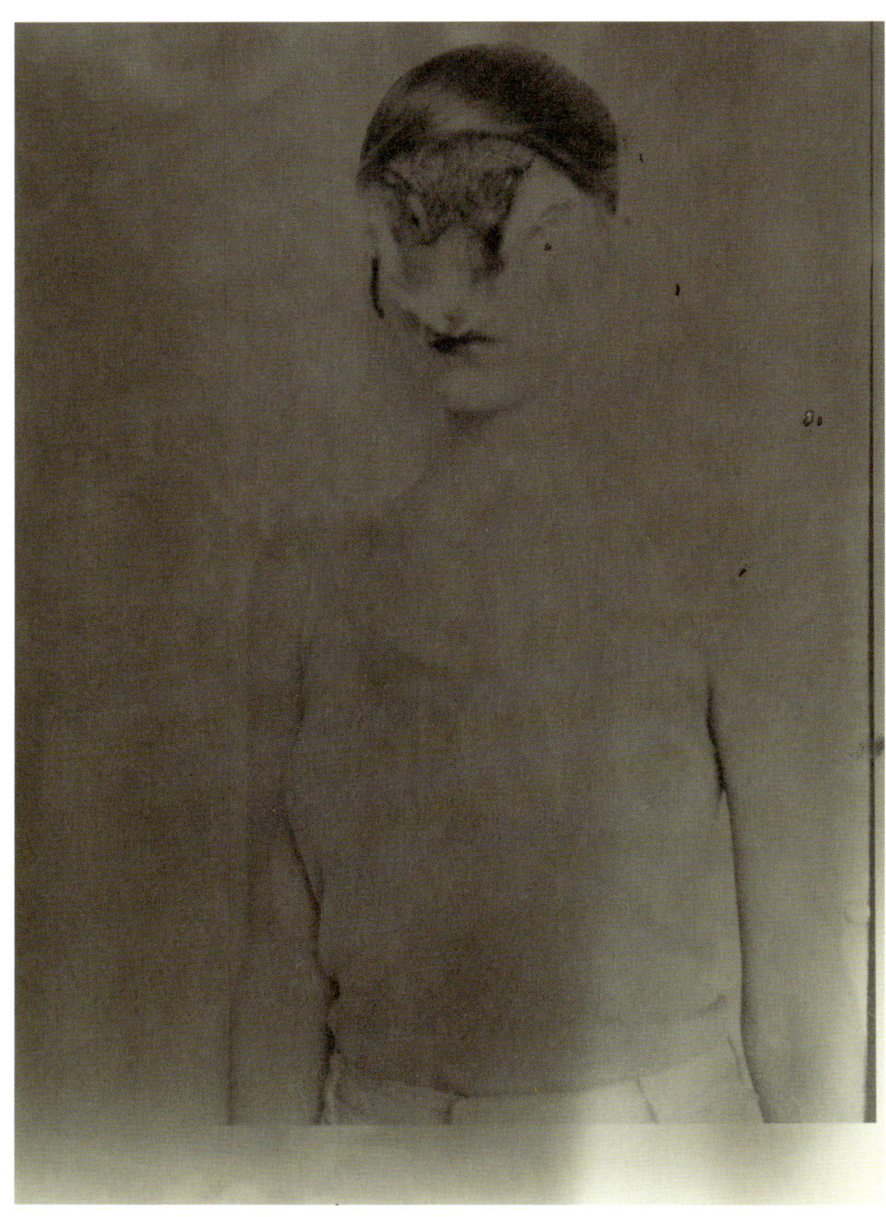

127 *Ohne Titel (Selbst mit Fellchen)* 1974
Untitled (Self with Little Fur)

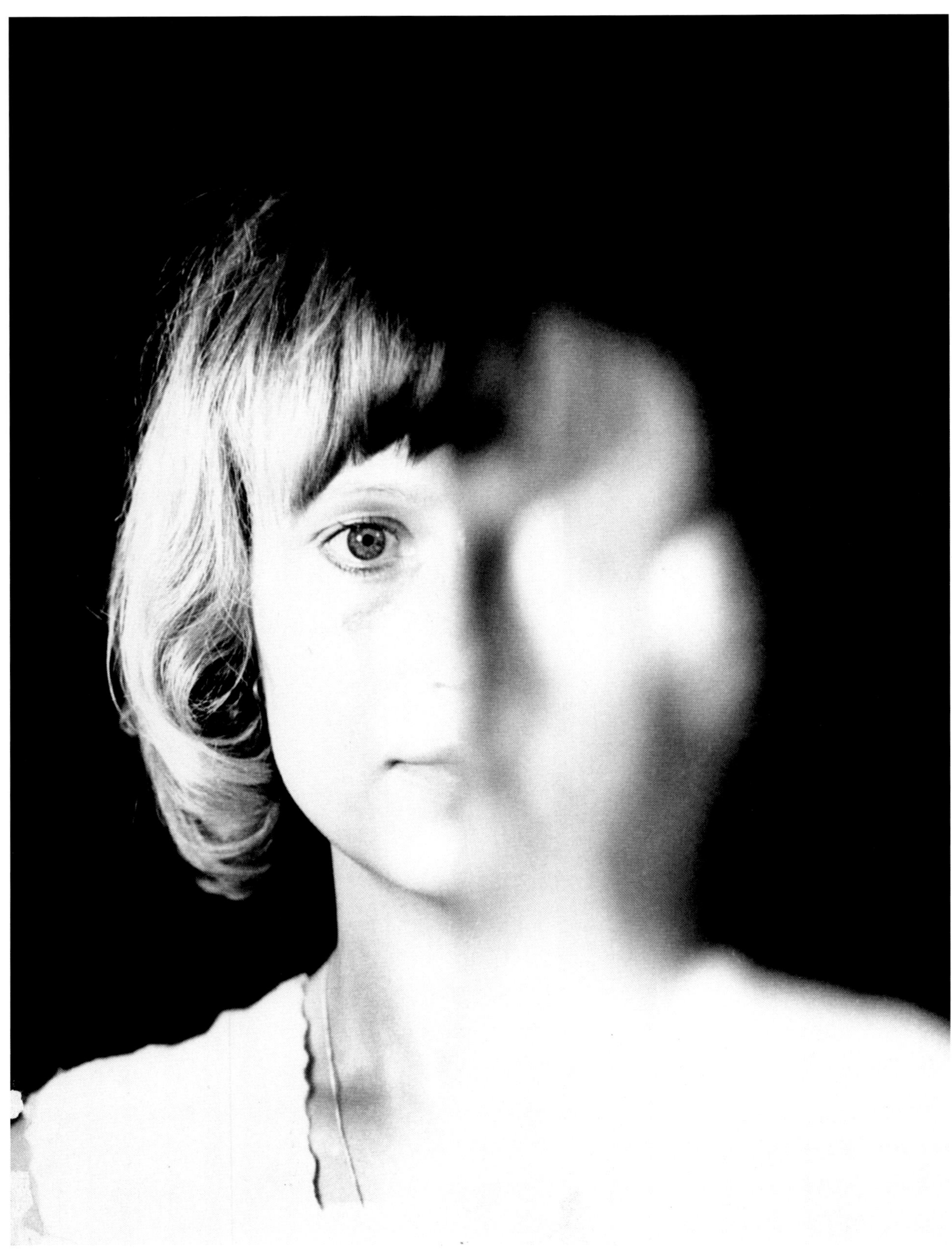

128   *Ohne Titel* 1972
       Untitled

Femishism:
Birgit Jürgenssen
in conversation with
Maurizio Cattelan

Maurizio Cattelan
in collaboration with
Marta Papini

sind wir jetzt?
ove is all about space: it's about desiring the space where
o people would like to meet. Sex is all about erasing
it space. So I guess you can't have love and sex
gether. You can only take turns; every man kills
e things he loves." Maurizio Cattelan
au Luc Godard: „Tous disent la règle, personne ne dit
exeption, il est de la règle de l'Europe, de la
lture, que d'organiser la mort de l'art de vivre
i fleurissait encore à nos pieds."

How did you become an artist?
As I recall, at the age of eight or nine,
I started drawing stories, using schoolbooks
of my brother's that he had left some
empty pages in. I grew up very much within
role clichés and really did not know how
to deal with that. I was in a quandary, not
knowing how far I could go with my artistic
expression. So I just drew or photographed
my everyday life. I operated in a very
spontaneous way, because I'm very much
opposed to the posture of »So now I'm
doing art.«

What influenced you most?
I first encountered surrealism aged sev-
enteen. I had friends in Paris who worked
in the theater and organized readings of
works by authors like Artaud. But I saw my
work as closer to that of Meret Oppenheim
and Louise Bourgeois, who were more
poetic, less direct, and more subversive.
I always liked the idea of going beyond
realistic depiction to create something fictional and perplexing.

What do you think art should do today?
Art serves to stimulate other ways of thinking and to foster awareness. It has to hit
the spot.

So art has meaning only as a critique
of power?
Not at all. My work relates to perception.
Using manipulative mechanisms, pictures,
and the values and norms they convey
can have a subversive status. This is help-
ful in analyzing what is behind them and
how certain images (an image in the sense
of the objectuality/paradox of the woman)
are used to conceal or support social
interrelations according to their (patriarchal) liking.

Is it a quest for answers or questions?
We all want to get some kind of response.
My interest is not in the representation
of things themselves, because they are only
intriguing when the relationships they
are in come to the fore.

I usually disguise by running away, while it
seems you are disguising yourself by wearing masks. Standing in front of a camera,
even if covered, seems quite an ineffective
strategy for creating a disguise … Yours
is a selfie apology, like Cindy Sherman's
profile on Instagram?
I wouldn't call it disguise. It is more of
a surreal practice, making things visible by
concealing them. I mask myself because
it is less about me and more about the situ-
ations in which I present myself, the
stories that become visual. And, of course,
it is about slipping into different roles
and identities.

I would have loved to see a performance
by you, but I missed out …
You know, at the beginning, performance
seemed too direct to me, and I was simply
too shy to appear in public: the drawings
and then the photographs and objects had,
of course, come out of a private performance, and I then converted them into the
respective medium. For me, performance
is an opportunity to put a specific issue into
a dramatic form and use the presentation
of it to elicit a direct response. The worst
thing for me is isolation; an action or public
performance is a communicative act,
a learning process.

There are works of art by young artists
sold for astronomical prices today—cases
like Oscar Murillo, etc. How much do
»likes« on Facebook, Instagram, and Twitter
count today?
Personal achievements are what count.
We're still looking in the milk pot of
the Holy Trinity of *seller-gallerist-artist*.
Maybe, though, there's a separation
between the art business and that which
has content and is a new intellectual/
artistic movement.

Speaking of the future, how do you see
art today, the explosion of art that makes
use of computer screens?
I would like there to be more real collectors and fewer speculators. And no separation between gold invitations and normal
invitations to a vernissage!

We share a passion for shoes, don't we?
Shoes seemed to be the right objects
for me to give free rein to my erotic and
cynical fantasies and all other possible
interpretations too. I began to explore this
theme when I was still a student, and
it took several years before I started getting
annoyed by being called »the woman
with the shoes.« I was looking for a neutral
object that everyone was familiar with.
In 1975 I drew a line under this theme with
an environment with shoe objects and
drawings in the Nuremberg Kunsthalle.

What is fetishism for you?
To touch is to make contact. *Do not touch*
as an interdiction is the greatest temptation. One has to break prejudices and
taboos—as de Sade says, *happiness is
only ever possible inasmuch as there are
prohibitions to be broken, and all happiness ceases when one takes away its trans-
gressiveness.*

How are fetishism and feminism linked?
Fetishism, the obsessive interest in objects,
has always fascinated me, as is evident,
for example, in the photos I took with dis-
torting mirrors in 1979 and 1980, where
all that we can see is an amorphous impression of shining leather. These pictures
are not so much about it being me that is
fragmented and rendered with anamor-
photic distortion. They are more about the

object. The identity of the woman is made to disappear, leaving just the fetishized object, the focus of male wishful thinking.

So, are you a femishist?
In the sense of becoming conscious of, analyzing, and deconstructing dominant theories and representational systems … Yes.

Are feminist movements today, such as #MeToo, effective? What is still missing for them to become effective?
Self-irony, although we wanted the result of our work together to be taken very seriously. Like women and humor, women and irony is still very much a taboo topic. The price for this is not being taken seriously to a large degree. For me, self-irony is a form of autobiographical strategy, a means to more easily convey a subversive and deconstructive potential.

Are there any other examples of this kind of approach in recent art history?
In New York I met the Gorilla Girls, and we—DIE DAMEN—then asked ourselves how we wanted to deal with the questions of commitment, struggle, and radical politics. In Austria we saw that feminist actions just led to processes of exclusion, and we wanted to reach a very broad and diverse audience. To gain attention here, we needed an entertainment factor.

What do you think of the new generation of artists, such as Wu Tsang, that seems to reject the simplistic confines of identification?
For several years now there has been gender discourse, and it seems that gender is no longer a barrier for a career as an artist. Today, all things flow into, condition, and permeate one another … I like it when there's an active feminism operating in parallel. But I don't think one should make a career out of it.

Do you mean that these artists are using their identity as a tool to get to artistic success?
Quite simply, what's necessary is to produce convincing work. Maybe artists should respond *more artistically* at times. I hoped that time would be on my side, and that the conditions for art by women would change. Eventually, the concept of art was redefined, through crossover and the use of new media. Today's gender discourse consists precisely in addressing concepts like »typically male« versus »typically female« art.

Is there an achievement you're proud of, outside the artworks?
When I was a student, I noticed that there was not a single German-language anthology of women artists. I even wrote to the Dumont publishing house and complained about this. Two years later an encyclopedia of women artists was then indeed published.

One could say that your work is at a crossroads between the non-acceptance of reality as a given and a form of resistance to official power …
Let me quote Mae West: »It is better to be looked over than overlooked.«

How do you think the world will end?
I go to bed and can't (don't want to) sleep. Aladdin's lamp, adorned with a thousand eyes, sits on my chest. The lamp is still sealed but the beings inside it are restless. Angels and demons need no passports.

Can you imagine a world without art?
I don't think I can.

Why aren't you still with us?
Because less is more.

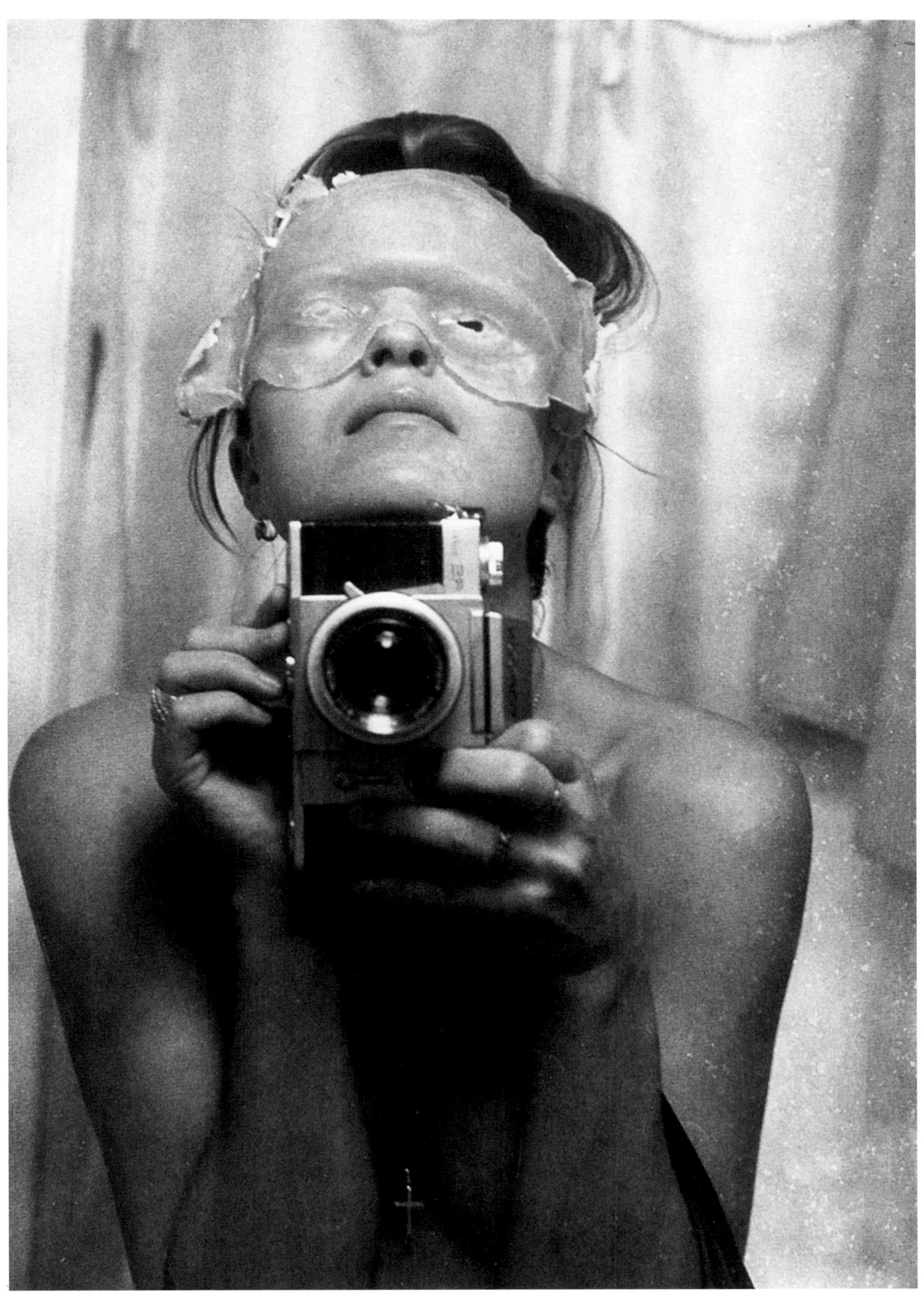

129 *Ohne Titel* 1976
Untitled

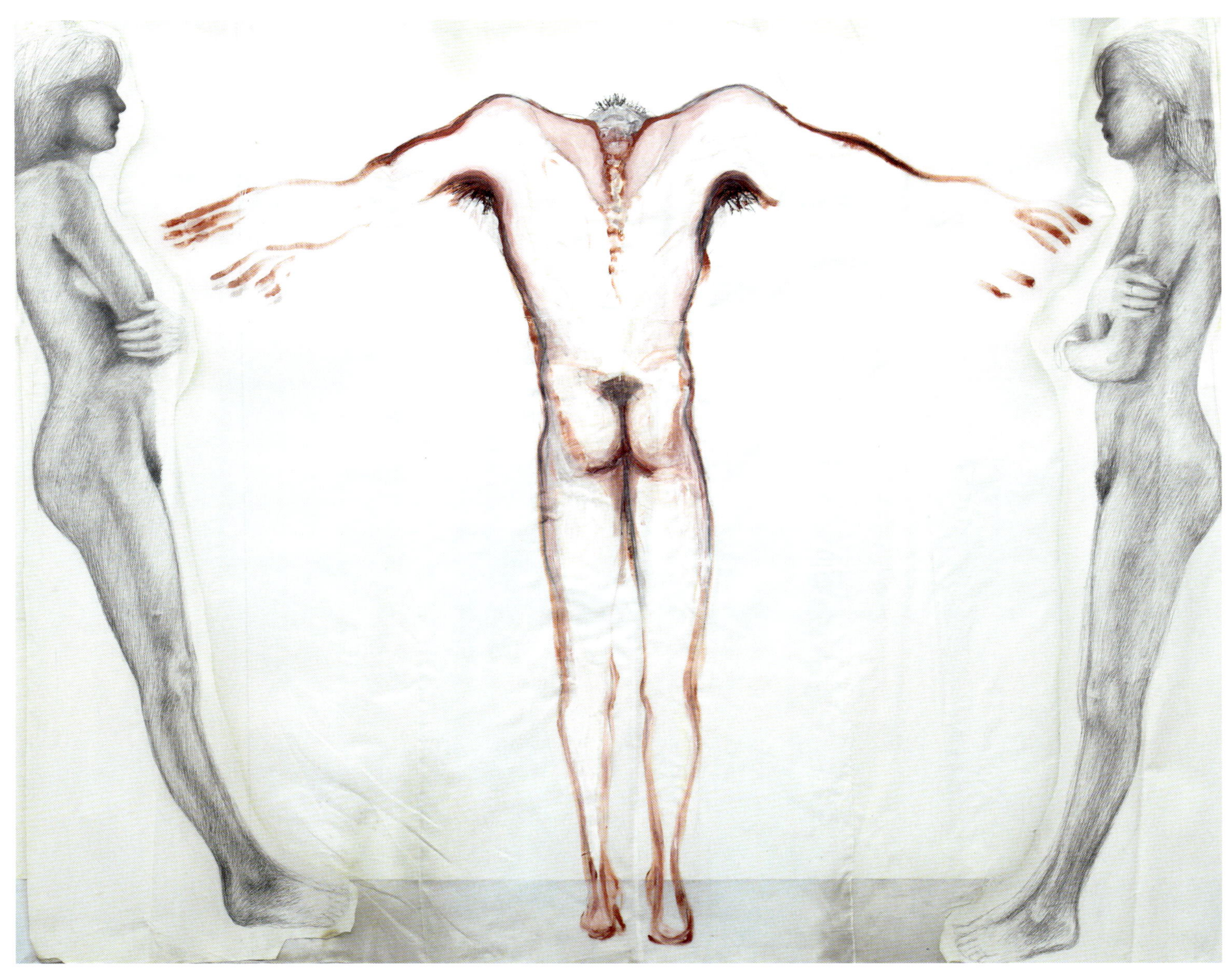

<u>130</u> *Ohne Titel* 1978
Untitled

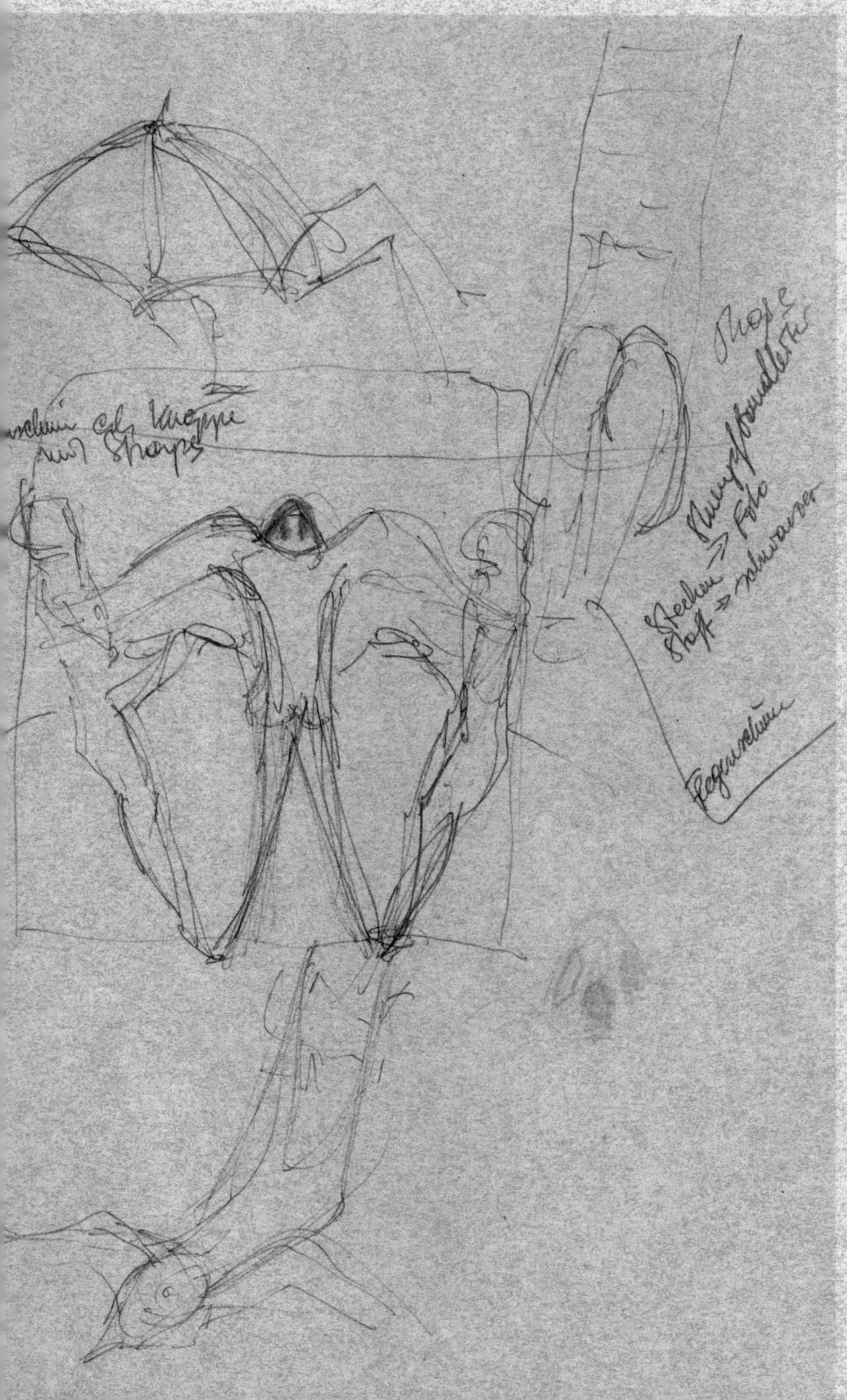

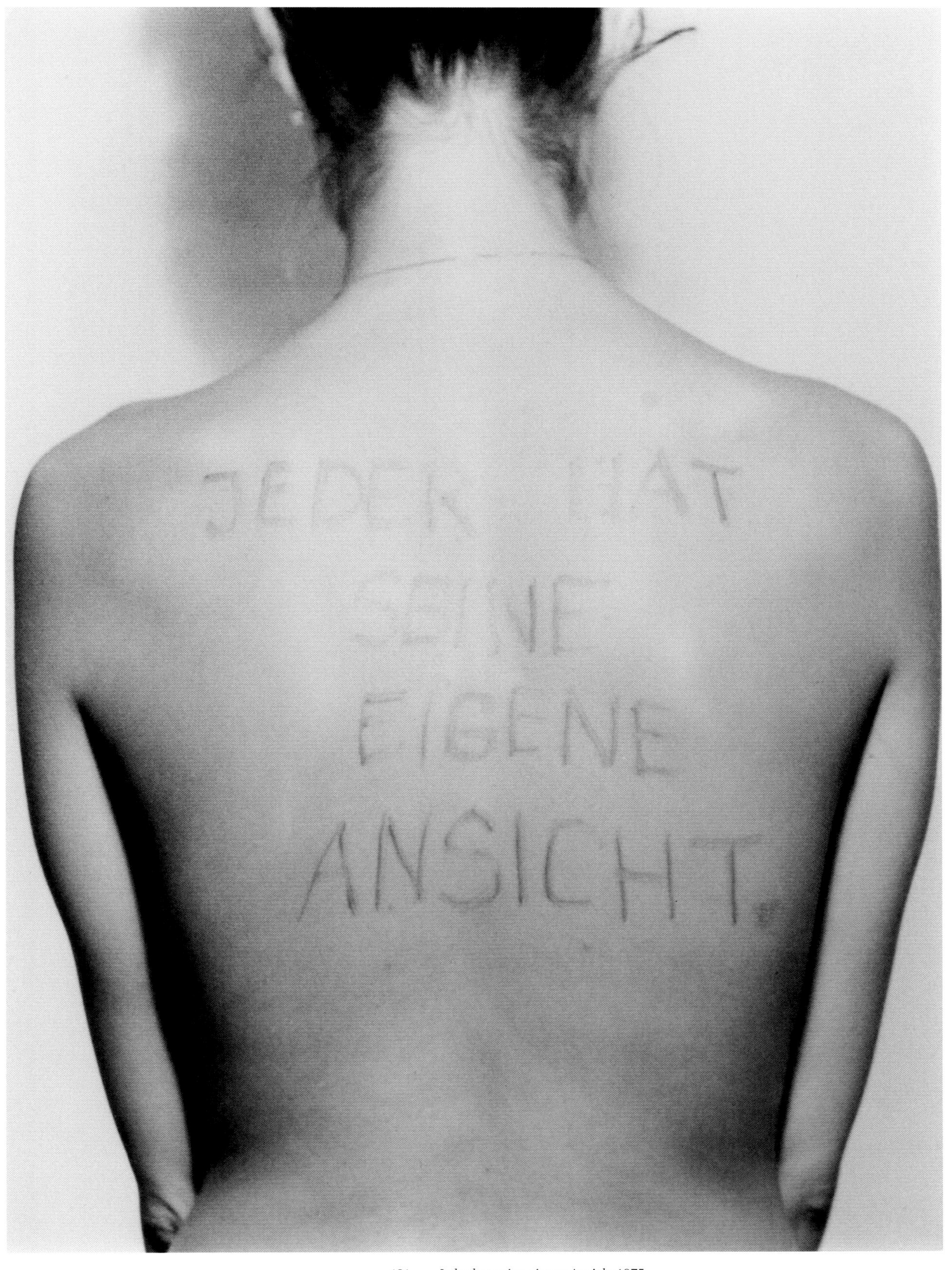

131 *Jeder hat seine eigene Ansicht* 1975
Everyone Has His Own Point of View

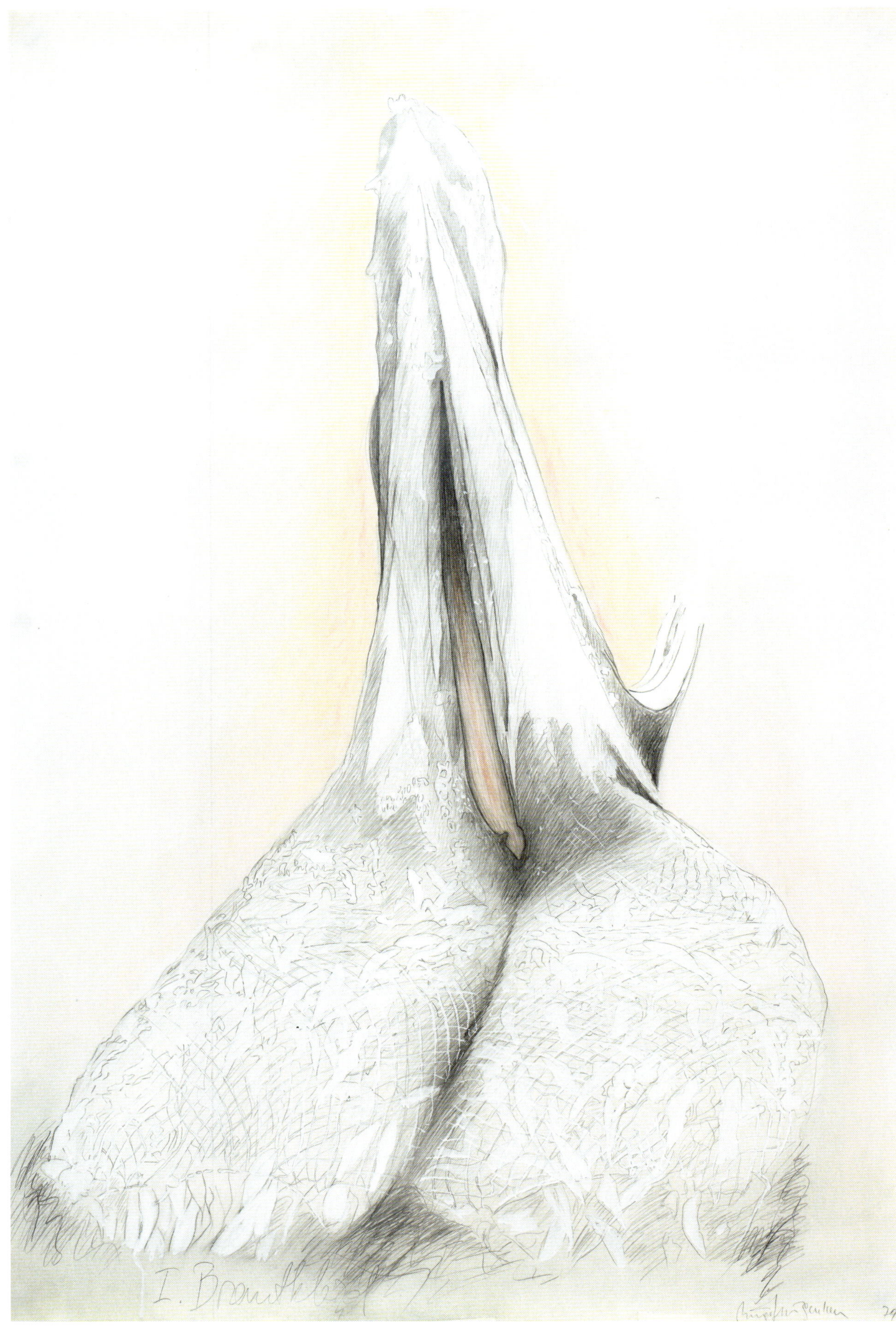

132 *I. Brautkleid* 1979
I. Wedding Dress

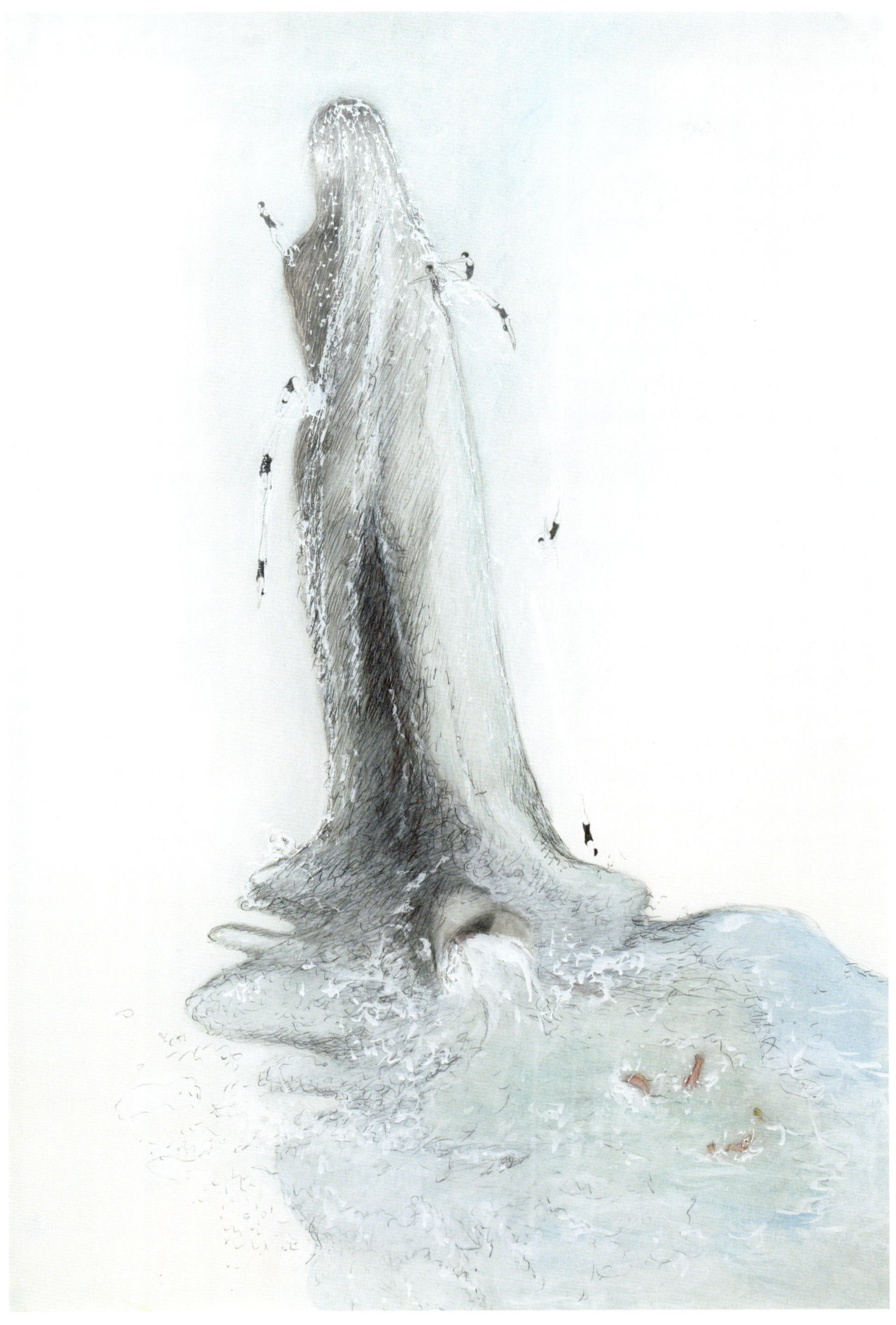

133 *Ohne Titel (Brautkleid)* 1979/1980
Untitled (Wedding Dress)

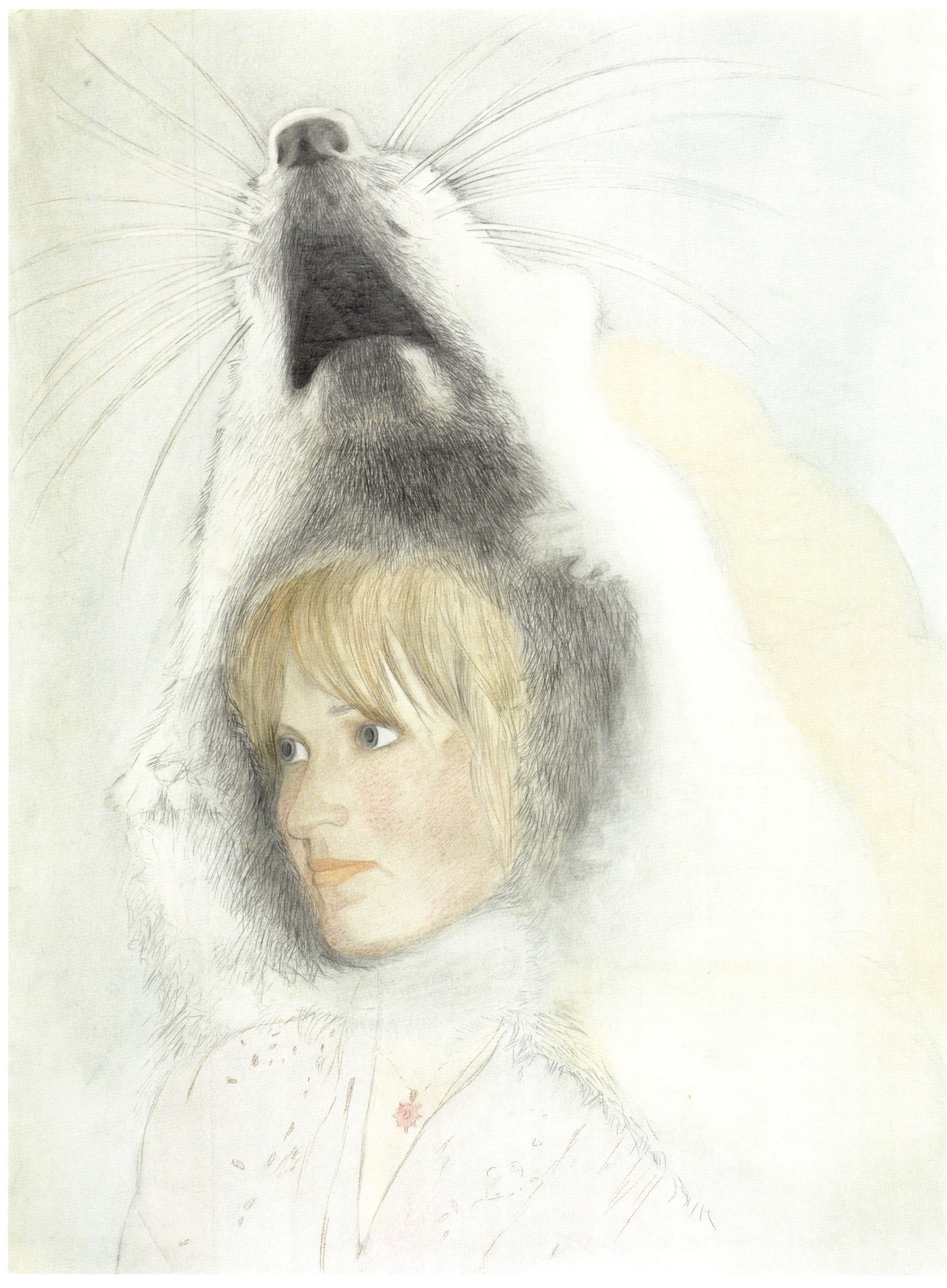

134 *Ohne Titel* 1977/1978
     Untitled

Birgit Jürgenssen,
Seen through the Anthropocene

Abigail Solomon-Godeau

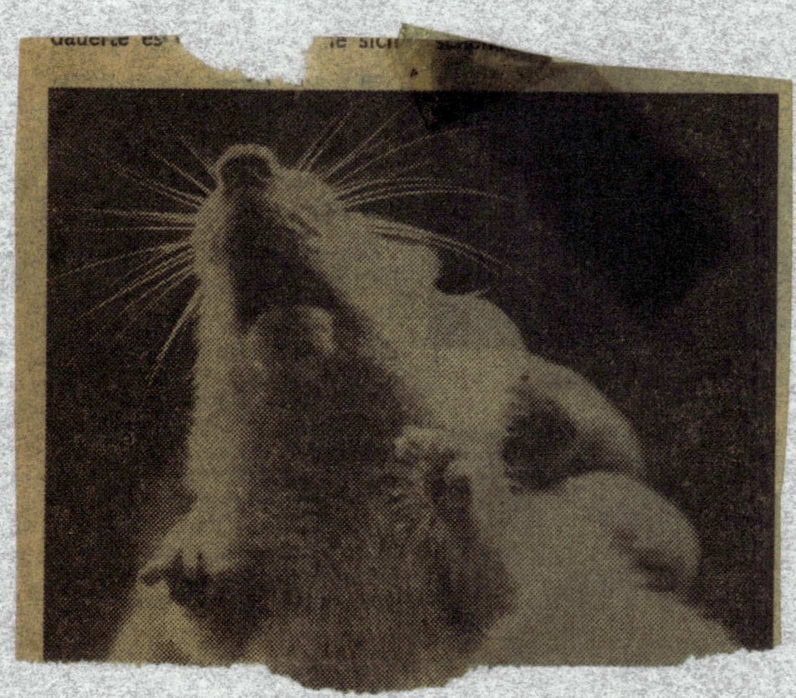

*The confusion of all nonhuman living creatures with the general
and common category of the animal is not simply a sin against rigorous thinking,
vigilance, lucidity, or empirical authority; it is also a crime. Not against
animality precisely, but a crime of the first order against the animals, against animals.*[1]

[1] Jacques Derrida, *The Animal That Therefore I Am*, ed. Marie-Louise Mallet, trans. David Wills (New York: Fordham University Press, 2008). Cited in Donna Haraway, *When Species Meet* (Minneapolis: University of Minnesota Press, 2008), p. 417.

It could be a close-up photographic view of a patch of leopard skin, and it measures 49.5 × 32 cm (ill. 137). But looking at it more closely and touching its surface, it seems to be a kind of laminated paper with a slightly raised texture, not at all furry but somehow heightening the illusion of an actual leopard's skin. Obviously, a »found« object, and one upon which Birgit Jürgenssen had written in black marker the following phrase: *Auf der Lauer* (»Lying in Wait«). When Jürgenssen includes phrases within the literal space of her artworks or, in other instances, gives them titles, these are anything but arbitrary, and they often echo, supplement, or pun on the meaning of a given work. But in terms of the phrase she has inscribed on this unidentifiable object, one wonders what it is that is lying in wait here? Is it a synecdoche for the feline predator lurking in the jungle? Or is it she, the artist who lurks, perpetually on the alert to capture what she finds, giving it a meaning that permits it to signify differently?

Lying in Wait prefaces this essay insofar as it is one of Jürgenssen's numerous works that engage with both the concept and the figuration of animality, not as something »other« to the human being but among their diverse attributes, as an otherness within

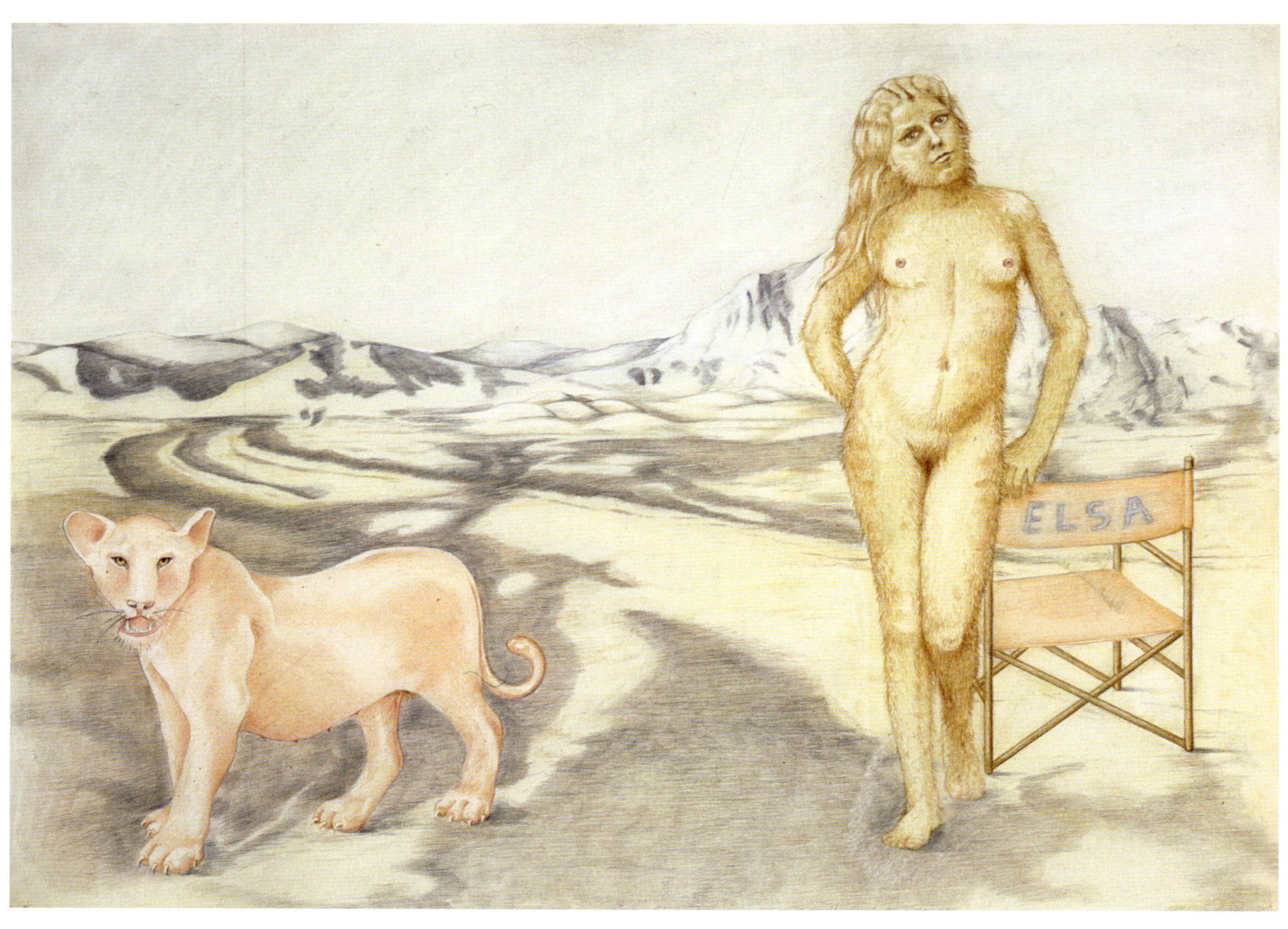

135   *Elsa* 1973

[2] As in many works by Jürgenssen, earlier drawings or photographs become templates for later transformation.
[3] »Becoming-animal,« an imaginative process, derives from the Tenth Plateau described in Gilles Deleuze and Felix Guattari's *A Thousand Plateaus: Capitalism and Schizophrenia*, trans. and foreword by Brian Massumi (London: The Athlone Press,1999). For a concise summary of this new multidisciplinary field, see Harriet Ritvo, »On the Animal Turn,« *Daedalus* 136, no. 4 (2007), pp. 118–22. There is however, a substantial bibliography in the arts, in the social sciences, and in feminist theory that interrogates (and critiques) the division of the world into human and nonhuman. In this regard, the work of Donna Haraway is foundational, as is the work of Jacques Derrida, especially *The Animal That Therefore I Am*.

[4] See the eponymous essay in which Freud laid out his concept of »Fetishism,« in *The Standard Edition of the Complete Psychological Works of Sigmund Freud*, vol. 21, trans. James Strachey (London: The Hogarth Press, 1961).

the human being. Thus, as early as 1973, Jürgenssen produced a drawing *Elsa* (ill. 135), a hirsute female nude with a director's chair, accompanied by a puma or mountain lion, where the woman-as-animal and the animal-as-animal cohabit in an inhospitable and mountainous landscape. Similarly, her crouching dog-woman of 1978 (ill. 95), equally hirsute, is beckoned forward by one disembodied hand, her foot yanked back by another, and her spine pressed downward by a third.[2] Is the lot of the pet dog to be likened to that of the domesticated woman? Conversely, in certain of her graphic and photographic works (but not only) where the nonhuman is figured, it is effectively denaturalized. In some drawings, strange amalgams of skeletal structures are grafted onto bodies, both animal and human, morphing into flora or fauna; in other drawings, rats are merged with female genitalia, the claws of a lobster erupt from the side of a young man, nattily dressed for sport. In one of her *Body Projections*, aboriginal representations of Australian mammals are projected on her torso (ill. 136). This topos of animality in Jürgenssen's art, including her variants on »becoming-animal« both anticipate and run parallel to what has come to be called since the 1990s »the animal turn.«[3] Well before this received its philosophical/academic/institutional formulations in the 1990s, it would seem that one of the intuitive insights (*avant la lettre*) of many feminist artists and writers was that the manifestations of patriarchal domination were not limited to the oppression of women but included that of the natural world, an observation that inspired eco-feminism. In the Judeo-Christian origin myth of Genesis, God gives Adam sovereignty over all that is considered *natura naturans*. Eco-feminism, one of the ethical and political outgrowths of feminism and environmentalism, is thus based on the notion that the domination of nature and women are aspects of the same compulsion to control, dominate, and possess, animated by the patriarchal desire to transcend the materiality, physicality, and ephemerality of creaturely existence.

In this respect, I would suggest that while artists do not necessarily read philosophers, and philosophers do not necessarily attend to contemporary art, in their respective domains both register seismic changes in consciousness: this includes questioning the absolutism of the human/nonhuman divide.

As all those who are familiar with the work of Birgit Jürgenssen are aware, one of its most striking characteristics is its remarkable diversity of media. These encompass traditional forms such as drawing and painting and extend to the most recent image-making technologies, such as the digitally generated or manipulated imagery with which she worked in the last years of her life. Throughout the four decades of her art-making, she produced sculptural objects (for example, her shoe series *Schuhwerk*, the *Kitchen Apron* (ill. 199), and other three dimensional objects), photographic and graphic imagery of all kinds (e.g., Polaroids, slide projections, cyanotypes, analogue photographs in b/w and color, collages, photograms, and so forth), modified ready-mades such as *Lying in Wait*—the list can be readily expanded. Many of these are hybridized inventions employing various media within the same work. With the exception of pencil drawings, her approach to materials was essentially experimental and acutely sensitive to their respective haptic qualities.

Notwithstanding the variety of her objects and images, there are, however, certain thematic preoccupations that regularly recur throughout her artistic production. Fetishism, in its Freudian formulation, was clearly one of her enduring preoccupations, exemplified also in the *Schuhwerk*, but equally, in drawings such as *Wedding Dress* (ill. 132, 133), and *Untitled* (ill. 71) or installations such as *Elevin* (ill. 221). These function as a kind of de-sublimation or demystification of the sovereign phallus, exposing, as it were, its compensatory relation to (unconscious) castration fears prompted by the male child's perception of female genitalia.[4] Jürgenssen's feminism, which freely incorporated this and other psychoanalytic concepts, is part of a shared critique equally evident in the work of a number of her female contemporaries in Austria, artists such as VALIE EXPORT, Ulrike Ottinger, Renate Bertlmann, Ulrike Rosenbach, and others. Doubtless, to one degree or another, the feminist orientation of their work was honed and sharpened in reaction to the previous generation of Actionists, an all-male formation

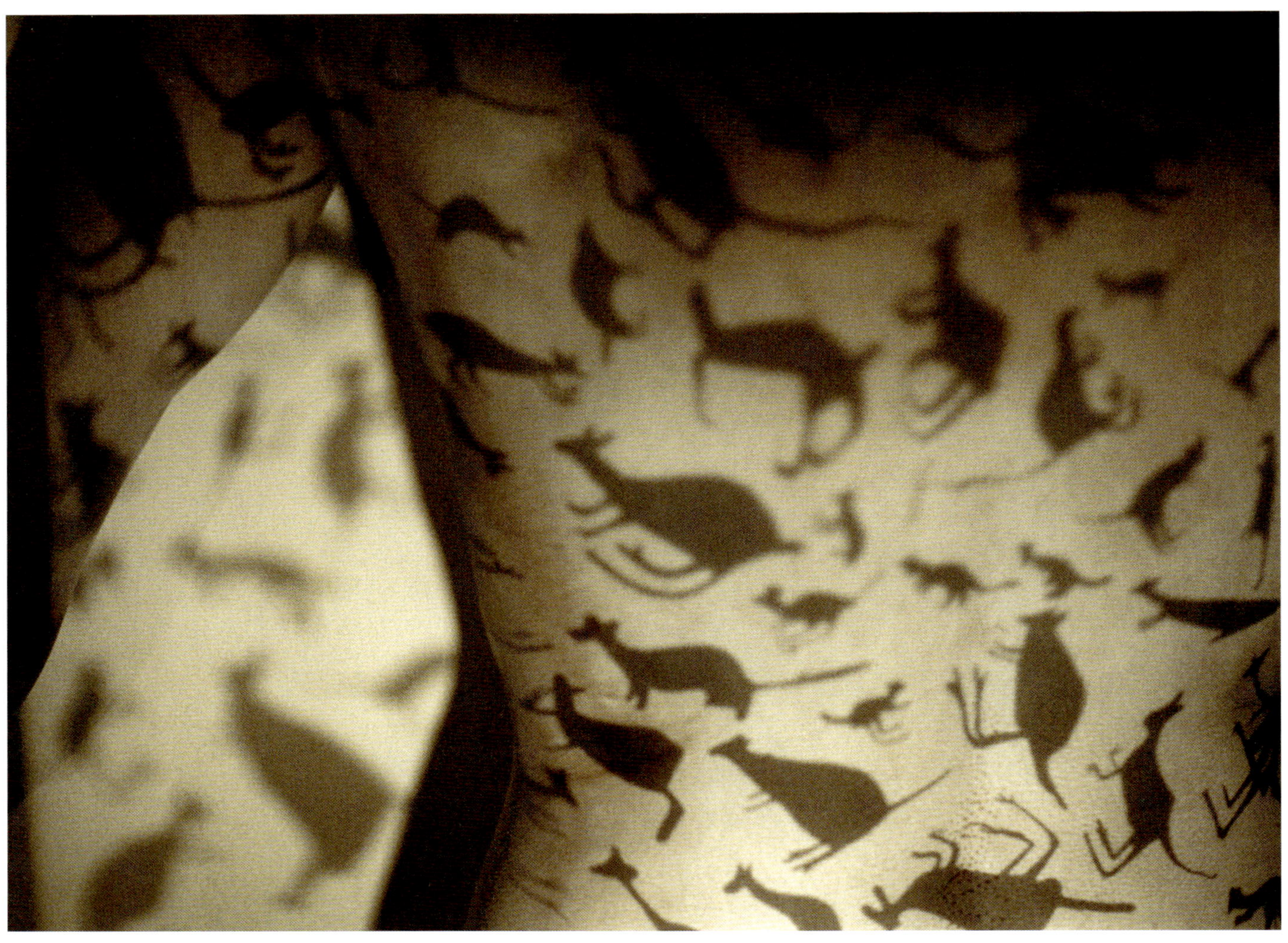

136 *Ohne Titel (Körperprojektion)* 1988
Untitled (Body Projection)

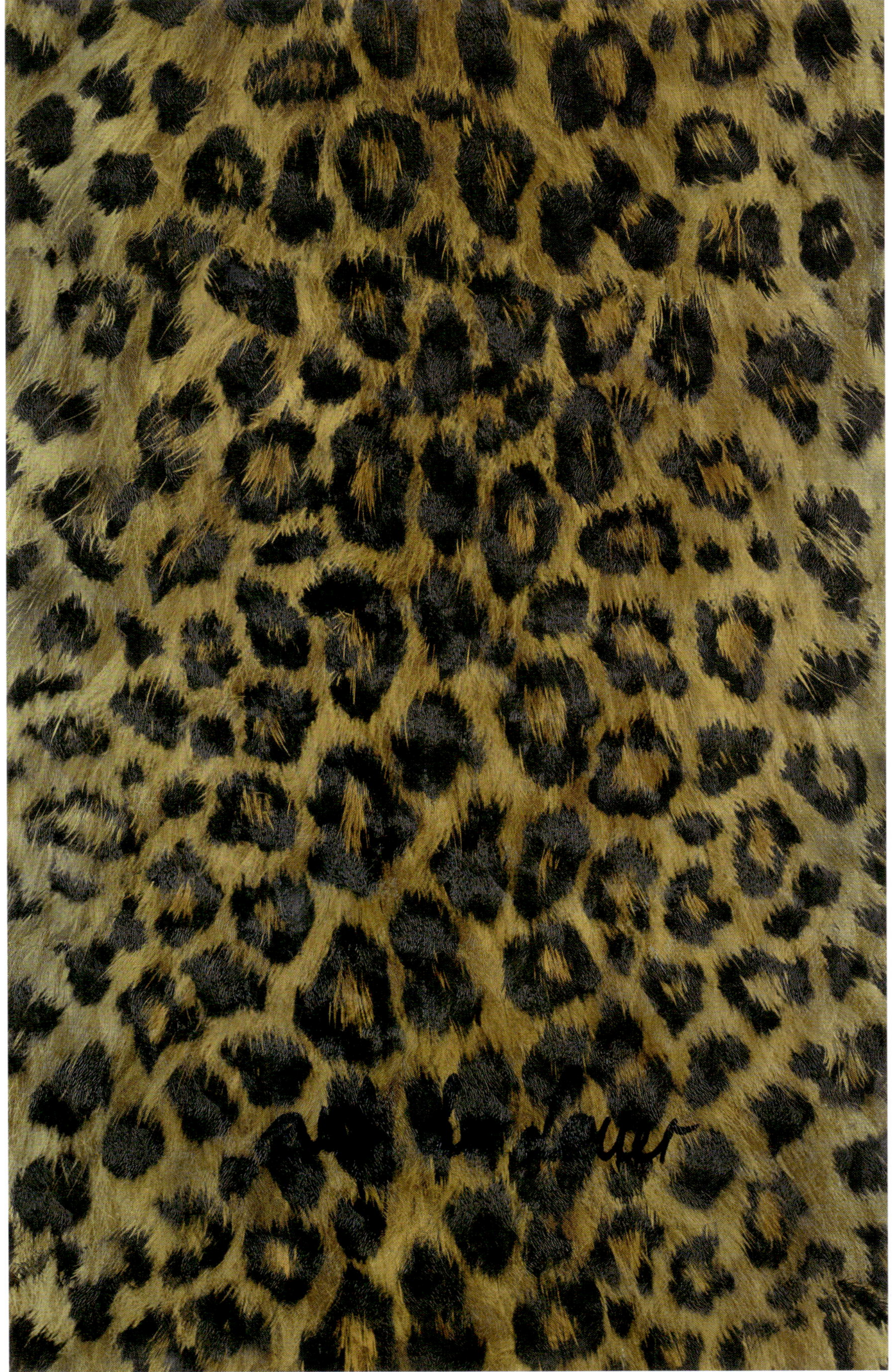

137   *Auf der Lauer* 1985
Lying in Wait

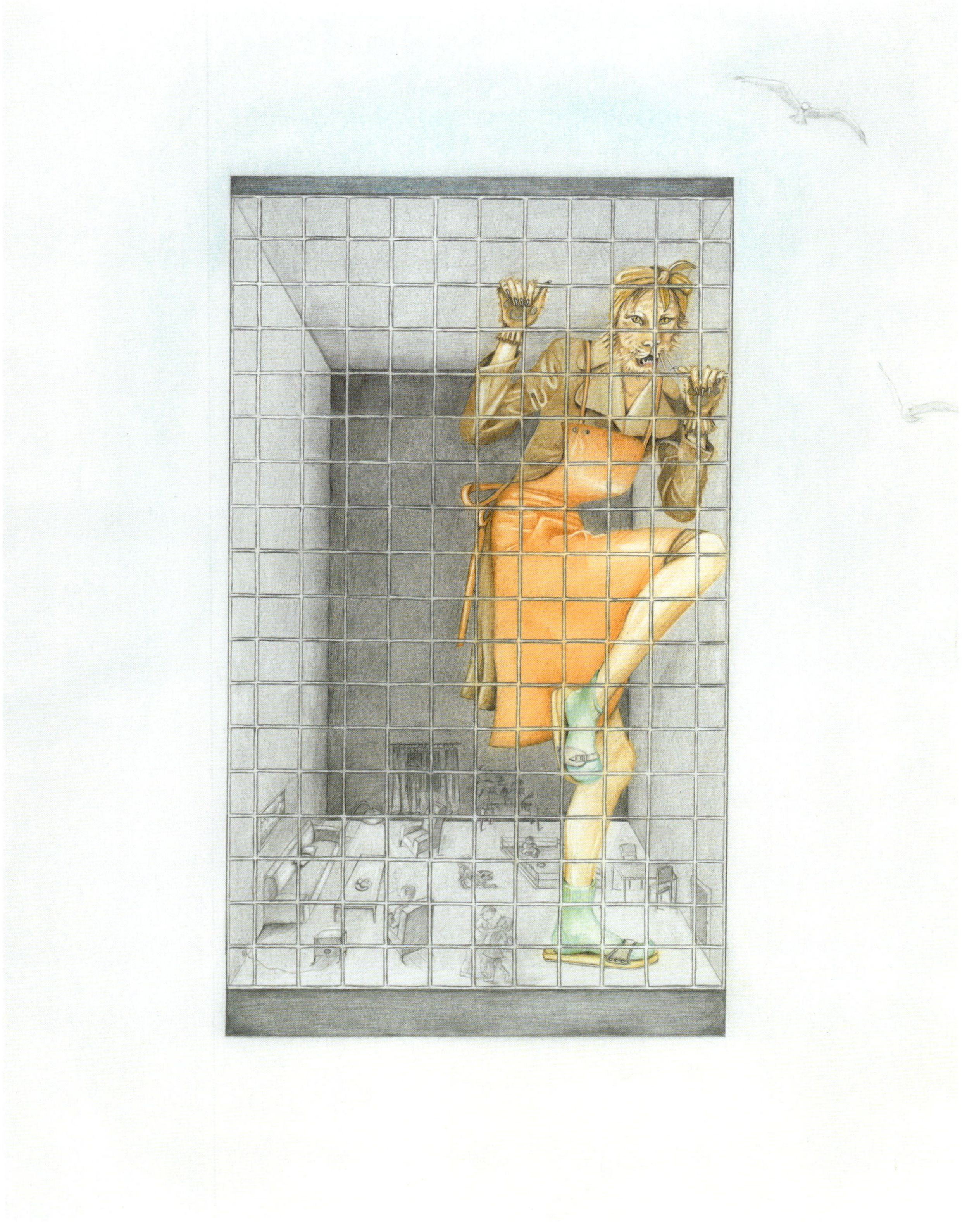

138   *Hausfrau* 1974
       Housewife

that received international recognition and came to exemplify the »radical,« as well
as to the performative direction of postwar Austrian art. In a number of cases, these artists
were professors in the art schools where some of these women had studied, during
which time there existed not a single woman professor of art in an Austrian art school.[5]
Jürgenssen, for example, was teaching assistant of Arnulf Rainer, and although he is not
necessarily categorized as an Actionist, his expressionist work centers on the exploration
of his own subjectivity and angst.

[5] The first woman to be given a chair at Vienna's School of Applied Arts was Maria Lassnig in 1980, then aged sixty-one. The second was Elizabeth von Samsonow, at the Vienna Academy of Fine Arts in 1996. Birgit Jürgenssen had applied in 1994 for a full-time teaching position at the Vienna Academy of Fine Arts.

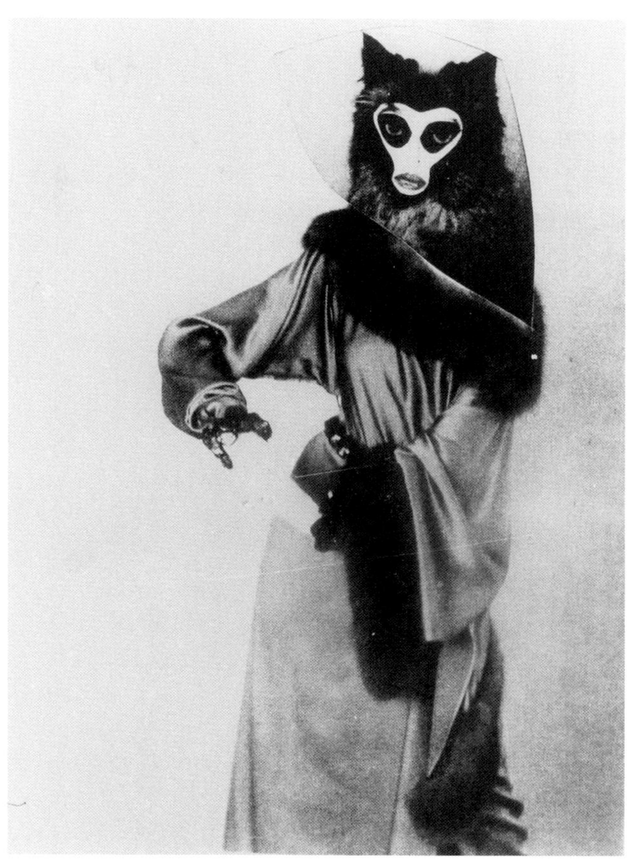

139   *Ohne Titel* 1980
       Untitled

⁶ Cf. Sigrid Schade,
» ›The Corpse Lives‹:
Pictorial Tradition and
Gender Construction
in the *Totentanz* Series
by Birgit Jürgenssen,«
in Gabriele Schor, Abigail
Solomon-Godeau, eds.,
Birgit Jürgenssen,
(Ostfildern: Hatje Cantz,
2009), pp. 179–189.;
Gabriele Schor »›I Want
Out of Here!‹: Birgit
Jürgenssen's Art of the
1970s«, in Gabriele Schor
(ed.), *Donna: Avanguardia
femminista negli
anni '70 dalla Sammlung
Verbund di Vienna*,
Milan 2010, pp. 196–213;
Peter Weibel, »Birgit
Jürgenssen and the Night
of Pyschoanalysis,«
in Heike Eipeldauer,
Gabriele Schor (eds.):
Birgit Jürgenssen. exh. cat
Bank Austria Kunstforum,
(Munich: Prestel, 2010),
pp. 111–123; Giovanna Zap-
peri, »Formen von
Weiblichkeit: Birgit
Jürgenssens Metamorpho-
sen,« in Heike Eipel-
dauer, Gabriele Schor (eds.):
Birgit Jürgenssen.
pp. 79–91.

⁷ In referring to her
use of the body as a screen
of projection, I am referring to those works in which
35 mm slides made
by Jürgenssen were pro-
jected on her own
body and then subsequently
made into positive
photographic prints (ill.
195–198).

As I have argued elsewhere—and has been elaborated by many other commentators—another of Jürgenssen's motifs was her exploration of the mythologies and ideologies of femininity.⁶ This aspect of her work, however, requires an acknowledgment of the distinction between Jürgenssen's gender—that is, her identity as a woman artist—and the myriad incarnations of the feminine she explored as phantasmatic projections of masculine fears and desires, rooted in the patriarchal *imaginaire*. For all that Jürgenssen used herself exclusively as a model, and employed her body quite literally as a screen for projection, there is nothing noticeably »personal« or »autobiographical« in her work.⁷ Impersonality, however, does not preclude the registration of an artist's subjective experience in the world. Which is only to say that Jürgenssen's subjectivity can be considered as itself a form of conceptual material that informed and mobilized her art, just as it determined her receptiveness to feminist critique.

Accordingly, early work by Jürgenssen that took as its subject the imprisonment of women in the role of *Housewife* reflects one of the initial recognitions of 1970s' feminism, although this domestic servitude was not necessarily the situation of the women artists who, like Jürgenssen, addressed it in their art. It is worth noting, however, that even in her early *Housewife* work, the becoming-animal imagery is present, as it is in *Elsa*. Consider, for example, the aproned housewife, climbing her cage, whose head and hands are those of a wild feline (ill. 138). In this respect, I want to enlarge upon Jürgenssen's use of animal imagery, which has received less attention than it merits. As I think is amply demonstrated in the current exhibition, we can observe her manifest fascination, even in some instances her identification, with the creaturely world. And following that, there is a related tendency to »animalize« the human as opposed to anthropomorphizing the animal. These two tropes appear in her early drawings of dung beetles or in fusions of flora and fauna, and later, in photographs where animal skulls cover her face. They are equally manifest in her human/animal hybrids produced in diverse media, in her female masks on cats, and cat masks on her own face, her collaged cat-woman with a claw-like hand (ill. 139), and in several of her most emblematic self-representations. I refer here to those photographs—*Self with Little Fur* (ill. 9)—where a fox head hides her upper face. And in one of her most elaborate and startling drawings her features emerge from the thorax of a rat, whose gaping (and toothless) mouth suggests a scream or howl (ill. 134).[8]

There are different approaches we might employ in order to better understand the meanings of Jürgenssen's iconography, which functions, in these particular instances, to put the human and the animal—often the female human being—in some kind of intimate relation or, alternatively, in physical conjunction with other species. It is important, however, to maintain the distinction between an artist's iconography, which may be personal or impersonal, and iconology, where figurative elements have particular, recognizable cultural meanings that circulate within specific sociocultural formations. In Erwin Panofsky's definition, iconology is defined thus: »The discovery and interpretation of these ›symbolical‹ values (which are often unknown to the artist himself and may even emphatically differ from what he consciously intended to express) is the object of what we may call ›iconology.‹«[9] Insofar as Jürgenssen perpetually and, apparently, intuitively assimilated (and also collected) vast amounts of art historical as well as mass cultural imagery and references, it would be possible, at least in theory, to locate at least some of this iconography in pre-existing sources. For example, perhaps we might identify certain correspondences in the work of artists such as Frida Kahlo (ill. 141) that might be compared with Jürgenssen's 1980 *Venery – Maiden* (ill. 140) or in imagery from medieval bestiaries (for example, the manuscript illumination depicting the *Siren from Les Abus du monde*).[10]

This kind of research is what many art historians do professionally as they seek to pin down, so to speak, the genealogy of an artist's imagery. In graduate school we called this »source mongering.« Be that as it may, this methodology does not seem a particularly fruitful approach to Jürgenssen's art, in which, as far as I can discern, her human / animal imagery seems to have few prototypes in twentieth century art and no real equivalents in the work of her contemporaries. Even in the example of Kahlo's *The Wounded Deer*—and from a purely formal perspective—Kahlo's is a conventional easel painting, and Jürgenssen was far more attracted to more experimental (and contemporary) media. Consequently, I want to suggest that her deployment of animal imagery, certainly by the late 1980s, was contemporaneous with what I previously indicated has emerged in Anglo-American scholarship as »the animal turn.«

The ongoing expansion of this ethical, philosophical and scientific field was prompted by the animal rights movement, launched by the Australian philosopher Peter Singer in his 1974 book *Animal Liberation*. This »animal turn« has also contributed to the growth of a newly minted academic field, Human-Animal Studies, within which the concept of an ontological binary between human and animal is taken as a problem, not as a given. In his 1994 book *The Animal That Therefore I Am*, Jacques Derrida argued that one function of the universalizing category of *the* animal serves to secure definitions of *the* human. (By analogy, we might argue that other essentializing categories, *the* Woman, like *the* Other, function to secure the primacy of the male subject as the representative human being). Where feminist theory works to decenter and dislodge the equivalence of the human with the masculine, so too does the philosophical interrogation of the animal/human divide serve to question the sovereignty of the (male) human. As Marie-Louise Mallet notes in her preface to Derrida's text, »The violence done to the animal begins as [Derrida] says, with this pseudo-concept of ›the animal,‹ with the use of this word in the singular, as though all animals from the earthworm to the chimpanzee constituted a homogeneous set to which ›the human‹ would be radically opposed.«[11] Which is effectively to observe that against the multiplicity of animal species, the (male) human being presides as the One. Throughout Jürgenssen's œuvre, there are numerous works that implicitly reject the binarism of man / animal, or for that matter, of the human and the botanical. Consider, for example, the drawing *Footrace* (ill. 142), which twins the male runner with a gorilla, or the *Slave of the Heart* series (ill. 154, 155), in which animal and human are inextricably conjoined.

[8] There exist at least two preliminary versions of the final, most elaborate version, made in 1977/1978
[9] Erwin Panofsky, *Meaning in the Visual Arts* (New York: Doubleday, 1955), p. 31.
[10] *The Abuses of the World*, Rouen, France, ca. 1510, The Morgan Library & Museum, New York, MS M.42, fol. 15r.
[11] Marie-Louise Mallet, foreword, in Derrida, *The Animal That Therefore I Am*, p. viii.

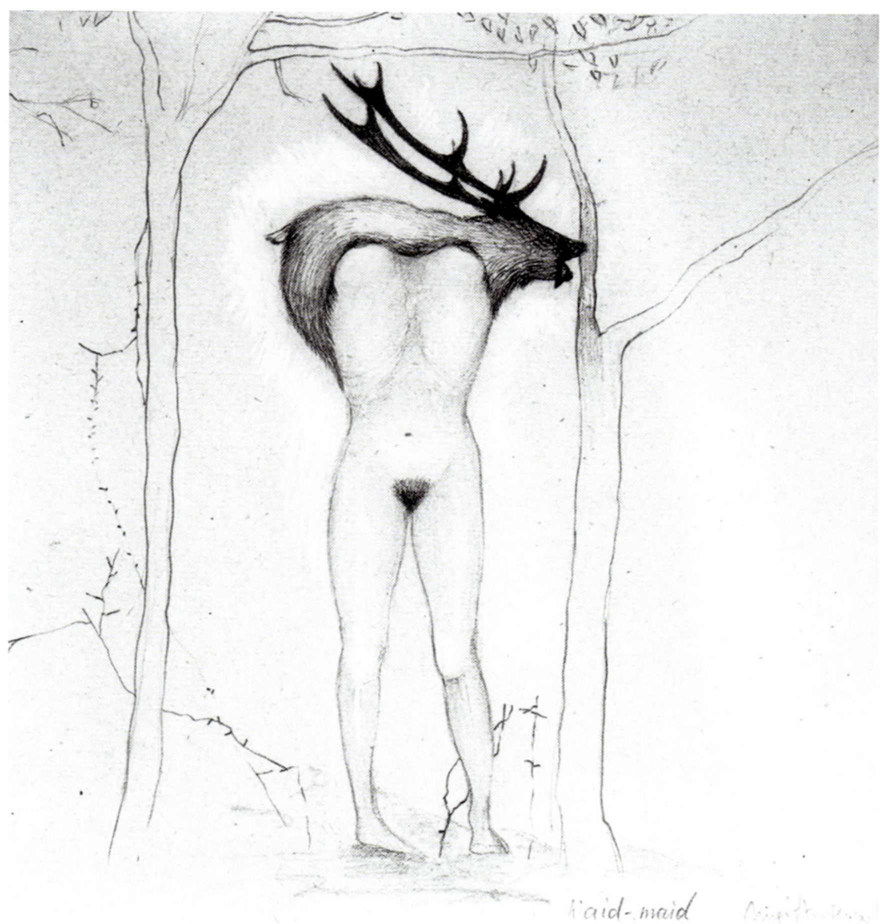

140   *Waid – Maid* 1980
       Venery – Maiden

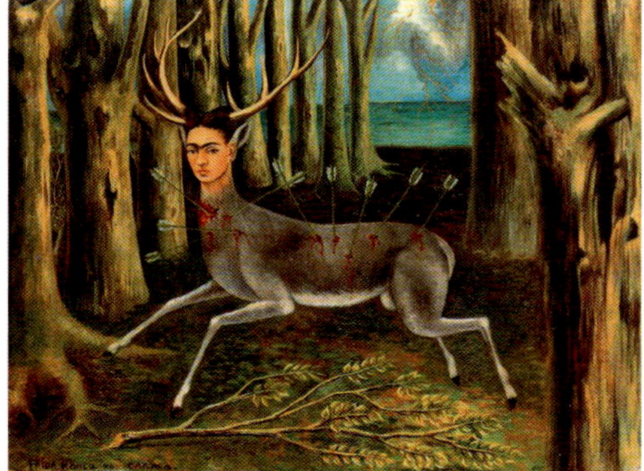

141   Frida Kahlo *El venado herido* /
       The Wounded Deer 1946
       © Banco de México Diego Rivera & Frida Kahlo
       Museums Trust, México D.F. / Bildrecht, Vienna 2018

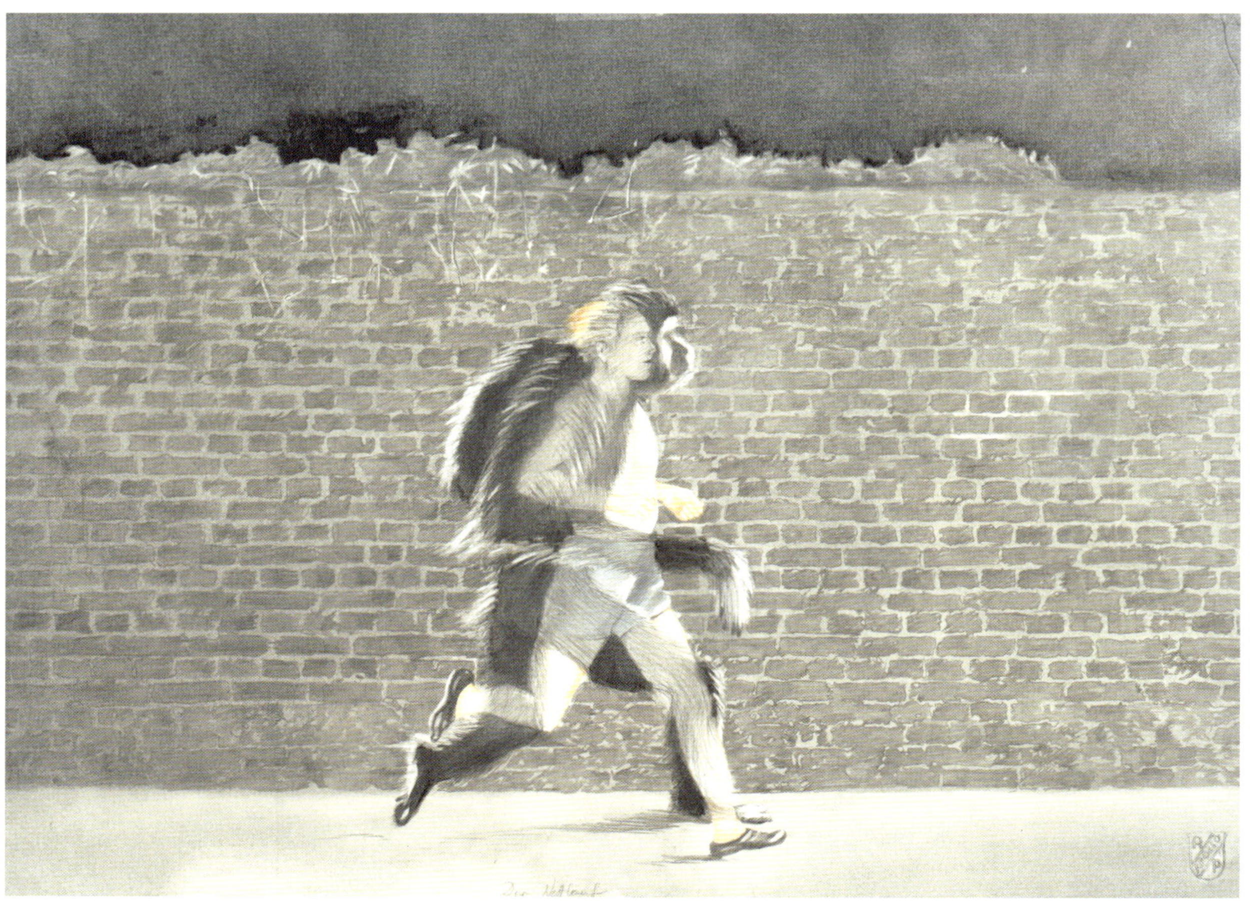

142 *Der Wettlauf* 1975
Footrace

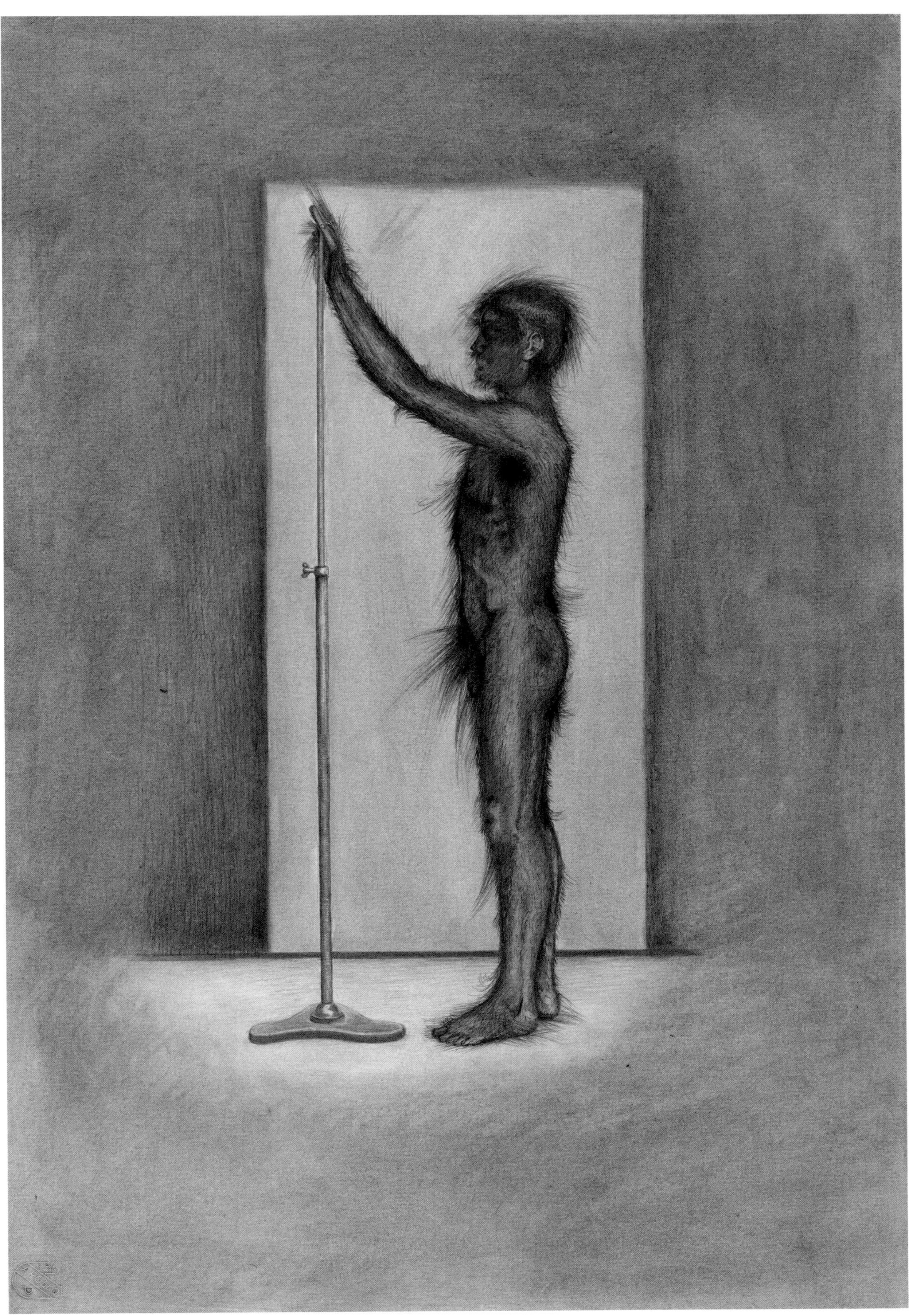

143   *Ohne Titel* 1975
Untitled

Although, at least since Aristotle, it has been long accepted that human beings are themselves animals, the essentialist concept of *the* animal, like *the* human being (who is generically white and male), or for that matter *the* woman has profound ramifications. The sovereignty that God gives to Adam over the entire animal kingdom thus provides the alibi for all that is done to them. Animal liberation, in Peter Singer's eponymous work, thus has important connections to the ecological and environmental consequences of what is now generally accepted as the era of the Anthropocene.[12]

All of which suggests that Jürgenssen's artistic exploration of the animal realm was not only prompted by her love of animals but, consciously or not, was registered in her perception of the problem of the animal/human divide, and indeed, the wholesale domination of nature that characterizes the Anthropocene as well as its catastrophic consequences. Jürgenssen's deployment of animal imagery falls into several discrete categories irrespective of the medium she employs. There are works in which the recognizably human form is bestialized, as in the drawings of the dog-woman, or the bristled male figure (ill. 143). There are works in which the female body is linked to the nest and eggs of avian reproduction, alluding (among other things) to the biology of women, who, needless to say, also produce eggs (ill. 220). There are works in which Jürgenssen transforms herself into a kind of totem of the vegetal, as in her leaf woman, or uses her body to conjure the form of a spider (ill. 144).

In reflecting on these themes throughout Jürgenssen's artistic career, a few other observations are in order. Although Jürgenssen can be playful in these works, she manifests little sentimentality with respect to the nonhuman. (She does not ignore the relations of predator and prey, as in *Diagonal from Top Left to Bottom Right – Falling*). Nor have I wished to imply that there is any programmatic, much less polemical intention in her disruptions or subversion of what is now termed »speciesism.«[13] But certainly Jürgenssen was fully cognizant of the venerable belief in women's animality, their presumed closeness to nature, and even the learned medieval debates as to whether women possessed souls. »Woman is natural, therefore abominable,« wrote Baudelaire, and this by no means isolated consignment of femininity to an abjected nature might be thought of as the territory claimed, or reclaimed, by Jürgenssen. For hers is a concept of nature and a living, if imperiled world where—as in *Untitled* (ill. 145), a manipulated SX-70 Polaroid—the leaf, the sex-neutral human, and the dog coexist in no particular hierarchy (the leaf is larger than both) and whose substance, as the scientists claim, derives from stardust.

[12] This term, which entered *The Oxford Dictionary of the English Language* only in 2014, is defined as follows: »*Geology.* A. n. Chiefly with *the.* The era of geological time during which human activity is considered to be the dominant influence on the environment, climate, and ecology of the earth. The Anthropocene is most commonly taken to extend from the time of the Industrial Revolution to the present, but is sometimes considered to include much or all of the Holocene.«

[13] The term is associated with the British psychologist Richard Ryder, first in a privately published pamphlet, and subsequently in an anthology of essays edited by his graduate students, entitled »Animals, Men and Morals.« As he wrote: »Inasmuch as both ›race‹ and ›species‹ are vague terms used in the classification of living creatures according, largely, to physical appearance, an analogy can be made between them. Discrimination on grounds of race, although most universally condoned two centuries ago, is now widely condemned. Similarly, it may come to pass that enlightened minds may one day abhor ›speciesism‹ as much as they now detest ›racism.‹ The illogicality in both forms of prejudice is of an identical sort. If it is accepted as morally wrong to deliberately inflict suffering upon innocent human creatures, then it is only logical to also regard it as wrong to inflict suffering on innocent individuals of other species. [...] The time has come to act upon this logic.« See the Wikipedia entry for »Speciesism,« in https://en.wikipedia.org/wiki/Speciesism#Origin_of_the_term, accessed September 30, 2018.

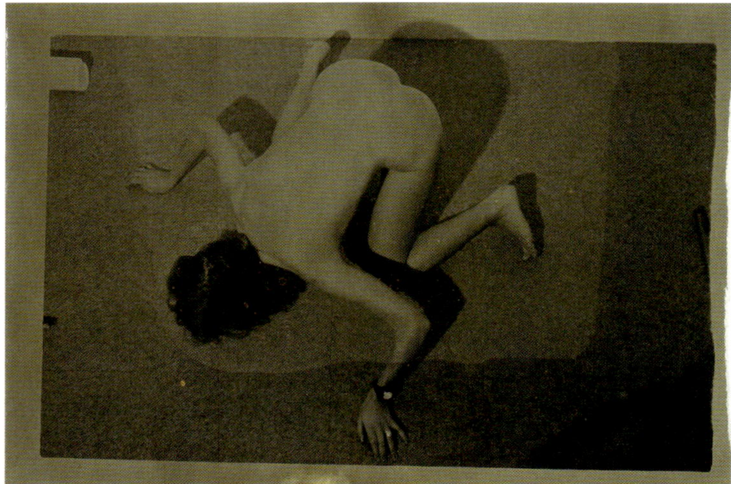

144   *Spinne* 1979
     Spider

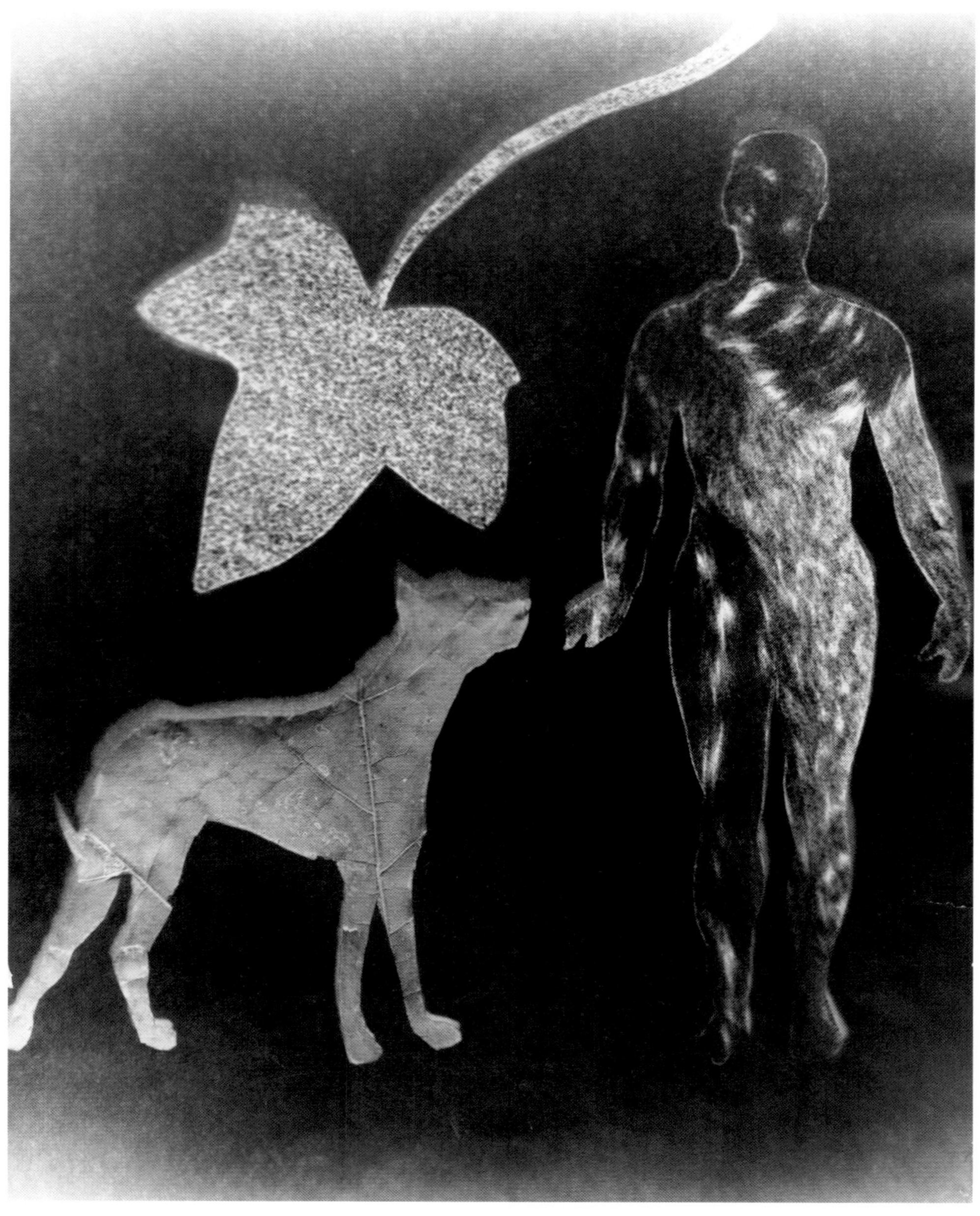

145   *Ohne Titel* 1975
       Untitled

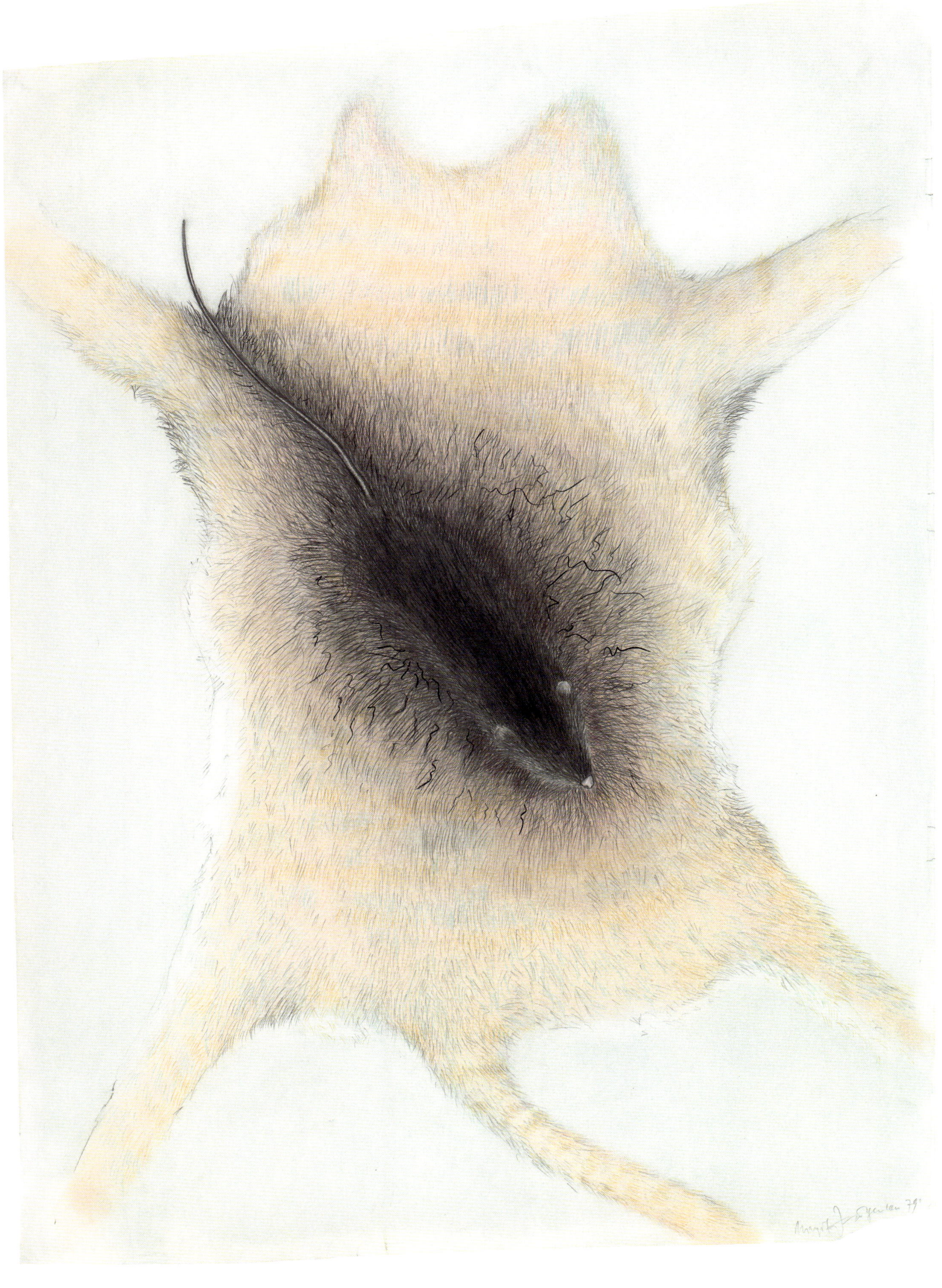

146   *Ohne Titel* 1979
       Untitled

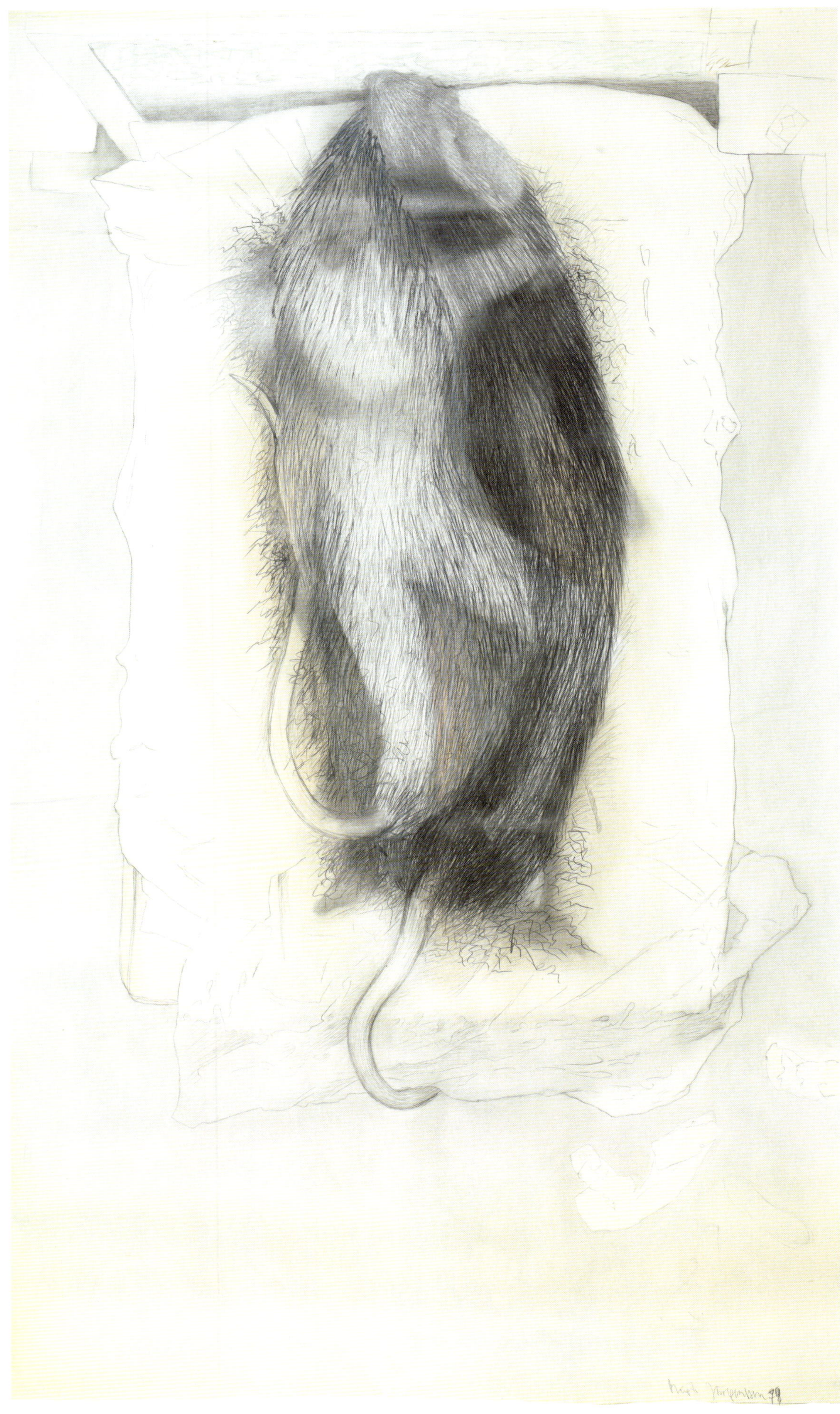

147 *Ohne Titel (2 Mäuse)* 1979
Untitled (2 Mice)

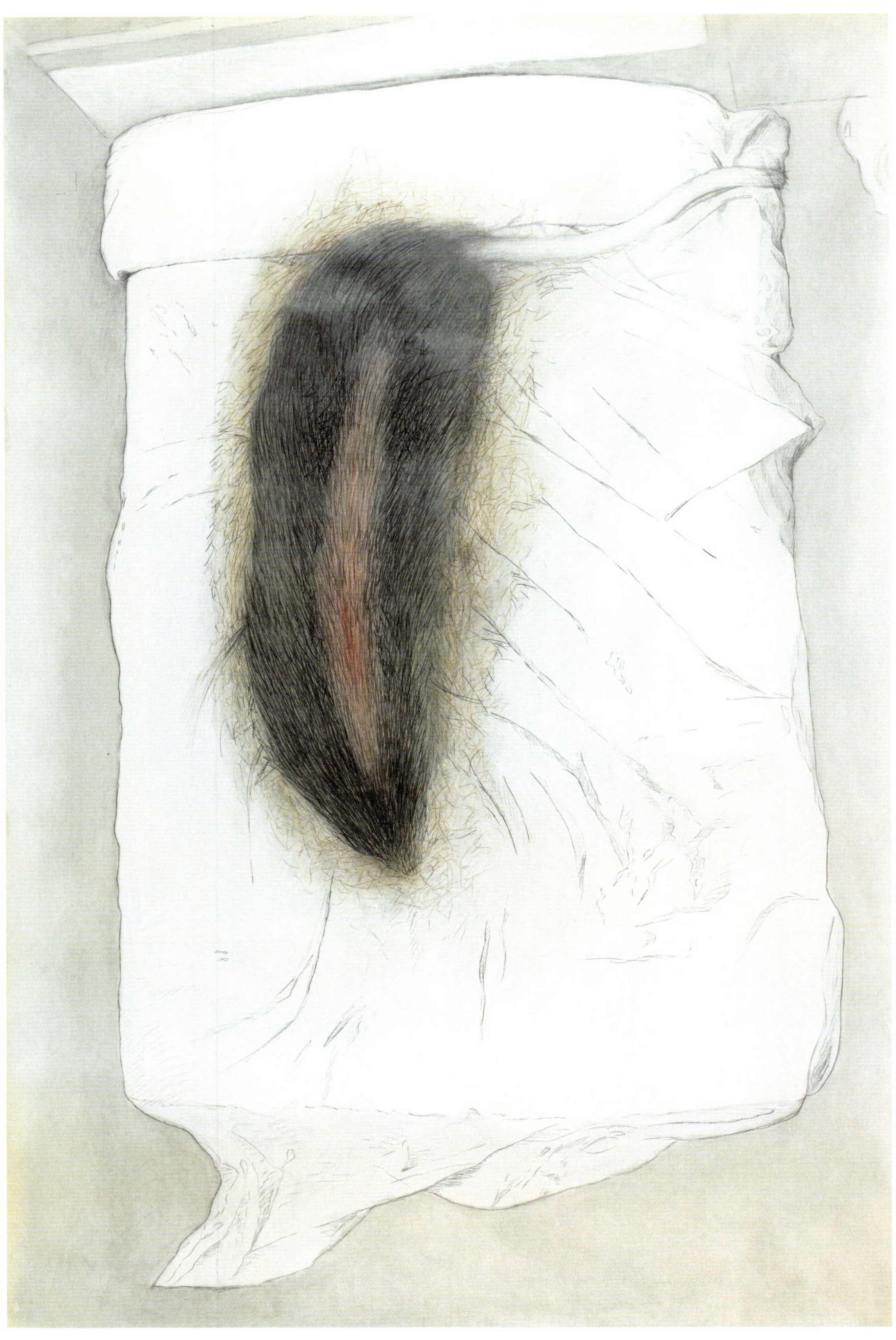

148 *Ohne Titel 1979*
Untitled

The Rat in the Bed

Louisa Buck

What an arresting and deeply unsettling image this is. Freud meets Feminism in a colored pencil drawing of a hybrid mouse-vagina, which is either emerging out of or burrowing into a pristine white bed. We don't see the face of the creature, but its thick tail snakes along the edge of the pillow and loops down around the side, firmly anchoring the furry form to the crisp top sheet. At the same time, a force field of fine wispy lines drawn in colored pencil around the edges of the otherwise sleek pelt gives a sense of restless, quivering agitation. Then there are the unmistakably sexual associations triggered by the pink wound-like opening running along its back.

The many metamorphoses of the female form underpin Birgit Jürgenssen's work. Steeped from an early age in surrealism, psychoanalysis, and feminist theory as well as being widely versed in literature and art history, over nearly four decades she devoted herself to destabilizing and dismantling time-honored notions of the feminine. Through text and image, using photography, drawing, painting, printing, collage, object making, performance, and video, Jürgenssen was tirelessly experimental in playing with and off the multitude of accrued preconceptions and stereotypes associated with the representation of women and their bodies.

One of the most powerful ways she did this was by blending the animal with the human. Here, in one of her most audacious works (ill. 148), Jürgenssen transforms the mouse from a symbol of furtive timidity into a powerful sexually charged protagonist. Commonly known as the traditional terrorizer of women, this scuttling creature now becomes the fiercely assertive sex of woman herself. There's nothing meek or mild about this new and blatantly genital incarnation. The work measures almost two meters in height and this large scale, along with its subject, also seems disquietingly at odds with the modest, childlike connotations of a colored crayon drawing, even one as technically accomplished as this.

The drawing is one of a number produced by Jürgenssen in the years 1978–80, a period in which she explored her dual fascination with animal pelts and anthropomorphism in a more explicit way, often in the form of finely executed, distinctively illustrative crayon drawings. Many of these feature hair, that most suggestively bestial and also magically symbolic substance. Jürgenssen was also all too aware of the Freudian notion of the uncanny, which Freud defined as *unheimlich*, or »uncanny.« The frisson of the familiar rendered extraordinary reoccurs right from the beginning in her work.

Throughout, nothing in Jürgenssen's art is fixed or finite: all readings are left purposefully open-ended and often contradictory. And nowhere do we find her messages more mixed or her humor more sardonic than in this unforgettable depiction of the bedroom as a site of psychosexual drama, presided over by a chimerical female presence whose intentions are not necessarily benign.

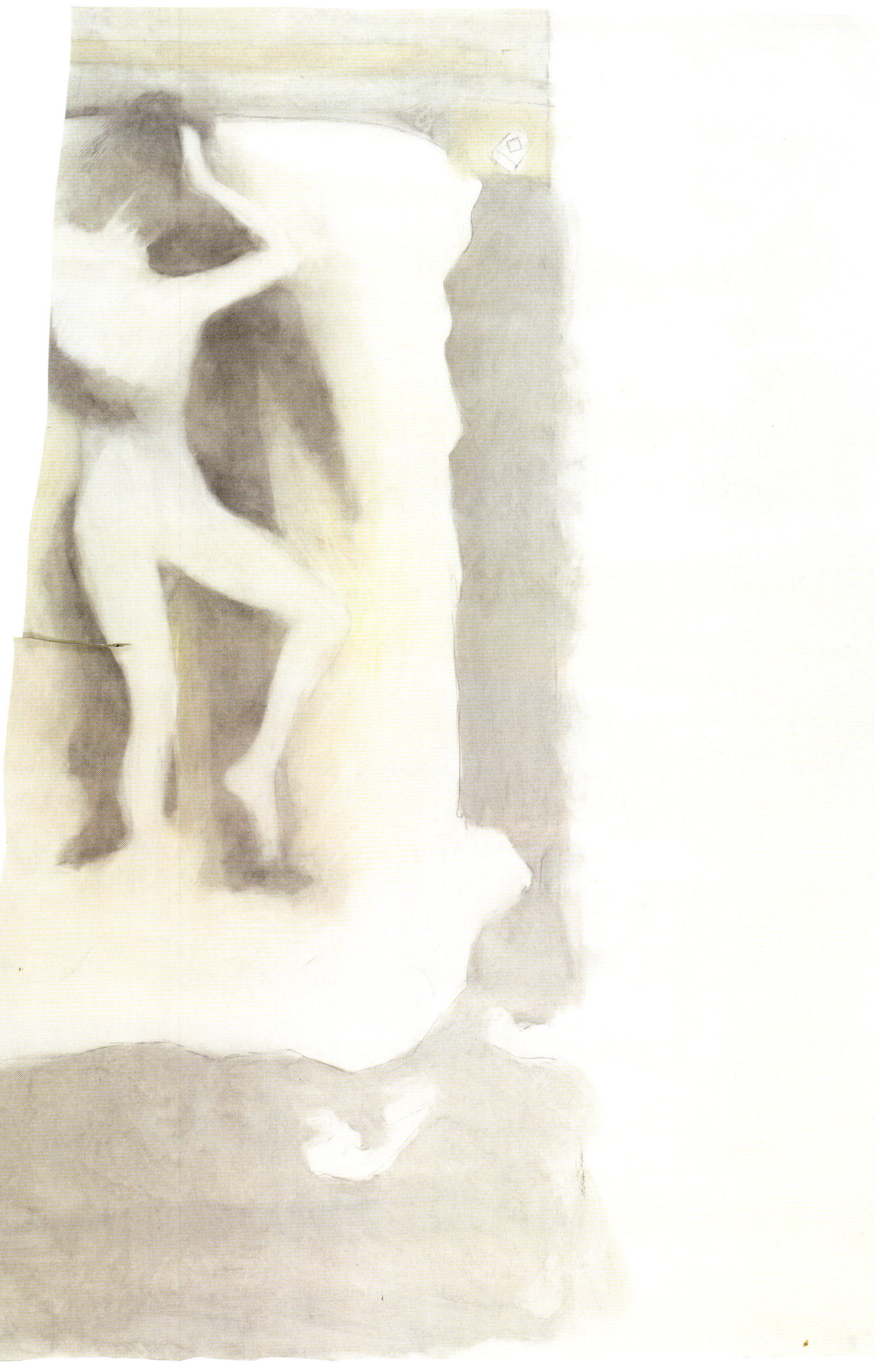

149 *Ohne Titel* 1979
     Untitled

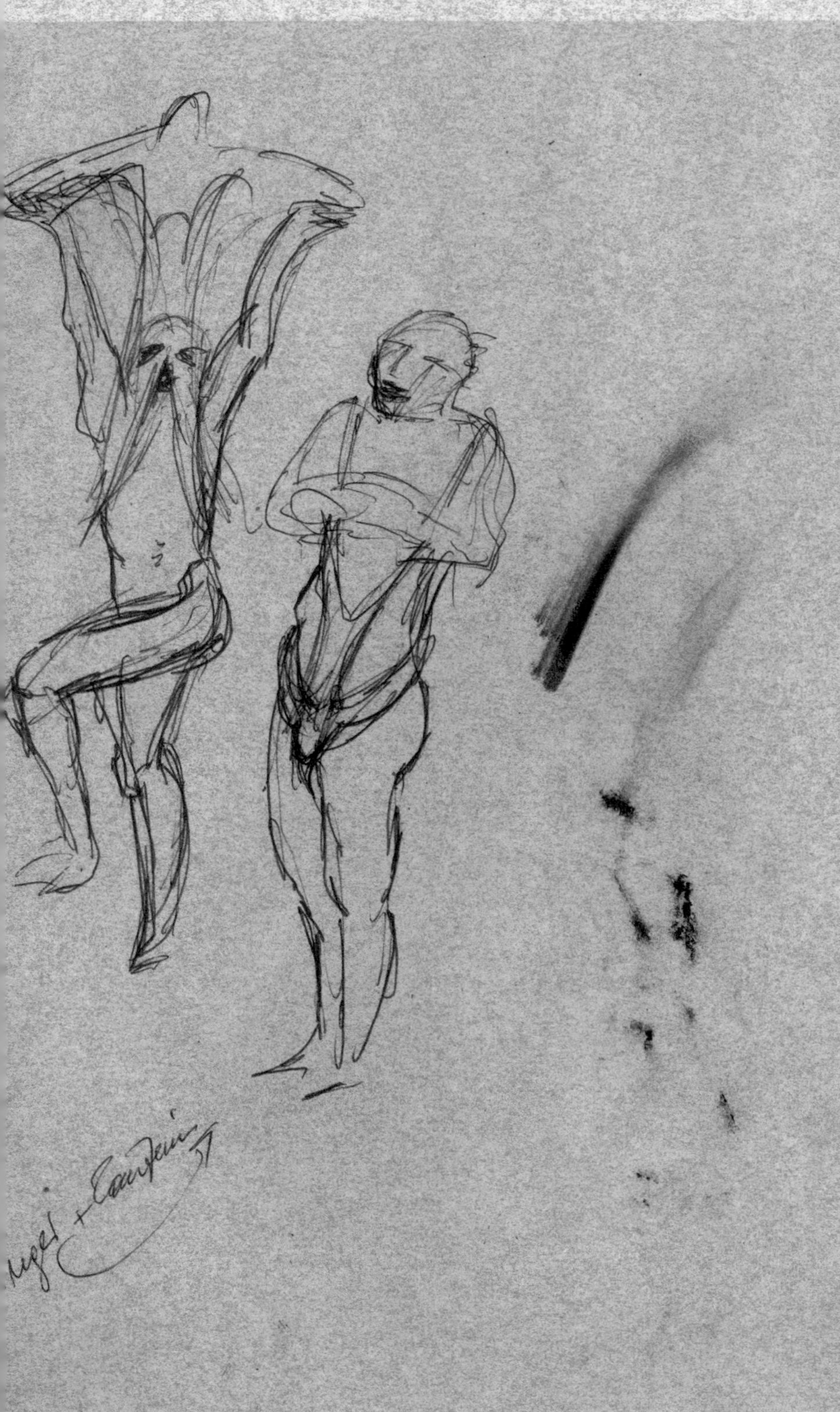

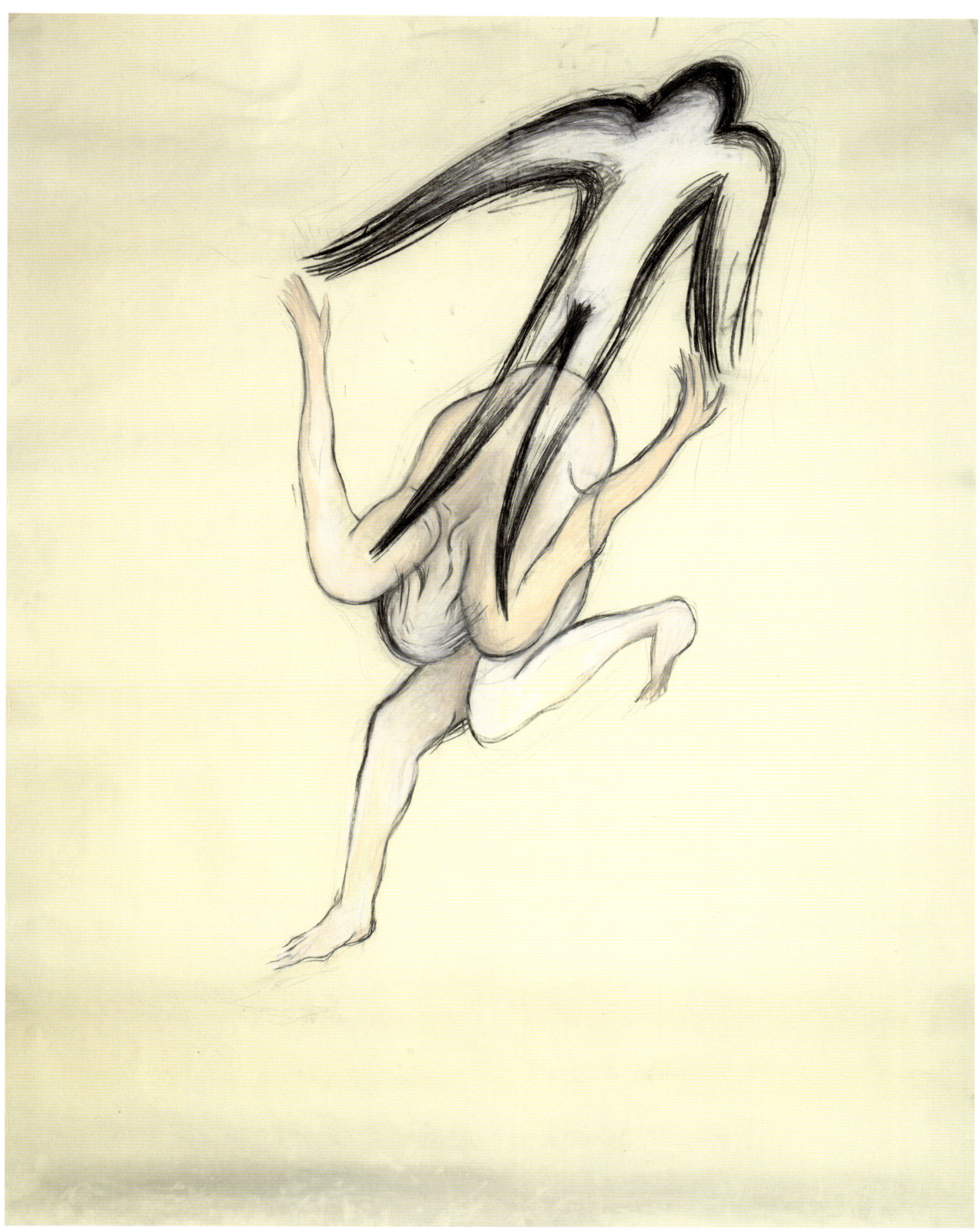

150   *Ohne Titel* 1983
       Untitled

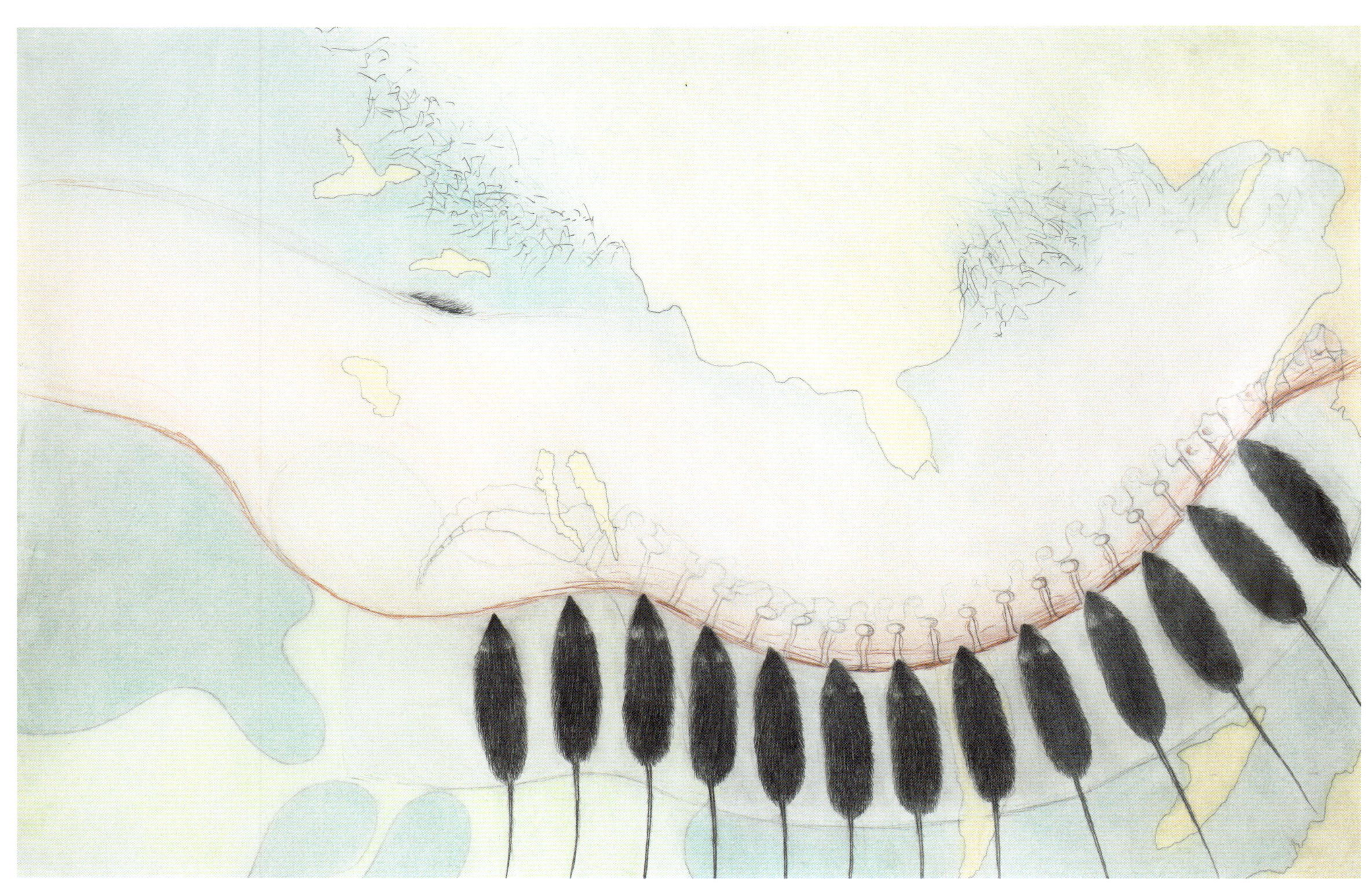

151 *Ohne Titel* 1979
Untitled

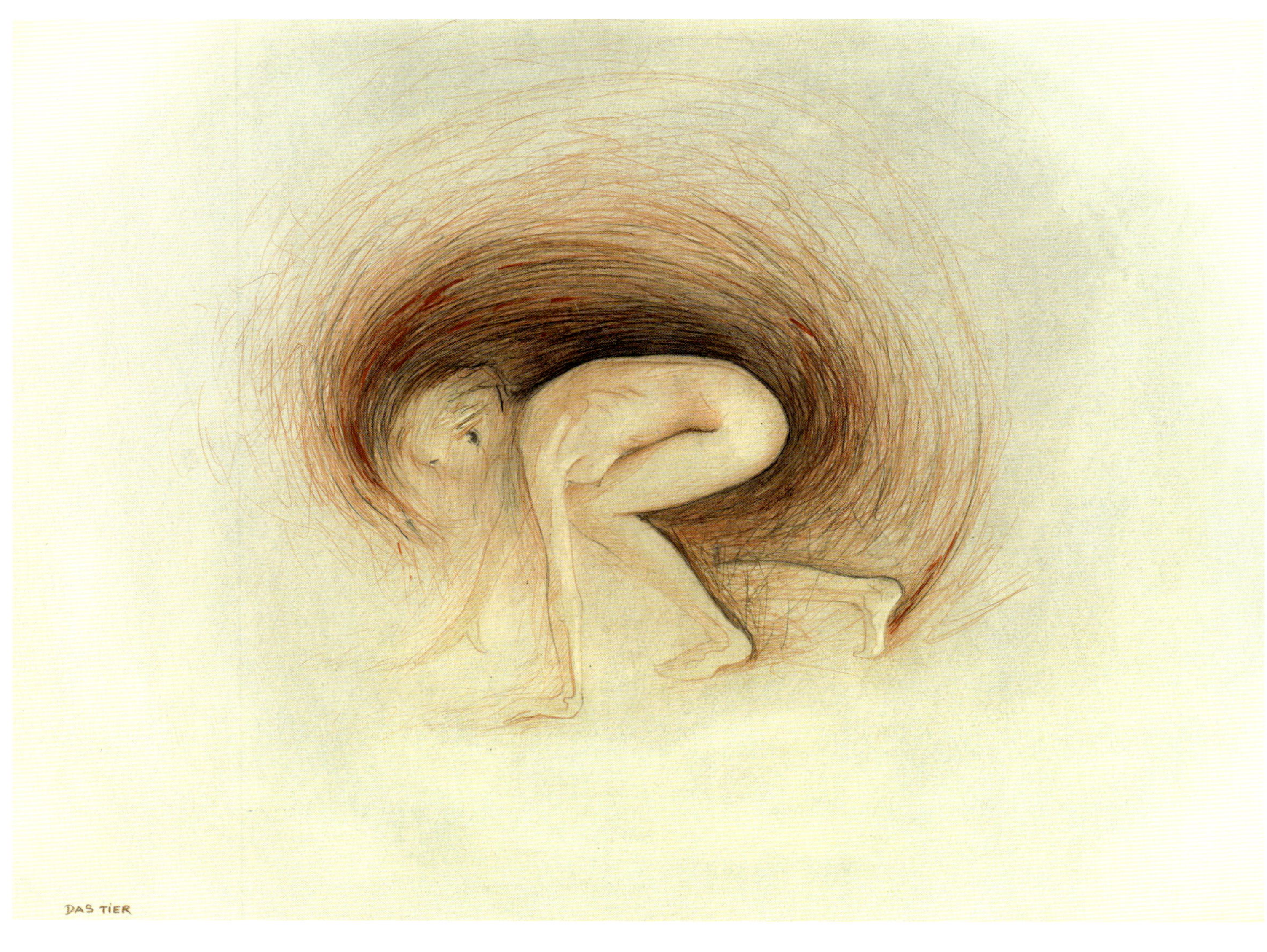

  Das Tier 1978
The Animal

The Woman
Does (Not) Exist

Marta Dziewańska

»The woman does not exist,« Jacques Lacan states in 1971, in one of his notorious seminars given at the Saint Anne Hospital Center in Paris—an assertion advanced in the context of his musings about feminine sexuality: phallus-less, the woman is »not-whole«; the lack of the *signifier* places her *jouissance* beyond language, making it inaccessible, »different.« Lacan's inflammatory contention has led to much fervid discussion, confrontation, and rupture.

The drawing *The Animal* (ill. 152) by Birgit Jürgenssen (1978) can be seen as an interesting commentary and subversive riff on that—provocative—assertion.

The female figure, drawn with a gentle touch, has been captured mid-movement; she may be about to straighten up or bend down, spring forth or lower herself to the ground to take a rest. She is encased in a glittering film that seems to be growing out of her very body, both deforming and highlighting its contours. This is not the classical, motionless pose of a model in a live-drawing class—the artist has set out to capture the figure in its ambiguous state of transformation. The title reinforces the message, which points to the hidden elements: the animalistic nature of femininity, with its subconscious desires and instincts.

Within these slight transpositions, the artist playfully sets in motion Lacan's proposition. With this drawing, Birgit Jürgenssen appears to be saying, *The Woman*— as a homogeneous, ready-made and easily definable entity, with socially allocated traits and roles—*does not exist*. By the same token, she rejects the cultural construct of »femininity« or »female nature«—revealing her figure as an unstable hybrid, whose identity is in motion, in an indeterminable state of flux.

In blurring the contours and making the figure ambiguous, the artist also seems to be questioning the phantasm of objectivity. With this subtle gesture she has made the academic stereotype go awry; in the context of the resolutely bourgeois and deeply patriarchal imagination and culture of her time, this is synonymous with creating art on her own terms. *The woman does not exist*, Jürgenssen appears to be saying, *because the identikit that describes her has been imposed on her by men*. Precisely in that sense, her drawing becomes a demand, a sui generis postulate: women must begin to speak in their own authentic voices, from their own perspective, about their own needs and desires, and only then can there exist equality.

The Animal can thus be seen as an affirmation of woman-as-subject. If voiced by Birgit Jürgenssen, Lacan's allegation would rather be *The Woman does (not) exist*—not a negation but, on the contrary, a mobilization of pent-up potential.

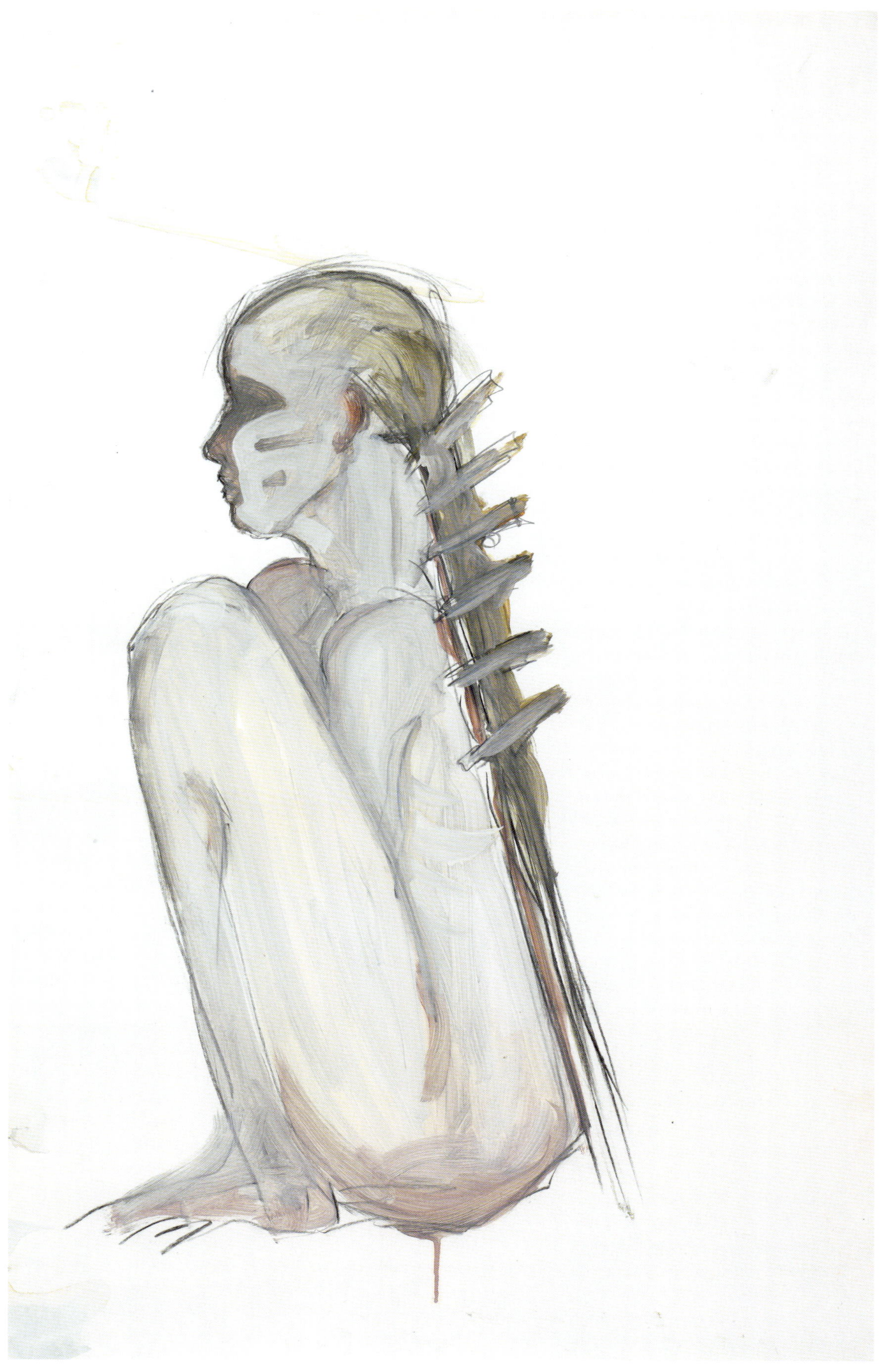

153 *Ohne Titel* 1982/1983
Untitled

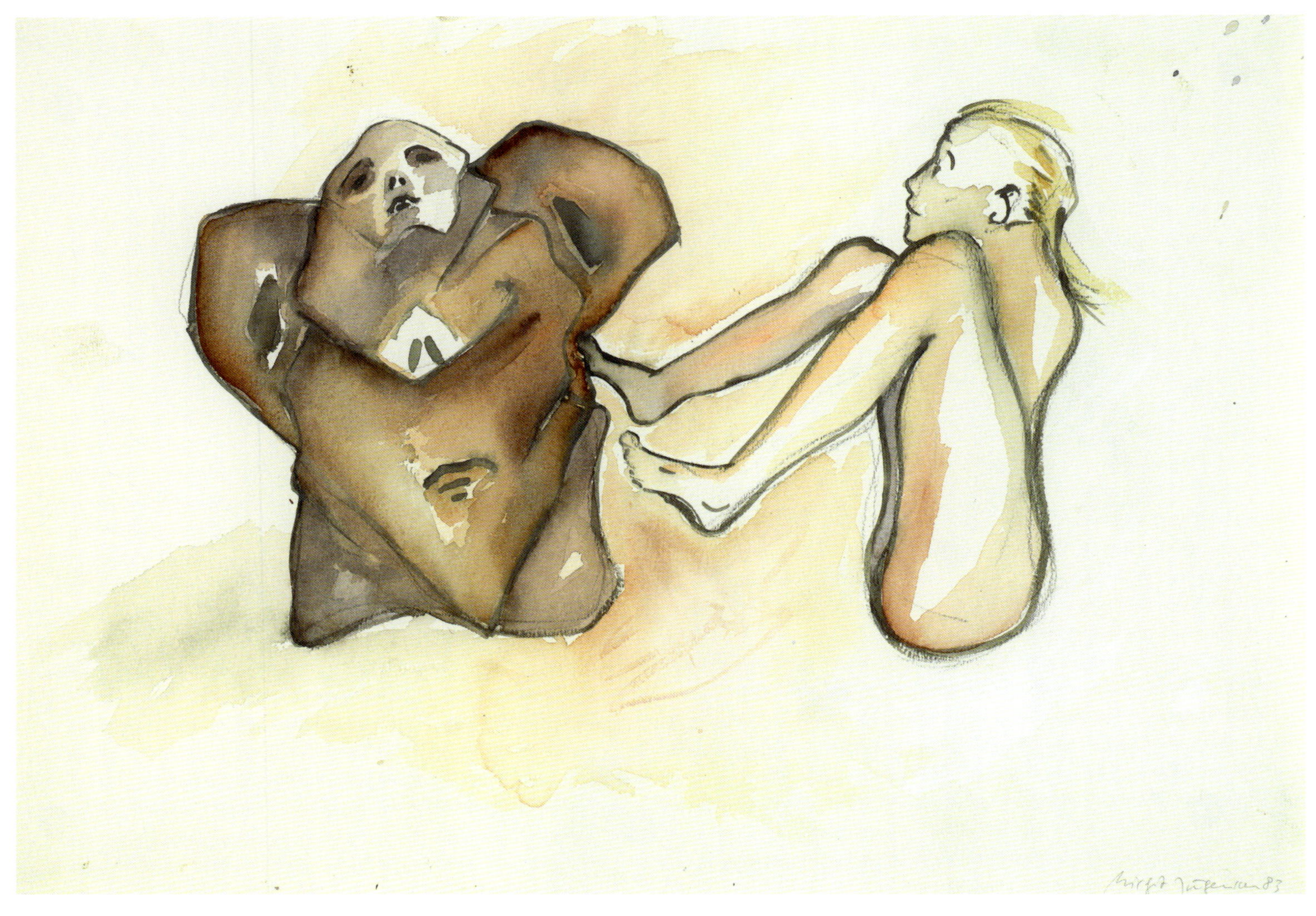

154 *Sklavin des Herzens* 1983
Slave of the Heart

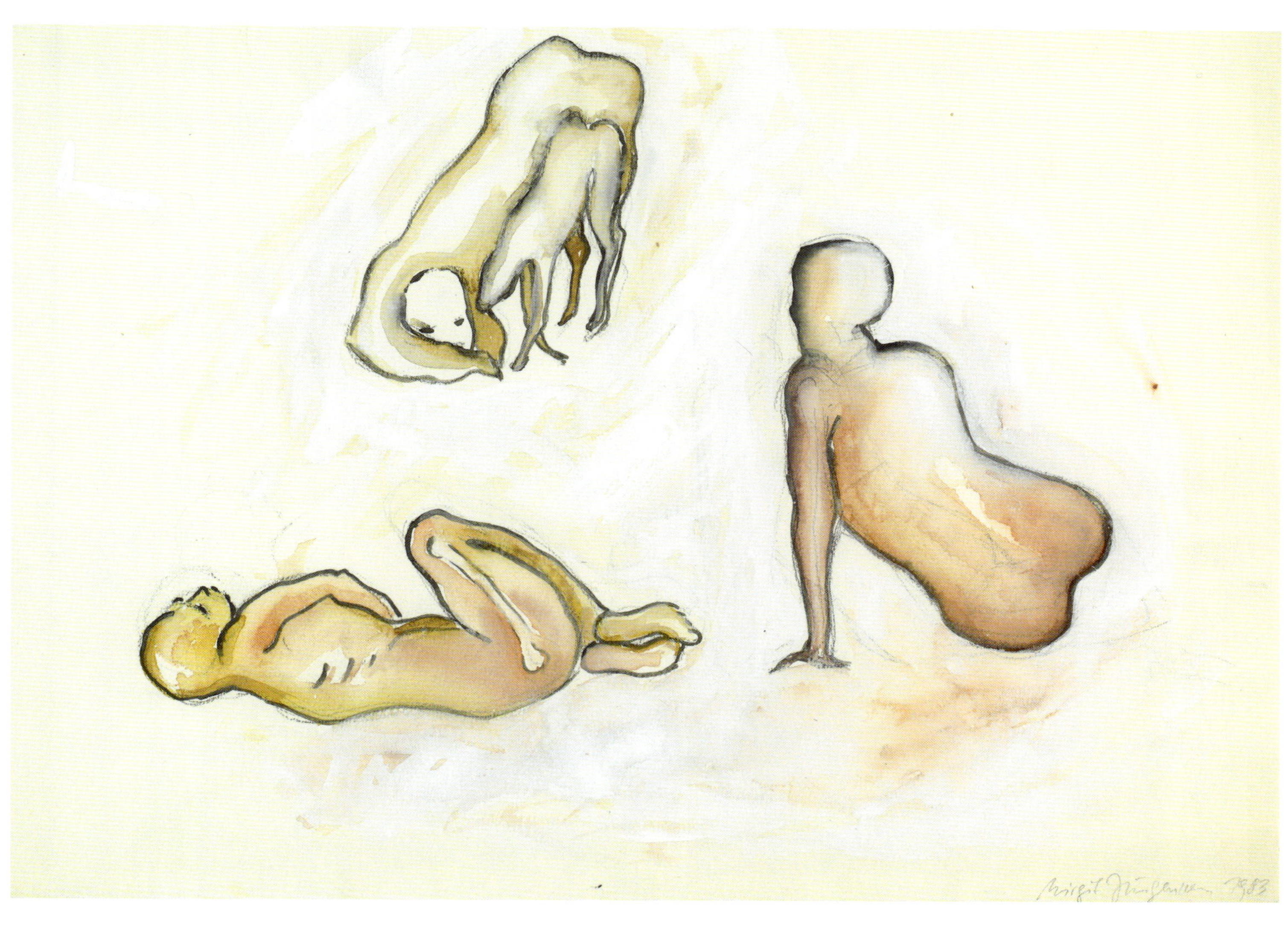

154   *Sklavin des Herzens* 1983
Slave of the Heart

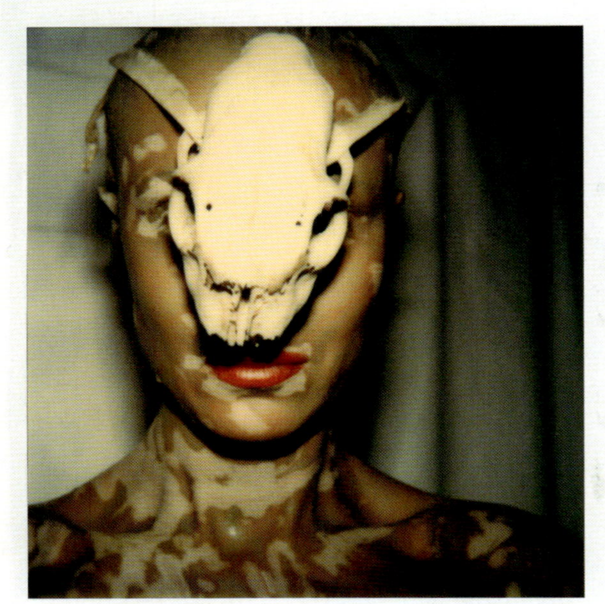
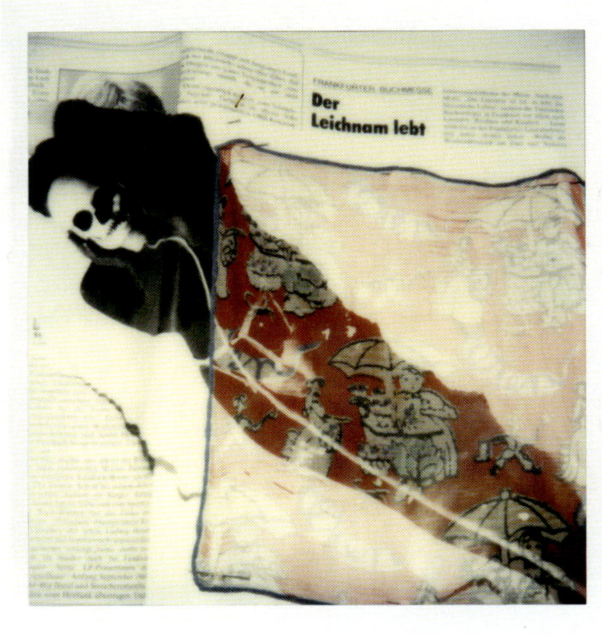

156   *Ohne Titel* 1979
       Untitled
157   *Ohne Titel (Der Leichnam lebt)* 1979
       Untitled (The Corpse Lives)

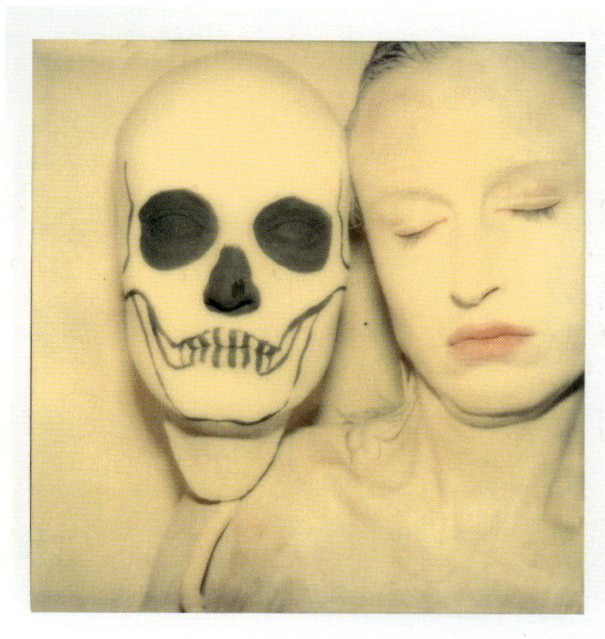

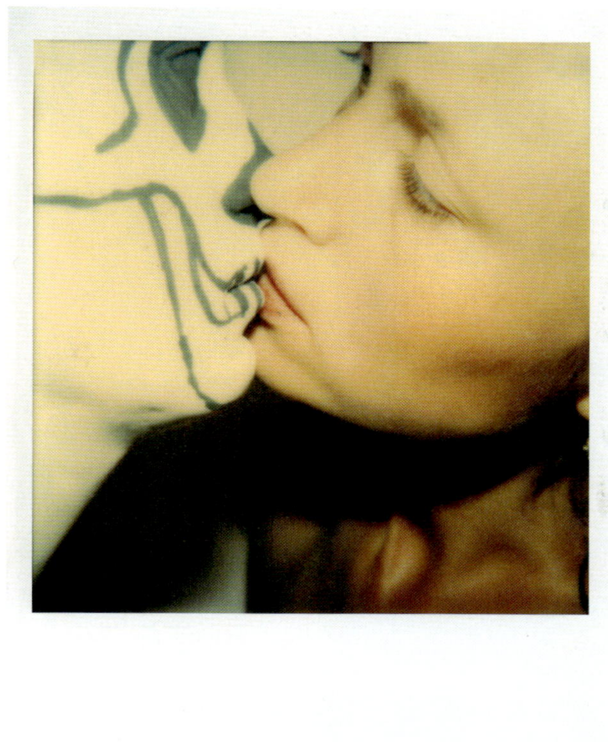

158   *Ohne Titel* 1979
       Untitled
159   *Ohne Titel* 1979
       Untitled

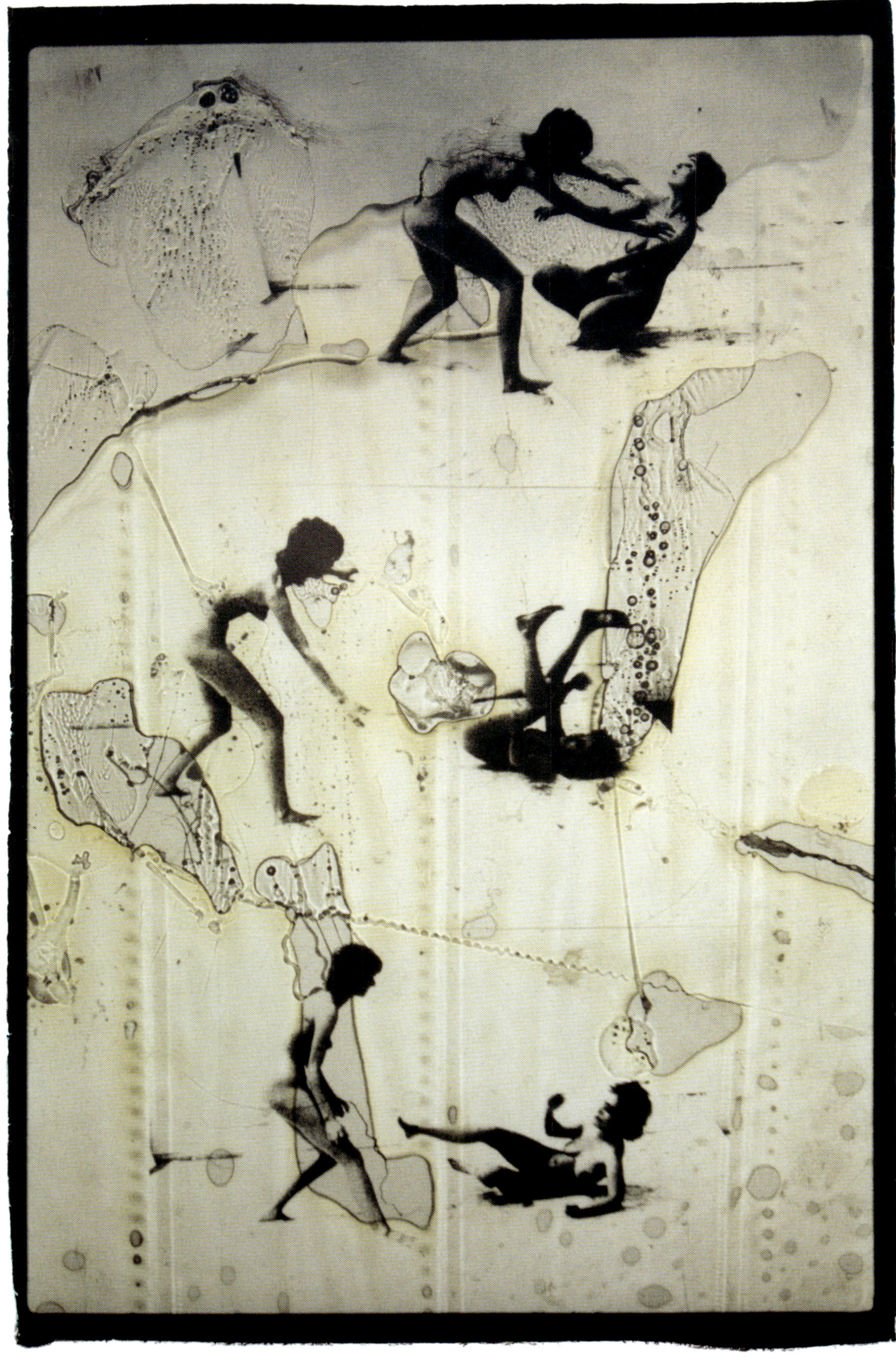

160 *Ohne Titel (Ranking)* 1999
Untitled (Ranking)

Freed from Any Constraint

On Birgit Jürgenssen's Photographic Experiments

Ninja Walbers

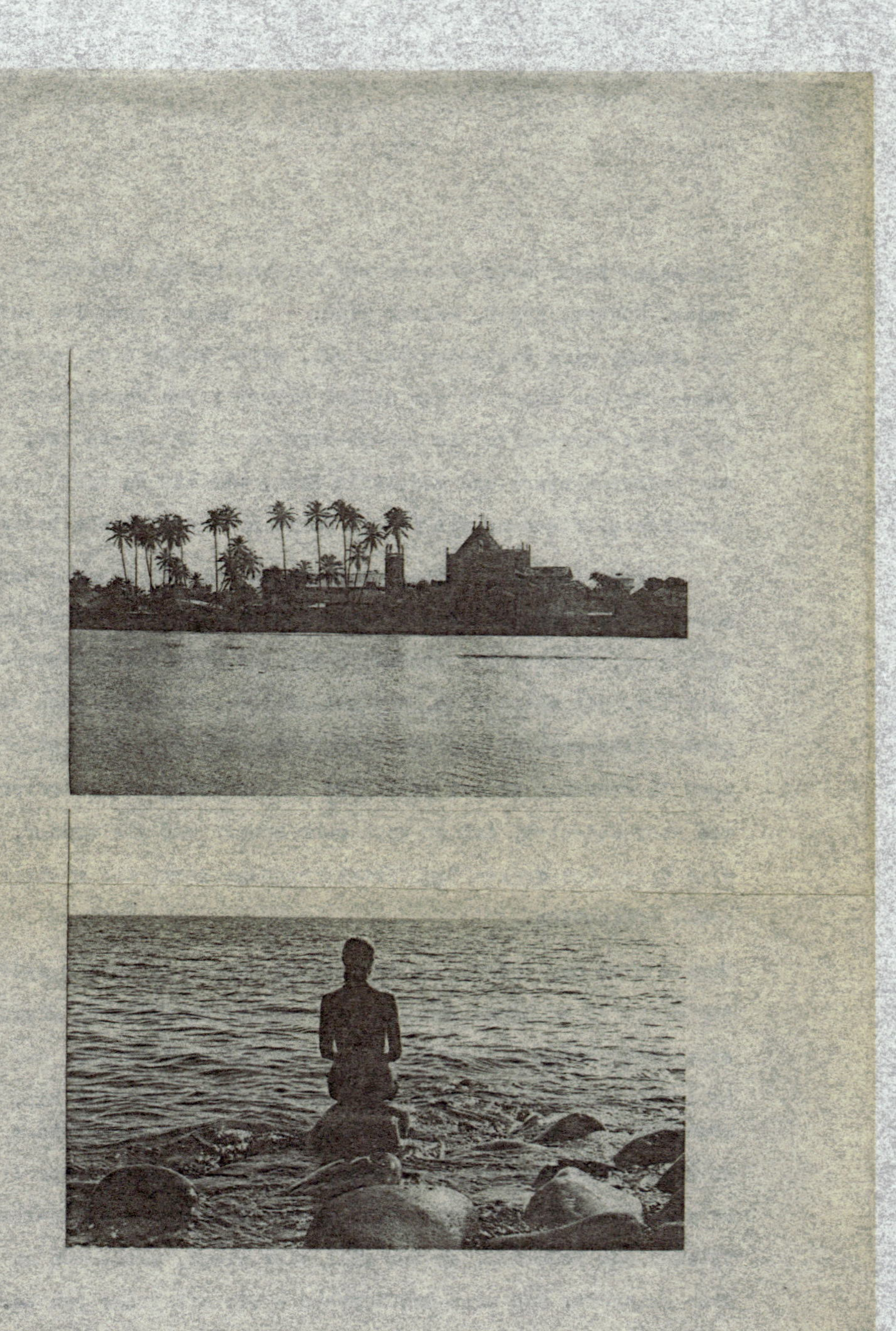

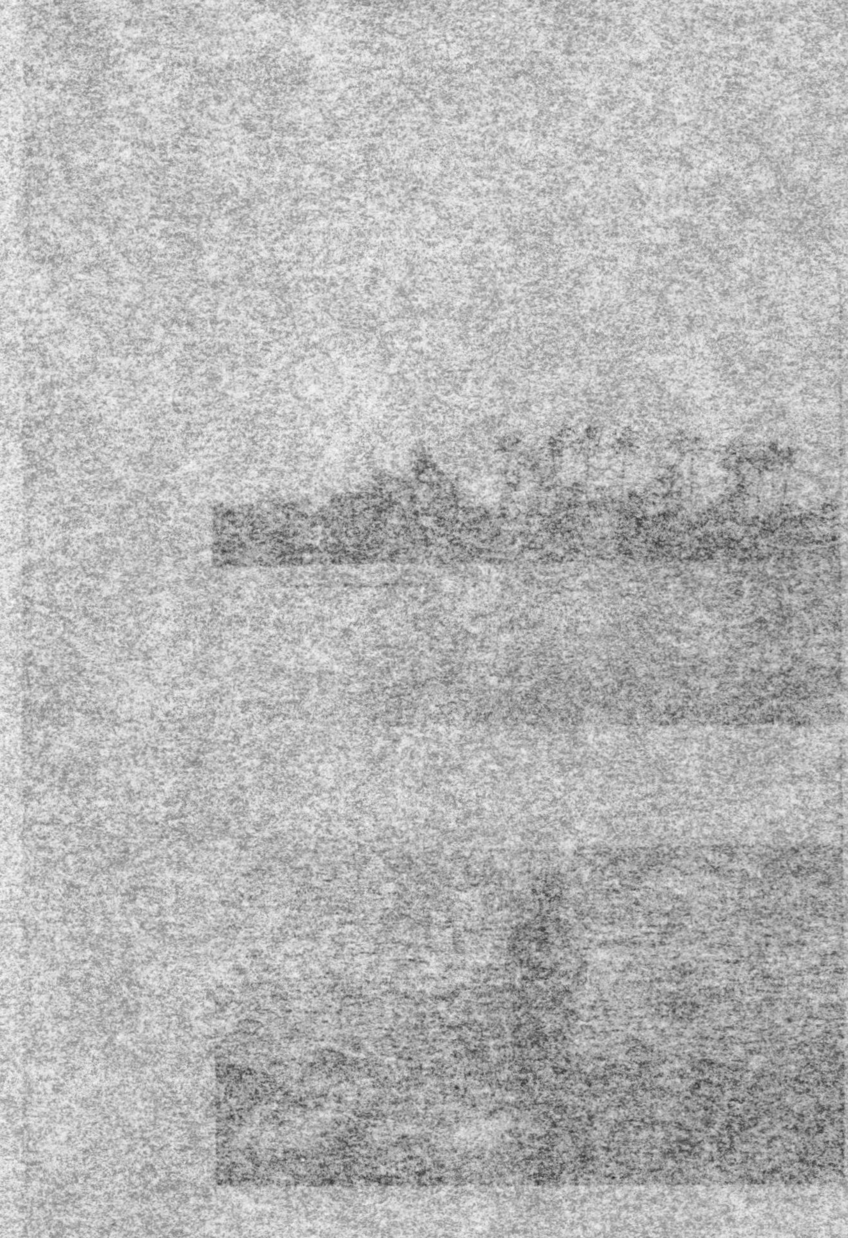

[1] Birgit Jürgenssen in conversation with Heidemarie Seblatnig (quotation slightly changed, while retaining the meaning), in Heidemarie Seblatnig, *Einfach den Gefahren ins Auge sehen: Künstlerinnen im Gespräch* (Vienna: Böhlau, 1988), pp. 158–61, here: p. 159.
[2] See Abigail Solomon-Godeau, »The Fine Art of Feminism,« in *Held Together with Water: Art from the Sammlung Verbund*, ed. Gabriele Schor, exh. cat., MAK Vienna (Ostfildern: Hatje Cantz, 2007), pp. 32–45, here: p. 40.
[3] See Wolfgang Kemp, *Geschichte der Fotografie: Von Daguerre bis Gursky*, 2nd ed. (Munich: Beck, 2014), p. 92 [translated].
[4] See Doris Linda Psenicnik, *Identität, Geschlecht und Konstruktion: Künstlerische Interventionen im Spektrum feministischer Strategien zu Fragen nach der Geschlechtsidentität; Mit einem Schwerpunkt auf dem fotografischen Œuvre Birgit Jürgenssens*, diploma thesis, University of Graz, 2001, p. 122.
[5] See Gabriele Schor »›I Am‹: On the Flux of the Artistic Self in the Works of Birgit Jürgenssen,« in *Birgit Jürgenssen*, ed. Gabriele Schor and Abigail Solomon-Godeau (Ostfildern: Hatje Cantz, 2009), pp. 13–64, here: p. 62.

»I am much more interested in experimenting than in finding a brand for myself,« Birgit Jürgenssen said in an interview in 1988.[1] This was not just a statement of her own view of herself as an artist but also of her way of working, typical of her entire œuvre. The pleasure of experimentation leads to a very broad form of crossover, particularly in her photographs. Around 2,500 works make for a complex corpus, with black-and-white and color photos, photograms, Polaroids, solarizations, cyanotypes, sometimes drawn over, painted over, collaged, or scratched. Birgit Jürgenssen took a deliberately manipulative approach to photography, aiming to probe deeper levels of the unconscious—on the basis of her own experience of the world. In terms of content, her work ranges from an exploration of feminist and socially critical issues to the treatment of themes drawn from art history and the creation of new fictional realities.

Jürgenssen developed her work on the margins of the international art scene.[2] Although the art world took very little notice of this Austrian artist, her photographic œuvre is closely related to the avant-garde of the 1970s and 1980s, characterized by conceptual performative and serial photography. New contexts were also derived from combinations of image and text and through »image recycling.«[3] With great variety, Jürgenssen expanded the options for photography, transferring it into other media like painting. Unconventionally, she tended to always use photography as a complementary medium whenever it seemed the right approach for a specific work.[4] She also moved easily from style to style, linking her work to the history of prewar photography, and also working very much in the spirit of her own time, as evidenced by her use of Polaroids. According to Gabriele Schor, Birgit Jürgenssen's work is located at the threshold between modernism and postmodernism, a thesis that can be confirmed when looking at the artist's photographic cosmos.[5]

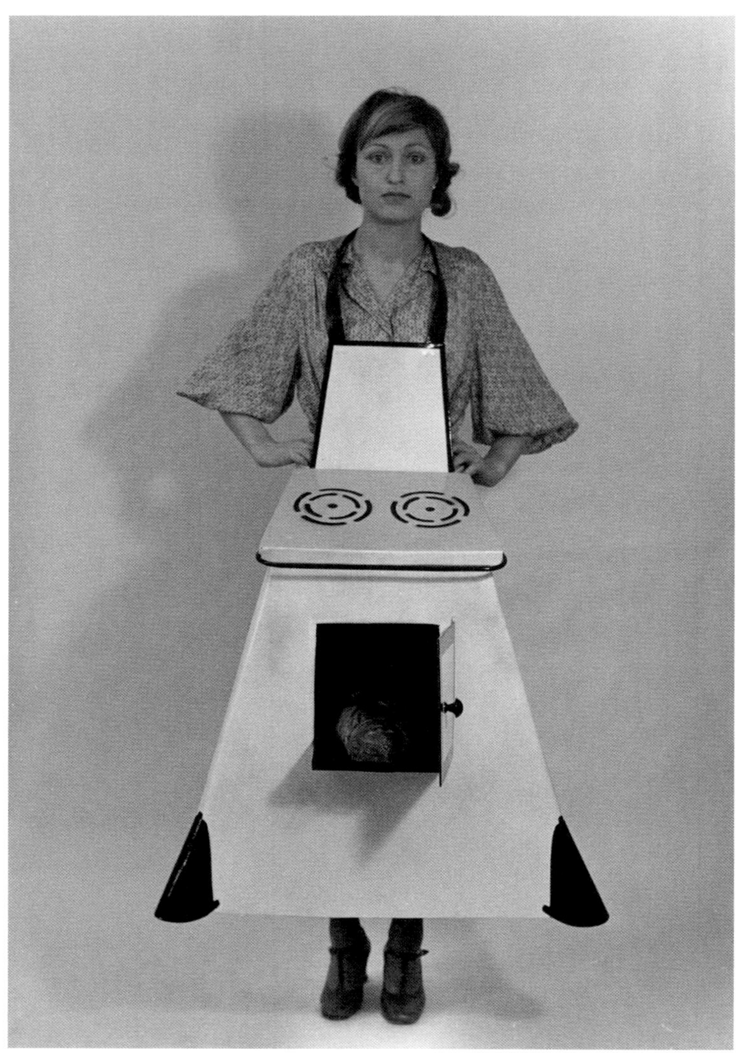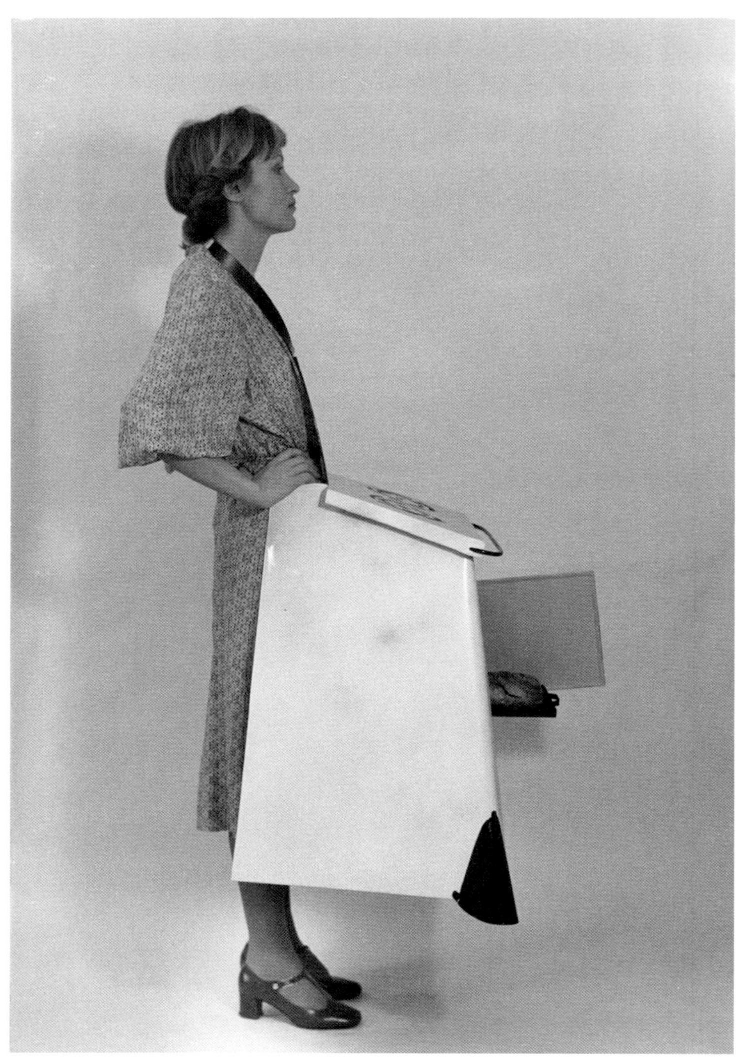

<u>161</u>   *Hausfrauen – Küchenschürze 1975*
Housewives' Kitchen Apron

Art with Photography

[6] See Birgit Jürgenssen in conversation with Heidemarie Seblatnig (see n. 1), p. 158.
[7] See Margit Zuckriegl, ed., *Österreichische Fotografie seit 1945* (Salzburg: Pustel, 1989), p. 13.
[8] On this, see the text by Heike Eipeldauer on p. 267 in this volume.
[9] See Gabriele Schor, »Sklavin des Herzens‹: Von der Liebe im Werk von Birgit Jürgenssen,« in *Birgit Jürgenssen*, Gabriele Schor and Heike Eipeldauer, ed., exh. cat., Kunstforum Vienna (Munich: Prestel, 2010), pp. 11–27, here: p. 11.
[10] See Susan Sontag, *On Photography* (New York: Farrar, Straus & Giroux, 1973), p. 16.
[11] Psenicnik, »Identität« (see n. 4), p. 26 [translated].
[12] See Schor, »I Am,« (see n. 5), p. 14.
[13] Jürgenssen, cited in Gabriele Schor, »Pulsebeat of a Sensuality‹: Introductory Remarks,« in Schor and Solomon-Godeau, *Birgit Jürgenssen* (see n. 5), pp. 6–10, here: p. 8.
[14] Psenicnik, »Identität« (see n. 4), p. 132.
[15] See Betty Friedan, *The Feminine Mystique* (New York: W.W. Norton, 1963).

Birgit Jürgenssen was given her first camera at the age of fourteen, and she intuitively saw photography as an artistic medium. She made small objects and then photographed them in staged setups,[6] thereby already trying out in her youth what would become one of the defining features of enacted photography in the 1970s. This was the period in which Jürgenssen, a student of graphic arts at the University of Applied Arts, taught herself photography and professionalized her skills in the field. By creating constructed realities for the camera, she reacted to photography's promise of »reality« and in this context explored the question of the relationship between the photographic image and reality, which was a major theme in both artistic and theoretical discourse at the time. There was also plenty of lively discussion about the status of the medium of photography.

More and more artists were integrating photography into their visual repertoires. By using photography as a medium of artistic expression in tandem with other media, Jürgenssen was making »art with photography,« as it would have been put at the time in an attempt to define all the different uses of photography. This was a way of working that only slowly found any recognition within the established Austrian cultural scene, right up into the 1990s. Cultural policy in Vienna and the entire »island« of Austria (as it was known up to the mid-1980s) was to a greater or lesser extent repressive. Photography exhibitions were understood as mere documentation, and the few art exhibitions such as *Creative Photography from Austria* (1974) remained exceptions.[7] There was no place for photography in conventional art exhibitions. This was changed in 1975 by VALIE EXPORT, in the spectacular exhibition that she curated and showed at the Galerie nächst St. Stephan, *MAGNA – Feminism: Art and Creativity*. Here Birgit Jürgenssen, twenty-five years old at the time, presented her object *Kitchen Apron* (ill. 199),[8] seen today as one of the key feminist artworks of the 1970s,[9] as well as the accompanying photographs (ill. 161). It is particularly ironic that three years later the artist was not allowed to show photographs alongside her drawings in her solo exhibition *Lineaturen* at the graphic arts collection at the Albertina.

Of Housewives and Women Criminals

With her analytical and ironic approach, Birgit Jürgenssen questions the social function and uses of photography. In one of her first triptychs from 1972 (ill. 163) she presents herself in frontal view, looking very serious, and also in profile, recalling the police mugshots that had been in use since the nineteenth century (ill. 162). By citing this kind of image, Jürgenssen exposes functional and symbolic structures. To this day, photographs serve as instruments of power in the form of evidence and information. They are the formulation of a bureaucratic view of the world, in which photographs gain validity through the information they carry. Identity documents, for example, only become valid when they include a photographic likeness.[10] These pictures may seem objective, but such photographs confirm the identity of a person and thus have an important function in the social order. Here, for Jürgenssen, photography is a »concrete and at the same time conceptual medium used to critically review verified and anchored ways of seeing,«[11] an approach that runs through all her photography.

Jürgenssen again uses the aesthetics of criminal photography, together with caustic irony, for a photograph of herself and her object in *Kitchen Apron*. Here she parodies the traditional roles embedded in patriarchal social structures.[12] As a feminist artist, »in the sense of becoming aware of, analyzing, and deconstructing dominant theories and systems of representation,«[13] she visualizes and deconstructs the »sign of woman.«[14]

This photograph can be read as a visual comment on American author Betty Friedan, who in 1963 debunked the voluntary submission of women to lives as housewives as an image of femininity propagated by the media.[15] Jürgenssen's artistic answer to this misogynistic social image is her black-and-white photograph *I Want Out of Here!* (ill. 165).

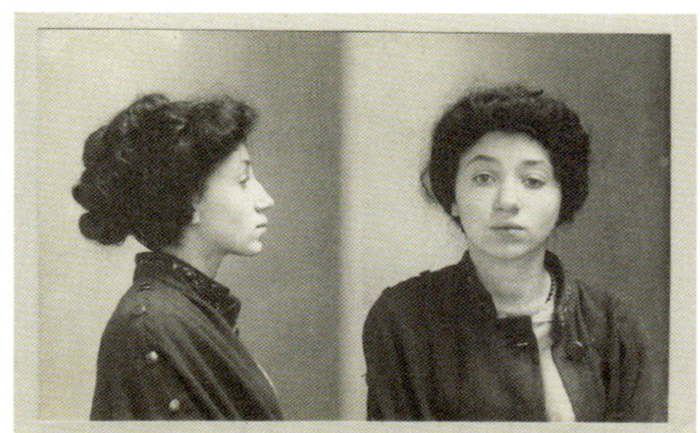

162 Bertillon card: Esther Ginsberg, June 1, 1910
NYPD Crime Scene Photograph Collection
Courtesy New York City Municipal Archives

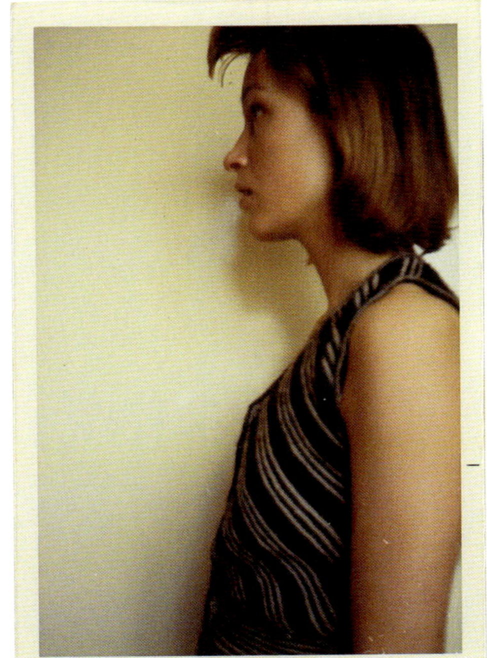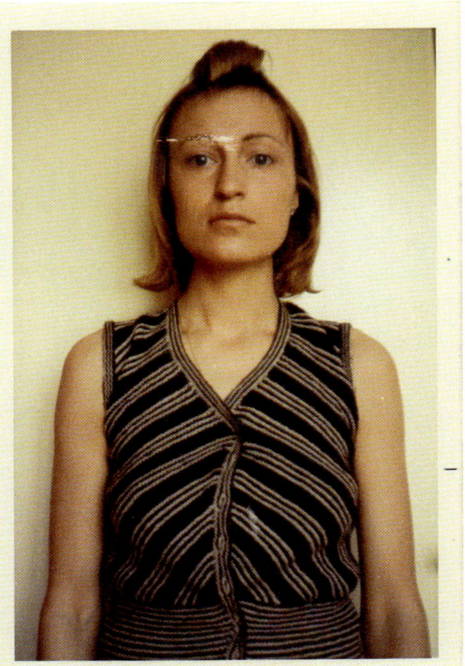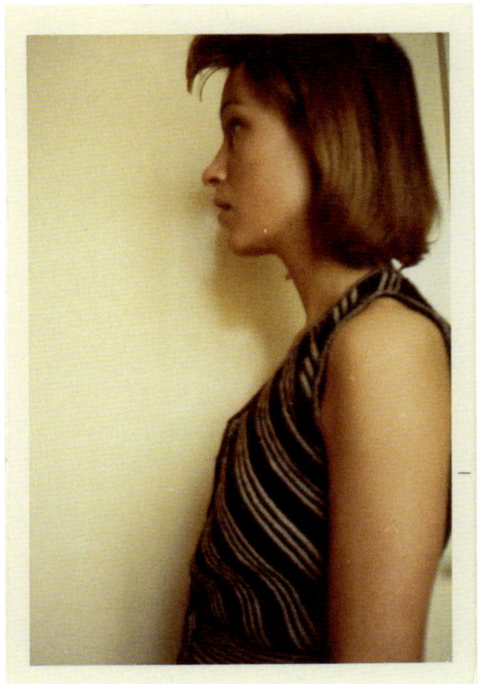

163   *Ohne Titel* 1972
       Untitled

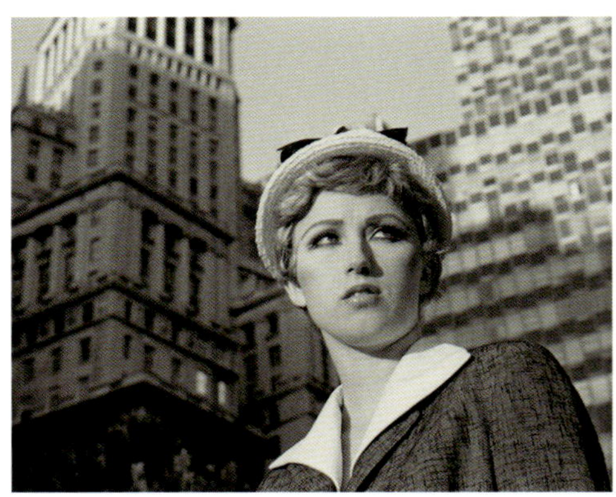

164   Cindy Sherman *Untitled Film Still #21* 1978
       Gelatin silver print
       20.3×25.4 cm
       Courtesy of the Artist and Metro Pictures, New York

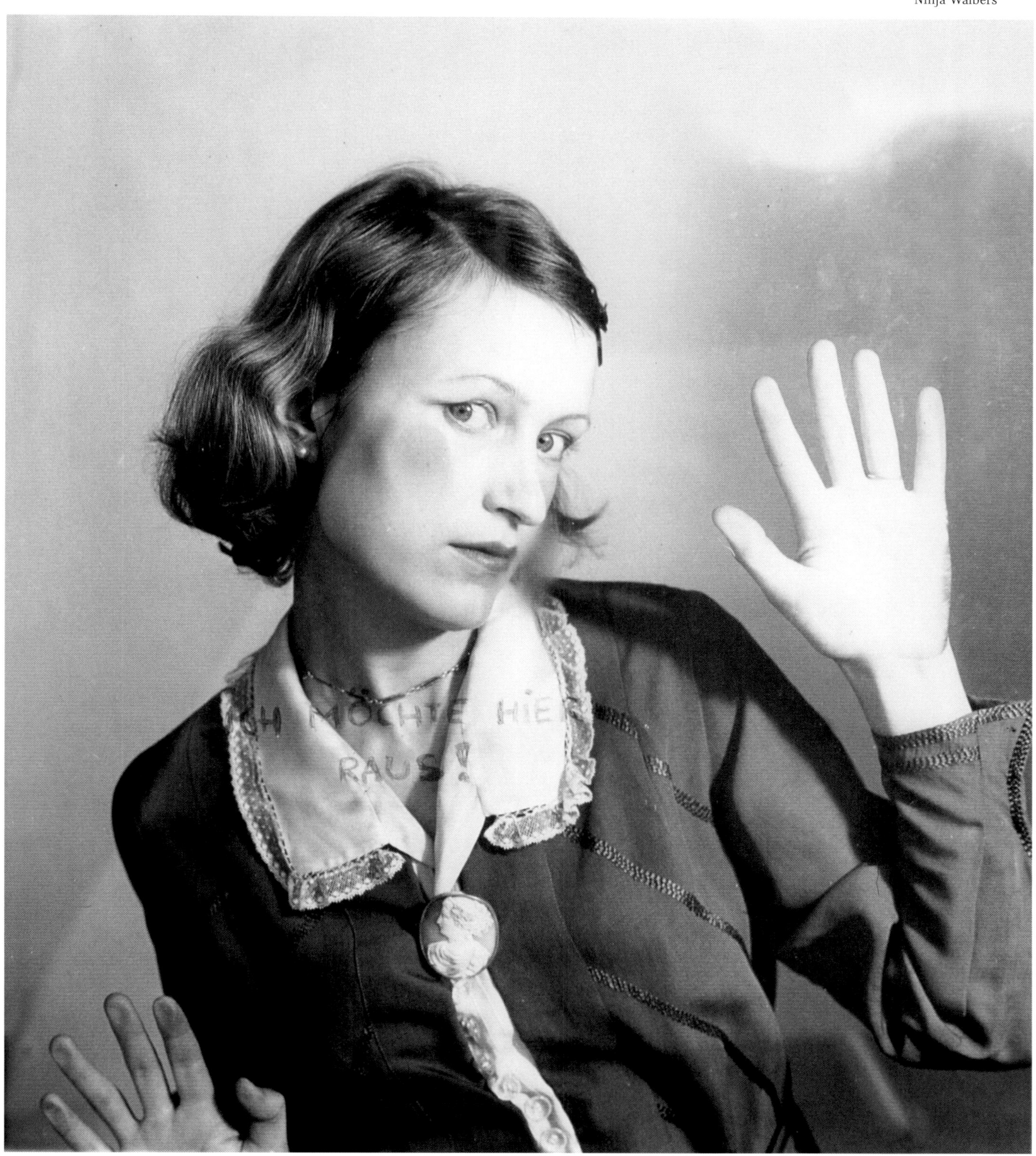

165   *Ich möchte hier raus!* 1976
        I Want Out of Here!

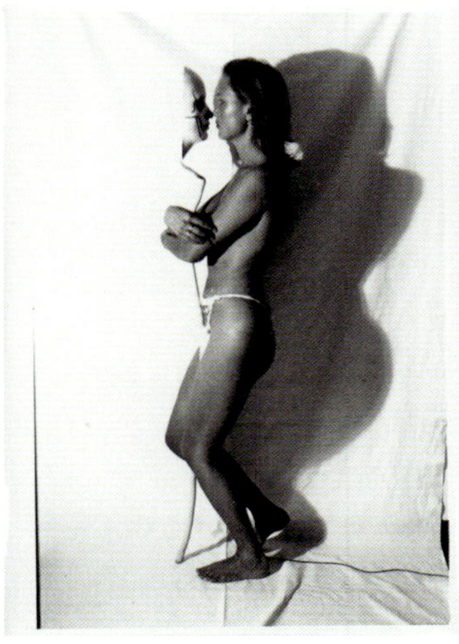 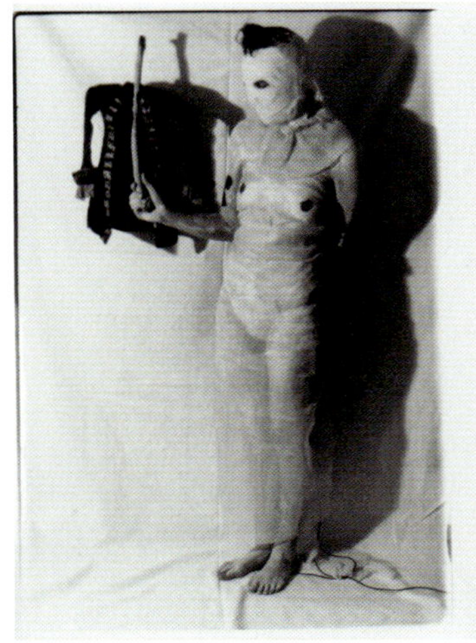 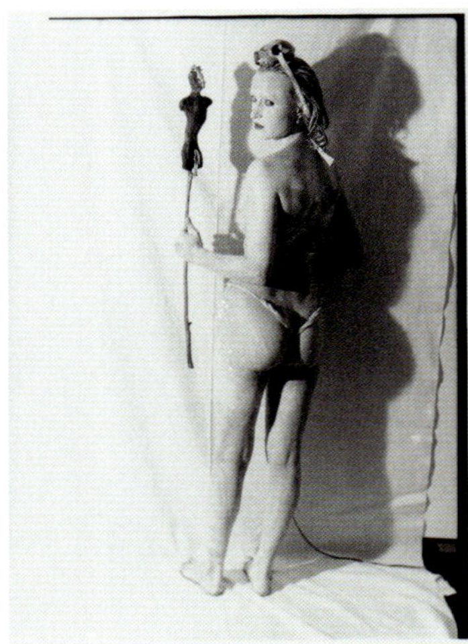 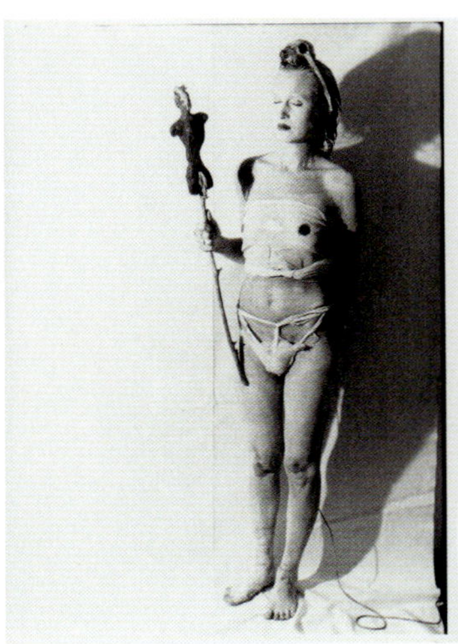

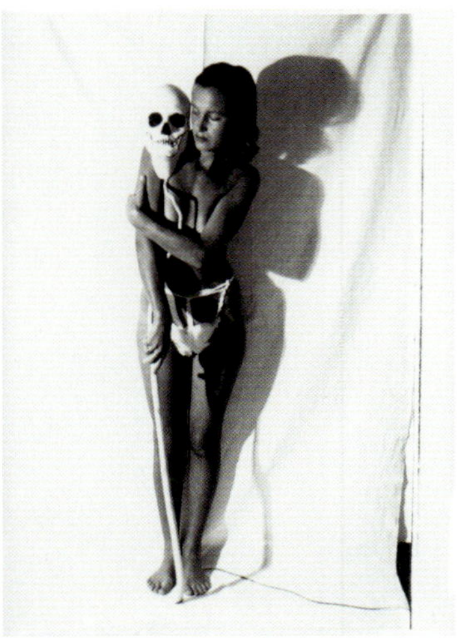 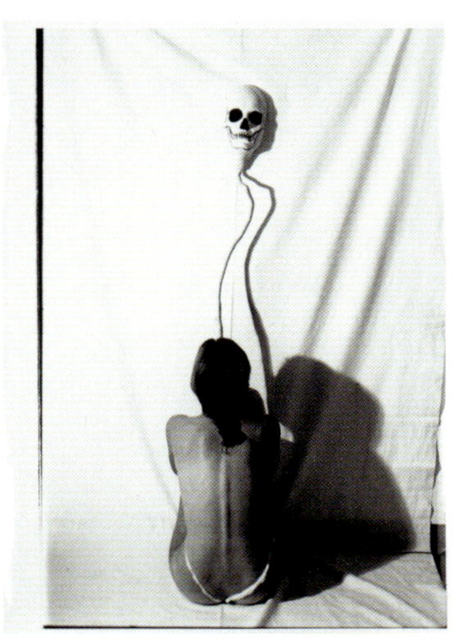 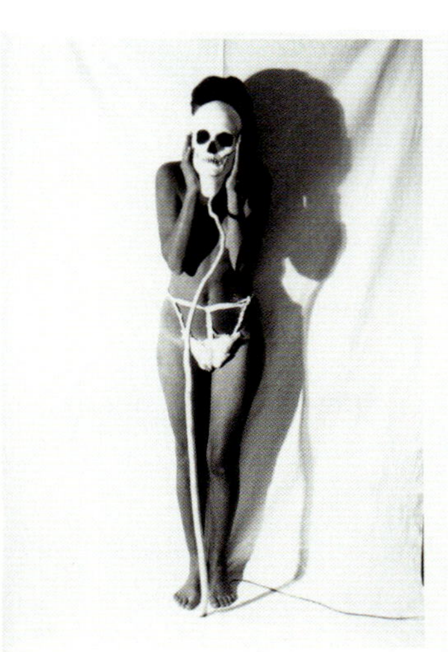 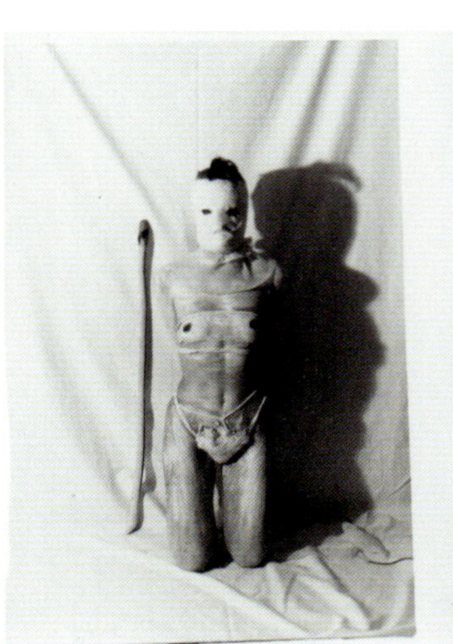

166 *Totentanz mit Mädchen* 1979/1980
Death Dance with Maiden

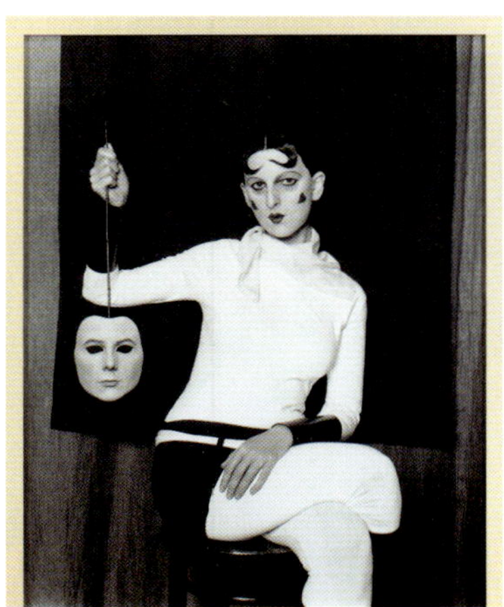

167 Gillian Wearing *Me as Cahun Holding
a Mask of My Face* 2012
Framed bromide print
157.3 × 129 × 3.3 cm
© Gillian Wearing, courtesy Maureen
Paley, London, Tanya Bonakdar
Gallery, New York, and Regen Projects,
Los Angeles

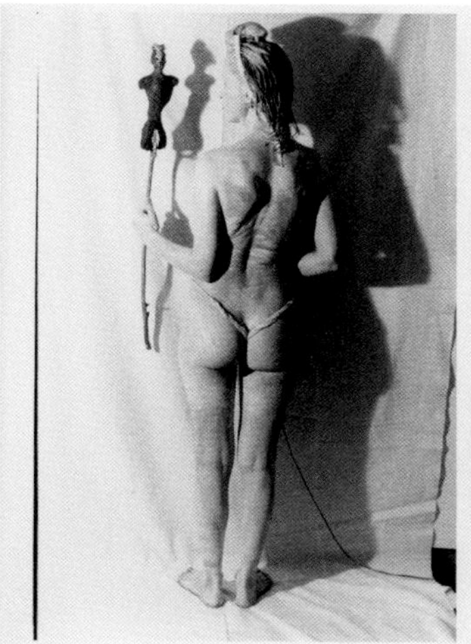
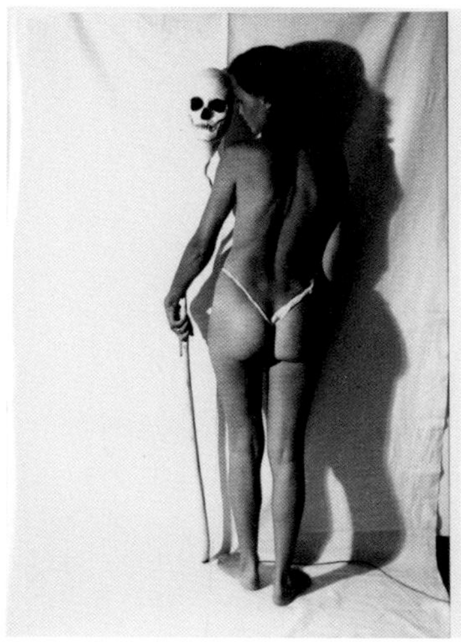
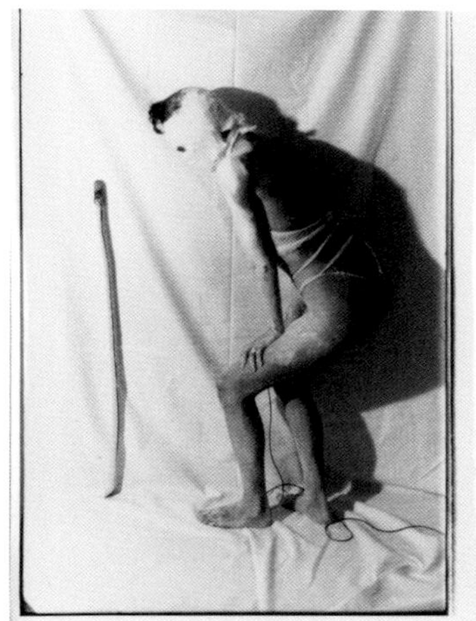
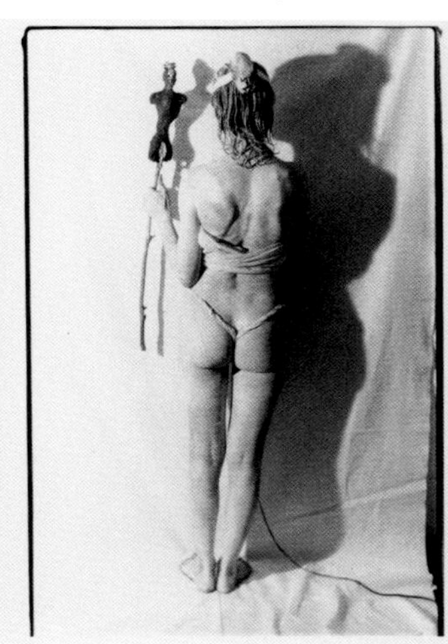

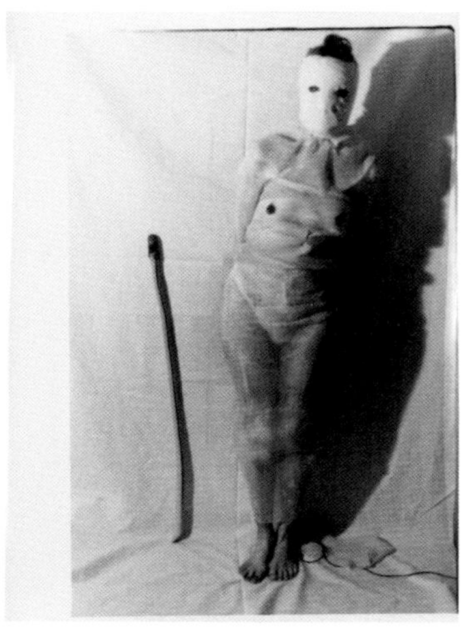
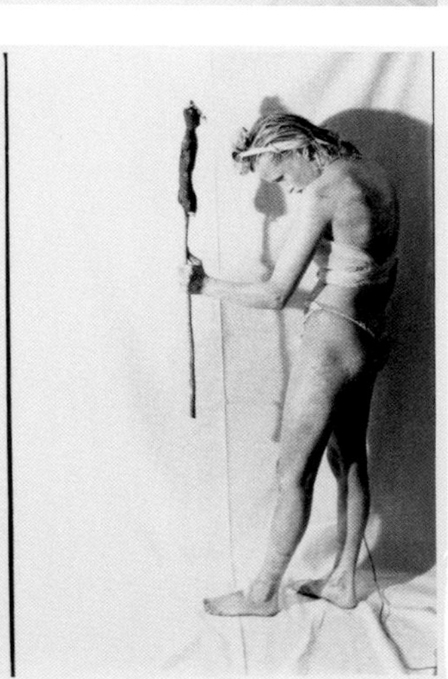

[16] Hans Belting, *An Anthropology of Images: Picture, Medium, Body*, trans. Thomas Dunlap (Princeton, NJ: Princeton University Press, 2014), p. 154.
[17] Edith Futscher, »Clowning Instead of Masquerading: Birgit Jürgenssen's Photographs of the 1970s,« in Schor, *Held Together with Water* (see n. 2), pp. 106–13, here: p. 112.

Here she theatrically stages herself as a well-dressed woman with a ruched collar and a brooch. Her cheeks and hands are pressed against a pane of glass, on which her plea for a way out is written. Similar to Cindy Sherman's *Untitled Film Stills* (ill. 164), Jürgenssen's performative photographs have narrative structures. They consciously aim at our »mental image production,«[16] which integrates them into our pictorial memories of images of women from films. In her text »Clowning Instead of Masquerading,« Edith Futscher looks at the clown-like elements of Jürgenssen's specific pictorial humor, in which she uses her various masks in the same way as Sherman, both of them dancing like »fools on the stage of patriarchy.«[17]

Performative Photography

Like Cindy Sherman, and above all like surrealist artist Claude Cahun, an early pioneer of performative photography, as is evident from her reception—demonstrated here by Gillian Wearing's *Me as Cahun Holding a Mask of My Face* (ill. 167)—Birgit Jürgenssen always staged and enacted her own body, taking pictures of it with a self-timer. All three artists use sophisticated role plays and masquerades to undermine social stereotypes, thereby employing a photographic language that they very deliberately keep simple.

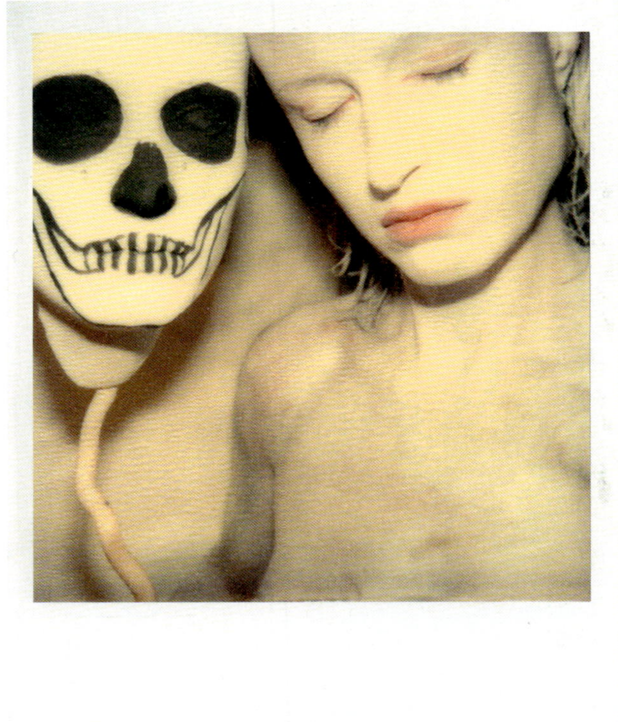

168   *Ohne Titel* 1979
      Untitled

The appearance of the artist in her own work is the »paradox of a reproduction without self-portrait, without self-representation.«[18] The depicted body is thus a transfer or
projection surface for ideas and not representative of the personality of the artist. The
images show the artist, but the artist is not meant.

    Death Dance with Maiden (ill. 166) is a large black-and-white series of tableaux
vivants and is typical of Jürgenssen's experimental and conceptual approach. It is also
a good example of her spectrum of themes, which go deep into spaces of existential experience. Like the first performers in totemic theater, Jürgenssen takes on the role
of a dead person, painted in white and her body wrapped in bandages and gauze. With
her props—a fetish doll she made herself and a »death mask« that she took of her own
face—Jürgenssen enters into a symbolic dialogue with death in front of a white sheet.
She quite literally faces up to her own death. This is in fact an unimaginable event,
only possible in a fictional game. The performative enactment for the photographic image
is thus also consciously shown, not least by leaving the cable of the self-timer visible.

[18] Martina Weinhart, *Selbst-
bild ohne Selbst:
Dekonstruktionen eines
Genres in der zeit-
genössischen Kunst* (Berlin:
Reimer, 2004), p. 10
[translated].

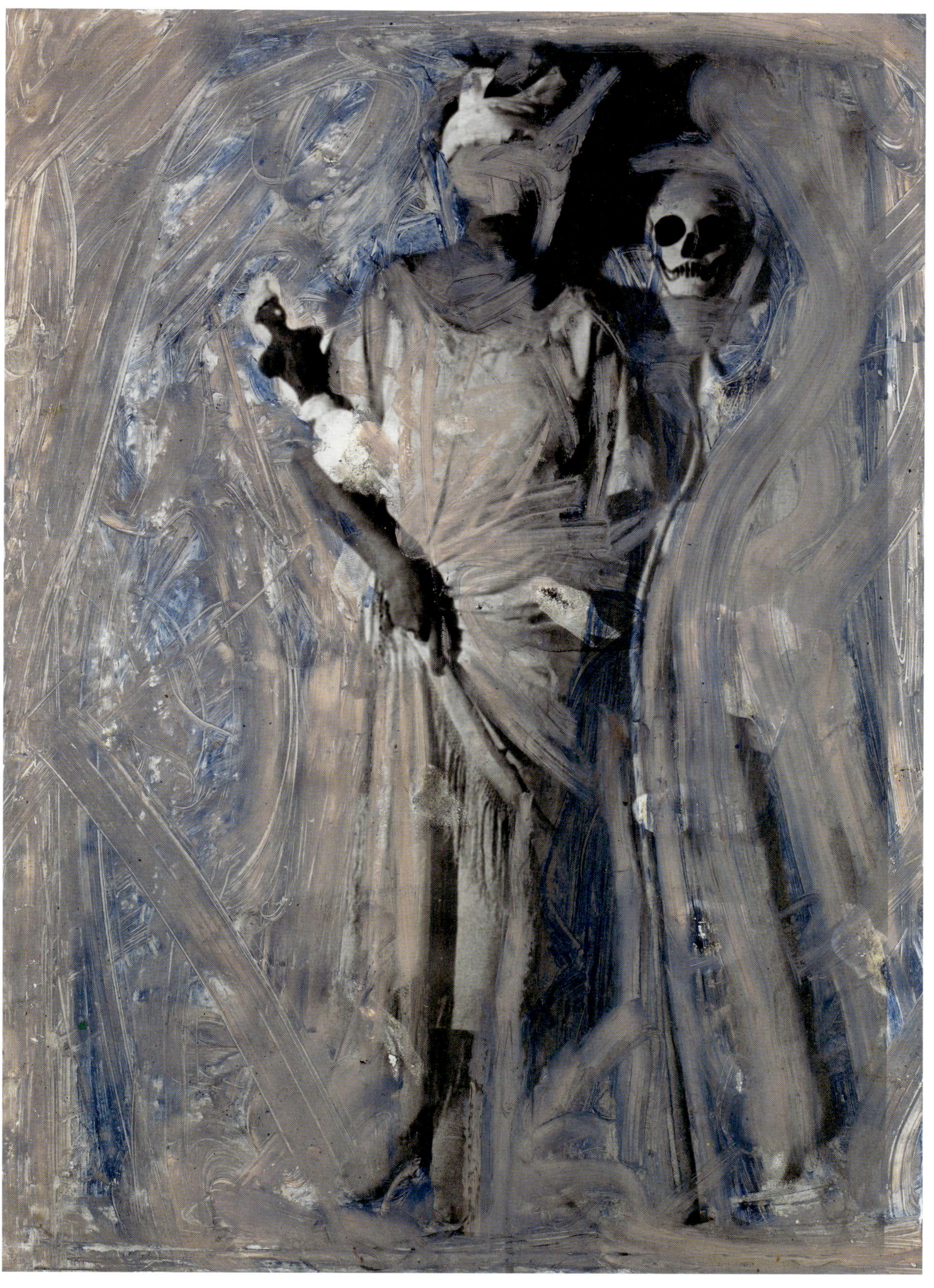

169   *Ohne Titel (Aus der Serie »Totentanz mit Mädchen«) 1979/1980*
Untitled (From the Series »Death Dance with Maiden«)

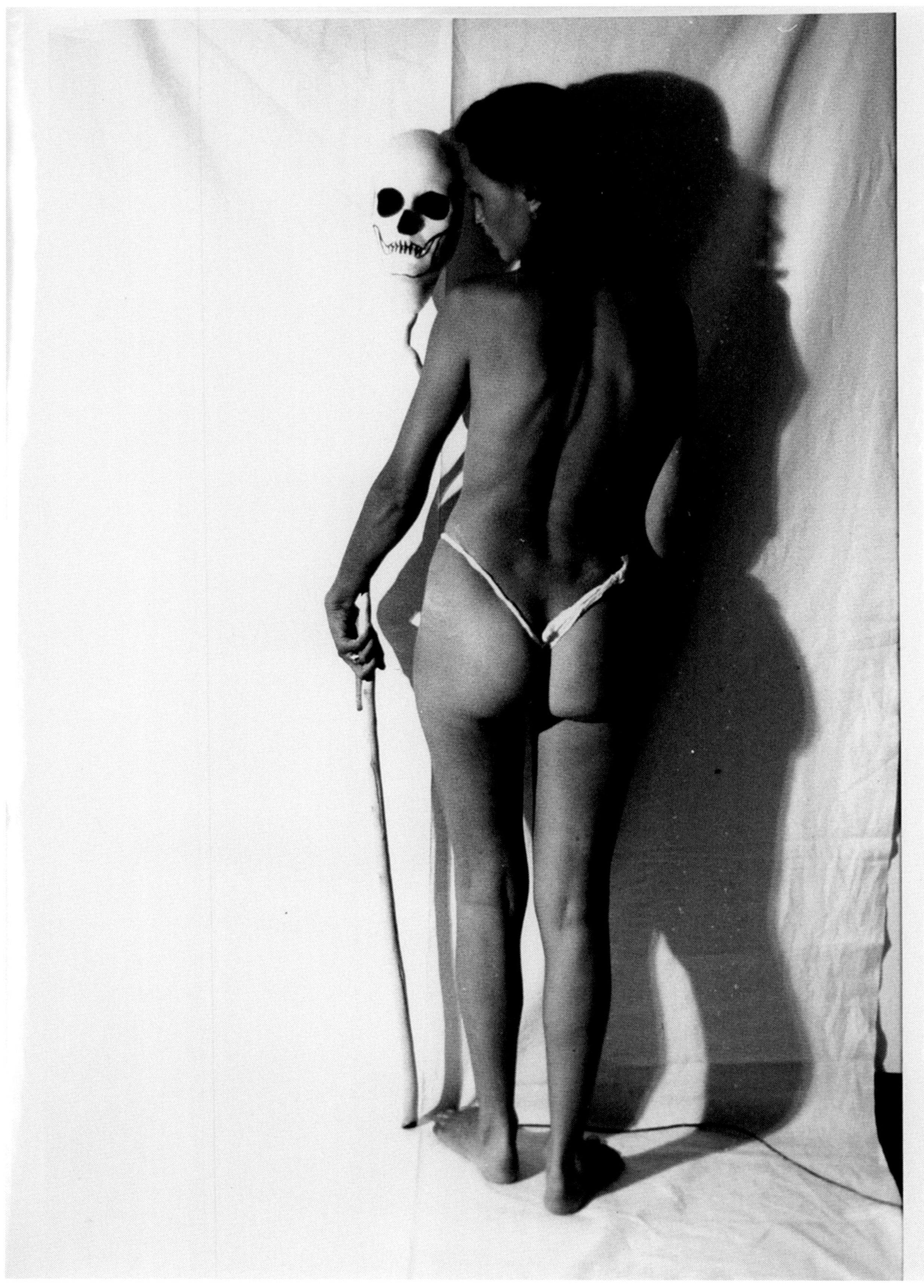

170 *Ohne Titel (Aus der Serie »Totentanz mit Mädchen«)* 1979/1980
Untitled (From the Series »Death Dance with Maiden«)

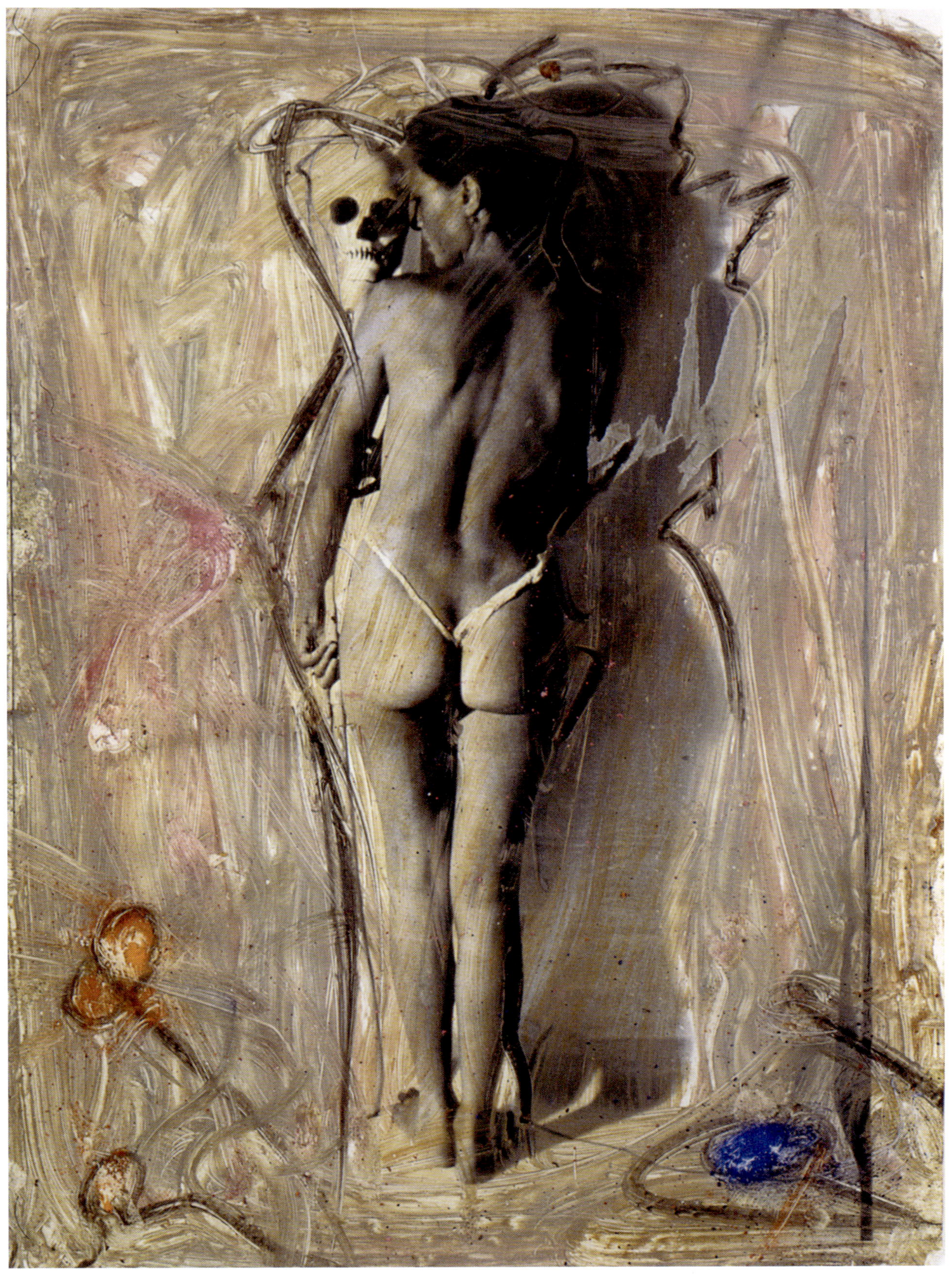

171 *Ohne Titel (Aus der Serie »Totentanz mit Mädchen«)* 1979/1980
Untitled (From the Series »Death Dance with Maiden«)

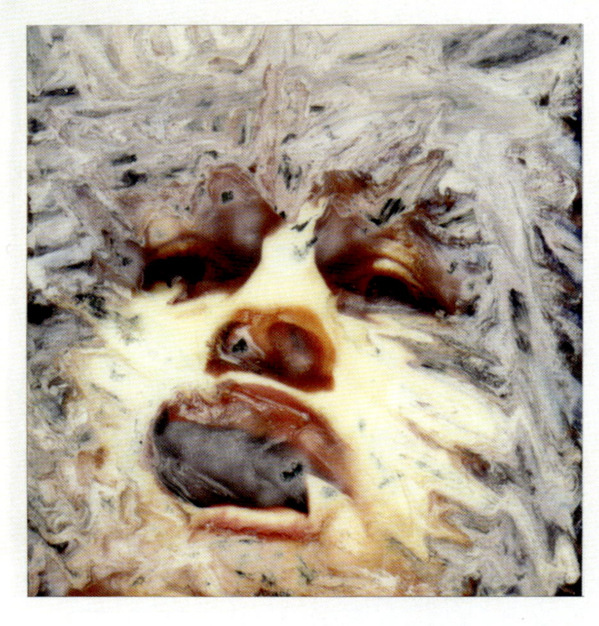

172 *Ohne Titel* 1978
Untitled

[19] Roland Barthes, *Camera Lucida: Reflections on Photography*, trans. Richard Howard (New York: Hill and Wang, 1965), p. 14.
[20] Sigrid Schade, »›The Corpse Lives‹: Pictorial Tradition and Gender Construction in the *Totentanz* Series by Birgit Jürgenssen,« in Schor and Solomon-Godeau, *Birgit Jürgenssen* (see n. 5), pp. 179–89, here: p. 180.
[21] See Meike Kröncke and Rolf F. Nohr, »Polaroids und die Ungewissheit des Augenblicks,« in *Polaroid als Geste – über die Gebrauchsweisen einer fotografischen Praxis*, Sigrid Schade and Barbara Lauterbach, eds., (Ostfildern: Hatje Cantz, 2005), pp. 6–17, here: p. 12.
[22] See Barbara Hitchcock, »When Land Met Adams,« in *The Polaroid Book: Selections from the Polaroid Collections of Photography*, ed. Steve Crist (Cologne: Taschen, 2005), pp. 12–17, here: pp. 16–17.

[23] See Zuckriegl, *Österreichische Fotografie seit 1945* (see n. 7), p. 28.
[24] The installation *10 Tage – 100 Photos* was first shown in 1981 in the Galerie Hubert Winter. This exhibition marked the beginning of a close collaboration and today the gallery holds the estate of Birgit Jürgenssen.
[25] Silvia Eiblmayr, »Der Gedanke auf dem Bad in einem spiegellosen Raum: Die *Bade*-Polaroids von Birgit Jürgenssen,« in *Birgit Jürgenssen: Früher oder später*, exh. cat., Oberösterreichische Landesgalerie Linz (Weitra: Bibliothek der Provinz, 1998), pp. 33–34, here: p. 34 [translated].
[26] See Schor, »Sklavin des Herzens« (see n. 9), pp. 20–21.

That Jürgenssen used photographs to depict this dance of death is relevant in two ways, as death seems to very much appertain to this medium. Posing for the camera transforms the living body into an image right from the outset. Photography, writes Roland Barthes, »represents that very subtle moment when [...] I am neither subject nor object but a subject who feels he is becoming an object.«[19]

Jürgenssen uses photography as a reflection on the medium, so as to present that passing moment of the transformation from subject to object—i.e., the process of becoming a picture. As an image of a living corpse, Jürgenssen also here inscribes herself into the art-historical tradition of the dance of death. In her comprehensive analysis of the *Death Dance* series, Sigrid Schade shows the many layers of meaning there—from the memento mori to erotic fantasies that are expressed in connection with the motifs of »death« and the »young girl.« In this European tradition, death is inextricably linked to the image of the woman, where »›femininity‹ appears as the signifier of various images of death and, vice versa, death appears as the signifier of the ›feminine.‹«[20] Jürgenssen's subtle game of transformation deconstructs this imagery. By making her own female body appear androgynous, she dissolves the parameters of clearly definable gender ascriptions. She also adds new original images to these tableaux vivants, picking out certain photos, which she paints over and condenses (ill. 169, 171, 179), while motifs are also produced by the selective nature of the square Polaroid format (ill. 168).

New Photographic Images

In the 1970s, the instant camera was a technical revolution that radically influenced the way images were used and the aesthetics, themes, and content of photography. This offered Jürgenssen a freedom to create that undermined the criteria and standards of professional photography and thus also the assessment of what constitutes a good picture.[21] In her use of this new technique, Jürgenssen was clearly among the avant-garde in Austrian contemporary photography at the time. In the USA, the Polaroid was celebrated by stars like Andy Warhol, and many artists saw it as a kind of canvas onto which they inscribed their individual styles.[22] In Austria, however, the Polaroid was still relatively unappreciated up until the 1980s.[23] For Jürgenssen it was the right way of experimenting with new elements of photographic style.

She utilized the specific features of the Polaroid image development process, manipulating these to create painterly photographic compositions. Once the shutter release has been pressed, the camera itself develops, fixes, and ejects the Polaroid. For a few moments, no image can be seen on the chemical coating of the paper, but gradually colors and shapes emerge. Like Greek American artist Lucas Samaras (ill. 173), who pressed down onto the developing color layers with a stylus to make distorted self-portraits, Jürgenssen also took the Polaroid image to the highest possible levels of painterly quality. While the photos were developing, she pushed and mixed the emulsion layers, leading to flowing color surfaces and trails. In a series of self-portraits from 1978, her faces dissolve into a dynamic and expressive chromatic play and are seen beneath layers of color, as if drowning (ill. 172). In these Polaroids Jürgenssen abandons the self to dissolution, revealing a sense of human vulnerability.

In the nine-part Polaroid tableau *Bath Series, Wounding* (ill. 174) she shows her body in fragments, corresponding to the format of the images. This work is directly related to the *Bath* Polaroids of the same year, which she incorporated into her installation *10 Days – 100 Photos* (ill. 175).[24] In the *Bath* Polaroids Jürgenssen re-enacts »the (media) appearance and disappearance of the female body, the fantasy of the erotic, fetishized, and fragmented female nude from a distance and close up at the same time.«[25] While Jürgenssen developed black-and-white photographs in her own darkroom, color films needed to be taken to the lab—but the artist was too shy to do this because of the nude images they contained.[26] Polaroids thus gave the artist the possibility to explore intimate themes such as pain and bodily and psychological injury.

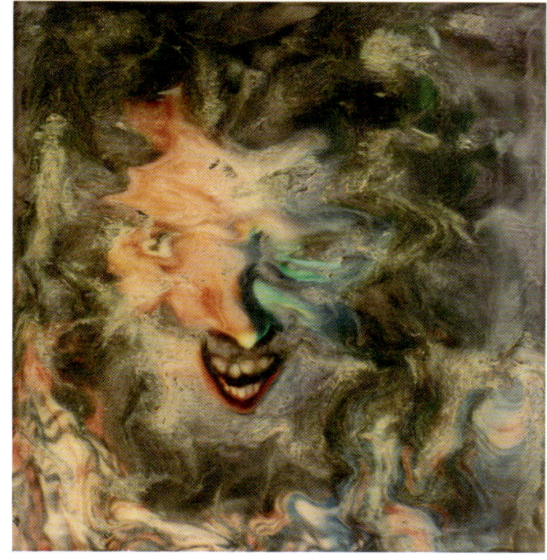

173   Lucas Samaras *Photo-Transformation, 12/13/73* 1973
Internal dye diffusion transfer print (SX-70 Polaroid)
10.8 × 8.9 cm
Photograph by Tom Barratt
© Lucas Samaras, courtesy Pace Gallery

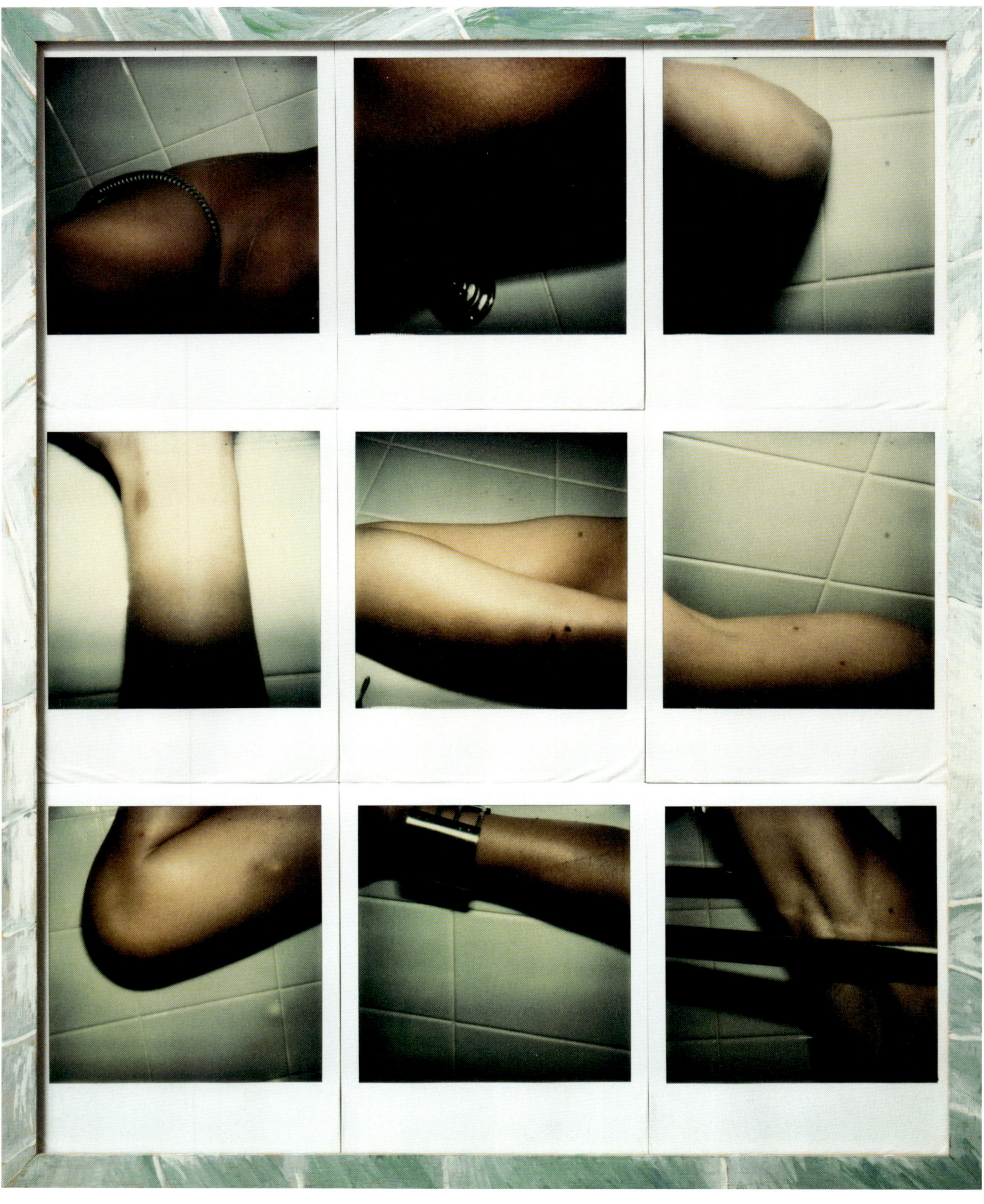

174 *Badeserie, Verletzung* 1980
Bath Series, Wounding

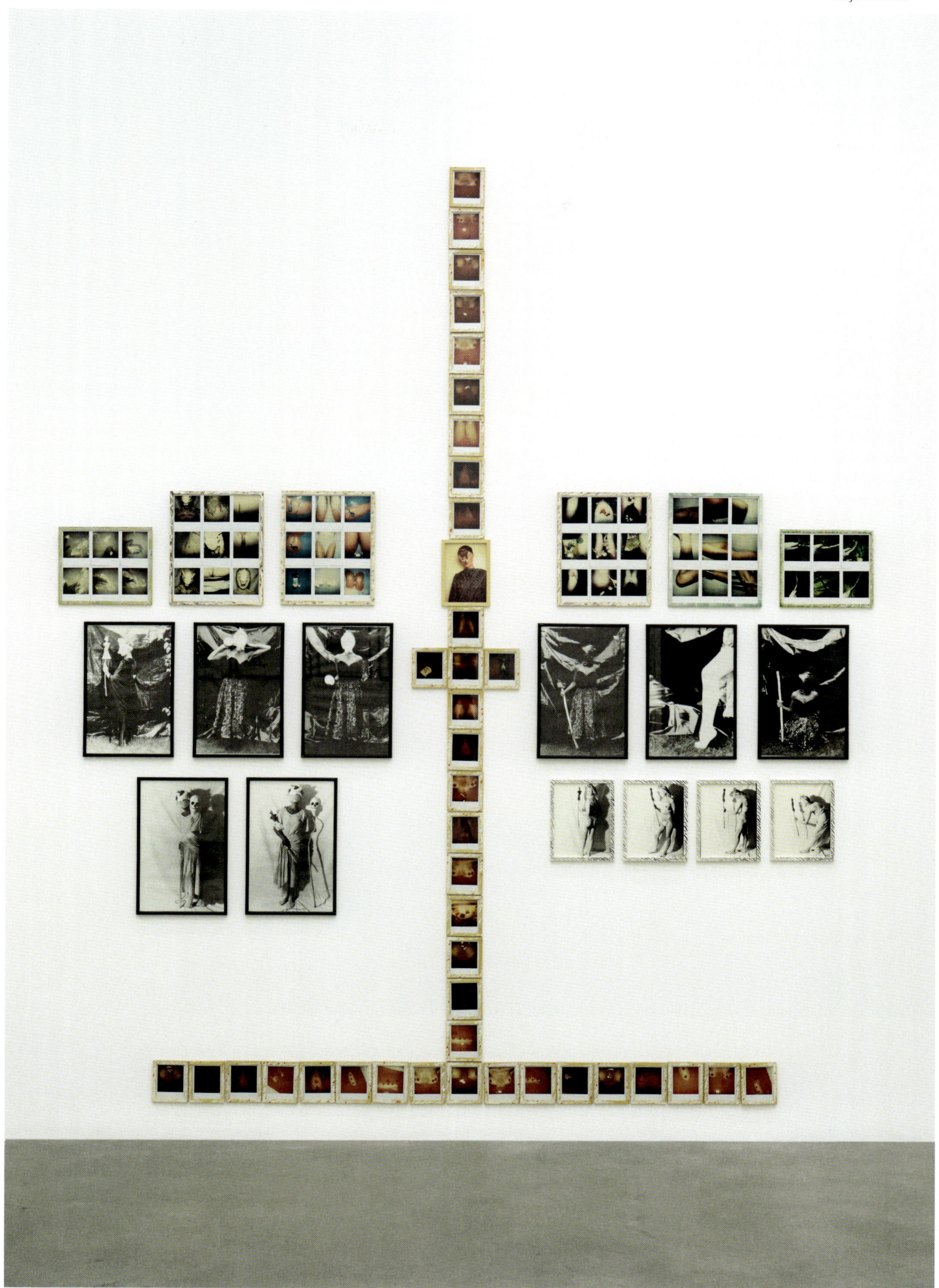

175   *10 Tage – 100 Photos* 1980/1981
       10 Days – 100 Photos

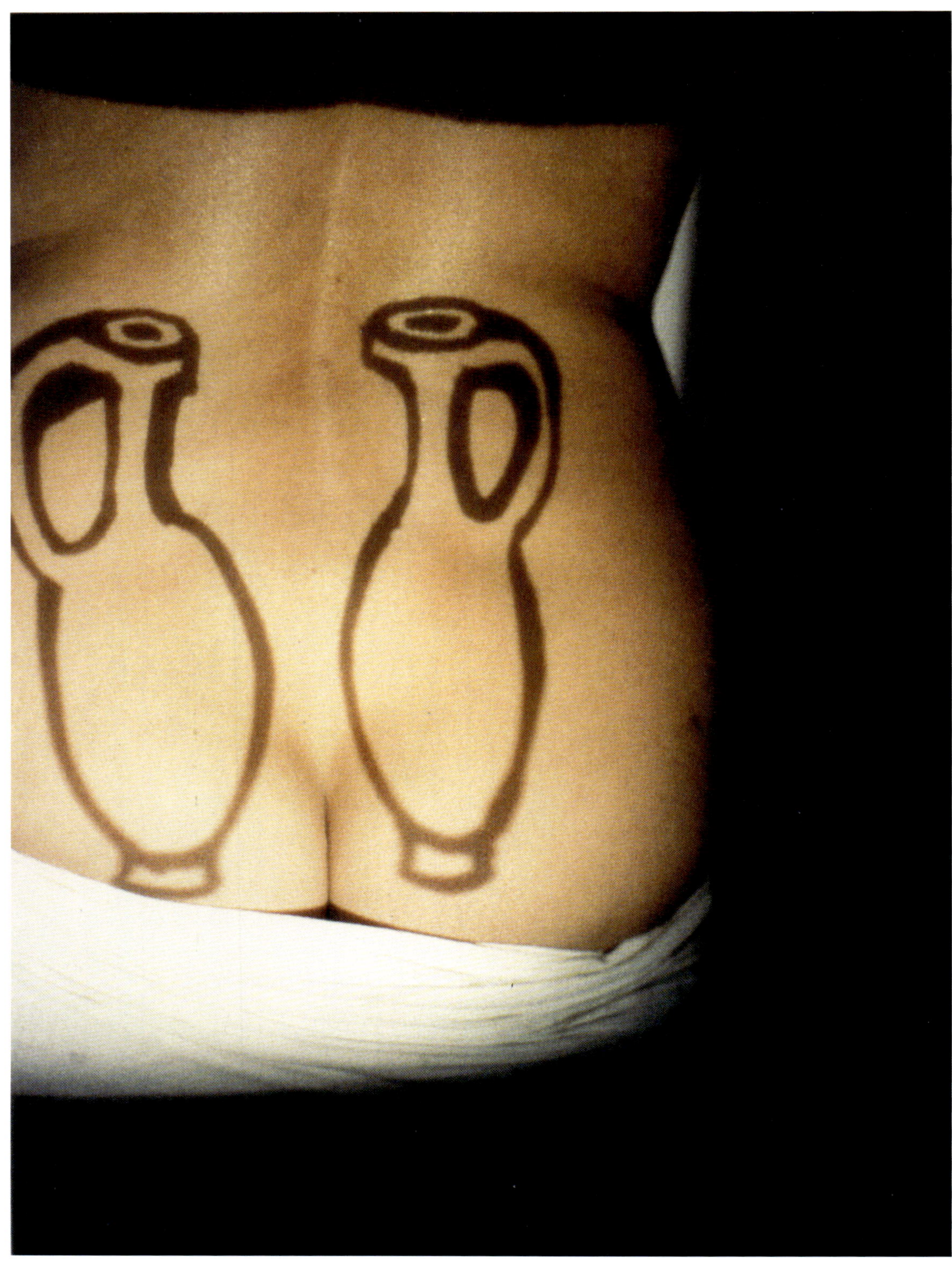

176   *Ohne Titel (Körperprojektion)* 1988
       Untitled (Body Projection)

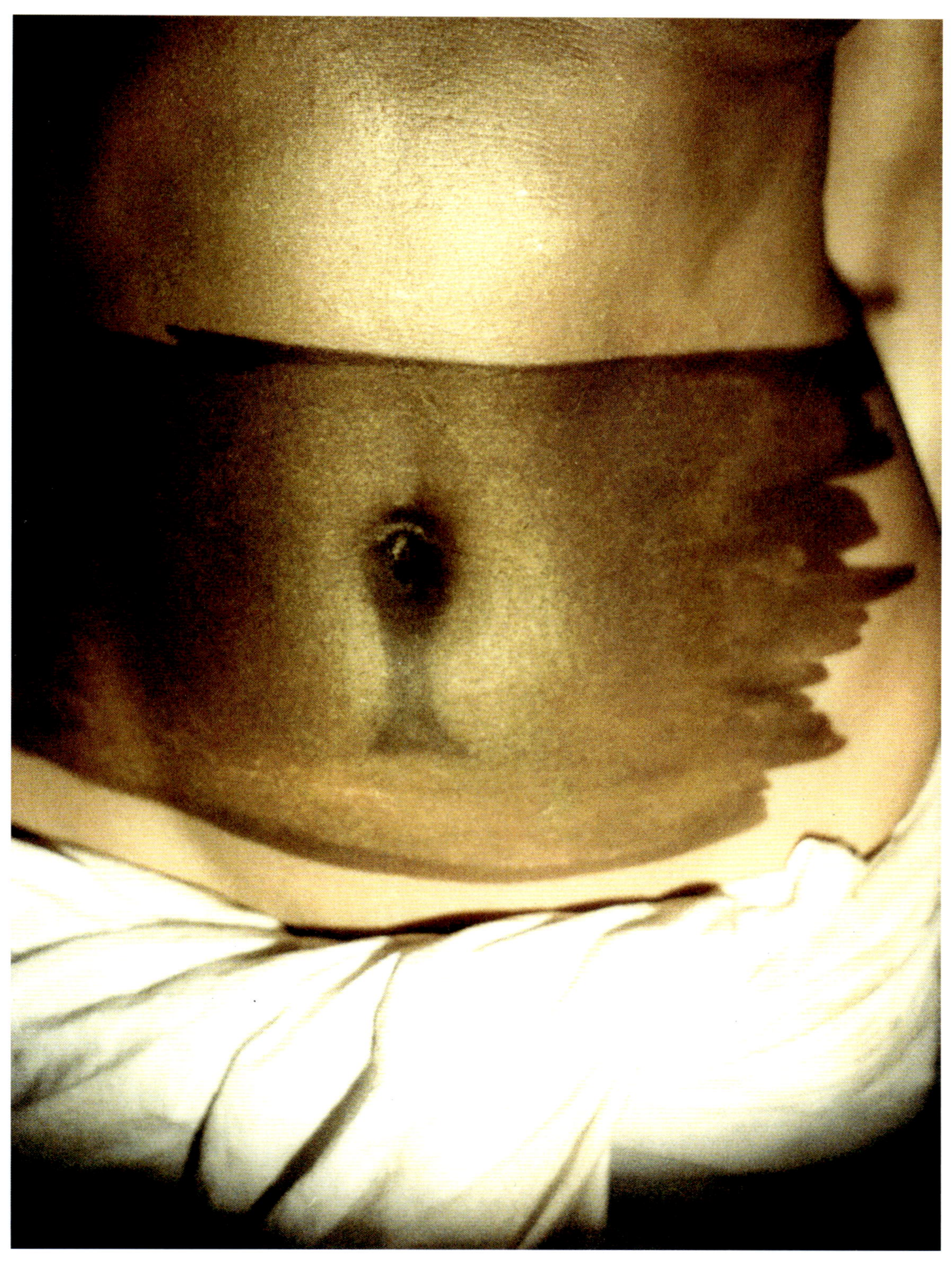

177   *Ohne Titel (Körperprojektion)* 1988
       Untitled (Body Projection)

Even if it did not come about as a result of the same kind of personal experience of the body, there is a further series that belongs to Jürgenssen's work on the experimental dissolution of the body. For the 1999 work *Ranking* (figs. 160, 19) Jürgenssen used documentary black-and-white photographs that she had taken during the action *Schauraufen* in the masterclass of Arnulf Rainer, whom she assisted at the Academy of Fine Arts for twenty years. By means of several processes of transformation, Jürgenssen situated the three female nudes in a new fluid space. She first isolated the photographed bodies from their original setting in the studio, copying them onto transparency and laying this on an overhead projector, where she covered them in liquid bath oils—before photographing this new scenario in color. The image is largely created by the chemical liquids that dissolved parts of the transparency, leading to organic shapes looking like micro-organisms seen under a microscope that seem, on the one hand, to be integrating the human bodies within themselves while also attacking certain parts of these bodies. The effects of these shifts in form and color are akin to the two elements of fire and water, which Jürgenssen connects with the human figures in a similar context. This is not only a playful modern version of the doctrine of the four elements[27] (as was the case in the *Bath* series too) but also a successful new kind of imagery based on the motifs of women fighting with each other, all of which transcended »the scope of what had hitherto been stored in the archives of the formulation of female pathos.«[28]

Expressive Gestures – Between Photography and Painting

The explosive power of Birgit Jürgenssen's approach pushes back the borders of photography. This is very clear in the expressive gestures of her overpainted photographs. The base material for *Untitled* (1979, ill. 179), a black-and-white photograph, is a female nude seen from the back, which Jürgenssen boldly overpainted with the complementary colors red and green. In this artistic move, the usual distance between object and photographer gives way to emotion. As in the expressionist painting of the early twentieth century, this picture shows an inner world of the imagination that transcends the function of photography as a mirror of visible reality. The black overpainting on the back of the nude's head can be seen as a mask-like face. And on the back of the women, Jürgenssen has painted female breasts. To the right, there is a vague impression of a second figure that seems to refer to Pablo Picasso's women in his painting *Les Demoiselles d'Avignon* (1907, ill. 178). By drawing on primitivism and the expressionist tradition in painting and thereby imitating the appropriation and deconstruction of woman by the painter, Jürgenssen exposes the structural power relations and the projection of male fantasies onto women. As Abigail Solomon-Godeau writes, »Her working method exposes the rhetorical language of expressionism, its status as just another representational and stylistic convention [...]. Jürgenssen's appropriation of this most ›masculine‹ of painterly or graphic procedures is another tactic of détournement.«[29] In this strategy, Jürgenssen not only cites expressionist modernism but also reveals power structures perpetuated in her own time. Her overpainted photographs are reminiscent of overpainted works from Arnulf Rainer's 1977 series *Cycle: Women's Language*, in which he painted over a number of often highly aggressive erotic and pornographic images. Rainer understood painting as a solely male form of art, and he said straight out that women could not paint.[30]

Between 1983 and 1987, Jürgenssen created a group of works in the darkroom she had set up in the Academy—large-format, square photograms in which she completely transferred photography into painting (ill. 180). These are abstract pictures on which individual abstracted motifs can be identified. Jürgenssen moved the light-sensitive photographic paper in the developing and fixing baths, leading to a flowing marbling effect in various gray tones. She poured chemicals onto these, which left dark traces.[31] Then she intervened directly into the material, damaging it by cutting slits in the surface and leaving the edges uneven, torn, or folded. Jürgenssen was a highly skilled draughtswoman. In her »painted photographs« she did not pursue the perfection typical of her drawings

[27] See Geraldine Spiekermann, »What She Saw in the Water: The *Bath*-Polaroids by Birgit Jürgenssen,« in Schor and Solomon-Godeau, *Birgit Jürgenssen* (see n. 5), pp. 207–218, here: p. 213.

[28] Elisabeth von Samsonow, »Birgit Jürgenssen: Sparta unterm Schminktisch,« *Eikon: Internationale Zeitschrift für Photographie und Medienkunst* 28 (1999), pp. 4–9, here: p. 4 [translated].

[29] Abigail Solomon-Godeau, »Birgit Jürgenssen: Between the Lines, beyond the Boundaries,« in Schor and Solomon-Godeau, *Birgit Jürgenssen* (see n. 5), pp. 107–44, here: p. 124. Here Solomon-Godeau also refers to Picasso's studies on *Les Demoiselles d'Avignon* in connection with Jürgenssen's painting *Mama 6* (p. 125).

[30] See »Birgit Jürgenssen in conversation with Rainer Metzger, 2003,« in Gabriele Schor and Heike Eipeldauer (eds.), *Birgit Jürgenssen*, exh. cat. Kunstforum, Vienna, (Munich: Prestel, 2010), p. 276.

[31] See Katharina Sykora, »Hautbild/Bildhaut oder ein Blatt wird gewendet,« in Schor and Eipeldauer, *Birgit Jürgenssen* (see n. 9), pp. 57–72, here: p. 65.

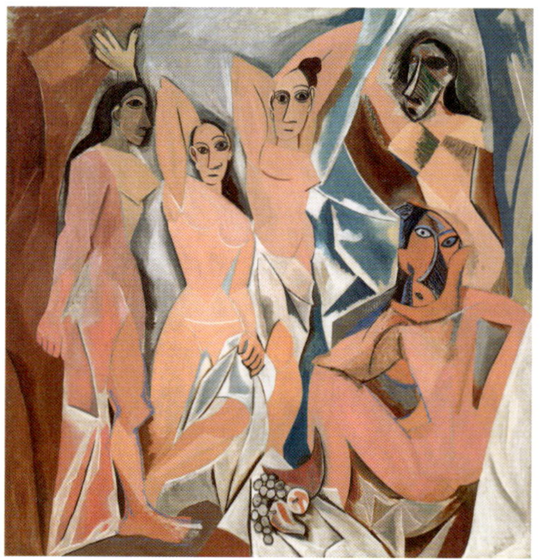

178   Pablo Picasso *Les Demoiselles d'Avignon* 1907
Oil on canvas
243.9 × 233.7 cm
MoMA – Museum of Modern Art, New York
Acquired through the Lillie P. Bliss Bequest. 333.1939
© 2018. Digital image, The Museum of Modern Art, New York/Scala, Florence

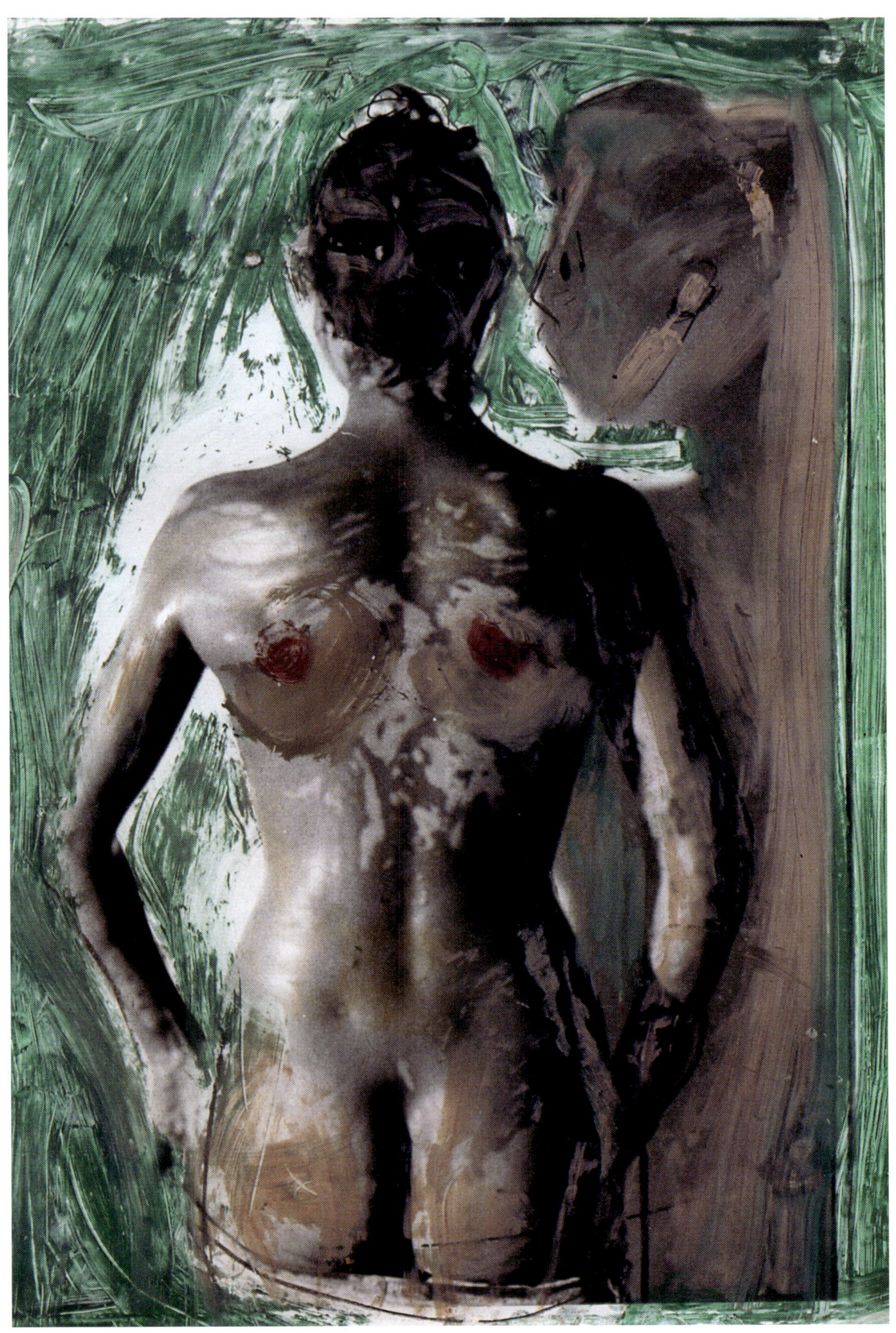

179   *Ohne Titel* 1979
        Untitled

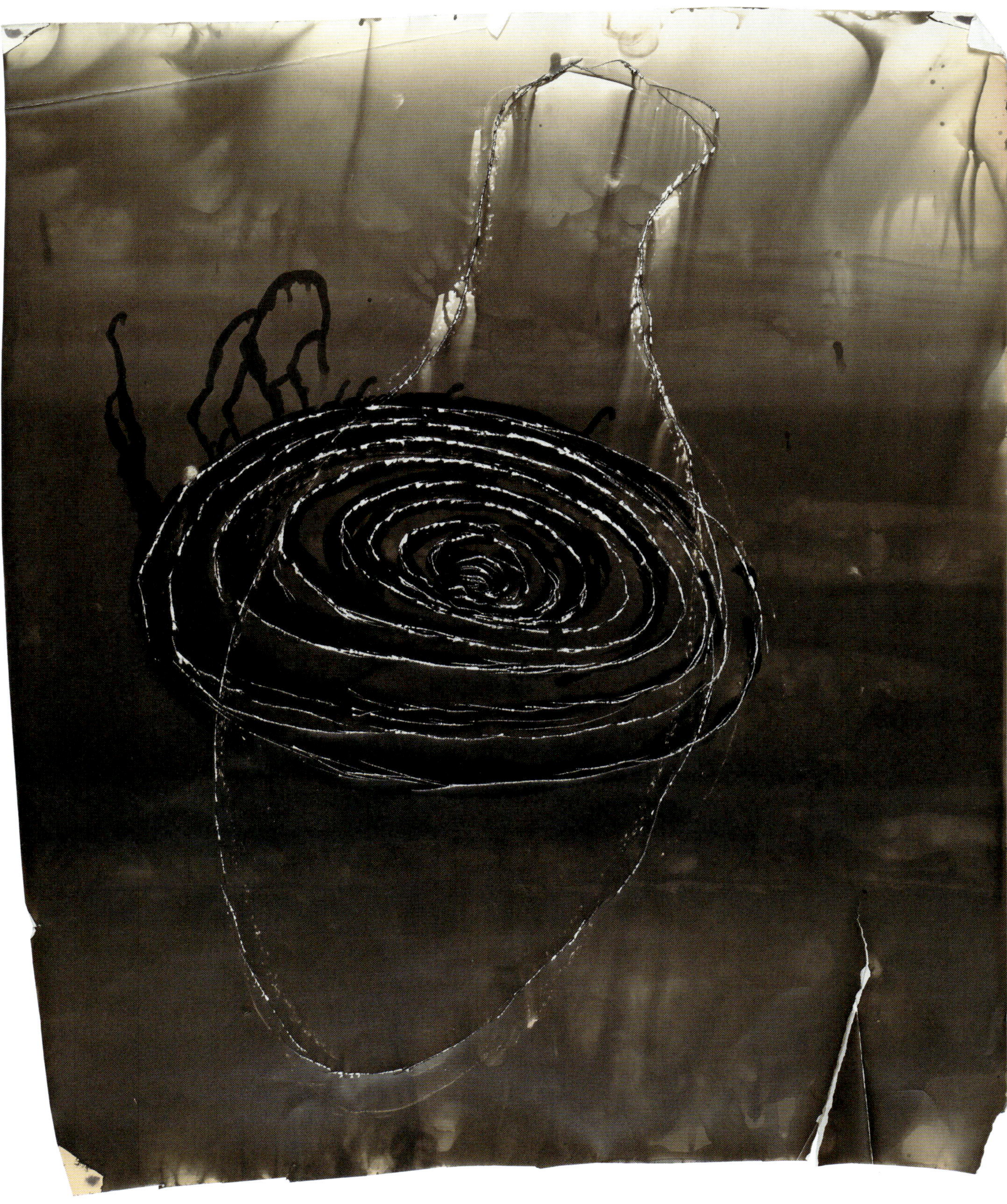

180 *Ohne Titel* 1983–1987
     Untitled

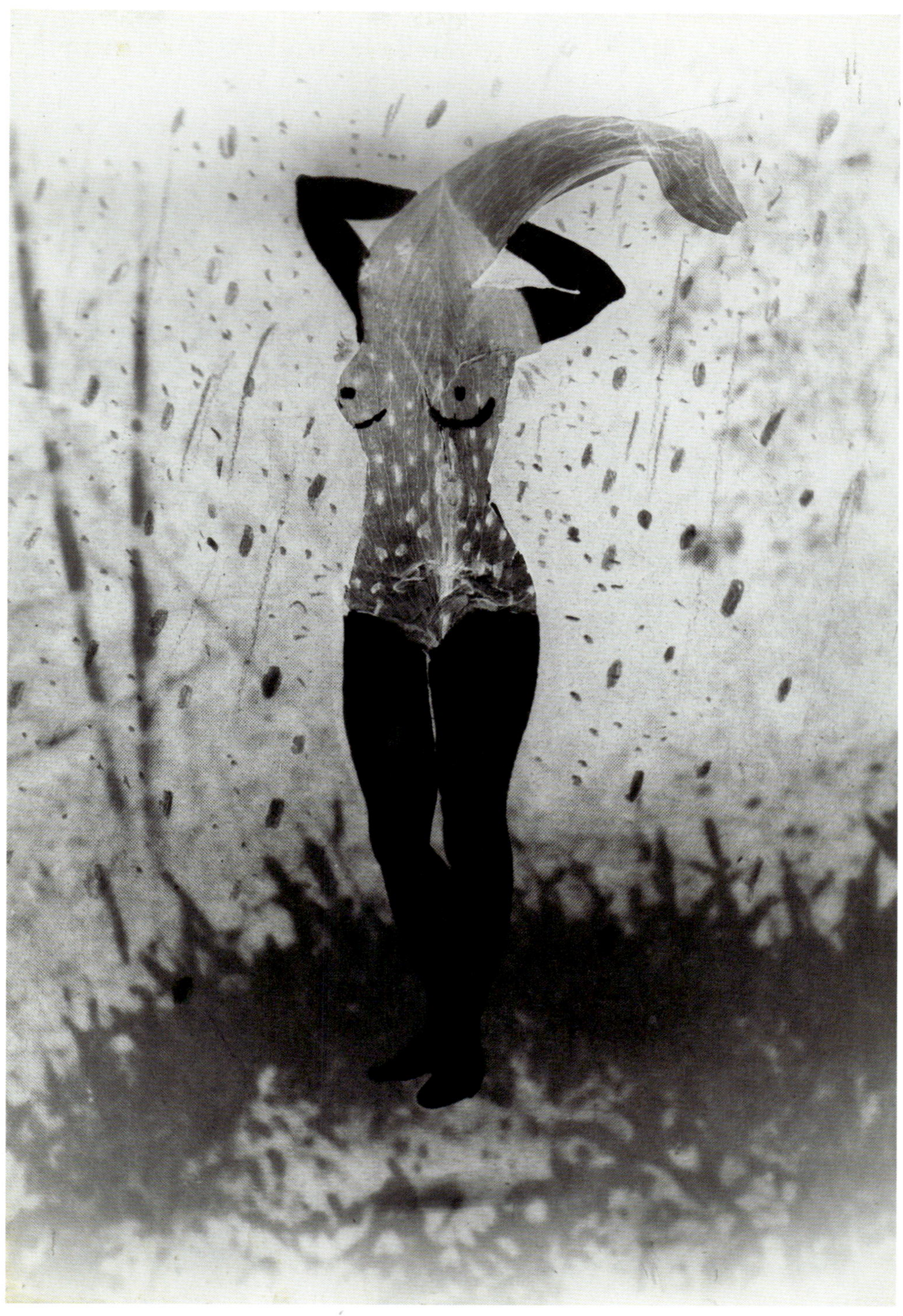

181   *Ohne Titel (Naturgeschichte)* 1975
       Untitled (Natural History)

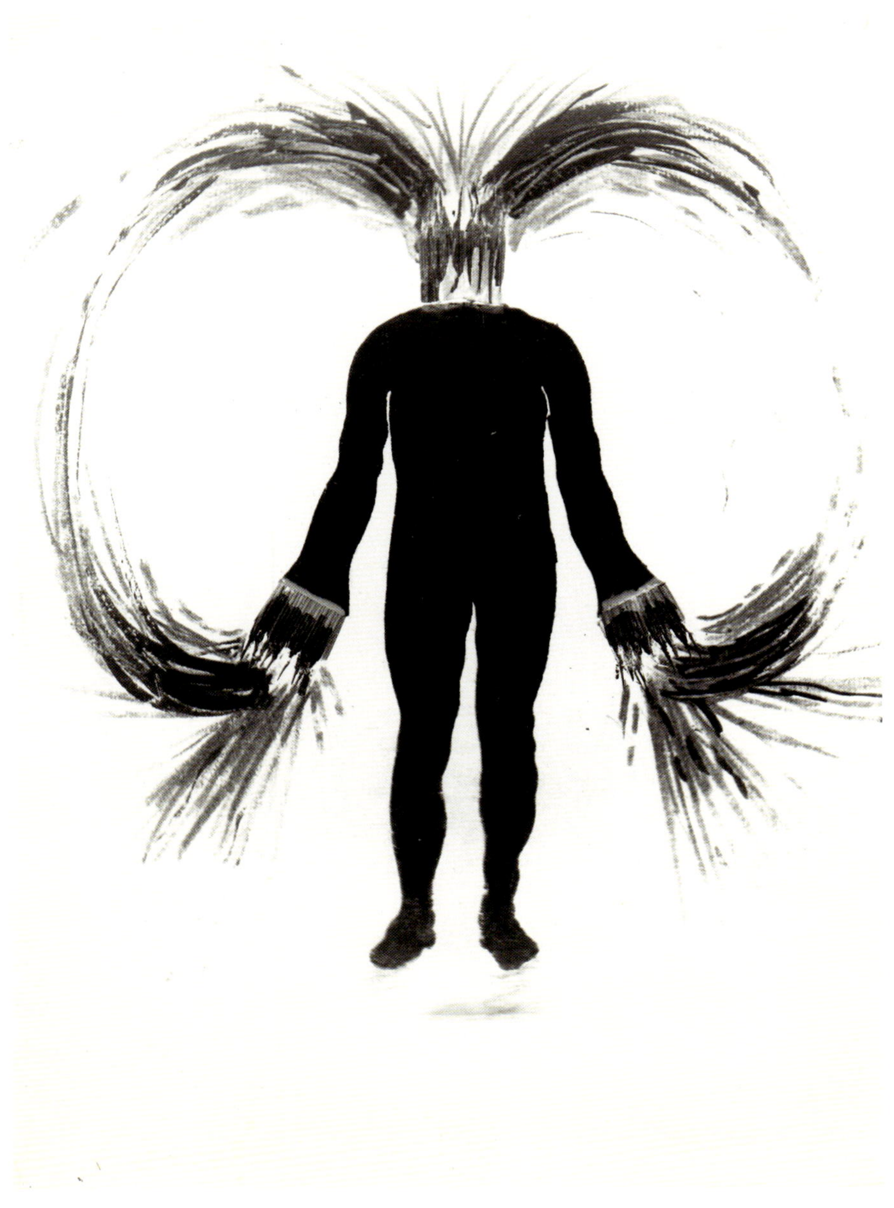

182   *Ohne Titel* 1975
       Untitled

[32] A comprehensive text by Margit Zuckriegl on the *Body Projections* is in the exhibition catalogue *Birgit Jürgenssen: Früher oder später* (see n. 25), pp. 69–73.

[33] Sykora, »Hautbild/ Bildhaut« (see n. 30), p. 65 [translated].

[34] Floris M. Neusüss, *Anwesenheit bei Abwesenheit: Fotogramme und die Kunst des 20. Jahrhunderts*, exh. cat., Kunsthaus Zürich (Zurich: Schweizerische Stiftung für die Photographie, 1990), p. 8 [translated].

[35] See Susan Sontag, *On Photography* (see n. 10), p. 40.

[36] See Emmanuelle de l'Ecotais, »Man Ray: Der Erfinder der surrealistischen Fotografie,« in *Man Ray 1890–1976*, exh. cat. (Cologne: Taschen, 2000), pp. 77–85, here: p. 81.

but instead consciously aimed at a more gestural form of expression. The compositions drew on existing movements, extending them and using lines as countering movements expressing tension. More peaceful areas were given scored textures. It is powers inherent to the body and to the inner psyche that are manifested here on paper. And these pictures remain symbolically tied up with the female body, such as when their abstraction leads to simplified figurative forms like vases—a container that Jürgenssen explores as an analogy to the female body, as Katharina Sykora has shown in her text »Hautbild/ Bildhaut« (Skin Picture/Picture Skin). In a photograph of her *Body Projections*, another of her experimental methods,[32] for example, Jürgenssen projected two vases directly onto her skin (ill. 176). In the painted photographs, vases become the general signifier of »a skin image that is written into or torn out of the picture skin against its own resistance.«[33] In this, Jürgenssen's drawings are like injuries or wounds. The surface texture is also marked by the figure of the house, an ambiguous and emotionally charged space that can symbolize both a sheltering refuge and also a place of imprisonment for the woman—as in the *Femme-Maison* works by Louise Bourgeois, whom Jürgenssen felt to be a kindred spirit in artistic terms.

Cameraless Methods

»Sketches from a world beyond the visible, hidden directly behind our everyday world.«[34] In her volume of essays *On Photography*, Susan Sontag wrote that surrealism was inherent to the nature of photography. For Sontag, photography creates a second-degree reality that we cannot see with our eyes.[35] It is this invisible reality that Birgit Jürgenssen explores. An appropriate medium for her surrealist-style pictorial worlds was the rayogram, a photographic procedure without a camera and without a lens. Objects are placed directly on photographic paper and then exposed to light. When the picture is developed, the dark and light values are exchanged, and bodies look like areas of shadow, removed from space and time. Like Man Ray, Jürgenssen transforms the well-known into a new unknown outward form, opening the mind up to a new reality.[36]

Jürgenssen is not interested in the realistic depiction of things but in the relations between them, which assume form in her rayograms. In these works, she opens up associative and narrative spaces that alternate between the imagination and reality. In her *Natural Histories*, for example, Jürgenssen transforms the human body, animals, and plants into dreamlike surrealist scenarios with strange hybrid creatures, telling the stories of an enchanted animistic world typical of fairy tales and popular stories. Through techniques of overlapping, she creates connections between the physical cycles of both human and vegetable life, making hidden structures visible and evoking ancient ideas of the microcosm and macrocosm. Drawing on the notion that the earth, like the human body, has internal organs, Jürgenssen turns the idea on its head and equates the human body with the system of veins on leaves (ill. 55). What we can see in these works is the fragile relationship between humanity and nature. Artists in particular were very aware of and reacted to the vulnerability of society in the 1970s, the fragility of civilizational and ecological systems. Jürgenssen's rayograms represent a view that emphasizes the inner connectedness of humanity and nature. In this, the *Natural Histories* (ill. 52–55) also refer to the knowledge and the rich associations of natural philosophy and encyclopedic thought, to the dualism of nature and culture, and also to clichéd correlations between woman and nature, such as when Jürgenssen draws stylized breasts on her natural creatures or sees a leaf as representing femininity (ill. 181). This is an image that is deeply anchored in our collective memory, and which becomes productive in the photographic work of Otto Steinert and in Floris Neusüss's photograms, for example (ill. 183).

Whereas Neusüss worked with female nude models, Jürgenssen used cuttings from magazines and newspapers, templates from her own collection of images that she playfully varied. Her rayograms are intensive reflections on the formal potential of the medium and the territory beyond it. In her work *Untitled* (1975, ill. 182), Jürgenssen presents

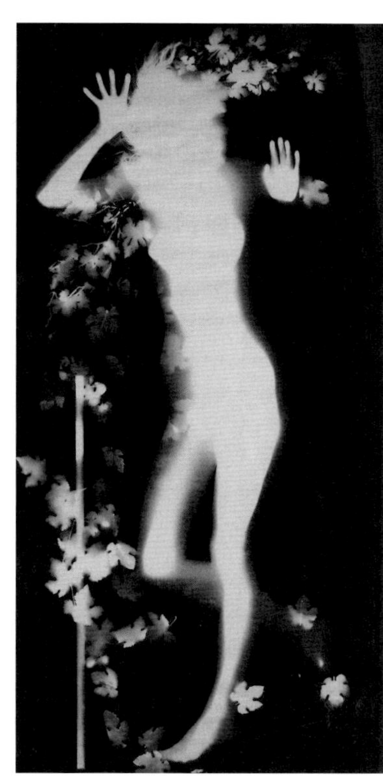

183   Floris Neusüss *Untitled* 1964
Photogram
200 × 103.5 cm
© Floris Neusüss, courtesy: Daniel Blau, Munich

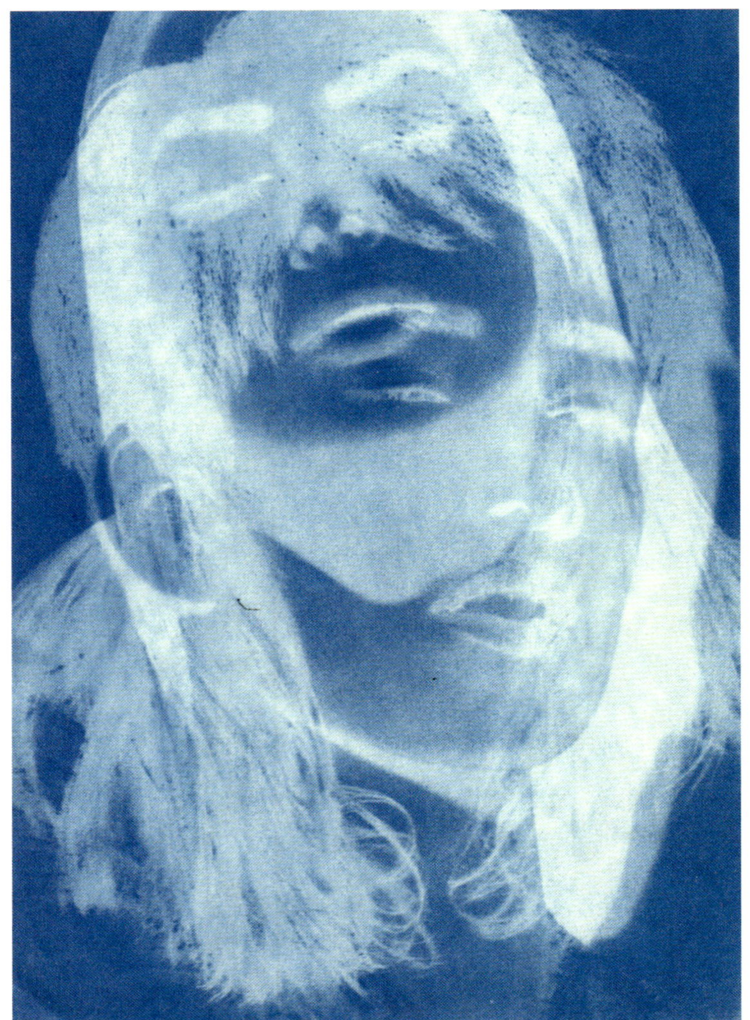 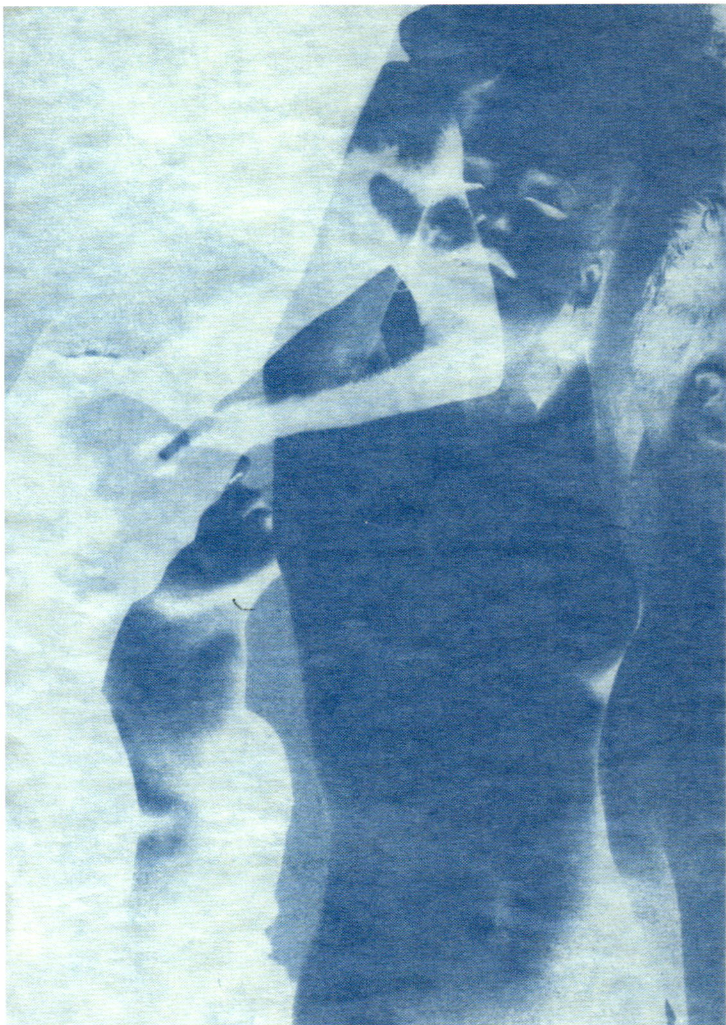

184   *Ohne Titel* 1988/1989
       Untitled
185   *Ohne Titel* 1988/1989
       Untitled

[37] See »Birgit Jürgenssen: Cyanotypes from the years 1988/89,« Estate Birgit Jürgenssen, accessed July 18, 2018, https://birgitjuergenssen.com/ausstellungen/einzelausstellungen/birgit-juergenssen-cyanotypien-von-1988-89.

[38] Wassily Kandinsky, *On the Spiritual in Art* (New York: Guggenheim, 1946), p. 55.

[39] In 1842 the English scientist and astronomer John Herschel developed the cyanotype process. The English botanist and early woman photographer Anna Atkins used Herschel's technique shortly thereafter in her books. For a long time, the cyanotype was not credited as an artistic method of producing high-quality photographic prints.

[40] See Iris Strohner, »Birgit Jürgenssen: Cyanotypes from 1988/89,« Estate Birgit Jürgenssen, accessed July 18, 2018, https://birgitjuergenssen.com/bibliographie/ausstellungskritiken/strohner2012.

the human figure as a living paintbrush in the most literal sense of the word. In a gestural movement, she links the head and the hands, which she has transformed into brushes. This is a picture that addresses the unity of mind and body as an active, executive whole. As in many of Jürgenssen's works, a painterly approach finds its way into the photograph as an emotional gesture. The source of light here is the tool that Jürgenssen guided across the paper. Like Man Ray, she uses this cameraless method to show that photography is no mere documentary medium but can be used for the presentation of artistic visions and ideas.

Jürgenssen's cyanotypes of 1988 and 1989 also seem like fragments of a dream (figs. 184, 185). This is a group of a total of 250 works in subtle blue tones. The figures are reminiscent of photos of ghosts from the nineteenth century, ephemeral, wraithlike, and undergoing transformation through a process of superimposition, as in the rayograms. They dissolve into color, light, surface, and structure. This group of works can serve particularly well to describe how Birgit Jürgenssen worked. When she discovered a new medium, she always worked intensively with it, testing all its formal options. Crossing over media, she would draw on and reuse motifs from her own personal iconography, leading to networks of connections. The motif of the animal-human, for example (ill. 95), which she used performatively in 1974 in her photograph *Self with Little Fur* (ill. 9), then again in the Polaroid series *Olga* (1979, ill. 23), and in a series of collages in 1980 (ill. 139), also featured in her cyanotypes. And there is the theme of self-analysis in front of a mirror, in which the self is now completely dissolved and beyond all identification. The fragility of these scenarios is heightened by the fine silky paper that Jürgenssen had sent from New York. Cyanotypes work on the basis of the paper being coated in a light-sensitive solution containing iron. The dried and sensitized paper is covered with negatives or objects and then exposed to ultraviolet light, which creates the characteristic blue that is embedded in the structure of the paper fibers. Located in the realm of metaphysics, for Jürgenssen the color blue symbolized eternity,[37] and, as Wassily Kandinsky put it in his text *On the Spiritual in Art*, it was a »principle of inner necessity«[38] that speaks deeply to the human soul.

By using this technique, which was invented back in 1842, the past and the present, reality and dreams all become one in the images, and in drawing on these cameraless techniques Jürgenssen was updating methods to which artists in the 1970s paid only little attention. Jürgenssen's love of experimentation not only led her to take up forgotten techniques; her rediscovery of women artists such as Anna Atkins[39] and Claude Cahun also led to greater visibility for the hidden traces of female creativity.[40]

Physicality and Materiality

In many respects, the work of Birgit Jürgenssen is about physicality, sensuality, and materiality. While the body plays a key role in her early work, and in the course of her œuvre it becomes more and more dissolved in photographic and chemical processes, in the 1990s it again »gained weight«—in two ways. Jürgenssen created a group of large-format photo works that she laminated onto canvas and combined to form tableaux. Framed individually in metal or wooden frames, these photos move from two dimensions into three, leading to new levels of perception. They are covered in transparent gauzes, giving them a haptic character. Reflecting light makes the flowing structures of the material visible, and here Jürgenssen adds remarkable sensuality to the coldness of the medium of photography.[41]

Untitled from 1991 (ill. 186) consists of six color photos that shimmer in gold through gauze and light. The four outer pictures are of soft textiles with folds. Modeled through the effects of light and shade, they have a great materiality to them. The lower central panel shows three lamps that seem to add further optical intensity to the shining textiles. While the movement of the textile on the lower left seems to be continued in the movement of the female figure seen from behind in the upper middle panel, the materials are also connected to the clothes of the male figure. The figures are Pygmalion

from Ovid's *Metamorphoses* and Galatea. According to the myth, Pygmalion created
an ivory sculpture that looked as if it were alive, which Aphrodite then breathed life into
in recognition of his love for it. Jürgenssen draws on a section of a painting by the
French artist Jean-Léon Gérôme, who focuses on the movements of the two bodies. The
selection of the excerpt and the representation of the material are inspired by the
Renaissance painting *Jupiter and Io* by Correggio, which was one of Jürgenssen's favorite
works in Vienna's Kunsthistorisches Museum. Mimicking a metamorphosis, she transforms photography into painting, and photographic painting into sculptural objects that
she endows with something active and organic. In this way, she gives the depicted
textiles their own materiality back. As the seduced, Jürgenssen, so she says, wishes
to seduce again, to make veiling visible by veiling, playing with illusion and reality. The
approach may be a surrealist practice, but Jürgenssen is more interested in a pictorial
attitude and in the relations that form and space have to other forms or colors.[42]

    This game with the repertoire of pictorial options runs through Birgit Jürgenssen's
entire photographic work, which displays a virtuoso and undogmatic artist's thirst for
knowledge, the enjoyment of reflection, and the affirmation of diversities. Jürgenssen's
approach to photography can be seen as being very much in line with Breton, who
wanted to see the »mechanisms of artistic creation [...] freed from any constraint.«[43]

[41] See Birgit Jürgenssen,
»Ich beschäftige mich
mit Fotografie …,« in Schor
and Eipeldauer, *Birgit
Jürgenssen* (see n. 9), p. 240.
[42] Ibid.
[43] André Breton, »The Art
of the Insane, the Door
to Freedom,« in *Free Rein
(La Clé des champs)*,
trans. Michel Parmentier
and Jacqueline d'Amboise
(Lincoln: University
of Nebraska Press, 1995),
pp. 217–20, here: p. 220.

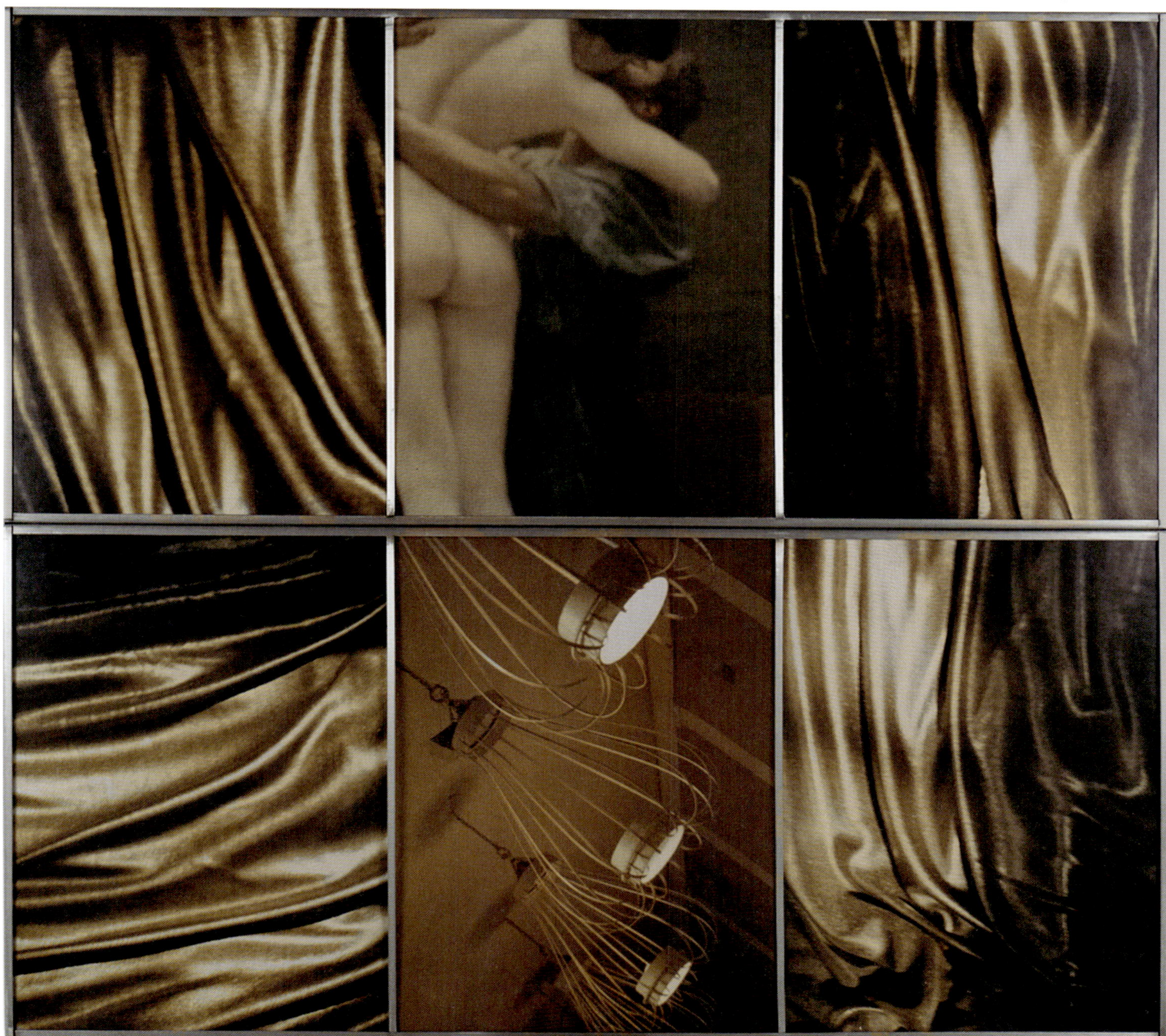

186   *Ohne Titel* 1991
       Untitled

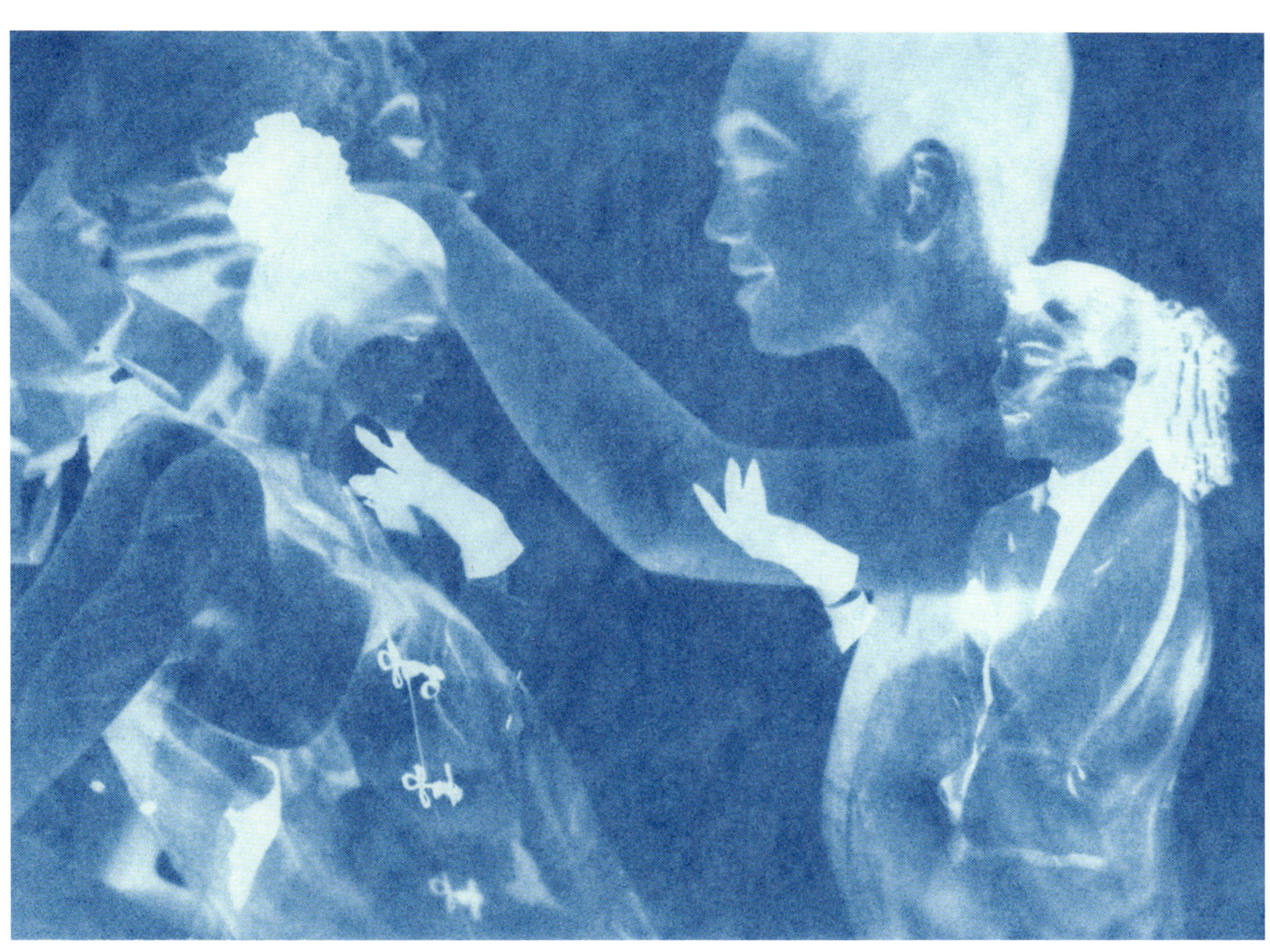

<u>187</u>   *Ohne Titel* 1988/1989
       Untitled

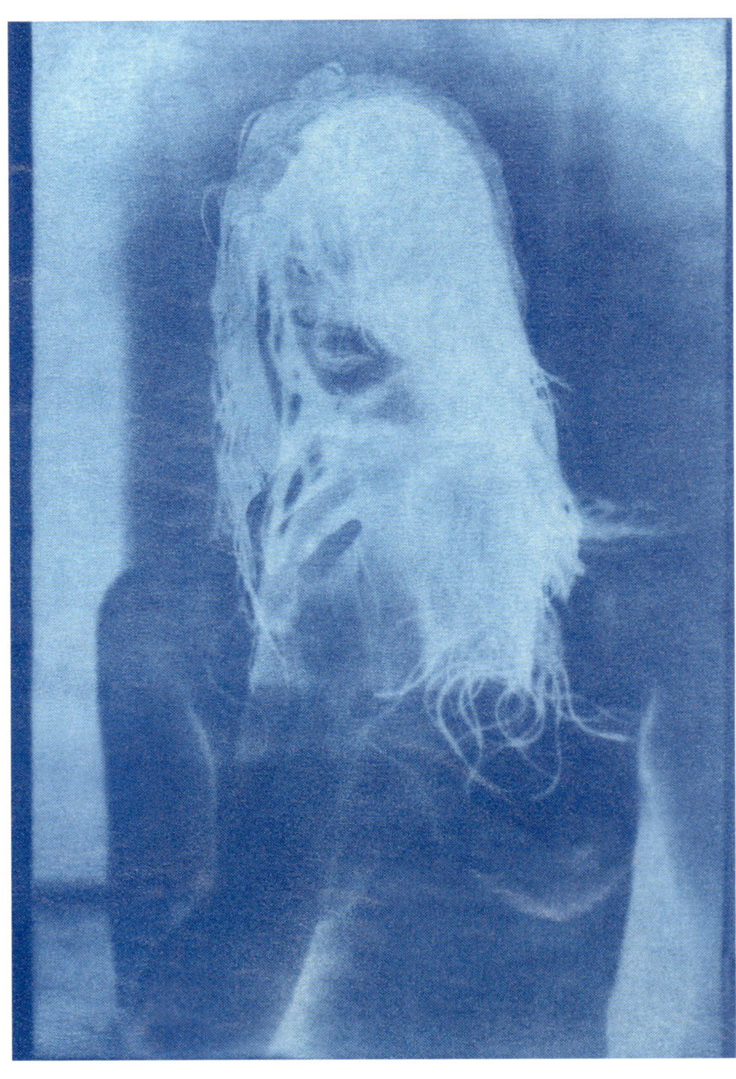

188 *Ohne Titel* 1988/1989
     Untitled

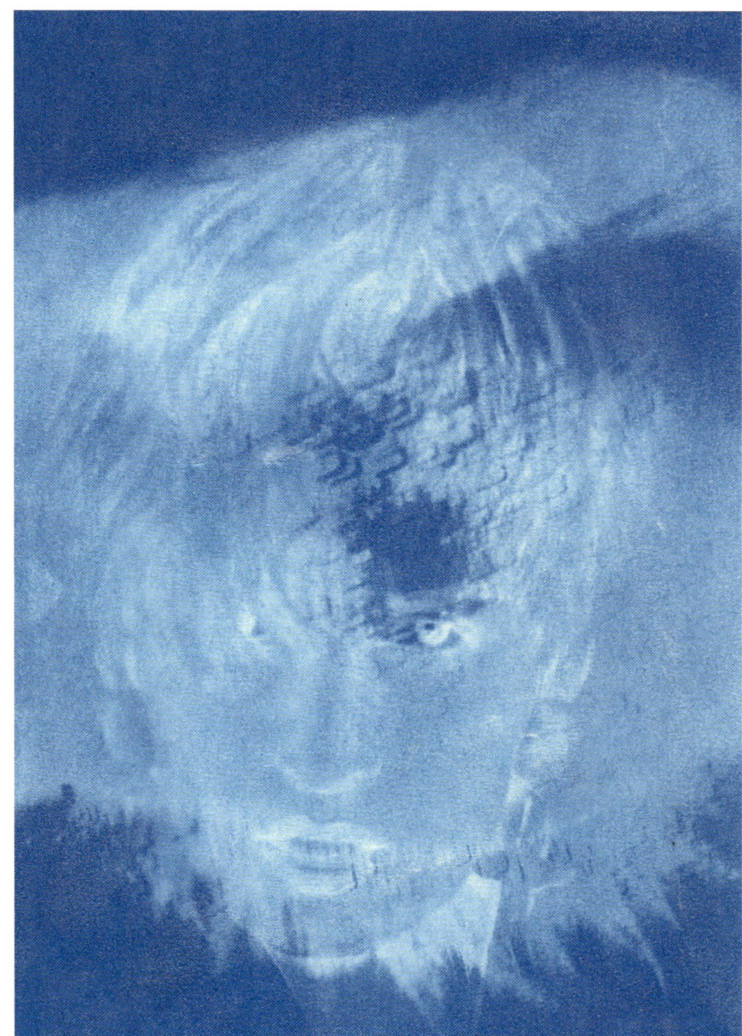
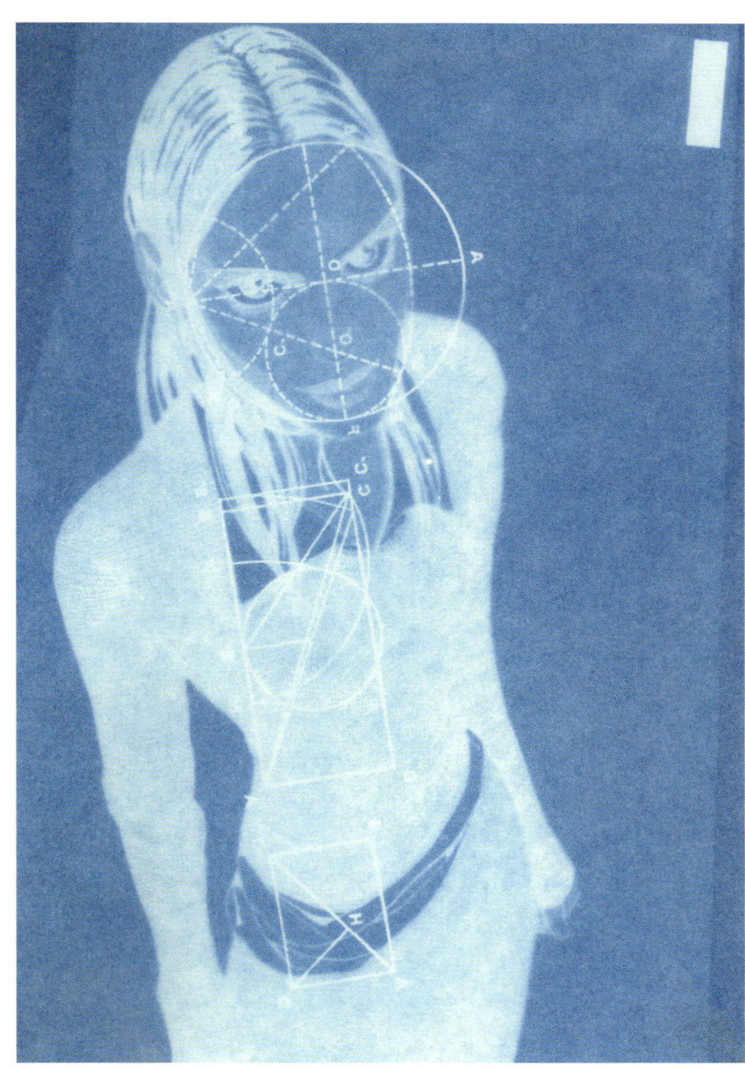

189 *Ohne Titel* 1988/1989
Untitled
190 *Ohne Titel* 1988/1989
Untitled

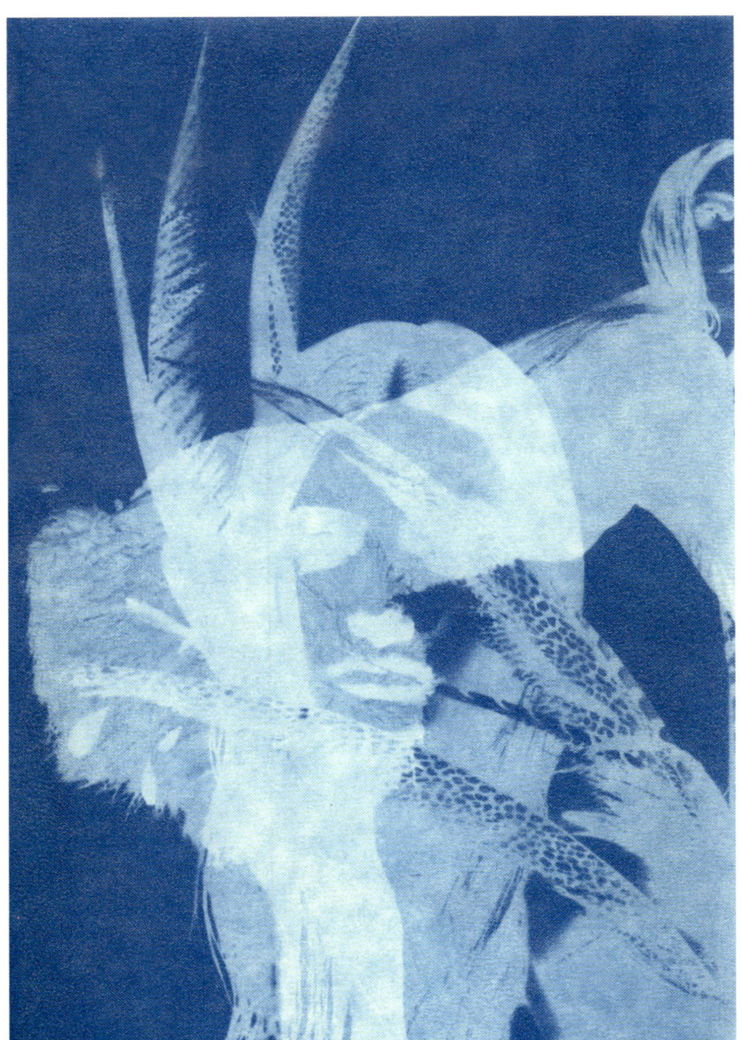 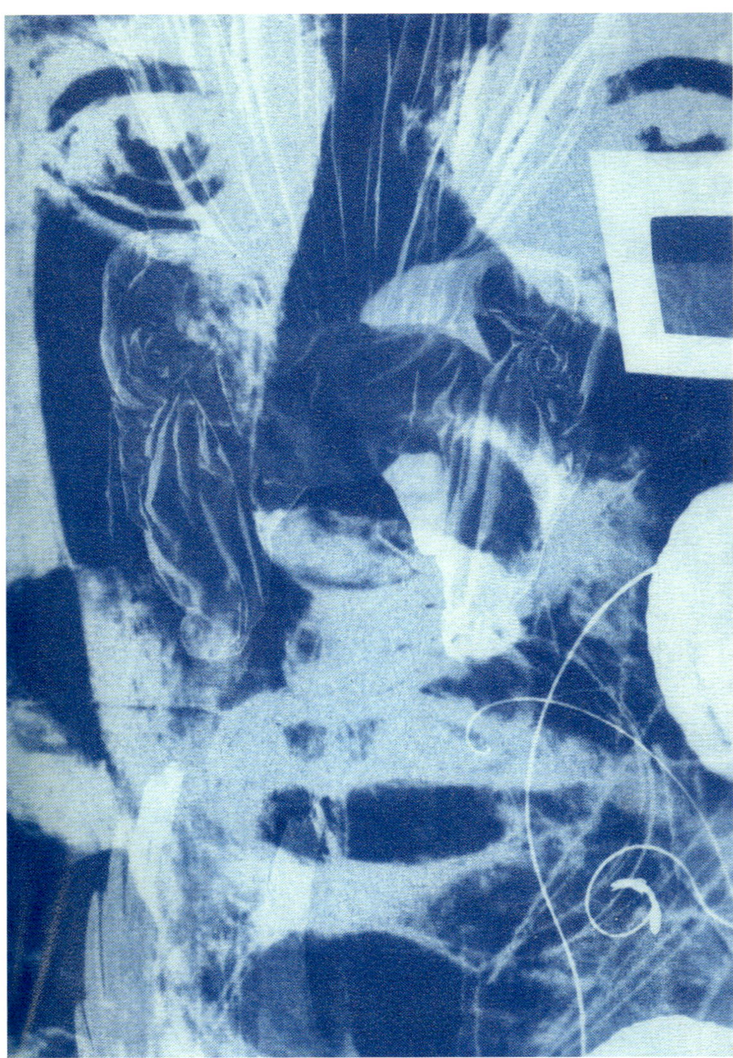

191 *Ohne Titel* 1988/1989
    Untitled
192 *Ohne Titel* 1988/1989
    Untitled

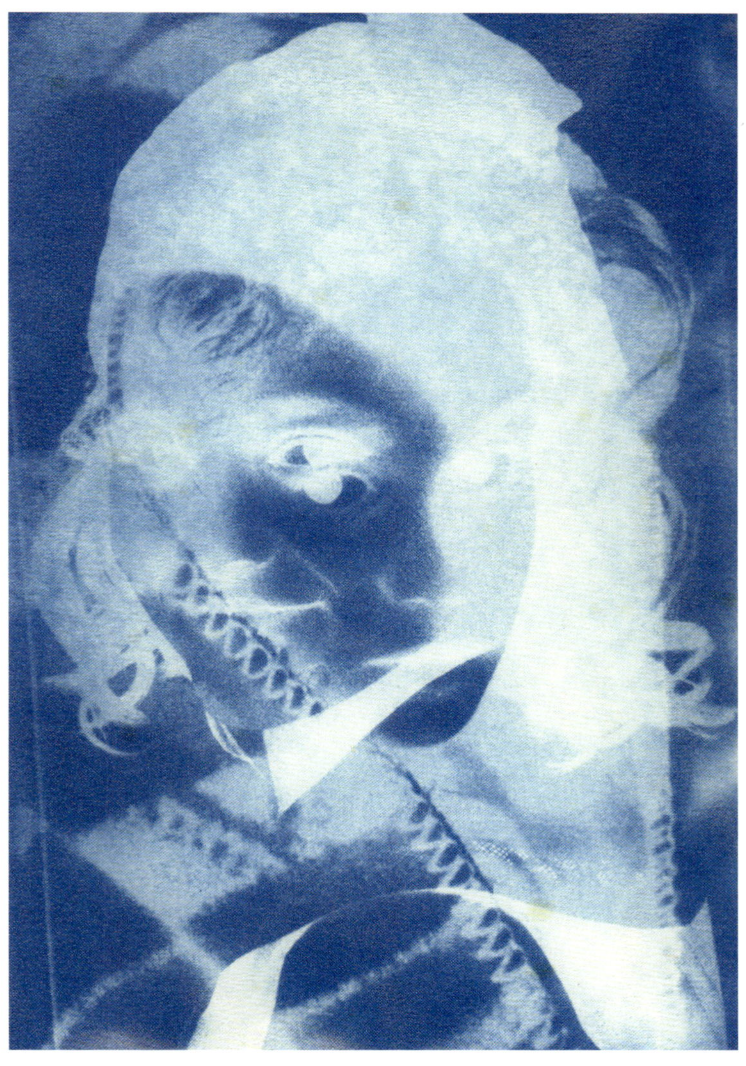

193   *Ohne Titel* 1988/1989
       Untitled

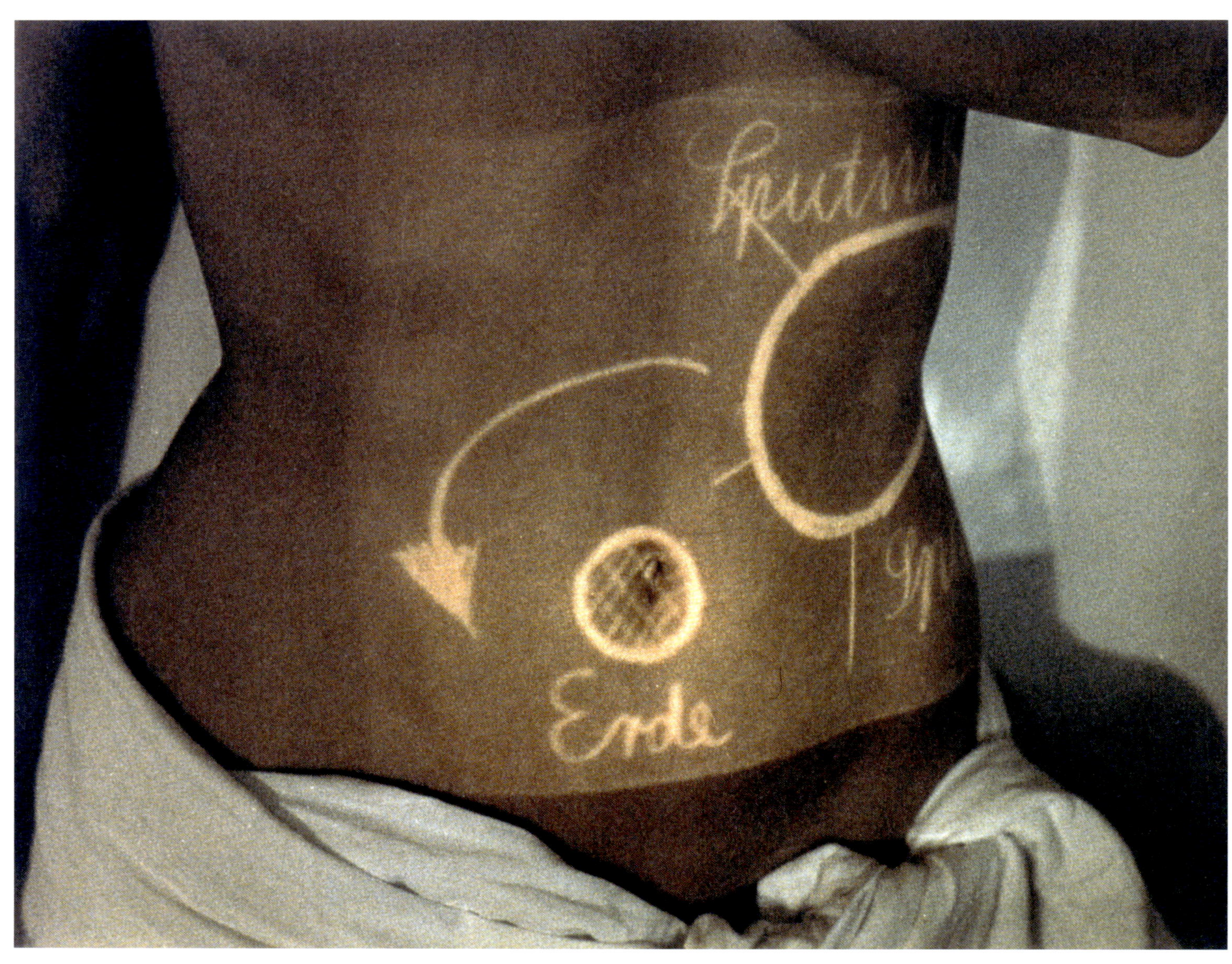

194 *Ohne Titel (Körperprojektion)* 1988
Untitled (Body Projection)

Lieblingsfarbe · Schwarz
bevorzugte Farbe

TABOO – TATOO
____
Projection

BASIC SENSE OF DESIRE

Body — "(no)reality" — essentially untouchable.
— and therefore transgressive. ˣ Projection auf
(Pornography a political issue) den Körper —
IS SHOCK THE BEST WAY TO BREAK THROUGH
bourgeois HABIT? — better breaking taboos
or transgressions — with both in form and in
content.

— hot subject — you'd see all the hypocrixy
and the real + political biases of the society.
Connection between power and society →
it's basically a world view. There's also the
use of non-social realist language and imagery
that is very involved with areas of the mind
which are not rational: It's almost like we
all have the same favorite color — black.

→ Liste von Surrealisten, Baudelaire, Rimbaud,
Lautremont, Bataille, Artaud, de Sade, Genet...
Breton, Leiris, Klossowski!
→ the idea that daily reality is partly a lie
covering up emotion and sexuality, the Body
generally. ???
— this art bios is about transcending limits.
— it's about seeing — seeing almost becomes

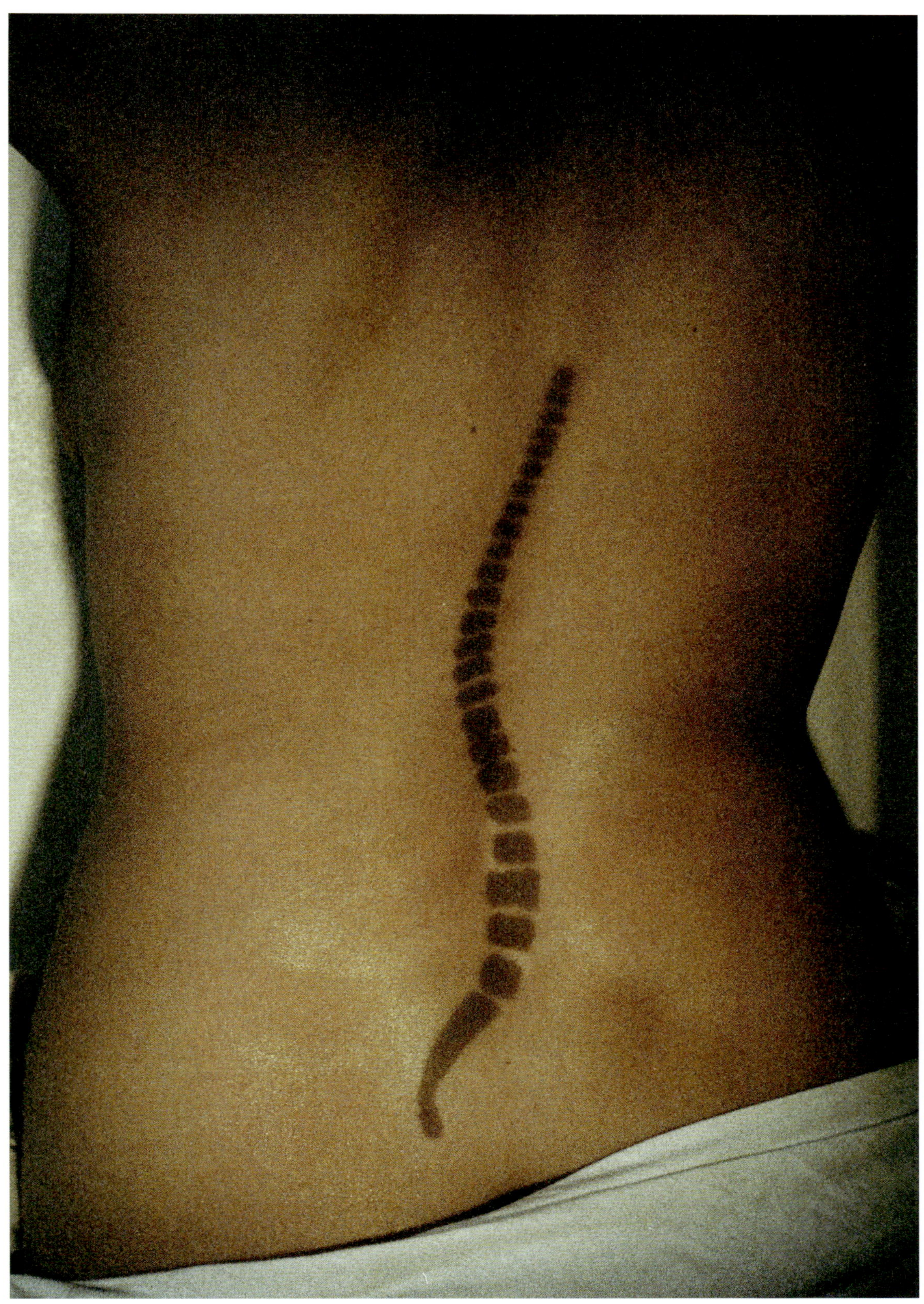

195   *Ohne Titel (Körperprojektion)* 1988
       Untitled (Body Projection)

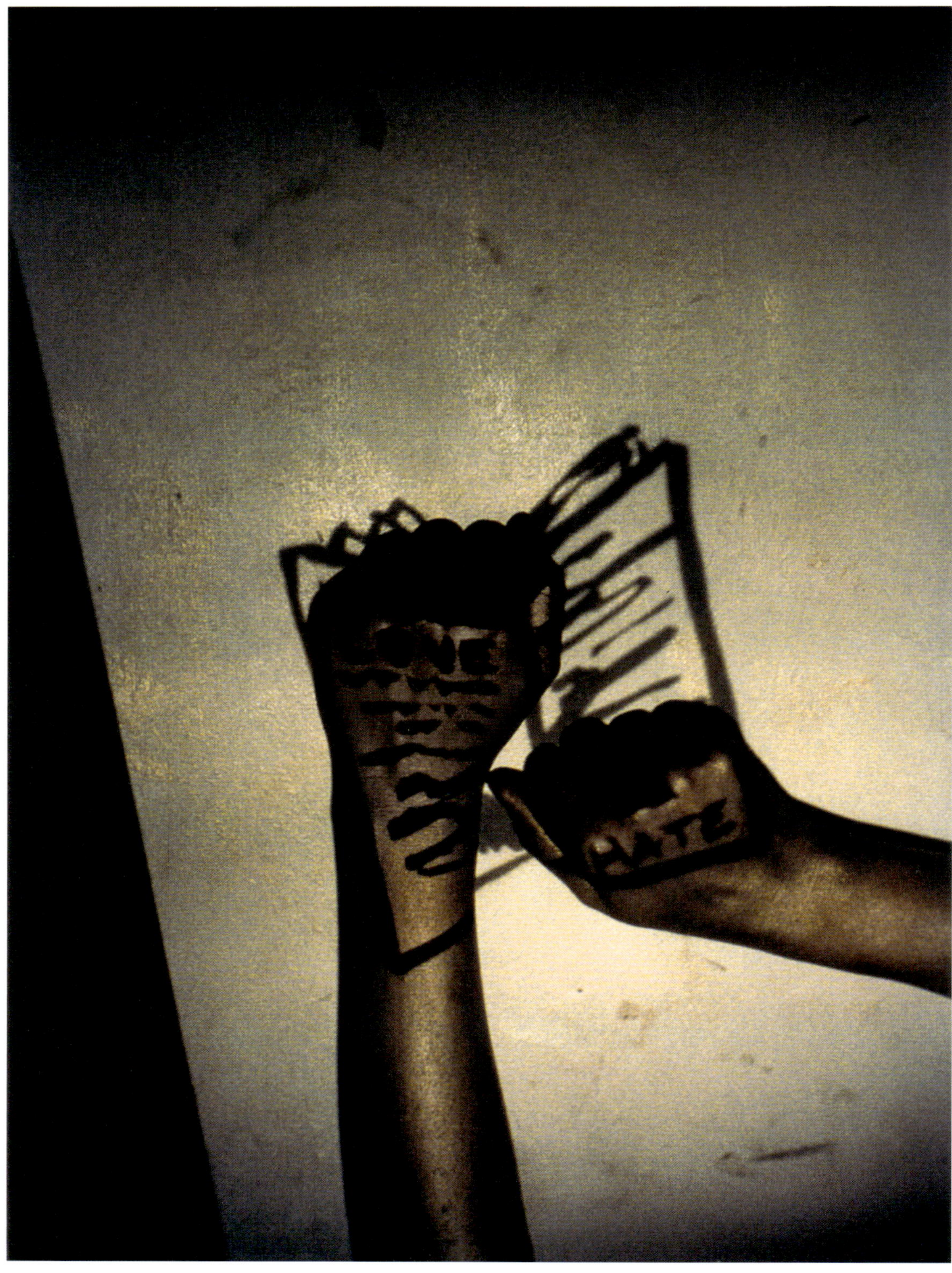

196   *Ohne Titel (Körperprojektion)* 1987
       Untitled (Body Projection)

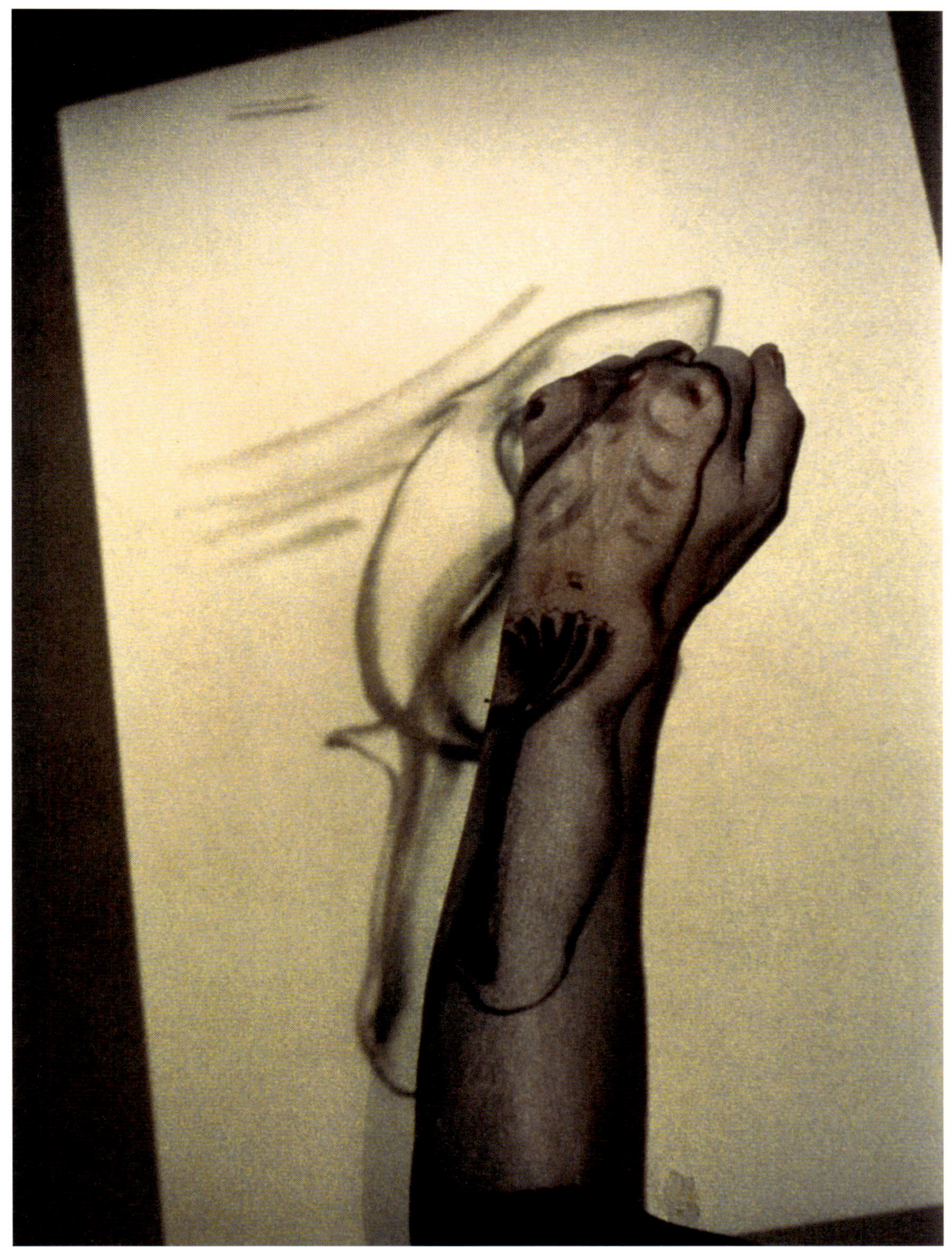

197 *Ohne Titel (Körperprojektion)* 1987
Untitled (Body Projection)

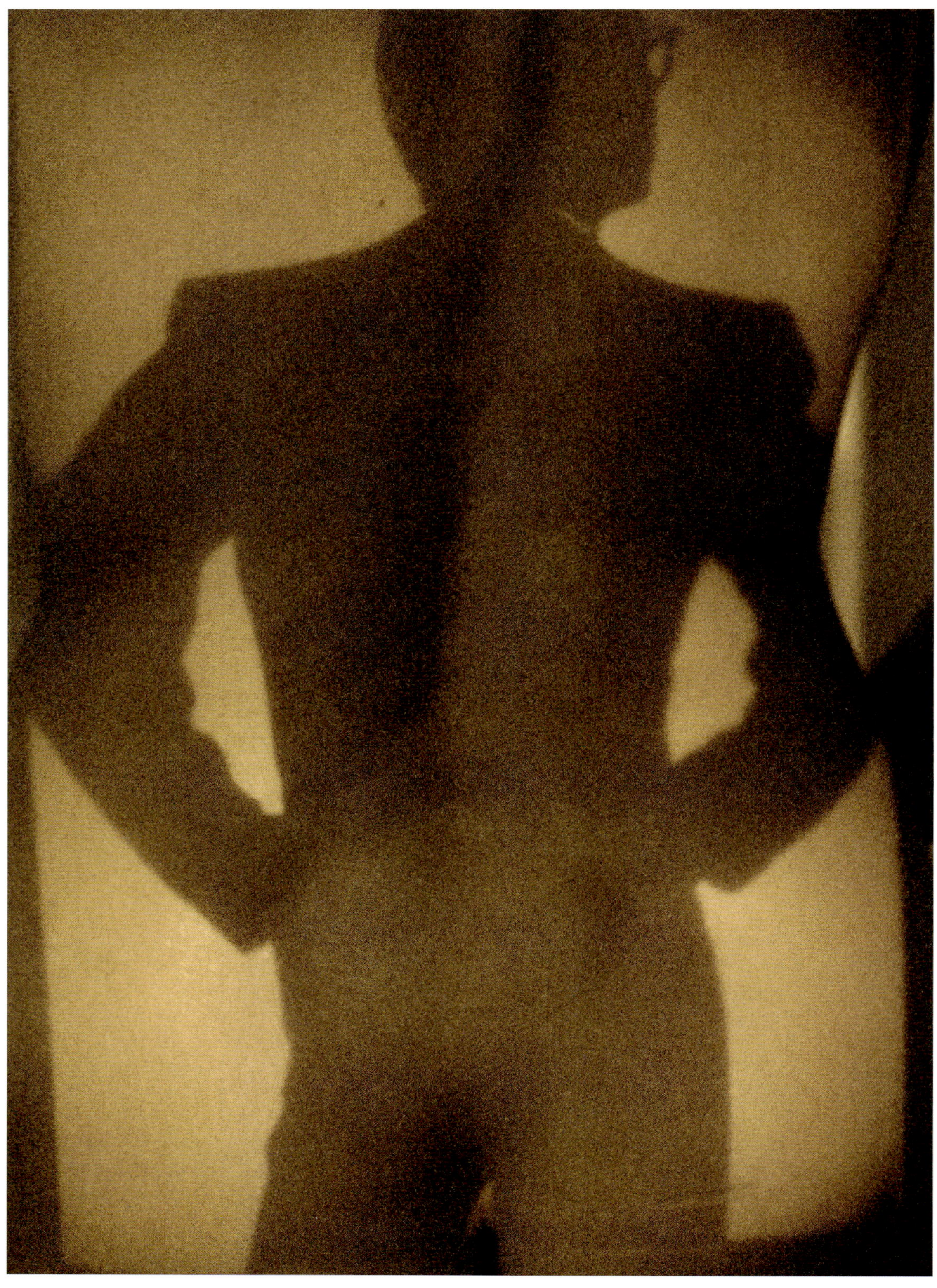

198   *Ohne Titel (Körperprojektion)* 1988
       Untitled (Body Projection)

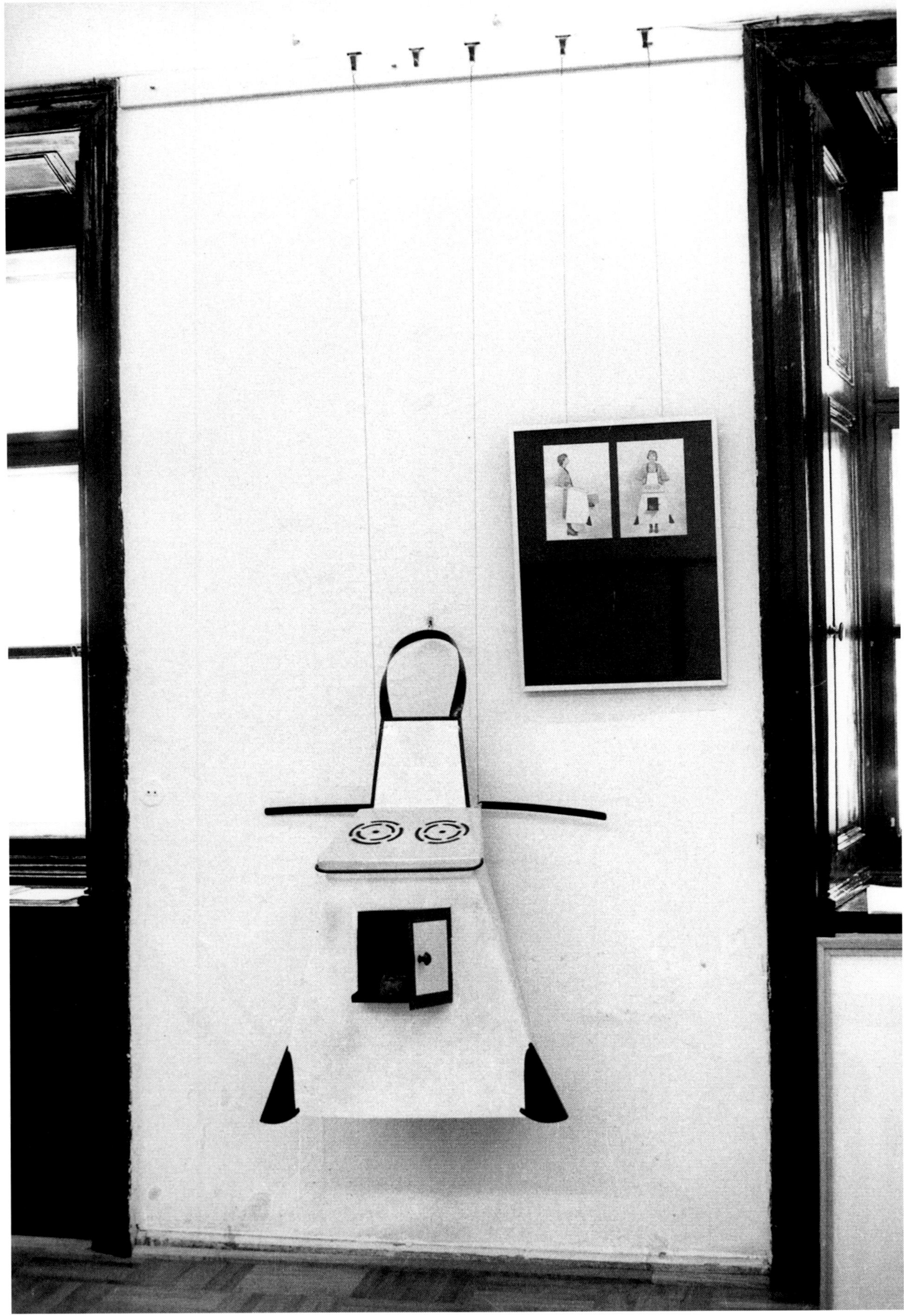

199 *Küchenschürze 1974/1975*
Kitchen Apron

»There is more advantage to separate home and body«[1]

Heike Eipeldauer

[1] See *Birgit Jürgenssen. Früher oder später*, exh. cat., Landesgalerie, Oberösterreichisches Landesmuseum, (Linz, 1998), p. 64.

[2] On the subversive potential of the link between housework and artwork in the art of Mary Kelly, Martha Rosler, Mierle Laderman Ukeles, and others, see Helen Molesworth, »House Work and Art Work,« *October* 92 (2000), pp. 71–97.

[3] In »Modernity and the Spaces of Femininity,« in Griselda Pollock, *Vision and Difference: Femininity, Feminism and the Histories of Art* (London, 1988), pp. 50–90, Griselda Pollock takes the interior as a point of departure for describing the dichotomy—paradigmatic of modernism—on the basis of which the difference between sexual and gender identity is defined.

[4] See Martina Löw, »Der Körperraum als soziale Konstruktion,« in *Geschlechter-Räume: Konstruktionen von »gender« in Geschichte, Literatur und Alltag*, ed. Margarete Hubrath (Cologne: Böhlau, 2001), pp. 211–22. This strategy is reminiscent of Louise Bourgeois's *Femme-Maison* works of the 1940s. Jürgenssen appreciated Bourgeois's works for their poetic and subversive qualities. See »Birgit Jürgenssen im Gespräch mit Rainer Metzger,« in *Birgit Jürgenssen*, ed. Gabriele Schor and Heike Eipeldauer, exh. cat. Kunstforum Vienna, (Munich: Prestel, 2010), p. 276.

[5] See Peter Weibel, in *La casa, il corpo, il cuore: Konstruktion der Identitäten*, exh. cat., Museum moderner Kunst Stiftung Ludwig Wien (1999), p. 300.

Birgit Jürgenssen's *Kitchen Apron* (ill. 199) is a three-dimensional kitchen stove that can be worn in front of the body like an apron. Not without reason, it is now considered an icon of feminist art that inquires into the cultural and sociopolitical aspects of things that are supposedly »private.« By turning its wearer into a service provider ready and willing to fulfill the functions imposed upon her—as a »housed-wife,« cook, nurturer, birth-giver, and mother as well as »culinarized« sex object—this mobile, performative art object lends paradigmatic expression to the feminist criticism of woman's literal »domestication« and the related mechanisms of social subjugation.

Executed in 1974 and 1975 within the context of the women's movement in Austria, *Kitchen Apron* was featured at the influential exhibition *MAGNA – Feminismus: Kunst und Kreativität* which, curated by VALIE EXPORT, took place in the spring of 1975 at the Galerie nächst St. Stephan in Vienna. There, Jürgenssen also presented a selection of her *Housewife Drawings* as well as a photo diptych reminiscent of a pair of mugshots. In the latter, the artist staged herself, once from the front and once from the side, sporting the *Kitchen Apron* and thus demonstrating it as an expansion of her *own* body into the »scene of the crime«—the kitchen.[2] By literally incorporating domesticity, however, the work takes this association of female body and home—and the related dichotomy of public and private, inner world and outer world[3]—to a point of grotesquery; at the same time, it seems to be parodying the imago of the female body as a (uterine) »receptacle space.«[4] In the *Kitchen Apron*, the reproductive work of the house/wife yields the loaf of bread seen sticking out of the oven. A literal interpretation of the expression »to have a bun in the oven,« this element alludes to the childbearing role of the housewife, while at the same time unmistakably evoking a phallus. Fetishization has turned the homely stove from a familiar everyday appliance into a disturbing, libidinously charged object doomed to collapse in its multifunctional polyvalence and become something monstrous.[5]

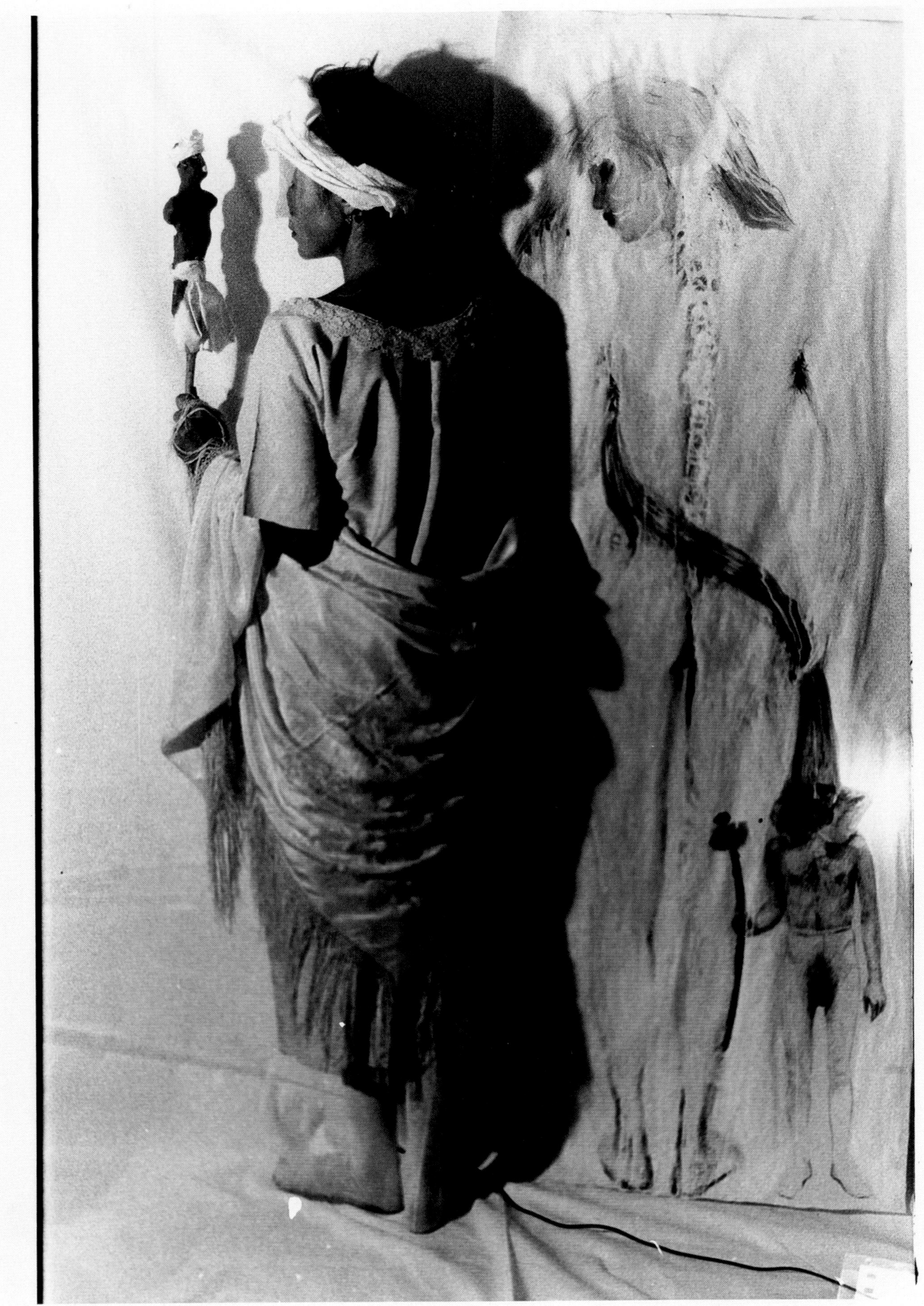

200 *Ohne Titel (Aus der Serie »Totentanz mit Mädchen«)* 1979/1980
Untitled (From the Series »Death Dance with Maiden«)

dolf LOOS: "A cultivated man does not look out of the
window; his window is a ground glass; it is
there only to let the light in, not to let the
gaze pass throught."

___

KÖRPER & RAUM

PER SONT (Hindurchtönen)

STRONG OPINIONS

CAPUT MORTUUM

SYNTONIC (gleiche Wellenlänge)

BODY FLUIDS / SHIFTED STIMULI

DEFENITLEY MAYBE

PLEASE STAND A LITTLE BIT CLOSER APART.

Man kennt nur die Dinge, die man bezähmt."
        (R.)
    sagt der Fuchs zum kleinen Prinzen (Saint-Exupéry)

Titel . . . . .
Künstler namen
+ 2 oder 3 Sätze genügen für den Folder.

                        Birgit J.

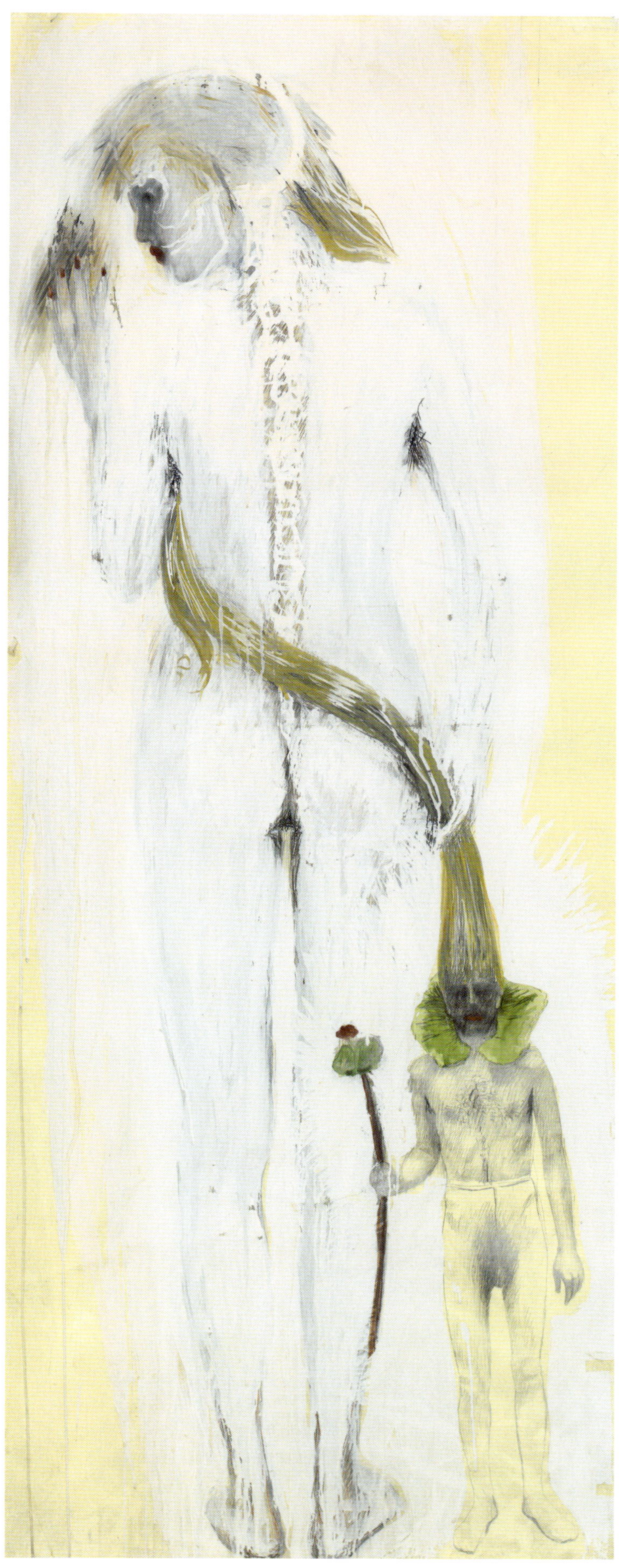

201   *Ohne Titel* 1978
       Untitled

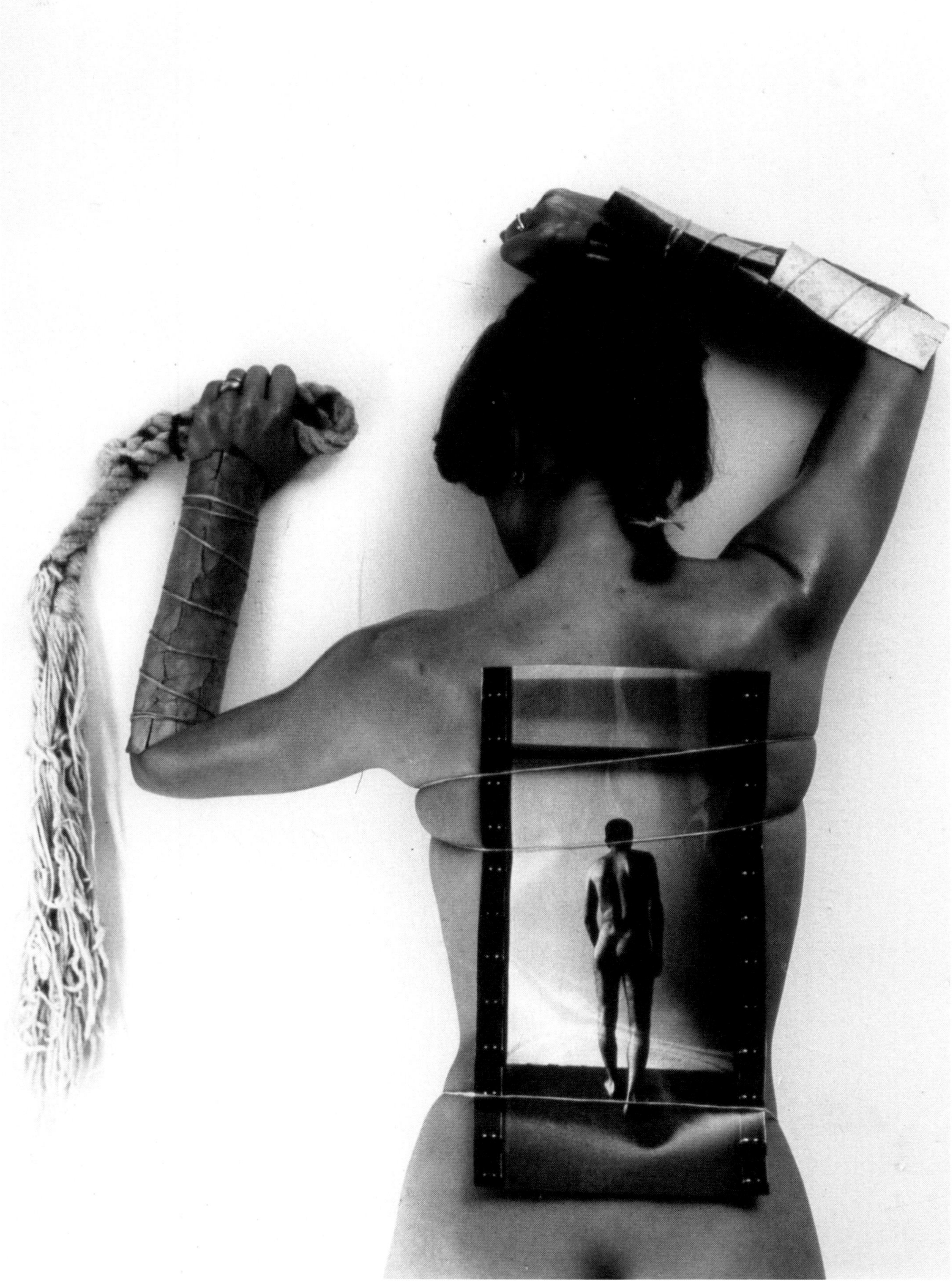

202 *Gladiatorin* 1980
Gladiatrix

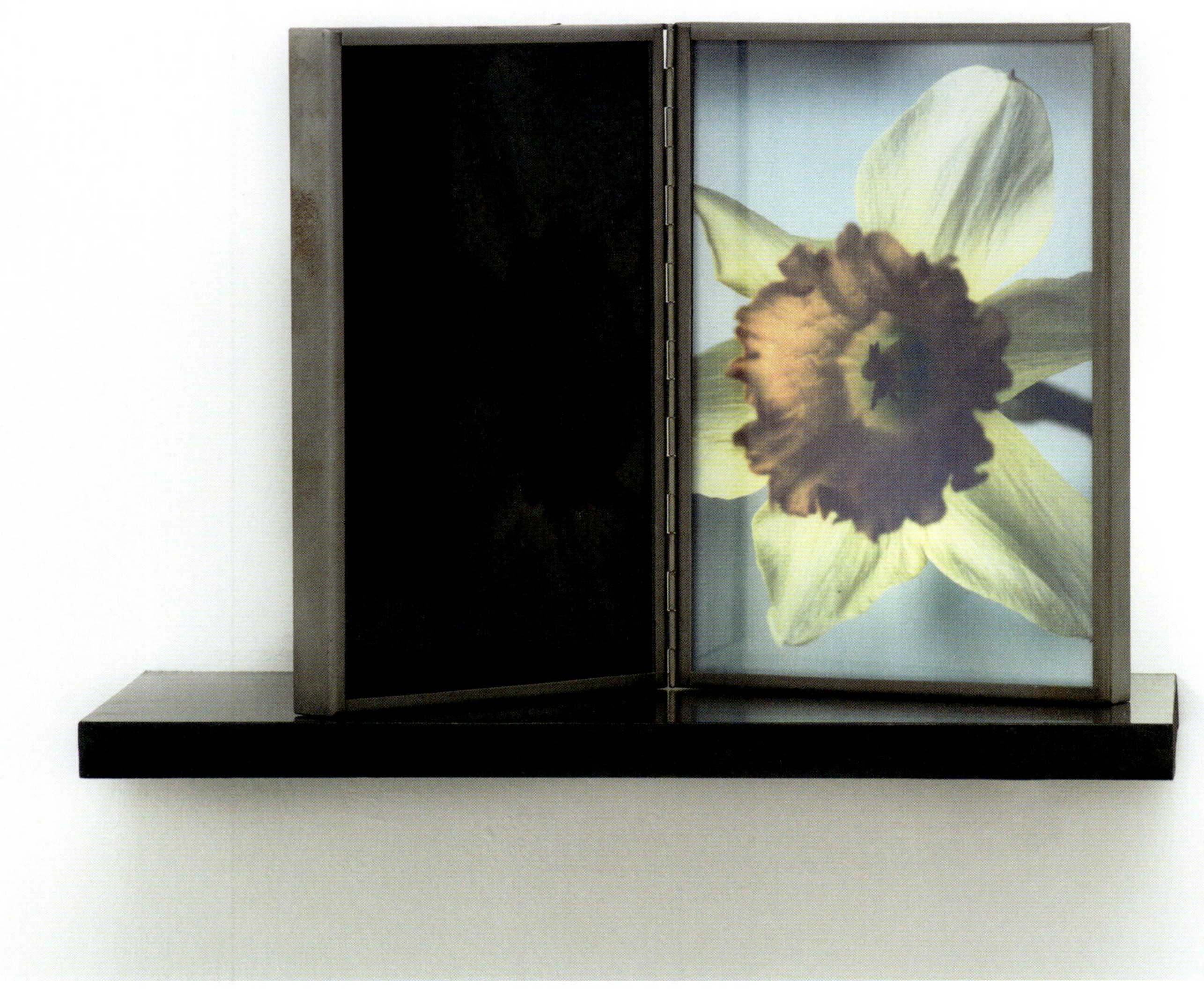

203　*Narziß und Echo 1991*
Narcissus and Echo

Narcissus and Echo

Jasper Sharp

A small, framed photograph of a narcissus flower sits on a wooden shelf (ill. 203). Its deep golden, trumpet-shaped cup reaches out from a crown of pale yellow petals as if to usher us inside. Illuminated from behind by a small lamp, the image casts an indistinct reflection onto the matching pane of dark glass to which it is hinged. One moment it is there, the next it is gone.

The work belongs to a series of six closely related objects that Jürgenssen produced in 1991 for an exhibition at the Flecha Gallery in London. Sitting on their shelves tight to the wall, their electrical wires hanging loosely beneath them like roots burrowing down into the ground, they resemble a collection of family photographs.

With characteristic economy, the works weave together a number of ideas and motifs that appear frequently in Jürgenssen's work: mirroring and reflection, ephemerality, myth and legend, regeneration and fertility, flowers and organic materials, and the use of light to cast shadows and ethereal apparitions. A restless and inventive spirit, she experimented from an early age with a broad range of photographic techniques from Polaroid and rayogram to photo collage and, in this case, a rudimentary light box.

The story of Narcissus and Echo, the hunter and the nymph, is recounted in Ovid's epic narrative poem *Metamorphoses*. A tragic tale of unreciprocated love, heartbreak, vanity, and, ultimately, revenge, it has inspired paintings by Caravaggio, Poussin, Turner, and Dalí, poems by Rilke, and novels by Stendhal and Wilde. The flower which was given his name has itself appeared in literature and the visual arts since the Middle Ages as a symbol both of death and of resurrection, due to its reappearance each year at Easter time. An avid reader, Jürgenssen would have been aware of its mythological origins and continuing cultural significance.

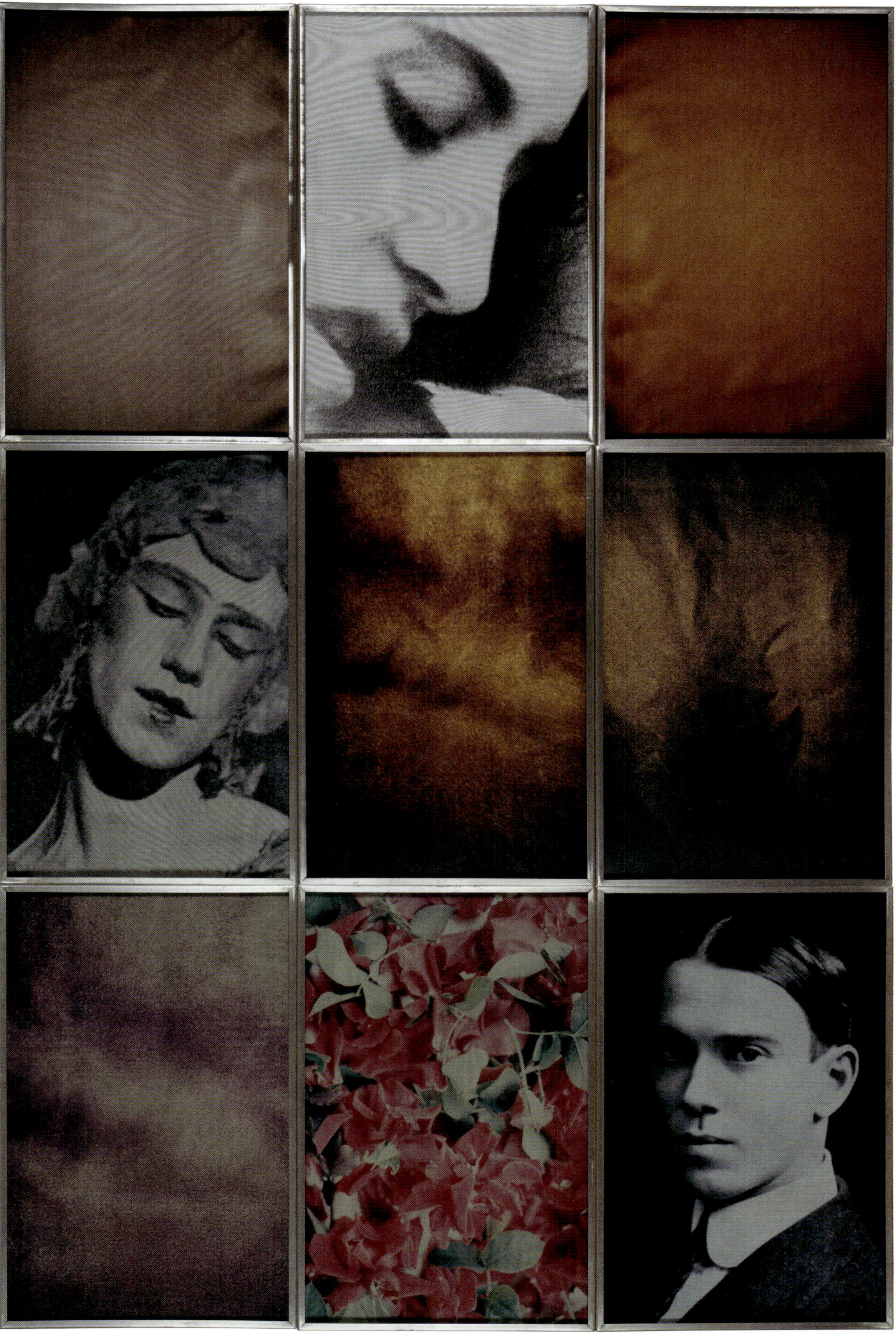

204   *Fragmente einer Rose (Nijinski)* 1989
        Fragments of a Rose (Nijinsky)

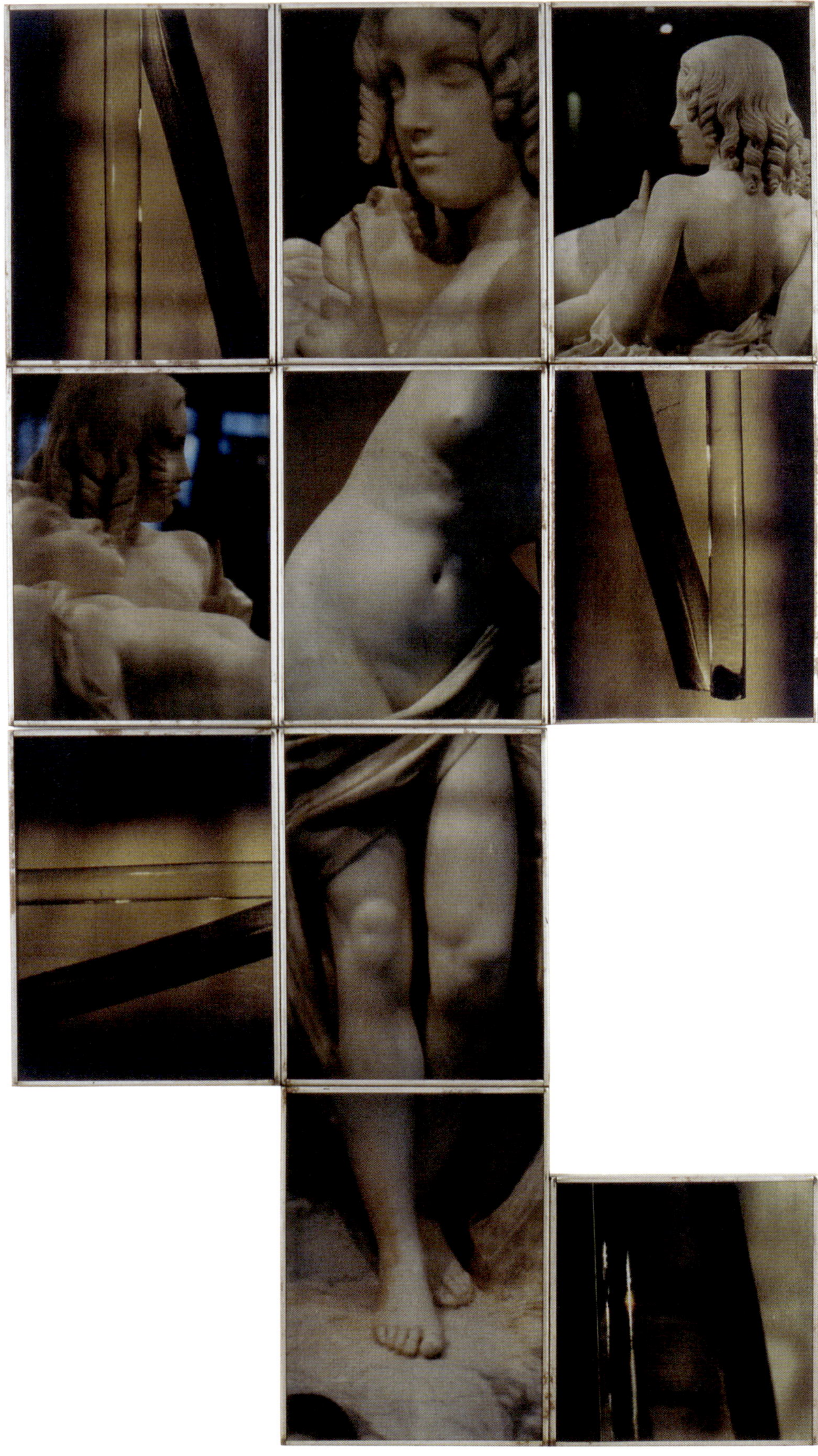

<u>205</u> *Ohne Titel* 1995
Untitled

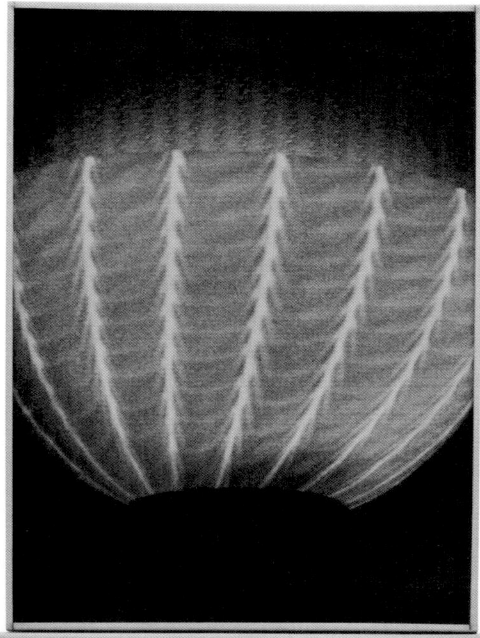

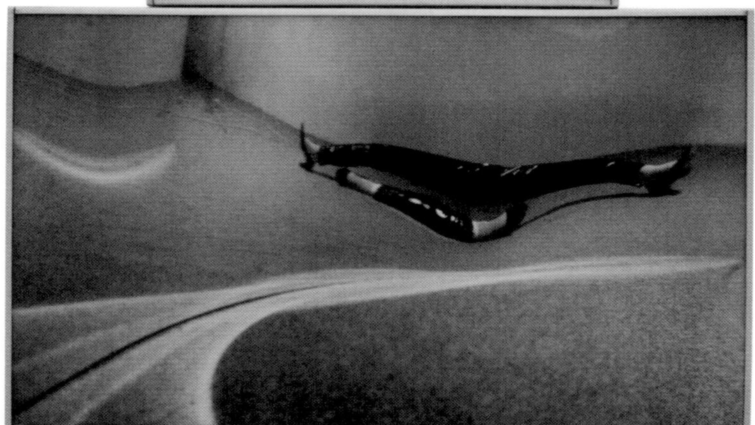

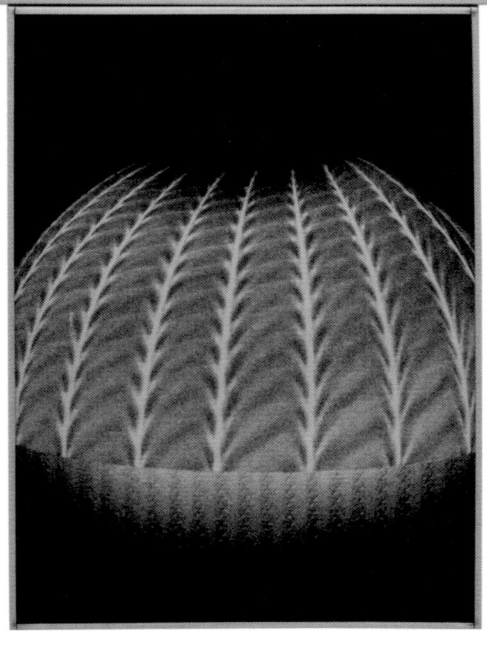

<u>206</u>   *Selbstportrait mit Lampe* 1979/1991
Self-Portrait with Lamp

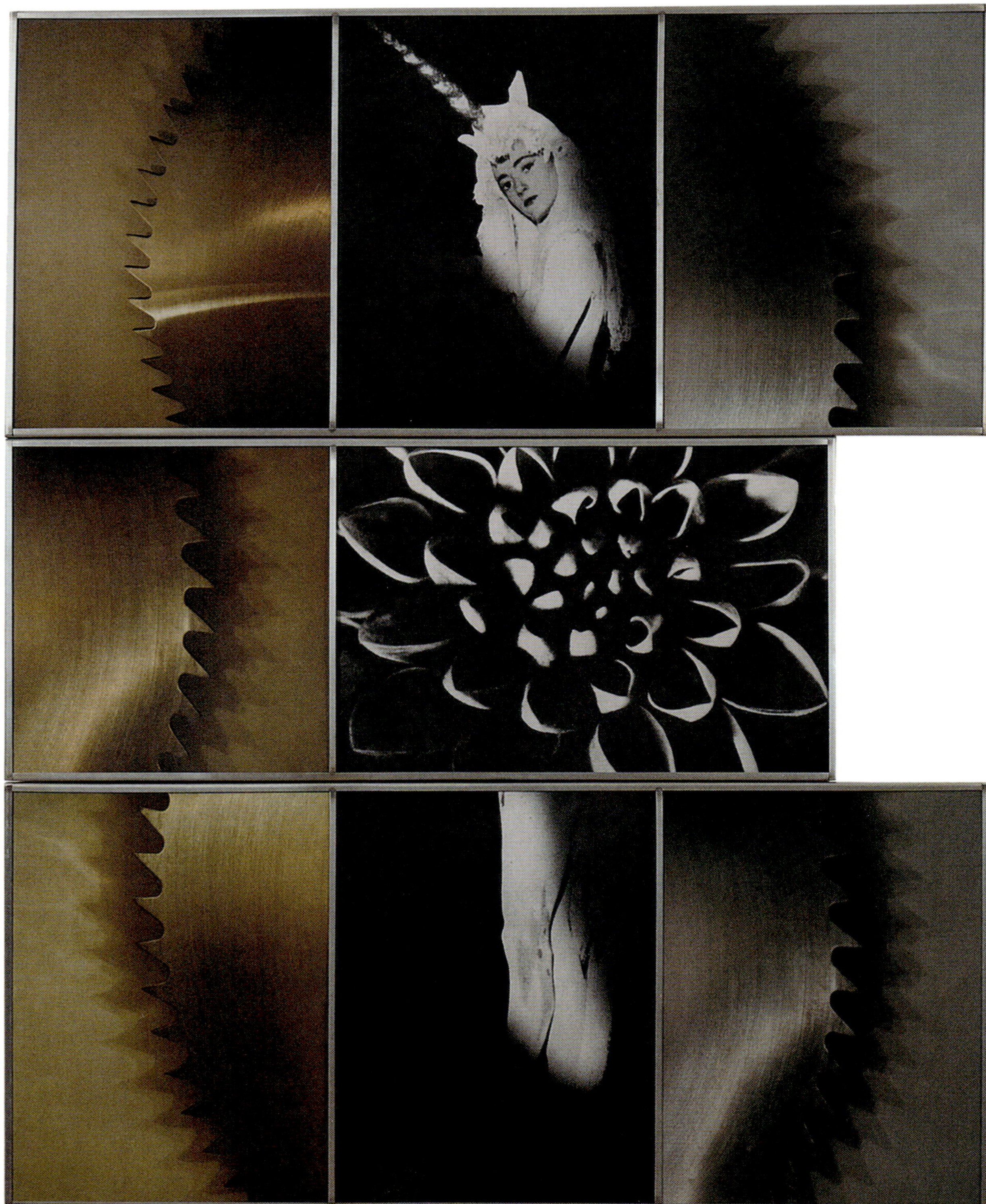

207   *Einhorn* 1991
      Unicorn

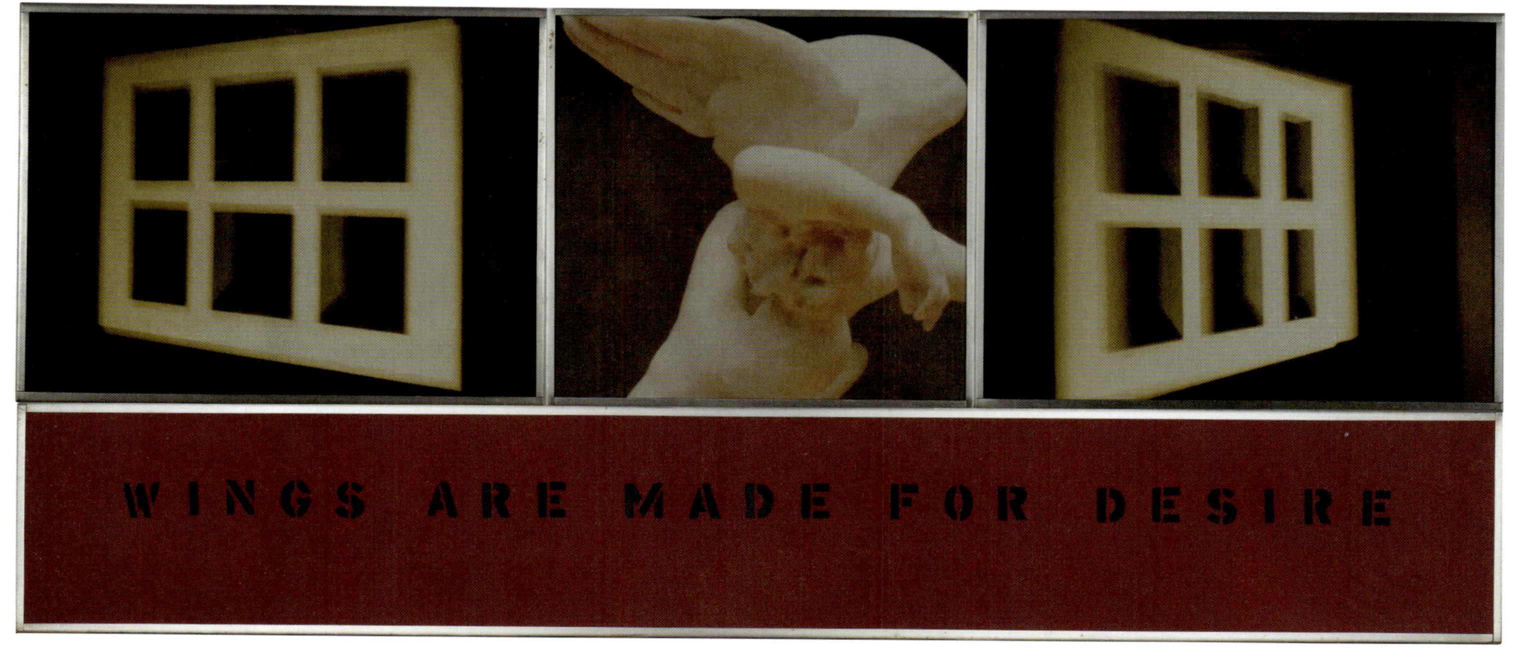

208   *Wings Are Made for Desire* 1989

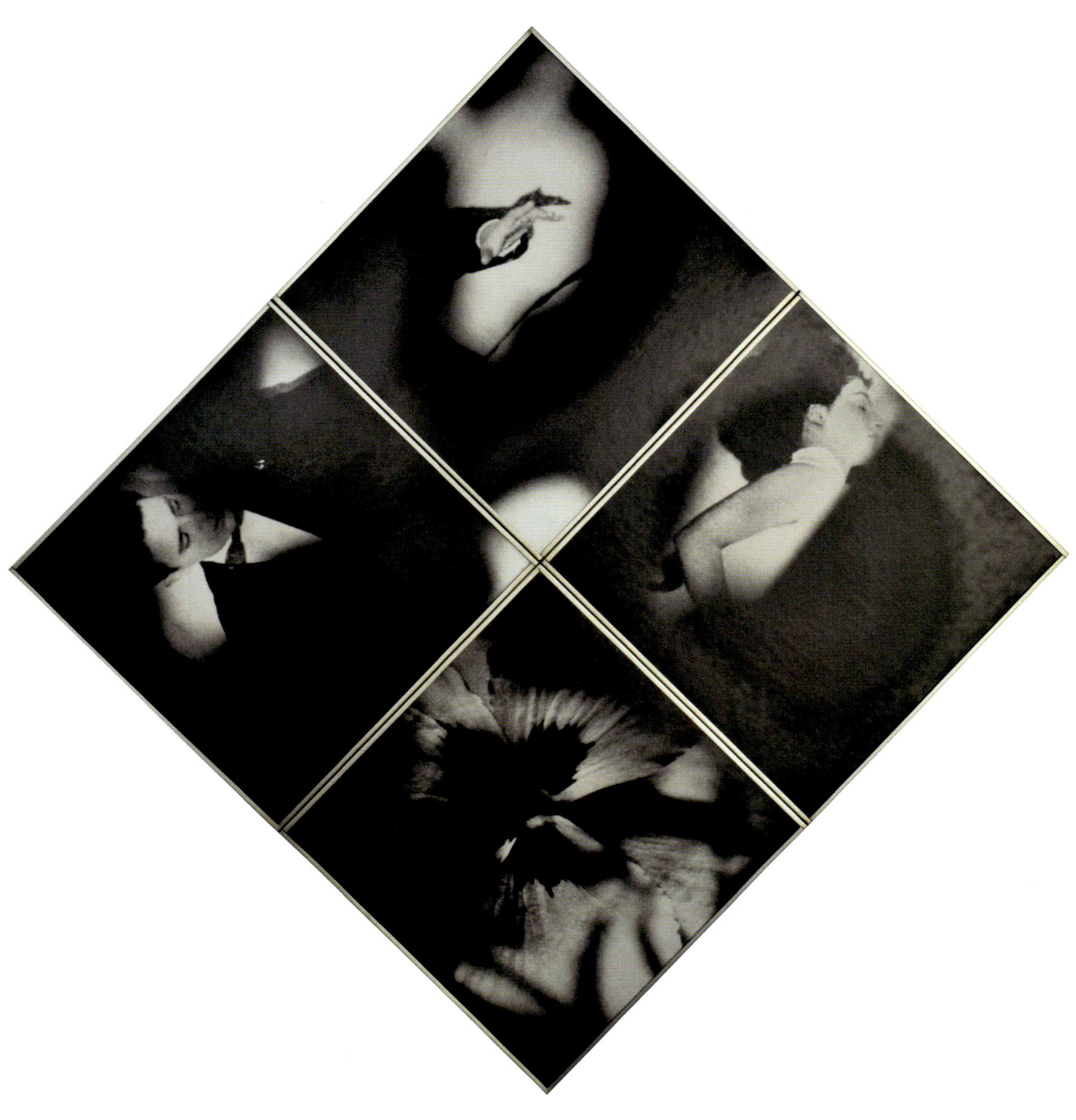

209   *Houdini* 1990

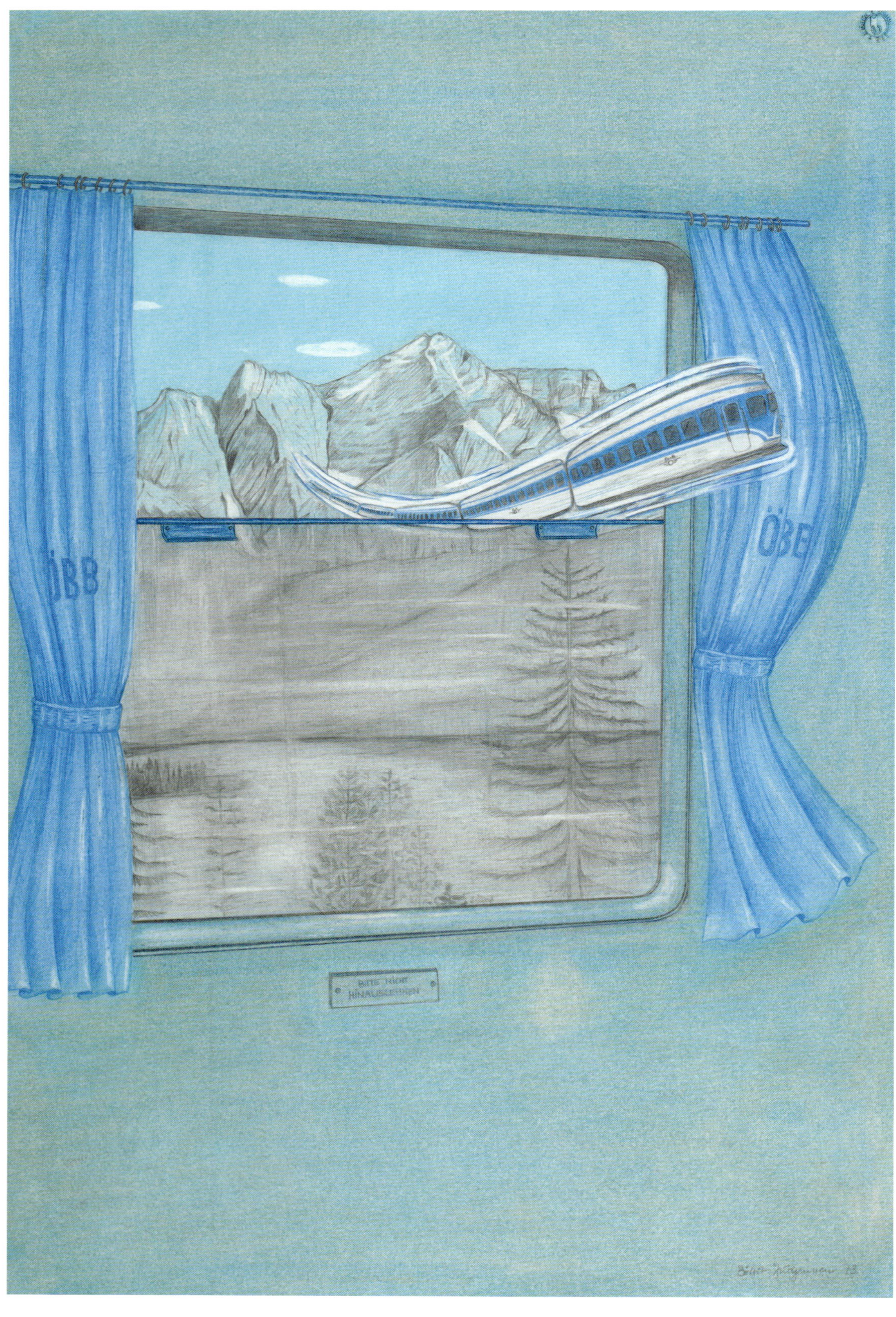

<u>210</u>   *Ohne Titel* 1973
      Untitled

Trans-Europe Express

Michael Bracewell

[1] Cited in Felicitas Thun-Hohenstein, »»Everything Flows, Conditions and Permeates Itself ...‹ Felicitas Thun-Hohenstein in an Interview with Birgit Jürgenssen,« in *Let's Twist Again: If You Can't Think It, Dance It; Performance in Vienna from 1960 until Today*, ed. Carola Dertnig and Stefanie Seibold (Gumpoldskirchen: de'A Buch- und Kunstverlag, 2006), pp. 272–79.

This portrait-format drawing depicts the interior of a train that is traveling through a mountain landscape (ill. 210). The window is lowered and the curtain on the right-hand side is blowing inward. Another train is flying down from the distant mountains at great speed and entering into the carriage through the open window. Beneath the window is a small sign that reads »BITTE NICHT HINAUSLEHNEN« (Please do not lean out).

Shades of blue, turquoise, and green-blue dominate this drawing, creating a sense of magical realism. The atmosphere seems dreamlike and enigmatic—intense yet calm. There is a sense of fantasy or modern fairy tale: a playful allegory of the Romantic spirit. Only the scenery visible through the bottom half of the drawing is gray—the foothills and some scattered trees. The »magical« train entering the carriage could almost be a visual pun on the phrase »train of thought.« At the same time, it could be a familiar spirit— a symbol—in the mythical world envisaged by the artist.

Accordingly, there is a literary quality to this drawing—a sense of narrative and psychology. Jürgenssen said of her artistic relationship to literature, »I started to deal with surrealistic literature and art at a very early point in my life and my pieces of work developed from the interplay between reading and every-day life. It was impossible for me to draw without having literature in my mind.«[1]

During 1973 Birgit Jürgenssen made several drawings depicting trains. They all share an insinuation of Romantic allegory and modern fairy tale—the artist depicting escape from one world into another. The train becomes a modern symbol of transcendence and flight yet is also slightly ambiguous—hinting at mortality. This drawing might be a European rendition of an American myth—the need to move on, to take flight into real life.

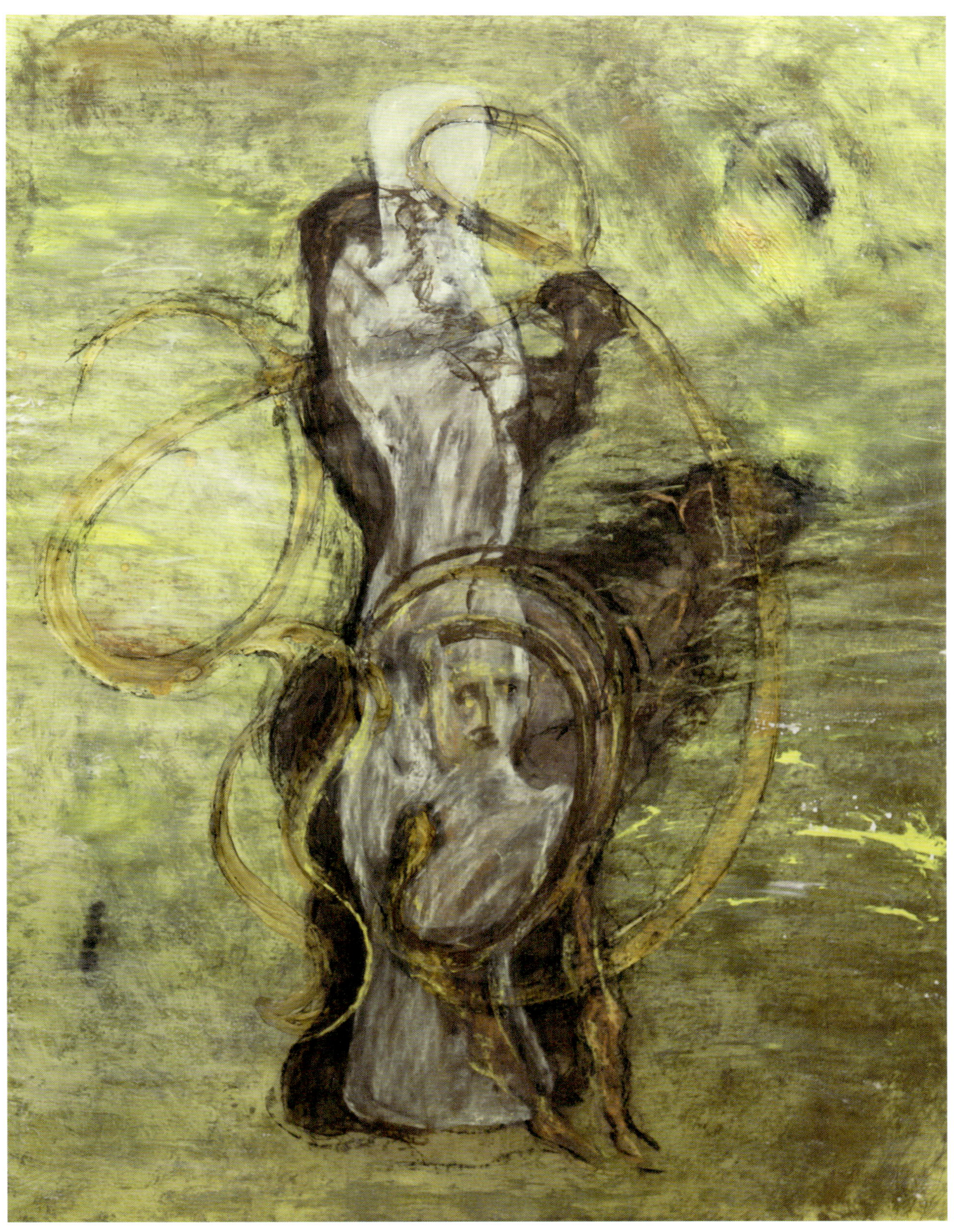

211   *Forbidden Morning* 1986

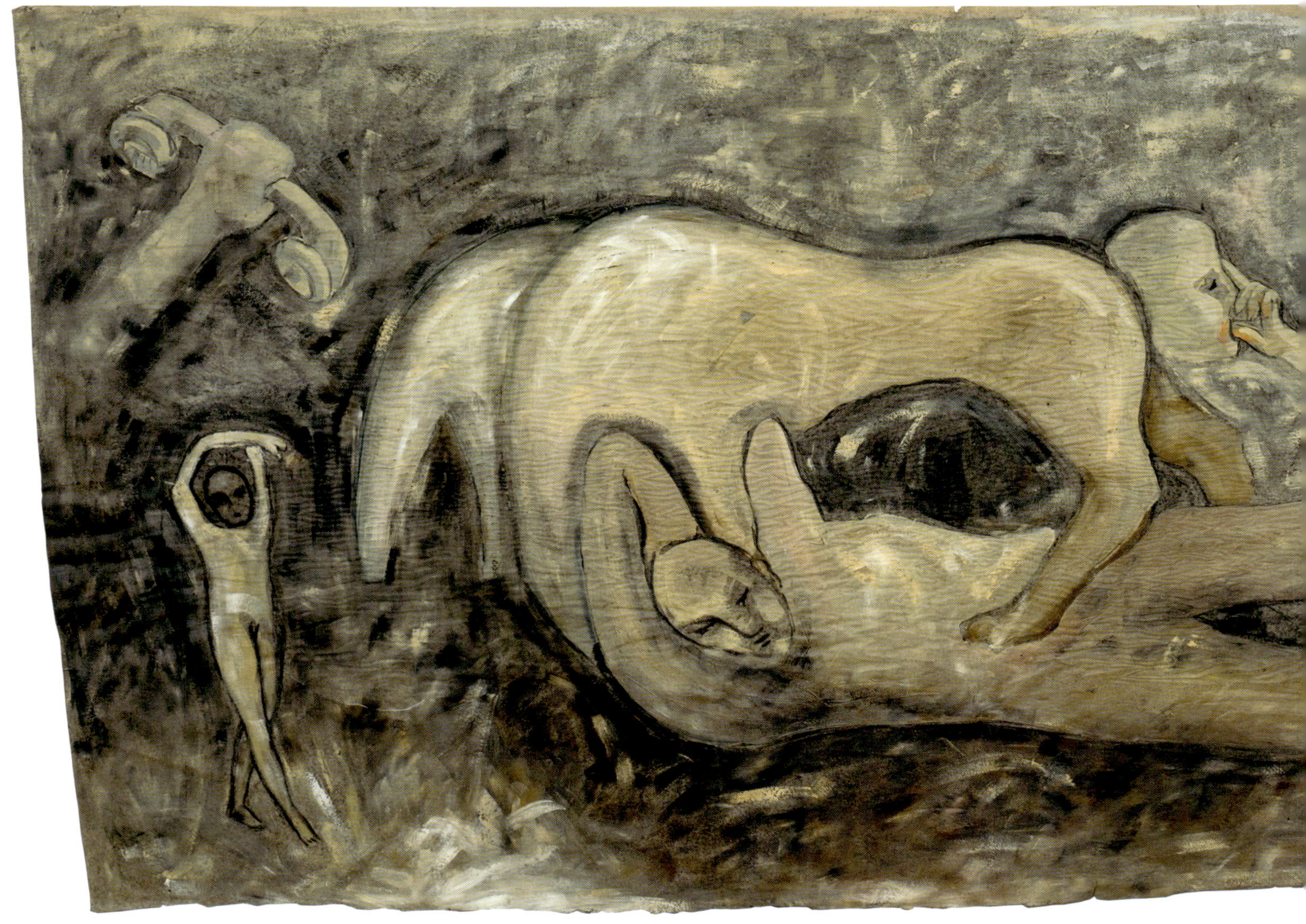

212 *Ohne Titel* 1984
Untitled

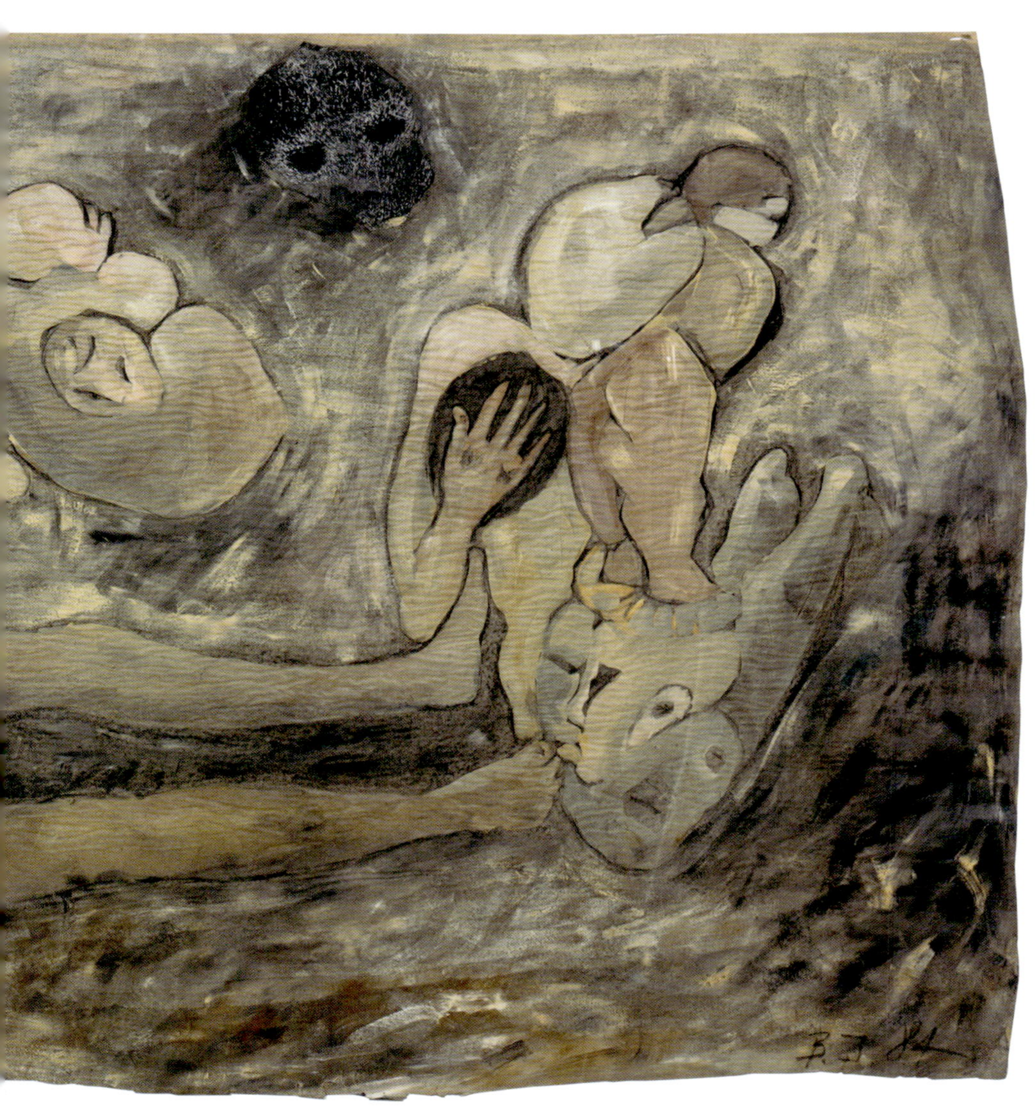

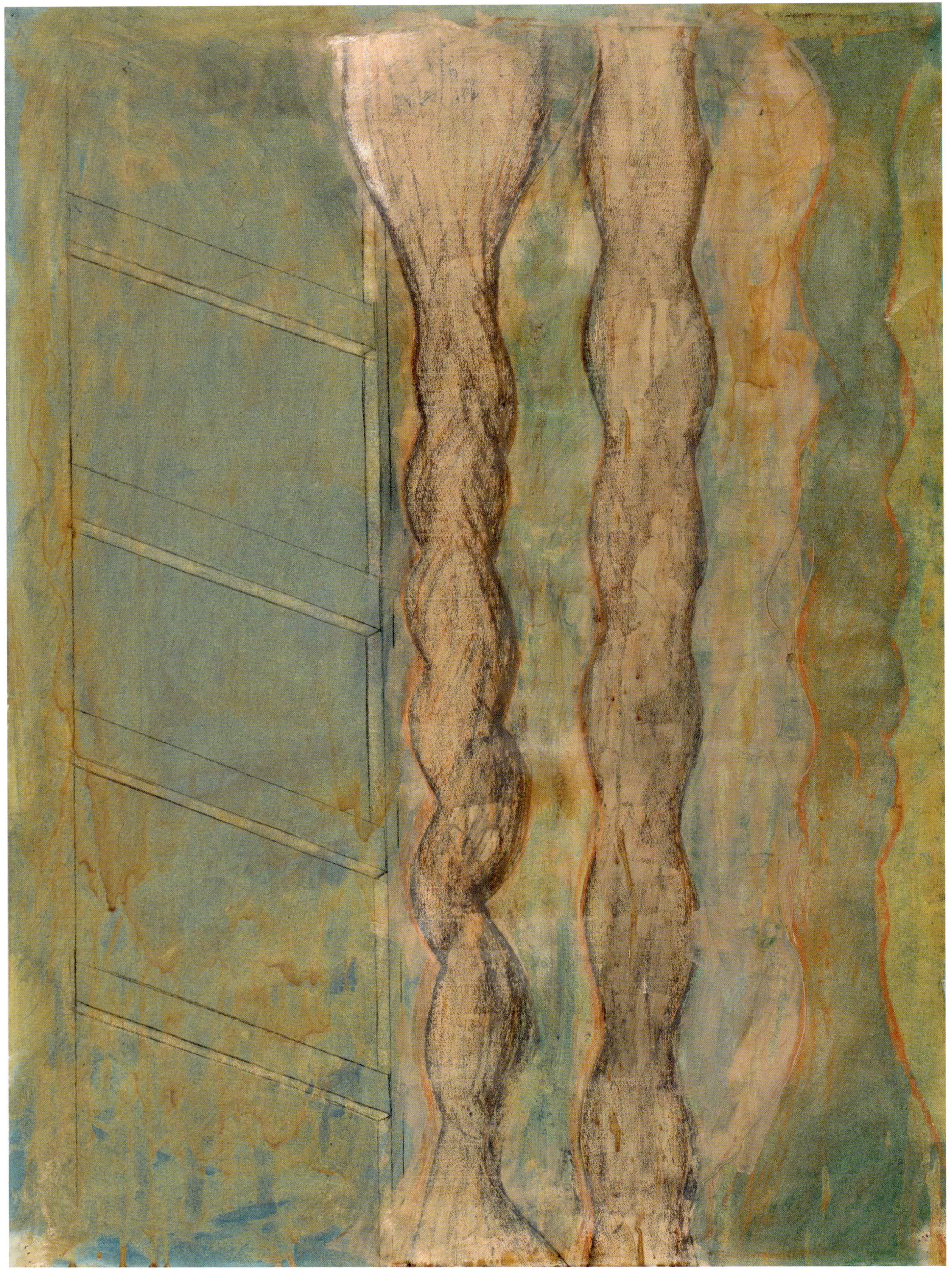

213   *Ohne Titel* 1989/1990
      Untitled

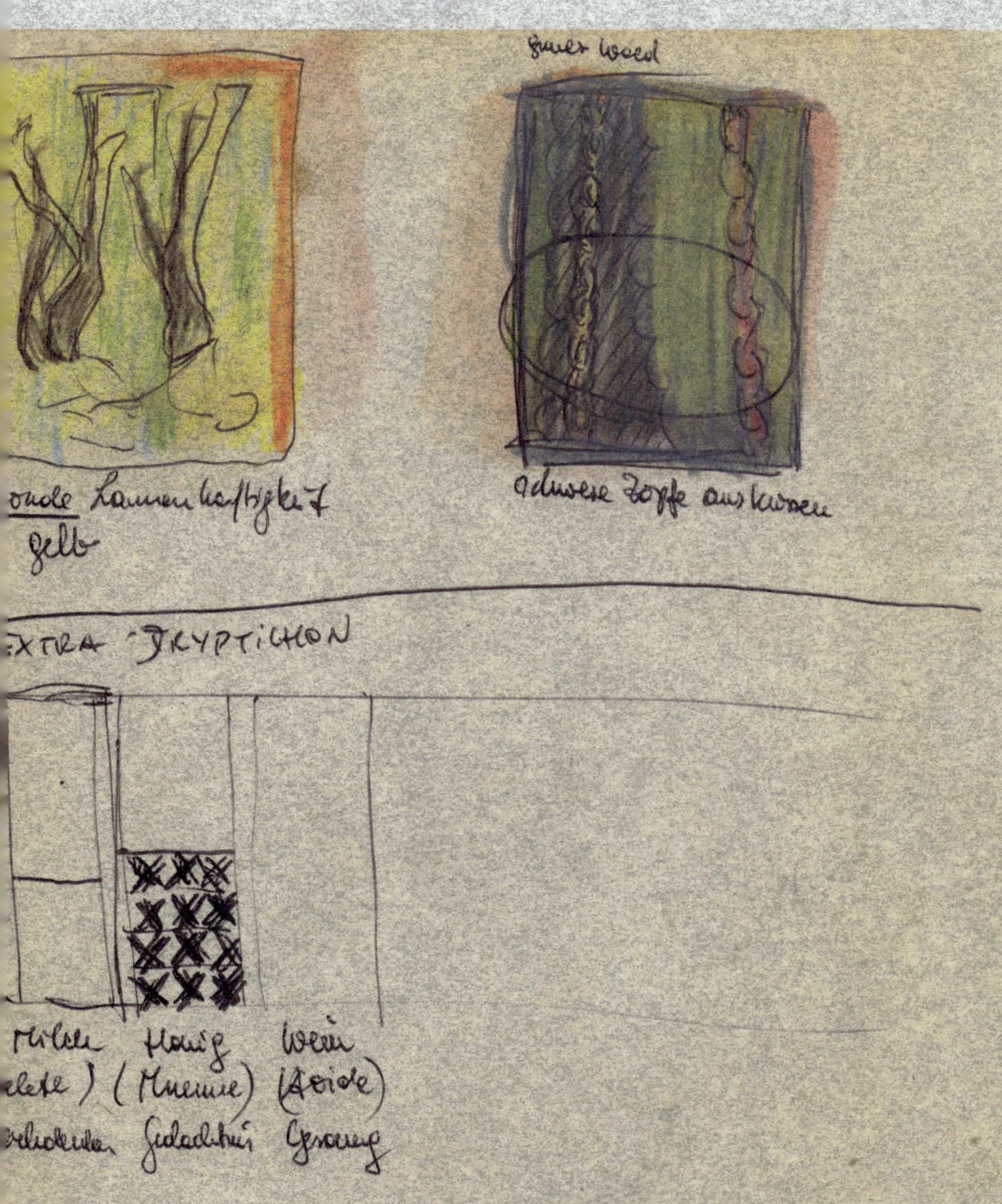
zwei wood
onde Lannenhaftigkeit
gelb
schwere Zöpfe aus Kissen
EXTRA 'TRYPTICHON
Milch   Honig   Wein
...lete)   (Mnemie)   (Seide)
...lichden   Gedächtnis   Gesang

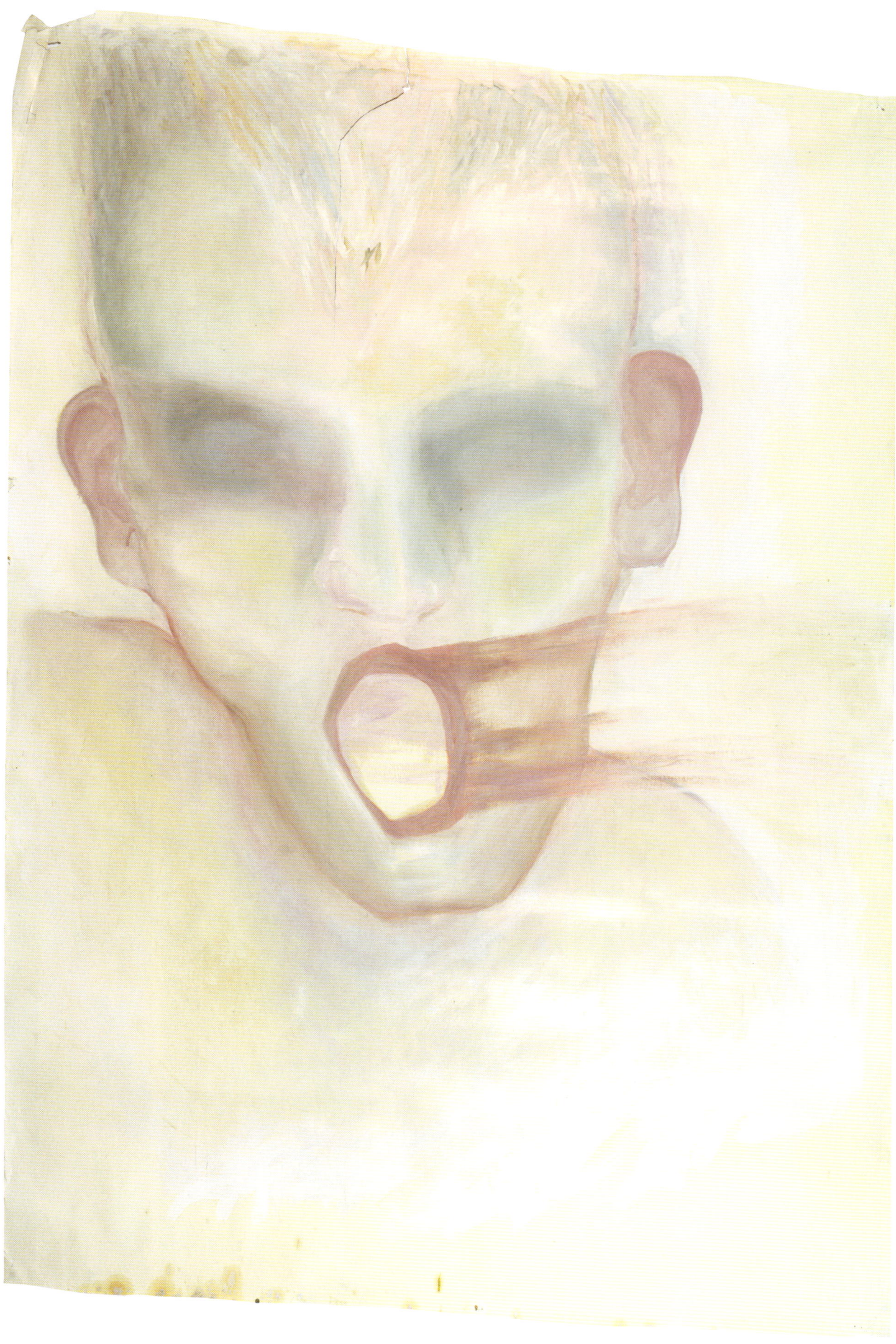

214 *Ohne Titel* 1983
Untitled

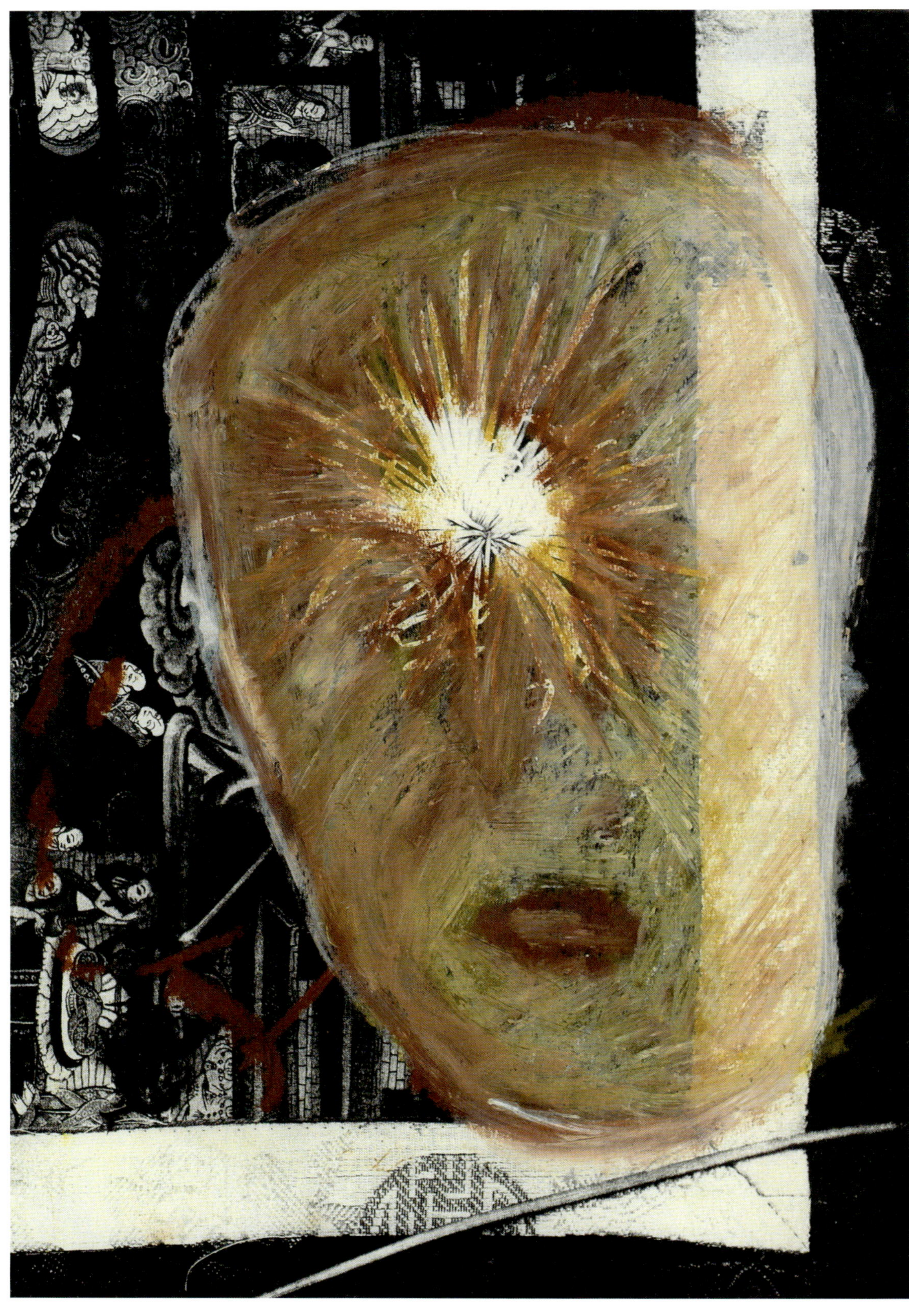

215　*Ohne Titel (Aus der Serie »Kopfalarm«) 1985*
Untitled (From the Series »Head Alert«)

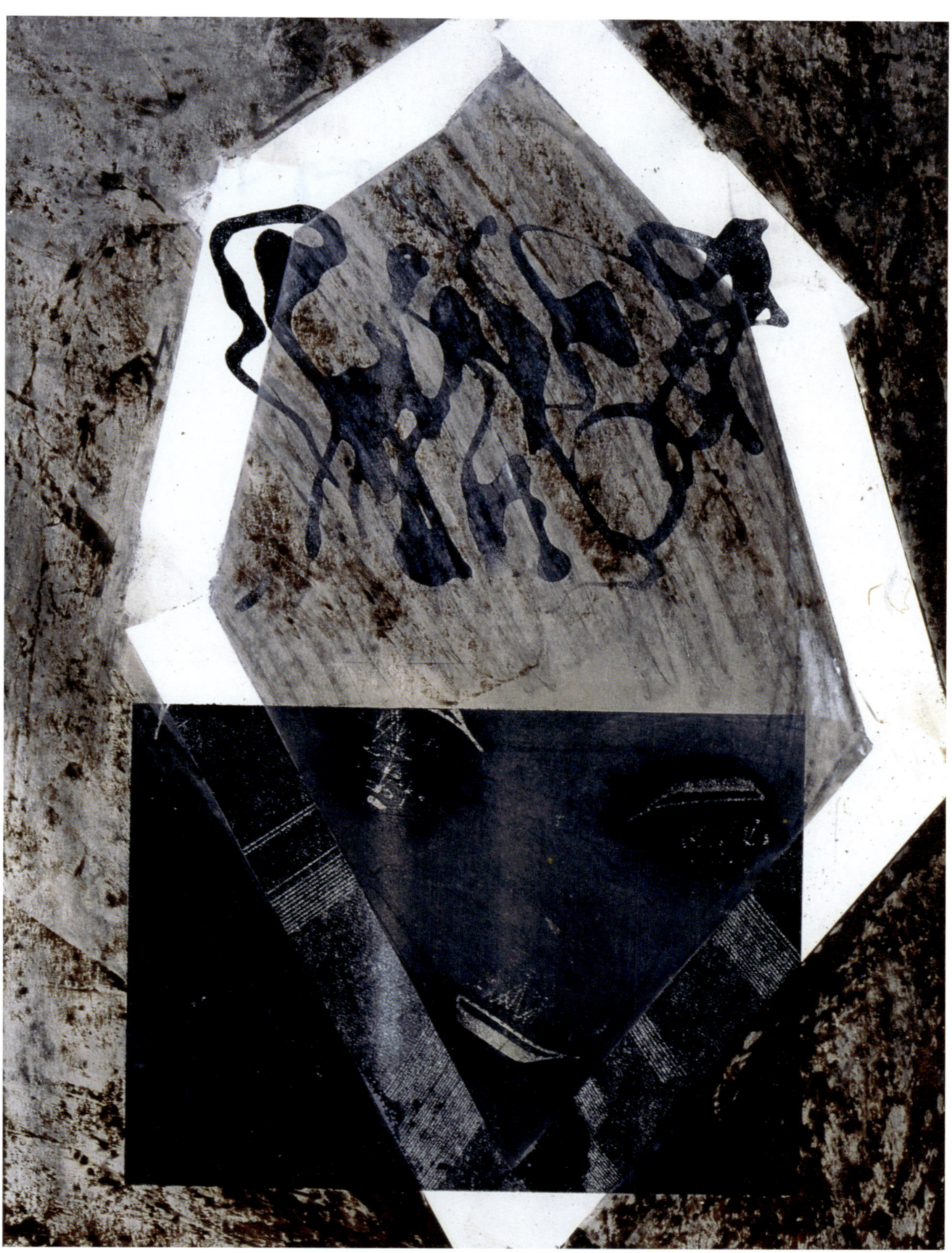

216　*Ohne Titel (Aus der Serie »Kopfalarm«)* 1985
　　Untitled (From the Series »Head Alert«)

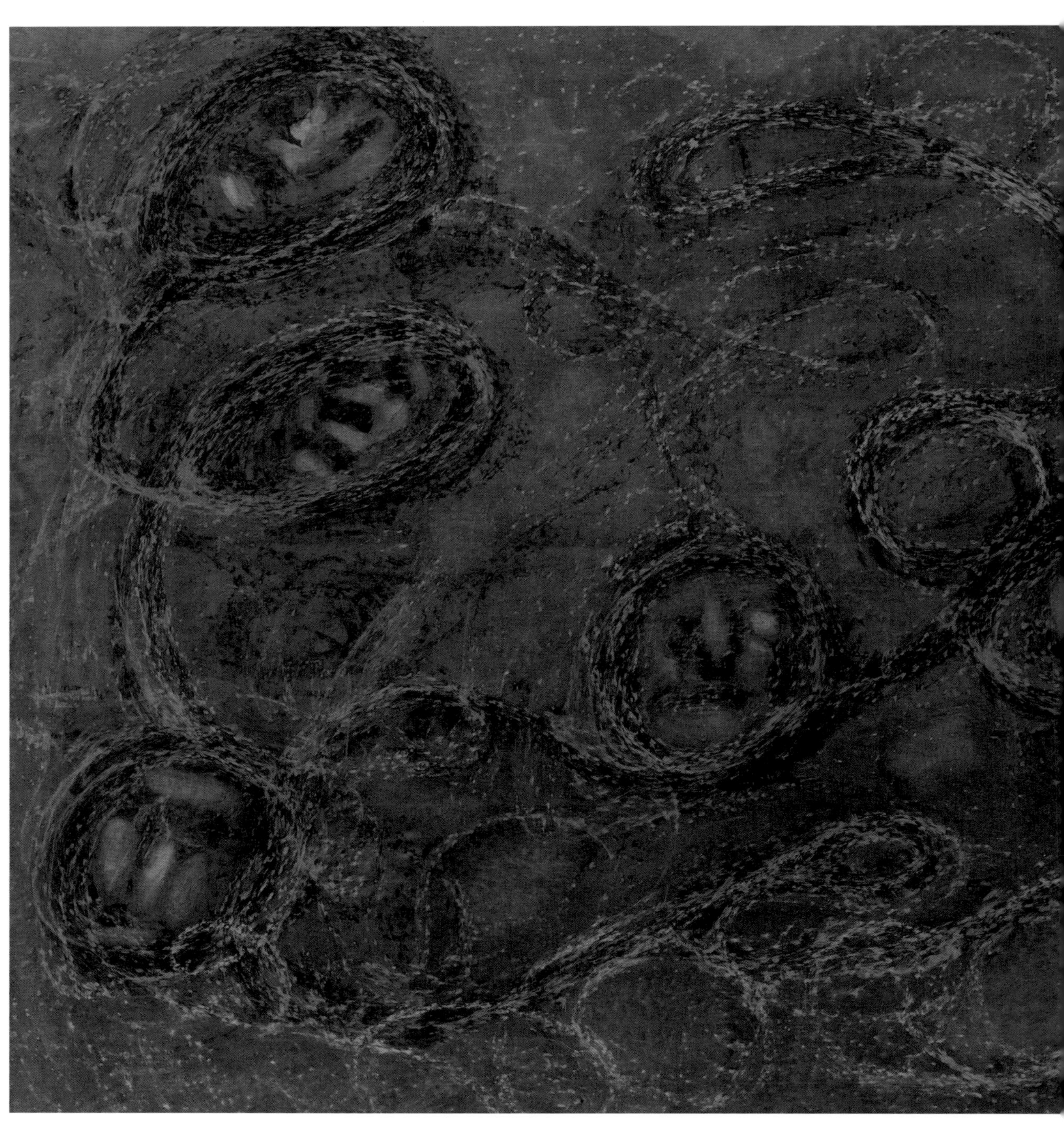

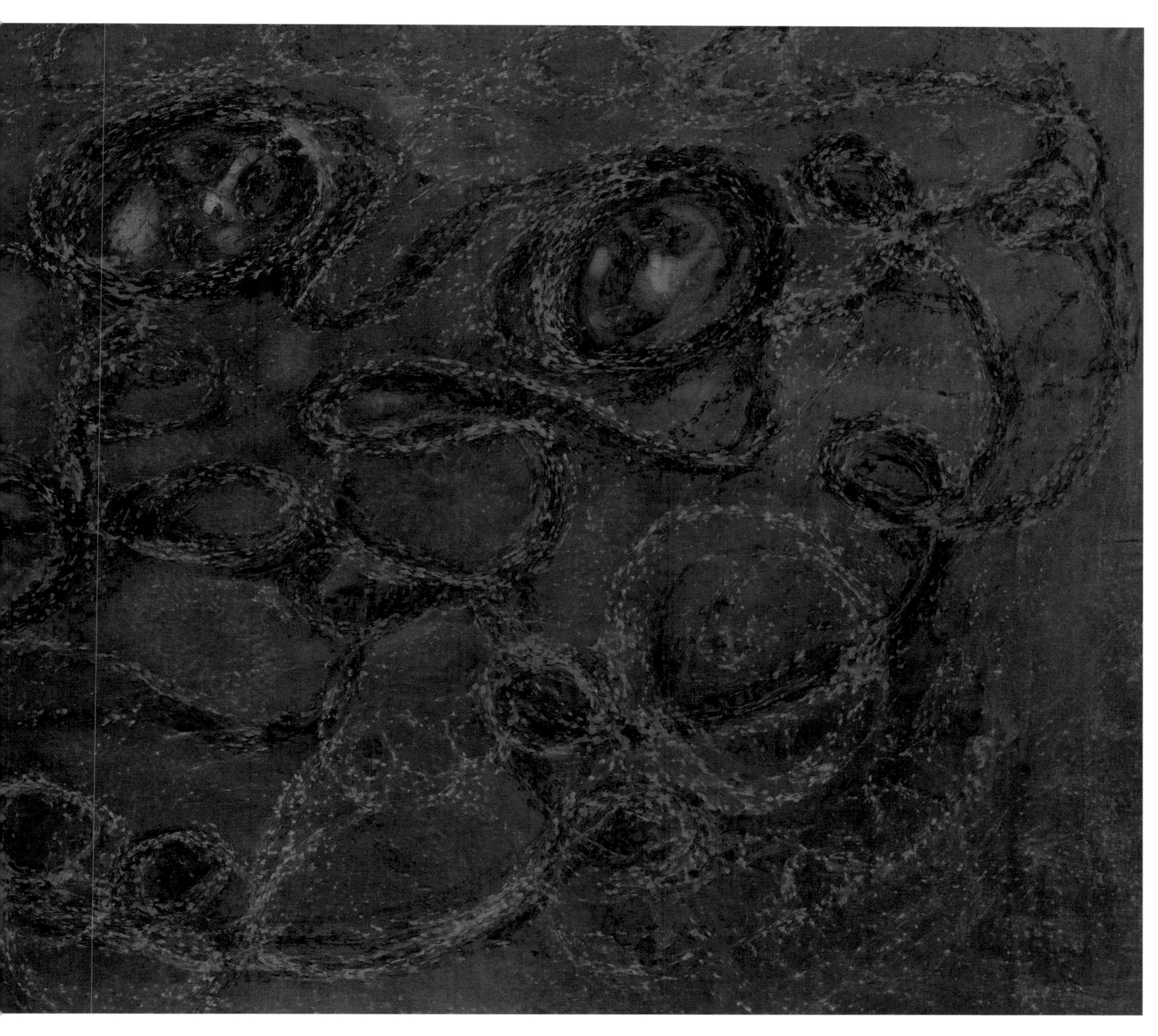

217   *The Tediousness of the Connoisseurs* 1985

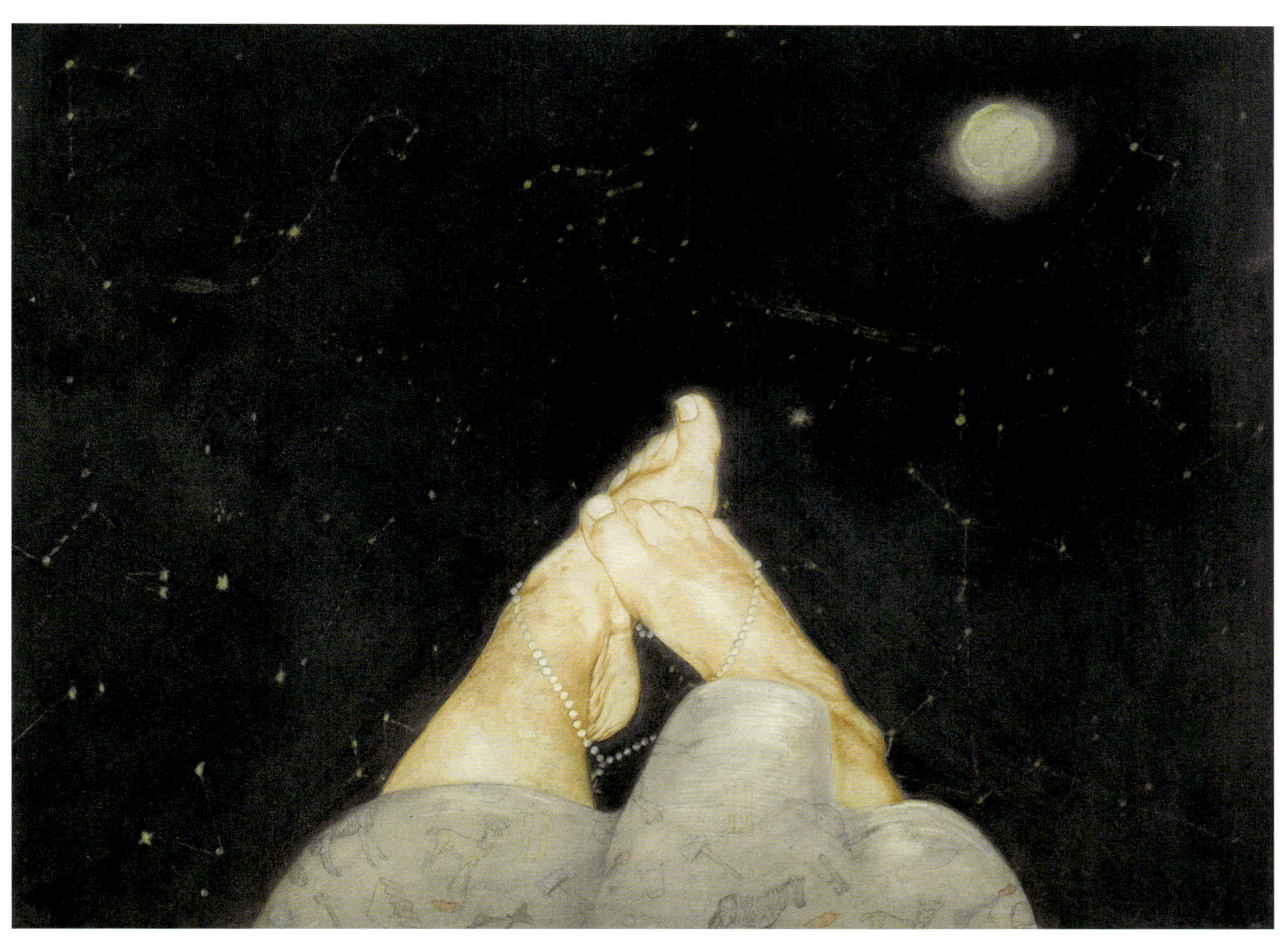

218 *Ohne Titel* 1977
Untitled

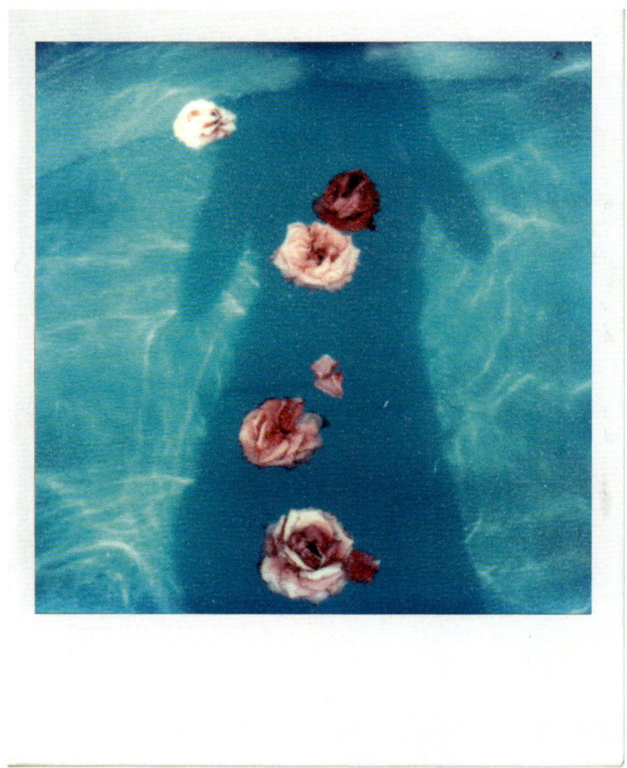

219 *Ohne Titel* 1979
Untitled

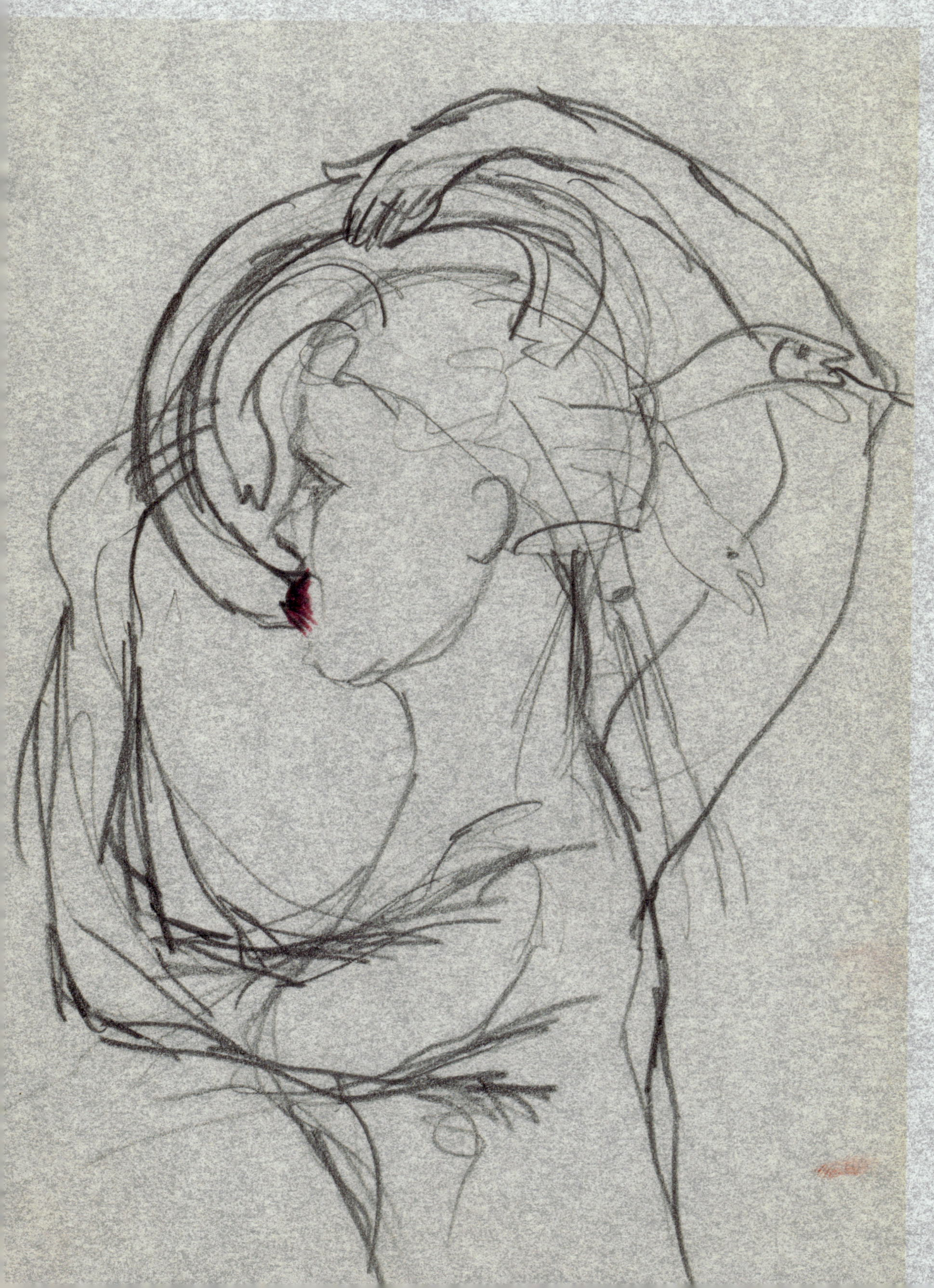

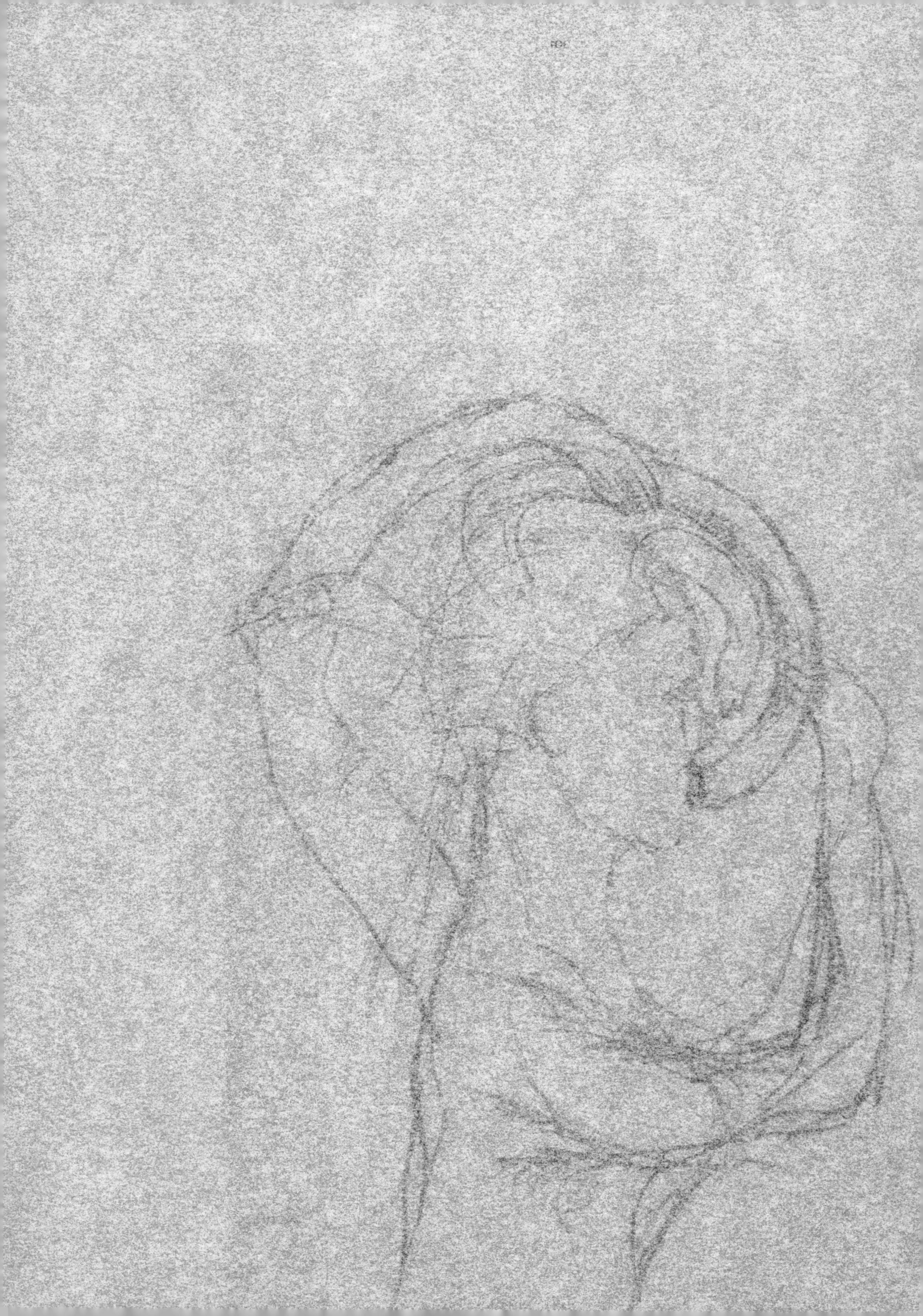

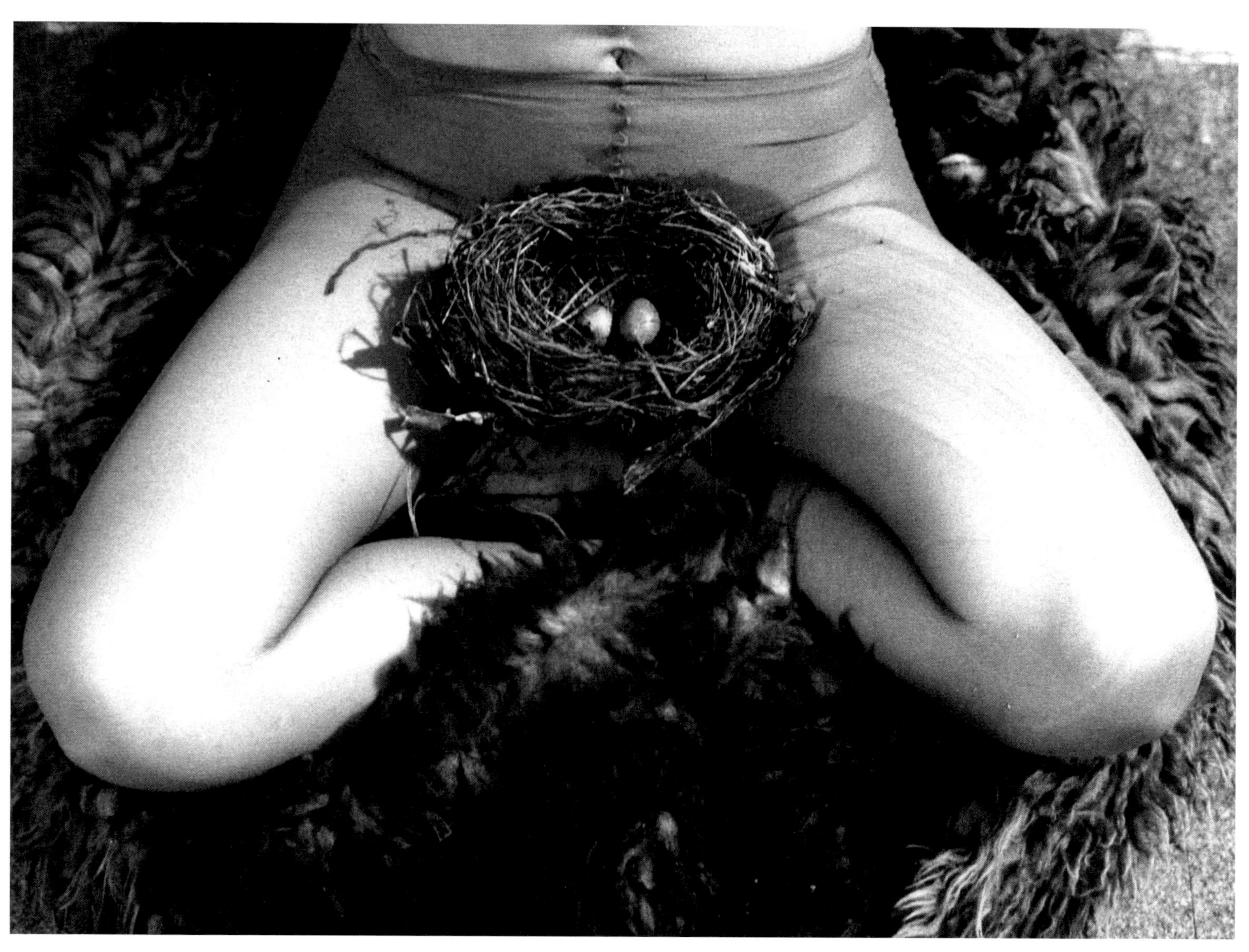

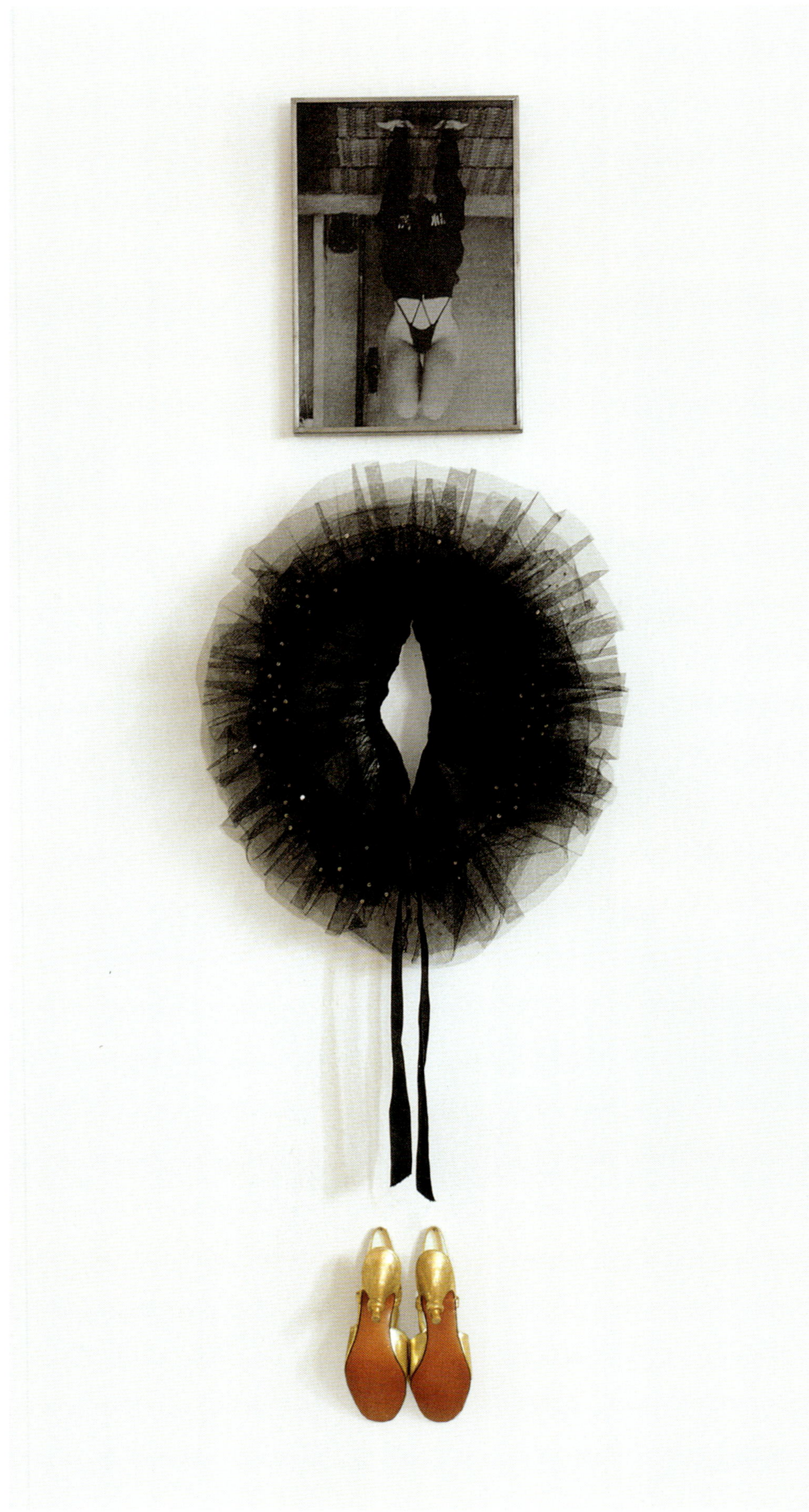

221   *Elevin* 1993

Biography

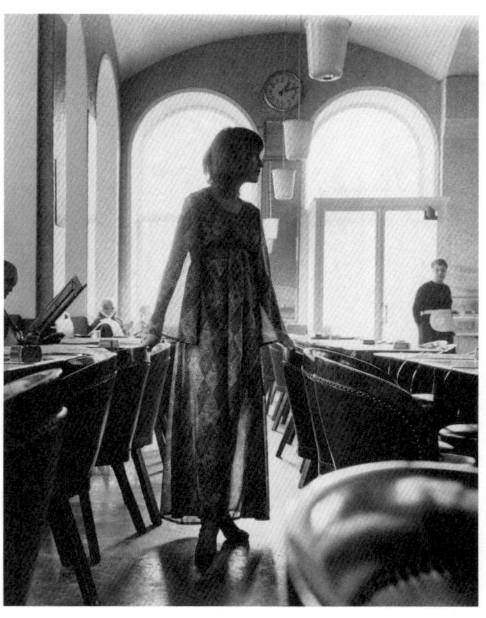

1949

Birgit Jürgenssen is born on April 10 in Vienna.

1957

At the age of eight, she begins to draw copies of works by Pablo Picasso in a school exercise book. Her signature »BICASSO Jürgenssen« is a combination of the name of the Spanish master and her own name. As a child she is called »Bi« by family and friends.

At fourteen she is given her first semi-automatic camera. Most of her photographs are of small objects she has made herself. As a teenager, she dances ballet and is a fan of Rudolf Nureyev.

»As far as I remember, I began to draw stories at the age of eight or nine in my brother's unused school exercise books. Some of my parents' friends were artists and people who lived unconventional lives. The stories my parents told me about them and about the large Picasso exhibition in Paris, as well as a book with pictures by Paul Klee we had at home, made me very curious, and so I tried to draw copies of everything that interested me. At the age of 14 I got my first semi-automatic camera and most of my photos were of small objects that I made myself. The aim was to do most of them in just one color.«

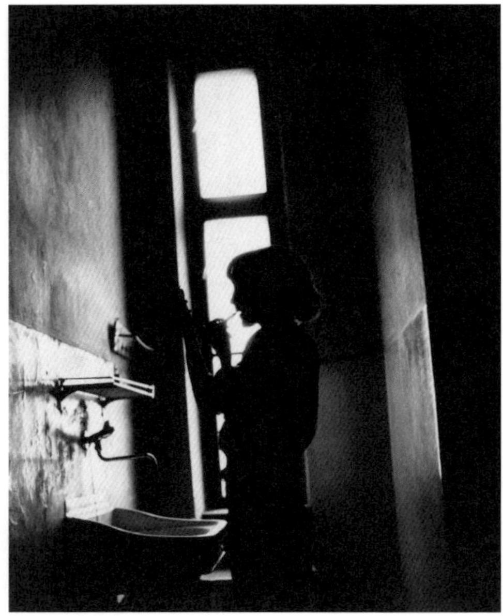

1967

On May 30, 1967, Jürgenssen completes middle school.

She spends several extended periods in France and becomes acquainted with French literature, the theater of Antonin Artaud, and the »inspirational poetry« of surrealism. She then takes an interest in psychoanalysis, structuralism, the ethnology of Claude Lévi-Strauss, and the socially critical discourses of her generation. This intellectual horizon was to shape her art.

Although she has not taken a foundation course, she is admitted to Franz Herberth's master class in graphic art at the Academy of Applied Arts. She was to speak of Herberth with great admiration throughout her life.

1971

On June 30, Jürgenssen completes her studies at the Academy of Applied Arts in Vienna with her diploma project *zipfeln* (a comprehensive, bound portfolio of 42 drawings). For her diploma project, she receives a prize to promote young artists from the Ministry of Education, Science, and Research and also the Wolfgang Hutter Prize.

After finishing her studies, Jürgenssen applies for scholarships abroad at the Hochschule für bildende Künste in Berlin, the École ABC de Paris, and for a Fulbright scholarship in the USA (Parsons School of Design, NY; Pratt Institute, Brooklyn; Cooper Union, NY). The British Council also has her name on the reserve list for the 1972/73 academic year.

»After finishing at the Academy, I immediately applied for scholarships in New York, Berlin, and London. I met the application requirements for all three. But in that year no artists were accepted for New York and Berlin, only scientists, and I was one year too young for London. So, unfortunately, I was unable to go abroad.«

1972

Jürgenssen registers as a master student in Herberth's class in graphic art *»to allow me to continue lithographing at the university«* and teaches herself to take black-and-white art photographs. She sets up a dark room in her studio.

1974

On April 1, Jürgenssen sends a letter to the DuMont publishing house, challenging them to publish a book about female artists: *»Women are so frequently the objects of art, but it is only on rare occasions that they are grudgingly allowed to express themselves in words and images. I would like to have the opportunity to compare myself with women artists and colleagues, and not just men.«* She finds kindred spirits in the artists Meret Oppenheim and Louise Bourgeois, whose work she considers »more poetic, less direct, and more subversive« than that of other women artists. DuMont rejects Jürgenssen's suggestion and also rejects a second request on June 6, 1979.

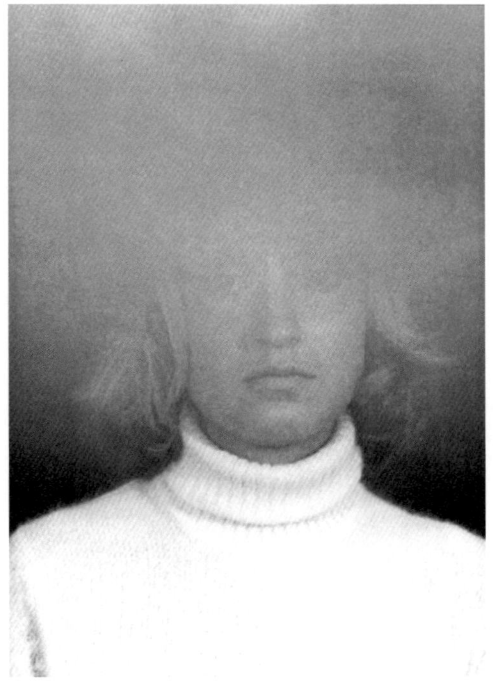

1975

From March 7 to April 5, Jürgenssen participates in the exhibition *MAGNA – Feminism: Art and Creativity*, curated by VALIE EXPORT at Galerie nächst St. Stephan, Vienna.

To mark International Women's Year, Austrian women artists are invited to take part in an exhibition at the Museum of Ethnology. The jury consists entirely of men, against which a group of prominent women protest, among them Birgit Jürgenssen, Doris Reitter, Meina Schellander, and VALIE EXPORT. When the protest is ignored, forty-six artists refuse to take part in the exhibition.

»In the early 1970s, the women's movement gained ground in Austria. Some of us committed to this at an early stage and were talking about the need to present women artists in galleries much more frequently. Then suddenly some of these women became gallery owners themselves, and this was all forgotten. [...] I approve of active feminism, in parallel, but not of using it to make a career. It is necessary to just produce convincing work, and perhaps women artists sometimes need to respond in more artistic ways.«

1976

Rejection of Jürgenssen's application for an Austrian state scholarship for the fine arts.

1978

Solo exhibition *Lineaturen* in the Albertina Museum's Graphic Art Collection in Vienna.

1980

On October 1, Jürgenssen begins work as the only assistant teacher in Prof. Maria Lassnig's master class at the University of Applied Arts. On June 25, 1981, students publish a flyer protesting against the fact that *»assistant teacher Birgit Jürgenssen has been fired in a disgraceful manner«* and demanding *»the immediate reinstatement of Birgit Jürgenssen as an assistant teacher for the 1981/82 academic year.«* Jürgenssen's position at the University of Applied Arts is terminated on September 30, 1981.

1981

On January 22, the exhibition *10 Tage – 100 Photos* (10 Days – 100 Photos) opens at Galerie Hubert Winter, then still located in Seilergasse 19, from which a continuing collaboration between the artist and the gallery will emerge.

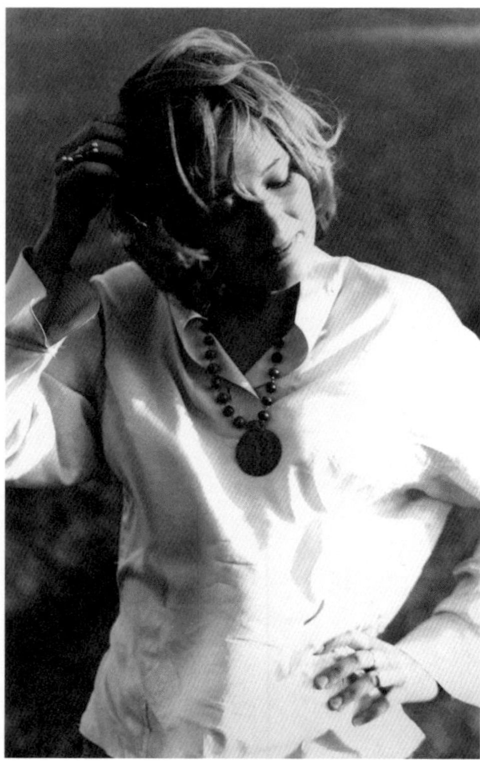

1982

On March 1, Jürgenssen begins teaching in Arnulf Rainer's master class at the Academy of Fine Arts Vienna. She initiates and establishes courses in photography and teaches at the Academy for more than twenty years.

»The problems and questions in the feminist movement in the seventies have now become those of the eighties. The simple and accepted fact that women today can express themselves in all areas of art makes things different and is a positive development. This is part of a social change in which the role and image of women have been transformed.«

1988

Foundation of the women artists' group DIE DAMEN with Birgit Jürgenssen, Ona B., Evelyne Egerer, and Ingeborg Strobl. In 1993 Lawrence Weiner replaces Ingeborg Strobl. The group performs together up until 1996.

1994

Birgit Jürgenssen curates the exhibition *Wenn die Kinder sind im Dunkeln …* at the Vienna Secession.

On September 24, she applies for »full-time« employment as a teacher at the Academy of Fine Arts Vienna.

1996

Artist's book *I MET A STRANGER*, together with Lawrence Weiner.

1998

Sooner or Later exhibition at TZ'Art Gallery in New York, and also the retrospective show *Earlier or Later* at the Oberösterreichisches Landesmuseum in Linz.

2001

Birgit Jürgenssen curates the Austrian contribution to the 8th International Biennale in Cairo.

2003

Birgit Jürgenssen dies on September 25 in Vienna.

»It is personal achievements that count. In the end, there are only good drawings, good photos, good pieces of work.«

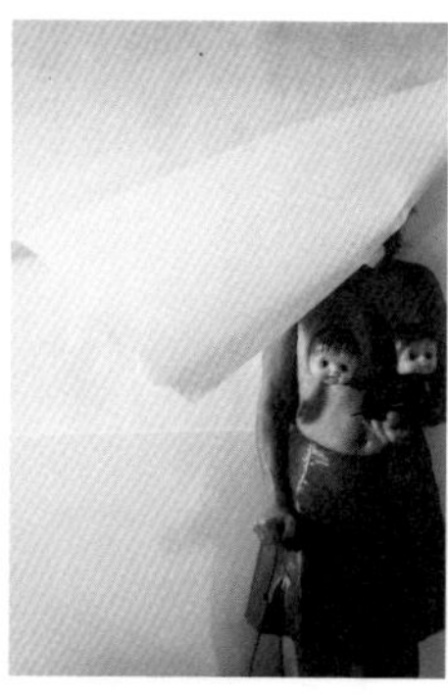

1

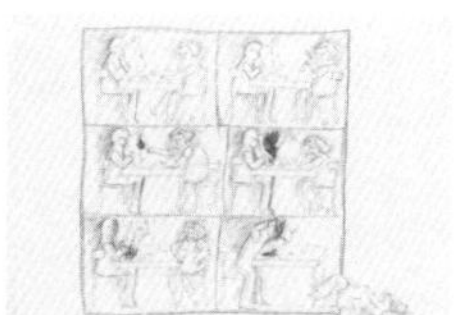

2

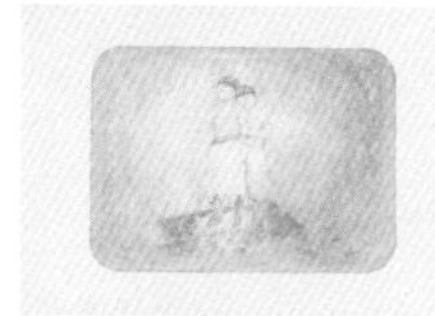

3

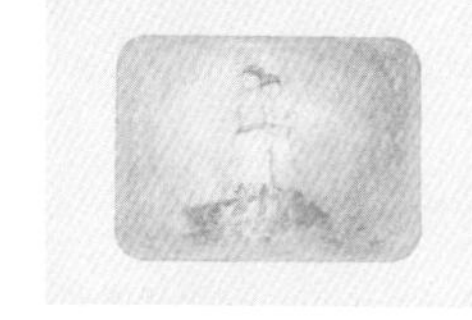

4

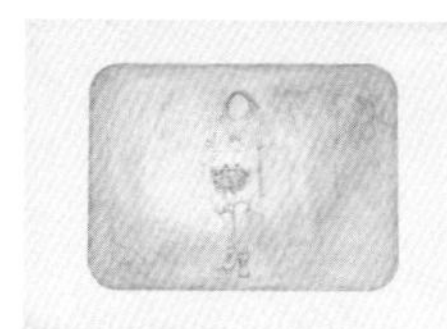

5

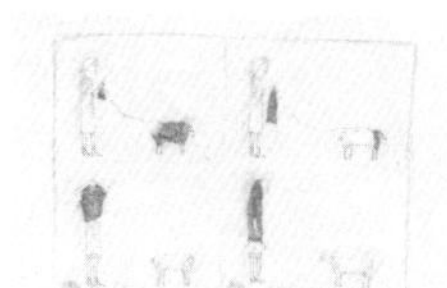

6

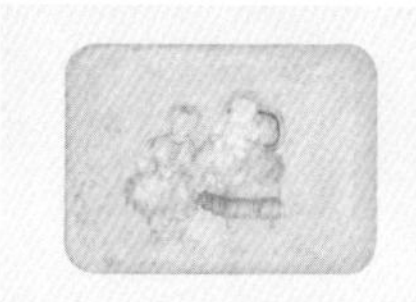

7

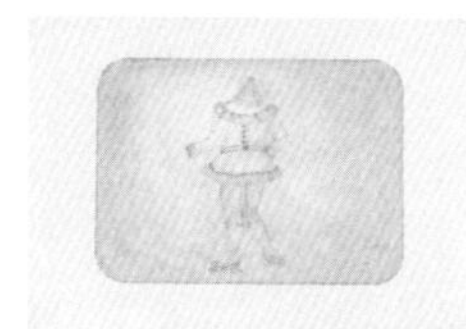

8

Catalogue of works

1
Ohne Titel | *Untitled* 1997
Color photograph
70 × 50 cm
SAMMLUNG VERBUND, Vienna (ph750)

2
Ohne Titel | Untitled 1969
Pencil, colored pencil on handmade paper
43.9 × 62.6 cm
Estate Birgit Jürgenssen (z167)

3
Ohne Titel | Untitled 1969
Pencil, colored pencil on handmade paper
43.5 × 62.7 cm
Estate Birgit Jürgenssen (z166)

4
Ohne Titel | Untitled 1969
Untitled
Pencil, colored pencil on handmade paper
43.7 × 62.4 cm
Estate Birgit Jürgenssen (z160)

5
Ohne Titel | Untitled 1971
Pencil, colored pencil on handmade paper
43.8 × 62.1 cm
Estate Birgit Jürgenssen (z24)

6
Ohne Titel | Untitled 1971
Pencil, colored pencil on handmade paper
43.8 × 62.1 cm
Estate Birgit Jürgenssen (z27)

7
Ohne Titel | Untitled 1971
Pencil, colored pencil on handmade paper
43.9 × 62.4 cm
Estate Birgit Jürgenssen (z269)

8
Ohne Titel | Untitled 1971
Pencil, colored pencil on handmade paper
43.8 × 62.1 cm
Estate Birgit Jürgenssen (z26)

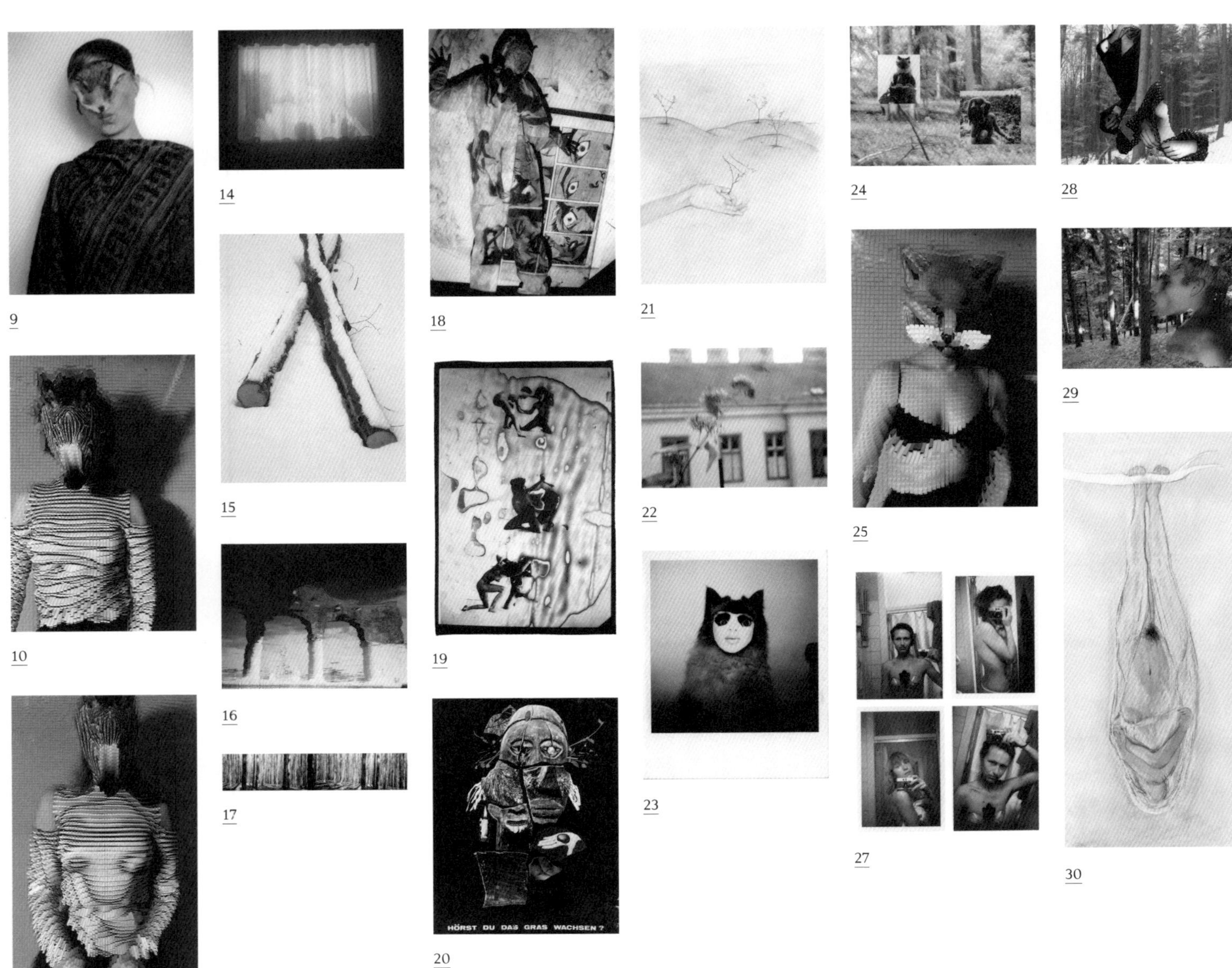

9   *Ohne Titel (Selbst mit Fellchen) | Untitled (Self with Little Fur)* 1974/1977
Color photograph
18 × 13 cm
Estate Birgit Jürgenssen (ph679)

10   *Zebra 1* 2001
Color photograph on aluminum behind acrylic glass
60 × 40 cm
SAMMLUNG VERBUND, Vienna (ph125)

11   *Zebra 2* 2001
Color photograph on aluminum behind acrylic glass
60 × 40 cm
Private collection, Vienna (ph126)

14   *Schneegewitter | Snow Storm* 2000/2001
Video
8 min.
Estate Birgit Jürgenssen (v2)

15   *X-Mahl* 2001
Digital photograph on canvas board
200 × 150 cm
Estate Birgit Jürgenssen (ph2205)

16   *Venedig | Venice* 2001
Digital photograph on canvas board
133 × 176 cm
Estate Birgit Jürgenssen (ph 2214)

17   *Purkersdorf* 2001
Digital photographs on aluminum behind acrylic glass, diptych
80 × 204 cm each
Estate Birgit Jürgenssen (ph2206)

18   *Ohne Titel | Untitled* 2001
Digital photograph on aluminum behind acrylic glass
104 × 77 cm
Estate Birgit Jürgenssen (ph124)

19   *Ohne Titel (Ranking) | Untitled (Ranking)* 1999
Color photograph, laminated
69 × 50.5 cm
Estate Birgit Jürgenssen (ph1559)

20   *Hörst du das Gras wachsen? | Can You Hear the Grass Grow?* 1968
Collage
62 × 48.8 cm
Estate Birgit Jürgenssen (z524)

21   *Lebenslinien-Bäumchen | Lifelines – Little Trees* 1977
Pencil, colored pencil on handmade paper
62 × 45 cm
Estate Birgit Jürgenssen (z44)

22   *Ohne Titel | Untitled* 2003
Color photograph
Unpublished photographic material
Estate Birgit Jürgenssen

23   *Ohne Titel (Olga) | Untitled (Olga)* 1979
SX-70 Polaroid
10.5 × 8.7 cm
SAMMLUNG VERBUND, Vienna (ph385)

24   *Ohne Titel | Untitled* 2002
Digital collage
Unpublished photographic material
Estate Birgit Jürgenssen

25   *Ohne Titel | Untitled* 2001
Digital collage
Unpublished photographic material
Estate Birgit Jürgenssen

27   *Ohne Titel | Untitled* 1973
Polyptych, Color photograph
25.3 × 18.1 cm
Estate Birgit Jürgenssen (ph673)

28   *Ohne Titel | Untitled* 2002
Digital collage
Unpublished photographic material
Estate Birgit Jürgenssen

29   *Ohne Titel | Untitled* 2002
Digital collage
Unpublished photographic material
Estate Birgit Jürgenssen

30   *Ohne Titel | Untitled* 1979
Pencil, colored pencil, oil crayon on paper, heightened with white
179 × 80 cm
Grażyna Kulczyk Collection (z913)

31   *Ohne Titel | Untitled* 1977
Pencil, colored pencil on handmade paper
56 × 39.5 cm
Estate Birgit Jürgenssen (z177)

32   *Du Jane, Ich Tarzan | You Jane, Me Tarzan* 1974
Pencil, colored pencil on handmade paper
62.5 × 43.5 cm
Estate Birgit Jürgenssen (z412)

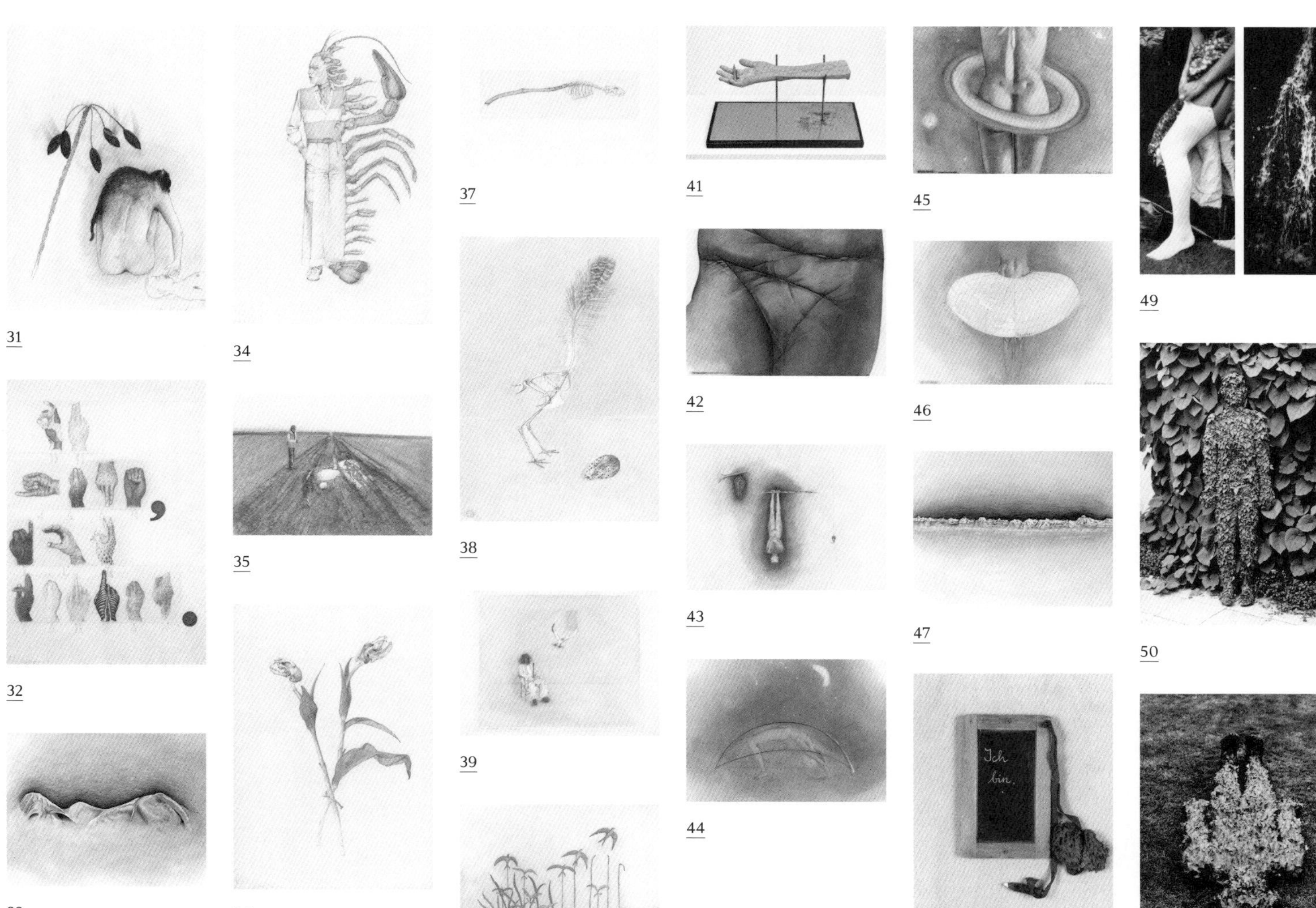

33   *Rückenlinie eines Tieres* / *Dorsal Line of an Animal* 1978
Pencil, colored pencil on handmade paper
44.9 × 62.6 cm
Estate Birgit Jürgenssen (z265)

34   *Fehlende Glieder* / *Missing Limbs* 1974
Pencil, colored pencil on handmade paper
62.5 × 43.5 cm
SAMMLUNG VERBUND, Vienna (z413)

35   *Ohne Titel* / *Untitled* 1977
Pencil, colored pencil on handmade paper
44 × 62 cm
SAMMLUNG VERBUND, Vienna (z104)

36   *Verwelkte Blümchen* / *Withered Little Flowers* 1974
Pencil, colored pencil on handmade paper
62.2 × 44 cm
SAMMLUNG VERBUND, Vienna (z55)

37   *Metamorphose I* / *Metamorphosis I* 1974
Pencil, colored pencil on handmade paper
44 × 62.2 cm
S. Hannae Brand Collection (z54)

38   *Ohne Titel* / *Untitled* 1974
Pencil, colored pencil on handmade paper
62.3 × 43.6 cm
Estate Birgit Jürgenssen (z53)

39   *Verwandtschaft mit der Möwe* / *Kinship with a Seagull* 1977
Pencil, colored pencil on paper
44.5 × 62 cm
Estate Birgit Jürgenssen (z1190)

40   *Ohne Titel* / *Untitled* 1974
Pencil, colored pencil on handmade paper
43.6 × 62.2 cm
Estate Birgit Jürgenssen (z130)

41   *Ohne Titel* / *Untitled* 1974
Iron, colored pencil, graphite, wood, earthenware
45 × 18 × 20 cm
Private collection (s49)

42   *Handlinien / Lebenslinie / Karte für Wahrsager* / *Palm Lines / Lifeline / Map for the Fortune Tellers* 1978
Pencil, colored pencil, charcoal on handmade paper
44.9 × 62.7 cm
SAMMLUNG VERBUND, Vienna (z185)

43   *Ohne Titel* / *Untitled* 1975/1976
Pencil on handmade paper
45 × 62.5 cm
Estate Birgit Jürgenssen (z70)

44   *Fluglinie der Sterne* / *Trajectory of the Stars* 1978
Pencil, colored pencil on handmade paper
44.5 × 62.3 cm
Estate Birgit Jürgenssen (z724)

45   *Kreisring (Schwimmgürtel)* / *Annulus (Life Belt)* 1978
Pencil, colored pencil on handmade paper
44.9 × 62.7 cm
Estate Birgit Jürgenssen (z184)

46   *Krinoline* / *Crinoline* 1978
Pencil, colored pencil on handmade paper
44.8 × 62.5 cm
Estate Birgit Jürgenssen (z171)

47   *Ohne Titel* / *Untitled* 1978
Pencil, colored pencil on paper
44.9 × 62.5 cm
Estate Birgit Jürgenssen (z249)

48   *Ich bin.* / *I am.* 1995
Chalk, blackboard, sponge mounted on wooden panel, behind acrylic glass
30.9 × 25.3 cm
Estate Birgit Jürgenssen (s46)

49   *Ohne Titel (Sonderbare Regenfälle)* / *Untitled (Peculiar Rainfalls)* 1992
B/W photographs, diptych
85 × 40 cm each
Estate Birgit Jürgenssen (ph766)

50   *Ohne Titel* / *Untitled* 1979
Color photograph
70 × 50 cm
Private collection (ph783)

51   *Ohne Titel* / *Untitled* 1979/1980
B/W photograph
40 × 30.4 cm
Estate Birgit Jürgenssen (ph770)

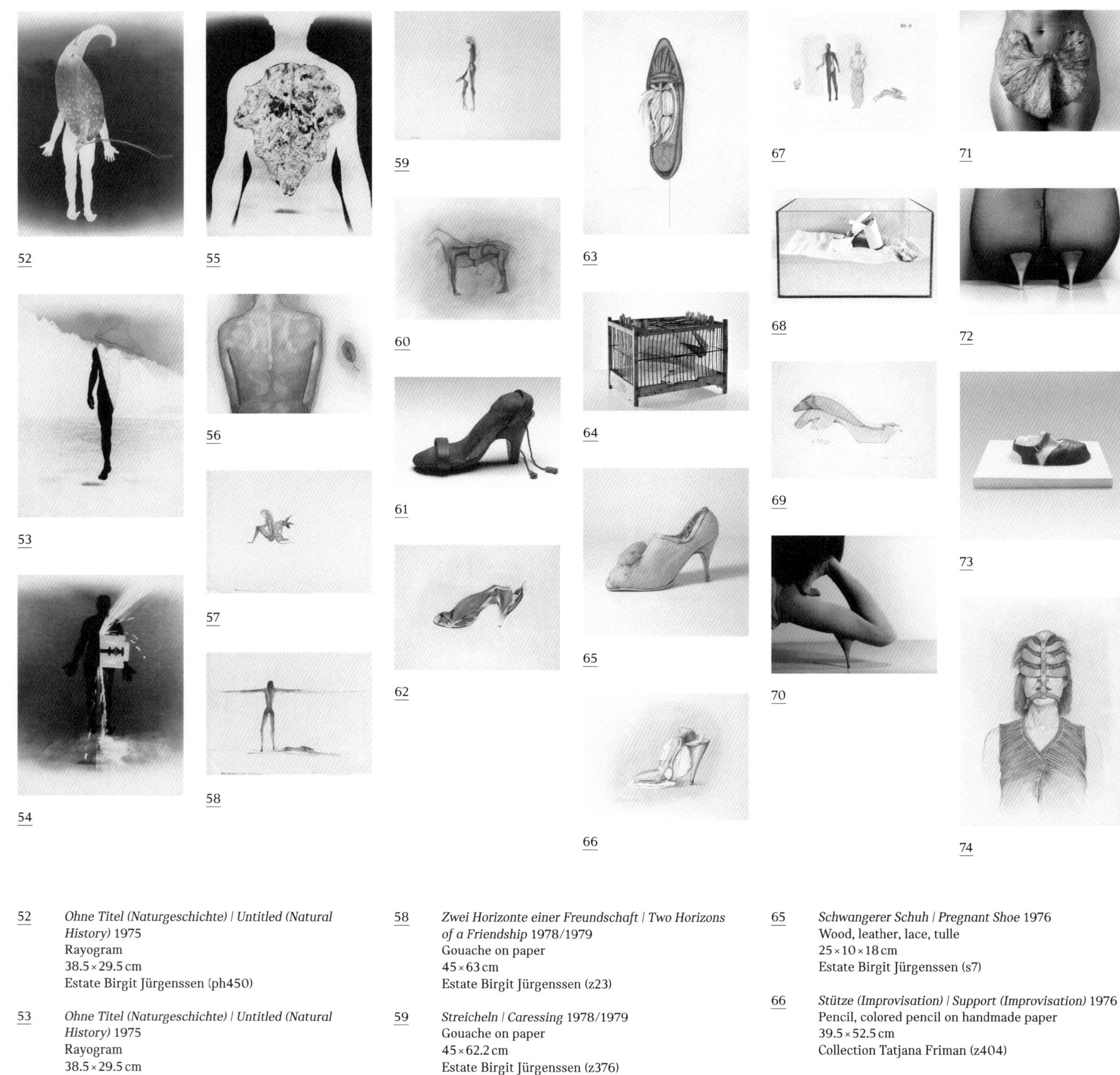

52 | *Ohne Titel (Naturgeschichte)* | *Untitled (Natural History)* 1975
Rayogram
38.5 × 29.5 cm
Estate Birgit Jürgenssen (ph450)

53 | *Ohne Titel (Naturgeschichte)* | *Untitled (Natural History)* 1975
Rayogram
38.5 × 29.5 cm
Estate Birgit Jürgenssen (ph451)

54 | *Ohne Titel (Naturgeschichte)* | *Untitled (Natural History)* 1975
Rayogram
38.5 × 29.5 cm
Private collection (ph453)

55 | *Ohne Titel (Naturgeschichte)* | *Untitled (Natural History)* 1975
Rayogram
38.5 × 29.5 cm
Estate Birgit Jürgenssen (ph454)

56 | *Verwandtschaft mit einem Blatt. Keimzeichnung* | *Kinship with a Leaf: Germ Drawing* 1978
Pencil, colored pencil, collaged leaf on handmade paper
44.9 × 62.7 cm
Estate Birgit Jürgenssen (z189)

57 | *Rücken an Rücken sitzen* | *Sitting Back to Back* 1978/1979
Gouache on paper
45 × 63 cm
Estate Birgit Jürgenssen (z22)

58 | *Zwei Horizonte einer Freundschaft* | *Two Horizons of a Friendship* 1978/1979
Gouache on paper
45 × 63 cm
Estate Birgit Jürgenssen (z23)

59 | *Streicheln* | *Caressing* 1978/1979
Gouache on paper
45 × 62.2 cm
Estate Birgit Jürgenssen (z376)

60 | *Ohne Titel* | *Untitled* 1978
Pencil, colored pencil on handmade paper
43 × 61 cm
Estate Birgit Jürgenssen (z527)

61 | *Zungenleckschuh* | *Lick-Tongue Shoe* 1974
Leather, metal, beef tongue
20 × 15 × 18 cm
Estate Birgit Jürgenssen (s16)

62 | *Muskelschuh* | *Muscle Shoe* 1976
Pencil, colored pencil on handmade paper
31 × 44 cm
Estate Birgit Jürgenssen (z476)

63 | *anna-tommie* 1976
Pencil, colored pencil on handmade paper
52.4 × 39.5 cm
Estate Birgit Jürgenssen (z474)

64 | *Gefangene Fröhlichkeit* | *Caught Happiness* 1982
Found cage, wooden clips, oil on cellophane
35.5 × 49 × 36 cm
Estate Birgit Jürgenssen (s43)

65 | *Schwangerer Schuh* | *Pregnant Shoe* 1976
Wood, leather, lace, tulle
25 × 10 × 18 cm
Estate Birgit Jürgenssen (s7)

66 | *Stütze (Improvisation)* | *Support (Improvisation)* 1976
Pencil, colored pencil on handmade paper
39.5 × 52.5 cm
Collection Tatjana Friman (z404)

67 | *Spiegelblick – Häschenerlebnis – Wem gehört der Mädchenhandschuh?* | *Mirror gaze – Bunny Experience – Who Does the Girl's Glove Belong To?* 1977
Pencil, colored pencil on handmade paper
45 × 62.4 cm
Estate Birgit Jürgenssen (z94)

68 | *Ohne Titel (Hochzeitsschuh)* | *Untitled (Wedding Shoe)* 1976
Glass cabinet, artificial flowers, leather, sand, tulle
44.7 × 17.6 × 30.5 cm
Private collection, New York (s57)

69 | *Netter Raubvogelschuh* | *Nice Bird of Prey Shoe* 1972
Pencil, colored pencil on handmade paper
31 × 44 cm
Estate Birgit Jürgenssen (z467)

70 | *Schuhroulade* | *Shoe Roulade* 1977
B/W photograph
23.9 × 30.2 cm
Private collection (ph1670)

71 | *Ohne Titel* | *Untitled* 1988
Color photograph
22 × 30.4 cm
SAMMLUNG VERBUND, Vienna (ph962)

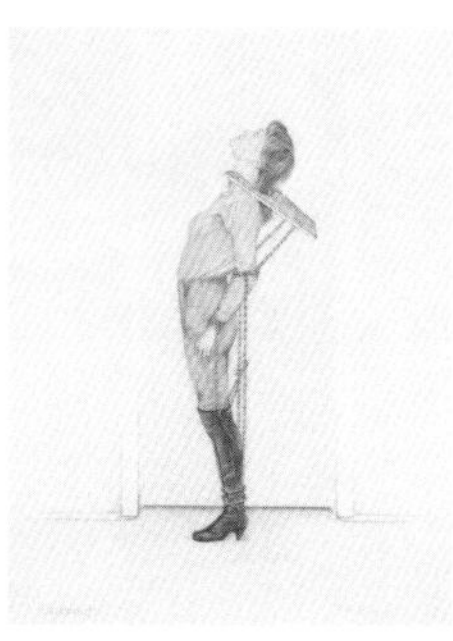

75

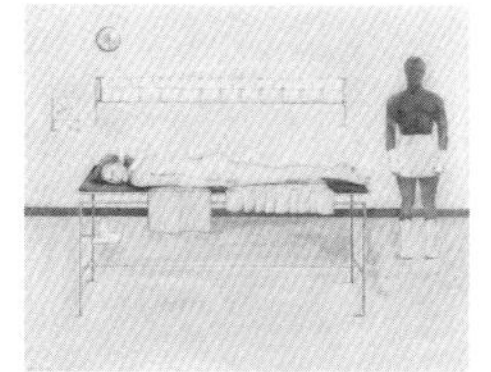

78

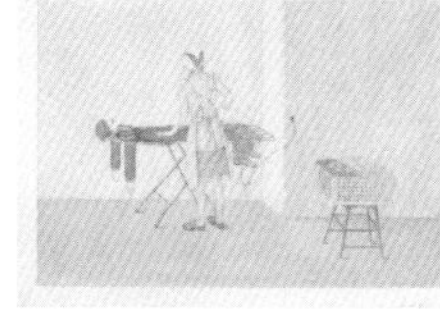

81

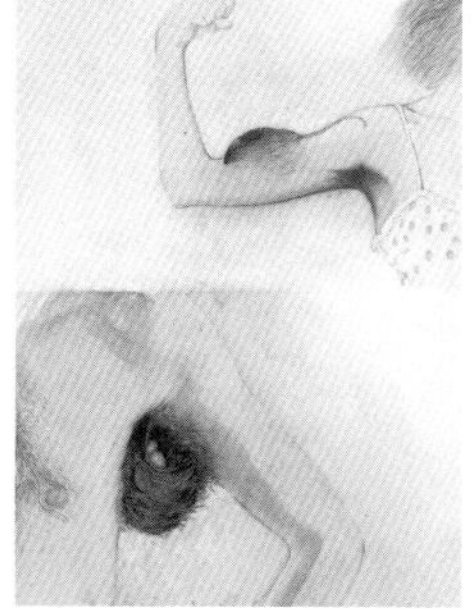

82

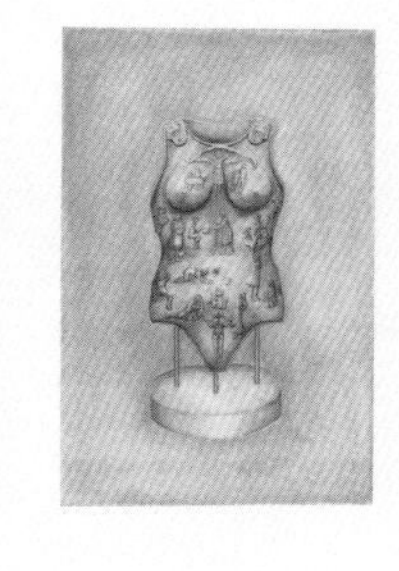

85

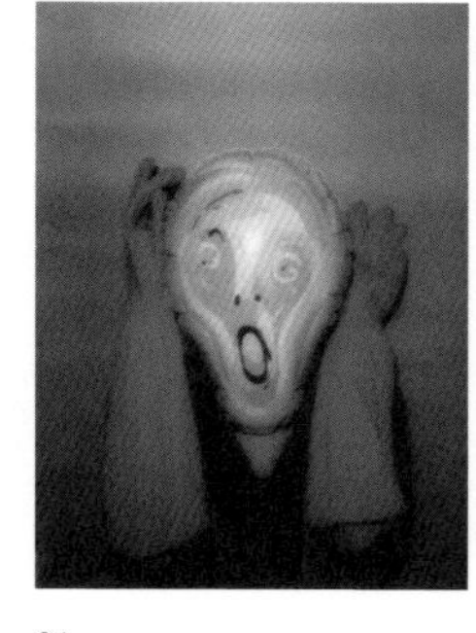

91

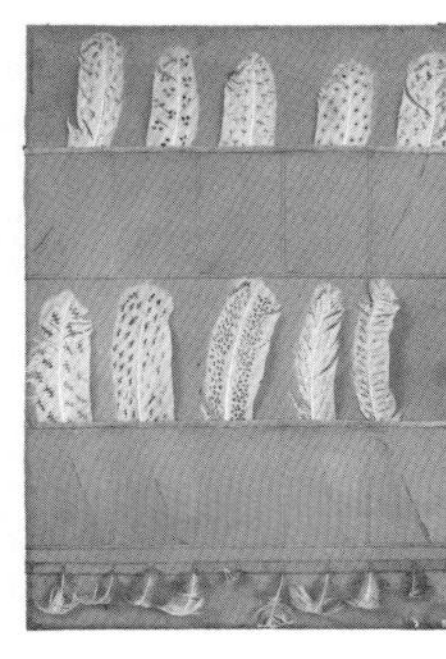

76

79

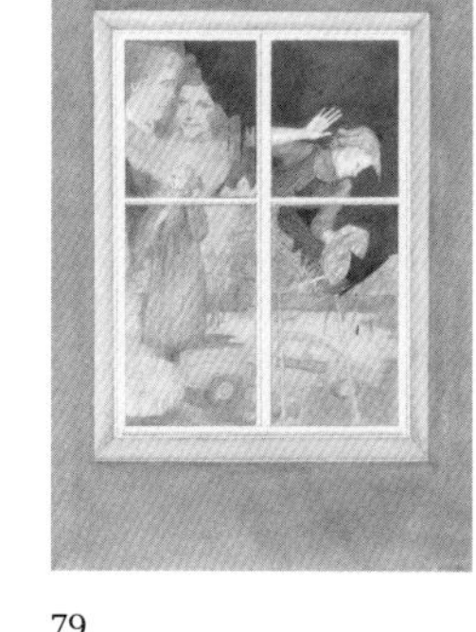

80

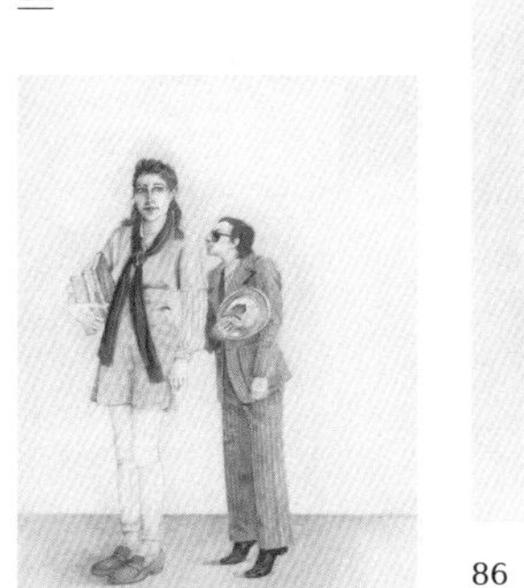

86

83

84

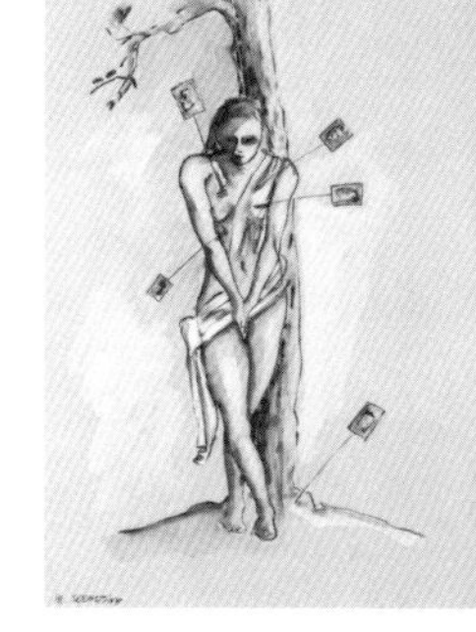

89

92

87

90

77

88

72   *Ballonschuh* / *Balloon Shoe* 1976
B/W photograph
24 × 30.3 cm
SAMMLUNG Hainz, Vienna (ph1658)

73   *Kopfsandale* / *Head Sandal* 1976
Plaster, leather
32.5 × 30 × 10 cm
Estate Birgit Jürgenssen (s11)

74   *Schuhmaske* / *Shoe Mask* 1976
Colored pencil on handmade paper, heightened
with white
52.5 × 39.5 cm
SAMMLUNG VERBUND, Vienna (z406)

75   *Stiefelknecht* / *Bootjack* 1976
Pencil, colored pencil on handmade paper
52.5 × 39.5 cm
MoMA – Museum of Modern Art, New York (z417)

76   *Stütze* / *Crutch* 1976
Pencil, colored pencil on handmade paper
62.5 × 45 cm
MoMA – Museum of Modern Art, New York (z98)

77   *Ohne Titel* / *Untitled* 1975
Mixed media (leather, labelled feathers mounted
on stretcher frame)
70 × 50 × 5 cm
Estate Birgit Jürgenssen (s42)

78   *Ohne Titel (The Hour of the Feather)* / *Untitled
(The Hour of the Feather)* 1976
Pencil, colored pencil on handmade paper
45 × 55.5 cm
Estate Birgit Jürgenssen (z99)

79   *Fensterputzen* / *Window Cleaning* 1975
Pencil, colored pencil on handmade paper
62.5 × 43.5 cm
Estate Birgit Jürgenssen (z400)

80   *Hausfrau* / *Housewife* 1974
Colored pencil on handmade paper, heightened
with white
62.5 × 44.6 cm
Estate Birgit Jürgenssen (z966)

81   *Hausfrauenarbeit* / *Housewives' Work* 1973
Pencil, colored pencil on handmade paper
44.6 × 62.3 cm
Estate Birgit Jürgenssen (z681)

82   *Bodenschrubben* / *Scrubbing the Floor* 1975
Pencil, colored pencil on handmade paper
43.5 × 62.5 cm
SAMMLUNG VERBUND, Vienna (z402)

83   *Großes Mädchen* / *Big Girl* 1975
Pencil, colored pencil on handmade paper
62.5 × 43.5 cm
Estate Birgit Jürgenssen (z399)

84   *Ohne Titel* / *Untitled* 1979
Gelatin silver print
24 × 30 cm
Estate Birgit Jürgenssen (ph23)

85   *Ohne Titel* / *Untitled* 1977
Pencil, colored pencil on handmade paper,
heightened with white
56 × 39.5 cm
Estate Birgit Jürgenssen (z176)

86   *Mrs. Churchill* 1976
Pencil, colored pencil on handmade paper
62.5 × 45 cm
Private collection (z716)

87   *Ohne Titel (Frau)* / *Untitled (Woman)* 1979
B/W photograph, overpainted
29.6 × 39.9 cm
Private collection, Vienna (ph1096)

88   *Demenstration* 1978/1979
Gouache, gauze, blotting paper, fabric, cotton wool,
thorns on paper
113 × 78 cm
Estate Birgit Jürgenssen (z408)

89   *Der Panzer der Augustina* / *Augustina's Armor* 1974
Pencil on handmade paper
62.3 × 44.5 cm
Estate Birgit Jürgenssen (z107)

90   *Das Dreieck* / *The Triangle* 1976
Pencil on handmade paper
43.9 × 62.4 cm
Estate Birgit Jürgenssen (z173)

91   *Ohne Titel* / *Untitled* 1994/1995
3D photograph
11.3 × 8.9 cm
Estate Birgit Jürgenssen (ph2169)

92   *Hl. Sebastine* / *St. Sebastine* 1983
Gouache, felt-tip pen on paper
40 × 30 cm
Estate Birgit Jürgenssen (z639)

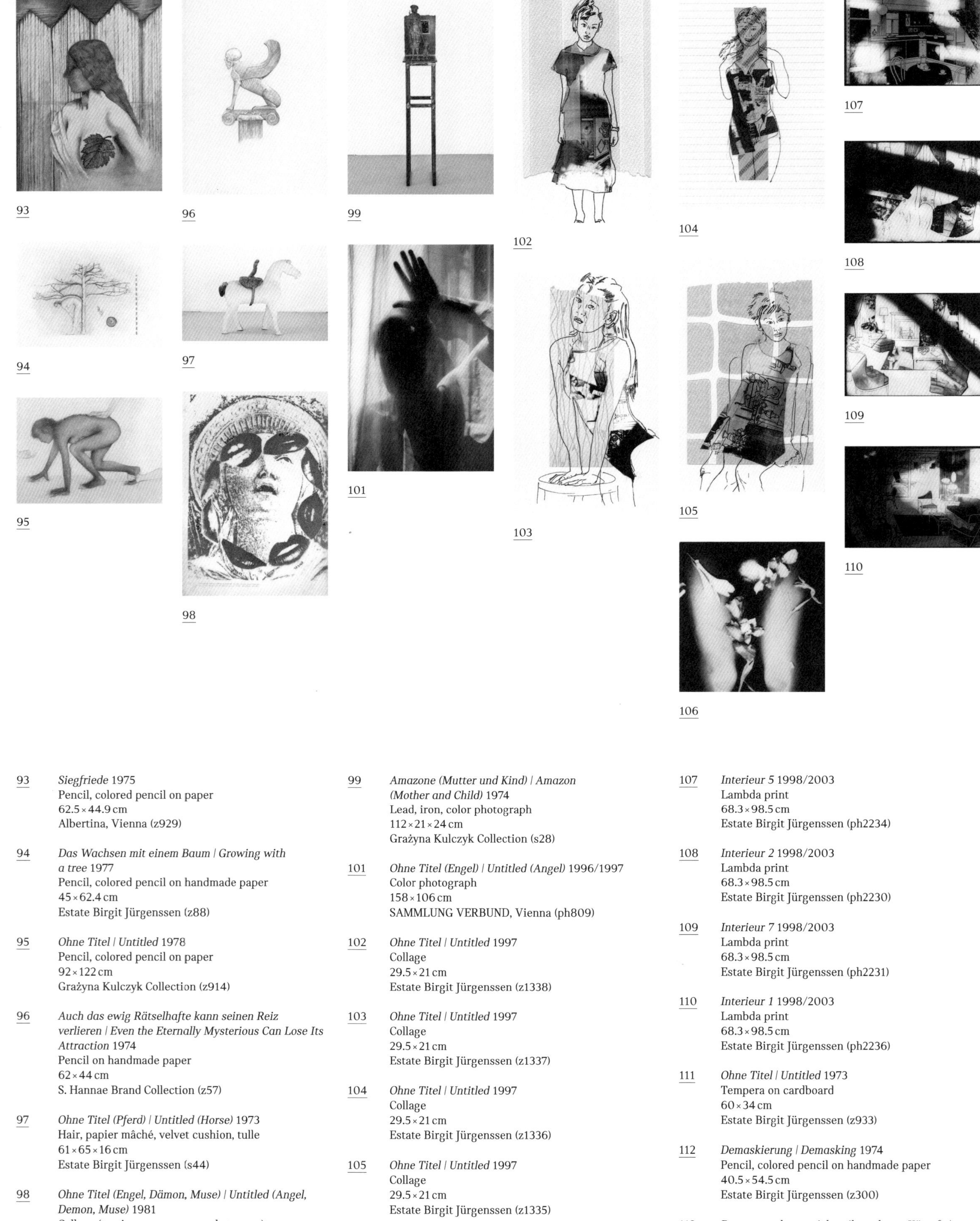

93

96

99

102

104

107

94

97

108

95

101

103

109

98

105

110

106

93   *Siegfriede* 1975
Pencil, colored pencil on paper
62.5 × 44.9 cm
Albertina, Vienna (z929)

94   *Das Wachsen mit einem Baum | Growing with a tree* 1977
Pencil, colored pencil on handmade paper
45 × 62.4 cm
Estate Birgit Jürgenssen (z88)

95   *Ohne Titel | Untitled* 1978
Pencil, colored pencil on paper
92 × 122 cm
Grażyna Kulczyk Collection (z914)

96   *Auch das ewig Rätselhafte kann seinen Reiz verlieren | Even the Eternally Mysterious Can Lose Its Attraction* 1974
Pencil on handmade paper
62 × 44 cm
S. Hannae Brand Collection (z57)

97   *Ohne Titel (Pferd) | Untitled (Horse)* 1973
Hair, papier mâché, velvet cushion, tulle
61 × 65 × 16 cm
Estate Birgit Jürgenssen (s44)

98   *Ohne Titel (Engel, Dämon, Muse) | Untitled (Angel, Demon, Muse)* 1981
Collage (tracing paper, paper, photocopy)
30.4 × 21 cm
Estate Birgit Jürgenssen (z812)

99   *Amazone (Mutter und Kind) | Amazon (Mother and Child)* 1974
Lead, iron, color photograph
112 × 21 × 24 cm
Grażyna Kulczyk Collection (s28)

101   *Ohne Titel (Engel) | Untitled (Angel)* 1996/1997
Color photograph
158 × 106 cm
SAMMLUNG VERBUND, Vienna (ph809)

102   *Ohne Titel | Untitled* 1997
Collage
29.5 × 21 cm
Estate Birgit Jürgenssen (z1338)

103   *Ohne Titel | Untitled* 1997
Collage
29.5 × 21 cm
Estate Birgit Jürgenssen (z1337)

104   *Ohne Titel | Untitled* 1997
Collage
29.5 × 21 cm
Estate Birgit Jürgenssen (z1336)

105   *Ohne Titel | Untitled* 1997
Collage
29.5 × 21 cm
Estate Birgit Jürgenssen (z1335)

106   *Ophelia* 1979
Color photograph
30 × 30 cm
Estate Birgit Jürgenssen (ph22)

107   *Interieur 5* 1998/2003
Lambda print
68.3 × 98.5 cm
Estate Birgit Jürgenssen (ph2234)

108   *Interieur 2* 1998/2003
Lambda print
68.3 × 98.5 cm
Estate Birgit Jürgenssen (ph2230)

109   *Interieur 7* 1998/2003
Lambda print
68.3 × 98.5 cm
Estate Birgit Jürgenssen (ph2231)

110   *Interieur 1* 1998/2003
Lambda print
68.3 × 98.5 cm
Estate Birgit Jürgenssen (ph2236)

111   *Ohne Titel | Untitled* 1973
Tempera on cardboard
60 × 34 cm
Estate Birgit Jürgenssen (z933)

112   *Demaskierung | Demasking* 1974
Pencil, colored pencil on handmade paper
40.5 × 54.5 cm
Estate Birgit Jürgenssen (z300)

113   *Bevor man das erreicht, gibt es harte Kämpfe | You Have a Tough Struggle on Your Hands Before You Get There* 1974
Pencil, colored pencil on handmade paper
44.2 × 62 cm
Estate Birgit Jürgenssen (z148)

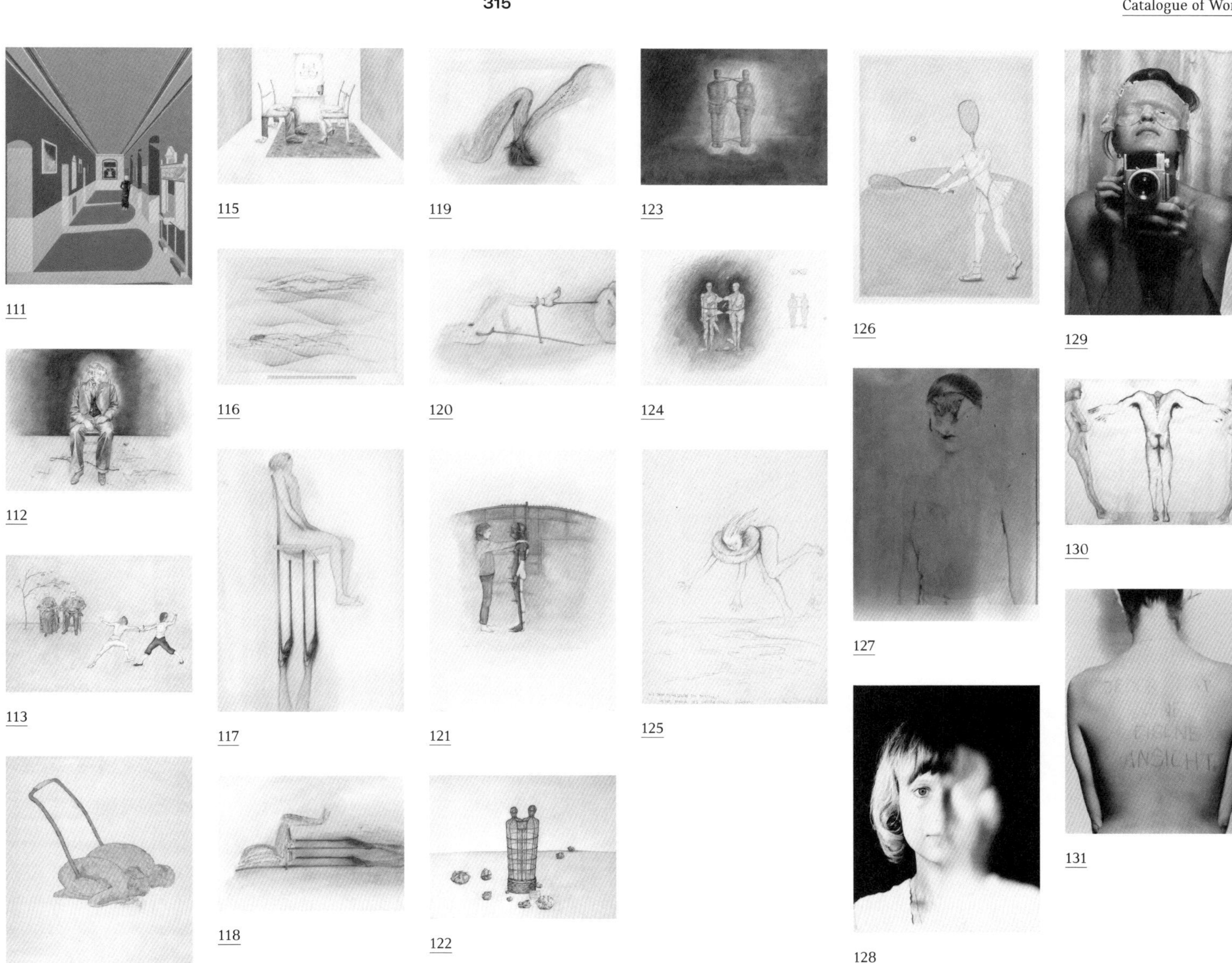

114　Ohne Titel | Untitled 1972
Gouache, pencil, colored pencil on paper
(grounded with emulsion paint)
151×136 cm
Estate Birgit Jürgenssen (z902)

115　Ohne Titel (The Party) | Untitled (The Party) 1973
Pencil on handmade paper
44×60.6 cm
Estate Birgit Jürgenssen (z705)

116　Gleiche Wellenlänge? | On the Same Wavelength? 1976
Pencil, colored pencil on handmade paper
44.9×62.5 cm
Estate Birgit Jürgenssen (z253)

117　Ohne Titel | Untitled 1979/1980
Pencil, colored pencil on tracing paper
54×39 cm
Estate Birgit Jürgenssen (z159)

118　Andersrum | The Other Way Round 1979
Gouache, pencil, colored pencil on tracing paper
39.1×53.4 cm
Estate Birgit Jürgenssen (z484)

119　Unsere | Ours 1979
Gouache, pencil, colored pencil on tracing paper
39.1×53.4 cm
Estate Birgit Jürgenssen (z483)

120　Me Do! 1979
Gouache, pencil, colored pencil on tracing paper
39×54.6 cm
Estate Birgit Jürgenssen (z482)

121　Eiserne Jungfrau | Iron Maiden 1976
Pencil, colored pencil on handmade paper
62.5×44.4 cm
Estate Birgit Jürgenssen (z97)

122　Gewächshaus zur Pflege zwischenmenschlicher
Beziehung | Greenhouse to Nurture Interpersonal
Relationship 1974
Pencil, colored pencil on handmade paper
44.6×62.4 cm
Estate Birgit Jürgenssen (z255)

123　Ohne Titel | Untitled 1978
Pencil, colored pencil on handmade paper
45×62.3 cm
Estate Birgit Jürgenssen (z74)

124　Ohne Titel | Untitled 1975
Pencil, colored pencil on handmade paper
44×62 cm
Estate Birgit Jürgenssen (z72)

125　Mit dem Mühlstein um den Hals in das Meer des
Vergessens stürzen | Plunging into the Sea of Forget-
fulness with a Millstone around One's Neck 1983
Pencil, colored pencil on handmade paper, heightened with white
44.8×32.6 cm
Estate Birgit Jürgenssen (z313)

126　Das Match das trag ich mit mir selber aus | I'll Play
the Match with Myself 1973
Pencil, colored pencil on handmade paper
62.2×45 cm
Estate Birgit Jürgenssen (z30)

127　Ohne Titel (Selbst mit Fellchen) | Untitled (Self
with Little Fur) 1974
B/W photograph, solarization
24×18 cm
Private collection (ph1594)

128　Ohne Titel | Untitled 1972
24×18 cm
Unpublished photographic material
Estate Birgit Jürgenssen

129　Ohne Titel | Untitled 1976
B/W photograph
12.6×9.1 cm
Private collection, Vienna (ph2435)

130　Ohne Titel | Untitled 1978
Collage (Pencil, oil on fabric, pencil on paper;
mounted on paper)
190×243 cm
Estate Birgit Jürgenssen (z512)

131　Jeder hat seine eigene Ansicht | Everyone's Got His
Own Point of View 1975
Gelatine silver print
34.3×26.5 cm
Estate Birgit Jürgenssen (ph1815)

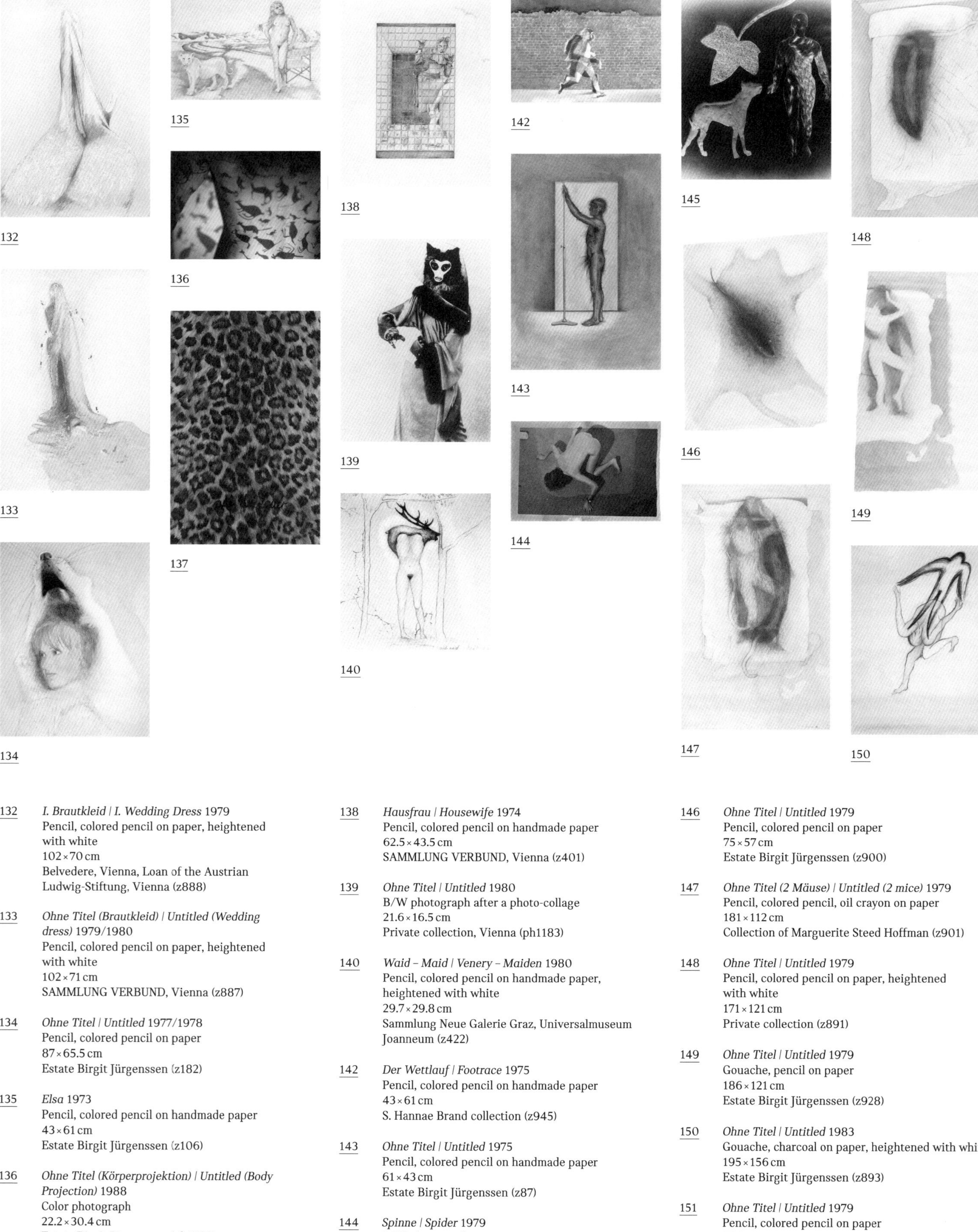

135

138

142

132

136

145

148

133

137

143

139

146

149

144

147

150

140

134

132   *I. Brautkleid / I. Wedding Dress* 1979
Pencil, colored pencil on paper, heightened
with white
102×70 cm
Belvedere, Vienna, Loan of the Austrian
Ludwig-Stiftung, Vienna (z888)

133   *Ohne Titel (Brautkleid) / Untitled (Wedding
dress)* 1979/1980
Pencil, colored pencil on paper, heightened
with white
102×71 cm
SAMMLUNG VERBUND, Vienna (z887)

134   *Ohne Titel / Untitled* 1977/1978
Pencil, colored pencil on paper
87×65.5 cm
Estate Birgit Jürgenssen (z182)

135   *Elsa* 1973
Pencil, colored pencil on handmade paper
43×61 cm
Estate Birgit Jürgenssen (z106)

136   *Ohne Titel (Körperprojektion) / Untitled (Body
Projection)* 1988
Color photograph
22.2×30.4 cm
Estate Birgit Jürgenssen (ph1729)

137   *Auf der Lauer / Lying in Wait* 1985
Marker on structured paper
49.5×32 cm
Estate Birgit Jürgenssen (z718)

138   *Hausfrau / Housewife* 1974
Pencil, colored pencil on handmade paper
62.5×43.5 cm
SAMMLUNG VERBUND, Vienna (z401)

139   *Ohne Titel / Untitled* 1980
B/W photograph after a photo-collage
21.6 × 16.5 cm
Private collection, Vienna (ph1183)

140   *Waid – Maid / Venery – Maiden* 1980
Pencil, colored pencil on handmade paper,
heightened with white
29.7×29.8 cm
Sammlung Neue Galerie Graz, Universalmuseum
Joanneum (z422)

142   *Der Wettlauf / Footrace* 1975
Pencil, colored pencil on handmade paper
43×61 cm
S. Hannae Brand collection (z945)

143   *Ohne Titel / Untitled* 1975
Pencil, colored pencil on handmade paper
61×43 cm
Estate Birgit Jürgenssen (z87)

144   *Spinne / Spider* 1979
B/W photograph
18.6 × 24.6 cm
Estate Birgit Jürgenssen (ph2452)

145   *Ohne Titel / Untitled* 1975
Rayogram
36 × 29.4 cm
Estate Birgit Jürgenssen (ph1075)

146   *Ohne Titel / Untitled* 1979
Pencil, colored pencil on paper
75×57 cm
Estate Birgit Jürgenssen (z900)

147   *Ohne Titel (2 Mäuse) / Untitled (2 mice)* 1979
Pencil, colored pencil, oil crayon on paper
181×112 cm
Collection of Marguerite Steed Hoffman (z901)

148   *Ohne Titel / Untitled* 1979
Pencil, colored pencil on paper, heightened
with white
171×121 cm
Private collection (z891)

149   *Ohne Titel / Untitled* 1979
Gouache, pencil on paper
186×121 cm
Estate Birgit Jürgenssen (z928)

150   *Ohne Titel / Untitled* 1983
Gouache, charcoal on paper, heightened with white
195×156 cm
Estate Birgit Jürgenssen (z893)

151   *Ohne Titel / Untitled* 1979
Pencil, colored pencil on paper
57,5×90,5 cm
Estate Birgit Jürgenssen (z912)

152   *Das Tier / The Animal* 1978
Pencil, colored pencil on handmade paper
44.5×62.3 cm
Estate Birgit Jürgenssen (z725)

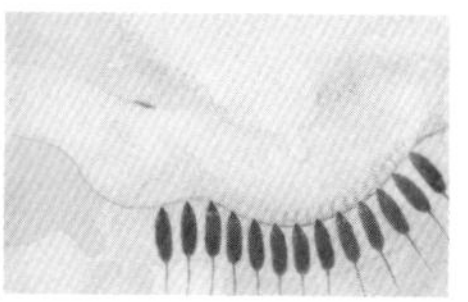

151

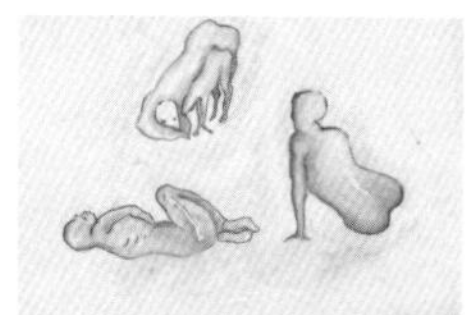

155

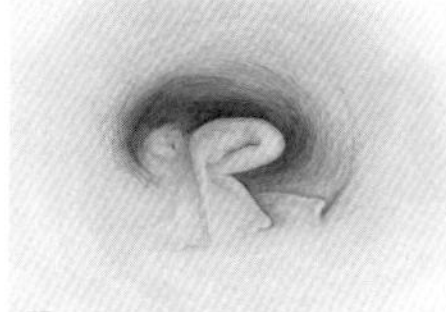

152

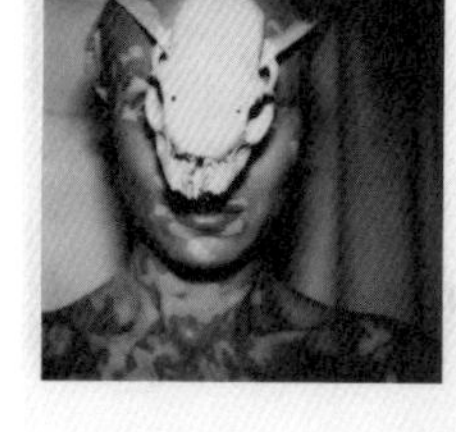

156

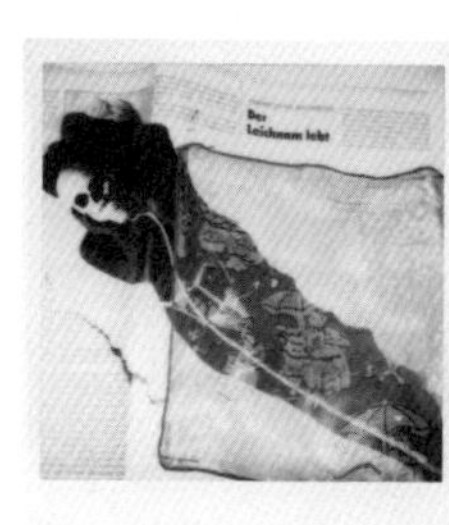

153

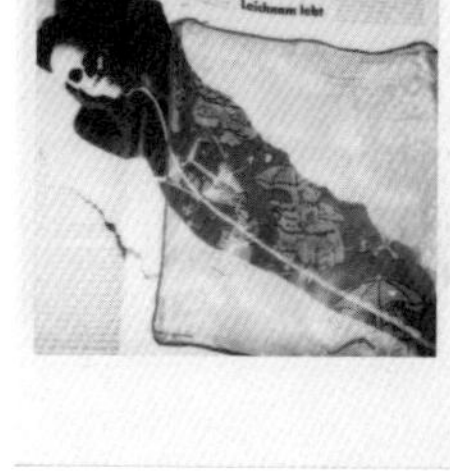

157

154

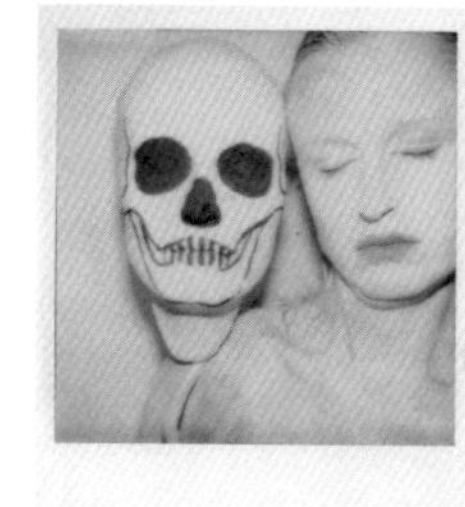

158

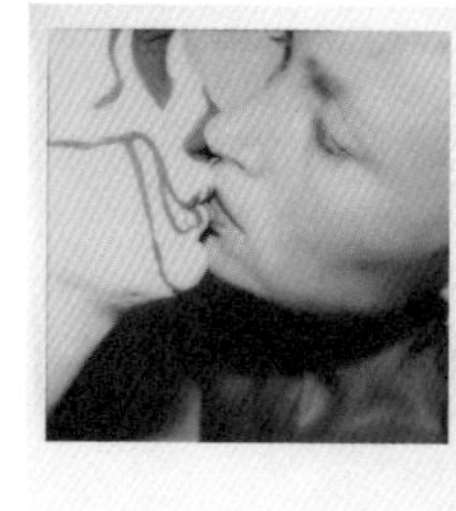

159

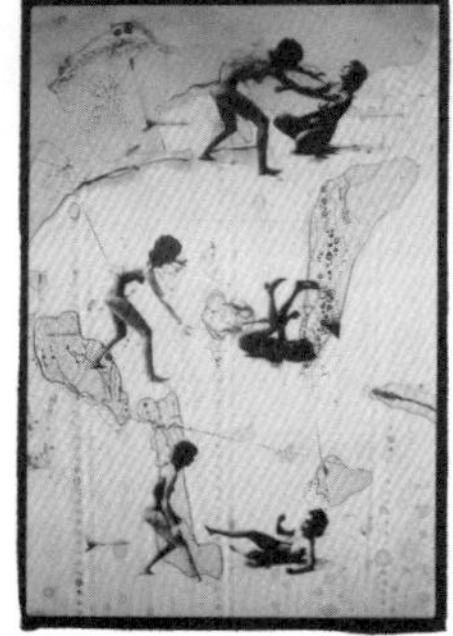

160

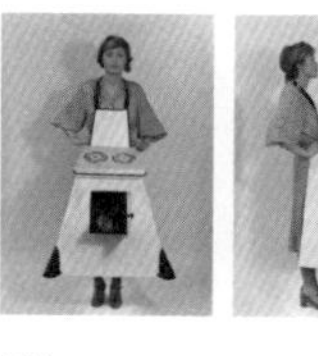

161

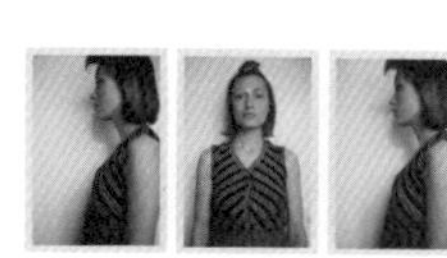

163

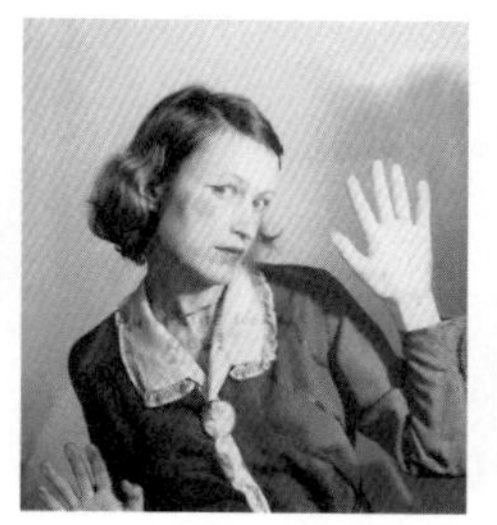

165

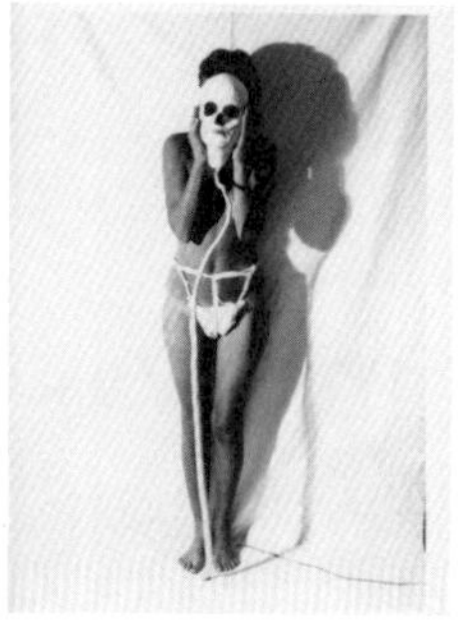

166

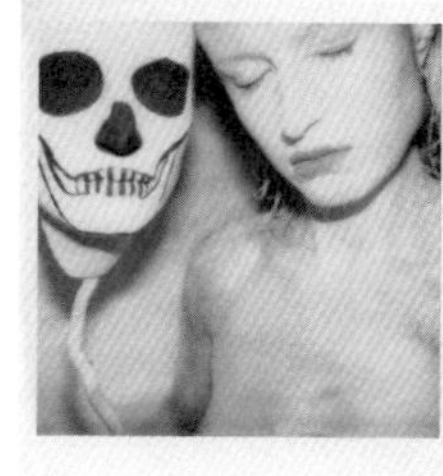

168

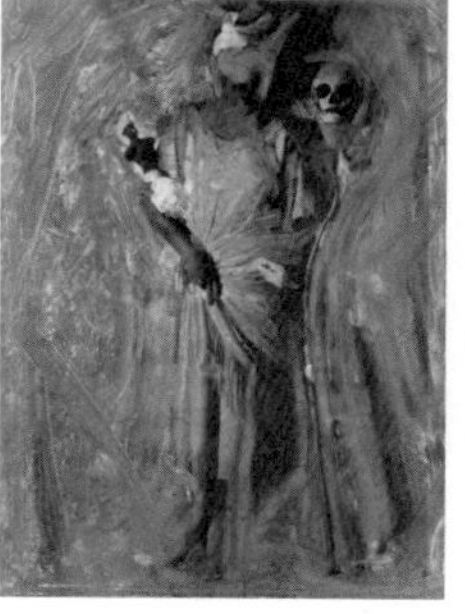

169

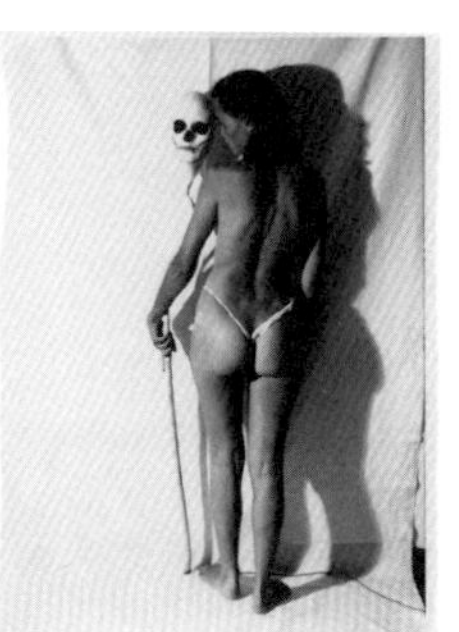

170

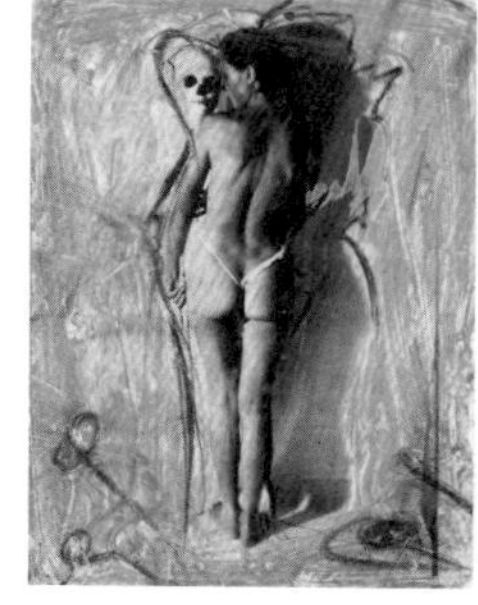

171

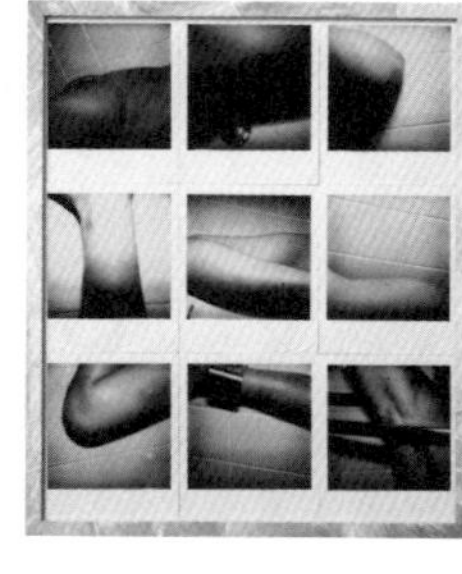

172

174

153   *Ohne Titel | Untitled* 1982/1983
Gouache, charcoal, oil on paper
100×65 cm
Estate Birgit Jürgenssen (z911)

154   *Sklavin des Herzens | Slave of the Heart* 1983
Gouache, pencil on handmade paper,
heightened with white
38×56.4 cm
Estate Birgit Jürgenssen (z454)

155   *Sklavin des Herzens | Slave of the Heart* 1983
Gouache, pencil on handmade paper,
heightened with white
38×56.4 cm
Estate Birgit Jürgenssen (z452)

156   *Ohne Titel | Untitled* 1979
SX-70 Polaroid
10.5×8.7 cm
Estate Birgit Jürgenssen (ph153)

157   *Ohne Titel (Der Leichnam lebt) | Untitled
(The Corpse Is Alive)* 1979
SX-70 Polaroid
10.5×8.7 cm
Estate Birgit Jürgenssen (ph422)

158   *Ohne Titel | Untitled* 1979
SX-70 Polaroid
10.5×8.7 cm
Estate Birgit Jürgenssen (ph146)

159   *Ohne Titel | Untitled* 1979
SX-70 Polaroid
10.5×8.7 cm
Estate Birgit Jürgenssen (ph147)

160   *Ohne Titel (Ranking) | Untitled (Ranking)* 1999
Color photograph, laminated
69×50.5 cm
Estate Birgit Jürgenssen (ph1554)

161   *Hausfrauen-Küchenschürze | Housewife's Kitchen
Apron* 1975
B/W photographs
39.3×27.5 cm each
Estate Birgit Jürgenssen (ph1578)

163   *Ohne Titel | Untitled* 1972/2001
Color photographs, triptych
11.2×26.1 cm
Estate Birgit Jürgenssen (ph671)

165   *Ich möchte hier raus! | I Want Out of here!* 1976/2006
B/W photograph
40×30 cm
Estate Birgit Jürgenssen (ed2)

166   *Ohne Titel (Totentanz mit Mädchen) | Untitled (Death
Dance with Maiden)* 1979/1980
B/W photographs, polyptych
39×24.9 cm each
Estate Birgit Jürgenssen (ph1334–ph1347)

168   *Ohne Titel | Untitled* 1979
SX-70 Polaroid
10.5×8.7 cm
Estate Birgit Jürgenssen (ph272)

169   *Ohne Titel (Aus der Serie »Totentanz mit
Mädchen«) | Untitled (From the Series »Death Dance
with Maiden«)* 1979/1980
B/W photograph, overpainted
39.5×29.5 cm
Estate Birgit Jürgenssen (ph2040)

170   *Ohne Titel (Aus der Serie »Totentanz mit
Mädchen«) | Untitled (From the Series »Death Dance
with Maiden«)* 1979/1980
B/W photograph
39.5×29.5 cm
Estate Birgit Jürgenssen (ph1343)

171   *Ohne Titel (Aus der Serie »Totentanz mit
Mädchen«) | Untitled (From the Series »Death Dance
with Maiden«)* 1979/1980
B/W photograph, overpainted
40×30 cm
Anne & Wolfgang Titze Collection (ph1540)

172   *Ohne Titel | Untitled* 1978
SX-70 Polaroid, manipulated
10.5×8.7 cm
Estate Birgit Jürgenssen (ph371)

174   *Badeserie, Verletzung | Bath Series, Wounding* 1980
SX-70 Polaroids, artist's frame
32.4×26.7 cm
Estate Birgit Jürgenssen (ph1405)

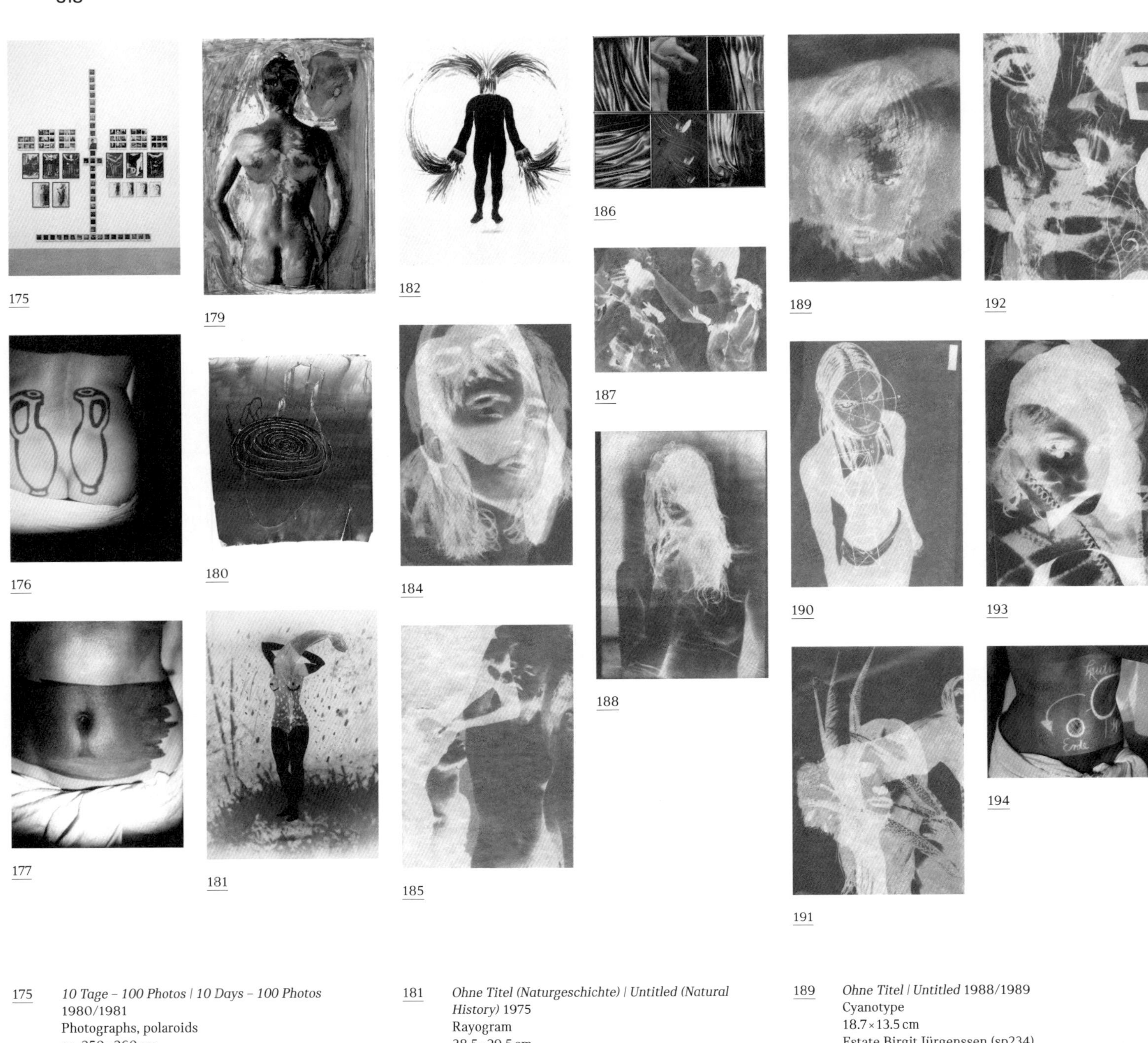

175

179

182

186

187

189

192

176

180

184

190

193

177

181

185

188

194

191

175   *10 Tage – 100 Photos / 10 Days – 100 Photos*
1980/1981
Photographs, polaroids
ca. 250 × 260 cm
Estate Birgit Jürgenssen (s29)

176   *Ohne Titel (Körperprojektion) / Untitled (Body Projection)* 1988
Color photograph
37 × 26.9 cm
Estate Birgit Jürgenssen (ph71)

177   *Ohne Titel (Körperprojektion) / Untitled (Body Projection)* 1988
Color photograph
30.4 × 22 cm
Estate Birgit Jürgenssen (ph964)

179   *Ohne Titel / Untitled* 1979
B/W photograph, overpainted
40 × 30 cm
Anne & Wolfgang Titze Collection (ph1532)

180   *Ohne Titel / Untitled* 1983–1987
Painted photograph, scratch marks
74 × 64 cm
Estate Birgit Jürgenssen (ph2050)

181   *Ohne Titel (Naturgeschichte) / Untitled (Natural History)* 1975
Rayogram
38.5 × 29.5 cm
Estate Birgit Jürgenssen (ph456)

182   *Ohne Titel / Untitled* 1975
Rayogram
40 × 30 cm
Estate Birgit Jürgenssen (ph1073)

184   *Ohne Titel / Untitled* 1988/1989
Cyanotype
18.9 × 13.6 cm
Estate Birgit Jürgenssen (sp199)

185   *Ohne Titel / Untitled* 1988/1989
Cyanotype
19.1 × 13.3 cm
Estate Birgit Jürgenssen (sp196)

186   *Ohne Titel / Untitled* 1991
Color photographs, fabric
80 × 90 cm
Estate Birgit Jürgenssen (ph1470)

187   *Ohne Titel / Untitled* 1988/1989
Cyanotype
13.4 × 18.7 cm
Estate Birgit Jürgenssen (sp179)

188   *Ohne Titel / Untitled* 1988/1989
Cyanotype
18.8 × 13.1 cm
Estate Birgit Jürgenssen (sp9)

189   *Ohne Titel / Untitled* 1988/1989
Cyanotype
18.7 × 13.5 cm
Estate Birgit Jürgenssen (sp234)

190   *Ohne Titel / Untitled* 1988/1989
Cyanotype
19 × 13.2 cm
Estate Birgit Jürgenssen (sp239)

191   *Ohne Titel / Untitled* 1988/1989
Cyanotype
18.7 × 13.5 cm
MoMA – Museum of Modern Art, New York (sp22)

192   *Ohne Titel / Untitled* 1988/1989
Cyanotype
18.9 × 13.3 cm
Estate Birgit Jürgenssen (sp178)

193   *Ohne Titel / Untitled* 1988/1989
Cyanotype
19.2 × 13.4 cm
Estate Birgit Jürgenssen (sp177)

194   *Ohne Titel (Körperprojektion) / Untitled (Body Projection)* 1988
Color photograph
30.4 × 45.3 cm
Estate Birgit Jürgenssen (ph34)

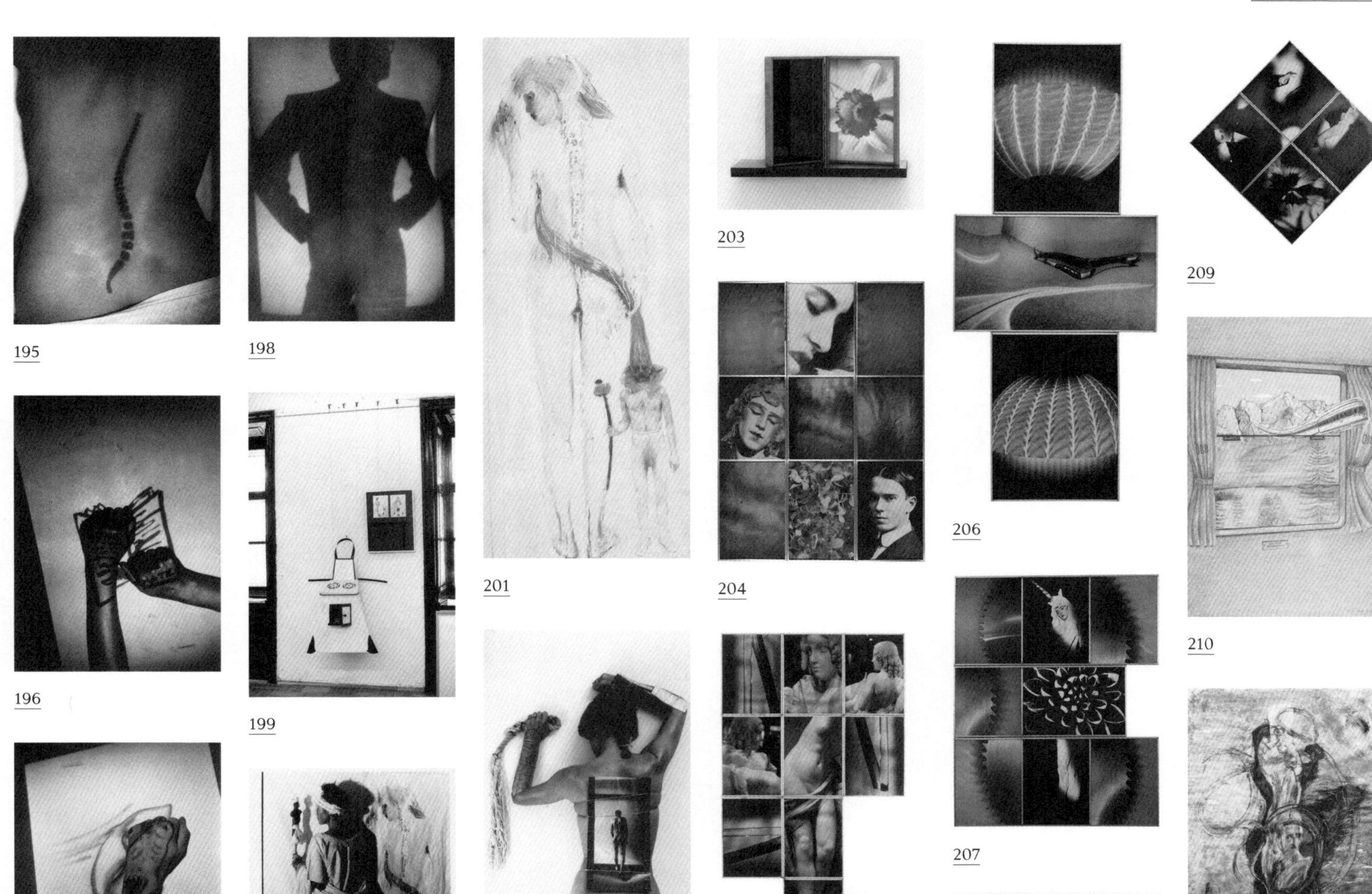

195

198

196

199

201

203

204

206

209

210

197

202

205

207

208

211

200

195   *Ohne Titel (Körperprojektion) / Untitled (Body Projection)* 1988
        Color photograph
        30.4 × 22.1 cm
        Estate Birgit Jürgenssen (ph1732)

196   *Ohne Titel (Körperprojektion) / Untitled (Body Projection)* 1987
        Color photograph
        37.6 × 25.4 cm
        Estate Birgit Jürgenssen (ph50)

197   *Ohne Titel (Körperprojektion) / Untitled (Body Projection)* 1987
        Color photograph
        37.6 × 25.4 cm
        Estate Birgit Jürgenssen (ph53)

198   *Ohne Titel (Körperprojektion) / Untitled (Body Projection)* 1988
        Color photograph
        29.5 × 22 cm
        Estate Birgit Jürgenssen (ph1730)

199   *Küchenschürze / Kitchen Apron* 1974/1975
        Plate, bread
        115 × 76 × 48 cm
        Museum moderner Kunst Stiftung Ludwig Wien (s51)

200   *Ohne Titel / Untitled* 1979
        B/W photograph, overpainted
        40 × 30 cm
        Estate Birgit Jürgenssen (ph1054)

201   *Ohne Titel / Untitled* 1978
        Gouache, pencil, coating paint on paper
        175.5 × 71 cm
        Private collection

202   *Gladiatorin / Gladiatrix* 1980
        Gelatine silver print
        23 × 17.5 cm
        SAMMLUNG VERBUND, Vienna (ph24)

203   *Narziß und Echo / Narcissus and Echo* 1991
        Mixed media (diapositives, glass, wood, lamps, foldable metal frame)
        Diptych 30 × 43.6 cm each
        Private collection (s48)

204   *Fragmente einer Rose (Nijinski) / Fragments of a Rose (Nijinsky)* 1989
        Color photographs beneath fabric
        120 × 90 cm
        Estate Birgit Jürgenssen (ph882)

205   *Ohne Titel / Untitled* 1995
        Color photographs beneath fabric
        160 × 90 cm
        The Rachofsky Collection (ph740)

206   *Selbstportrait mit Lampe / Self-portrait with lamp* 1979/1991
        B/W photographs, fabric
        162 × 74 cm
        Private collection (ph716)

207   *Einhorn / Unicorn* 1991
        B/W photographs, Color photographs, fabric
        110 × 90 cm
        Estate Birgit Jürgenssen (ph737)

208   *Wings Are Made for Desire* 1989
        B/W photographs, fabric
        47 × 112.5 cm
        Estate Birgit Jürgenssen (ph903)

209   *Houdini* 1990
        B/W photographs, fabric
        120 × 120 cm
        Estate Birgit Jürgenssen (ph735)

210   *Ohne Titel / Untitled* 1973
        Pencil, colored pencil on handmade paper
        62.5 × 43.6 cm
        Estate Birgit Jürgenssen (z126)

211   *Forbidden Morning* 1983
        Mixed media on paper
        155 × 130 cm
        Estate Birgit Jürgenssen (z1227)

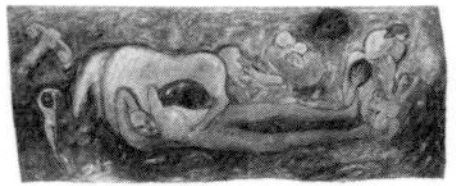

212

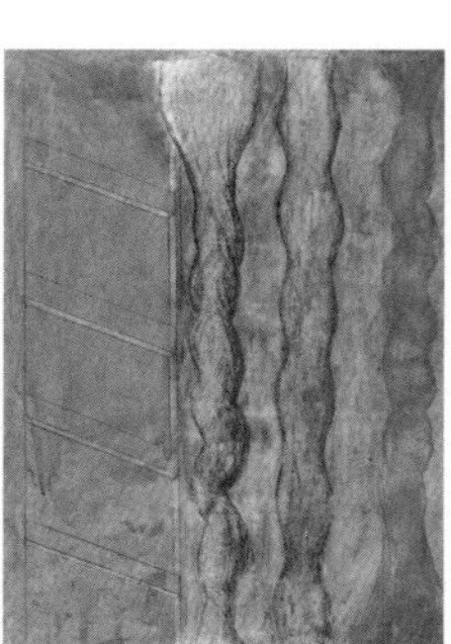

213

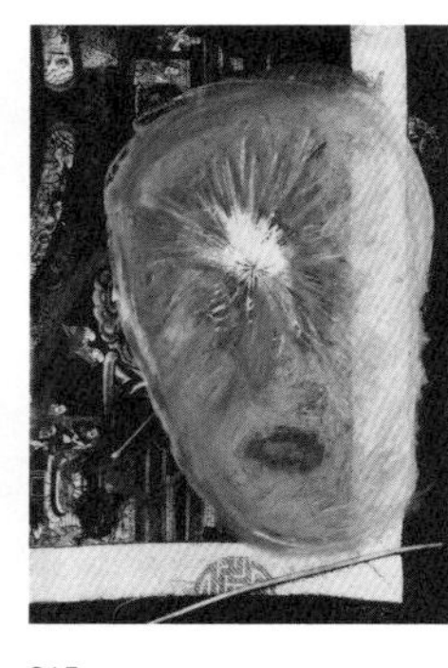

215

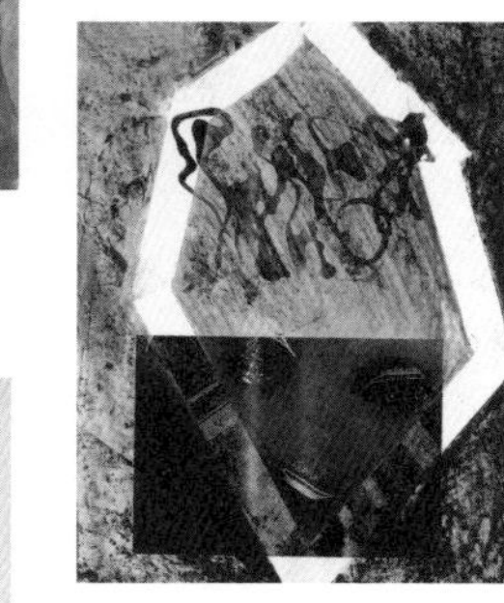

216

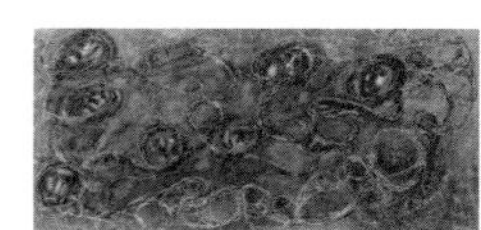

217

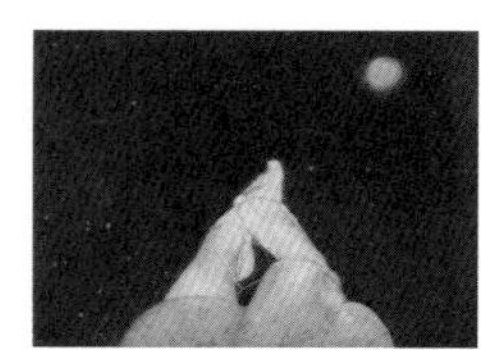

214

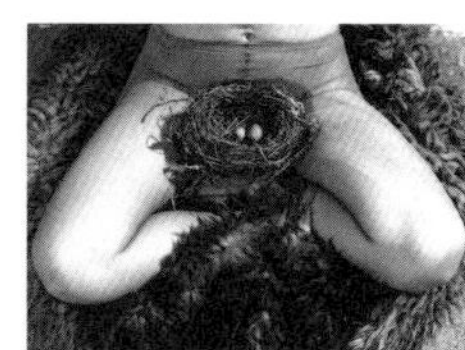

219

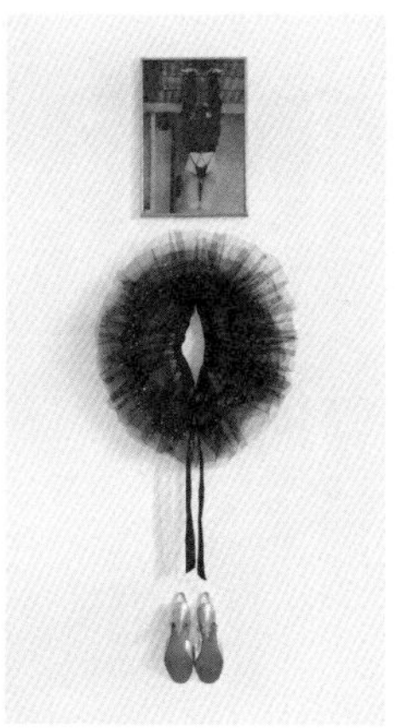

220

218

221

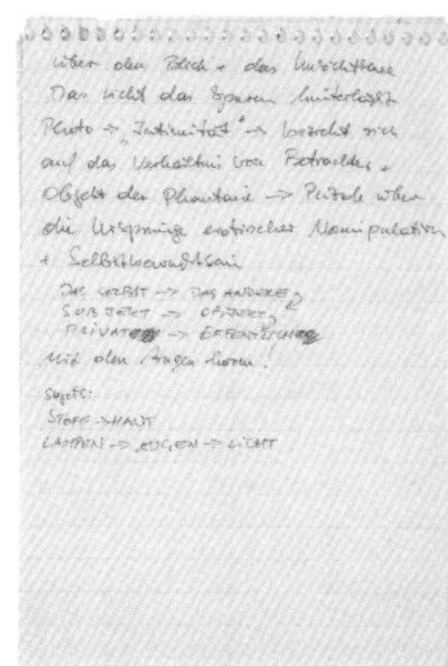

p. 19

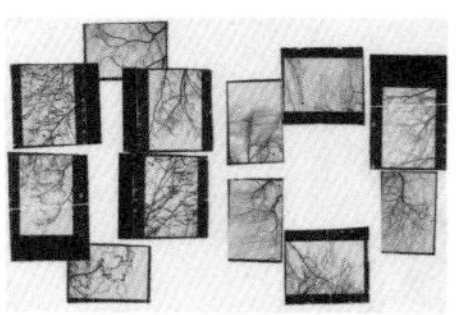

p. 29

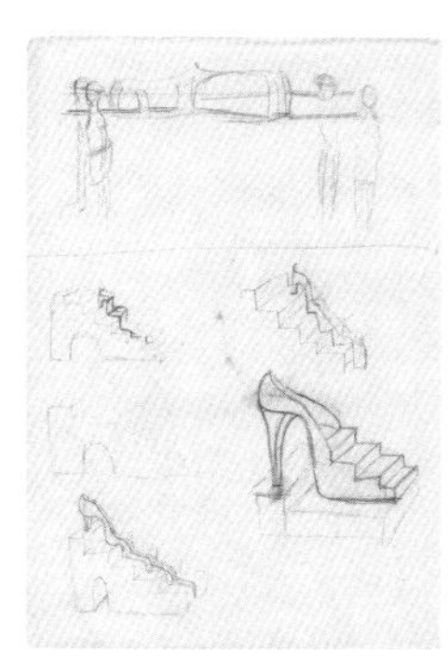

p. 85

212   *Ohne Titel | Untitled* 1984
Mixed media on Paper
98.4 × 220 cm
Estate Birgit Jürgenssen (la59)

213   *Ohne Titel | Untitled* 1989/1990
Mixed media on handmade paper (gouache,
charcoal, pastel)
107 × 79 cm
Estate Birgit Jürgenssen (z809)

214   *Ohne Titel | Untitled* 1983
Oil on paper
227 × 190 cm
Estate Birgit Jürgenssen (z894)

215   *Ohne Titel (Aus der Serie »Kopfalarm« | Untitled
(From the Series »Head Alert«)* 1985
Mixed media on photocopy
29.7 × 20.9 cm
Estate Birgit Jürgenssen (z270)

216   *Ohne Titel (Aus der Serie »Kopfalarm« | Untitled
(From the Series »Head Alert«)* 1985
Mixed media on photocopy
29.7 × 20.9 cm
Estate Birgit Jürgenssen (z275)

217   *The Tediousness of the Connoisseurs* 1985
Mixed media on canvas
90 × 190 cm
Estate Birgit Jürgenssen (z991)

218   *Ohne Titel | Untitled* 1977
Pencil, colored pencil on handmade paper
43.5 × 62.5 cm
Estate Birgit Jürgenssen (z964)

219   *Ohne Titel | Untitled* 1979
SX-70 Polaroid
10.5 × 8.7 cm
Estate Birgit Jürgenssen (ph262)

220   *Nest* 1979/2011
Lambda print
27 × 39.1 cm
Estate Birgit Jürgenssen (ed42)

221   *Elevin* 1993
Mixed media (tutu, golden shoes, B/W photograph)
172 × 53 × 20 cm
Grażyna Kulczyk Collection (s32)

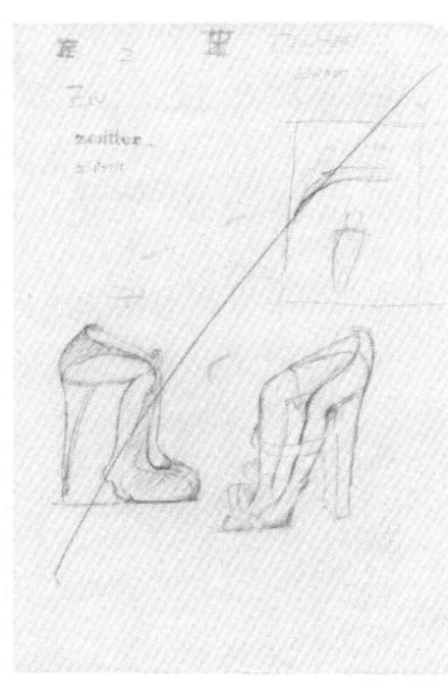

p. 91

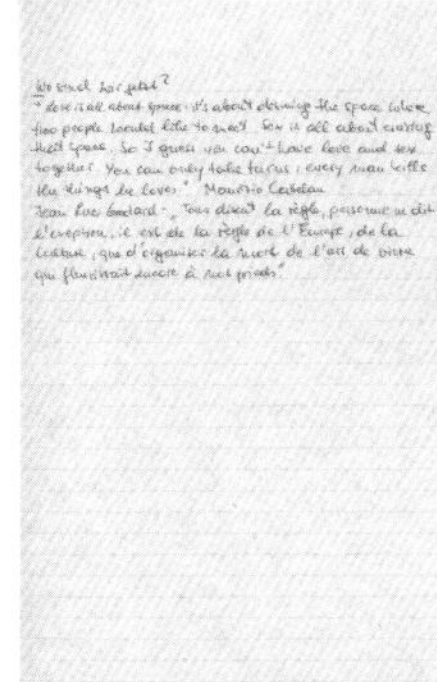

p. 123

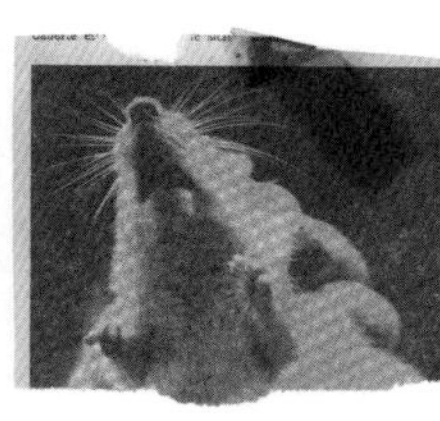

p. 187

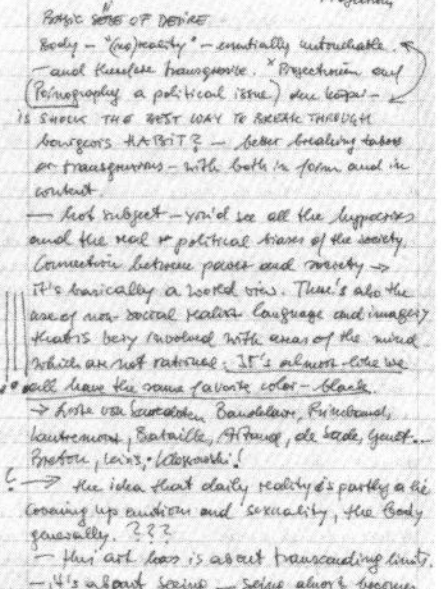

p. 259

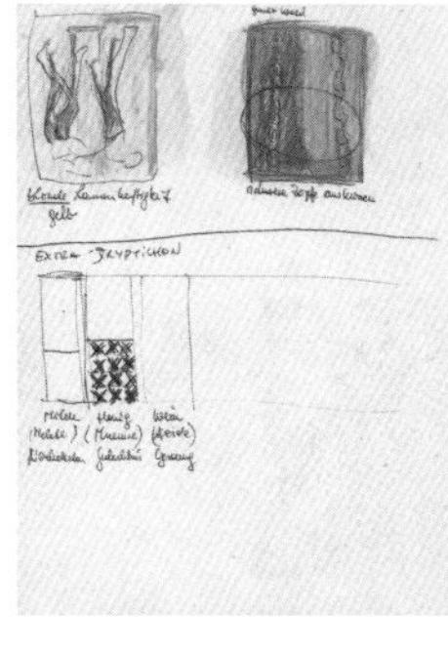

p. 291

p. 173

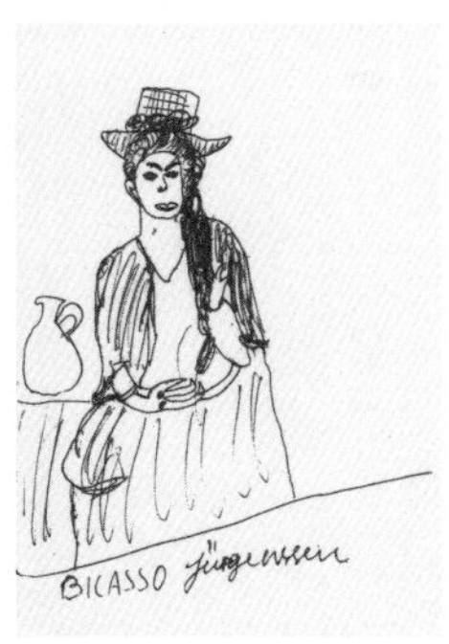

p. 117

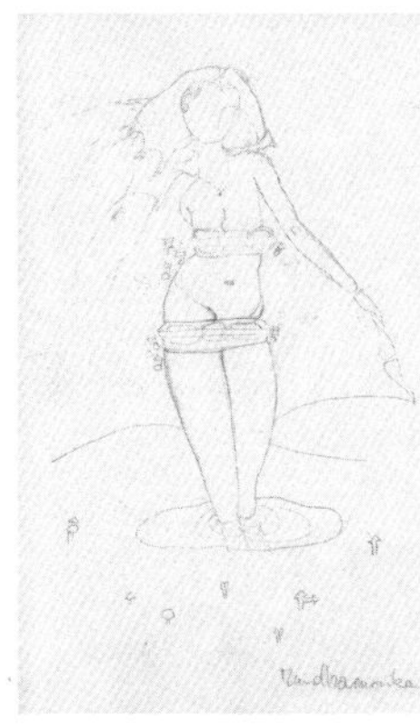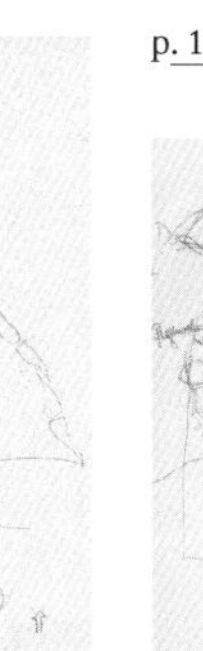

p. 163

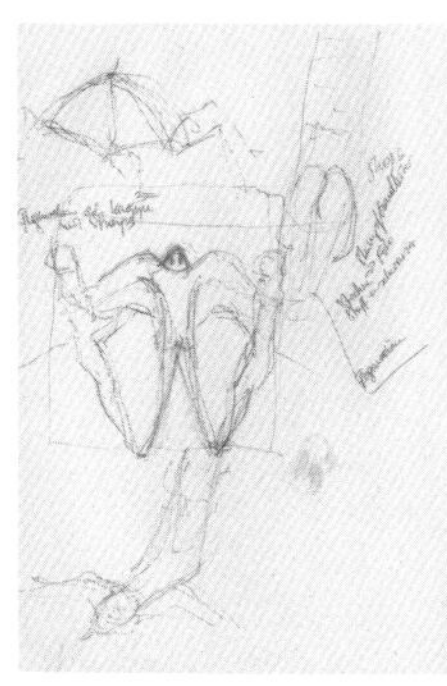

p. 181

p. 209

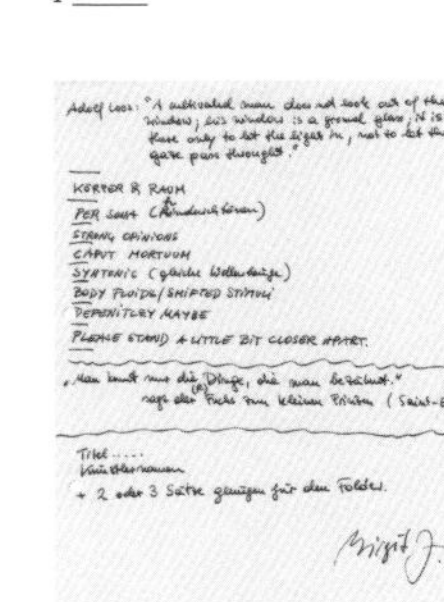

p. 269

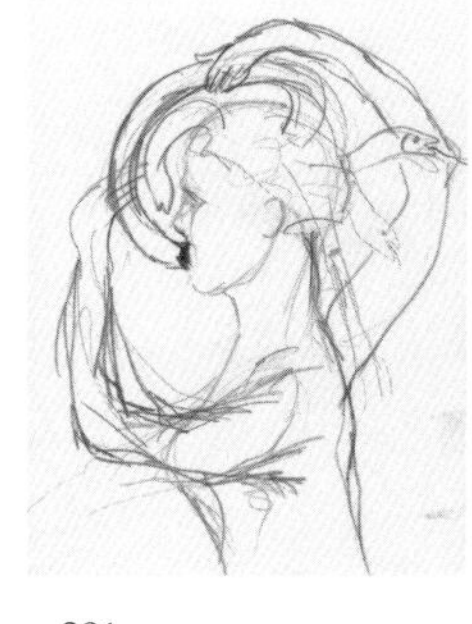

p. 301

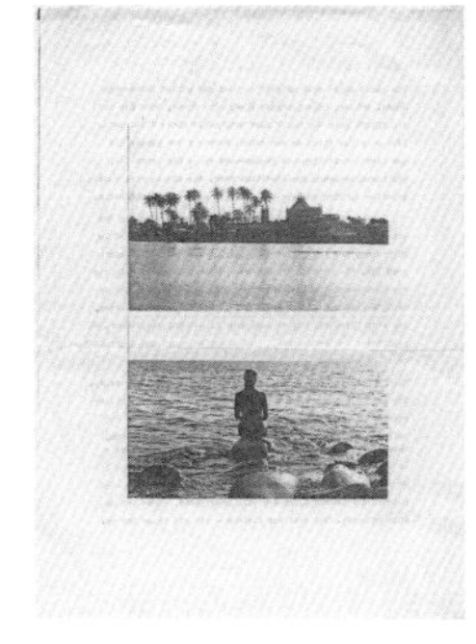

p. 223

Notebook pages

p. 19   Notebook, undated
Unpaginated
16 × 12 cm
Estate Birgit Jürgenssen (sk24)

p. 29   Notebook, undated
Unpaginated
13.5 × 20.5 cm
Estate Birgit Jürgenssen (sk78)

p. 85   Notebook 1974
Unpaginated
21 × 29.6 cm
Estate Birgit Jürgenssen (sk68)

p. 91   Notebook 1974
Unpaginated
21 × 29.6 cm
Estate Birgit Jürgenssen (sk68)

p. 117   *BICASSO Jürgenssen* 1957/1994
Unpaginated
20.8 × 14.8 cm
Estate Birgit Jürgenssen (b5)

p. 123   Notebook, undated
Unpaginated
21.4 × 15 cm
Estate Birgit Jürgenssen (sk13)

p. 163   Notebook, undated
Unpaginated
25.4 × 18 cm
Estate Birgit Jürgenssen (sk67)

p. 173   Notebook (*Three Subject Notebook*) 2000/2001
Unpaginated
24.4 × 18.5 cm
Estate Birgit Jürgenssen (sk43)

p. 181   Notebook 1982
Unpaginated
20.9 × 15.5 cm
Estate Birgit Jürgenssen (sk8)

p. 187   Notebook, undated
Newspaper clipping
7.5 × 9 cm
Estate Birgit Jürgenssen

p. 209   Notebook 1982
Unpaginated
20.9 × 15.5 cm
Estate Birgit Jürgenssen (sk8)

p. 223   Notebook, undated
Unpaginated
31 × 22 cm
Estate Birgit Jürgenssen (sk73)

p. 259   Notebook, undated
Unpaginated
24.6 × 17.6 cm
Estate Birgit Jürgenssen (sk18)

p. 269   Notebook, undated
Unpaginated
31 × 22 cm
Estate Birgit Jürgenssen (sk73)

p. 291   Notebook, undated
Unpaginated
15 × 21 cm
Estate Birgit Jürgenssen (sk77)

p. 301   Notebook, undated
Unpaginated
21.4 × 15 cm
Estate Birgit Jürgenssen (sk13)

Selected Exhibitions

Solo Exhibitions

2019
I am. LOUISIANA Museum of Modern Art, Humlebæk.

Io sono. GAMeC – Galleria d'Arte Moderna e Contemporanea di Bergamo.

2018
Ich bin. Kunsthalle Tübingen.

Birgit Jürgenssen. Barbara Gladstone, Brussels.

Birgit Jürgenssen. Fergus McCaffrey, Tokyo.

Birgit Jürgenssen: Nocturnal Light. Alison Jacques Gallery, London.

NEKYIA: NACHT SEH FAHRT / NIGHT SEE CROSSING. Galerie Hubert Winter, Vienna.

2017
Ungesehenes. Galerie Hubert Winter, Vienna.

2016
Birgit Jürgenssen. Fergus McCaffrey, St. Barth.

Jürgenssenweg: Birgit Jürgenssen, Astrid Nylander, & Stine Olgod. Galerie Hubert Winter, Vienna.

2015
Birgit Jürgenssen: Rankings. Galerie Hubert Winter, Vienna.

2014
Das Alphabet der Birgit Jürgenssen: Arbeiten aus den Jahren 1970/72. Galerie Hubert Winter, Vienna.

2013
Birgit Jürgenssen. Alison Jacques Gallery, London.

Birgit Jürgenssen. Fergus McCaffrey, New York.

Birgit Jürgenssen. Stoffarbeiten. Galerie Hubert Winter, Vienna.

2012
Birgit Jürgenssen: Körperprojektionen. Galerie Jordanow, Munich.

Birgit Jürgenssen: Cyanotypien von 1988/89. Galerie Hubert Winter, Vienna.

2011
Birgit Jürgenssen. Österreichisches Kulturforum, Bratislava.

Birgit Jürgenssen: Gemalte Fotografie. Galerie Hubert Winter, Vienna.

2010
Birgit Jürgenssen: Retrospektive. Bank Austria Kunstforum, Vienna.

Birgit Jürgenssen: Körperprojektionen aus den 1980er-Jahren. Galerie Hubert Winter, Vienna.

2009
Birgit Jürgenssen, »Pulsschlag einer Sinnlichkeit«. Vertikale Galerie SAMMLUNG VERBUND, Vienna.

Birgit Jürgenssen: Arbeiten aus den 1980er-Jahren. Galerie Hubert Winter, Vienna.

2008
Birgit Jürgenssen: 20 Zeichnungen aus den Jahren 1973–1979. Galerie Hubert Winter, Vienna.

2006
Birgit Jürgenssen: Fotos, Rayogramme, Polaroids und Solargrafiken aus den 1970er-Jahren. Galerie Hubert Winter, Vienna.

2004
Schuhwerk: Subversive Aspects of »Feminism.« MAK – Österreichisches Museum für angewandte Kunst, Vienna.

2003
The Mind Is a Muscle. Galerie Matthias Kampl, Munich.

2001
ich weiß nicht. Galerie Hubert Winter, Vienna.

2000
Ranking. Galerie Schafschetzy, Graz.

1999
formlos. Galerie Hubert Winter, Vienna.

1998
Birgit Jürgenssen: Früher oder später. Landesgalerie, Oberösterreichisches Landesmuseum, Linz.

Arbeiten 1973–1976 und 1997. Galerie Hubert Winter, Kontorhaus, Berlin.

1997
Sooner or Later. TZ-Art Gallery, New York.

Galerie Hubert Winter, Kontorhaus Berlin (with Mary Ellen Carroll).

1996
I Met a Stranger – Installation zur Präsentation des Künstlerbuches B. Jürgenssen / L. Weiner. Secession, Vienna.

1994
Kirschblüten in Siena / Man kennt nur die Dinge, die man zähmt. Galerie Hubert Winter, Vienna.

Das Echo im Silberstreif. Galerie Schafschetzy, Graz.

1991
Mario Flecha Gallery, London.

Kunst-Europa, Kunstkreis Schenefeld.

Galerie Hubert Winter, Vienna.

1990
Galerie Paradigma, Linz.

1989
Galerie Hubert Winter, Vienna.

1988
Graeme Murray Gallery, Edinburgh.

1987
Sehen, was ist – Living Room, Private Room. Galerie Hubert Winter, Vienna.

Nekyia, Nacht Seh Fahrt, Night See Crossing. John Hansard Gallery, Southampton.

Van Gogh mise en scène: Malen ist wie Säen – Installation zum Dädalus-Projekt »Journal der Orte«. Museum des 20. Jahrhunderts, Vienna.

1986
Quintessenzen. Galerie Bismarck, Bremen.

Group Exhibitions (Selection)

1985
Wie erfährt man sich im Anderen, das Andere in sich? Galerie Hubert Winter, Vienna.

1984
Jack Tilton Gallery, New York.

Galerie Hubert Winter, Vienna.

1981
10 Tage – 100 Photos. Galerie Hubert Winter, Vienna.

1980
Der Untergang des Römischen Reiches. Galerie Hofstöckl, Linz.

1978
Lineaturen. Grafische Sammlung, Albertina, Vienna.

1976
Kulturzentrum bei den Minoriten, Graz.

1974
Birgit Jürgenssen. Zeichnungen und Objekte 1971–1973. Galerie Schottenring, Vienna.

1972
Forum Stadtpark, Graz (with Ingeborg Strobl).

2018
Freak. Codex Berlin.

WOMAN The Feminist

2018
DRAG: Self-Portraits and Body Politics. Hayward Gallery Project Space, London.

Avant-Garde of the 1970s. Works from the SAMMLUNG VERBUND Collection, Vienna. Museum Stavanger.

Freak. Codex Berlin.

Spiegelungen/FlächenTiefenSelbstbetrachtungen. Projektraum in der alten Feuerwache, Berlin.

Ordination, Ordination Garnisongasse 11, Vienna.

The Provisional City. Spazio Murat, Bari.

Virginia Woolf: An exhibition Inspired By Her Writings. Pallant House, Chicheste.

Zeig mir deine Wunde. Dom Museum Wien, Vienna.

The Shape of Time. Kunsthistorisches Museum, Vienna.

WOMAN HOUSE. National Museum of Woman in the Arts, Washington.

Glaube, Liebe, Hoffnung. Kunsthaus Graz.

2017
Meret Oppenheim and her artist friends. MASILugano.

Pro(s)thesis. Akademie der bildenden Künste, Vienna.

The Beguiling Siren Is Thy Crest. MoMA Warsaw.

Art Links To My Near Death Singularity. Bratislava, Österreichisches Kulturforum, Bratislava

HYPOKEIMENON, en Dessous du SANG. GNF Gallery, Brussels.

WOMAN. mumok, Vienna.

Ich weiß nicht. MAK – Museum für angewandte Kunst, Vienna.

We Love Animals. Kunstmuseum Ravensburg.

Sterne. LENTOS Kunstmuseum, Linz.

Sex Work. FRIEZE LONDON.

WOMAN HOUSE. La Monnaie de Paris.

Feministische Avantgarde der 1970er Jahre aus der SAMMLUNG VERBUND Vienna. ZKM | Zentrum für Kunst und Medientechnologie Karlsruhe.

2016
Identitiy Revisited. The Warehouse, Dallas.

Priere de Toucher. Museum Tinguely, Basel.

ICH. Schirn Kunsthalle, Frankfurt.

Das imaginäre Museum. MMK Museum für Moderne Kunst, Frankfurt.

Die zu sein scheint, die ich bin. Galerie Thomas Schulte, Berlin.

Feminist Avant-Garde of the 1970s. The Photographers Gallery, London.

2015
Schlaflos – Das Bett in Geschichte und Gegenwartskunst. 21er Haus, Belvedere, Vienna.

Love & Loss. Mode und Vergänglichkeit. LENTOS Kunstmuseum, Linz.

Feministische Avantgarde der 1970er Jahre. Hamburger Kunsthalle.

All Back in the Skull Together. Maccarone, New York.

Picasso in der Kunst der Gegenwart. Deichtorhallen, Hamburg.

Wirkliches Leben? Ein Panorama der Sammlungen. Museum der Moderne Mönchsberg, Salzburg.

Die achtziger Jahre in der Sammlung des MUSA. MUSA – Museum auf Abruf, Vienna.

SHOEting Stars: 5 Sinne & mehr. Stadtgalerie Klagenfurt.

Francesca Woodman & Birgit Jürgenssen. Kunst Merano Arte

Ich bin eine Pflanze. Naturprozesse in der Kunst. Kunstmuseum Ravensburg.

The Great Mother. Fondazione Nicola Trussardi, Milan.

Feets, Dont Fail Me Now. Belmacz, London.

Torso. Ursula Blickle Stiftung, Kraichtal.

Rabenmütter. LENTOS Kunstmuseum, Linz.

All Men Become Sisters. Muzeum Sztuki, Łódź.

Für Gaderobe wird nicht gehaftet. AIL – Angewandte Innovation Laboratory, Vienna.

2014
Die andere Sicht: Sammlerin und Künstlerin. Essl Museum, Vienna.

Call Me on Sunday. As a part of CCC – Curators Collectors Collaboration. Krinzinger Projekte, Vienna.

Aktionistinnen. Forum Frohner, Krems.

SHOEting Stars: Der Schuh in Kunst und Design. Kunst Haus Wien, Vienna.

Selbstauslöser. Austrian Cultural Forum, New York; Museum der Moderne, Mönchsberg, Salzburg; MUSAC, Leon.

Die andere Seite: Spiegel und Spiegelungen in der zeitgenössischen Kunst. 21er Haus, Belvedere, Vienna.

Artevida:corpo / artevida: politica. Casa Franca-Brasil / Museu de Arte Moderna, Rio de Janeiro.

Gwangju Biennale 2014: Burning Down the House. 10th Gwangju Biennale.

Tod und Sterben. MAG3 Projektraum.

WOMAN. The Feminist Avant-Garde of the 1970s: Works from the SAMMLUNG-VERBUND, Vienna. Mjellby Art Museum, Halmstad.

CORPUS. Zacheta-National Gallery of Art, Warsaw.

2D23D: Photography as Sculpture / Sculpture as Photography. OstLicht. Galerie für Fotografie, Vienna.

Sigmar Polke / Birgit Jürgenssen. Fergus McCaffrey, New York.

2013
BODY I AM: Birgit Jürgenssen, Ana Mendieta & Hannah Wilke. Alison Jacques Gallery, London.

Through a Glass Darkly: Faces Past and Present. Mucsarnok Kunsthalle, Budapest.

Revolution from Within. Kaufmann Repetto, Milan.

Starker Auftritt! Experimentelles Schuhdesign. Grassi Museum, Leipzig.

CORPI IN AZIONE/ CORPI IN VISIONE: Body Action-Body Vision. Museo Pecci, Milan.

XL: 19 New Acquisitions in Photography. MoMA – The Museum of Modern Art, New York.

Mujer: La vanguardia feminista de los anos 70 Obras de la SAMMLUNG VERBUND, Vienna. Circulo de Bellas Artes, Madrid.

Die Sammlung #3. 21er Haus, Belvedere, Vienna.

Self, Model, and Self as Other. MFAH – The Museum of Fine Arts, Houston.

Ask for Haydn: Blicke aus der Gegenwart. Landesgalerie Burgenland, Projektraum, Eisenstadt; Austrian Cultural Forum, Washington.

2012
BODY.ACTION: Collected #2. Tresor im Bank Austria Kunstforum,Vienna.

Röcke tragen: Die Inszenierung von Kleidung in der zeitgenössischen Fotografie und Plastik. Museum der Moderne, Mönchsberg, Salzburg.

Plus ou moins sorcières 2/3: Epréuves ritualisées. Maison Populaire, Montreuil.

Reflecting Fashion: Kunst und Mode seit der Moderne. mumok, Vienna.

Die Nacht im Zwielicht: Kunst von der Romantik bis heute. Unteres Belvedere, Vienna.

Privat. Schirn Kunsthalle, Frankfurt.

re.act.feminism #2: A Performing Archive. Fundacio Antoni Tapies, Barcelona; Akademie der Künste, Berlin.

Gnadenlos: Künstlerinnen und das Komische. Kunsthalle Vogelmann, Heilbronn; Paula Modersohn-Becker Museum, Bremen.

2011
Obsessions and Intimacy.
Theocharakis Foundation,
Athens.

Beauty Contest. Austrian
Cultural Forum New York
and MUSA – Museum
auf Abruf, Vienna.

2010
*elles@centrepompidou:
Artistes femmes dans
les collections du Musée
national d'art moderne.*
Centre Pompidou, Paris.

*Brave New World: New
Concepts in Austrian Photo-
graphy.* The Austrian
Cultural Forum, London.

Les Femmes Fatales. Forum
Frohner, Krems.

*Anna Artaker/Lilla Khoór,
Renate Bertlmann, Marita
Fraser, Eva Grubinger, Kathi
Hofer, Birgit Jürgenssen,
Tatiana Lecomte, Ulrike
Lienbacher, Lone Haugaard
Madsen, Lisa Ruyter,
Patricia Reinhart, Eva
Schlegel, Maja Vukoje,
Astrid Wagner.* Engholm
Galerie, Vienna.

*raum_körper einsatz: Posi-
tionen der Skulptur.* MUSA
Museum auf Abruf, Vienna.

*DONNA: Feminist Avant-
garde of the 1970s from
Sammlung Verbund, Vienna;
200 works by 17 artists.*
Galleria nazionale d'arte
moderna, Rome.

2009
Wir sind Maske. Kunsthistorisches Museum, Vienna.

*Rebelle. Feminism & Art
1969–2009.* Museum voor
Moderne Kunst, Arnhem.

Double Face. Vertikale
Galerie Sammlung Verbund,
Vienna.

2008
*Female Trouble: Die Kamera
als Spiegel und Bühne
weiblicher Inszenierungen.*
Pinakothek der Moderne,
Munich.

*Suyun Bir Arada Tuttuğu:
Verbund Koleksiyonu'ndan
Sanat – HELD TOGETHER
WITH WATER. Art from the
Sammlung Verbund.* Museum
of Modern Art, Istanbul.

*Matrix: Geschlechter, Ver-
hältnisse, Revisionen.* MUSA
Museum auf Abruf, Vienna.

2007
*Conceptual Photography
1964–1989.* Zwirner &
Wirth, New York.

*HELD TOGETHER WITH
WATER: Kunst aus der
Sammlung Verbund.* MAK –
Österreichisches Museum
für angewandte Kunst,
Vienna.

*Role Play: Feminist Art Re-
visited 1960–1980.* Galerie
Lelong, New York.

*Ich bin keine Küche: Gegen-
wartsgeschichten aus dem
Nachlass von Margarete
Schütte-Lihotzky.* Universität
für Angewandte Kunst,
Heiligenkreuzer Hof, Vienna.

*Passion for Art: Ausstellung
aus Anlass des 35-jährigen
Bestehens der Samm-
lung Essl.* Sammlung Essl,
Klosterneuburg.

2006
*L'Inventaire – Inventaire au
5 novembre 2006 de tous les
artistes et de toutes les œuv-
res de la collection du Musée
Cantonal des Beaux-Arts de
Lausanne.* Palais de Rumine,
Lausanne.

Der Schuh in der Kunst. Galerie im Traklhaus, Salzburg.

2004
Mühlviertler Festspiele,
Schwertberg.

*Ulysses: Die unausweichliche
Modalität des Sichtbaren.*
Atelier Augarten, Österrei-
chische Galerie, Vienna.

Gegen-Positionen. Museum
Moderne Kunst Stiftung
Wörlen, Passau.

Andererseits: Die Phantastik.
Landesgalerie Linz, Ober-
österreichisches Landes-
museum.

2003
*Mimosen – Rosen – Herbst-
zeitlosen.* Kunsthalle Krems.

Phantom der Lust. Neue
Galerie, Graz.

*Human Stories: Fotoarbeiten
und Malerei aus der Samm-
lung Essl.* Museum Ludwig,
Budapest.

2002
*Let's Twist Again. If You
Can't Think It, Dance It.
Performance in Vienna from
1960 until Today.* Kunsthalle
Exnergasse, Vienna.

frieden weltwärts. Österrei-
chisches Studienzentrum für
Frieden und Konfliktlösung,
Burg Schlaining.

Hic et Nunc. Villa Manin
di Passariano, Udine.

Just Remember: It's Vienna.
Galerie Hubert Winter,
Vienna.

2001
Retratos Efémeros. Municipal Council, Macau.

*Produkt Muttertag: Zur
rituellen Inszenierung eines
Festtages.* Österreichisches
Museum für Volkskunde,
Vienna.

2000
Dum, têlo, srdce. Národni
galerie v Praze, Prague.

*Der anagrammatische
Körper.* ZKM | Zentrum für
Kunst und Medien-
technologie, Karlsruhe.

Träume. Historisches
Museum der Stadt Wien,
Vienna.

kunst hautnah. Künstlerhaus, Vienna.

Chile – Austria. Museo
de Bellas Artes, Santiago
de Chile.

1999
foul play. Thread Waxing
Space, New York.

Die Farben Schwarz.
Joanneum, Graz.

Dreams 1900–2000. Equita-
ble Art Gallery, New York.

Jahrhundert der Frauen.
Bank Austria Kunstforum,
Vienna.

*Calendar 2000 (in colla-
boration with art for art's
sake).* Center for Curatorial
Studies Museum,
Bard College, Annandale-
on-Hudson, New York.

*Wirklichkeit: Zur Situation
künstlerischer Fotografie
in Österreich.* Kunsthaus,
Bregenz.

*La casa, il corpo, il cuore:
Konstruktion der Identitäten.*
Museum moderner Kunst
Stiftung Ludwig 20er Haus,
Vienna.

My house is your house ….
Galerie Hubert Winter,
Vienna.

Chile – Austria. Kärntner
Landesgalerie, Klagenfurt.

1998
Lifestyle. Kunsthaus
Bregenz.

*»Enthüllt«: Ein Jahrhundert
Akte Österreichischer Künstlerinnen.* Frauenbad, Baden.

*Sarajevo 2000: Schenkungen
von Künstlern für ein neues Museum in Sarajevo.* Museum moderner Kunst Stif-
tung Ludwig, Vienna; Palais
Liechtenstein, Vienna.

A Visão Austríaca. Fundação
Calouste Gulbenkian,
Lisbon.

*Positionen, Hedendaagse
Oostenrijkse Kunst.* Cultureel
Centrum »Schaarpoord,«
Knokke-Heist.

Sisi, Sisismus, Sisismen.
Galerie Menotti, Baden.

The Search Within. Kloster
Pernegg; National Gallery
of Modern Art, New Delhi;
National Gallery of Modern
Art, Mumbai.

*La Visión Austríaca: Posi-
ciones del arte contempo-
ráneo.* Museo Nacional de
Bellas Artes, Buenos Aires.

1997
*The Austrian Vision: Posi-
tions of Contemporary Art.*
Denver Art Museum, Denver.

Angel, Angel. Galerie Rudolfinum, Prague.

Engel, Engel. Kunsthalle,
Vienna.

1 Herz für Tiere. Kärntner
Landesgalerie, Klagenfurt.

1996
Sammlung Speck. Museum
Ludwig, Cologne.

*Kunst aus Österreich
1896–1996.* Kunst- und Aus-
stellungshalle der Bundesre-
publik Deutschland, Bonn.

Elements. Hugh Lane Municipal Gallery of Modern Art,
Dublin.

1995
Auf den Leib geschrieben.
Kunsthalle im Museums-
quartier, Vienna.

*Art Contemporain Autrichien,
Festival Ouverture.* FRAC
Fonds régional d'art contem-
porain de Basse-Normandie,
Abbaye-aux-Dames, Caen.

*Fiktion / non-fiction: Welt-
anschauungen zwischen
Vorstellung und Realität.*
Landesgalerie Linz, Ober-
österreichisches Landes-
museum.

3-D-Emotional. Galerie
Hubert Winter, Vienna.

1994
Light. ARTprop, New York.

Photo Album (Austria).
ARTprop, New York.

*La Visión Austriaca: Tres
generaciones de artistas.*
Fundación »La Caixa,«
Madrid.

Oh Boy, It's a Girl. Kunstverein Munich; Kunstraum,
Vienna.

*Positionen zum Ich: Kamera-
bilder.* Kunsthalle Kiel.

*Selbstporträts von Foto-
grafinnen.* Kunstverein
Eislingen.

1993
Die verlassenen Schuhe.
Rheinisches Landesmuseum,
Bonn.

Radical Surface. Heiligen-
kreuzerhof, Vienna.

*Ideas, Imágenes, Identi-
dades – Aspectos del Arte
Austriaco Contemporáneo.*
Tecla Sala, L'Hospitalet,
Barcelona.

Konfrontationen. mumok,
Vienna.

The Seventh Wave. John
Hansard Gallery, South-
ampton.

1992
Radical Surface. LA Art,
Los Angeles.

LagerFeuer. Galerie Hubert
Winter, Vienna.

Integrierte Fotografie,
Galerie im Taxispalais,
Innsbruck.

*2. Internationale Foto-
Triennale.* Esslingen.

1991
*Kunst Europa: Junge Kunst
aus Österreich.* Kunstverein
in Hamburg; Deichtorhallen,
Hamburg; Galerie Rähnitz-
gasse, Dresden.

1990
Ursprung der Moderne.
Neue Galerie, Linz.

*Foto-Sammeln. Österreichi-
sche Fotografie von privaten
Leihgebern.* Stift Altenburg.

Vision Vienna. Galerie
van Esch, Eindhoven; Kunstverein Zwolle.

High Season II. Galerie
Hubert Winter, Vienna.

1989
*32 Porträts: Photography
in Art.* Contemporary Art
Foundation, Amsterdam.

Vienna–Vienna: 1960–1990.
Museum für Moderne Kunst,
Bolzano.

Kunst der letzten 10 Jahre.
mumok, Vienna.

Ornamenta I. Reuchlinhaus,
Pforzheim.

The Age of Woman. Jack
Tilton Gallery, New York.

*Installation – Konzeption –
Imagination.* Kulturhaus,
Graz.

*Moskau – Vienna – New
York.* Wiener Festwochen im
Messepalast, Vienna; Galerie
van Esch, Eindhoven.

1988
Aktuelle Kunst in Österreich.
Musée de l'Etat, Luxemburg.

Erinnerungen. Fotogalerie
WUK, Vienna.

Geisterspuk und Elfenzauber.
Niederösterreichische
Gesellschaft für Kunst und
Kultur, St. Pölten.

Jugendwerke. Akademie der
bildenden Künste, Vienna.

*Maler und Zeichner aus
Österreich.* Musée Cantonal
des Beaux-Arts, Lausanne.

Der pornographische Blick.
Kunstverein Salzburg.

Fotografie aus Österreich.
The Finnish Museum
of Photography, Helsinki.

1987
*Ein drittes Geschlecht:
Mythos oder Chance.* Schles-
wig-Holsteinisches Landesmuseum, Schleswig.

*Europalia – Aktuelle Kunst
aus Österreich.* Museum van
Hedendaagse Kunst, Ghent.

*Oostenrijkse fotografie
in de 20ste eeuw – Europalia
87 Österreich.* Cultureel
Centrum Hasselt; Provinciaal
Museum voor Fotografie,
Antwerp.

*Zeichen am Körper: Phäno-
men Schmuck; Forum
Design.* Museum Francisco-
Carolinum, Linz.

1986
*Fotokurs – Vienna
1979–1986.* Galerie Hubert
Winter, Vienna.

Das Andere Ich. Galerie
Hubert Winter, Vienna.

1985
*Kunst mit Eigen-Sinn:
Internationale Ausstellung
aktueller Kunst von Frauen.*
Museum des 20. Jahrhun-
derts, Vienna.

*Austria Felix: La nuova
Pittura Austriaca.* Palazzo
Costanzi, Trieste.

Zeichen zu Modigliani.
Theseustempel, Vienna.

Dinge des Menschen. Kunsthalle Recklinghausen.

*»Subjektives« Viennaer
Fotografie Teil 2.* Fotogalerie
WUK, Vienna.

Durch die Wüste. Galerie
Hubert Winter, Vienna.

1984
*Private Symbol: Social
Metaphor.* The 5th Biennale
of Sydney, Art Gallery of
New South Wales, Sydney.

*1984 – Orwell und die Gegen-
wart.* Museum des
20. Jahrhunderts, Vienna.

Märchen-Gestalten. Hochschule für Angewandte
Kunst, Vienna.

1983
Neue Fotografie aus Vienna.
Fotogalerie WUK, Vienna.

*Künstlerinnen: Österreich
20. Jahrhundert.* Neue Galerie, Linz.

1982
9&9. Galerie Hubert Winter,
Vienna.

1981
Erweiterte Fotografie.
Secession, Vienna.

Traum. Galerie Hubert
Winter, Vienna.

1980
*Künstlerfotografien
in Österreich 1965–1980.*
Art 11, Basel.

Eros. Kunsthandlung
Hummel, Vienna.

*Aspekte der Zeichnung
in Österreich.* Kunstverein
Bremen.

1979
*Jugendtriennale der Zeich-
ner.* Kunsthalle, Nürnberg.

Mail-Art. Künstlerhaus
Stuttgart.

1978
*Positionen der Zeichnung
in Österreich.* Kunsthalle
Baden-Baden; Neue Galerie,
Linz.

1977
*Künstlerinnen International
1877–1977.* Schloss Charlot-
tenburg, Neue Gesellschaft
für Bildende Kunst, Berlin;
Frankfurter Kunstverein.

1976
*Schuh-Werke: Aspekte
zum Menschenbild.* Kunst-
halle Nürnberg.

Bilder. Kulturzentrum bei
den Minoriten, Graz.

1975
*MAGNA – Feminismus: Kunst
und Kreativität.* Galerie
Nächst St. Stephan, Vienna;
Kunsthal Charlottenborg,
Copenhagen

1974
Galerie Freund, Klagenfurt.

Aspekte des Realistischen.
Galerie Bloch, Innsbruck.

1973
*Bildnerische Tatbestände
österreichischer Kunst
heute.* Neue Galerie, Linz;
Badischer Kunstverein,
Karlsruhe.

1970
Musée d'Art Moderne
de la Ville de Paris.

Grafikbiennale. Tiroler
Landesmuseum Ferdinan-
deum, Innsbruck.

2001
Austrian Participation,
8th International Biennal,
Cairo (Christoph Hinter-
huber, Franz Vana, Eva
Wohlgemuth).

1994
*Wenn die Kinder sind im
Dunkeln,* Secession, Vienna
(Karen Dolmanisth, Drew
Dominick, Nicole Eisenman,
Andres Serrano, Violet Suk).

1992
Die schwangere Muse (with
Elisabeth Schweeger) on
the occasion of the 300th
anniversary of the Academy
of Fine Arts, Vienna.

1988
*Der Hund in mir / The
Dog Within,* Galerie Hubert
Winter, Vienna (Jennifer
Bolande, Christian
Boltanski, Valie Export,
Fischli + Weiss, General
Idea, Urs Lüthi, Annette
Messager, Peter Weibel,
Lawrence Weiner, et al.).

1988-1995
Cooperations with the artist
group DIE DAMEN: Ona B.,
Evelyne Egerer, Ingeborg
Strobl (until 1993), since
1993 with Lawrence Weiner.

Bibliography

Catalogues Solo Exhibitions / Artist Books

Birgit Jürgenssen zipfeln. Vienna: Galerie Hubert Winter, 2011.

Gabriele Schor, Heike Eipeldauer, eds., *Birgit Jürgenssen.* Exhibition catalogue. Bank Austria Kunstforum, Vienna. Munich: Prestel, 2010.

Gabriele Schor, Abigail Solomon-Godeau, eds., *Birgit Jürgenssen.* Ostfildern: Hatje Cantz, 2009

Peter Noever, ed., *Birgit Jürgenssen: Schuhwerk. Subversive Aspects of ›Feminism.‹* Vienna: MAK, 2004.

Birgit Jürgenssen. *Birgit Jürgenssen: Früher oder später.* Exhibition catalogue. Linz: Oberösterreichisches Landesmuseum, 1998.

Birgit Jürgenssen, Lawrence Weiner: *I Met a Stranger.* Artist book. Vienna: Folio, 1996.

Birgit Jürgenssen: *BICASSO Jürgenssen* (1957). Vienna: Galerie Hubert Winter, 1994.

Birgit Jürgenssen. Exhibition catalogue. Edinburgh: Graeme Murray Gallery, 1988.

Birgit Jürgenssen: NEKYIA: NACHT SEH FAHRT / NIGHT SEE CROSSING. Exhibition catalogue. Southampton: John Hansard Gallery, 1987.

Birgit Jürgenssen: Quintessenzen. Exhibition catalogue. Bremen: Galerie Bismarck, 1986.

Birgit Jürgenssen: Loves Blindness. Exhibition catalogue. Vienna: Galerie Hubert Winter, 1984.

Birgit Jürgenssen. Exhibition catalogue. Vienna: Galerie Hubert Winter, 1984.

Birgit Jürgenssen: 10 Tage – 100 Photos. Exhibition catalogue. Vienna: Galerie Hubert Winter, 1981.

Birgit Jürgenssen: Zeichnungen und Objekte 1971–1973. Exhibition catalogue. Vienna: Galerie Schottenring, 1974.

Catalogues Group Exhibitions (Selection)

Jasper Sharp, Sabine Haag, eds., *The Shape of Time.* Exhibition catalogue. Kunsthistorisches Museum Vienna. Cologne: Verlag der Buchhandlung Walther König, 2018, pp. 41–45.

Roxana Azimi. *La Guide Hazan de l'Art Contemporain.* Paris: Editions Hazan, 2017, pp. 110–111.

Camille Morineau, Lucia Pesapane, eds., *Woman House.* Exhibition catalogue. National Museum of Woman in the Arts, Washington, La Monnaie de Paris. Paris: Manuella Editions, 2017, pp. 55–58, pp. 76–79.

Teresa de Marco: Art Links To My Near Death Singularity. Exhibition catalogue. Bratislava: Österreichisches Kulturforum Bratislava, 2017, pp. 24–27.

Guido Comis, Maria Giuseppina di Monte, eds., *Meret Oppenheim.* Exhibition catalogue. MASI Lugano. Milan: Skira, 2016, p. 107.

Lisa Anette Ahlers, Lars Blunck, Kathleen Bühler, Constance Classen, eds., *Prière de Toucher. Der Tastsinn der Kunst.* Exhibition catalogue. Museum Tinguely Basel. Weitra: Bibliothek der Provinz, 2017.

Kacha Szaniawska. *The Beguiling Siren Is Thy Crest.* Exhibition catalogue. Warsaw: Museum of Modern Art in Warsaw, 2017, pp. 29, 51.

Sabine Fellner, Elisabeth Nowak-Thaller. *Sterne: Kosmische Kunst von 1900 bis heute.* Exhibition catalogue. Linz: LENTOS Kunstmuseum Linz, 2017, S.117, pp. 136–137.

Martina Weinhart, Max Hollein, eds., *Ich: Das Selbst als Politikum.* Exhibition catalogue. Schirn Kunsthalle Frankfurt. Cologne: Verlag der Buchhandlung Walther König, 2016, p. 85.

Patricia Allmer, ed., *Intersections: Woman artists/surrealism/modernism.* Manchester: Manchester University Press, 2016, pp. 241–256.

Massimo Gioni, Roberta Tenconi, eds., *The Great Mother.* Exhibition catalogue. Fondazione Nicola Trussardi, Milan. Milan: Skira Editore, 2015, pp. 286–289.

Photography at MoMA. 1960–Now. Exhibition catalogue. New York: The Museum of Modern Art, 2015, p. 179.

Schlaflos: Das Bett in Geschichte und Gegenwartskunst. Exhibition catalogue. Vienna: 21er Haus, 2015, pp. 268–269.

Stella Rollig, Elisabeth Nowak-Thaller, Sabine Fellner, eds., *Rabenmütter: Zwischen Kraft und Krise; Mütterbilder von 1900 bis heute.* Exhibition catalogue. LENTOS Kunstmuseum Linz. Vienna: Verlag für moderne Kunst, 2015, p. 39.

Dirk Luckow, ed., *Picasso in der Kunst der Gegenwart.* Exhibition catalogue. Deichtorhallen, Hamburg. Cologne: Snoeck, 2015.

Gabriele Schor, ed., *Feministische Avantgarde: Kunst der 1970er-Jahre aus der Sammlung Verbund, Vienna.* Exhibition catalogue. Hamburger Kunsthalle. Munich: Prestel, 2015, pp. 312–355.

Love & Loss: Mode und Vergänglichkeit. Exhibition catalogue. LENTOS Kunstmuseum Linz. Vienna: Verlag für moderne Kunst, 2015, pp. 62–63.

Nicole Fritz, ed., *Ich bin eine Pflanze: Naturprozesse in der Kunst.* Kunstmuseum Ravensburg. Bielefeld: Kerber 2015, pp. 89–98.

Aktionistinnen. Exhibition catalogue. Kunsthalle Krems, Forum Frohner, Krems, 2014, pp. 20–21.

The Feminist Avant-Garde of the 1970s. Exhibition catalogue. Brussels: BOZAR – Centre for Fine Arts, 2014, pp. 38–43.

Agnes Husslein-Arco, Edelbert Köb, Thomas Miessgang (eds.): *Die andere Seite*. Exhibition catalogue. Belvedere, Vienna. Melk: Gugler, 2014.

Photography as Sculpture / Sculpture as Photography. Exhibition catalogue. Vienna: Ostlicht. Galerie für Fotografie, 2014, pp. 26–31.

Jessica Morgan. *Burning Down the House*. Exhibition catalogue. Gwangju Biennale 14. Bologna: Damiani, p. 216.

Die Damen. Exhibition catalogue. Zeitkunst Niederösterreich, St. Pölten. Nuremberg: Verlag für moderne Kunst, 2013.

Eva Maria Hoyer, ed., *Starker Auftritt! Experimentelles Schuhdesign*. Exhibition catalogue. GRASSI Museum für Angewandte Kunst, Leipzig. Bielefeld: Kerber Verlag, 2013, p. 139.

Arttirol: Kunstankäufe des Landes Tirol 2010-2012. Innsbruck: Land Tirol, 2013, pp. 28–29.

Martina Weinhart, Max Hollein, eds., *Privat/Privacy*. Exhibition catalogue. Schirn Kunsthalle, Frankfurt. Berlin: Distanz Verlag, 2012, pp. 62–65.

Susanne Neuburger, Barbara Rüdiger (eds.) *Reflecting Fashion: Kunst und Mode seit der Moderne*. Exhibition catalogue. mumok Stiftung Ludwig, Vienna. Cologne: Verlag der Buchhandlung Walther König, 2012, pp. 88–89.

Andreas Stadler, Georg Bauer (eds.) *Beauty Contest*. Exhibition catalogue. Austrian Cultural Forum, New York; MUSA, Vienna. Vienna: Passagen Verlag, 2012, pp. 10, 19, 52–53.

Rita E. Täuber (ed.) *Gnadenlos: Künstlerinnen und das Komische*. Exhibition catalogue. Kunsthalle Vogelmann; Städtische Museen Heilbronn. Cologne: Wienand Verlag, 2012, pp. 180–187.

Agnes Husslein-Arco, Brigitte Borchhardt-Birbaumer, Harald Krejci, ed., Exhibition catalogue. Österreichische Galerie, Belvedere, Vienna. Munich i. a.: Prestel, 2012, pp. 24, 119, 135, 246.

Gabriele Schor, ed., *DONNA: Avanguardia femminista negli anni'70 dalla Sammlung Verbund di Vienna*. Exhibition catalogue. Galleria nazionale d'arte moderna, Rome. Milan: Electa S. p. A., 2010, pp. 196–213.

Mirjam Westen, ed., *Rebelle: Art & Feminism*. Exhibition catalogue. Museum voor Moderne Kunst Arnhem. Arnhem: De Rijn, 2009, pp. 166–167.

Sylvia Ferino-Pagden, ed., *Wir sind Maske* Exhibition catalogue. Milan: Silvana Editoriale, 2009, pp. 358–359, 367–368.

Peter Noever, ed., *MAK-Sammlung Gegenwartskunst*. Nuremberg: Verlag für moderne Kunst, 2009, pp. 120–123.

Inka Graeve Ingelmann, ed., *Female Trouble: Die Kamera als Spiegel und Bühne weiblicher Inszenierungen*. Exhibition catalogue. Pinakothek der Moderne, Munich. Ostfildern: Hatje Cantz, 2008, pp. 148–159.

Sabine Mostegl, Gudrun Ratzinger, eds., *MATRIX: Geschlechter/Verhältnisse/ Revisionen*. Exhibition catalogue. MUSA, Vienna. New York: Springer, 2008, pp. 136–137.

Gabriele Schor, Levent Çalıkoğlu (Hrsg.) *Suyun Bir Arada Tuttuğu: Verbund Koleksiyonu'ndan Sanat. – HELD TOGETHER WITH WATER: Art from the Sammlung Verbund*. Istanbul: Istanbul Museum of Modern Art, 2008, pp. 28, 63–87.

Gabriele Schor, ed., *HELD TOGETHER WITH WATER: Kunst aus der Sammlung Verbund*. Ostfildern: Hatje Cantz, 2007, pp. 20, 39–42, 106–125.

Passion for Art: Ausstellung aus Anlass des 35-jährigen Bestehens der Sammlung Essl. Klosterneuburg: Edition Sammlung Essl Privatstiftung, 2007, pp. 56–57.

Carola Dertnig, Stefanie Seibold, eds., *Let's Twist Again. If You Can't Think It, Dance It. Performance in Vienna from 1960 until Today*. Gumpoldskirchen/ Vienna: D.E.A., 2006, pp. 272–279.

Vladimir und Estragon, eds., *Monat der Fotografie: Wien 2006*. Exhibition catalogue. Salzburg: Fotohof Edition, 2006, pp. 180–183.

Der Schuh in der Kunst. Exhibition catalogue. Salzburg: Galerie im Traklhaus, 2006.

Dieter Bechtloff, ed., *Kunstforum International*, Bd. 172. Roßdorf: TZ-Verlag, 2004, p. 382.

Hans Peter Wipplinger, ed., *Frau im Bild: Gegen-Positionen und Frauenbilder*. Passau: MMK Stiftung Wörlen, 2004, pp. 22–23.

Silvie Aigner, Brigitte Borchhardt-Birbaumer, eds., *Mimosen – Rosen – Herbstzeitlosen. Künstlerinnen: Positionen 1945 bis heute*. Exhibition catalogue. Krems: Kunsthalle Krems, 2003, pp. 142, 257.

Peter Weibel, ed., *Phantom der Lust: Visionen des Masochismus in der Kunst*, vol. 2. Graz: Neue Galerie, 2003, pp. 238–241.

Alexander Boesch, Birgit Bolognese-Leuchtenmüller, Hartwig Knack, eds., *Produkt Muttertag: Zur rituellen Inszenierung eines Festtages*. Vienna: Österreichisches Museum für Volkskunde, 2001, pp. 206–207.

Katharina Blaas-Pratscher, ed., *Public Art – Veröffentlichte Kunst: Kunst im öffentlichen Raum*. Vienna: Springer, 2000, pp. 172–173.

Veronika Schwarzinger, ed., *Kunst hautnah*. Exhibition catalogue. Vienna: Künstlerhaus, 2000, pp. 72–73.

Der Spaziergänger: Artothek und Fotosammlung; Eine Ausstellung der Kunstsektion im Bundeskanzleramt. Exhibition catalogue. Vienna: Kunst BKA, 2000.

Peter Weibel, ed., *Der anagrammatische Körper: Der Körper und seine mediale Konstruktion*. Cologne: Verlag der Buchhandlung Walther König, 1999.

Peter Assmann, Arnulf Rohsmann, eds., *Chile-Austria: Ein künstlerischer Dialog*. Exhibition catalogue. Weitra: publication N 1, 1999, pp. 104–107.

Ingried Brugger, ed., *Jahrhundert der Frauen*. Exhibition catalogue. Vienna: Residenz, 1999, pp. 284–288.

La casa, il corpo, il cuore: Konstruktion der Identität. Exhibition catalogue. Vienna: Museum Moderner Kunst Stiftung Ludwig Vienna, 1999, pp. 300–303.

Tina Kosak, Goschka Gawlik, eds., *Sisi, Sisismus, Sisismen. Geschichte–Mythos–Gegenwart*. Vienna: Triton, 1998, pp. 30–32.

Positionen – hedendaagse Oostenrijkse kunst. Knokke-Heist: Cultureel Centrum, 1998, pp. 38–39, 80.

Sarajevo 2000: Schenkungen von Künstlern für ein neues Museum in Sarajevo. Exhibition catalogue. Vienna: Museum moderner Kunst Stiftung Ludwig Vienna, 1998, pp. 42, 45, 186–189.

The Search Within: Art between Implosion and Explosion. Exhibition catalogue. Vienna: Österreichisch-Indische Gesellschaft, 1998, pp. 76–80.

A Visao Austríaca. Exhibition catalogue. Vienna: Museum moderner Kunst Stiftung Ludwig Vienna, 1998, pp. 84–85.

La Visión Austríaca: Posiciones del arte contemporáneo – The Austrian Vision: Positions of Contemporary Art. Exhibition catalogue. Vienna: Museum moderner Kunst Stiftung Ludwig Vienna, 1997, pp. 25, 41, 108–111.

Cathrin Pichler, ed., *Engel: Engel – Legenden der Gegenwart*. Exhibition catalogue. Kunsthalle Vienna, Rudolfinum Prague. Vienna, New York: Springer, 1997, p. 273.

Arnulf Rohsmann, ed., *1 Herz für Tiere*. Exhibition catalogue. Klagenfurt: Kärntner Landesgalerie, 1997, p. 27.

Friedrich Achleitner, ed., *Kunst aus Österreich 1896–1996*. Exhibition catalogue. Bonn: Prestel, 1996, p. 155.

Georg Eisler, Kristian Sotriffer, eds., *elements: Austrian Paintings since 1980*. Exhibition catalogue. Vienna: Löcker, 1996, pp. 42–43.

Alfred M. Fischer, ed., *Sammlung Speck*. Exhibition catalogue. Cologne: Oktagon, 1996.

Peter Assmann, Peter Kraml, eds., *Fiktion / non-fiction: Weltanschauungen zwischen Vorstellung und Realität*. Exhibition catalogue. Linz: Residenz, 1995, pp. 282–287.

Seamus Farrell, Robert Fleck, eds., *On peut bien sûr tout changer: Art autrichien 1960–1995*. Exhibition catalogue. Rouen: Édition médianes, 1995, pp. 84–85.

Auf den Leib geschrieben. Exhibition catalogue. Vienna: Kunsthalle im Museumsquartier, 1995, pp. 73–80.

La Visión Austríaca: The Austrian Vision. Exhibition catalogue. Vienna: Museum moderner Kunst Stiftung Ludwig, 1995, pp. 132–135.

Hans-Werner Schmidt, ed., *Positionen zum Ich: Kamerabilder*. Exhibition catalogue. Kiel: Kunsthalle, 1994, pp. 30–33.

Oh Boy, It's a Girl! Feminismen in der Kunst. Exhibition catalogue. Munich: Kunstverein, 1994, p. 51.

Photo Album Austria. Exhibition catalogue. New York: ARTprop, 1994.

Selbstporträts von Fotografinnen. Exhibition catalogue. Eislingen: Kunstverein, 1994, pp. 33–35.

Klaus Honnef, Brigitte Schlüter, Barbara Kückels, eds., *Die verlassenen Schuhe*. Exhibition catalogue. Heidelberg: Edition Braus, 1993, p. 42.

Lóránd Hegyi, ed., *Konfrontationen: Neuerwerbungen 1990–1993*. Exhibition catalogue. Vienna: Museum moderner Kunst Stiftung Ludwig Vienna, 1993, pp. 228–229.

Gue Schmidt, ed., *Austria – Korea*. Exhibition catalogue. Vienna: edition ausart, 1993.

ideas, imagenes, identidades. Exhibition catalogue. Barcelona: Centro cultural Tecla Sala, 1993, pp. 30–31.

The Seventh Wave. Exhibition catalogue. Southampton: John Hansard Gallery, 1993, pp. 40–41.

Radical Surface: Individuelle Positionen in der zeitgenössischen österreichischen Kunst. Exhibition catalogue. Vienna: Museum Moderner Kunst Stiftung Ludwig, 1992, pp. 56–57.

Manfred Schmalriede, Silke Schmalriede, eds., *2. Internationale Foto-Triennale Esslingen 1992. Erfundene Wirklichkeiten*. Exhibition catalogue. Stuttgart: Edition Cantz, 1992, pp. 106–109.

Integrierte Fotografie. Exhibition catalogue. Vienna: BKA Kunst, 1991.

Kunst, Europa. Junge Kunst aus Österreich. Exhibition catalogue. Cologne: Arbeitsgemeinschaft Deutscher Kunstvereine, 1991, pp. 32–33.

Rupertinum Fotopreis 1991 des Landes Salzburg. Exhibition catalogue. Salzburg: Österreichische Fotogalerie Salzburg, 1991, p. 11.

Unbedingt: Spirituelle Tendenzen in der jungen Kunst Österreichs. Exhibition catalogue. Salzburg, 1990.

Andreas Bee, Christmut Präger, eds., *BLAU: Kaleidoskop einer Farbe*. Exhibition catalogue. Heidelberg: Kunstverein, 1990, p. 79.

Kristian Sotriffer, Othmar Rychlik, eds.,: *Wien–Wien 1960–1990*. Exhibition catalogue. MUSEION Bolzano. Milan: Mazotta, 1990, p. 59.

Foto Sammeln. Exhibition catalogue. Wolkersdorf: Fluss Niederösterreichische Fotoinitiative, 1990, p. 27.

Progetto 1990 Civitella d'Agliano. Exhibition catalogue. Bolsena: Progetto Civitella d'Agliano, 1991, p. 67.

Ursprung und Moderne: Oberösterreichische Landesausstellung 1990. Exhibition catalogue. Linz: Neue Galerie, 1990, p. 231.

Vision Wien: Gegenwartskunst aus Österreich. Exhibition catalogue. Eindhoven: Gallery van Esch, 1990, pp. 52–54.

Minna Antova, ed., *Konfrontationen.* Exhibition catalogue. Vienna: Österreichische Hochschülerschaft, 1989, pp. 102–103.

Erika Billeter, ed., *Chefs-d'Œuvre du Musée cantonal des Beaux-Arts Lausanne.* Exhibition catalogue. Lausanne: Musée cantonal des Beaux-Arts, 1989, pp. 286, 340–341.

Wolfgang Drechsler, ed., *Kunst der letzten 10 Jahre.* Exhibition catalogue. Vienna: Museum moderner Kunst Vienna, 1989, pp. 124–125.

Margit Zuckriegl, ed., *Österreichische Fotografie seit 1945.* Exhibition catalogue. Salzburg: Universitätsverlag Anton Pustet, 1989, pp. 144–145.

32 Portraits: Photography in Art. Exhibition catalogue. Amsterdam: SDU/Contemporary Art Foundation, 1989, pp. 49–52.

Moskau–Wien–New York. Exhibition catalogue. Vienna: Wiener Festwochen, 1989, p. 48 ff.

Ornamenta 1. Internationale Schmuckkunst. Exhibition catalogue. Munich: Prestel, 1989, pp. 252–253.

Erika Billeter, ed., *Peinture et dessin en Autriche.* Exhibition catalogue. Lausanne: Musée cantonal des Beaux-Arts, 1988, pp. 100–107.

Birgit Flos, Michael Freund, eds., *Hinter den Wänden: Zeitschrift der blau-gelben Galerie Nr. 1.* Exhibition catalogue. Vienna: NÖLR / Kulturabteilung, 1988, p. 29.

Erinnerung. Fotobuch Nr. 9. Exhibition catalogue. Vienna: Fotogalerie, 1988.

Gustav Peichl, ed., *Jugendwerke vom Schillerplatz.* Exhibition catalogue. Vienna: Akademie der bildenden Künste Wien 1988, p. 176.

Schmuck: Zeichen am Körper. Exhibition catalogue. Linz: Falter, 1987, p. 200, 234–235.

Austria.Ferix. *Juliet Art Magazine Special Issue.* 1985, pp. 16–17.

Wiener Fotografie, Teil 2: Subjektives. Exhibition catalogue. Vienna: Fotogalerie, 1985.

The Fifth Biennale of Sydney: Private Symbol, Social Metaphor. Exhibition catalogue. Sydney: Biennale of Sydney, 1984.

Neue Fotografie aus Wien. Exhibition catalogue. Vienna: Fotogalerie, 1983.

Sammlung Mobil. Exhibition catalogue. Vienna: E. V., 1983, p. 58.

9 & 9. Exhibition catalogue. Vienna: Galerie Hubert Winter, 1982.

Julius Hummel, ed., *Eros.* Exhibition catalogue. Vienna: Julius Hummel Kunsthandlung, 1980, p. 40.

Künstlerinnen International 1877–1977. Exhibition catalogue. Berlin: Neue Gesellschaft für Bildende Kunst, 1977, p. 322.

MAGNA – Feminismus: Kunst und Kreativität. Exhibition catalogue. Vienna: Galerie nächst St. Stephan, 1975.

Catalogues for Exhibitions Curated by Birgit Jürgenssen

Wenn die Kinder sind im Dunkeln, … Exhibition catalogue. Vienna: Wiener Secession, 1994.

Die schwangere Muse. Exhibition catalogue. Vienna: Akademie der Bildenden Künste, 1992.

Der Hund in mir / The Dog Within. Exhibition catalogue. Vienna: Galerie Hubert Winter, 1988.

Texts by Birgit Jürgenssen

»Dolce Tocco« [2002], unpublished. Estate Birgit Jürgenssen.

»Fragebogen zur Ausstellung Muttertag« [2002], unpublished. Estate Birgit Jürgenssen.

»Von Birgit Jürgenssen zu ›Love & Peace‹« [2001], www.mip.at/attachments/367/; accessed September 30, 2018.

»Selbst hartgesottene Wissenschaftler …« [2000], unpublished. Estate Birgit Jürgenssen.

»Badeschluß« [1998], unpublished. Estate Birgit Jürgenssen.

»The Inner Passage,« in *The Search Within: Art between Implosion and Explosion.* Exhibition catalogue. Vienna: Österreichisch-Indische Gesellschaft, 1998, p. 76.

»Dem Fremden sich entfernend nähern …,« in *Minerva – Die Buchhandlung im MAK. Herbst 96* Vienna: Minerva, 1996, p. 37.

»Kann Sehnsucht dreidimensional werden? Sehnsucht: 3-D emotional?,« in Peter Assmann, Peter Kraml, eds., *Fiktion / non-fiction. Weltanschauungen zwischen Vorstellung und Wirklichkeit.* Exhibition catalogue. Linz: Oberösterreichisches Landesmuseum, 1995, pp. 282–287.

»Antwort auf eine Umfrage der Zeitschrift Springer vom 21.7.1995,« unpublished. Estate Birgit Jürgenssen.

»Wie erfährt man sich im Anderen, das Andere in sich?,« in *Selbstporträts von Fotografinnen.* Exhibition catalogue. Eislingen: Kunstverein, 1994, p. 34.

»Vorwort,« in *Wenn die Kinder sind im Dunkeln, …* Exhibition catalogue. Vienna: Wiener Secession, 1994, p. 6.

»Die Beschreibung der Ausstellung,« in *Die schwangere Muse.* Exhibition catalogue. Vienna: Akademie der bildenden Künste Wien, 1992, pp. 15–16.

»Ich beschäftige mich mit Fotografie …,« in Manfred Schmalriede, Silke Schmalriede, eds., *2. Internationale Foto-Triennale Esslingen 1992. Erfundene Wirklichkeiten.* Exhibition catalogue. Stuttgart: Edition Cantz, 1992, p. 109.

»Unendlichkeit …,« in Andreas Bee, Christmut Präger, eds., *Blau. Kaleidoskop einer Farbe.* Exhibition catalogue. Heidelberg: Kunstverein, 1990, p. 79.

»Der Mittelbau,« in *Akademie der Bildenden Künste.* Vienna: Akademie der Bildenden Künste, 1989, pp. 127–129.

»Bruchstücke …,« in *32 Portraits: Photography in Art.* Exhibition catalogue. Amsterdam: SDU / Contemporary Art Foundation, 1989, p. 49.

»Letter to J. R.« [1988], unpublished. Estate Birgit Jürgenssen.

»Was hast du getan …,« in *Erinnerung. Fotobuch Nr. 9.* Exhibition catalogue. Vienna: Fotogalerie, 1988.

»The Place of Images …,« in *Birgit Jürgenssen.* Exhibition catalogue. Vienna: Galerie Hubert Winter, 1988, pp. 10–14.

»Pulsschlag einer Sinnlichkeit,« in *Schmuck: Zeichen am Körper.* Exhibition catalogue. Vienna: Falter, 1987, p. 234.

»Going to Bed without Sleeping« [1986], in: Erika Billeter, eds., *Chefs-d'Œuvre du Musée cantonal des Beaux-Arts Lausanne.* Exhibition catalogue. Lausanne: Musée cantonal des Beaux-Arts, 1989, p. 340.

»Kunst aus dem Zwischenreich …,« in *9 & 9.* Exhibition catalogue. Vienna: Galerie Hubert Winter, 1982.

»Mein Spiegelbild suchend …,« in *Birgit Jürgenssen. 10 Tage – 100 Photos.* Exhibition catalogue. Vienna: Galerie Hubert Winter, 1981.

»Brief an Fr. A.,« in *Das Pult* 44, 1977, p. 72.

»Über Schuhe,« in *Das Pult* 44, 1977, p. 77.

Interviews with Birgit Jürgenssen

Felicitas Thun-Hohenstein. »»Everything Flows, Conditions and Permeates Itself …‹« Felicitas Thun-Hohenstein in an Interview with Birgit Jürgenssen." In *Let's Twist Again: If You Can't Think It, Dance It; Performance in Vienna from 1960 until Today*, edited by Carola Dertnig, Stefanie Seibold. Exhibition catalogue. Gumpoldskirchen/Vienna: D.E.A., 2006, pp. 272–279.

»Birgit Jürgenssen. ›Wie erfährt man sich im Anderen, das Andere in sich?‹ Ein Gespräch mit Rainer Metzger,« in *Kunstforum International* 64, March–May 2003, pp. 234–247.

Interview with Doris Linda Psenicnik, Vienna, 1998, unpublished. Estate Birgit Jürgenssen.

»Frauen-Bilder: Bilder-Frauen; Birgit Jürgenssen, Mario-Jo Lafontaine, Gundula Schulze el Dowy«, Radio report by Rudij Bergmann in Südwestrundfunk, 1995.

»Drawings of the Sky. Birgit Jürgenssen interviewed by Kevin Henderson,« in *Birgit Jürgenssen: Früher oder Später.* Exhibition catalogue. Linz: Oberösterreichisches Landesmuseum, 1998, p. 116; erstmals erschienen in: *Alba*, 12, 1989, p. 41.

»Birgit Jürgenssen,« in Heidemarie Seblatnig, eds., *Einfach den Gefahren ins Auge sehen. Künstlerinnen im Gespräch.* Vienna: Böhlau, 1988, pp. 158–161.

<u>Works by
Birgit
Jürgenssen
for Publica-
tions</u>

»Icônes,« in *multitudes* 4,
2001, pp. 128–129.

»1949 / Unser Morgen hat
eine neue Zukunft. 1999 ...
etc. ...,« in *Freibord.
Zeitschrift für Literatur
und Kunst* 107/108, 1999,
pp. 76–84.

»Heimliche Bärenfrüchte,
die man im Dunklen frißt ...,«
in *PlantSüden* 6, 1997, pp.
76–79.

»Kann Sehnsucht dreidimen-
sional werden? Sehnsucht:
3-D emotional?,« in Peter
Assmann, Peter Kraml, eds.,
*Fiktion / non-fiction. Welt-
anschauungen zwischen
Vorstellung und Wirklichkeit*
Exhibition catalogue. Linz:
Residenz, 1995, pp. 282–287.

»Schon als Tier hat der
Mensch Sprache ...,«
in *PlantSüden* 3, 1994,
pp. 58–61, 79.

Adam Bronstein. »Die ent-
scheidende Seite 1« und
Wolfram Knorr / »Die neuen
Wörter,« in *Diners Club
Magazin* 4, 1990,
pp. 168–180 illustrations.

Jeffrey Rian. »Cosimo's
Sleep,« Vienna: Galerie
Hubert Winter, 1989, unpa-
ginated, illustrations.

*Konkursbuch: Zeitschrift
für Vernunftkritik – Nummer
Sechs: Erotik*, 1979, pp. 59,
65, 109, 131, 147, illustrations.

Authors' Biographies

<u>Patricia Allmer</u>
is a leading scholar of surrealism. Her books include *Lee Miller: Photography, Surrealism, and Beyond* (MUP, 2016), *René Magritte: Beyond Painting* (MUP, 2009), and a biography, *René Magritte* (Reaktion Press, 2019) as well as the edited volumes *Intersections: Women Artists / Surrealism / Modernism* (MUP, 2016) and the *Dada / Surrealism* special issue *Wonderful Things – Surrealism and Egypt* (2013). She curated *4 Saints in 3 Acts: A Snapshot of the American Avant-Garde in the 1930s* (2017; MUP) and *Taking Shots: The Photography of William S. Burroughs* (2014; Prestel), both at the Photographers' Gallery, and the groundbreaking *Angels of Anarchy: Women Artists and Surrealism* (Manchester Art Gallery, 2009; Prestel). She has lectured at London's Freud Museum (2016), The Hepworth (2018), and Princeton University (2018), and was the guest speaker for the 2017–18 Chaire Internationale Émile Bernheim program in Brussels. She is senior lecturer in art history at the University of Edinburgh.

p. 151

<u>Michael Bracewell</u>
is a British writer and novelist. Between 1988 and 1999 he published three novels and three novellas. He has since written extensively on modern and contemporary art and culture and is a contributor to *The Burlington Magazine*.

His more recent writings include *Kai Althoff* (contributor; Michael Werner, 2012), *The Rise of David Bowie 1972–1973* (with Mick Rock and Barney Hoskyns; Taschen, 2016), and *Paul Nash: British Visionary Modernism* (Fondation Vincent Van Gogh, 2018.)

His selected writings on art, *The Space Between*, edited by Doro Globus, were published by Ridinghouse, London, in 2011.

p. 285

Louisa Buck
is a writer and broadcaster on contemporary art. She has been London contemporary art columnist for *The Art Newspaper* since 1997 and is a regular reviewer on BBC radio and TV. She writes a weekly visual arts column for *The Telegraph Luxury*.

She is the author of a number of catalogue essays for institutions including Tate, Whitechapel Gallery, ICA London, and the Stedelijk Museum in Amsterdam.

Her books include *Moving Targets 2: A User's Guide to British Art Now* (Tate, 2000), *Market Matters: The Dynamics of the Contemporary Art Market* (Arts Council England, 2004), and *Owning Art: The Contemporary Art Collector's Handbook* (co-authored with Judith Greer; Cultureshock Media, 2006). *Commissioning Contemporary Art : A Handbook for Curators, Collectors and Artists* was published by Thames & Hudson in October 2012, and in 2016 she authored »The Going Public Report« commissioned by Museums Sheffield.

Louisa Buck was a judge for the 2005 Turner Prize.

p. 207

Natascha Burger
studied art history in Vienna, Münster, and Aix-en-Provence. She has been executive director of the Estate Birgit Jürgenssen since 2009 and is director of Galerie Hubert Winter, Vienna. Responsible for the entire archive, she is involved as curator and editor in the upcoming comprehensive Birgit Jürgenssen retrospective *Ich bin. / I Am.* at the Kunsthalle Tübingen, Germany, with subsequent showings at the GAMeC in Bergamo, Italy, and the Louisiana Museum of Modern Art in Denmark.

Born 1980 in Vienna, Austria. Lives and works in Vienna, Austria.

p. 19

Maurizio Cattelan
(born in Padua in 1960) is one of the most popular and controversial artists on the contemporary art scene. Drawing freely on the real world of people and objects, his works are an irreverent operation aimed at both art and institutions. His playful and provocative use of materials, objects, and gestures set in challenging contexts forces commentary and engagement. He first achieved notoriety on an international scale in New York with *La Nona Ora* (The Ninth Hour), a wax statue of Pope John Paul II hit by a meteorite, which was first exhibited in 1999 at the Kunsthalle Basel. *L.O.V.E.* (2010), a public art intervention permanently installed in Piazza Affari, Milan, triggered the re-appropriation by citizens of a square that had otherwise been forgotten. In the same year, Cattelan started a biannual, picture-based publication co-created with the photographer Pierpaolo Ferrari. In 2011, he provoked a lively debate with an installation of two thousand stuffed pigeons presented at the 54th edition of the Venice Biennale. He also had a one-man show at the Guggenheim in New York, with all his works suspended from the ceiling. In 2016, he replaced the toilet in the Guggenheim restroom with a fully functional replica cast in 18-karat gold, making it available to the public; in the same year he was invited to exhibit a selection of his most important works at Le Monnaie de Paris, resulting in a retrospective titled after one of his works, *Not Afraid of Love*. He has exhibited in major European and American museums and participated in the major international exhibitions of contemporary art.

p. 173

Melissa Destino
(born in Bari in 1984; lives and works in Vienna) is a PhD candidate in the Department of Art Theory and Cultural Studies at the Academy of Fine Arts in Vienna and an independent curator. She currently works at Galerie Hubert Winter, Vienna. With a background in visual arts and curating, as well as design and photography of cultural heritage, she has worked in various contemporary art galleries (Office Baroque, Antwerp; Sprüth Magers,

London; Sassa Trülzsch, Berlin) and has assisted curator Elena Filipovic on several publishing projects, including *The Artist as Curator*, (Mousse Publishing). She has worked as production manager of Marinella Senatore's »The School of Narrative Dance« in Brussels within the framework of the Parckdesign 2016 Urban Biennial. She recently curated *The Provisional City* at Spazio Murat, Bari.

p. 95

Marta Dziewańska
is curator and head of research at the Museum of Modern Art in Warsaw, a PhD candidate in philosophy at the Polish Academy of Sciences, also in Warsaw.

She has curated and co-curated several exhibition projects, including *The Other Trans-Atlantic: Kinetic and Op Art in Eastern Europe and Latin America, 50s–70s* (MoMA Warsaw and Sesc Sao Paulo, Brazil, 2017/18), *Alina Szapocznikow: Human Landscapes* (The Hepworth Wakefield, UK), *Andrzej Wróblewski: Recto/Verso* (MoMA Warsaw and Museo Reina Sofia in Madrid, 2015/16), *Maria Bartuszova: Provisional Forms* (MoMA Warsaw, 2015). She was curatorial advisor for documenta 14 (2017).

Her editorial and co-editorial credits include *MIRIAM CAHN: I AS HUMAN,* (upcoming, 2019), *Maria Bartuszova: Provisional Forms* (2015), with André Lepecki; *Points of Convergence: Alternative Views on Performance* (2017), with Claire Bishop; *1968–1989: Political Upheaval and Artistic Change* (2009). Her writings have appeared in numerous catalogues and art magazines.

p. 215

Heike Eipeldauer,
born 1978, studied art history and law with a focus on law and cultural affairs in Vienna and Dijon. She is head of collections and curator at the Leopold Museum Vienna. From 2001 to 2004 she worked as an academic assistant at the Museum moderne Kunst Stiftung Ludwig Vienna, and from 2004 to 2017 she was curator for

classical modernism and contemporary art at Kunstforum Wien, where she was responsible for pioneering monographic exhibitions, including *Georges Braque* (2008), *Meret Oppenheim* (2013/14, also shown at the Martin-Gropius-Bau, Berlin, and LaM, Lille), *Birgit Jürgenssen* (2010/11, together with Gabriele Schor), *Georgia O'Keeffe* (2016/17, also shown at Tate Modern, London, and AGO, Toronto), and most recently *Gerhard Rühm* (2017), as well as thematic exhibitions like *A Feast for the Eyes: Food in Still Life* (2010) and *Love in Times of Revolution: Artist Couples of the Russian Avant-Garde* (2015/16 and 2017). Teaches at the University of Vienna.

p. 267

Nicole Fritz

has been director and board member at Stiftung Kunsthalle Tübingen since January 1, 2018. From 2011, she was founder director of Kunstmuseum Ravensburg, which was awarded Museum of the Year 2015 by the International Association of Art Critics, AICA. She studied art history and empirical cultural studies in Tübingen, gaining her doctorate in 2002. From 2002 to 2004, she was a member of the academic staff at Staatliche Kunsthalle Baden-Baden; from 2008 a freelance curator, working for Städtische Galerie Ravensburg, Cobra Museum in Amstelveen (Amsterdam), and others. From 2010 to 2011, she was curator at the Kunsthalle in Krems (Austria). Since 2007, teaching positions at the State Academy of Fine Arts in Stuttgart and Reinwardt Academie, Amsterdam. Since 2018 curator of the Collection LBBW. Nicole has been a member of various juries and appointments committees (including the Cultural Foundation of Hesse in 2017; the Innovation Fund of the State of Baden-Württemberg, the Oskar Schlemmer Prize, the Grand State Prize of the State of Baden-Württemberg (2014); and the Hans Thoma Prize (2017/2013). Numerous publications on twentieth- and twenty-first-century art.

p. 117

Lorenzo Giusti

is the director of GAMeC – Galleria d'Arte Moderna e Contemporanea di Bergamo. From 2012 to 2017 he has been director of the MAN Museum in Nuoro and in 2016 part of the curatorial team of the 3rd Shenzhen Animation Biennale. In his projects he focuses both on leading figures in 20th-century avant-gardes and international contemporary artists, such as Ragnar Kjartansson, Julian Rosefeldt, Maria Lai, Thomas Hirschhorn, Michael Höpfner, Roman Signer, Michel Blazy, Jennifer West, and others.

p. 77

Jessica Morgan

joined Dia as director in January 2015 and was named Nathalie de Gunzburg Director in October 2017. At Dia, Morgan is responsible for strengthening and activating all parts of Dia's multivalent program, including its pioneering land art projects, site-specific commissions, and collections and programs at Dia:Beacon, as well as reinvigorating its artistic and intellectual presence in New York City. Under Morgan's directorship Dia has grown and diversified its collection, adding substantial bodies of work by Mary Corse, Nancy Holt, Mario Merz, Robert Morris, Dorothea Rockburne, Kishio Suga, Anne Truitt, and Lee Ufan among others. Prior to assuming her position at Dia, Morgan was the Daskalopoulos Curator, International Art, at Tate Modern in London from 2010 to 2014, and was curator at Tate from 2002 to 2010. At Tate, she organized a number of important exhibitions including the group shows *The World Goes Pop* (2015/16) and *Common Wealth* (2003) and retrospectives of *Saloua Raouda Choucair* (2013), *Gabriel Orozco* (2011), *John Baldessari* (2009/10), and *Martin Kippenberger* (2006). In addition to her work on exhibitions, Morgan played a key role in the growth of Tate's collection—helping develop the museum's holdings of mid-century and emerging art from North America, the Middle East, North Africa, and South Asia. Morgan served as the artistic director of the 10th Gwangju Biennale in 2014 and has published extensively in *Artforum* and *Parkett* as well as other journals and scholarly publications.

p. 143

Marta Papini

(born in Italy in 1985) is a curator based in Italy. She recently worked as associate curator on *The Artist Is Present*, curated by Maurizio Cattelan, Yuz Museum, Shanghai. Prior to that she was assistant curator to Cecilia Alemani for the Italian Pavilion at the Venice Biennale (2017). In 2016, she curated the show *Lo stato delle cose*, as part of the 16th Rome Quadriennale. In 2014, she curated *Shit and Die* with Maurizio Cattelan and Myriam Ben Salah in Palazzo Cavour in Turin. Since 2014, she has been curator and head of research and public programs at the Centre for Contemporary Art Luigi Pecci in Prato, Tuscany. From 2011 to 2014 she was project manager of *TOILETPAPER* magazine founded by Maurizio Cattelan and Pierpaolo Ferrari in Milan. She graduated in history of art at DAMS in Bologna and then attended CAMPO12 at the Fondazione Sandretto Re Rebaudengo in Turin. She has co-curated, edited, and coordinated several publications and catalogues, such as *Il mondo magico* (Marsilio Editori, 2017), *Shit and Die* (Damiani editore, 2014), and *1968: Radical Italian Design* (Deste Foundation, 2014).

p. 173

Gabriele Schor

studied philosophy and art history in Vienna and San Diego. She worked at the Tate Gallery in London, was art correspondent for the *Neue Zürcher Zeitung* and taught modern art as well as the theory and practice of art criticism at universities.

Since 2004 she has directed the SAMMLUNG VERBUND Collection, Vienna, which she has built up from the beginning with two main focuses: the perception of spaces and places as well as feminist art of the 1970s.

Schor coined the term »Feminist Avant-Garde« and established it as part of the art-historical discourse in order to highlight the pioneering role of these artists. Her numerous publications include the first Birgit Jürgenssen monograph (with Abigail Solomon-Godeau; 2009), a catalogue raisonné on the early works of Cindy Sherman

(2012), a catalogue on Francesca Woodman (with Elisabeth Bronfen; 2014), a compendium on the feminist avant-garde (2015), the first monograph on Renate Bertlmann (with Jessica Morgan; 2016), and a catalogue on Louise Lawler (2018).

p. 67

Jasper Sharp

(born in 1975) is a British curator and art historian. He worked at the Peggy Guggenheim Collection, Venice, from 1999 to 2005 before moving to Austria. He is the curator for modern and contemporary art at the Kunsthistorisches Museum in Vienna, for whom he developed a new program of exhibitions, including retrospectives of Lucian Freud, Joseph Cornell, and Mark Rothko (2019). He was commissioner of the Austrian Pavilion at the 55th Venice Biennale in 2013, and founding curator of the talks program at Frieze Masters. In September 2014, he was nominated by *Apollo* magazine as one of the ten most promising museum curators in Europe under the age of 40.

p. 275

Abigail Solomon-Godeau

is Professor Emerita, Department of Art History, University of California, Santa Barbara, and now lives and works in Paris. She is the author of *Photography at the Dock: Essays on Photographic Histories, Institutions, and Practices* (1992), *Male Trouble: A Crisis in Representation* (1997), *Chair à Canons: Photographie, discours, féminisme* (2015), and *Photography after Photography: Gender, Genre, History* (2017). She has also written a monograph on the Australian artist *Rosemary Laing* (2011) and coauthored the monograph *Birgit Jürgenssen* (with Gabriele Schor; 2013). Her essays on photography, 18th- and 19th-century art, feminism, and contemporary art have been widely anthologized and translated.

p. 187

Ninja Walbers

gained her master of arts in art studies, German studies, and psychology at the Art Academy and University of Kassel, focusing on the art of the twentieth and twenty-first centuries and on photography. After a period as a volunteer at Kunstmuseum Ravensburg, she worked freelance there on the exhibition *I Am a Plant: Natural Processes in Art*. At present, she works as an art consultant and is the assistant to the director of the Gargonza Arts Award, an artist-in-residence scholarship. She publishes on classical modernism, contemporary art, and feminist positions.

p. 223

Acknowledgements

Our special thanks go to

Anja Besserer
Simone Borghi
Jonathan M. Brand
Michael Brzezinski
Christoph Bueble
Melissa Destino
Ivan Fauri
Patrizia Filippig Gießler
Thomas Gebauer
Kristof Georgen
Werner N. Greiner
Zita Hartel
Miciah Hussey
Alison Jacques
Maria Kanzler
Adrian Kovac
Manfred Kostal
Nina Krick
Fergus McCaffrey
Irmgard Müller
Peter Noever
Sami Örcün
Boris Palmer
Corinna Pickart
Silvia Reiber
Robert Suitner
Mathias Ussing Seeberg
Melanie Wagner
Ninja Walbers
Silvia Weimer
Stefanie Wenzel
Franziska Winter
Wolfgang Woessner

as well as all contributing authors
and lenders.

Flaubert & Luise
Olga & Josephine

Colophon

This catalogue is published at the occasion of the exhibition *Birgit Jürgenssen. Ich bin.*

Curators
Natascha Burger, Estate Birgit Jürgenssen
Nicole Fritz, Kunsthalle Tübingen

Kunsthalle Tübingen, Germany November 10, 2018 – February 17, 2019

KUNSTHALLE TÜBINGEN

GAMeC – Galleria d'Arte Moderna e Contemporanea di Bergamo, Italy
March 8 – May 19, 2019

GAMeC

LOUISIANA Museum of Modern Art, Humlebæk, Denmark
Summer 2019

LOUISIANA MUSEUM OF MODERN ART

Catalogue

Editors
Natascha Burger
Nicole Fritz

Managing Editor
Philipp Wagner

Translations
Angela Arnone (Giusti)
Greg Bond (Foreword, Burger, Schor, Walbers, Biography Jürgenssen)
Pauline Cumbers &
Anna McSherry (Fritz)
Anda McBride (Dziewańska)
Judith Rosenthal (Eipeldauer)

Copyeditor
Simon Cowper

Graphic design and typesetting
Marie Artaker

Typeface
Catalog
GT America

Paper
Profibulk
Pergamenata
Popset

Reproductions
Pixelstorm, Wien

Project management, Prestel
Anja Besserer

Production, Prestel
Corinna Pickart

Print and binding
Holzhausen Druck & Medien GmbH, Vienna

Prestel Verlag, a member of Verlagsgruppe Random House GmbH
Neumarkter Straße 28
81673 Munich
Germany

Prestel Publishing Ltd.
14-17 Wells Street
London W1T 3PD
United Kingdom

Prestel Publishing
900 Broadway, Suite 603
New York, NY 10003
USA

In respect to links in the book, the publisher has no influence at all over the current and future design, content or authorship of the linked sites. For this reason Verlagsgruppe Randomhouse expressly disassociates itself from all content on linked sites that has been altered since the link was created and assumes no liability for such content.

© 2018 Prestel Verlag, Munich, London, New York, Estate Birgit Jürgenssen, Vienna and authors.

Photo Credits
For the reproduced works of Birgit Jürgenssen:
© Estate Birgit Jürgenssen, Vienna / Bildrecht, Vienna 2018; p. 239 Photo: Courtesy Michael Brzezinski (Alison Jacques Gallery).

For the reproduced works of the other artists: p. 23 Courtesy Photobibliothek.ch; p. 25 Foto: © bpk Berlin / Charles Wilp, © The Estate of Yves Klein / Bildrecht, Vienna 2018; p. 41 © bpk / S. Fischer Stiftung / Leonore Mau; p. 133 © Bildrecht, Vienna 2018; p. 197 © Banco de México Diego Rivera & Frida Kahlo Museums Trust, México D.F. / Bildrecht, Vienna 2018; p. 227 Courtesy NYC Municipal Archives; p. 228 Courtesy of the artist and Metro Pictures; p. 230 © Gillian Wearing, courtesy Maureen Paley, London, Tanya Bonakdar Gallery, New York and Regen Projects, Los Angeles; p. 237 © Lucas Samaras, Courtesy Pace Gallery; p. 242 ©2018. Digital image, The Museum of Modern Art, New York/ Scala, Florence; p. 247 © Floris Neusüss, courtesy Daniel Blau, Munich.

Every effort was made to find all copyright holders of the works illustrated. Should it have omitted to contact any artists, photographers, or their legal successors, the rightful copyright holders are asked to notify the Estate Birgit Jürgenssen.

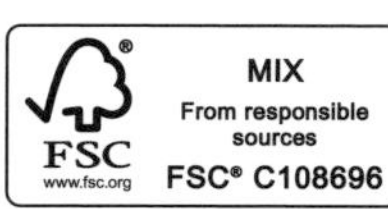

Verlagsgruppe Random House FSC® N001967
Printed in Austria

ISBN 978-3-7913-5833-8 (English Edition)
ISBN 978-3-7913-5832-1 (German Edition)
ISBN 978-3-7913-6911-2 (Italian Edition)

Cover illustration
Birgit Jürgenssen *Untitled* 1980 (ph1619)

Frontispiece
Birgit Jürgenssen *Emancipation* 1973 (z109)

Galerie Hubert Winter
Breite Gasse 17
1070 Vienna
Austria

GALERIE

HUBERT

WINTER

www.galeriewinter.at
www.birgitjuergenssen.com

www.prestel.com

With friendly support by

≡ Bundeskanzleramt